Volcano and Geothermal Tourism

Volcano and Geothermal Tourism

Sustainable Geo-Resources for Leisure and Recreation

Edited by Patricia Erfurt-Cooper and Malcolm Cooper

from Routledge

First published by Earthscan in the UK and USA in 2010

For a full list of publications please contact:

Earthscan
2 Park Square, Milton Park, Abingdon, Oxfordshire OX14 4RN
711 Third Avenue, New York, NY 10017

First issued in paperback 2015

Earthscan is an imprint of the Taylor & Francis Group, an informa business

ISBN 13: 978-1-138-99411-9 (pbk)
ISBN 13: 978-1-84407-870-7 (hbk)

Typeset by Domex e-Data, India
Cover design by Clifford Hayes

A catalogue record for this book is available from the British Library

Library of Congress Cataloging-in-Publication Data

Volcano and geothermal tourism : sustainable geo-resources for leisure and recreation / edited by Patricia Erfurt-Cooper and Malcolm Cooper.
        p. cm.
    Includes bibliographical references and index.
    ISBN   978-1-84407-870-7 (hardback)
    1.   Ecotourism. 2.   Geotourism. 3.   Volcanoes. 4.   Geothermal resources.   I.   Erfurt-Cooper, Patricia II.   Cooper, Malcolm.
    G156.5.E26V65   2010
    338.4'75521–dc22

                                                                    2010000820

CONTENTS

List of Figures, Tables and Boxes

Figures

List of Contributors

Ted Brattstrom has a BA in Chemistry, an MEd in Secondary Education and an MSc in Geology and Geophysics. An earth science teacher living on the Big Island of Hawai'i, Ted has journeyed south three times to visit Antarctica and/or various sub-Antarctic islands to pursue his passion for Antarctic history, geology and wildlife.
ted@ Hawaii.edu

Brian Brogan is a keen amateur photographer who took up photography after an accident resulting in severe spinal damage. He rewarded himself with a trip to Australia after he learnt to walk again and contributed the colour photo of the basalt columns in Mt Kaputar National Park.
bbrogan@talktalk.net

Malcolm Cooper PhD is vice president (research) and holds the position of professor of tourism management in the Graduate School of Asia Pacific Studies at Ritsumeikan Asia Pacific University, Japan. Professor Cooper has published over 80 books, refereed articles and book chapters. His research interests include tourism development and planning, sustainable development and management of environmental resources.
cooperm@apu.ac.jp

Ross Dowling PhD is foundation professor of tourism at Edith Cowan University, Perth, Australia. Professor Dowling is advisor to the United Nations Educational, Scientific and Cultural Organization's (UNESCO) Global Network of National Geoparks, a board member of the Indian Ocean Tourism Organisation, and founder and advisor for the Global Geotourism Conference held every two years.
r.dowling@ecu.edu.au

Jerry Eades PhD is currently professor and dean, College of Asia Pacific Studies and Graduate School of Asia Pacific Studies, Ritsumeikan Asia Pacific University, Beppu, Japan, and senior honorary research fellow, Department of Anthropology and Conservation, University of Kent, Canterbury, United Kingdom. His current research interests include migration, urbanization, the environment and tourism.
jerryeades@gmail.com

Jens Edelmann originally trained as a lawyer, but has been interested in volcanoes since his childhood. He specialized in geology and geotourism and has authored three books focusing on geology and travel, as well as numerous paleontological publications for a rockhound magazine. His travels usually take him to Africa, Iceland and the volcanoes of south-east Asia. He organizes and leads geotouristic travel projects to Morocco and southern Europe.
Jens.Ed@t-online.de

Patricia Erfurt-Cooper lectures in tourism planning and resource management at Ritsumeikan Asia-Pacific University, Japan, and is currently completing her PhD through James Cook University, Australia. Patricia has co-edited with Malcolm Cooper a book about Hot Spring Tourism and her research interests include geothermal resources for human use and geotourism in volcanic and geothermal environments with a focus on risk management and sustainability.
Patricia.Erfurt@jcu.edu.au

John Fletcher PhD is professor of tourism, director of the International Centre for Tourism and Hospitality Research and head of Bournemouth University Graduate School. Professor Fletcher is an economist who has pioneered the development of economic impact models for countries throughout the Caribbean, The Indian Ocean, the South Pacific and Europe. He is editor in chief of the International Journal of Tourism Research and a member of the International Academy for the Study of Tourism and a fellow of the Tourism Society. jefletch@bournemouth.ac.uk

Henry Gaudru PhD is a French volcanologist and the president of the European Volcanological Society (Geneva, Switzerland). As scientific adviser to the United Nations International Strategy for Disaster Reduction (UNISDR) for volcanic risk mitigation, he carried out many missions around the world during recent eruptions about hazards assessment, crisis management and public awareness in coordination with local scientists, local and national authorities. He is member of the International Association of Volcanology and Chemistry of the Earth's Interior (IAVCEI) international commission 'Cities and Volcanoes'. hgaudru@sveurop.org

Tanner Heggie is a research assistant with the Astronomical Instrumentation Group at the University of Lethbridge, Canada. tanner.heggie@uleth.ca

Tracey M. Heggie MS lectures at the University of North Dakota and is affiliated with the Recreation & Tourism Studies Program. tracey.heggie@und.edu

Travis W. Heggie PhD is a professor in the Recreation and Tourism Studies program at the University of North Dakota. Dr Heggie is also the co-director of the Great Plains Injury Prevention Research Initiative at the University of North Dakota. travisheggie@mail.und.nodak.edu

Tom Hose PhD is a principal lecturer in heritage and tourism management at Buckingham Chilterns University in the UK. He initially trained as an Earth scientist and is a fellow of the Geological Society of London. Dr Hose has authored chapters for Geological Society books and numerous geotourism and geological interpretation journal papers and

articles. Tom has extensive experience as a field geologist and naturalist and considerable expertise in natural heritage conservation and environmental education. He is a consultant on geotourism and geology-focused interpretative provision. those01@bucks.ac.uk

Associate Professor **Edmund Bernard Joyce PhD** is honorary principal fellow at the School of Earth Sciences of the University of Melbourne. For 40 years he has worked on the Newer Volcanics of Victoria, and he is currently studying volcanic landforms of Western Victoria to see what they can tell us about volcanic eruption risk, and also how best to look after the landscape heritage of the new Kanawinka Global Geopark. ebj@unimelb.edu.au

Jonathan Karkut is a specialist in project development, design and management for London Metropolitan University, who has helped to successfully deliver substantial EU funded tourism and heritage projects in the geographical contexts of the Balkans, Mediterranean and India. Sparked off by initial research concerning tourism development around active volcanic sites, he is now studying for his PhD by combining an earlier career in exploration geology with more recent experience in the anthropology of tourism to provide a critical analysis of the rapidly expanding geoparks global network. j.karkut@londonmet.ac.uk

Lisa M. King holds a MEd in secondary education with further degrees in biology and ecotourism and is currently pursuing her PhD in tourism at James Cook University in Cairns, Australia. A third generation field geologist married to an Earth science high school teacher, Lisa's research interests include geotourism, world heritage national parks, remote islands, visitor monitoring and capacity building. volcanolisa@hotmail.com

Yeganeh Morakabati PhD is a lecturer in services marketing, research methodology and tourism at Bournemouth University and has undertaken extensive research into travel and tourism risk and risk perceptions. Dr Morakabati has undertaken research for the Commonwealth Tourism Centre and local authorities in the UK, as well as an

examination of the economic impact of Gibraltar on the economy of the Campo de Gibraltar.
ymora@bournemouth.ac.uk

David Newsome PhD is an associate professor in the School of Environmental Science at Murdoch University, Perth, Western Australia and holds degrees in botany, soil science and geomorphology. His research activities focus on the sustainable use of landscapes and the assessment and management of recreational activity in protected areas. His research interests focus on the environmental impacts of tourism in national parks and nature reserves and geotourism. David is the lead author of two books – *Natural Area Tourism: Ecology, impacts and management* and *Wildlife Tourism* – and, along with Ross Dowling, co-editor of *Geotourism*, a book which lays the foundation for the emergence of geotourism.
D.Newsome@murdoch.edu.au

Nick Petford PhD is pro vice-chancellor (research and enterprise) at Bournemouth University. He is a geologist by training and has worked on academic and commercial research projects throughout the world, most recently as a consultant to the Department for International Development (DFID) on the management of volcanic hazard monitoring on Montserrat. He is former council member of the Geological Society, London, former vice-president of the Mineralogical Society of Great Britain and Ireland and current section chair of IAVCEI. He has held visiting professor appointments at the University of Vermont (USA) and Macquarie University (Australia).
npetford@bournemouth.ac.uk

Richard Roscoe PhD is currently working as a patent examiner at the European Patent Office Munich in the biotechnology field. Dr Roscoe's spare time is dedicated to the study and photographic documentation of volcanoes and geothermal areas, as made available on his scientifically detailed website www.photovolcanica.com
rr@photovolcanica.com

Alfred Kazadi Sanga-Ngoie PhD is doctor of science (geophysics: environmental and atmosphere science), Kyoto University, Japan. Now professor of environmental geoscience, Graduate School of Asia

Pacific Studies, Ritsumeikan Asia Pacific University, Beppu, Japan, professor emeritus, Mie University, Japan and visiting professor, Faculty of Science, Kinshasa University, Dem. Rep. of Congo.
sangank@apu.ac.jp

Young Kwan Sohn PhD is a professor in the Department of Earth and Environmental Sciences at the Gyeongsang National University in Jinju, Republic of Korea. His research interest and field of expertise is classic sedimentology.
yksohn@gnu.ac.kr

Ariane Struck is presently finalizing her PhD thesis at the University Duisburg-Essen (Germany), Department of Geography, which is most likely the first PhD covering the aspects of volcano tourism. Ariane is also managing a tourism company with 20 employees focusing on short trips within Germany.
Ariane.Struck@verwoehnwochenende.de

Kazem Vafadari PhD is currently involved in a JSPS-UNU postdoctoral programme with United Nations University Institute of Advanced Studies Operating Unit Ishikawa Kanazawa (UNU-IAS OUIK) and Kanazawa University. Dr Vafadari's research focuses on the role of rural tourism in rural revitalization and conservation of natural resources in so-called rural landscapes of Satoyama and Satoumi in Japan.
kazemv@gmail.com

Christoph Weber contributed facts and images to this book. His background is electronic engineering, but he also operates the German based travel agency VEI (Vulkanexpeditionen International, www.v-e-i.de). His research interests take him all over the world, usually in the wake of erupting volcanoes such as Ol Doinyo Lengai in Tanzania, Krakatau in Indonesia, Pinatubo in the Philippines and Santa Maria in Guatemala, which are just a few of the sites he has visited.
mail@v-e-i.de

Kyung Sik Woo PhD is a professor in the Department of Geology at the Kangwon National University in Chuncheon, Republic of Korea. Dr Woo's research interests and fields of expertise are carbonate sedimentology, cave geology and palaeoclimatology.
wooks@kangwon.ac.kr

Preface

Every year large numbers of people are attracted to volcanic and geothermal areas. With over 1500 volcanoes currently classed as active worldwide, part of this attraction is the unpredictable and potentially hostile phenomena connected to volcanic activity. In fact, heightened activity seems to correlate with an increase in visitor numbers as many of the papers in this book show.

Active and dormant volcanoes and their associated unique landforms have fascinated humans throughout history, however, to date, there has been very little research into volcano tourism and no literature recognizing the importance of volcanic and geothermal tourism as an independent sub-sector of various types of nature-based tourism including adventure and extreme tourism. This book is the first to identify key issues of relevance to tourism in volcanic and geothermal environments.

While planning this book special consideration was given to the sustainability and risk management side of tourism in active volcanic and geothermal areas. In many regions, risk management planning and policies presently include only local residents and communities who are living close to active volcanoes. Temporary visitors, although they number millions each year, are generally ignored despite the fact that they contribute significantly to the economy in many countries where volcano tourism constitutes one of the main sources of revenue from tourism.

This book provides a source of reference material for a number of significant volcanic and/or geothermal destinations, in both chapter and in case study format, although it is impossible to cover every destination worldwide in one book as there are simply too many to choose from. It will take several publications to do justice to an emerging tourism sector which offers so much for the study of natural, cultural, historical and geological heritage as well as extreme tourism experiences.

Trips to volcanoes are often independent from seasons and climate, offer unique natural environments and are destinations with a wide range of recreation and leisure opportunities. The more recent trend towards nature based *geotourism* has caused an increase of interest in volcanic and geothermal destinations and their rich environmental heritage. The unique landforms of highly active volcanoes and geothermal areas are especially of interest to travellers who enjoy a more adventurous holiday.

For a number of years we have observed people visiting active and dormant volcanoes. Over time it became evident that volcano tourism, although not generally (or not as yet) known by this name, is a rather popular sub-sector of nature-based geotourism and ecotourism. What also became obvious is the apparent lack of safety guidelines and recommendations for visitors in many of these active environments. Although many national parks and other protected areas provide information for visitors, including warning signs, announcements and educational videos, these are not always made available in more than the local language. This omission makes it difficult to raise the level of awareness of every tourist regarding possible accidents and emergencies because danger is either ignored or not perceived as such due to a lack of comprehensive information. In fact tourists may not even be aware that they are visiting an active environment.

As a tourism sector with the potential for sustainability of the environment under favourable conditions and best practice management volcano tourism has much to offer for future development, with many untapped markets like smaller island communities in the process of developing volcano and geothermal tourism sites. However, the risk management aspects related to temporary visitors discussed in this book need to be addressed as a matter of urgency and applied at an international level before these destinations become a tourism reality so that the problems faced by existing destinations in this regard are not replicated elsewhere.

The close relationship of volcanic tourism with hot spring and spa tourism is also used as a marketing tool in many areas where the volcanic environment is the cause of renewable geothermal resources. Worldwide, natural hot springs are used for both their visual impact as well as their role in health and wellness. In combination with volcanic landscapes and geothermal 'wonderlands' these are powerful tourist drawcards with increasing visitor numbers and good prospects for future development on the condition that safety issues are appropriately addressed and suitable risk management strategies for visitors are implemented.

We hope that this first contribution to the literature on volcano tourism provides some valuable insights for the reader and encourages further research into the area of volcano and geothermal tourism.

Patricia Erfurt-Cooper
Malcolm Cooper
January 2010

List of Acronyms and Abbreviations

AAPIT	Azienda Autonoma Provinciale per l'Incremento Turistico
ADAS	automatic data acquisition system
APT	Provincial Tourism Agency of Catania
BGS	British Geological Survey
CDEM	Civil Defence Emergency Management
CONAF	Corporation Nacional Forestal
COPD	chronic obstructive pulmonary disease
DCP	Development Concept Plan
DOT	Department of Tourism
DRC	Democratic Republic of the Congo
ECVP	European Cenozoic Volcanic Province
EIS	Environmental Impact Statement
EPA	Environmental Protection Agency
ERLAWS	Eastern Ruapehu Lahar and Warning System
GDP	gross domestic product
HACE	high altitude cerebral edema
HAPE	high altitude pulmonary edema
IAVCEI	International Association of Volcanology and Chemistry of the Earth's Interior
IDNDR	International Decade for Natural Disaster Reduction
IGN	National Geographic Institute
ISDR	International Strategy for Disaster Reduction
JMA	Japan Meteorological Agency
LAC	Limits of Acceptable Change
LGA	Lochaber Geopark Association
MAV	Museo Archeologico Virtuale
MCDEM	Ministry of Civil Defence & Emergency Management
MINAE	Ministerio de Ambiental y Energia
MVO	Montserrat Volcano Observatory
NEPVA	National Emergency Plan for the Vesuvian Area
NN	Nicolosi Nord (Etna tourist station)
NPS	National Park Service
NRA	National Recreation Area
PHIVOLCS	Philippine Institute of Volcanology and Seismology
PNR	parc naturel régional
PP	Piano Provenzana (Etna tourist station)
SNH	Scottish Natural Heritage
TVZ	Taupo Volcanic Zone
UNESCO	United Nations Educational, Scientific and Cultural Organization
UNISDR	United Nations International Strategy for Disaster Reduction
UNWTO	United Nations World Tourism Organization
USGS	United States Geological Survey
VEI	Volcanic Explosivity Index
VIM	Visitor Impact Management
VMSG	Volcanic and Magmatic Studies Group
VNP	Virunga National Park
WHO	World Health Organization
WOVO	World Organization of Volcanic Observatories

Part I

Introduction

1

Introduction

Patricia Erfurt-Cooper

Introduction to volcano and geothermal tourism
The context of volcano and geothermal tourism

This book presents a first collection of chapters looking more closely at a tourism sector that includes travelling to volcanic and geothermal destinations as part of the new quest for sustainable tourism. Volcano tourism is particularly popular in combination with recreational activities such as skiing, hiking, trekking, climbing and visiting hot springs, as well as many other outdoor activities (Erfurt-Cooper and Cooper, 2009), and with the need for the strengthening of attitudes and practices relating to environmentally sound tourism. Volcano and geothermal tourism as a whole are under-reported in the literature as yet, but the tourist numbers for this special interest area are rising, with study tours and field trips being offered to volcanic destinations worldwide. While in fact volcano tourism has been widespread in European countries such as Italy, Greece and Iceland for centuries, greater mobility and a personal desire for more information about these unique and active landforms are key motivations behind the growing interest of 21st century tourists in volcanic and geothermal environments.

Volcano tourism comes in many different guises – in some cases people are not even aware that they could be close to active volcanism, while for others touring active volcanic and geothermal environments is part of the trip agenda and many visitors will undertake a short side trip to volcanic landscapes to fill in a day – or sometimes less – depending on the location as part of a tour to a specific destination. For the purpose of this book we define volcano tourism as follows:

> *Volcano tourism involves the exploration and study of active volcanic and geothermal landforms. Volcano tourism also includes visits to dormant and extinct volcanic regions where remnants of activity attract visitors with an interest in geological heritage.*

Volcanoes are described as 'awesome and spectacular examples of natural change' (Simkin et al, 1981, pvii) and as 'nature's most exciting and deadly shows' with 'their unpredictability and intensity matched only by their visibly stunning bursts of activity' (Bourseillier and Durieux, 2002). Volcanic eruptions are portrayed by Sigurdsson and Lopes-Gautier (2000, p1289) as 'one of nature's most awesome spectacles' with some volcanoes being exciting and dramatic symbols for a nation, for example, Vesuvius in Italy and Fuji in Japan (Fisher et al, 1997). A variety of benefits from volcanoes result in sustainable livelihoods in some locations (Kelman and Mather, 2008); these include thermal springs and geothermal energy, tourism, geothermally based agriculture and mining, whereby income can be combined with visiting hot springs or a geothermal power station (Iceland, New Zealand). Sigurdsson et al (2000) provide a summary of the literature promoting volcanic benefits like geothermal resources and tourism resulting from volcanism. Perry and Lindell (1990) suggested nearly 20 years ago that risks from volcanism are directly related to the beauty and recreational quality of an area and its power to attract visitors.

Volcano tourism is an important sector of geotourism, which includes the geodiversity and the geological heritage of unique landscape features (Dowling and Newsome, 2006), but in particular the attractions of active volcanic and geothermal environments, and it is not uncommon that some tourists, who are looking for a more adventurous getaway, are increasingly planning their travels around active volcanoes (Brace, 2000). Between 550 volcanoes with historically recorded activity (Edelmann, 2000; Schmincke, 2006) and possibly up to 1500 volcanoes in total which are believed to have erupted historically and/or during the Holocene (Smithsonian, 2009) are currently classed as active (Figure 1.1 indicates major locations); subaqueous volcanoes are not included in these figures.

The attraction of volcanoes can be appreciated from the fact that they are included in 18 of Japan's 28 national parks (Sakaguchi, 2005). A large number of these fascinating landforms have gained in worldwide popularity for a variety of reasons. Firstly, volcano tourism generally synergizes well with other forms of tourism such as hot spring

tourism (health and wellness), ecotourism and adventure tourism (Erfurt-Cooper and Cooper, 2009). Secondly, volcano tourism includes several specific leisure and recreational activities such as skiing (e.g. Hokkaido, New Zealand), hiking and trekking, mountaineering (e.g. Cascades, Andes), and camping – all of which form a perfect combination with exploring adventurous or unique destinations. Also, natural hot springs with or without spa and resort facilities are often associated with and in close proximity to volcanic and geothermal activity, and many volcano tourists enjoy a relaxing soak in natural hot spring pools. Sampling of the local cuisine is generally one of the additional selling points. A third reason for an increase in volcano tourist numbers is the growing ease of access to remote destinations and the affordability for budget travellers (e.g. backpackers in Mesoamerica, New Zealand). A fourth reason is the growing interest in the natural environment, which includes not only the biosphere or ecosphere, but also the geosphere with an extraordinary natural heritage increasingly protected in national parks (e.g. Yellowstone, Tongariro, Mt Fuji) and

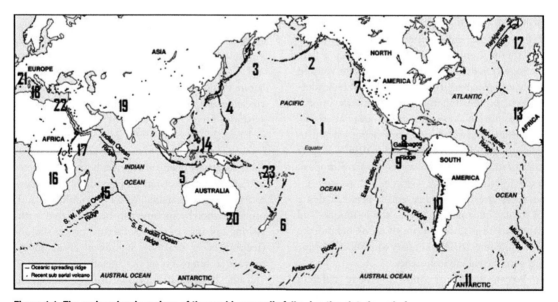

Figure 1.1 The main volcanic regions of the world, generally following the plate boundaries

Notes: The numbers indicate tourist destinations of significance: 1) Hawai'i, USA; 2) Aleutians, Alaska; 3) Kamchatka, Russia; 4) Japan; 5) Indonesia; 6) New Zealand; 7) Cascades, USA; 8) Galapagos, Ecuador; 10) Andean Volcanoes, Chile, Argentina, Peru, Bolivia, Colombia; 11) Deception Island, Antarctica; 12) Iceland; 13) Cape Verde, Independent; Canary Islands, Spain; Azores and Madeira, Portugal; 14) Philippines; 15) Reunion, Africa; 16) Congo and Tanzania; 17) Ethiopia; 18) Italy; 19) Iran; 20) Australia; 21) Germany and France (dormant); 22) Greece and Turkey.

world heritage sites, and as national or global geoparks (e.g. China, Europe, Australia). For a list of world heritage sites including active and dormant volcanic landforms please see Table 1.1.

The volcano tourist

Although volcano tourism is becoming increasingly popular in many countries worldwide (Hansell and Oppenheimer, 2004), the academic and general literature covering volcanic and geothermal environments rarely mentions tourism in volcanic regions. Nevertheless, volcano viewing in active and dormant areas and the exploration of geothermal landscapes are frequently included as sightseeing activities and part of the trip agendas for many travellers every year. Quite often the visit to an active or dormant volcano or to a geothermal park is a choice made spontaneously closer to the destination and depends on various factors such as how much time is involved, the current state of volcanic or geothermal activity, the weather, ease of access, transport and distance to cover, plus possible requirements for special equipment. Level of fitness is also an important factor, as people often overestimate their personal endurance levels.

To attract visitors of different interest groups, tourism operators offer a diversity of tours with varying degrees of difficulty and risk factors. The most sought after attractions are glowing lava flows, strombolian eruptions and fissure eruptions. Night tours to popular viewing spots are organized for maximum effect. Associated activities range from trekking, hiking, climbing and skiing on or around active and dormant volcanoes, to canoeing, water skiing and fishing on crater lakes, depending on the state of environmental protection in individual areas.

Three main categories have been identified in which visits to volcanic and geothermal environments can be broadly classed with varying degrees of background information, knowledge and experience by the volcano tourist, as well as current activity levels of the destination, and any time frames involved:

1   Tours or day trips
    • organized for the majority of general sightseeing tourists of all ages, interests and backgrounds;
    • involve no strenuous exercise, easy to manage;
    • often included in travel and sightseeing itinerary, transport by bus or cruise ship (e.g. Iceland, Japan); and
    • are very casual about safety issues, but this group presents the majority of 'volcano tourists'.

2   Excursions and field trips
    • organized by or for interest groups, e.g. scientists and students, photographers;
    • can be day tours, several weeks or even longer;
    • involve awareness of potential risks and dangers at varying degrees; and
    • are a growing market segment of geotourism with special interests in volcanic and geothermal environments.

3   Expeditions and exploration
    • for experienced and fit participants able to cope with 'unusual experiences' along the way and prepared to go where only few or even nobody went before (e.g. Erta Ale, Nyiragongo, Kamchatka, Antarctica);
    • can be ultra-extreme, partly also depending on climate and season, and need special equipment and provisions;
    • involve a high awareness of potential dangers; and
    • are a minority group amongst tourists.

The first group most likely represents the majority of visitors to active volcanic and geothermal environments and has the lowest level of awareness about safety and potential hazards. The second group is a fast growing market sector with a medium level of awareness and the third group, although representing currently the minority of travellers, has probably the highest level of risk awareness. The fact that specially organized volcano tours and expeditions exist reflects the sheer determination of a growing number of people to visit areas with unusual volcanic or geothermal features.

Visitor motivations

The vast number of active volcanoes worldwide presents a huge potential for volcano tourism and is attracting many different types of visitors from all age groups and all socio-cultural and educational backgrounds. Apart from people with a general interest in nature and outdoor activities the following list gives a brief overview of tourist types generally encountered in volcanic and geothermal environments:

- tour groups and individuals (*domestic and international visitors*);
- couples, families and retirees;
- adventurers and thrill seekers;
- scientists and students;
- hikers, trekkers, climbers, skiers;
- repeat visitors (*mountain collectors*);
- geotourists and ecotourists; and
- photographers, writers.

Volcanoes are described by Lawrence (1997, p209) as having an incalculable aesthetic value with some people seeking spiritual renewal in their presence. The motives for visiting volcanic and geothermal environments are as varied as the visitor types and commonly there is a combination of more than one reason given by volcano tourists. The reasons listed below reflect some of the possible visitor motivations:

- sightseeing, part of trip agenda, leisure activity;
- mountain climbing, hiking, general outdoor activities;
- ambition and curiosity, photography;
- collecting information, field research;
- scientific interest, study, education; and
- collecting rock samples.

Other reasons may include the spontaneous decision to do something unusual to fill in time or the opportunity to gain access to an area that was inaccessible/out of bounds at a previous time. Travel to and within remote regions has become easier, information is more readily available and people are looking for a different experience. Some countries have opened their borders, while political instability in others is sealing off access to places of interest. Some countries and regions have built part of their economy on the revenue from tourism, often based on or including visits to volcanic and geothermal areas, for example, Iceland, New Zealand, Japan, Hawai'i and Central America.

In active regions volcanoes are among the primary drawcards for visitors, whereas in dormant areas they possibly play a more secondary role and are often combined with other attractions to increase visitor numbers and length of stay. Wildlife viewing (Yellowstone National Park), skiing (New Zealand) and hot spring bathing (Japan) are some examples which add extra value to volcano tourism.

During interviews at various sites with volcano tourists domiciled in non-volcanic areas several main attitudes towards volcanic hazards were identified: a) an active volcano is a must-see destination at least once in a lifetime; b) [they hope] nothing will happen while they are there [near an active volcano]; c) they rely on having enough time to get to a safer area in case of an eruption; d) they would not live near an active volcano if they had a choice. The last finding is in direct contrast to many residents in volcanic regions who either choose to live close to an active volcano or who have no choice at all in where they live.

A research paper by Gaillard (2008) confirms that what is written about risk management measures relates either to community-based disaster and risk management (Bankoff et al, 2004) or is based on citizens' risk perception of natural hazards in general (Davis and Ricci, 2004). Both types of assessment leave out millions of temporary visitors (e.g. volcano tourists) to active volcanic and geothermal environments every year.

The top ten attractions in volcanic and geothermal areas

The most sought after visitor attractions in volcanic environments include observing active lava flows from as close as possible, preferably after dark for the visual effect, and strombolian eruptions from a reasonably safe distance; both desires adding to the problems of risk management around active volcanoes. The risk perception of individuals can be severely influenced by the excitement of being close to an active volcano and may reduce alertness, as well as the level of necessary caution that they should observe. Listed below are ten popular volcanic and geothermal attractions which are most appealing to visitors of these unique natural environments:

1 active lava flows;
2 strombolian eruptions;
3 geysers and hot springs;
4 lava lakes;
5 crater lakes;
6 boiling ponds;
7 fumaroles and vents;
8 boiling mud pools;
9 hot rivers and streams;
10 sinter terraces.

Volcanic and geothermal manifestations often occur in clusters including several features, although on occasion it is only one particular attraction that draws the crowds to a location. In the case of geysers some famous names like *Old Faithful* (Yellowstone National Park) and the original *Geysir* (Iceland) come to mind, both of them located in areas that offer other geothermal attractions as well. Geothermal tourism is very closely related to volcano tourism and has an equally long tradition of attracting visitors to active environments with spectacular visual displays. Hot springs are a common by-product in volcanic areas and are used either as visual attractions such as geysers and boiling lakes, or as hot springs for spas and resorts. Bubbling mud pools and other geothermal features like sinter terraces (e.g. Pamukkale – Turkey, Mammoth Hot Springs – USA, Bai Shui Tai – China, Whakarewarewa – New Zealand) are known to attract large visitor numbers – but so do dormant volcanic features like crater lakes and old lava flows (e.g. Vulkaneifel – Germany).

For tourists interested in geological evidence of former volcanic activity there are many regions where they can observe basalt columns, bedded pyroclastic formations, rhyolitic tuffs, granite intrusions, rock faces containing flow banding, volcanic breccia, obsidian and pillow lava. Dormant or extinct volcanic areas have a lot to offer in the form of unique landscapes in many countries worldwide.

Volcano and geothermal tourism

Unique landscape features or geosites are attractions for tourists, either for passive recreation (Dowling

and Newsome, 2006) involving time spent among geological attractions without engaging in adventurous activities, or they are used by thrill seekers who want to take full advantage of active volcanic and geothermal destinations. For both visitor types volcanic environments such as national parks are playing an important role in modern education about volcanoes (Sigurdsson and Lopes-Gautier, 2000). In recent times geoparks on a national and global scale have been added to the protected zones containing volcanic and geothermal landforms, with a number of these also recognized as world heritage sites. Several of these sites are located in regions with volcanic and geothermal landforms as their main characteristics. Some of these have been previously known as national parks and have been nominated in order to protect them for future generations (Table 1.1).

Quite a few of these listed sites include currently dormant volcanic regions with remnants of volcanic activity, which nevertheless present a visual attraction and evidence of a more violent geophysical past. The trend towards geotourism includes the volcanic heritage of a region as a valuable learning tool and is in many cases supported by interpretive visitor centres, which are an option for people who do not want to physically venture close to active craters or climb summits such as Mt Teide in Spain (Hunt and Sanger, 2006), or Mt Aso and the new global geoparks of Mt Unzen and Mt Usu in Japan (see Chapters 9 and 10). Although world heritage sites are not always listed because of their geological heritage, this particular aspect is still part of the equation when considering the growing interest in geotourism. The overlap into other important tourism sectors includes the cultural and religious significance of volcanoes for local communities in countries such as Indonesia or Japan, symbolizing the spiritual connection between humans and the environment.

Expectations of possible eruptions and heightened activity appear to draw larger numbers of tourists to eruption centres (Sigurdsson and Lopes-Gautier, 2000; Morella, 2007). On the other hand remnant volcanic landforms, including presently dormant regions or areas assumed extinct located either in national parks or other designated areas are marketed as family friendly destinations

Table 1.1 This table lists some examples of world heritage sites including active and dormant volcanic landforms

World heritage site	Number	Country	Year listed
Galapagos Islands	1	Ecuador	1978
Yellowstone National Park	28	United States	1978
Ngorongoro Conservation Area	39	Africa	1979
Lord Howe Island Group	186	Australia	1982
Sangay National Park	260	Ecuador	1983
Rock Sites of Cappadocia	357	Turkey	1985
Gondwana Rainforests	368	Australia	1868
Giant's Causeway	369	Ireland	1986
Garajonay National Park	380	Canary Islands, Spain	1986
Kilimanjaro National Park	403	Kenya	1987
Hawai'i Volcanoes National Park	409	USA	1987
Tongariro National Park	421	New Zealand	1990
Pamukkale – Hierapolis	485	Turkey	1988
Mt Huangshan	547	China	1990
Ujung Kulon National Park	608	Indonesia	1991
Komodo National Park	609	Indonesia	1991
Joya de Cerén	675	El Salvador	1993
Rapanui National Park	715	Easter Islands, Chile	1995
Volcanoes of Kamchatka	765	Russian Federation	1996
Pompeii and Herculaneum	829	Italy	1997
Aeolian Islands	908	Italy	2000
Pico Island	1117	Azores, Portugal	2004
Tropical Rainforest Heritage	1167	Sumatra, Indonesia	2004
Teide National Park	1258	Tenerife, Spain	2007
Jeju Volcanic Island	1264	Korea	2007
Surtsey Island	1267	Iceland	2008

Note: The sites are listed in order of their inclusion in the world heritage list by year.
Source: Compiled by author

Table 1.2 National parks in the United States that include mainly volcanic and geothermal features

Destination examples (US)	Annual visitor numbers (2008)
Yellowstone National Park	3,066,580
Hawai'i Volcanoes National Park	1,270,538
Hot Springs National Park	1,238,147
Haleakala National Park	1,185,068
Mt Rainier National Park	1,163,227
Crater Lake National Park	415,686
Lassen Volcanic National Park	377,361
Devil's Tower National Monument	336,303
Devil's Postpile National Monument	134,005
Lava Beds National Monument	120,076
North Cascades National Park	18,725

Source: Compiled by the author from National Park Service (2009)

Table 1.3 National parks and other protected areas worldwide incorporating volcanic and geothermal heritage

Destination Examples (Worldwide)	Annual Visitor Numbers
Fuji-Hakone-Izu National Park, Japan	103,000,000 (2004)
Teide National Park, Spain	3,540,195 (2004)
Vesuvius National Park, Italy	1,000,000 (2004)
Tongariro National Park, New Zealand	1,000,000 (2004)
Giants Causeway, Ireland	500,000 (2004)
Etna Provincial Park, Italy	240,000 (2004)
Geyser, Iceland	122,000 (2004)
Arenal Volcano National Park, Costa Rica	840,000 p/a

Source: Compiled by the author from various sources

offering recreation and outdoor activities for everybody. The volcanic and geothermal destinations in Tables 1.2 and 1.3 give an indication of the importance of national parks with volcanic and geothermal landforms. Judging by the visitor numbers volcano tourism offers attractions for visitors on an impressive scale.

While a figure between 103 and 105 million annual visitors to the Fuji-Hakone-Izu National

Park in Japan may seem excessive, for destinations of great national interest this is completely normal considering the travel patterns of Japanese people. The cultural and religious significance of Mt Fuji evokes interest among artists and scholars as well as among the global scientific community in addition to the millions of short-term, mainly domestic, visitors. Of the well over 100 million visitors per year, on average approximately 300,000 actually climb to the top of Mt Fuji, with about one third of these being foreign visitors. However, the vast majority of visitors to the Fuji-Hakone-Izu National Park enjoy the view of Mt Fuji either from a distance or hike around the lower areas for brief recreational activities. Many visitors come for the hot spring resorts, the cherry blossoms in spring or the autumn season.

The demand for volcano and geothermal tourism

The fascination of people with active volcanoes and their occurrence worldwide has created a growing demand for volcano tourism, and this increases with heightened volcanic activity that paradoxically encourages longer stays, unless of course it becomes too dangerous. Geotourism could therefore well be the new medium for raising awareness about potentially dangerous environments without decreasing visitor numbers, as well as for education about risks and hazards in volcanic environments. Destination promotion through information exchange via the Internet (travel logs, blogs, articles, reports etc.) contributes to a raised awareness about volcanic and geothermal environments. As a result some areas are now specializing in catering exclusively for volcano tourists, and accommodation is made available as close to the volcanic activity as possible (i.e. Arenal Observatory Lodge, Costa Rica; Ruapehu Chalet, New Zealand; Mt Aso Ryokans, Japan; Etna B & Bs, Italy).

New volcano sports are also emerging on the slopes of more or less active mountains such as 'volcano boarding' or 'volcano surfing' (e.g. Cerro Negro, Nicaragua), which is promoted through virtual tourism on the Internet to give volcano tourists some ideas about what to expect at different destinations. Whether active, dormant or extinct – volcanoes are therefore major tourist magnets in many regions, because for many countries the revenue from nature-based tourism including volcano tourism means a substantial contribution to the economy. However, the objective should be to make volcano tourism as safe as possible with existing safety guidelines for residents in active volcanic and geothermal regions to be analysed as to how they can be adapted for temporary visitors.

Volcanoes in history and culture

Volcano and geothermal tourism possibly goes back much further than we think, although most reliable documentation in the West points to the onset of the European 'Grand Tour' around 1660 to 1670, when volcanoes were included in the trip agenda. However, it is now known that the people of earlier civilizations settled close to active volcanoes (Grattan, 2006), in many cases most likely to benefit from the hot springs commonly found in the proximity of active volcanoes worldwide (Erfurt-Cooper and Cooper, 2009, pp49–59). The Romans for example, are known to have used geothermal springs on islands like Ischia or visited the Campi Flegrei for leisure and recreation, similar to their neighbours in Greece and Turkey, where volcanic hot springs provided attractive destinations. Volcanoes such as Vesuvius attracted visitors throughout the 17th and 18th centuries, when young and affluent Europeans undertook the 'Grand Tour', which saw them travelling, learning and socializing for extended periods of time (Fisher et al, 1997; Sigurdsson and Lopes-Gautier, 2000). Consequently volcano tourism is not new but has emerged as a separate tourism sector which is attracting increasing numbers of visitors worldwide. Japan, New Zealand, Iceland, Greece and Italy are a few examples of countries with a longstanding tradition in volcano tourism, although in Italy the legacy of Herculaneum and Pompeii is a grim reminder of the destructive power of volcanic eruptions (Fisher et al, 1997). And Krakatau, Indonesia also has a fixed place in the dramatic history of volcanic eruptions; visitors were fascinated by the unusual spectacles displayed before the mountain erupted in 1883 in a final cataclysm (Furneaux, 1964). These forms of epic volcanic events are described by De Boer and Sanders (2002) in several case studies examining the relationship of humans and volcanoes in history.

In ancient times volcanoes were seen by many cultures as the entrance to the underworld or hell, ruled by subterranean forces, and were thus regarded with suspicion and awe (Bullard, 1977; Fisher et al, 1997; Edelmann, 2000; Sigurdsson and Lopes-Gautier, 2000; Cashman and Cronin, 2008; Dove,

2008). Myths about demons and religious worship of volcanoes are still widespread (Schmincke, 2006) and it is therefore not surprising that all sorts of sacrificial offerings have been considered beneficial in the appeasement of ill-tempered spirits (Fisher et al, 1997; Lawrence, 1997; Davison, 2003; Holland, 2004; Dalton, 2005; Marti and Ernst, 2005; Cochrane, 2006; Wockner, 2006; Marshall, 2008a) thought to inhibit active volcanoes in many countries. Even human sacrifices were in some regions included in the past (Henderson, 2007; Cashman and Giordano, 2008; Alvarado and Soto, 2008; Viramonte and Incer-Barquero, 2008; Encyclopaedia Britannica, 2009; Montgomery, n.d.) to influence the mood of the volcano gods in order to avoid a disaster. The success rate of such activities undoubtedly left a lot to be desired!

Volcanoes in the literature

Numerous books have been published about volcanoes and their various geophysical backgrounds, with descriptions generally including a range of popular locations, their eruption history, the numbers of fatalities over time, and frequent references to potential dangers for people living close to active volcanoes. Some publications are meant to encourage further research and interest in volcanism (Wood and Kienle, 1990) or to introduce non-geologists to the history of certain volcanic or geothermal areas (Fritz, 2004), while others are directed at the general reader who is interested in volcanoes and the earth sciences (Rosi et al, 2003; Lopes, 2005). Over the last few years a number of books have been published because according to some authors millions of people find 'super volcanoes' especially fascinating (Savino and Jones, 2007). Some of these 'super volcanoes' have been used in recent publications in a rather sensationalist style: on the one hand raising awareness of a potential danger, on the other the fear factor is used to sell books with catchy subtitles mentioning '*ticking time bombs*'. While this categorization of certain volcanoes may well be the case – the preferred option is to have experienced scientists and volcanologists to determine this, not travel agents or media outlets. Without relevant qualifications in appropriate fields of science to give such publications some weight, the marketing of scare tactics and doomsday

Figure 1.2　Examples of informative guides to volcanic regions worldwide, although many focus on individual countries or areas

Source: Collected by author

scenarios does not offer any solutions to potential risk problems, or contribute in a constructive way to risk management.

It appears that, with a few exceptions, such as Leonard et al (2008), not much scholarly research has been carried out related to the field of tourism in volcanic areas – in particular not with regards to the potential risk situation of millions of annual visitors to active volcanoes and associated landforms like geothermal features. The sector of volcano and geothermal tourism does however receive attention from authors of guidebooks (see Figure 1.2). Visual and interpretive visitor guides covering volcanic regions for the general public (Fisher et al, 1997; Edelmann, 2000; Kelsey, 2001; Rosi et al, 2003; Frank, 2003; Forst, 2004; Fritz, 2004; Fritsch, 2005; Lopes, 2005; Secor, 2005) abound, and there are a number of field guides for people with a basic knowledge in geology or volcanology (Guðmundsson and Kjartansson, 1996; Kilburn and McGuire, 2001; Scarth and Tanguy, 2001; Thordarson and Höskuldsson, 2002). Coffee table style books which showcase the unique landforms of volcanic and geothermal environments (Bourseillier and Durieux, 2002; O'Meara, 2008) are used to create additional interest in these areas.

Popular ways of sharing knowledge about a certain area are the walking and climbing guides, for example, by Kelsey (2001); Dungey and Whytlaw (2007); and Secor (2005), or books covering suitable routes for field trips into volcanic and geothermal environments by authors such as Kilburn and McGuire (2001), and Thordarson and Höskuldsson (2002). Most of these cover the basic geology necessary to understand and interpret the landforms of a chosen area. Depending on the current state of activity these books contain warnings and occasionally guidelines for personal safety as well as suggestions as to the right equipment needed depending on altitude, season and climate. In the case of dormant environments books describe the geological heritage of an area, thereby revealing the episodes of former volcanic activity (Gannon, 2008).

Books and the Internet do offer advice on risk prevention, but only to those people who access these sources; the majority of travellers do not collect books about volcanoes worldwide or search the Internet for safety guidelines, but it is this majority that needs the extra information to be on the safe side when travelling in volcanic and geothermal areas.

Volcanic activity is generally covered in the media when people's lives are in danger or infrastructure is damaged (Schmincke, 2006), but journalists also describe their own experiences on volcanoes, adding information and advice through their articles, which either appear in local or regional newspapers or globally online, for example, Carter (2002) reporting about Cotopaxi in Ecuador. Articles in travel journals encourage visits to volcanoes and hot springs and magazines such as *National Geographic* have repeatedly featured volcanic regions (e.g. Holland, 2004; Marshall, 2008a, 2008b), each time increasing awareness about destinations with volcanic activity, like for example, Hawai'i or Indonesia. But although the dangers inherent to active volcanoes and the number of fatalities in the past are discussed, more emphasis is placed on interesting socio-cultural relationships and the religious ceremonies carried out to appease the temperamental mountains '. . . where the slaughtering of goats is still considered a ceremony effective in preventing volcanoes like Merapi from erupting. . .' (Marshall, 2008a). Offerings are also commonly made by locals and visitors to Hawaiian volcanoes who come to worship and leave a variety of gifts for the goddess Pele, from chants and prayers to groceries and fake money (Holland, 2004).

The Internet also provides a vast amount of information related to volcanoes, in fact there is so much to choose from that it becomes increasingly difficult to locate the right information, as not all websites are updated and reliable. The number of websites featuring organized volcano tours from Alaska to Vanuatu, including most known volcanic regions worldwide is a clear indicator of the growing interest in volcano tourism, especially under the guidance of experienced tour operators (Heelan, 2004). Other websites use the Internet for promoting destinations like Vanuatu's island of Tanna where volcano tours are described as the most popular activity (Wantok Environment Centre, 2009). The most valuable information comes from sources such as the US Geological Survey in the form of online fact sheets and booklets giving an overview of the various volcanic hazards for visitors (US Geological Survey, 2000a; Hawai'i Volcano Observatory, 2005), an example for many regions elsewhere to use as a role model.

This type of information is important, because one of the main aims of this book is to point out the various risk factors from active volcanoes. Currently dormant environments have their own risk, not so much depending on volcanic activity, but more on the recreational interests of tourists. However, many volcanoes presently dormant are classed as active with varying degrees of potential for future eruptions. Even in Australia, where people generally think volcanic activity is not an issue, at least not on the mainland, scientists are suggesting to be prepared for a reawakening of some former volcanic centres where earthquakes have indicated tectonic activity.

Geophysical background: Volcanic and geothermal processes

The geophysical background to volcanoes will be only briefly mentioned here, because this book is not about the geology of volcanoes, but about their attraction for tourism. A short overview of the relevant landforms of volcanic and geothermal environments with examples of destinations where these can be found is considered as sufficient information.

Four main types of volcanoes are generally distinguished: shield volcanoes, composite or strato-volcanoes, cinder cones and lava domes. Because this book is looking at the tourism side of volcanic and geothermal environments the following list also includes volcanic landforms that are of interest for tourists, in alphabetical order with a number of examples for each of them:

- **Caldera** [Spanish for cauldron] – formed by the collapse of the roof of an empty magma chamber (*Aso and Aira Caldera, Japan; Ngorongoro Crater, Tanzania; Blake River Mega Caldera, Canada; Vilama Caldera, Argentina/Central Andes; Caldera de las Canadas/Teide, Tenerife/Spain; Santorini, Greece; Crater Lake, Oregon*).
- **Cinder cones/scoria cones** – commonly straight-sided cone-shaped hills built from airfall deposits of fragmented pyroclastic material such as particles from congealed lava (*Pu'u O'o, Hawai'i; Paricutin, Mexico; Eldfell, Iceland; Red Rock and Mt Scoria, Australia; Wizard Island, Crater Lake/Oregon; Cerro Negro, Nicaragua; Kometsuka/Aso, Japan*).
- **Composite or strato-volcanoes** – symmetrical and steep-sided cones built up of alternating layers of lava, ash and other pyroclastic material (*Snaefellsjökull, Iceland; St Helens and Mt Baker, Washington; Shasta, California; Mt Hood, Oregon; Mt Fuji and Mt Usu, Japan; Cotopaxi, Ecuador; Shishaldin, Alaska; Mayon, Philippines; Vesuvius and Stromboli, Italy; Nevado del Ruiz, Colombia; Damavand, Iran; Merapi, Indonesia*).
- **Crater** – bowl-shaped or funnel-like openings at the mouth of a volcano, created by volcanic activity, e.g. summit craters, pit craters, maars, diatremes.
- **Crater rows** – can be produced along fissures (*Leirhnjúkur and Laki, Iceland; Waimangu Valley, New Zealand*).
- **Decade volcanoes** – selection of active volcanoes chosen for more in-depth research to raise the awareness about volcanoes and their potential hazards (*Avachinsky-Koryaksky, Kamchatka; Colima, Mexico; Etna, Italy; Galeras, Colombia; Mauna Loa, Hawai'i; Merapi, Indonesia; Nyiragongo, Democratic Republic of the Congo; Mt Rainier, Washington; Sakurajima, Japan; Santa Maria/Santiaguito, Guatemala; Santorini, Greece; Taal, Philippines; Teide, Canary Islands, Spain; Ulawun, Papua New Guinea; Unzen, Japan; Vesuvius, Italy*).
- **Hydrothermal vent or black smoker** – continuously spouting under water at high temperatures enriched with minerals, first discovered in 1977 (*commonly found along mid-ocean ridges*).
- **Igneous province and flood basalt** – regions where large volcanic eruptions have deposited thick layers, usually basalt, covering expansive surface areas (*Siberian Traps, Ethiopian Highlands; Deccan Traps, India; Brazilian Highlands; Newer Volcanic Provinces, Australia; North Atlantic Igneous Province; Columbia River Plateau*).
- **Island arc volcanoes** – see volcanic arc.
- **Lava cave, lava tube** – remaining cave which forms after lava flows stop and leave behind a lava tunnel (tube) which can be up to several kilometres long (*Undara Volcanic National Park, Australia; Hawai'i Volcanoes National Park; Jeju Island, Korea; Canada; Iceland; Chile; New Zealand*).
- **Lava dome** – created by slow extrusion of viscous lava from a volcanic vent (*El Chichón, Mexico; Unzen, Tsurumi, Yufudake, Showashinzan, Japan; Soufrière Hills, Montserrat; Novarupta, Redoubt and Augustine, Alaska; Bezymianny, Kamchatka, St Helens, Washington; Santa Maria, Guatemala; Tarawera, New Zealand*).
- **Lava lake** – molten lava held in a volcanic crater; active lava lakes, especially permanent ones, are very rare (*Ambrym, Vanuatu; Erta Ale, Ethiopia; Kilauea, Hawai'i; Erebus, Antarctica; Nyiragingo, D.R. of the Congo; Villarica, Chile*).
- **Lava plateau** – formed by sheets of lava flows pouring from fissures and creating broad plateaus or flood basalts; compare igneous provinces (*Iceland, North America, Argentina, Japan, New Zealand*).
- **Maars, tuff rings and diatremes** – volcanic craters formed as a result of violent phreato-magmatic eruptions, often filled with water (*Germany, Vulkaneifel; France, Auvergne; Australia, North Queensland, Victoria and South Australia; Ethiopia; Turkey; New Mexico; North America; Alaska; Patagonia, South America; Israel; Iran; Japan; Indonesia; Chile; Bolivia; New Zealand; Krashenninikov, Kamchatka*).

- **Mud volcanoes** – similar to magma volcanoes, they can erupt by channelling boiling water, steam or pressurized gas to the surface. They can be related to oil and gas reserves and sometimes erupt in flames (Gallagher, 2003) (*Iran, Indonesia, Japan, New Zealand, Russia, Italy, China, Pakistan, Romania, Canada, North America, Colombia, Venezuela*).
- **Moberg or tuya** – see sub-glacial volcano.
- **Pseudo craters** – also known as rootless cones formed by exploding steam when lava flows over wetlands (*Skútustaðagígar, Iceland*).
- **Rift valley** – see volcanic rift.
- **Shield volcanoes** – built mainly from multi-directional lava flows of Hawaiian type eruptions into gently sloping landforms comparable to a broad shield (*Mauna Loa, Mauna Kea, Hawai'i; Cascades, Oregon; Erta Ale, Ethiopia; Easter Islands; Hierro, Canary Islands; Skjaldbreiður, Iceland; Newer Volcanic Provinces, Australia; Santorini, Greece; Tolbachik, Kamchatka; Rangitoto, New Zealand; Fernandina, Galapagos*).
- **Sub-glacial volcano** – table mountain created by a volcanic eruption underneath a glacier (*Tuya Butte, Canada; Herðubreid, Iceland; Viedma, Argentina*).
- **Sub-marine or subaqueous volcanoes** – occur frequently along mid-ocean ridges, sometimes producing islands (*Surtsey – Iceland; Hawaiian Emperor Seamount Chain; Tonga – Home Reef*).
- **Super volcanoes** – according to some scientists it is only a matter of time until one of them will erupt and cause a disaster of great magnitude (Cas, 2005; Watts, 2007) (*Mt Toba, Sumatra/Indonesia; Aniachak, Alaska; Taupo, New Zealand; Yellowstone, Wyoming; Tambora, Indonesia; Vilama Caldera, Argentina/Central Andes*).
- **Volcanic arc** – chain of volcanic islands, usually with strong seismic activity related to underlying tectonic processes (*Japanese island chains; Aleutian Volcanic Arc; Marianas Arc; Kuril Island Arc; Lesser Antilles; Kermadic Islands; Tonga Islands; Sunda Island Arc; Solomon Islands; Philippine Islands*).
- **Volcanic belt** – region of volcanic and geothermal activity (*Pacific Ring of Fire; Garibaldi VB, Canada; Andean VB; Trans-Mexican VB; Taupo VB; Okhotsk-Chukotka VB; Pontide VB, Turkey; Wrangell VB, Alaska; Central Iranian VB*).
- **Volcanic field** (*Auckland VF, New Zealand; Oku VF, Cameroon; Tuya VF, British Columbia/Canada; Clear Lake VF, California*).
- **Volcanic fissure** – fissure vent, fissure volcano, linear or elongated fracture of the ground from which lava, pyroclastics or gas are erupting, can be up to several kilometres long (*Krafla, Eldgjá, Laki – Iceland; Hawai'i; Great Rift Valley; Tobalchik – Kamchatka; Ethiopia; Komagatake – Japan*).
- **Volcanic rift** – a region marked by volcanic action, e.g. long linear cracks in the Earth's crust which occur where magma reaches the surface (Ritchie and Gates, 2001) (*Canary Islands; Hawai'i; Iceland; East African Rift; Tonga Arc; Antarctica*).

The volcanic features listed above include quite a few interesting volcanic destinations for tourists, although not all of them are accessible to the general public – for example, submarine hydrothermal vents or black smokers. Fascinating as the latter are, access to these is only possible via submersible observation crafts, which are in the exclusive service of science.

Besides volcanic landforms, geothermal features are visual attractions in their own right and are commonly found either in the neighbourhood of volcanoes, both active and dormant, or they originate from artesian springs and bores (e.g. Guarani Aquifer, South America; Great Artesian Basin, Australia). Hot springs do not need magma bodies to acquire their high temperatures. As water passes through subterranean rocks, the geothermal temperature gradient combined with time and pressure at depth play a role in the formation of hot springs rich in minerals and metallic trace elements. The effects of heated rocks below the surface can cause a number of processes, some of which manifest themselves as geothermal phenomena such as hot springs, fumaroles, geysers, boiling lakes, heated streams and bubbling mud ponds (Erfurt-Cooper and Cooper, 2009, pp130–155). Some examples below highlight the most interesting geothermal features with some examples of destination countries:

- geysers (*Iceland, New Zealand, USA, South and Central America, Japan*);
- boiling lakes and ponds (*Japan, USA, New Zealand, Iceland*);

- hot streams and waterfalls (*New Zealand, Central America, Japan, Iceland, USA*);
- boiling and bubbling mud pools (*New Zealand, Japan, Iceland, USA*);
- hydrothermal mud ponds (*Japan, Iceland, New Zealand, USA*);
- sinter terraces (*China, Turkey, New Zealand, USA*);
- steam vents and fumaroles (*USA, New Zealand, Italy, Alaska, Hawai'i, South and Central America, Iceland, France*); and
- hot springs for spas and pools (*worldwide*).

Although geothermal areas may not include the same potential risk as active volcanoes, visitors to these environments should also be considered in risk management strategies.

Risk management: How great is the risk factor?

Demographic changes and urbanization have led to increased exposure of people to volcanic hazards, with many large cities around the world located close to volcanoes classed as active. In fact 9 per cent of the global population (between 450 and 500 million people) live within 100km of active volcanoes (Chester et al, 2001; Small and Naumann 2001; Mayell, 2002; Grattan, 2006; Hansell et al, 2006; Horwell and Baxter, 2006) and are presently considered to be at risk from volcanic hazards. While the preference of residents for the quality of life in a certain area often outweighs the volcanic risk (Gregg et al, 2004), temporary visitors or tourists are not always aware of any potential dangers from volcanic activity. While much is done to educate the local public about any potential volcanic hazards in the vicinity of their cities or villages, some thought should be directed at the millions of annual visitors to volcanic regions. With volcano viewing often on the sightseeing agenda, visitors to these destinations may not all be going close to active volcanic areas, but they certainly are in the vicinity of possible volcanic hazards. The hot spring town of Baños in Ecuador, for example, lies in a high danger zone in the case of a major eruption of the nearby volcano Tungurahua, which has been constantly active since 1999 (Ecuador-Travel.Net, 2009; Seach,

2009a; The Best of Ecuador.com, 2009). After Baños had been evacuated for a considerable time in 1999, the community leaders organized the return of the residents despite a still-standing evacuation order and started to promote tourism again to revive the economy, although public safety for both residents and for tourists was compromised (Lane et al, 2003).

In 2006 in the Philippines extremely heavy rainfall remobilized volcanic debris on the slopes of Mt Mayon causing major lahars which caught most people unawares, taking over 1200 lives and destroying property in communities and urbanized areas downstream. The massive lahar flows arrived suddenly, carrying large boulders, and buried houses and left fields barren (Paguican et al, 2009). These two examples show the contrasting sides of volcanic hazards; the danger a community is prepared to live with and the sudden and rather unexpected event that does not leave any choice. In both cases temporary visitors can get caught up in catastrophic situations, but in cases like this not being a local resident also has the added disadvantage that important information in case of volcanic activity is generally not available for visitors. Language barriers often exacerbate any problems, as well as the possible exclusion from local emergency, rescue and evacuation systems that do not account for tourists, as their numbers fluctuate. The following list provides some examples (in alphabetical order, not in order of potential danger) of small and large cities close to active volcanoes:

- Auckland, New Zealand (*Auckland Volcanic Fields*)
- Anchorage, Alaska (*Redoubt*)
- Baños, Ecuador (*Tungurahua*)
- Goma, DR Congo (*Nyiragongo*)
- Jogjakarta, Indonesia (*Merapi*)
- Kagoshima, Japan (*Sakurajima*)
- Kumamoto, Japan (*Aso and Unzen*)
- Managua, Nicaragua (*Masaya*)
- Manila, Philippines (*Pinatobu*)
- Mexico City, Mexico (*Popocatepetl*)
- Nagasaki and Shimabara, Japan (*Unzen*)
- Naples, Italy (*Vesuvius*)
- Oita and Beppu, Japan (*Tsurumi*)
- Pasto, Colombia (*Galeras*)

- Quito, Ecuador (*Cotopaxi, Guagua Pichincha, Pululagua*)
- Rotorua, New Zealand (*Mt Edgecumbe, Tarawera*)
- San Jose, Costa Rica (*Arenal*)
- Seattle, USA (*Mt Rainier*)
- Tokyo, Japan (*Fuji*)
- Toya, Japan (*Usu*)

In some regions more than one active volcano presents potential hazards for residents and visitors. This often includes regions where volcano tourism is one of the major sources of economic revenue and visitors accept a certain risk in exchange for unique and adventurous experiences on an active volcano. Destructive natural events such as volcanic eruptions are a risk factor with catastrophic potential which is particularly high in developing countries (Chester et al, 2001), where the tourism sector is highly vulnerable to natural disaster (Méheux and Parker, 2006), for example, through the destruction of tourism infrastructure as has happened on Montserrat (Government of Montserrat, 2008).

Every year millions of tourists visit active volcanic and geothermal environments, quite commonly without sufficient awareness regarding the potential dangers they could face in an emergency situation such as an unexpected eruption. Informative texts about volcanic regions rarely focus on safety guidelines for tourists, although some books (e.g. Fisher et al, 1997; Edelmann, 2000; Lopes, 2005; Rosi et al, 2003) do offer recommendations on what type of safety precautions should be taken before setting out into hazardous locations. The Geological Survey of the United States (USGS, 2000b) and the National Park Service offer educational fact sheets via the Internet for visitors of active volcanic areas such as Hawai'i, for example, because the popular activity of lava viewing can be hazardous and common sense alone is not enough for a safe experience. In these cases people have the opportunity to get valuable information before they arrive, but in most other situations the required information is buried in local planning schemes or just does not exist.

Potential risk factors around volcanoes

Volcanic eruptions may not be as common as other types of natural hazards such as extreme weather or floods (Johnston and Ronan, 2000; Chester et al, 2001; Seach, 2009b), which can happen anywhere to unsuspecting tourists, or the risks and hazards broadly applying to mountain regions in varying degrees – for example, hiking and climbing accidents, hypothermia and altitude sickness, avalanches of snow or rocks, sudden fog and getting lost. However, by adding volcanic and geothermal activity the scenario can change significantly and at least another handful of potential problems should be considered seriously before venturing into unknown territory. Volcanic hazards refer to ash and tephra fall, pyroclastic flows and lahars (Blong, 2000), with the hazard of lahars continuing for months or even years after an eruption, as they can be triggered by rainfall at any time (Table 1.4).

In the case of an unexpected eruption, ballistic objects in various sizes and at various temperatures can inflict serious injury or even death. Lava flows as seen in documentaries from Hawai'i may be the least threatening event due to their comparatively slow movement although lava from Nyiragongo (Chapter 2) and Piton de la Fournaise (Furnace Peak) can flow at higher speeds due to its low viscosity. Pyroclastic flows and pyroclastic density currents, however, (avalanches of glowing ash and rocks), cannot be outrun or hidden from with a reasonable chance of survival, and have caused the most deaths and injuries in volcanic eruptions (Marti and Ernst, 2005; Schmincke, 2006). They can travel at speeds up to several hundred kilometres per hour and can reach temperatures of up to 800–1000°C. While pyroclastic flows seem to follow gullies and valleys downhill, pyroclastic surges can move uphill and over ridges, which makes them extremely dangerous and unpredictable (Wright and Pierson, 1992; Myers and Brantley, 1995).

Other unpleasant and life threatening experiences can originate from glacier bursts or jökulhlaups when subglacial volcanoes erupt and release melt water across the countryside. Unexpected eruptions, ashfall, lahars, mudslides, landslides, gas emissions and toxic fumes, earthquakes and thermal burns from hot springs

Table 1.4 Volcanic hazards

Type of volcanic hazard	Potential dangers and effects
Acid rain	Rain turns acidic when falling through clouds of volcanic gas or acid particle emissions. Eye and skin irritant, affects vegetation and water quality (Hansell et al, 2006).
Ash	Of all eruptive hazards ashfall can affect the most people because of the wide areas that can be covered (Blong, 1996). Ash is a collective term for fine pyroclasts of a size <2mm diameter, that can affect the respiratory and cardiovascular systems and is irritating to eyes and skin (Hansell et al, 2006). Ash can also destroy vegetation, crops, block roads, block drains, watercourses and cause damage to equipment. In large eruptions, the danger to aircraft is considerable and particles can impact on climate and weather (Chester et al, 2001).
Ballistics, bombs, blocks	Rocks and lava lumps ejected during major and minor eruptions causing injuries from impact and burns (Hansell et al, 2006).
Gas emissions	Volcanic gases present hazards to human health and vegetation. The effects of SO_2, HCl, CO_2 and H_2S are at their most severe close to a volcano or a hydrothermal vent. Hydrogen sulphide (H_2S) also occurs near some hot springs and has caused fatalities in several countries.
Jökulhlaup	Icelandic name for glacier burst, causing severe flooding by melt water, when a volcano erupts underneath a glacier or an ice cap.
Lahar, landslide, mudslide	Gravity-controlled mudflows carrying volcanic debris and ash mixed with water downhill. Dangerous because of their great speed, embedded large boulders and ability to wash away foundations of bridges and buildings. They can be triggered a long time after a volcanic eruption through heavy rainfall.
Lava flows	Lava flows are molten rock and generally move slowly along paths determined by topography and do not normally threaten life, because they allow time for evacuation. Lava flows cause destruction through burial and burning of property and vegetation and can cause thermal burns.
Laze (Lava haze)	HCl gas clouds form when lava flows enter the ocean and come in contact with seawater. Affects the respiratory system, irritates eyes and skin.
Pyroclastic flows	Pyroclastic flows and surges (Schmincke, 2006), can travel at several hundred km per hour and can even jump over ridges uphill. Maximum temperatures in such flows can reach over 800°C and can cause death, injury, destruction of buildings, impact damage and burial. They are usually caused by either a dome collapse or the collapse of an eruption column or a lateral blast.
Tephra, air fall deposits	They are created when blocks, bombs and lapilli are ejected from a volcanic eruption column or plume and can be deposited over long distances. The particle size can range from ash (<2mm) and lapilli (>2mm) to blocks and bombs (>greater than 64mm). Hazard can be severe, depending on the proximity to the volcano. Injuries and death through impact are possible.
Tsunami	Also known as 'sea wave' or 'harbour wave' and is caused by the displacement of water in the ocean by an earthquake or subaqueous eruption. A tsunami is not a tidal wave but can inundate vast stretches of low lying coastal areas.

Source: Compiled by author from various sources including Chester et al, 2001; Francis and Oppenheimer, 2004; Hansell et al, 2006

or steam vents, acid rain and ground deformation can make for rather unpleasant experiences. In some areas unreliable and unqualified tour guides offer mountain tours with great views, assuring the tourists that there is no danger involved and halfway up the mountain everybody has to run for their lives. These things have happened on various occasions and it is therefore paramount to err on the side of caution to avoid unpleasant or even life threatening experiences.

It is not just tourists that can get caught by unexpected eruptions; this has happened in the past to experienced and trained scientists working on active volcanoes because essential information appears to have been either misinterpreted or even ignored (Bruce, 2001), resulting in the death of several scientists as well as tourists and with severe injuries for the survivors. This makes it clear that even qualified and experienced scientists are not safe from fatal accidents, as another tragic event has shown at Mt Unzen (Japan, June 1991) when 43 people, including volcanologists Katia and Maurice Krafft, Harry Glicken and 40 journalists and taxi drivers perished in a pyroclastic surge that suddenly jumped over of ridge that was considered as safe. For untrained visitors to active volcanic areas even more so their inexperience or errors of judgement can be the cause of serious accidents and injuries, with personal risk assessment often built only on the basic information sought before travel.

According to Rosi et al (2003) injuries happen regularly when people visit natural environments they are not familiar with and misjudge potential dangers including the concentration of gas, thermal activity, avalanches and falling rocks. Serious injuries are generally caused by going too close to the action and not being 'dressed for the occasion'. The right footwear is very important when visiting lava fields or other volcanic and geothermal locations. Toxic emissions are a further danger; not every tourist is aware of chemical reactions which take place, for example, when hot lava enters the ocean and reacts with seawater to form hydrochloric acid (HCl), which burns the skin and affects the respiratory system, in some cases with a fatal outcome. HCl in the form of volcanic air pollution poses a local environmental hazard along Hawai'i's coast to people who visit the sites where lava flows enter the ocean (Sutton et al, 2000). Hydrogen sulphide (H_2S) is another potentially lethal gas, an asphyxiant which affects the respiratory system, and which can occur near hot springs and volcanic vents. It is also common that people venture out after dark to take photos of glowing lava or strombolian activity and a number of tourists lose their footing when they focus their attention on volcanic activity instead of where they put their feet (Erfurt-Cooper and Heggie, 2008; Erfurt-Cooper, 2009).

As mentioned earlier, lahars pose a particular danger as it does not take a volcanic eruption to trigger these particular types of mudflows; heavy rain is sufficient to move loosely compacted volcanic debris, resulting in lahars that sweep down channels of rivers and streams or down into secluded valleys

(Harris, 2006). More detailed accounts of hazards associated with volcanic phenomena are described in Blong (1989; 2000), Myers and Brantley (1995), Chester et al (2001), Hill (2004), Myers et al (2004) and Hansell et al (2006).

Even in areas of geothermal activity there is a possibility of hydrothermal eruptions and other dangers, which can occur in any high-temperature geothermal field but do not necessarily mean that a volcano will erupt or has erupted in the traditional way (Nairn, 2002). Only a small minority of tourists may be aware of this factor without adequate information. The frequency of such explosions in geothermal areas is also difficult to estimate, although small eruptions are unlikely to cause more damage than creating craters a few metres across (Christiansen et al, 2007). Nevertheless, in the case of tourists standing nearby, injuries can be expected. Larger hydrothermal eruptions, however, clearly represent a threat to visitors of geothermal parks and their infrastructure (Christiansen et al, 2007). Some accidents in geothermal areas can also result in thermal burns from stepping into extreme hot springs (Iceland Review, 2007), which has happened to people hiking over unknown terrain. In Japan the popular *Jigoku* (Japanese for hells, usually featuring boiling ponds and steam vents) are quite clear about what happens if visitors get too close to extreme hot springs (Figure 1.3). Finally, the increased interest in volcano and

Figure 1.3 One of the ten Jigoku in Beppu on the southern island of Kyushu has a clear warning sign in Japanese and English, predicting the outcome of getting too close to one of the boiling ponds.

geothermal tourism may also result in a growing potential for accidents and injuries near such active environments, as has been noticed by Callander and Page (2003), and Bentley et al (2007) with certain types of adventure tourism in New Zealand, simply because visitors are more interested in observing activity than in taking reasonable precautions for their personal safety.

Critical questions about risk management

Hazard and risk management in volcanic environments is extremely challenging due to the varying degrees of imminent danger from active volcanoes and geothermal fields, which can generate different types of hazards. Also, remoteness, difficult terrain and adverse climate conditions often present additional complications in an emergency situation. In addition, individual risk perception and risk assessment are significant factors in both risk *creation* and risk *prevention* as people are influenced in different ways when deciding responsibility and preparedness for their personal protection (Paton et al, 2001) while visiting hazardous environments. A number of questions (Erfurt-Cooper, 2010a) relating to safety issues and the overall risk management in areas of volcanic activity will be discussed to highlight the need for international guidelines for visitor safety in volcanic and geothermal active regions. The first question that may come to mind is whether tourism close to active volcanoes should be encouraged and promoted? The answer is a cautious yes, providing that acceptable risk management strategies are in place and visitor numbers do not put the surrounding natural environment under additional pressure. The next question is whether the economic benefits from tourism outweigh the potential risks? This is a question for the host communities and the local authorities who are in charge of deciding whether to open potentially dangerous areas to the public or not. However, not all volcanoes are closely monitored. Which raises the next question – whether visits to currently and/or potentially active volcanoes are a disaster waiting to happen? Unfortunately there is no answer to this as much depends on events out of our control. How much

is done to raise awareness about the potential danger of volcanic environments? Is every volcano tourist informed about rescue services and how to contact them through guidelines and instructions for emergencies? Who is responsible and in charge in case of an unexpected emergency and how to contact rescue services?

An important sub-question here is whether visitors to volcanic environments are seeking or are able to obtain enough information about individual destinations from available sources like the Internet and guidebooks, as local guidelines and instructions for emergencies are not available everywhere. To be aware of the potential dangers in volcanic environments visitors need to know beforehand how to prevent accidents and who is in charge and/or responsible in an emergency. Impacting strongly on this situation is one of the most important issues in risk prevention: the language barriers that often exist. Signage, announcements and warnings – do they reach *every* visitor or tourist and are they understood sufficiently to encourage safe behaviour? In many countries signage is only in one language – this is clearly not enough (Figure 1.4). Communication can also be a problem in remote areas, as people increasingly rely on their mobile phones to cover the risk of isolation. While in some countries such as Iceland the most remote areas have exceptional mobile phone cover, this is *not* the case everywhere and electronic communication barriers can cause significant problems if relied upon in the case of

Figure 1.4 Interpretive signage and signs that contain warnings should be in more than one language

Note: In areas with many foreign visitors, images or pictograms should be used for immediate visual recognition.

accidents and emergencies, sometimes with dire consequences for both the tourist and the host community.

One of the remaining questions is, what and how much is done to prevent accidents? This brings us to the range of initial risk prevention measures, both by the volcano tourist and the local authorities in charge. Whereas local residents in active volcanic regions are generally made aware of any potential dangers and hazards, travellers rarely have this information and are not always aware of local safety guidelines, emergency shelters and evacuation procedures should the need for them arise. These considerations open the discussion as to whether there should be international standard guidelines about safety on volcanoes which can be adapted for individual regions.

Despite these sobering thoughts people will not be stopped by disasters happening in other areas; on the contrary, catastrophic events unfortunately seem to have the opposite effect of drawing attention to a certain region. The first objective therefore should be to make tourism in every volcanic and geothermal area *as safe as possible*. The second objective should be to provide essential information to all people who visit active volcanic environments, and the third objective to develop international guidelines for visitor safety in active volcanic and geothermal environments.

Suggestions for international safety guidelines for visitors

While a number of individual regions, national parks and other designated natural areas have developed their own strategies for dealing with potential hazards for visitors, it is very important to advance from risk management plans only for local residents to the inclusion of temporary visitors. In order to make important information available to every visitor a simple fact sheet of one page, printed on both sides, which offers visual recognition of signs, maps and symbols to avoid language barriers, may prove sufficient. A fact sheet (Appendix 3) can be divided into four sections to display the necessary information on half a page for each of the following:

1 a hazard zone map which highlights areas to avoid;
2 possible escape routes;
3 symbols and pictograms to indicate key points (*shelters, first aid, emergency phones etc*);
4 emergency contacts.

These could be developed as a general template and applied to every region – which would also create familiarity with the use of such information. Hazard mapping is considered as one of the most effective ways to reduce hazard exposure and therefore casualties in high-risk zones (Blong, 2000; Calvache, 2001; Chester et al, 2001; Francis and Oppenheimer, 2004; Marti and Ernst, 2005; Leonard et al, 2008) and an essential tool in the communication of volcanic risk between scientists, the local authorities and the public (Felpeto et al, 2007; Haynes et al, 2007; Nakamura et al, 2008).

Japanese authorities, for example, have developed a number of similar maps and booklets for local residents and visitors to volcanic areas. These areas have designed individual disaster prevention handbooks, available on the Internet, with only some of them already available in more than one language (Figure 1.5). In the case of no imminent danger volcano tourists are more likely to ignore warnings and safety information, if they are given any at all, behavioural patterns which have been established through observation of tourist behaviour as well as personal communication with volcano tourists in several countries (Erfurt-Cooper and Heggie, 2008; see also Faulkner, 2001).

By now it is rather obvious that most regions have an individual approach to risk and disaster management. Dealing with increased volcanic activity can include the closure of a national park for a period of time, as has happened in the Volcán Poás National Park in Costa Rica, where the most visited and most economically important park in the country had visitation limited for three weeks by the park administration (Aguirre and Ahearn, 2007). New Zealand is another country where volcanic eruptions have affected tourism in the past. Every time Mt Ruapehu erupts, surrounding communities, agricultural land, air and road traffic are affected (Paton et al, 1998), and this of course affects the tourism industry through loss of revenue from winter sports and general sightseeing (Miller et al, 1999).

Figure 1.5 Japanese risk maps are for everybody, although only a small number of maps have been translated into other languages to date

Note: The maps and booklets are very colourful, which is not necessary. Simple fact sheets following a generic template and containing essential information including emergency phone numbers, danger zones, escape routes, shelter locations and collecting points, which could largely be based on pictograms for easy visual recognition may be a solution to the lack of information in many volcanic areas (Erfurt-Cooper, 2007a,b; 2008a,b ; Erfurt-Cooper and Heggie, 2008; Erfurt-Cooper, 2009a).

In this situation of individual risk management the Internet presently offers local communities and the general public (usually tourists or potential tourists) a range of information for health and safety around volcanoes; however, this is only useful if people are actually looking for information and advice. Both the US Geological Survey and IAVCEI have recommendations for safety in case of a volcanic disaster, but these are mainly developed for scientists and local residents. Aramaki et al (1994) developed recommendations for scientists working on volcanoes, and the public living in the vicinity of active mountains; temporary visitors such as tourists are not mentioned. What's more, these guidelines were developed 15 years ago and it may now be the right time to review such previous safety recommendations and make some provision for the millions of annual visitors in active volcanic and geothermal environments. Leonard et al (2008) are among the very few scientists including in their research findings transient populations such as tourists (in popular skiing areas such as the slopes of Mt Ruapehu, New Zealand). Risk management assessments are valuable contributions towards *adapting* existing general warning systems and emergency management models for the use of the temporary visitors of any volcanic region. If people realize that they may be vulnerable in active environments they are more likely to undertake protective measures (Johnston et al, 1999).

Existing guidelines need to be adapted for and made available to temporary visitors, as they do not have access to the same information as the local population. While residents may not be in the habit of visiting their volcanoes in great numbers, they are generally aware of emergency and evacuation plans. They are also familiar with the area, which means they can follow designated escape routes and know how to find refuge locations. Tourists do NOT have this advantage. Millions of visitors who travel to active volcanos and geothermal environments every year are relying on what is available to them either a) on the Internet, b) through publications in the general literature or c) what they are told at their destination. This does not necessarily reflect real-time updates, which are rather important in active volcanic regions.

Even with major national parks (e.g. Yellowstone or Hawai'i Volcanoes National Park)

offering sufficient information for visitors, it is still the personal risk perception and risk acceptance thresholds (Figure 1.6) of the individual tourist that can present potential problems in risk management. What is needed is a commitment from all the relevant authorities like tourism boards and associations, volcano observatories and the scientific communities, local governments and tour operators to accept the fact that there are between 100 and 150 million people every year visiting volcanic and geothermal environments, with many of these visitors being rather unaware of potential risks. All stakeholders should consider joining forces and working towards making volcano tourism as safe as possible with safety guidelines for *all* visitors of active volcanic areas

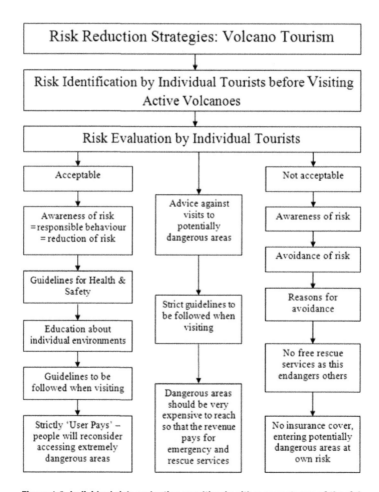

Figure 1.6 Individual risk evaluation resulting in either acceptance of the risk or avoidance

worldwide as a priority. This would be a step in the right direction by invoking responsible tourist behaviour focusing on risk prevention as well as educating people about the unpredictable and potentially hostile nature of some volcanic and geothermal areas. Risk mitigation, starting with risk prevention, has become a priority for the tourism sector, and must be encouraged among visitors as accidents and injuries are increasing among 'adventure tourists'. The achievement of this is an important issue for further investigation and research. Recommendations for safety guidelines for tourism in active volcanic environments are included in Chapter 22.

Summary: The New Frontier – volcanic and geothermal destinations

Specialized tour operators (Heelan, 2004) such as Volcano Discovery Tours, Volcano Expeditions International (VEI) and Volcano Travel offer their customers what they are looking for: an adventurous trip to volcanic regions with guaranteed activity under the guidance of trained volcanologists. Attracting tourists with scenic beauty (Harris, 2006), volcano and geothermal tourism includes accommodation (from budget to luxury) at the destination, often as close as possible for eruption viewing, which is seen as an added plus. Thanks to infrastructure development near active volcanoes visitors can enjoy volcanic landscapes from either their hotel balconies or from the verandah of a bungalow with uninterrupted views (Dunlop et al, 2000), whereby the combination with local hot springs for relaxation frequently offers a further highlight, all courtesy of volcanic activity. On the other hand, places with a very recent history of volcanic activity like Montserrat in the Caribbean are looking at attracting visitors again by replacing destroyed infrastructure as soon as possible (Swanson, 2005) in the remaining safe areas.

With expeditions in Bolivia the focus is on trekking volcanoes such as Tunupa and Licancabur combined with watching condor nests (Bolivia Contact, 2008), and thermal springs which are also considered an added bonus for the volcano tourist. Nicaragua advertises volcanoes, lakes and rainforests to be explored by hiking, kayaking or by plane (MEA, 2008). Horse riding to volcanic craters like San Cristobal is another option and snowboarders and skiers go to Cerro Negro for a spot of volcano boarding on the flanks of the scoria cone to enjoy an unusual adrenalin rush (Taylor, 2009).

In Asian countries like the Philippines and Indonesia volcanoes are also becoming major tourist attractions – often not far from world heritage listed sites, as in the case of Borobodur in central Java where the rather notorious Mt Merapi is located – amongst other more or less active volcanoes. Action Asia (2009) is a website that offers advice for hiking volcanoes with a 'hotlist of must-do peaks'. Island tourism is combined with volcano tourism in the form of Anak Krakatau, based on the historic eruption events from 1883, which lure visitors to this Indonesian island to see for themselves the location of the cataclysmic eruption of Krakatau. The island is generally accessible for tourists, unless Indonesian authorities prohibit access due to renewed activity (Decker and Decker, 1998).

The African volcano Nyiragongo has been described as 'an exceptional volcano' by Tazieff (1979) who repeatedly visited this mountain despite the extreme difficulties that face every tourist who wants to get close to one of the few craters in the world with an active lava lake. These do not however stop determined volcano tourists from setting out on expeditions to Nyiragongo but unfortunately this sometimes can end with an accident. A Chinese volcano tourist died in 2007 while attempting to take photographs without the protection of ropes, ignoring warnings from tour guides, and falling over 100m into the crater (ABC News, 2007). Further to the north in Tanzania is the volcano Ol Doinyo Lengai which has been described by Belton (2006) as very dangerous for inexperienced tourists. Belton maintains a website where he lists the risk factors in detail, mentioning his own close calls during repeated visits. Lengai tours and safaris are however promoted on several travel sites on the Internet.

Most volcanic destinations worldwide endeavour to let visitors see as much as possible; for example, the geological features along Crater Rim Drive in the Hawai'i Volcanoes National Park include spectacular views of exposures of ash layers and tree moulds, lava tubes and lava flows, sulphur banks with fumaroles and steam vents, earthquake and devastation trails, and the Volcano Observatory and Thomas A. Jaggar Museum (Hazlett and Hyndman, 1996). Safety is a great issue here and sufficient information is available, although some tourists do not heed the warnings and end up in trouble when they try to walk on recent lava flows at Kiluaea volcano.

Europe has volcanic areas both dormant and active. The dormant regions are used by volcano tourists to gain an insight into the geological heritage of former activity including regions in Scotland, Ireland, Germany, France, Turkey and Spain. In Turkey the region of *Cappadocia* (Kapadokya) bears witness to immense volcanic activity which resulted in tephra deposits composed of rhyolitic and dacitic ignimbrite layers covering an area of approximately 1000km² (Temel et al, 1998). Unique landforms such as the 'Fairy Chimneys' or the 'Rose Valley' attract tourists throughout the year, although the area is not promoted as a volcanic destination but as more of a generalized geological and cultural experience.

One of the greatest adventures, however, is viewing the volcanic landscape of Cappadocia from one of the many hot air balloons which take passengers for flights early every morning (Figure 1.7).

In Scotland, Arthurs Seat near Edinburgh is a popular destination for people who want to get out of town into a natural environment. Fingal's Cave is another volcanic landform and one of the attractions visitors to Scotland often include in their field trips or excursions into geoparks. The dormant volcanoes in France contribute interesting geological features with locations in the Central Massif (Graveline and Chabanne, 2002; Chapter 17 this volume), but also down on the Mediterranean coast with the ancient volcano of Cap d'Agde (Bousquet, 2006). Interestingly, before 1750 the volcanoes of the Chaîne des Puys in the Auvergne were thought to be 'heaps of mining waste or gigantic furnaces from Roman forges' (Krafft, 1991, p56).

Maars or maar craters are used for water-based recreational purposes, but for most people they are notching more than a picturesque lake, often with a perfectly circular shape, not an obvious reminder of the violent past which created them. Examples

Figure 1.7 Hot air balloons travel over the volcanic landscape in Cappadocia, Turkey

Note: Flights start very early in the morning and up to 30 balloons are usually seen above the unique landscape of Göreme.

of maars can be found in many areas: Alaska, Africa, Australia, Canada, France, Germany, Indonesia, Iran, Israel, Japan, New Zealand, North, Central and South America and Turkey. In Germany the 'Vulkaneifel' draws many visitors to the volcanic landscape with maars and other remnants of volcanoes.

In Asia and Oceania active and dormant volcanic regions often include geothermal fields with features like sinter terraces as colourful tourist attractions. The coexistence of volcanic and hot springs is a common occurrence in many countries, even where volcanic activity has long ceased.

The structure of this book

This book is designed to contribute a balanced view of the sustainable use of active volcanic and geothermal environments for geotourism on a global scale. It is a pioneer in the fusion of tourism, geography/geology, sustainable environments and the tourist quest for knowledge about the environments they visit. For most people it may come as a surprise that there are over 1300 active volcanoes worldwide and many more dormant or extinct. While not all of them can be reached this still means an abundance of destinations waiting for people with an interest in volcanic environments (with varying ease of access). Some are developed as tourist destinations; others are not (or not yet). The diversity of complementary landscape features also makes volcanic landforms very attractive to a broad spectrum of visitors.

No other major academic publications are as yet available covering volcano tourism, and this book provides an abundance of information from volcanic regions all over the world, brought together by a number of authors familiar with individual destinations and their particular management as a tourism attraction. The contributing authors predominantly have backgrounds in geology, risk management, environmental science and other relevant disciplines, can relate to volcanic and geothermal environments, and have the expertise to present important topics associated with sustainable geothermal-based tourism.

Volcano and Geothermal Tourism is organized in five parts. The 22 chapters and 19 independent case studies deal with a wide range of issues, providing analyses of volcanic and geothermal tourism in many important contexts, and investigate the range of existing and necessary risk-management policies that are needed for the further development of this subsector of geotourism. As the editors show in detail in the first and last chapters, the work presented here makes a substantial contribution to the better understanding of this emerging sector of tourism, while identifying some gaps in management capabilities in relation to sustainable tourism practices in volcano and geothermal tourism. Unless otherwise stated, figures and tables are supplied by the individual authors of each chapter; where material has been contributed by third parties full reference is made.

Part I is made up of this introductory chapter which examines the background to the most important issues of this growing tourism sector and reflects relevant global research undertaken on volcano tourism to date. As well as discussing recommendations for international safety guidelines and sustainable management, the chapter undertakes a review of the existing literature related to the use of volcanic and associated forms of geothermal activity for leisure and recreation purposes. The theme of risk management for both tourists and the local environment of host communities and the volcanoes themselves is taken up in all subsequent chapters and case studies.

Part II covers volcano and related forms of tourism in Africa. The two main chapters and three case studies show that Africa is a continent rich in volcanic and geothermal environments, with some well-known areas of interest for geotourists along the Rift Valley, including the volcanoes Nyiragongo and Nyamuragira in the Democratic Republic of the Congo and Erta Ale in Ethiopia. The African Rift Valley also includes mountains like Tanzania's Mt Kilimanjaro, Ngorongoro Crater, Mt Meru and Ol Doinyo Lengai, all of which are currently prominent tourist destinations although the local political situation can occasionally be an obstacle to safe travel in certain areas.

The four chapters and six case studies of Part III detail volcano and geothermal tourism in the

Americas. South, Central and North America and off-shore islands are represented by examples. For many people around the world the first place with volcanic activity that comes to mind is probably Hawai'i and the benevolent flowing and glowing lava which can often be viewed from relatively close up without any risk to the curious visitor. Although this may be the case in a controlled environment accompanied by trained guides or rangers this can lead to fatal errors in judgement when tourists are venturing out on their own, especially after dark. Another problem is that people often associate volcanism elsewhere with the gently flowing lava in Hawai'i, a perception that cannot be applied to completely different volcanic regions. The impression that it is possible to outrun a lava or pyroclastic flow could not be further from reality in other areas.

Volcano tourism in Asia, as described in the six chapters and three case studies of Part IV, includes the opportunity to visit highly active and potentially dangerous volcanic and related geothermal landforms within the close vicinity of active volcanoes. These chapters allow for a deeper insight into a tourism sector which to date has not been researched and described in greater depth. The visitors to this particular region include not only international volcano lovers, scientists and geotourists, but also local residents, who, in many highly active regions, have a very close cultural connection to their local fire mountains.

Part V discusses Europe where both dormant as well as very active volcanic regions can be found and volcano tourism has been practiced for several centuries. Iceland, for example, offers volcano tourism all over the country within its unique landforms and spectacular scenery offering insights into the Earth's geologic processes that continue to this day. Several volcanic regions of Europe are presented here as an important sector within mainstream geotourism in five chapters. An additional four short case studies cover areas well known for their volcanic and geothermal activity, including world heritage listed sites.

Oceania is discussed in Part 6, in three chapters and three case studies. This part of the world has some of the most active volcanic and geothermal areas to be found on Earth and therefore attracts a growing number of tourists who have the desire to come face to face with powerful displays of nature at work. Finally, the book is completed by Part 7, which contains one chapter. In this the editors summarize, map and synthesize the analyses and findings of 21 contributors, and identify priorities for further research in this rapidly developing area of geotourism.

References

ABC News (2007) 'Tourist killed after falling into volcano', abc.net.au/news/stories/2007/07/08/1972776.htm, accessed 4 October 2008

Action Asia (2009) 'Volcano hikes: Having a blast – Asia's 10 best volcano hikes', www.actionasia.com/actionasia/Articles/index.jsp?aid=3056, accessed 24 July 2009

Aguirre, J.A. and Ahearn, M. (2007) 'Tourism, volcanic eruptions, and information: lessons for crisis management in National Parks', Costa Rica, 2006, in *Revista de Turismo y Patrimonio Cultural*, Vol. 5, No 2. Pp. 175-191 Alvarado, G. E. and Soto, G. J. (2008) 'Volcanoes in the pre-Columbian life, legend, and archaeology of Costa Rica', *Journal of Volcanology and Geothermal Research*, vol 176, pp356–362

Aramaki, S., Barberi, F., Casadevall, T. and McNutt, S. (1994) 'Safety recommendations for volcanologists and the public', *Bulletin of Volcanology*, vol 56, pp151–154

Bankoff, G., Frerks, G. and Hilhorst, D. (eds) (2004) *Mapping Vulnerability: Disasters, Development and People*, Earthscan, London

Belton, F. (2006) 'Ol Doinyo Lengai - the Mountain of God', Online Document: frank.mtsu.edu/~fbelton/lengai.html, accessed 7 January 2010

Bentley, T. A., Page, S. J. and Macky, K. A. (2007) 'Adventure tourism and adventure sports injury: The New Zealand experience', *Applied Ergonomics*, vol 38, no 6, pp791–796

Blong, R. A. (1989) 'Volcanic hazards', in R. W. Johnson (ed) *Intraplate Volcanism in Eastern Australia and New Zealand*, Cambridge University Press, Cambridge

Blong, R.J. (1996) Volcanic hazards risk assessment. In: Scarpa, R. and R.I. Tilling (eds.), Monitoring and Mitigation of Volcano Hazards. Springer-Verlag, Berlin. p. 675-700.

Blong, R. (2000) 'Volcanic hazards and risk management', in Sigurdsson, H., Houghton, B., McNutt, S., Rhymer, H. and Stix, J. (eds) *Encyclopedia of Volcanoes*, Academic Press, An Imprint of Elsevier, San Diego, CA

Bolivia Contact (2008) 'Expeciones incahuasi: Volcanoes itinerary', www.boliviacontact.com/uyuni/en/volcanes.php, accessed 27 July 2009

Bourseillier, P. and Durieux, J. (2002) *Volcanoes*, Harry N. Abrams, Inc., New York

Bousquet, J. C. (2006) *Geologie du Languedoc-Roussillon*, Les Presses du Languedoc, Sete, France

Brace, M. (2000) 'Ring of fire', travel.guardian.co.uk/print/0,,3962210-104895,00.html, accessed 28 July 2009

Bruce, V. (2001) *No Apparent Danger – The True Story of Volcanic Disaster at Galeras and Nevado Del Ruiz*, Harper Collins Publishers, New York

Bullard, F. M. (1977) *Volcanoes of the Earth*, revised edition, University of Queensland Press, Brisbane, Australia

Callander, M. and Page, S. J. (2003) 'Managing risk in adventure tourism operations in New Zealand: A review of the legal case history and potential for litigation', *Tourism Management*, vol 24, no 1, pp13–23

Calvache, M. L. (2001) 'Volcanic hazard map as a tool of city planning: Experiences at Galeras Volcano and the County of Pasto', Colombia, American Geophysical Union, Fall Meeting 2001, www.adsabs.harvard.edu/abs/2001AGUFMED42 B0186C, accessed 20 June 2009

Cas, R. (2005) 'Super-volcanoes greatest hazard on earth', www.monash.edu.au/news/newsline/story/341, accessed 20 June 2009

Cashman, K. V. and Cronin, S. J. (2008) 'Welcoming a monster into the world: Myths, oral tradition, and modern societal response to volcanic disasters', *Journal of Volcanology and Geothermal Research*, vol 176, pp407–418

Cashman, K. V. and Giordano, G. (2008) 'Volcanoes and human history', *Journal of Volcanology and Geothermal Research*, vol 176, pp325–329

Carter, K. (2002) 'Volcanic view', www.theglobeandmail.com/life/volcano-views/article501204/, accessed 28 July 2009

Chester, D. K., Degg, M., Duncan, A. M. and Guest, J. E. (2001) 'The increasing exposure of cities to the effects of volcanic eruptions: A global survey', *Environmental Hazards*, vol 2, pp89–103

Christiansen, R. L., Lowenstern, J. B., Smith, R. B., Heasler, H., Morgan, L. A., Nathenson, M., Mastin, L. G., Muffler, L. J. P. and Robinson, J. E. (2007) 'Preliminary assessment of volcanic and hydrothermal hazards in Yellowstone National Park and vicinity', *Open-file Report 2007–1071*, U.S. Department of the Interior, U.S. Geological Survey, Washington DC

Cochrane, J. (2006) 'Indonesian national parks: Understanding leisure users', *Annals of Tourism Research*, vol 33, no 4, pp979–997

Dalton, B. (2005) 'Far from tsunami, climbing an Indonesian volcano', Travel Watch – National Geographic Traveller, www.news.nationalgeographic.com/news/2005/01/0121_050121_rinjani.html, accessed 28 July 2009

Davis, M. S. and Ricci, T. (2004) 'Perceptions of risk for volcanic hazards in Italy: A research note', *International Journal of Sociology and Social Policy*, vol 24, nos 10/11

Davison, P. (2003) *Volcano in Paradise: Death and Survival on the Caribbean Island of Montserrat*, Methuen Publishing, London

De Boer, J. Z. and Sanders, D. T. (2002) *Volcanoes in Human History: The Far-Reaching Effects of Major Eruptions*, Princeton University Press, New Jersey

Decker, R. and Decker, B. (1998) *Volcanoes*, 3rd edn, W. H. Freeman and Company, New York

Dove, M. R. (2008) Perception of volcanic eruption as agent of change on Merapi volcano, Central Java, *Journal of Volcanology and Geothermal Research* 172 (2008) 329–337

Dowling, R. and Newsome, D. (eds) (2006) *Geotourism*, Elsevier Butterworth Heinemann, London

Dunlop, F., Pendle, C., Eggington, J. and Watkins, S. (2000) *Central America: Expert Guides for the Adventure Traveller*, AA Publishing, Basingstoke

Dungey, K. and Whytlaw, J. (2007) *Tropical Walking Tracks of North Queensland*, Footloose Publications, Kuranda, North Queensland

Ecuador-Travel.Net. (2009) 'Volcanoes of the Andes: Tungurahua', www.ecuador-travel.net/andes.volcano.tungurahua.htm, accessed 28 July 2009

Edelmann, J. (2000) *Vulkane Besteigen und Erkunden*, Reise Know How Verlag Peter Rump GmbH. Bielefeld, Germany

Encyclopaedia Britannica (2009) 'Tungurahua', www.britannica.com/EBchecked/topic/609122/Tungurahua, accessed 20 July 2009

Erfurt-Cooper, P. (2007a) 'Volcanic environments: Tourism destinations with a risk factor?', presented as Poster to the *Cities on Volcanoes 5 Conference*, Shimabara, Japan, 19–23 November

Erfurt-Cooper, P. (2007b) 'Volcanic environments: Geothermal phenomena as tourist attractions', presented to the *ERE Conference*, James Cook University, Cairns, Australia, 1–3 December

Erfurt-Cooper, P. (2008a) 'Geotourism: Active geothermal and volcanic environments as tourist destinations', presented to *The Inaugural Global Geotourism Conference*, Perth, Australia, 17–20 August

Erfurt-Cooper, P. and Heggie, T. (2008) 'Risk perception, prevention, management and mitigation in volcanic environments', Workshop held at *The Inaugural Global Geotourism Conference*, Perth, Australia, 17–20 August

Erfurt-Cooper, P. (2008b) 'Geotourism in volcanic environments: Destinations with a risk factor?', Poster presentation at *The Inaugural Global Geotourism Conference*, Perth, Australia, 17–20 August

Erfurt-Cooper, P. (2009a) 'Volcano tourism: A disaster waiting to happen?', Keynote presentation at *The VMSG Conference*, University of Bournemouth, Bournemouth, 4–6 January

Erfurt-Cooper, P. and Cooper, M. (2009) Health and Wellness Tourism: Spas and Hot Springs, Channel View Publications, Bristol, UK

Erfurt-Cooper, P. (2010a) 'Geotourism – Active Geothermal and Volcanic Environments as Tourist Destinations', In: Dowling, R.K. & Newsome, D. (eds) *Global Geotourism Perspectives*, Goodfellow Publishers, Oxford, UK. (Forthcoming)

Faulkner, W. (2001) 'Towards a framework for tourism disaster management', *Tourism Management*, vol 22, pp135–147

Felpeto, A., Martí, J. and Ortiz, R. (2007) 'Automatic GIS-based system for volcanic hazard assessment', *Journal of Volcanology and Geothermal Research*, vol 166, pp106–116

Fisher, R. V., Heiken, G. and Hulen, J. B. (1997) *Volcanoes: Crucibles of Change*, Princeton University Press, New Jersey

Forst, B. (2004) *Auvergne: Cévennen Massif Central. Reise Know-How: Das komplette Reisehandbuch für Reise, Freizeit und Kultur in einer der ursprünglichsten Regionen Frankreichs*, Reise Know-How Verlag Peter Rump, Bielefeld, Germany

Francis, P. and Oppenheimer, C. (2004) *Volcanoes*, 2nd ed, Oxford University Press, Oxford

Frank, F. (2003) *Handbuch der 1350 aktiven Vulkane der Welt*, Ott Verlag, Thun, Switzerland

Fritsch, L. (2005) *Vulkane erleben: Outdoor Handbuch*, Conrad Stein Verlag GmbH, Welver, Germany

Fritz, W. J. (2004) *Roadside Geology of the Yellowstone Country*, Mountain Press Publishing Company, Missoula, MT

Furneaux, R. (1964) *Krakatoa*, Secker and Warburg. London

Gaillard, J. C. (2008) 'Alternative paradigms of volcanic risk perception: The case of Mt. Pinatubo in the Philippines', *Journal of Volcanology and Geothermal Research*, vol 172, pp315–328

Gallagher, R. (2003) 'Mud volcanoes: Mysterious phenomena fascinate scientists and tourists', *Azerbaijan International*, Summer 2003, vol 11, no 2, pp44–49

Gannon, P. (2008) *Rock Trails Snowdonia: A Hillwalker's Guide to the Geology and Scenery*, Pesda Press, Caernarfon, Gwynedd

Government of Montserrat (2008) 'Montserrat', www.gov.ms/?page_id=11, accessed 4 June 2009

Grattan, J. P. (2006) Volcanic eruptions and Archaeology: cultural catastrophe or stimulus?, *Quaternary International* 151, 10–18.

Graveline, F. and Chabanne, J. (2002) *Couleur Massif Central*, Éditions du Miroir, Clermont Ferrand, France

Gregg, C. E., Houghton, B. F., Paton, D., Swanson, D. A. and Johnston, D. M. (2004) Community preparedness for lava flows from Mauna Loa and Hualalai volcanoes, Kona, Hawai'I, *Bulletin of Volcanology*, Volume 66, Number 6 / August, 2004

Guðmundsson, A. T. and Kjartansson, H. (1996) *Land im Werden: Ein Abriß der Geologie Islands*, Vaka-Helgafell, Reykjavik, Iceland

Hansell, A. and Oppenheimer, C. (2004) 'Health hazards from volcanic gases: A systematic literature review', *Archives of Environmental Health*, vol 59, no 12, pp628–639

Hansell, A. L., Horwell, C. J. and Oppenheimer, C. (2006) 'The health hazards of volcanoes and geothermal areas', *Occupational Environmental Medicine*, vol 63, pp149–156

Harris, S. L. (2006) *Fire Mountains of the West: The Cascades and Mono Lake Volcanoes*, 3rd edn, Mountain Press Publishing Company, Missoula, MT

Hawai'i Volcano Observatory (2005) 'Volcanic hazards: Types of volcanic hazards on the Island of Hawai'i', US Geological Survey, www.hvo.wr.usgs.gov/hazards/types/main.html, accessed 29 July 2009

Haynes, K., Barclay, J. and Pidgeon, N. (2007) Volcanic hazard communication using maps: An evaluation of their effectiveness, *Bull Volcanol*, vol 70, pp123–138

Hazlett, R. W. and Hyndman, D. W. (1996) *Roadside Geology of Hawai'i*, Mountain Press Publishing Company, Montana, MT

Heelan, C. A. (2004) 'Tourism eruptions: Vacationing with a volcano', www.frommers.com/articles/2464.html, accessed 19 August 2008

Henderson, M. (2007) 'Incas fattened up their children before sacrifice on the volcano', *The Times Online*, www.timesonline.co.uk/tol/news/world/us_and_americas/article2570682.ece, accessed 30 July 2009

Hill, R. L. (2004) *Volcanoes of the Cascades: Their Rise and their Risks*, Falcon – Globe Pequot Press, Guildford, CT

Holland, J. S. (2004) 'American landscapes: Red hot Hawai'i Volcanoes National Park', *National Geographic*, October, pp2–25

Horwell, C. J. and Baxter, P. J. (2006) The respiratory health hazards of volcanic ash: A review for volcanic risk mitigation, *Bull Volcanol*, vol 69, pp1–24

Hunt, L. and Sanger, A. (2006) *Hotspots: Tenerife*, Thomas Cook Publishing, Peterborough

Iceland Review (2007) 'Two men choppered to hospital with burns', Iceland Review Online, Daily News, 13 July 2007, www.icelandreview.com/ icelandreview/daily_news/?cat_id=165398ew_o_ a_id=285263, accessed 14 July 2007

Johnston, D. M., Bebbington, M. S., Lai, C.-D., Houghton, F. F. and Paton, D. (1999) 'Volcanic hazard perceptions: comparative shift in knowledge and risk', *Disaster Prevention and Management* vol 8, No2, pp.118–126.

Johnston, D. and Ronan, K. (2000) 'Risk Education and Intervention', in Sigurdsson, H. , Houghton, B., McNutt, S., Rhymer, H. and Stix, J. (eds) *Encyclopedia of Volcanoes*, Academic Press, An Imprint of Elsevier, San Diego, CA

Kelman, I. and Mather, T. A. (2008) 'Living with volcanoes: The sustainable livelihoods approach for volcano-related opportunities', *Journal of Volcanology and Geothermal Research*, vol 172, pp189–198

Kelsey, M. R. (2001) *Climber's and Hiker's Guide to the World's Mountains and Volcanoes*, Kelsey Publishing Provo, Utah

Kilburn, C. and McGuire, B. (2001) *Italian Volcanoes*, Terra Publishing, Harpenden

Krafft, M. (1991) *Volcanoes – Fire from the Earth*, Thames and Hudson, London

Lane, L. R., Tobin, G. A. and Whiteford, L. M. (2003) 'Volcanic hazard or economic destitution: Hard choices in Baños, Ecuador', *Environmental Hazards*, vol 5, issues 1–2, pp23–34

Lawrence, B. S. (1997) *Restless Earth: Nature's Awesome Powers*, National Geographic Society, Washington DC

Leonard, G. S., Johnston, D. M., Paton, D., Christianson, A., Becker, J. and Keys, H. (2008) 'Developing effective warning systems: Ongoing research at Ruapehu volcano, New Zealand', *Journal of Volcanology and Geothermal Research*, vol 172, pp199–215

Lopes, R. (2005) *The Volcano Adventure Guide*, Cambridge University Press, Cambridge

Marshall, A. (2008a) 'The Gods must be restless: Living in the shadow of Indonesia's volcanoes', *National Geographic*, January, pp34–57

Marshall, A. (2008b) 'Drowning in mud: An unnatural disaster erupts with no end in sight', *National Geographic*, January, pp58–63

Marti, J. and Ernst, G. G. J. (eds) (2005) *Volcanoes and the Environment*, Cambridge University Press, Cambridge

Mayell, H. (2002) 'Volcanoes loom as sleeping threat for millions', *National Geographic News*, www.news. nationalgeographic.com.au/news/ 2002/ 06/ 0614_volcanoes_recov.html, accessed 20 July 2009

MEA (2008) Travel with MEA to: Nicaragua - Volcanoes, Lakes and Rainforests, Online Document: www.travelwithmea.org/itin_nic_vol. htm?nav=Nicaragua, accessed 7 January 2009

Méheux, K. and Parker, E. (2006) 'Tourist sector perceptions of natural hazards in Vanuatu and the implications for a small island developing state', *Tourism Management*, vol 27, pp69–85

Miller, M., Paton, D. and Johnston, D. (1999) 'Community vulnerability to volcanic hazard consequences', *Disaster Prevention and Management*, vol 8, no 4, pp255–260

Montgomery, C. (n.d.) *How to Survive a Volcano Eruption*, Secretsof Survival.com, www.secretsofsurvival. com/survival/volcano.html, accessed 20 June 2009

Morella, C. (2007) 'RP attempts to sell deadly volcanoes to tourists', ABS-CBN *News Online*, Special Reports, 14 October 2007, www.abs-cbnnews.com/storypage.aspx?StoryID=96798, accessed 25 July 2009

Myers, B. and Brantley, S. R. (1995) 'Volcano hazards fact sheet: Hazardous phenomena at volcanoes', *USGS Open-File Report* 95-231, www.vulcan. wr.usgs.gov/Hazards/Publications/OFR95-231/ OFR95-231.pdf, accessed 22 July 2009

Myers, B., Brantley, S. R., Stauffer, P. and Hendley II, J. W. (2004) 'What are volcano hazards?', *Reducing the Risk from Volcano Hazards*, USGS Fact Sheet-002-97, U.S. Department of the Interior, U.S. Geological Survey, www.pubs.usgs.gov/fs/fs002-97/fs002-97. pdf, accessed 22 July 2009

Nairn, I. A. (2002) *Geology of the Okataina Volcanic Centre*, Institute of Geological and Nuclear Sciences, Lower Hutt, New Zealand

Nakamura, Y., Fukushima, K., Jin, X., Ukawa, M., Sato, T. and Hotta, Y. (2008) 'Mitigation systems by hazard maps, mitigation plans, and risk analyses regarding volcanic disasters in Japan', *Journal of Disaster Research*, vol 3, no 4, 297–304

National Park Service (2009) *NPS Stats*, National Park Service Public Use Statistics Office, Washington DC

O'Meara, D. (2008) *Volcano: A Visual Guide*, Firefly Books, Buffalo, NY

Paguican, E. M. R., Lagmay, A. M. F., Rodolfo, K. S., Rodolfo, R. S., Tengonciang, A. M. P., Lapus, M. R., Baliatan, E. G. and Obille Jr, E. C. (2009) 'Extreme rainfall-induced lahars and dike breaching, 30 November 2006, Mayon Volcano, Philippines', *Bulletin of Volcanology*, published online 24 February 2009

Paton, D., Johnston, D. and Houghton, B. F. (1998) 'Organisational response to a volcanic eruption', *Disaster Prevention and Management*, vol 7, no 1, pp5–13

Paton, D. et al (2001) 'Direct and vicarious experience of volcanic hazards: implications for risk perception and adjustment adoption', *Australian Journal of Emergency Management*, vol 15, no 4, pp58–63

Perry, R. W. and Lindell, M. K. (1990) *Living with Mount St. Helens: Human Adjustment to Volcano Hazards*, Washington University Press, Pullman, WA

Ritchie, D. and Gates, A. E. (2001) *Encyclopedia of Earthquakes and Volcanoes*, Checkmark Books, An Imprint of Facts On File, Inc, New York

Rosi, M., Papale, P., Lupi, L. and Stoppato, M. (2003) *Volcanoes: A Firefly Guide*, Firefly Books Ltd, Buffalo, New York

Sakaguchi, K. (2005) 'Volcanoes as Tourism Resources: Marvellous Views and Hot Springs', in *Volcanic Eruptions and the Blessings of Volcanoes – The Front Line of Volcanic Research by AIST*, National Institute of Advanced Industrial Science and Technology (AIST), March, Tokyo, Japan

Savino, J. and Jones, M. D. (2007) *Supervolcano: The Catastrophic Event that Changed the Course of Human History – Could Yellowstone be Next?*, New Page Books, A Division of The Career Press, Inc, Franklin Lakes, NJ

Scarth, A. and Tanguy, J. C. (2001) *Volcanoes of Europe*, Oxford University Press, Oxford

Schmincke, H. U. (2006) *Vulkanism*, Springer Verlag, Berlin

Seach, J. (2009) 'Tungurahua Volcano', www.volcanolive. com/tungurahua.html, accessed 26 July 2009

Seach, J. (2009) 'Volcano safety: How safe are volcanoes? Risk zones around an active volcano', www. volcanolive.com/safety.html, accessed 3 July 2009

Secor, R. J. (2005) *Mexico's Volcanoes: A Climbing Guide*, 3rd edn, The Mountaineers Books, Seattle, WA

Sigurdsson, H. and Lopes-Gautier, R. (2000) 'Volcanoes and tourism', in Sigurdsson, H. (ed.) *Encyclopedia of Volcanoes*, Academic Press, pp1283–1299

Sigurdsson, H., Houghton, B., McNutt, S., Rhymer, H. and Stix, J. (eds) (2000) *Encyclopedia of Volcanoes*,

Academic Press, An Imprint of Elsevier, San Diego, CA

Simkin, T., Siebert, L., McClelland, L., Bridge, D., Newhall, C. and Latter, J. H. (1981) *Volcanoes of the World: A Regional Directory, Gazetteer, and Chronology of Volcanism During the Last 10,000 Years*, Hutchinson Ross Publishing Company, Stroudsburg, PA

Small, C. and Naumann, T. (2001) 'Holocene volcanism and the global distribution of human population', *Environmental Hazards*, vol 3, pp93–109

Small, C., and Naumann, T. (2002) 'The global distribution of human population and recent volcanism', *Environmental Hazards*, vol 3, pp93–109

Smellie, J. L., Lopez-Martinez, J., Headland, R. K., Hernandes-Cifuentes, F., Maestro, A., Millar, I. L., Rey, J., Serrano, E., Somoza, L. and Thomson, J. W. (2002) *Geology and Geomorphology of Deception Island*, BAS GEOMAP Series, Cambridge, British Antarctic Survey 2002

Smithsonian (2009) 'How many active volcanoes are there in the world?', *Global Volcanism Program*, Smithsonian National Museum of Natural History, Washington DC, www.volcano.si.edu/fac/index. cfm?faq=03, accessed 28 July 2009

Sutton, J., Elias, T., Hendley II, J. W. and Stauffer, P. H. (2000) 'Volcanic air pollution: A Hazard in Hawai'i', *Fact Sheet 169-97*, US Geological Survey, www. pubs.usgs.gov/fs/fs169-97/, accessed 27 July 2009

Swanson, D. (2005) 'Out from under the volcano', special to *The Globe and Mail*, www.theglobeandmail. com/life/out-from-under-the-volcano/ article892675/, accessed 27 July 2009

Tazieff, H. (1979) *Nyiragongo: The Forbidden Volcano*, Barron's/Woodbury, New York

Temel, A., Gundogdu, M. N., Gourgaud, A. and Le Pennec, J. L. (1998) 'Ignimbrites of Cappadocia (Central Anatolia, Turkey): Petrology and geochemistry', *Journal of Volcanology and Geothermal Research*, vol 85, nos 1–4, pp447–471

The Best of Ecuador.com. (2009) 'Tungurahua Baños: Volcanic activity', www.thebestofecuador.com/ banos.htm#climbing, accessed 22 July 2009

Thordarsson, T. and Höskuldsson, A. (2002) *Classic Geology in Europe 3: Iceland*, Terra Publishing, Harpenden

US Geological Survey (USGS) (2000a) 'Viewing Hawai'i's lava safely: Common sense is not enough', *USGS Fact Sheet 152-00*, version 1.1, December, www.pubs.usgs. gov/../fs152-00.pdf, accessed 28 July 2009

US Geological Survey (2000b) 'Hazard-zone maps and volcanic risk', Cascades Volcano Observatory, Vancouver, www.vulcan.wr.usgs.gov/Vhp/C1073/ hazard_maps_risk.html, accessed 28 July 2009

Viramonte, J. G. and Incer-Barquero, J. (2008) 'Masaya, the "Mouth of Hell", Nicaragua: Volcanological interpretation of the myths, legends and anecdotes', *Journal of Volcanology and Geothermal Research*, vol 176, pp419–426

Wantok Environment Centre (2009) 'Tanna, much more than Yasur', www.positiveearth.org/bungalows/ TAFEA/tanna.htm, accessed 25 July 2009

Watts, K. (2007) 'Yellowstone and Heise: Supervolcanoes that lighten up', *Geotimes*, www.geotimes.org/ nov07/article.html?id=feature_yellowstone.html, accessed 20 June 2009

Willmott, W. (2006) *Rocks and Landscapes of the National Parks of Central Queensland*, Geological Society of Australia, Queensland Division, Brisbane

Wisner, B., Blaikie, P., Cannon, T. and Davis, I. (2004) *At Risk: Natural Hazards, People's Vulnerability, and Disasters,* 2nd edn, Routledge, London

Wockner, C. (2006) 'Flowing volcano of mud can't be stopped', *The Advertiser Newspaper,* 30 December, Adelaide, Australia

Wood, C. A. and Kienle, J. (1990) *Volcanoes of North America, United States and Canada,* Cambridge University Press, New York

Wright, T. L. and Pierson, T. C. (1992) 'Living with Volcanoes', *USGS Circular 1973*, p39, www. vulcan.wr.usgs.gov/Vhp/C1073/, accessed 27 July 2009

Part II

Africa

Introduction

Africa is a continent rich in volcanic and geothermal environments with some well-known areas of interest for geotourism along the Rift Valley. This includes the active volcanoes Nyiragongo and Nyamulagira in the eastern Democratic Republic of the Congo, Ol Doinyo Lengai in Tanzania and Erta Ale in Ethiopia. The African Rift Valley also includes currently dormant mountains like Mt Kilimanjaro (Tanzania), Ngorongoro crater (Tanzania) and Mt Meru (Tanzania), all of which are prominent tourist destinations and have been for many decades, although the political situation can occasionally be an obstacle to safe travel in certain areas. Other volcanic regions on the continent or within the oceans surrounding Africa include Mt Cameroon, the Cape Verde Islands, St Helena and Ascension Island on the western side in the southern Atlantic Ocean, and Reunion on the eastern side in the Indian Ocean. The following chapters and case studies will provide some examples of these regions.

2

Africa's Great Volcanoes of the Albertine Rift Valley

Alfred Kazadi Sanga-Ngoie

Introduction

The Virunga National Park (VNP) (0°55′N, 1°35′S and 29°10′E, 30°00′E) is that spectacular blend of vast grasslands, high plateaus and towering high mountains and peaks, many of them covered with eternal snowcaps or rumbling with volcanic activities, that surrounds the northern part of the Albertine Rift Valley from just south of Lake Albert in the north to the scenic city of Goma on the northernmost tip of Lake Kivu in the south. All this dreamland, entirely located within Democratic Republic of the Congo (DRC) territory, stretches about 500km along the country's north-eastern border with Rwanda and Uganda (Diallo, 1975; Tazieff, 1979; Charlier, 1998; Stuart and Stuart, 1995).

Here, a very mild climate that is temperate throughout the year offers to the visitor, and to the local people alike, a very comfortable environment characterized by large an exceptionally rich and diverse flora and fauna. This is also the land targeted by large numbers of explorers for millennia. Since Greco-Roman times, this mountain range was known as the *'Lunaes Montes: Mountains of the Moon'*, where the source of the River Nile was supposed to be found, or, since European colonial times as a wildlife sanctuary of exceptional beauty and rich biodiversity, that had been, and still is, attracting thousands of scientists, tourists, naturalists, sportsmen (mountain climbing) and adventurers from all over the world.

Virunga National Park

The Albertine Rift Valley is the western branch of the Great Rift Valley, the 6000km-long tectonic fault stretching from Lebanon (Middle East) through the Red Sea and the Ethiopian highlands to Malawi, along which the African continent is being torn apart (Figure 2.1). The Albertine Rift Valley is the locus of the following African Great Lakes: Albert, Rutanzige (ex-Edward), Kivu and Tanganyika. Two big mountain ranges stand like huge stumbling blocks across the northern part of this rift valley: the Ruwenzori between Lake Albert and Lake Rutanzige, and the Virunga between Lake Rutanzige and Lake Kivu. The latter range is the natural divide between two great river basins: the River Nile (6700km) and the Congo River (4700km). Lakes Albert and Rutanzige are part of the River Nile basin, while Lakes Kivu and Tanganyika are within the Congo River Basin (Diallo, 1975; Boaz et al, 1992; Charlier, 1998; Saundry, 2009).

Lake Rutanzige is fed by some big streams, the Rutshuru River being one of them, flowing from the highlands in the south. This river is also considered to be the highest 'source of the Nile' as compared to the Ruvubu River in Burundi, the southernmost 'source of the Nile' (Diallo, 1975). Lake Rutanzige waters drain into Lake Albert through the Semliki River. The Uganda Nile flowing from Lake Victoria enters into Lake Albert through a broad delta located at the lake's northern end, just close to the exit of what is called the White Nile. This river flows northward on its

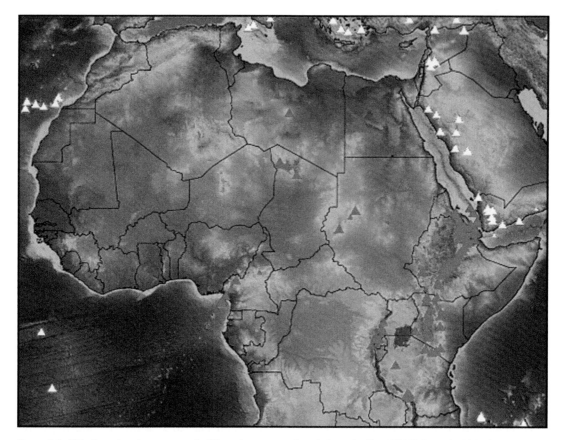

Figure 2.1 Africa's main volcanoes: most of the volcanoes are found along the Great Rift Valley, of which the western branch is known as the Albertine Rift Valley

Source: Global Volcanism Program, Smithsonian National Museum of Natural History

long journey across the deserts, bringing the waters from the Mountains of the Moon toward the Mediterranean Sea. To the south of the Virunga range, Lake Kivu waters flow into Lake Tanganyika through the Rusizi River, and then into the majestic Congo River toward the Atlantic Ocean.

These lands of spectacular beauty and diversity consist of three main areas, each one with its specific landscapes, ecosystems and natural habitats. At the centre is found the Rutanzige Lake depression (916m) with the swamps and grasslands of the Rwindi, the Rutshuru and Ishasha rivers to the south, and the forested valley of the Semliki River to the north. The forested granitic Ruwenzori range stands to the north-east of Lake Rutanzige, with its many snow-covered peaks, including the Peak Margherita (5119m), the third

highest of the African continent. The volcanic Virunga Massif is found in the south, comprising eight volcanoes along the Congo–Rwanda border, among them two still exceptionally active: Nyamulagira and Nyiragongo (Diallo, 1975; Tazieff, 1979).

These mountain ranges and the surrounding scenic lands and lakes, as well as the rich wildlife are all part of VNP, one of the most spectacular wildlife sanctuaries in the world. This park is also a very successful man-biosphere (MAB) reserve where conservation of nature coexists with daily use by the local population that live within its boundaries. Since its early days, the colonial power set rules to protect these lands against the poaching of the African elephant, then improved them into a national park in 1925, the first of its kind on the

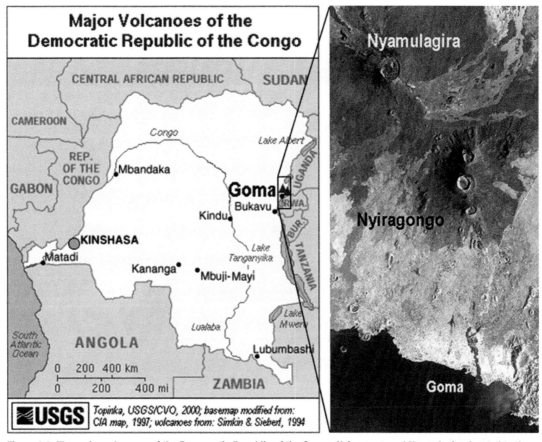

Figure 2.2 The major volcanoes of the Democratic Republic of the Congo: Nyiragongo and Nyamulagira, located to the north and north-north-east of Goma

Source: USGS, 2000 (map modified by author)

African continent. The park achieved its present borders in 1969, and was the first wildlife sanctuary to acquire world heritage status in DRC (in 1984). Its 800,000ha of lands were also designated a Ramsar site in 1996 (Diallo, 1975; Boaz et al, 1992; Charlier, 1998).

Ruwenzori range: The Mountains of the Moon

The quest for the source of the Nile had been an enigma that had eluded explorers since Homer's time (c. 850BC). Around 100BC Hipparchus drew a map of Africa showing the Nile as flowing out of three big lakes just north of the equator. Ptolemy (c. 100AD) improved the information by placing the lakes just south of the equator and

deep in central Africa, with the Nile flowing out of springs to be found in the Lunaes Montes (Mountains of the Moon).

Among the many 19th century explorers who scrambled for the Lunaes Montes, H. M. Stanley was the first to get the glimpse of their shining peaks – quite accidentally, because of the mist that almost permanently covers them. He located them on the map of Africa in 1885. Ruwenzori, the legendary 'Mountains of the Moon', were thus 'discovered'. This mountain range (Figure 2.4), which stretches over an area 120km long and 65km wide consists of a set of six massifs separated by deep ravines, among which Mt Stanley (with Peak Margherita, 5119m), Mt Speke (4890m) and Mt Baker (4843m) are the highest, and at the same

Figure 2.3 The volcanoes of the Central Virunga: Mikeno (3470m), Karisimbi (4507m) and Visoke (3711m) The snow-cap covered summit of Karisimbi can be seen in the lower centre

Source: Global Volcanism Program, Smithsonian National Museum of Natural History

time the third, fourth and fifth highest in Africa. These peaks are covered with permanent snow caps, especially on their western steep sides. The Duke of Abruzzi was the first European to climb up to its summit, in 1906 (Diallo, 1975).

The Ruwenzori mountain range is blessed with a very impressive variety of biomes, comprising lakes and water reservoirs at various heights, marshlands and peat bogs, saline soils and lava plains, lowland equatorial rainforests, mountain forests, alpine meadows, glaciers and snow caps. Its fauna and flora include forest elephants, primate species and many endemic birds, as well as giant lobelia and giant heater covered by moss. In fact the Ruwenzori range is noted to have the richest montane fauna in Africa because of its altitudinal ranges and its exceptional position just over the

equator, which result in constant climatic conditions (humidity, temperature and high insolation) all year round (McGinley, 2008). The Ruwenzori range is a world heritage site.

Because of the steep and inaccessible slopes, and their harsh weather conditions in their higher altitudes, the Ruwenzori range has been only marginally investigated. So far, no permanent scientific facility can be found in the area (McGinley, 2008). Some recent works (Taylor et al, 2006; Hastenrath, 2008) have shown that the glaciers in the Ruwenzori range have been sharply recessing both in number and in area: from 43 glaciers over 6 mountains with a total area of 7.5km² in 1906 when Abruzzi first climbed the mountain, to about half that number on 3 mountains covering about 1.5km² in 2005.

Figure 2.4 The snow-covered peaks of Mt Stanley, Ruwenzori mountain range

Source: Photo courtesy of Jurgen Wohlfarter (Peakware.com).

Virunga volcanic range: The belt of fire

The Virunga volcanic range is said to be one of the most spectacular volcanic areas on Earth. The range's volcanoes are all related to the African Great Rift system, in the same way as their well-known relatives on the Eastern Rift – Kilimanjaro, Mt Kenya and Ngorongoro – are (see Case Study 3). Tectonic hotspots and rifting or a combination of the two are pointed to as the major causes of most of the African volcanoes, from the highest to the lowest (Simkin et al, 1981).

The Virungas acquired much of their scientific and media exposure following intensive research by Haroun Tazieff, the French volcanologist (Diallo, 1975; Tazieff, 1979). This mountain range stands across the Albertine Rift Valley between Lakes Kivu and Rutazinge for a distance of 120km, thus separating the Nile and Congo basins. It consists of eight main volcanoes along the border between the Congo to the west and Rwanda and Uganda to the east: Nyamulagira, Nyiragongo, Karisimbi, Mikeno, Visoke, Sabinio, Mgahinga and Muhavura (from west to east; Figures 2.2, 2.3). All of these volcanoes are higher than 3000m, and the first six are located in the Virunga National Park. Karisimbi, the highest (4507m) of them has its round top covered by snow, while Nyiragongo and Nyamulagira are still strongly active, accounting for nearly 40 per cent of eruptions recorded in African history. Recently, in January 2002, about 40 per cent of Goma City on the shores of Lake Kivu was destroyed in an eruption of Nyiragongo, and later on in the same year, Nyamulagira erupted twice. More than a hundred other old craters and vents are found here and there all over the Virunga lava highland, testifying to its intense volcanic activity and the underlying tectonics. This range is also famous for the renowned mountain gorillas.

Nyiragongo

Nyiragongo (1°31′S, 29°15′E; 3470m) is one of Africa's most remarkable volcanoes. This strat-ovolcano in the Albertine Rift Valley, 20km north of Goma, DRC, has been erupting every three to five years since the early 20th century. However, for a long period of time during the 19th century it was thought that this volcano was dead. In fact, when the expedition by Von Goetzen climbed this mountain in 1894 for the first time ever, they found no sign of recent activity, except for some smoke from fumaroles. But this came to an abrupt end in 1928 when the lava lake in the crater was created (Diallo, 1975; Tazieff, 1979; GVP/USGS, 2008a).

Nyiragongo erupted in 1972, in 1975, in 1977, in 2002 and in 2006. Its eruptions are always preceded by strong tremors, according to which a state of emergency is declared by the Goma Geophysical Observatory. The 2002 eruption caused a lot of damage to Goma: more than 4500 houses were burned by, or buried under 2m-thick

lava flows from the 1.2km-wide crater. Similar destruction also occurred during the 1997 eruption, draining fluid lavas from the crater to the city in less than one hour (Allard et al, 2003).

Notwithstanding this damage Nyiragongo is seen as an exceptional resource for the people living in this area. For the local population its lavas bring forth rich soils of outstanding productivity that support their living, and for the tourists and climbers it has always been an exciting experience climbing the mountain and catching a view of the huge boiling lava lake from the crater rim. But sometimes at a great price: in July 2007, a Chinese tourist plummeted 120m to her death from the crater rim onto a ledge close to the lake of molten lava. She could not be rescued in time due to the unfavourable conditions inside the crater (ABC News, 2007; Polgreen, 2008).

Nyamulagira

Nyamulagira (1°24′S, 29°12′E; 3058m) is located about 25km north of Lake Kivu, and 13km

Figure 2.5 The stratovolcano Nyiragongo in the DRC

Source: Photo courtesy of Maik Bunschkowski (Wikimedia Commons)

north-north-west of Nyiragongo. This is Africa's most active volcano: it has erupted 34 times since 1882, each time spewing into the atmosphere large quantities of sulphur dioxide, and pouring flows of devastating molten lava that burn everything downhill. The 1938 lava flow created a lot of damage and continued until 1939. A recurrence cycle of about three to four years is observed, sometimes with extremely powerful blows of heated scoria, devastating lava flows, or both at the same time, but with the most recent eruption occurring on 4 July 1994 (ash and lavas). Destruction in the surrounding settlements was recorded only for the 1912–1913 eruptions. Nyamulagira's 2×2.3km wide truncated caldera, still with its floor partially covered with historic lava flows, is flanked by many subsidiary features: about 50 cones and 4 craters and vents (Diallo, 1975; GVP/USGS, 2008b).

The Karisimbi, Visoke and Mikeno group

This group of volcanoes, called the Karisimbi volcanic complex, is the highest of the Virunga volcanoes, and is dominated by Karisimbi (4507m). Sometimes snow falls over the Virunga, especially over the round top of Karisimbi, shining to the sun as 'white shells' (the meaning of *Karisimbi* in the local language). This is a dormant volcano having a pit crater (Muntango crater) south of the summit and still keeps a symmetrical shape notwithstanding more than 10,000 years of inactivity (Diallo, 1975; Andakar, 2005).

The very old Mikeno volcano (4000m) located north-west of Karisinbi is deeply eroded, while the perfectly symmetrical Visoke (3711m) to the north-east, contains a 450m-wide crater. These are volcanoes of the stratovolcano type. A mountain gorilla research centre named Karisoke was created by Dian Fossey on the Rwanda side between Karisimbi and Visoke. It has been abandoned since 1985 following Fossey's murder.

The Sabinyo, Mgahinga and Muhavura group

Mt Sabinyo (3645m) is an extinct volcano in the group of volcanoes located in the eastern part of the Virunga mountain range. Its summit marks the

intersection of the borders of three countries: DRC to the west, Rwanda to the south-east and Uganda to the north-east. Muhavura (4127m), a forested volcano, is the easternmost of the Virunga volcanoes. It is linked by a broad saddle on its western flank to Mgahinga (3474m). These volcanoes and parts of Sabinyo are part of the Volcanoes National Park in Rwanda, and the Mgahinga Gorilla National Park in Uganda. These two parks share with the Virunga National Park the remaining habitat for the world's mountain gorillas.

Biomes, wildlife and biodiversity
Biomes and ecosystems

The Virunga National Park biomes and ecosystems are strongly influenced by the climate, itself deeply linked to such physical elements as altitude, topography, temperature and rainfall. The overall land elevation in VNP goes from 680m in the north on the southern shores of Lake Albert, to 916m at the Rutanzige Lake, to 4507m at the top of Karisimbi in the Virunga massif in the south, and to 5109m at the snow-covered Peak Margherita in the north-eastern Ruwenzori range (see Figure 2.4).

As for rainfall, VNP has within its 800,000ha of land the driest (500mm of rain per year) and the wettest (more than 3000m) areas in the Congo, which are separated by less than 75km of distance. Average annual rainfall is around 500mm per year over Lake Rutanzige and its surroundings, 900–1500mm over the plains south of the lake, then decreasing with altitude, except for heavy orographic rains (>3000mm) over the western flanks of high peaks on the Ruwenzori mountains.

Notwithstanding the intensive deforestation by humans since they colonized this space, it still has innumerable species of fauna and flora, among which a very large quantity of endemic species. The park flora consists of five main ecosystems: swampy grasslands around Lake Rutanzige, savannas, lowland forests, forests in the volcanic Virunga massif, as well as mountain forests on the slopes of granitic Ruwenzori (McGinley, 2008).

The flora

VNP is blessed with the greatest diversity in habitats as compared to any other park in Africa, spreading from steppes on the lower lands to ice fields on the towering peaks. This significantly wide variety of wild vegetation types comprises such natural habitats as open grassland, lowland dry and humid mountain forests, savannas including swamps, and alpine vegetation. The open land habitats have evolved into steppe, savanna or swamps consequent to action by natural elements (low rainfall, soil type) or to animal or anthropogenic effects. Forest habitats include thickets around Rutanzige Lake, and dense forests in the mountains, while mountain habitats are characterized by transitional foothill forests to alpine zones (Stuart and Stuart, 1995; McGinley, 2008; Saundry, 2009).

The fauna

VNP is the natural habitat to some of the largest concentration of animals in Africa, most of them living along the streams in the grassland. Here live 218 species of mammals (23 of them endangered), including the African elephant, the lion and the leopard, and 22 species of primates, including the owl-faced monkey and the mountain gorilla. These rare and strongly endangered primates, found only on the slopes of the Virungas, have seen their populations decrease remarkably in recent years following the politico–military turmoil that prevailed in this region between 1994 and 2002. Seven hundred and six species of birds inventoried in the park are also endemic to the Virungas. As for reptiles and amphibians, 109 and 78 species, respectively, are found in this park. New species, discovered every year, still continue to add to these lists as research and scientific investigation continue (Stuart and Stuart, 1995; McGinley, 2008).

Human: Culture and settlements

Historically, this area was inhabited by a small number of pygmy hunters until the park was created. Because of the excellent climate and bountiful environment, and mostly because of the rich agricultural lands, immigrant populations started to increase very quickly from the early 1950s, to reach now more than 300 inhabitants per square kilometre, the highest density in the Congo. Population pressure is being felt along the park borders where many new towns with fast-increasing populations are located. Within the park territory, three fishing villages are found on the shores of Runtazige Lake: Kiavinonge, Nyakakoma and Vitshumbi. Their population has been increasing rapidly (Diallo, 1975).

The influx of about 500,000 Hutu refugees from Rwanda in 1994 and their accommodation in refugee camps within or close to the park brought about deep, and likely irreversible damage to this very sensitive environment. Vast tracks of protected forests were cleared for building the refugee camps, and for providing them with fuel wood for cooking their meals. It is reported that in a single day more than 600 tonnes of wood are felled by the refugees for this purpose. Moreover, rampant poaching and illegal traffic of bush meat by poachers, or hunting for living animals (baby mountain gorillas, rare animals or birds) to be sold as pets, have frequently put the rangers into clashes with the refugees. Quite a number of rangers have lost their lives in their commitment to protect the park (Sterling, 2010a, 2010b).

The Virunga National Park: Tourism and heritage

Notwithstanding all these problems VNP is the most visited park in DRC, with about 10,000 visitors per year. Accommodation is available at some specific places (Rwindi, Djomba, Mabenga and Kibali). Many tour itineraries are offered in order to satisfy the visitors' wishes: bird watching, safari for the big mammals, visiting the Vitshumbi fishing port where thousands of pelicans freely scavenge on the offal, or challenging the towering mountains to visit the mountain gorillas or some other exotic fauna and flora, or to have a first-hand glimpse of the boiling lava in the wide open smoking craters.

Goma and the Virunga mountains

For the majority of visitors Goma (population 150,000) is both the starting and finishing point of most of the tours. Goma is blessed with a fantastic physical setting on the northern tip of Kivu Lake, with a temperate climate all year long, day and night, and very nice hotels and other touristic accommodations. Nights in Goma are spectacular, under the glaring lights from two active volcanoes nearby. A panoramic view of the city, the lake and the Nyamulagira and Nyiragongo volcanoes can be the reward of climbing Mt Goma during the daytime.

Driving to the volcanoes will first take visitors through terraced fields clinging to the hills, at 1800–2000m. Banana fields, orchards and vegetable farms are all over, because of the rich volcanic soils. Normally, Nyamulagira and Nyiragongo are the most visited among the volcanoes. Sometimes visitors are also interested in going to snow-covered Karisimbi. Environmentalists and naturalists take special challenge in visiting the mountain gorillas on the slopes of the Sabinyo. The other volcanoes are almost left alone, with only some rare visits by especially interested people, mostly scientists.

Climbing Nyamulagira takes three days and Nyiragongo two days. Trained guides should be used to take care of visitors for a safe journey to the crater rim; however, catching a sight of the molten lava in the huge volcano crater is overwhelming. Airplane charters are also available for those who can afford it for a flight to the volcanoes and scenic Lake Makoto, 100km away from Goma. Elephants and hippopotami can be seen enjoying the lake water.

Rwindi Park

This has been the official entrance to VNP since 1925, from where the visitor gains access to the 800,000ha of protected flora, fauna, ecosystems, and the volcanoes. Many attractions are there to fulfill visitors' wishes: fishing along the Rwindi or the Rutshuru rivers or along Lake Rutanzige's banks, enjoying hot springs (some of them more than 90°C as at the Mayamoto hot springs), bird watching, spotting the herds of hippopotami wallowing on the Rutshuru riverbanks, and other mammals including herds of herbivores (elephants, antelopes, buffaloes), as well as their natural predators (lions, hyenas, leopards). All the animals found in continental Africa, except for the zebra, the giraffe and the rhinoceros, can be seen here in the wilderness and in large numbers. Under clear skies, the visitor can see the towering mountain ranges in the far east (Ruwenzori) and in the south (Virunga).

Beni-Ruwenzori

The visitor can reach Beni by plane or by road from Goma via Rwindi, and then get to Mutwanga, just at the foot of the impressive Ruwenzori mountain. Climbing this mountain is a very gruelling endeavour, requiring the expertise of very well trained guides. Enjoying the rich and various mountain biomes, fauna and flora at different altitudes, to end up in white glaciers and snow caps is a reward that only very few dedicated visitors can aspire to, but this unique experience of touching natural snow just under the equator is more than rewarding. From Beni, one can drive more to the north and reach Lake Albert, after visiting the very scenic Mt Hoyo (1450m) with its fantastic grottos and terraced waterfalls called 'Venus Stairs'.

Concluding remarks

The least that can be said is that the touristic potential of VNP, comprising the volcanoes and the other towering peaks of the Ruwenzori range, together with the exceptionally rich fauna, flora and ecosystems that can be found almost in pristine condition, are all under-developed and not used at their fullest capacity for tourism. Of course, very well trained rangers and tour guides are available for those tourists that do come, and this lessens the risk for travellers who take advantage of their services. However, the lack of tourism infrastructure, as well as the poor state of repair of the communication networks (routes, telecommunications) isolate this area and make it hard to visit and, therefore, difficult to enjoy.

The many kinds of hot springs and other geothermal resources found in the park could add new value and make volcano tourism more attractive in this area, especially to those people from coutries with a long tradition of enjoying hotsprings and spas (Korea and Japan). Other development-oriented use of these geothermal resources could propel VNP into an era of renewable and environmentally friendly energy that could sustain even more the economic growth of the people or institutions that own these precious, but dilapidated natural assets.

Visitor security, especially when climbing the active volcanoes, has to be assured. The case of the unfortunate Chinese visitor falling into the crater of Nyiragongo underlines the necessity of volcano tourism's security and hazard prevention and management. We would like to point here to the necessity of further research in order to establish a hazard map that can help in zoning the volcanoes in terms of security, and the need to develop ways and means to have the geo-touristic information conveyed in an easily understandable way to visitors.

References

ABC News (2007) 'Tourist killed after falling into volcano', www.abc.net.au/news/stories/2007/07/08/1972776.htm, accessed 21 November 2008

Allard, P., Baxter, P., Halbrawchs, M., Kasereka, M. and Komorowski, J. C. (2003) 'The most destructive effusive volcano of modern history: Nyiragongo 2003', *Geophysical Research Abstracts*, vol 5, p11970

Andakar, A. (2005) 'Ski-ing the Pacific Ring of Fire and beyond', www.skimountainer.com/ROF/ROF.php?name=Karisimbi, accessed 31 May 2009

Boaz, N. T., Bernor, R. L., Brooks, A. S., Cooke, H. B. S., de Heinzlein, J., Dechamps, R., Delson, E., Gentry, A. W., Harris, J. W. K., Meylan, P., Pavlakis, P. P., Sanders, W. J., Stewart, K. M., Verniers, J., Williamson, P. G. and Walker, A. J. (1992) 'A new evaluation of the significance of the Late Neogene Lusso Beds, Upper Semliki Valley, Zaire', *Journal of Human Evolution*, vol 22, pp505–517

Charlier, J. (1998) *Atlas du Congo*, Africa Editions, Kinshasa, DRC

Diallo, S. (1975) *Le Zaire aujourd'hui*, 2nd edn, Editions Jeune Afrique, Paris

GVP/USGS (2008a) Weekly volcanic activity report, http//volcano.oregonstate.edu/volcanoes/volc_images/africa/nyiragongo.html, accessed 21 November 2008

GVP/USGS (2008b) Weekly volcanic activity report, http//volcano.oregonstate.edu/volcanoes/volc_images/africa/nyamulagira.html, accessed 21 November 2008

Hastenrath, S. (2208) *Recession of Equatorial Glaciers: A Photo Documentation*, Sundog Publishing, Madison, WI

McGinley, M. (ed) (2008) 'Rwenzori Mountains National Park, Uganda', in Cleveland, J. (ed) *Encyclopedia of Earth*, www.eoearth.org/article/, accessed 29 May 2009

Polgreen, L. (2008) 'Some Congolese see hope in the caldron of liquid fire', *The New York Times*, Goma Journal, 22 September 2008

Saundry, P. (2009) 'Lake Edward, Africa, in Boukerou', L. (ed) *Encyclopedia of Earth*, www.eoearth.org.article/Lake_Edward,_Africa, accessed 11 January 2010.

Simkin, T., Siebert, L., McClelland, L., Bridge, D., Newhall, C. and Latter, J. H. (1981) *Volcanoes of the World: A Regional Directory, Gazetteer, and Chronology of Volcanism During the Last 10,000 Years*, Hutchinson Ross Publishing Company, Stroudsburg, PA

Smithsonian National Museum of Natural History (2009) Volcano of Africa and the Red Sea, *Global Volcanism Program*, www.volcano.si.edu/world/region.cfm?rnum=02, accessed 21 November 2009

Sterling, J. (2010a) 'Gorilla surviving warzone', *CNN.com International*, www.edition.cnn.com/2009/WORLD/Africa/01/12/gorilla.census/, accessed 14 January 2010

Sterling, J. (2010b) 'Slain Congolese ranger called "exceptional"', *CNN.com International*, www.edition.cnn.com/2009/WORLD/Africa/01/12/congo.slain.ranger/, accessed 14 January 2010

Stuart, C. and Stuart, T. (1995) *Africa: A Natural History*, Southern Book Publishers, Halfway House, South Africa

Taylor, R. G., Mileham, L., Tindimugaya, C., Majugu, A., Nakileza, R. and Muwanga, A. (2006) 'Recent glacial recession in the Rwenzori Mountains of East Africa due to rising air temperature', *Geographical Research Letters*, vol 33, L10402, doi:10.1029/2006GL025962

Tazieff, H. (1979) *Nyiragongo, the Forbidden Volcano*, Barrons Woodbury, New York

Wohlfarter, J. (2009) Mount Stanley, Peakware *World Mountain Encyclopedia*, www.peakware.com/peaks.html?pk=1084, accessed 21 November 2009

3

Volcano Tourism in Ethiopia and the Danakil Rift Zone

Jens Edelmann and Richard Roscoe

Introduction

Ethiopia, officially the Federal Democratic Republic of Ethiopia, is a landlocked country situated in the Horn of Africa. It is bordered by Eritrea to the north, Sudan to the west, Kenya to the south, Somalia to the east and Djibouti to the north-east. With an area of 1,100,000km² and an estimated population of over 85,000,000, it is Africa's second-most populous nation. The country capital Addis Ababa, is one of the oldest in the world, and the ancient city of Axum and the stunning monolithic rock churches of Lalibela are just two striking remnants of its past. It is also one of the earliest sites of human settlement. 'Lucy', discovered in the Awash Valley of Ethiopia's Afar region, is the world's oldest, most complete, and best preserved adult Australopithecine fossil at an estimated 3.2 million years old. At the beginning of the 1980s, a series of famines hit Ethiopia. These affected about 8 million people and left about 1 million dead, and the country is periodically affected by insurrections particularly in the hard-hit northern regions of Tigray and Eritrea. In May 1998, a border dispute with Eritrea, independent from Ethiopia since 1993, led to the Eritrean–Ethiopian war that lasted until June 2000.

Geological and structural outlines of Ethiopia

Ethiopia forms part of the large structural unit known to geoscientists as the Horn of Africa, which also encompasses the Arabian massif. This unit, which includes the present-day states of Ethiopia, Eritrea, Somalia, northern Kenya, the Red Sea and Gulf of Aden, and Arabia, has a complex geological history (Mohr, 1960).

Physiogeographically Ethiopia consists of two main plateaus, the Ethiopian and the Somalian, separated by the huge Ethiopian Rift Valley. The most famous rivers on the Ethiopian plateau are the Blue and White Nile, which are fed by numerous tributaries. The plateau rises to great heights in places, including the Simien Mounts massif in eastern Beghemeder, a Hawaiian-type volcanic pile now bounded by gigantic erosional precipices on almost all sides. This massif includes many summits reaching over 4000 metres above sea level, including the highest peak of Ethiopia, Ras Dashen, which is 4620m high (Mohr, 1960).

Though the focus within this chapter is on tourism at the active volcanoes of Ethiopia, the thick flood basalts (traps) in the central Ethiopian Highlands are certainly also worth a visit. These consist of intermediate and silicic lavas with interstratified pyroclastic sediments, which are superimposed on a highly folded basement of Pre-Cambrian rocks and mesozoic marine strata.

The Ethiopian Rift Valley

Separating the Ethiopian and Somalian plateaus, the Ethiopian Rift Valley (an extension of the East African Rift Valley), is a relatively sunken, faulted zone, which runs generally SSW–NNE from Lake Turkana (formerly Lake Rudolf) to the Danakil triangle where the African Rift System joins the

Red Sea and the Gulf of Aden Rifts. The northern part of the Afar Triangle is a topographically well defined depression, sharply limited on both sides by steep scarps of Paleozoic and Mesozoic origin: the Ethiopian escarpment to the west and the Danakil horst to the east, which runs parallel to the Red Sea coast of southern Eritrea. The Ethiopian rift floor rises to a height of over 1800m at the watershed north of Lake Ziwai and then descends northwards while spreading into a wide plain, areas of which in the Danakil Depression are below sea level (Mohr, 1960).

Due to the ongoing divergence of the African and Arabian Plates, Saudi Arabia has drifted away from the rest of the African continent, forming the Red Sea. Where the Red Sea meets the Gulf of Aden a spreading centre has been developing under Africa along the East African Rift Zone. Geologists believe that if spreading continues the three plates that meet at the edge of the present-day African continent will separate completely, allowing the Indian Ocean to flood the area and making the easternmost corner of Africa (the Horn of Africa) a large island.

Thus the Afar Region (or Danakil) depression is one of the key regions for the geology of East Africa, located as it is, at the intersection of three of the main structural units affecting the Earth crust in that zone – the Red Sea, the Gulf of Aden and the East African Rift. In spite of its geological importance, Afar has been neglected for a long time by geologists in favour of more hospitable regions of the rift zone, mainly because of difficulties with access and security. The first systematic field mapping and sample collecting were undertaken by a French-Italian geological team in the winter of 1967–68 (Barberi and Varet, 1970). Even until the 1980s the local Afars were considered to be hostile towards foreigners. Setting foot on their land without permission could even be fatal, since the Afar tribes were known as trophy hunters, mainly focusing on the male genitals.

Erta Ale: 'The glowing eye of the Danakil Desert'

Erta Ale is the most consistently active volcano in Ethiopia and the namesake and most prominent feature of the Erta Ale range. It is a huge basaltic shield volcano which rises to a height of more than 600m from a part of the barren Danakil depression which is below sea level. Erta Ale contains a 0.7×1.6km eliptical summit crater housing two steep-sided pit craters. Fresh-looking basaltic lava flows, coming from eruption fissures, have poured into the caldera and locally overflowed its rim (LeGuern et al, 1979; Acocella, 2006). During 1967–73 LeGuern et al (1979) documented overflows from the lava lake (70–200m across) that filled the north part of the 700×1600m summit-crater complex to a depth of 100m by January 1973. Continuous overflows from the southern lava lake (100m across) beginning in 1971 had covered the entire crater floor, and lava flowed down the south flank by late 1973.

One of the authors (Edelman) visited Erta Ale volcano in November 2002; between 1998 and 2001 this had been impossible due to the fact that the Danakil Desert was off-limits for tourists and foreign researchers because of hostilities between Ethiopia and Eritrea. During a six day stay on Erta Ale, members of the expedition descended onto the terrace adjoining the lava lake in the active southern pit crater in an attempt to obtain fresh lava samples and temperature data. Since the level of the lake was very low at this time the recovery of samples turned out to be difficult and finally had to be abandoned due to the dangerous instability of the crater walls. Several collapse events involving an estimated volume of 20,000m^3 were observed (Figure 3.1).

The lava lakes of Erta Ale

Just a handful of volcanoes in the world house active lava lakes. The most prominent example is Kilauea on the Big Island, Hawai'i which has frequently housed small lava lakes in recent years and indeed had the first touristically exploited lava lake, which was active in the huge Halema'uma'u crater until the powerful 1924 eruption. All other lava lakes are situated in poorly developed and/or very remote areas, such as those at Erta Ale and Nyiragongo (DRC), or at Mt Erebus in the Antarctic. The summit caldera of Erta Ale is renowned for two long-lived lava lakes (Figure 3.2) – a larger, currently inactive northern lava lake and a smaller, southern lava lake – located in two separate pit craters that have shown activity since at least 1967, or possibly since 1906 as reported by

Figure 3.1 Part of the crater wall is collapsing into Erta Ale's active lava pit

Source: Jens Edelmann

Pastori (Barberi and Varet, 1970; LeGuern et al, 1979). A significant change in the volcanic activity of the Erta Ale summit caldera from the 1960s until today has been documented.

Since the observations of LeGuern et al in 1967–68, lava lake activity at Erta Ale has clearly shifted from the former large eruptive centre in the northern pit to the smaller southern one. This is the place where a lava lake can be observed today. However, activity at the northern pit appears to be increasing again. Whilst it only showed strong fumarolic activity in November 2002, active spatter cones were observed therein in February 2009 (Weber et al, 2009). In November 2002, the lava lake was situated about 85 metres deep in the western side of the southern pit, with a distance down from the rim to the crater terrace on the eastern side of about 45 metres. In 2009 the lava lake surface was surprisingly on a much higher level (Figure 3.3), and the crater terrace was covered with fresh lava. These observations show the vitality of the outstanding volcanic system of Erta Ale.

During visits, the movement of the lake's crust can be easily observed. This is often likened to a small-scale model of plate tectonics. Molten lava frequently bursts out through the crust, resulting in often persistent small lava fountains that may be observed wandering across the surface of the lake. Occasionally, abrupt changes in the level of the lake may be observed, often accompanied by heightened activity. These fountains lead to the formation of 'Pelee's hair', thin filaments of basaltic magma, which are carried out of the crater in the hot sulphurous gases rising from within. Deposits of these are found strewn around its rim. Pelee's hair and the intense gases themselves present a hazard to the eyes and lungs of visitors, together with the ever-present risk that parts of the rim may fall into the crater.

Dallol

Dallol volcano is located in the Danakil Depression in north-eastern Ethiopia, in a remote area subject to the highest average temperatures on the planet. The volcano encompasses Dallol mountain (which

Figure 3.2 The craters of Erta Ale in November, 2002, viewed from the south-east from the helicopter that transported the expedition members

Source: Jens Edelmann

rises 50–60 metres above the surrounding salt plains and has approximate dimensions of 1.5 × 3km) and several other features in the vicinity, such as the 1926 crater near the 'Black Mountain' (which consists of manganese-rich halite), about 1.5km to the south-west.

Dallol is nested on top of a layer of quaternary evaporates including large potash (potassium salt) reserves, at least 1km thick. These massive evaporate deposits formed as the result of ongoing geological and tectonic processes in the region. Crustal spreading has resulted in repeated periods when the low-lying Danakil depression was connected to the sea. Subsequent geological events led to disconnection and eventual evaporation of the sea water, resulting in massive evaporate deposits. Dallol is a further result of the intrusion of basaltic magma into the oceanic crust covering the floor of the Danakil Depression, as a consequence of the rifting process. However, unlike at Erta Ale, the magma body appears to have caused an upwelling of the floor of the depression without actually reaching

the surface – at least no evidence of magmatic activity at the surface has been found to date.

The circular depression near the centre of Dallol Mountain is presumably a collapse crater, although neither its age nor the exact process which led to its formation are known. The south-west flank of Dallol Mountain harbours impressive salt canyons formed by erosion processes. Salt pillars up to 40 metres high are found rising above the canyon floors. The pillars consist of hundreds of layers of slightly pinkish (due to traces of KCl) halite (NaCl) salt deposits separated by thin layers of gypsum-like material. They are capped by gypsum anhydrite and clay beds which have protected them from the rainfall-induced erosion which formed the surrounding canyons.

A minor phreatic eruption was reported in Dallol in 1926 and formed a 30m wide crater. Since then, no significant volcanic activity has been reported. Currently, activity is only in the form of hot brine springs. As a result of these Dallol is one of the few places on Earth where significant

Figure 3.3 The raised level of the lava lake of Erta Ale in February 2009

Source: Photo courtesy of Hans-Jürgen Knoblauch

potash deposits are found near the surface. These are the result of upward transport of salts dissolved in geothermally heated groundwater from deep primary deposits. Secondary deposits form near the surface as the water that transported them evaporates. They include significant bodies of potash in the form of sylvite (KCl), carnallite ($MgCl_2$-KCl-$6H_2O$) and kainite ($MgSO_4$-KCl-$11/4H_2O$) salts. The main sylvite-bearing zones are between 15 and 40m in thickness (Hardie, 1991).

In 1906, the Italian T. Pastori recognized surface deposits of carnallite by the Black Mountains adjacent to the Dallol Mountain. Due to the economic value of potash, for example, in the fertilizer industry, this discovery resulted in several mining attempts at Dallol mound and in the surrounding area, remnants of which can still be seen today (Holwerda and Hutchinson, 1968). It was once estimated that a spring in the Black Mountain area was bringing around 1000 tonnes of potash to the surface in a single year and this was initially harvested by evaporation in salt pans.

Locals also tell stories of the existence of mine shafts dug into Dallol Mountain, probably in the 1930s, when the Italian company Compagnia Mineraria Coloniale was active in the area. However, no evidence for underground mining activities can be found today and it seems questionable whether mine shafts would have been driven into an active geothermal area.

Certainly, in the 1960s, the US Parsons Company drove exploratory mine shafts down to the 'Musley' sylvite strata west of Dallol at the base of the highlands. However, this site was many kilometres from the geothermal areas at Dallol Mountain. It is important to note that the terminology Dallol is often used to define a large surrounding area, which may cause confusion as to the exact location of historical mining operations. The primary (i.e. sedimentary) potash deposits in the salt plains surrounding Dallol mound are usually overlain with other evaporites, largely consisting of alternating layers of halite and mud to a depth of several metres. This crust results

Figure 3.4 Rectangular slabs of salt crust are loaded onto camels and donkeys for transport into the highlands after workers manually cut the crust into rectangular slabs

Source: Richard Roscoe

from periodic flooding of the area by sediment-rich waters out of the nearby highlands, and its subsequent dessication. South of Dallol, workers manually cut the crust into rectangular slabs which are then loaded onto camels and donkeys for transport into the highlands (Figure 3.4). This process and the near-endless salt caravans also attract tourists to the area. The salt slabs are sold in Mekele for processing into common salt.

Volcano tourism in the Danakil Desert

Visiting the Danakil Desert is a breathtaking experience. The first individual 'tourists' in Danakil were probably the group led by the German adventurer Rüdiger Nehberg, who crossed the depression on foot from south to north in the late 1970s. Today, expensive package tours offered by specialized international agencies frequently include the Danakil, and its prime volcanic features

of Dallol and Erta Ale, in their itineraries. American, French, Swiss and German tourist agencies are particularly active in the region, and their activities bring some money and work to the area. Small convoys of 4WD vehicles are the usual mode of transport. These can reach the base of Dallol Mountain and can cross the lava fields up to a point only about 10km from Erta Ale summit caldera, from which a path leads up to the volcano.

Before 2002 it was, however, very complicated to reach Erta Ale. The northern land route from Mekele was considered too dangerous due to the activity of armed groups in the area. On the southern route, the Afar people living around Lake Afdera didn't allow tourists to pass their villages, in spite of official papers and permits issued in Addis Ababa. It was virtually customary to be subjected to one or two days of enforced hospitality in an Afar village, which at least gave one the chance to improve one's negotiation skills before proceeding further.

Figure 3.5 Arrival on Erta Ale: The expedition in 2002 used an MI-8 military helicopter for transport to the crater

Source: Jens Edelmann

Thus, the easiest way to reach Erta Ale in those wild days was to charter an Ethiopian Army helicopter (Figure 3.5). The flight in the old Russian MI-8 from Mekele, a town in the north Ethiopian Highlands, into the depression already had an air of adventure about it, even before the main adventure started. The helicopter was fast and could carry a huge load of tourists, luggage and the water supplies made necessary by daytime temperatures of well over 40°C in the shade-free depression. It also was able to land within the Erta Ale caldera, less than 100 metres away from the active pit crater. The huge expense and limited availability of the helicopter are, however, problems that prevent its use today.

Multicoloured brine springs

The hot springs at Dallol Mountain are renowned for their stunning white, yellow and red colourations. As a result, tourism at the site is gradually increasing. While early visitors were scientists or photographers, Dallol is gradually being integrated in more mainstream adventure tourism itineraries. Although pure sylvite, karnalite and kainite and of course halite (NaCl) are relatively colourless, inclusion of various ions in the salt crystals is responsible for the variety of colours encountered in the Dallol area (Figure 3.6) which are in stark contrast to the predominantly white halite crust found in most of the depression. The colourful springs thus derive their colours mainly from ferrous chloride and iron hydroxide (both white-greenish), ferric chloride (yellow-brown) and iron oxide (brown). The active springs are usually white or yellow, whilst older inactive springs end up rust-coloured as the result of ongoing oxidation processes. The iron may be derived from the underlying basaltic intrusion.

Risk management

Development in the Danakil is still restrained by the constant threat of war, and famine and poverty remain an issue, irrespective of whether or not the volcano and lava lakes are active. Ethiopia still is one of the poorest countries in Africa, with the

Figure 3.6 A group of tourists visiting Dallol in February, 2009. Note the armed guards in the background

Source: Photo courtesy of Hans-Jürgen Knoblauch

Afar region being one of its least developed parts. Roads are few and in very bad shape. Jobs are rare and water is a scarce commodity. The war between Ethiopia and Eritrea, flaring up from time to time, deters further development of tourism in this remote region, as do sporadic armed attacks and kidnappings of tourist groups in the region. Despite this, volcano tourists are not deterred from visiting the two most stunning volcanoes in the Horn of Africa.

The local Afar authorities are now more cooperative in the development of tourism in the area, since it presents one of the few opportunities in the Danakil to earn some extra money for the family or to get temporary work. Use of armed Afar guards is mandatory and expensive. Tourist facilities, however, remain rudimentary, with the nearest comfortable accommodation in Mekele. Simple huts have been erected on the rim of Erta Ale using volcanic rocks, wood and straw. These provide protection from wind and sun and may be used for cooking or sleeping, although it is usually more comfortable to lie in the open gazing at the amazing number of stars visible on a clear night. The armed guards provide security and local camel drivers can assist in transporting material and even people to the volcano from the parking site. The northern approach into the depression, starting from Mekele, is arduous as the road is in part a rough track which may be virtually impassable during the rainy season. A first overnight stop is generally made in the village of Berehale, where local guides and guards must be engaged. Finally, after descending to the base of the depression one reaches the village of Amedale, which is only about 15 minutes drive across flat salt plains from Dallol. This village is also a transit point for salt caravans. A simple hut may be used as sleeping quarters but there are no other facilities.

Unfortunately, the area around Dallol remains subject to sporadic violent attacks on tourist convoys. Furthermore, there is the risk of mines on all tracks leading to the north, as evidenced by several recent incidents with injured soldiers and wrecked cars. Erta Ale lies further to the south, and is reached by driving cross-country through salt plains, sandy desert areas and finally over a rough track to the parking site. Orientation is difficult at times, especially when one of the frequent sand-storms is encountered. Hence, for many reasons the use of reputable local agencies is advisable. Most international agencies cooperate with these, but direct bookings are possible. One of the most recommendable tourist agencies in Ethiopia is Origin Ethiopia Tours and Travel, based in Addis Ababa (www.originsethiopiatours. com).

Conclusions

A significant boost to tourist development in the Danakil Depression would be the development of a road system. Work is in progress on a tarmac road from the south as far as Lake Afdera. It is possible that this road will eventually be extended as far north as the Dallol area, especially in view of renewed interest in the development of the natural resources at the site. This could lead to a substantial increase in tourism in the area, yet at the same time may remove much of its rugged charm.

Further, even today, tourist activities are beginning to damage the fine crystalline structures at Dallol, which raises questions about the sustainability of the area if tourism increases without a sound development strategy.

References

Acocella, V. (2006) 'Regional and local tectonics at Erta Ale caldera, Afar (Ethiopia)', *Journal of Structural Geology*, vol 28, no 10, pp1808–1820

Barberi, F. and Varet, J. (1970) 'The Erta Ale volcanic range (Danakil depression, Northern Afar, Ethiopia)', *Bulletin of Volcanology*, vol 34, no 4

Hardie, L. A. (1991) 'The roles of rifting and hydrothermal $CaCl_2$ brines in the origin of potash', *Annual Review of Earth and Planetary Sciences*, pp131–168

Holwerda, J. G. and Hutchinson, R. W. (1968) 'Potash-bearing evaporites in the Danakil area, Ethiopia', *Economic Geology,* vol 63, no 2, pp124–150

LeGuern, F., Carbonelle, J. and Tazieff, H. (1979) 'Erta Ale lava lake: Heat and gas transfer to the atmosphere', *Journal of Volcanology and Geothermal Research*, vol 6, pp27–48

Mohr, P. (1960) *The Geology of Ethiopia*, Poligrafico, Asmara, The University of Addis Ababa Press, Addis Ababa

Weber, C. (2009) 'Report on expeditions to Erta Ale and Dallol in 2002, 2008 and 2009', www.v-e-i.de, accessed 19 July 2009

Case Study 1

Reunion Island, France

Piton de la Fournaise Volcano

Henry Gaudru

Introduction

Reunion Island owes its impressive relief and landscapes to an active volcano (Piton de la Fournaise) and to three ancient cirques resulting from very large collapses (Salazie, Mafate, Cilaos). These two impressive mountain ranges are separated by two high plains (Plaine des Cafres and Plaine des Palmistes). The island, located in the western Indian Ocean is a favourite destination for hikers, mountain bikers and horse riders. Reunion Island provides many itineraries with the option of a night stay in a mountain lodge for the longer ones. Well-kept marked trails (including two for long treks) enable visitors to discover this beautiful volcanic landscape.

Piton de la Fournaise volcano (Furnace Peak)

The massive Piton de la Fournaise basaltic shield volcano (2631m) is one of the world's most active volcanoes. Much of its >530,000 year history overlapped with eruptions of the deeply dissected Piton des Neiges shield volcano to the north-west. Three calderas formed at about 250,000, 65,000 and less than 5000 years ago by progressive eastward slumping of the volcano. Numerous pyroclastic cones dot the floor of the calderas and their outer flanks. Most historical eruptions have originated from the summit and flanks of Dolomieu, a 400m high lava shield that has grown

within the youngest caldera, which is 8km wide and breached to below sea level on the eastern side (Smithsonian Institution, 2009). The eruptions of Piton de la Fournaise are generally of the Hawaiian style: fluid basaltic lava flowing out with fire fountaining at the vent. Occasionally, phreatic eruptions (groundwater steam-generated eruptions) occur. Lava flows crossing the Grand Brûlé can occasionally reach the sea, with spectacular results.

More than 170 eruptions, most of which have produced fluid basaltic lava flows, have occurred since the 17th century. Some eruptions, in 1708, 1774, 1776, 1800, 1977 and 1986, have originated from fissures on the outer flanks of the caldera. The most recent large-type eruption began on 2 April 2007 with rare intensity. Cracks opened at low altitude and emitted fountains of lava which poured into the ocean – several million cubic metres of incandescent rocks. The inhabitants of the village of Tremblet located in the vicinity, worried about lava flows in the Enclosure, which fortunately did not occur, nevertheless underwent bombardment from ash and lapilli, sulphur gas and acid diffusion, and forest fires. In addition, the withdrawal of the lava contained in the magmatic chamber present beneath the volcano caused a colossal collapse of the Dolomieu crater.

Volcanic activity of the Piton de la Fournaise is constantly monitored by geophysical sensors (tiltmeters, extensometers, differential GPS receivers, etc.). The data from those various sensors are sent to the volcanological observatory located in

Bourg-Murat north-west of the volcano. The Piton de la Fournaise Volcano Observatory, founded in 1978 following the Piton-Sainte-Rose flow, is one of several operated by the Institut de Physique du Globe de Paris. In Bourg-Murat there is an interesting volcano museum (La Maison du Volcan). It's a good way for tourists to be introduced to the volcano and to find out about the conditions before going up to it. This museum was conceived by the two famous French vulcanologists (Maurice and Katia Krafft), who died in 1991 during the Mt Unzen eruption in Japan. Many films of eruptions are from their personal collection. The museum is also very useful in understanding how the island was formed, or to learn about the different types of volcanoes around the world.

Access to the volcano is easy, as the mountain's frequent volcanic activity is a tourist attraction, so rides and tours are readily available. The whole area around the central crater is an amazing landscape of rocks, cinder and ash, devoid of vegetation, in deep shades of red-brown and black. The 13.4km hike to the volcano rim is not too difficult a walk but people must go prepared. Access to the summit is best by the road east to the volcano from Bourg-Murat (1560m), the starting point of the RF5 road, also called 'the volcano road (la route du volcan)'. It is about 30km long (20km sealed). Soon after starting, the scenery becomes increasing barren and finally is crossing the Plaine des Sables, with the remains of more ancient craters. The road ends at the Pas de Bellecombe, on the north-western rim of the caldera, where tourists can look out from the edge of a 300m cliff. Here there is parking for cars, then a path and a long stair which allows visitors to go down the cliff-face to the caldera floor, then cross the lava fields and ascend to the rim of the Dolomieu crater. This walk will take about four to five hours there and back. Visitors exploring the caldera should be in good physical condition, with hiking shoes and a supply of drinking water and food.

People must be prepared to exercise caution because the weather can change very quickly, moving from bright sunlight and heat (with risks of heatstroke) to dense fog with cold and rain. In dense fog, straying from paths is very risky. Visitors are advised to take the necessary precautions for sun, heat, cold and rain and not to stray from marked paths. Many white paint marks over rocks delimit a number of footpaths ascending the lava shield inside the caldera. There was completely free access during eruptions until 1998, now access is limited. Since the eruption of April 2007 during which the bottom of the Dolomieu crater collapsed to a depth greater than 300m, access in the Enclosure and to the crater rim has been temporarily prohibited to the public because the edges of the very destabilized summit craters continued to be detached frequently and suddenly. Also, this path is closed for safety reasons during seismic events that may precede eruptions, and during eruptions. Tourists can, however, take helicopter flights offered by commercial companies on the island and fly over the volcano when meteorologial conditions are good.

With a good road via Bellecombe the volcano is now a very popular natural site for tourists who want to observe an eruption. In 1972 at the time of the first eruption which followed the complete opening of the Road of the Volcano the local Préfect, anxious about the safety of important visitors, prohibited access to the Enclosure from 9 August 1972. The popular response was sharp and the Préfecture finally authorized access to small groups helped by guides. But meteorological conditions then were difficult and three people died of cold, with ten hospitalized. Since then the State, at the time of each eruption has introduced a device of regulation and organization of access to the sites of eruptions, while trying to find the formula which as much as possible reconciles public safety with the desire to see this impressive spectacle. In the light of the specific experiments for each eruption, the device-type has evolved over the years. Its application, however, never ceases to cause polemical debates relating to safety vs freedom to circulate. A gate has been put in place at the entry of the path to allow prefectoral closing of the Enclosure at the time of the eruptions.

During the eruption of 1998 the number of visitors caused congestion for several hours. Access was closed to vehicles and a system of paying shuttles was set up temporarily. Following this event, a feasibility study was undertaken on the desirability of replacing freedom of movement with a system of shuttles during eruptive phases. When an eruption is likely a regulation on Civil Security is engaged under the authority of the Préfect. This comprises several phases:

- promoting vigilance when an eruption in the short or medium term is becoming likely or probable;
- alarm level 1 when it becomes imminent; and
- alarm level 2 when the eruption is occurring.

These are communicated to the general population and to visitors by the authorities, and protection and prevention measures against death and injury phased in as required.

Reference

Smithsonian Institution (2009) 'Global volcanism program – Piton de la Fournaise', www.volcano.si.edu/world/volcano.cfm?vnum=0303-02=, accessed 4 May 2009

Case Study 2

Cape Verde Islands

Henry Gaudru

Introduction

The Cape Verde Islands are located in the mid-Atlantic Ocean some 450 kilometres (about 300 miles) off the west coast of Africa. This volcanic archipelago includes ten islands and five islets, divided into the windward (Barlavento) and leeward (Sotavento) groups. The main islands in the Barlavento group are Santo Antão, São Vicente, Santa Luzia, São Nicolau, Sal and Boa Vista; those of the Sotavento group include Maio, Santiago, Fogo and Brava. All the larger islands except Santa Luzia are inhabited. Three islands – Sal, Boa Vista and Maio – generally are level and very dry. Mountains higher than 1280m are found on Santiago, Fogo, Santo Antão and São Nicolau.

Fogo Island

Fogo (Portuguese for 'fire') is a volcanic island in the Sotavento group of Cape Verde. The population of the island is approximately 38,000. Fogo Island is sandwiched between the islands of Santiago and Brava. It is one of the southern-most islands of Cape Verde, but it is the most prominent of the group, rising to nearly 3000m above sea level at Mt Fogo, a single massive stratovolcano. Its largest feature is a 9km wide caldera, which has walls 1km high. The caldera has a breach in its eastern rim and a large peak rises in the centre. The central cone Pico de Fogo forms the highest point of Fogo island at 2829m. Its summit is about 100m higher than the surrounding wall of the caldera. This summit cone, capped by a 500m wide, 150m deep summit crater, was apparently in almost continuous activity from the time of Portuguese

settlement in AD1500 until around 1760. A violent eruption took place in 1680, visible over hundreds of kilometres and lasting for a few years. It was during this eruption that the island earned its name. Lava from the volcano has reached the eastern coast of the island within historical times.

Tourism

When tourists visit Fogo a trip to the volcano summit is recommended, but it is not for the faint hearted. Guides are there to help people with the trip to the volcano crater – the ascent of 1200m takes approximately five hours and the descent into the crater (180m) takes approximately two hours.

In the 20th century there were two eruptions. Lava spewed from one of the two chimneys on the southern side of the volcano in 1951 and also created cones to the north and south of the Pico – such as Monte Orlando, Monte Rendall and Monte Preto de Cima. These eruptions all began along a line of volcanic fissures extending from the flank of the Pico de Fogo summit cone across the floor of Cha das Caldeiras. The lava flows that issued from these vents spread over the northern and southern parts of Cha das Caldeiras and down the eastern flank of the island (Figure CS2.1). In 1995 the volcano erupted again, forming a new crater called Pico Pequeno. This eruption started on the night of 2 April 1995 when the flanks of Pico split apart as a line of fissures opened. The eruption began and a curtain of fire issued from the volcano and poured down into the crater. Thousands of inhabitants fled. The day after, the whole island was covered by a thick cloud of dark ash which extended 5km into the sky; lava bombs up to 4m wide landed half a kilometre from the eruption and a day later lava fountains were

Figure CS2.1 Fogo is an active volcanic island in the Sotavento group of Cape Verde

spurting 400m high. It is estimated that at the eruption's height the volcano ejected 4–8.5 million cubic metres of material per day. One month later the lava had thickened but was still flowing at 15cm per hour. It was another month before the flow stopped.

In February 2003, the volcano and the surrounding plateau became Cape Verde's first national park on an inhabited island. The economy of the island is based on agriculture and fishing, with coffee and wine among the main products but recently tourism has become steadily more popular. The government has pursued market-oriented economic policies since 1991, including an open welcome to foreign investors and a far-reaching privatization programme. It has established as top development priorities the promotion of the market economy and of the private sector, the development of tourism, light manufacturing industries and fisheries, and the development of transport, communications and energy facilities. Between 1994 and 2000 there were a total of about USD407 million in foreign investments made or planned, of which 58 per cent was in tourism,

17 per cent in industry, 4 per cent in infrastructure, and 21 per cent in fisheries and services.

Horse riding is provided at Cha das Caldeiras and this allows people to explore the volcano on horseback, when restrictions are not in force owing to increased volcanic activity. The volcano is the island's major attraction but many visitors also come to see relatives. The historic town of São Filipe and the Chã das Caldeiras in the volcanic crater receive the bulk of visitors. São Filipe's buildings are in the classic Portuguese colonial architectural style.

In Salina de Sao Jorge there is a natural swimming pool with black reefs which is worth a visit. Guides are also available to assist hikers. The slopes in the north-eastern part are green and grassy all-year round, but the rest of the mountain is dry and barren.

There are at least three volcanic tubes to explore on Fogo. The tubes are lava flows that solidify on the outside, after which the inner liquid flows away leaving them hollow inside. Inside they are beautiful, with frozen lava in streams down the inner walls.

Case Study 3

East Africa

Volcanoes, Glaciers and Safari Parks

Malcolm Cooper

Introduction

Simkin and Siebert (1994) note that West Africa is the only region other than the Mediterranean with a reliably dated eruption from ancient times, at Mt Cameroon, observed by a passing Carthaginian navigator in the 5th century BC. In the East written records only appear to have been kept or geological analysis carried out after the 15th century AD however, after the Portuguese exploration of Africa had begun, although there is undoubtedly material in earlier Arab and Chinese records that has not yet been published. In the next 370 years another 20 or so eruptions were recorded by European sources, but even this work did not really get underway until after 1870.

Most African volcanoes result from hotspots or the rifting that characterizes East Africa or a combination of the two (Simkin and Siebert, 1994). The East African Rift Valley, which runs from Ethiopia to Tanzania through Kenya, is one of the world's most dramatic geological structures, producing the continent's highest and lowest volcanoes, ranging from the massive Kilimanjaro to vents in Ethiopia's Danakil Depression that lie below sea level. While two volcanoes in the Democratic Republic of the Congo's Virunga National Park, Nyamuragira and Nyiragongo, have been responsible for nearly two-fifths of Africa's historical eruptions, these are part of the parallel West African or Albertine Rift Valley discussed in Chapter 2. To the East, the major volcanoes are Mt Meru, Mt Kilimanjaro, Mt Kenya and Ol Doinyo Lengai. Of these, Mt Kilimanjaro is the highest peak in Africa at 5895m, and is made up of three inactive volcanic cones, Kibo, Mawenzi and Shira. Mt Kenya, 150km north-north-east of the capital Nairobi is the second highest mountain in Africa, reaching 5182m, and is an extinct volcano that erupted around three million years ago with a few small glaciers amongst its peaks. Mt Meru is the third highest mountain in Africa at 4566m and is an active volcano that last erupted in 1910. Ol Doinyo Lengai is only 2903m, but this is an active volcano that last erupted in 2007–2008. The lava here is completely unique in composition to any other volcano (see below).

Geology

Table CS3.1 lists the active and dormant volcanoes to be found associated with the East African Rift Valley.

In East Africa, crustal spreading processes have already torn Saudi Arabia away from the rest of the African continent, forming the Red Sea. The actively splitting African Plate and the Arabian Plate meet in what is known as a triple junction (Afar, see Chapter 3), where the Red Sea meets the Gulf of Aden. A new spreading centre may be developing under Africa along the East African Rift Zone, and if spreading continues the three plates that meet at the edge of the present-day African continent will separate completely, allowing the Indian Ocean to flood the area and making the easternmost corner of Africa (the Horn of Africa) a large island (Kious and Tilling, 1996).

Table CS3.1 East African volcanoes

Volcano complex	Location	Elevation in metres	Last erupted
Igwisi Hills	Tanzania	–	Holocene
Izumbwe-Mpoli	Tanzania	1568	Holocene
Kieyo	Tanzania	2175	1800
Kilimanjaro	Tanzania	5895	–
Meru	Tanzania	4565	1910
Ngozi	Tanzania	2622	Holocene
Ol Doinyo Lengai	Tanzania	2962	2007
Rungwe	Tanzania	2961	Holocene
Usangu Basin	Tanzania	2179	Holocene
The Barrier	Kenya	1032	1921
Chyulu Hills	Kenya	2188	1855
Elementeita Badlands	Kenya	2126	Holocene
Emuruangogolak	Kenya	1328	1910
Homa	Kenya	1751	Holocene
Mt Kenya	Kenya	5199	–
Korosi	Kenya	1446	Holocene
Longonot	Kenya	2776	1863
Marsabit	Kenya	1707	Holocene
Menengai	Kenya	2278	6050BC
Namarunu	Kenya	817	6550BC
Nyambeni Hills	Kenya	750	Holocene
Ol Kokwe	Kenya	1130	Holocene
Olkaria	Kenya	2434	1770
Paka	Kenya	1697	6050BC
Segererua Plateau	Kenya	699	Holocene
Silali	Kenya	1528	5050BC
South Island	Kenya	800	1888

Source: Simpkin and Siebert, 1994

Kilimanjaro is an inactive stratovolcano in north-eastern Tanzania and Mt Kenya in Kenya is the same, created approximately three million years after the opening of the East African rift. It was covered by an ice cap for thousands of years, and this has resulted in very eroded slopes and numerous valleys radiating from the centre. There are currently 11 small glaciers and the mountain is an important source of water for much of Kenya. Today there are many walking routes, climbs and huts on the mountain, and an area of 715km² around the centre of the mountain is designated a national park and listed as a UNESCO world heritage site. The park receives over 15,000 visitors per year.

Mt Longonot is a 2776m high dormant stratovolcano located south-east of Lake Naivasha in the Great Rift Valley of Kenya. It is thought to have last erupted in the 1860s. Mt Longonot is protected by the Kenya Wildlife Service as part of Mt Longonot National Park. A trail runs from the park entrance up to the crater rim, and continues in a loop encircling the crater. The whole tour is only about 8–9km long but very steep, so that the round trip of park gate – Longonot Peak – park gate takes around five hours. The gate is around 2150m and the peak at 2780m, but following the jagged rim involves substantially more than the 630m vertical difference.

Menengai is a 2278m high shield volcano located in the Great Rift Valley, Kenya. Mt Meru is an active stratovolcano located 70km west of Mt Kilimanjaro in Tanzania. Much of its bulk was lost about 8000 years ago due to an eastward volcanic blast, similar to the 1980 eruption of Mt St Helens in the US. Mt Meru most recently had a minor eruption about a century ago. The several small cones and craters seen in the vicinity probably reflect numerous episodes of volcanic activity. Mt Meru is the topographic centerpiece of Arusha National Park.

The Crater Highlands are a region in Tanzania, and are so named for the many craters present. As common in spreading zones, magma in rising to fill the gaps reaches the surface and builds cones. Craters form if a volcano explodes or collapses and further spreading can fracture the volcanoes as well. Ol Doinyo Lengai (Figure CS3.1) is part of

Figure CS3.1 Ol Doinyo Lengai: Tourist attraction not without risk

these highlands but is unique among active volcanoes in that it produces *natrocarbonatite lava*, a unique occurrence of volcanic carbonatite (USGS, 2003), which means its lava flows at a temperature of only 510°C. This temperature is so low that the molten lava appears black in sunlight, rather than having the red glow common to most lavas. It is also much more fluid than silicate lavas. The sodium and potassium carbonate minerals of the lavas formed by Ol Doinyo Lengai are unstable at the Earth's surface and susceptible to rapid weathering, quickly turning from black to grey in colour. A few older extinct carbonatite volcanoes are located nearby, including Homa Mountain.

Tourism

Tourism in Tanzania and Kenya is probably more affected by civil unrest and ecosystem impact than by volcanism. Nevertheless, all the Eastern Rift Valley volcanoes are tourist attractions in their own right. National parks have been created based on these resources and tourism is fairly carefully regulated by national park regulations. Parks such as Amboseli immediately north-west of Mt Kilimanjaro, on the border with Tanzania are examples. Amboseli was established as a reserve in 1968 and became a national park in 1974. The park covers 244 square miles and forms part of the much larger 4828km² Amboseli ecosystem, which hosts large concentrations of wildlife in the dry season, making it a popular tourist destination. It is dominated by Kilimanjaro and its walking trails. In a similar fashion Tsavo West National Park has a varied topography including: open plains with Savannah bush and semi-desert scrub; acacia woodlands; rocky ridges, and more extensive ranges and isolated hills; belts of riverine vegetation; palm thickets and, on the Chyulu hills, mountain forest. Towards the Chyulu hills is the recent volcanic origin with lava flows and ash cones including the Shetani lava flow, an example of a recent volcanic event.

Risks and risk management

There are several routes by which to climb Mt Kilimanjaro, namely, Marangu, Rongai, Lemosho, Shira, Umbwe and Machame. Of all these Machame is by far the most scenic if steeper route up the mountain, and can be traversed in six or seven days, while the Rongai is the easiest camping route and the Marangu is also easy, but accommodation is in huts. As a result, this route tends to be very busy in season. Visitors wishing to climb Mt Kilimanjaro are advised to undertake appropriate research and ensure that they are both properly equipped and physically capable. Though the climb is technically very easy, the altitude and low temperature make this a difficult and dangerous trek. Acclimatization is essential, and even then most people suffer some degree of altitude sickness. About ten climbers die from this each year, together with an unknown number of local porters – figures for these are guessed at between 10 and 20 (Cymerman and Rock, n.d.).

Kilimanjaro summit is well above the altitude at which high altitude pulmonary edema (HAPE), or high altitude cerebral edema (HACE) can occur. All climbers will suffer considerable discomfort, typically shortage of breath, hypothermia and headaches, and though most young, fit people can make the Uhuru summit, a substantial number of trekkers abandon the attempt at a lower altitude (Cymerman and Rock, n.d.). The Tanzanian medical services around the mountain have expressed concern recently over the current influx of tourists that apparently perceive Kilimanjaro as an easy climb. Many individuals require significant medical attention during their attempts, and many are forced to abandon the climb. An investigation into the matter concluded that tourists visiting Tanzania are often encouraged to join groups heading up the mountain without being made aware of the significant physical demands the climb makes.

In Kenya, Mt Kenya National Park, established in 1949, protects the region surrounding the mountain. Initially it was a forest reserve before being announced as a national park. Currently the national park is within the forest reserve which encircles it. In April 1978 the area was designated a UNESCO biosphere reserve. The national park and the forest reserve, combined, became a UNESCO world heritage site in 1997. The Government of Kenya had four reasons for creating a national park on and around Mt Kenya, of which tourism was the most important. Apart from the importance of tourism for local and national economies the other reasons were the preservation of an area of great scenic beauty, conservation of the biodiversity within the park and the preservation of the water catchment for the surrounding area.

References

Briggs, P. (2006) *Bradt Northern Tanzania with Kilimanjaro and Zanzibar by 2006*, Bradt Travel Guides, Chalfont St. Peter, p194

Cymerman, A., and Rock, P. B. (n.d.) 'Medical problems in high mountain environments: A handbook for Medical Officers', *USARIEM-TN94-2*, US Army Research Inst. of Environmental Medicine Thermal and Mountain Medicine Division Technical Report, archive.rubicon-foundation.org/7976, accessed 5 March 2009

Kious, W. J. and Tilling, R. I. (1996) *This Dynamic Earth: The Story of Plate Tectonics*, USGS Online version 1.14, USGS Information services, Denver, pubs.usgs.gov/gip/dynamic/dynamic.html, accessed 4 August 2009

Simkin, T. and Siebert, L. (1994) *Volcanoes of the World*, Geoscience Press, Tucson, AZ

USGS (2003) 'World's coolest lava is in Africa', hvo.wr.usgs.gov/volcanowatch/2003/03_04_17.html, accessed 4 August 2009

Part III

The Americas

Introduction

For many people the first place with volcanic activity that comes to mind is probably Hawai'i and the benevolent flowing and glowing lava which can often be viewed from relatively close up seemingly without any risk to the curious visitors. Although this may be the case in a controlled environment accompanied by trained guides or rangers this can lead to fatal errors in judgement when tourists are venturing out on their own, especially after dark. Another problem is that people often associate volcanism elsewhere with the gently flowing lava in Hawai'i, a perception that cannot be applied to completely different volcanic regions. The impression that it is possible to outrun a lava flow could not be further from reality in most areas.

The chapters and case studies covering several countries and regions in North, South and Central America are examples highlighting the large number of regions with volcanic environments which are used to attract visitors and to increase the revenue from tourism. In some countries investment in necessary infrastructure and precautions for health and safety around active volcanoes do not match the economic benefit gained from volcano tourism and accidents, and fatalities do happen occasionally although statistics are not highly publicized.

In the northern Americas many national parks and other protected areas have systems and regulations for risk management in place, which give visitors enough information for their visit if they choose to look for it before they travel and abide by it when they arrive.

Most of the larger volcanic and geothermal national parks have information centres for visitors where educational videos with warnings and safety guidelines are offered. But there are still areas where information for visitors is either hard to find or language barriers are the cause for potential problems.

4

The Lure of Lava Tubes: Exploring Lava Tube Tourism on the Big Island of Hawai'i

Lisa M. King

Introduction

As one of the world's leading holiday destinations, the Hawaiian Islands are renowned for their tropical scenery, luxurious resorts, cultural and historical sites, laid-back lifestyle and diversity of outdoor recreational opportunities. Tourism and outdoor recreation are firmly linked with Hawai'i's iconic geologic features (King, 2010). The volcanic origins of the Hawaiian Islands has produced many well known and well marketed geomorphological attractions across the Hawaiian Islands including Diamond Head Crater, Haleakalā, Molokini Crater, Hanauma Bay, Mauna Kea, the Nā Pali Coast and the volcanoes of the Hawai'i Volcanoes National Park – Mauna Loa and Kīlauea. Ongoing volcanic activity on the Big Island of Hawai'i attracts visitors from all over the world to view active lava flows and volcanic landscapes. However, few visitors are familiar with Hawai'i's unique underground volcanic attractions – its lava tube caves.

This chapter introduces lava tube tourism on the Big Island (also known as Hawai'i Island or the Big Island of Hawai'i) and how small group adventure tours assist in promoting lava tube protection and conservation by fostering personal experiences with these unique environments. The chapter begins with a brief orientation to Big Island volcanoes and describes the processes which form lava tubes. The diverse values possessed by Big Island lava tubes are introduced and the human activities threatening these sites are presented. Key lava tubes open to the public and the types of tours offered by entrepreneurial cave entrance owners are discussed. The chapter concludes with a case study of the Pua Po'o adventure tour conducted by Hawai'i Volcanoes National Park staff and highlights how small group adventure tours can successfully transfer to tour participants the appreciation of, and conservation attitudes towards, Hawaiian lava tubes.

Introducing the 'Big Five' of the Big Island

The Big Island of Hawai'i is the youngest and largest of the Hawaiian Islands. The island is composed of five shield volcanoes: Mauna Kea, Mauna Loa, Kīlauea, Hualālai and Kohala, each created over a long series of eruptions consisting of fluid lavas, that over time, built upon themselves and coalesced into the Big Island as viewed today (Hazlett and Hyndman, 1996). Mauna Kea is the tallest volcano in the Hawaiian Islands with a height of 4205m. It last erupted between 6000 and 4000 years ago and may erupt again (United States Geological Survey [USGS], 2002). This massive shield volcano is home to an international collection of world-class astronomical observatories. The exceptional air quality, lack of extraneous ambient light sources, height and relatively easy access make Mauna Kea's summit the premier location for astronomical observation on Earth (University of Hawai'i Institute for Astronomy, 2009).

Mauna Loa, at 4170m, is the world's largest active volcano (USGS, 2006). Mauna Loa has erupted nearly 40 times since 1832 with its last eruption in 1984 (Hazlett and Hyndman, 1996).

Kīlauea volcano has erupted regularly since prehistoric times (USGS, 2009). Recognized as one of the most active volcanoes in the world (USGS, 2009), geotourism to the Big Island climbs dramatically whenever Kīlauea's eruption becomes more spectacular. Conversely, when Kīlauea's volcanic activity pauses for a short period, geotourism to the island declines markedly. Thus, the nature of Kīlauea's eruption is intimately intertwined not only with visitor attendance to Hawai'i Volcanoes National Park, but with the overall economic health of the Big Island.

Hualālai, at 2521m, is located on the western side of the island. Hualālai is considered to be a possibly dangerous volcano potentially erupting again within the next 100 years and menacing nearby resorts and residential areas (USGS, 2001).

An extinct volcano, Kohala at 1670m is the oldest volcano on the Big Island, with a last eruption dated at about 120,000 years ago (USGS, 1998). Major lava tube caves can be found on all of the island's volcanoes except Kohala (Halliday, 2004).

Lava tube formation

There are basically two types of basaltic lavas: 'a'a lava is rough, sharp and blocky and rarely makes lava tubes while pāhoehoe lava is smooth and ropey and frequently makes lava tubes (Bullard, 1977).

The first lava tube formation process begins when pāhoehoe lava creates a lava channel which crusts over from contact with the cooler surrounding air. The crust forms a roof beneath which molten lava continues to flow. Thermal and physical erosion deepens the channel. The lava within the channel core remains fluid and hot as the outer edges cool, thicken and solidify, forming

walls which insulate the core and create a conduit for the lava to continue flowing through (Cas and Wright, 1987). The hardened lava tube exterior insulates the still molten lava within its walls, enabling the lava to travel significantly farther than it would if exposed to cool air, broadening the flanks of the volcano. Thus, without lava tubes, the Big Island's volcanoes would be much steeper and would form much smaller islands (Hazlett and Hyndman, 1996). As an eruptive event wanes and the supply of lava stops, the molten lava drains away, leaving an empty tube similar to a water hose when the water is turned off. The size of a lava tube is influenced by the slope on which it flows, the rate the flow cools and the thickness and viscosity of the flow (Bullard, 1977).

The second lava tube forming process involves the inflation of leading edges of sheet flows of pāhoehoe lava. As the flow velocity decreases due to outbreaks of lava moving rapidly away from the source, a thin crust quickly forms over the slow moving, cooling lava. After the crust reaches a thickness of 2–5cm, it becomes rigid and is strong enough to retain incoming lava, thus increasing the hydrostatic head at the front of the flow (Hon et al, 1994). The 'increased hydrostatic pressure is distributed evenly through the liquid lava core of the flow, resulting in uniform uplift of the entire sheet-flow lobe... As the flow advances, preferred pathways develop in the older portions of the liquid-cored flow' (Hon et al, 1994, p351). These pathways can evolve into lava tube systems in only a few weeks. If the sheet flow stops advancing due to a decrease in eruption activity at the source, the tube remains filled with lava that hardens and blocks the tube, rather than draining to form a lava tube (Hon et al, 1994).

Big Island lava tube values

The Big Island of Hawai'i is the world's most important location for lava tube cave research and contains the world's most scientifically valuable lava tube systems (Halliday, 2004). The island also contains more lava tubes than any other Hawaiian island (Stone and Howarth, 2005). The two longest lava tubes in the world, Kazumura, with a length of at least 65.5km (Shick, 2008) and the Kīpuka Kanohina lava tube system, with a length of at least 25km (Cave Conservancy of Hawai'i [CCH], 2003), are both located on the Big Island. Smaller lava tubes of various sizes and accessibility are common and as land continues to be cleared and developed, new caves will be discovered (Stone and Howarth, 2005).

Big Island lava tubes contain a broad range of important resources and values (Stone et al, 2005). From a geologic point of view, the island's lava tubes contain a number of intriguing formations and features. For example, Kazumura contains stacked lava tubes, solidified lava falls up to 15m high (Halliday, 2004) with large plunge pools at their base, lava blades and draperies, sharktooth stalactites, drips, rafted breakdown (Allred and Allred, 1997; Hawai'i Speleological Survey, 1997) and many other formations (Shick, 2008). The Kīpuka Kanohina lava tube system consists of a complex of multilevel braided passageways containing many beautiful pāhoehoe flow features, along with large lava balls, blue stalactites, red gypsum curls and more unusual formations (CCH, 2003). The Pua Po'o lava tube, located in Hawai'i Volcanoes National Park contains a small unique feature which looks quite similar to a rooster's comb.

Big Island lava tubes contain the greatest number of cave organisms found anywhere in the Hawaiian Islands with over 44 known species, many more waiting to be described and new cave species still being discovered (Stone and Howarth, 2005). Blind underground tree crickets, plant hoppers, springtails, flightless flies, beetles, moths and cave adapted spiders (Howarth, 1972, 1987, 2004; Stone and Howarth, 1994) are just a few of the species adapted to life inside Hawaiian lava tubes. Studies show these specialized species find their way into a cave a few years after the surrounding lava flow cools, many living amongst root mats formed by surface vegetation extending into the cave. Roots provide food for a variety of cave species (CCH, 2003). Many of these species can only survive within the deeper cave environment of moist substrates, calm air saturated with water vapour and high carbon dioxide levels (Howarth, 2004). Slime molds, fungi, bacteria and other unusual microbes also live in the lava tubes (Figure 4.1) with an unknown number of these still waiting to be described by scientists (Harry Shick, personal communication, 2008).

Figure 4.1 Scientists collecting biological samples in Kazumura lava tube

Source: Photo courtesy of Rob Ratkowski

Big Island lava tubes are important sites for paleontologists. Some caves preserve the remains of extinct birds that once flourished on the islands including petrels, crows and flightless geese (CCH, 2003).

Native Hawaiians historically used lava tubes for a number of purposes including permanent and temporary shelter, water collection, religious ceremonies, and as refuges in times of war (Stone et al, 2005). Such caves are of interest to archeologists.

Aesthetically, lava tubes contain unique features and subterranean landscapes foreign to those living in surface environments which nonetheless captivate, inspire and awe those people who view them. Often encircled with ferns, large rock falls or gnarled tree roots, even cave entrances can be places of remarkable beauty.

And lastly, as a special interest pursuit, lava tubes provide recreational caving opportunities for those so inclined. Recreational caving is defined as 'caving purely for the joy of the experience' (Webb, 2004, p621). The popularity of caving is clearly revealed by the numerous cave-related sites and links on the web (Webb, 2004). Off-island spelunkers usually contact local cavers or 'grottos' (cave clubs) when planning such activities to enquire about permits needed and if a club member with local knowledge is available to accompany them.

Threats to Big Island lava tube caves

Big Island lava tubes face a variety of threats as subterranean environments are much more vulnerable to negative impacts than surface environments (Watson et al, 1997). Threats such as road works or land development activities may result in the complete destruction or partial collapse of particular lava tubes. Tree clearing or other changes to the surface environment above lava tubes (Figure 4.2) contribute to cumulative impacts that occur slowly over decades and potentially irreparably alter the cave environment while a careless moment by a clumsy cave visitor can damage or destroy a cave feature in an instant (Watson et al, 1997). Table 4.1 details the threats to Big Island lava tubes and their contents.

Though Table 4.1 is an extensive list, the principal threats to Hawaiian lava tubes are general land clearing, Ōhiʻa tree removal, pollution (Harry Shick, personal communication), vandalism and unrestricted entry by visitors. Hawaiʻi state law now protects lava tubes and their contents from vandalism, looting, pollution and disturbance of cave organisms. State law also outlines the requirements of lawful legal commercial entry (Hawaiʻi State Legislature, 2002). While spelunkers are aware that there are usually permissions required to enter caves, the casual cave visitor may be unaware of cave etiquette and lava tube cave protection laws.

In fact, when individuals or groups with little or no caving experience accidentally discover or seek out a cave entrance, and with no prior experience or knowledge 'explore the cave', the cave and its contents, as well as these 'casual cave tourists', are at risk from their activities (Webb, 2004). Sometimes casual cave visitors are Big Island residents who are unaware of the special values of Hawaiian lava tubes. Three examples illustrate the common problem of the Big Island casual 'cave tourist':

* In Hawaiʻi Volcanoes National Park, a group of 30 ill-informed Germans sought out and

Figure 4.2 A bulldozer unknowingly clearing land above a lava tube on the Big Island breaks through the roof and falls into the lava tube

Source: Photo courtesy of Orchidland Estates

Table 4.1 The range of human threats to Hawai'i Island lava tube resources

Category	Threat
Total or partial physical destruction	• Road works & construction • Subdivision development • New lava flows
Major land or hydrologic disturbance	• Ōhi'a tree removal & general land clearing • Hotter & more frequent fires from introduced grasses killing trees & causing erosion issues • Invasive species such as pigs, goats & fire tree that destroy or out compete surface vegetation and cause erosion
Pollution	• Raw sewage • Gray water • Solid waste dumps • Toxic & hazardous substances such as pesticides, herbicides, agricultural & automotive chemicals placed or leaked into lava tube
Physical impacts resulting directly from human visitation/alteration	• Vandalism of archaeological artifacts & cave features • Accidental destruction of tree roots & cave features • Tampering or trampling of archaeological artifacts & deposits • Trampling of cave flora & fauna • Introduction of invasive species including microbes • Creation of new entrances or the modification of existing entrances (addition of doors, etc) changing air flow and humidity in the cave causing deep cave areas to become drier; thus, further limiting habitat for deep cave species • Particle contamination (smoke, ash, dust, etc.)

Source: Table categories adapted from Watson et al's 1997 classification. Data compiled from Allred and Allred, 1997; Watson et al, 1997; Halliday, 2003; Hamilton-Smith, 2004; Mitchie, 2004; Stone and Howarth, 2005; Stone et al, 2005; Shick, 2008

visited a cave without park knowledge or permission and ignorantly trampled a section of fragile 'sand castle' deposits. They had read about the site in a German publication (Stone et al, 2005). This example illustrates the primary reason it is illegal to publish the location of any cave located on federal lands, as lack of knowledge of their exact location is a mechanism to protect cave sites from such situations.

• Unfamiliar with the famous Kazumura lava tube, a recreational caver wrote the word 'YES' between two large horizontal arrows in cave slime indicating the correct direction for cavers to travel (Shick, 2008). The graffiti was unnecessary and might take decades or longer for the cave 'slime' to obscure the unsightly mark. If the caver had visited Kazumura with

a local spelunker with prior experience in the cave, the situation could have been avoided.

• Many casual cave tourists tend to leave rubbish and other items in or near caves in ignorance and possibly indifference to the potential harm these items may eventually cause to the values of the site.

Stone and Howarth (2005) observe that many of these threats can be reduced through education and legislation. However, they note that there:

> is a dilemma posed with developing strategies for protecting cave resources: on one hand, one needs to make resources known so that they will be less likely to be destroyed through ignorance during land use changes; however, publicizing the resources can lead to increased visitation and subsequent increased rate of destruction'. (p24)

Developing guided interpretive tours for Big Island visitors and residents to experience and appreciate lava tube caves is one way to heighten awareness of these fragile environments and help foster interest in their protection while growing grassroots support for their conservation. Unfortunately, some of the lava tube experiences currently available on the Big Island could be greatly improved to better transfer appreciation of the fragility of lava tube environments.

The range of tourist lava tube experiences for visitors on the Big Island of Hawai'i

From self-guided to small group adventure tours, the Big Island offers a surprising range of lava tube cave experiences for visitors. Table 4.2 provides a list of key Big Island lava tube cave experiences available to visitors.

Kaūmana Cave

Located in a county park about five miles west of downtown Hilo is Kaūmana Cave. A large lava tube, Kaūmana Cave is one of the most accessible Big Island lava tube caves for geotourists to explore. The lava tube was formed in the main channel of the 1881 and 1882 Mauna Loa eruptions which nearly reached the town of Hilo (Hazlett and Hyndman, 1996; Halliday, 2003). Entry to Kaūmana is unrestricted and open to any visitor any time free of charge. County signage near the cave entrance advises visitors they explore the cave at their own risk and reminds them about cave hazards, the need to bring light, and to seek proper permissions if exploring beyond county parklands. The Kaūmana Cave car park area includes rest room facilities and a small picnic area.

The entrance to Kaūmana Cave is through a collapsed skylight (Hazlett and Hyndman, 1996), so it resembles entering a deep pit with nearly vertical walls. A cement staircase leads down to the picturesque cave entrance. Most visitors venture only a short distance downslope, but the adventurous can walk or crawl another 9000m. Kaūmana offers visitors the rare opportunity to move through a cave at their own pace unsupervised to pursue their own personal explorations.

Unfortunately, unsupervised 24-hour cave access also allows a small number of ignorant and ill-intentioned visitors the opportunity to vandalize the cave leaving graffiti, shattered glass and rubbish near and within the cave. Additionally, minimal interpretive signage at the cave entrance equates to minimal visitor awareness and appreciation of the unique values of Big Island lava tubes and may even encourage complacent attitudes towards their conservation.

Table 4.2 Key Big Island tourist lava tube caves, 2009

Lava tube	Tour provider	Tour types	Approx no. of visitors annually	Access
Kaūmana Cave	None	Self-guided	Unknown	Unrestricted
Nāhuku/Thurston	US National Park Service	Self-guided show cave segment and self-guided adventure tour	600,000–1,000,000	Unrestricted
Kazumura	Kazumura Cave Tours	Guided adventure	360	Restricted
	Kilauea Caverns of Fire	Guided tour and adventure tours	3000	Restricted
Kula Kai	Kula Kai Caverns	Guided show cave tour and adventure tours	1000	Restricted
Pua Po'o	US National Park Service	Ranger guided adventure tour	630	Restricted

Source: After King et al, 2008

Nāhuku

Most Hawai'i Volcano National Park visitors pay a visit to Nāhuku lava tube (also known as Thurston lava tube). Nāhuku is a park destination frequently highlighted in a variety of tourism media including TV programmes, travel books and guides, travel magazines, post cards, the park's official web site and a plethora of internet blogs. The well known lava tube is visited by between 600,000 (King et al, 2008) and one million tourists annually (Halliday, 2004). Nāhuku consists of two distinct segments. The first 120m 'show cave' segment is highly developed with a metal entrance bridge, a paved walking path, interior electric lighting and exit stairs (Halliday, 2004). The entrance is through the wall of a small pit crater while the exit is through a natural tube skylight (Hazlett and Hyndman, 1996). The lava tube can be quite crowded during peak hours and noise levels high as people socialize while walking through the cave.

Self-drive visitors walk through the cave at their own pace and with minimal interpretation. Of the numerous large commercial tour buses which stop at the lava tube, a few of the bus drivers accompany their group to the beginning of the Nāhuku trailhead and provide nominal interpretation before releasing their clients to walk onward and explore the show cave segment. Small group tours visiting the site receive significant interpretation about Big Island lava tube values from their generally well trained guides. The park service offers periodic small group interpretive tours through Nāhuku; however, only a small percentage of park visitors are able to participate in this opportunity.

The second segment of Nāhuku consists of about 330m of unlit lava tube. Visitors pass through an open chain link gate and down cave rubble to enter the dark side of Nāhuku. Visitors supply their own light to explore this part of Nāhuku. Approximately 85,000–90,000 visitors pass through the dark side gate unguided annually (King et al, 2008). Though undeveloped, this cave segment is also heavily impacted and must be cleaned regularly (Stone et al, 2005). The vast majority of visitors to the show cave side and the dark side of Nāhuku lava tube receive minimal interpretation and leave unaware of the significance of Big Island lava tubes and their contents.

Sites such as Nāhuku, damaged decades before cave conservation values were widely recognized, are frequently used by parks and others around the world as 'sacrificial' lava tubes to satisfy the public demand for an easily accessible cave experience, as well as for visitor education and appreciation purposes. However, more could be done at the Nāhuku site to better transmit Big Island lava tube values to the public.

Small group adventure tours promote cave conservation

Public understanding of and support for lava tubes and their protection is a vital element in long-term cave conservation efforts on the Big Island. Small group adventure tours into a few of these caves play an important role in fostering and maintaining this support. Carefully guided small group adventure tours are now offered by a handful of entrepreneurial cave entrance owners in a limited number of Big Island lava tubes.

Kula Kai

Located on the southern part of the island and along Mauna Loa's southwest rift zone is the Kīpuka Kanohina lava tube system of which Kula Kai Caverns (www.kulakaicaverns.com) is a part. Soluble minerals make the walls of Kula Kai much lighter in colour than most Hawaiian caves (Halliday, 2004). Kula Kai Caverns provides a show cave experience as well as a variety of adventure tours of various lengths through the braided passageways of this lava tube system. Owners of Kula Kai Caverns work closely with the Cave Conservancy of Hawai'i, whose mandate includes protecting the Kīpuka Kanohina lava tube system, to ensure proper management of their cave segment. The Kīpuka Kanohina lava tube system is currently the second longest lava tube in the world (CCH, 2003).

Kazumura

Kazumura lava tube, starting near the summit of Kīlauea and descending to the east, is currently the longest lava tube in the world (Halliday, 2004) and contains many beautiful and unusual features. Kīlauea Caverns of Fire (www.kilaueacavernsoffire.com), offers primarily two tours through different parts of Kazumura lava tube.

Kazumura Cave Tours (www.fortunecity.com/oasis/angkor/176/) takes visitors into different sections of the Kazumura lava tube system than the other tour company and offers outstanding adventure tours to some intriguing points of interest. The owner/tour guide for Kazumura Cave Tours is an avid spelunker with intimate knowledge of Kazumura and often guides visiting researchers and notables through the cave.

All three Big Island cave tour businesses market to potential customers through the occasional travel article, TV travel programme segment, newspaper stories and various web sites. Some advertise in travel magazines and work with distributors to place rack cards at appropriate venues while another relies primarily on word-of-mouth advertising.

Hawai'i Volcanoes National Park also offers a once a week small group adventure tour through a 'wild' lava tube not open to public for general visitation. The Pua Po'o adventure tour, guided by Hawai'i Volcanoes National Park staff is an example of a carefully planned and guided adventure tour helping promote cave appreciation and conservation, similar to the businesses above, and is detailed in the following case study.

Case study: The Pua Po'o adventure tour

In 1989, the Pua Po'o lava tube, known also as Cock's Comb Cave or the Wild Lava Tube, was discovered during the construction of a pig fence within Hawai'i Volcanoes National Park. According to official National Park Service procedures, Hawai'i Volcanoes National Park staff conducted a cultural assessment of the lava tube followed by a biological survey. Lava tube features were mapped and photographed. The Interpretation Department of the Park then applied for a permit to conduct limited guided tours through the lava tube (McDaniel, 2008, personal communication in King et al, 2008). With a ranger leading the group and a ranger or volunteer at the back of the group, park experts decided 12 visitors could be

Figure 4.3 Pua Po'o tour participants going down the ladder to the entrance of the lava tube

Figure 4.4 A member of the Pua Po'o tour squeezing out of the lava tube exit

guided through the lava tube with minimal impact on a weekly basis (Figures 4.3 and 4.4). Based on this information, Pua Po'o was opened up to a single public tour once a week (McDaniel, 2008, personal communication in King et al, 2008).

Pua Po'o tours are advertised on the park web site, as well as through word-of-mouth, travel guides, travel articles and internet blogs. Tour reservations can be made only one week in advance on a first come, first serve basis. Most reservations are made by phone, with a maximum of four people per call allowed to register for the tour. This restriction keeps commercial tour groups from dominating the 12 available slots. The registration system is biased towards visitors with a real interest in lava tubes as they must remember which day to call to ensure they will have a slot on the tour the following week (King et al, 2008).

The 'Wild Lava Tube' tour fills up quickly. During the initial phone call, park staff inform the tour participant to bring their own flashlight and water, wear long pants and closed-toed shoes, and bring a set of four AA batteries to replace the ones used in the headlamps provided by the park. Participants are also notified the walk to the lava tube is a fairly strenuous one-hour hike. Members of the tour meet the ranger at the designated location (King et al, 2008). The park ranger provides gloves, hardhats and headlamps to those that need them. The group then heads off to the entrance of Pua Po'o. Items, such as backpacks, that might shift while moving through the cave, are left hidden outside at the cave entrance in large plastic bags. Cave etiquette is discussed before visitors enter the lava tube. The park ranger discusses how lava tubes are formed, what tour participants will see inside and why it is important to limit the number of people visiting the site. During the tour, the ranger conducts a variety of activities, interprets cave features and questions are encouraged. Photography is allowed (King et al, 2008).

At the end of the tour, the ranger asks tour participants not to share the location of the lava tube with others, to please keep it secret. Notably, the vast majority of visitors do keep the secret of Pua Po'o as evidenced by the fact the location of the lava tube is not mentioned when the adventure is described on personal websites, internet blogs or to friends. Keeping the Pua Po'o secret infers a successful transfer of understanding and appreciation of wild lava tubes and the need to conserve them to tour participants (King et al, 2008).

Conclusion

The Big Island of Hawai'i holds the world's most valuable lava tubes containing an outstanding array of values. These lava tubes and their contents are endangered through major land and hydrologic disturbance such as land and tree clearing, pollution and human usage. Thus, it is vital to develop public appreciation and support for their preservation and conservation. Visitors experiencing Kaūmana and Nāhuku lava tubes, most receiving only the most minimal interpretation, leave these sites with little knowledge of why Big Island lava tubes should be conserved.

One means to grow support for cave protection is by offering carefully designed small group tours through lava tube environments. Kula Kai Caverns, Kīlauea Caverns of Fire, Kazumura Cave Tours and Hawai'i Volcanoes National Park's Pua Po'o tour provide in-depth interpretation which assists in transferring cave conservation values to visitors. In the case of the Pua Po'o tour, values transfer is clearly demonstrated by the park ranger guiding the tour asking tour participants not to share the location of the Pua Po'o lava tube with others, and the overwhelming majority abiding by this request. It is not unreasonable to assume that the other small group cave adventure tours mentioned above are also helping foster meaningful connections between cave visitors and Big Island lava tubes. Though visitor issues to such unique environments remain, thoughtful interpretive tour programmes such as those being offered by Hawai'i Volcanoes National Park and by other Big Island cave tour operators increase public awareness and work to help conserve Big Island lava tubes.

References

Allred, K. and Allred, C. (1997) 'Development and morphology of Kazumura cave, Hawai'i', *Journal of Cave and Karst Studies*, vol 59, no 3, pp67–80

Bullard, F. (1977) *Volcanoes of the Earth*, University of Queensland Press, St. Lucia

Cas, R. and Wright, J. (1987) *Volcanic Successions, Modern and Ancient: A Geological Approach to Processes, Products and Successions*, Allen & Unwin, London

Cave Conservancy of Hawai'i (2003) 'Kipuka Kanohina Cave Preserve management plan: May 15, 2003', www.Hawai'icaves.org/, accessed 27 April 2009

Halliday, W. (2003) 'Raw sewage and solid waste dumps in lava tube caves of Hawai'i Island', *Journal of Cave and Karst Studies*, vol 65, no 1, pp68–75

Halliday, W. (2004) 'Hawai'i Lava Tube Caves, United States', in Gunn, J. (ed) *Encyclopedia of Caves and Karst Science*, Fitzroy Dearborn, London, pp415–416

Hamilton-Smith, E. (2004) 'Tourist Caves', in Gunn, J. (ed) *Encyclopedia of Caves and Karst Science*, Fitzroy Dearborn, London, pp726–730

Hazlett, R. and Hyndman, D. (1996) *Roadside Geology of Hawai'i*, Mountain Press Publishing Company, Missoula, MT

Hawai'i Speleological Survey (1997) *The Kazumura Cave Atlas, Island of Hawai'i*, Hawai'i Speleological Survey, Honolulu

Hawai'i State Legislature (2002) 'Hawai'i Cave Protection Law 2002', Senate Bill No. 529. Twenty-Second State Legislature, State of Hawai'i, Honolulu

Hon, K., Kauahikaua, J., Denlinger, R. and MacKay, K. (1994) 'Emplacement and inflation of pahoehoe sheet flows: Observations and measurements of active lava flows on Kilauea volcano, Hawai'i', *Geological Society of America Bulletin*, vol 106, no 3, pp352–370

Howarth, F. (1972) 'Cavernicoles in lava tubes on the Island of Hawai'i', *Science*, vol 175, no 4019, pp325–326

Howarth, F. (1987) 'Evolutionary ecology of Aeolian and subterranean habitats in Hawai'i', *TREE*, vol 2, no 7, pp220–223

Howarth, F. (2004) 'Hawaiian Islands: Biospeleology', in Gunn, J. (ed) *Encyclopedia of Caves and Karst Science*, Fitzroy Dearborn, London, pp417–418

King, L. (2009) 'Geotourism in Hawai'i', in Dowling, R. and Newsome, D. (eds) *Geotourism: The Tourism of Geology and Landscape*, Goodfellow Publishing, Oxford, pp114–125

King, L. and Prideaux, B. (2010) 'Special interest tourists collecting places and destinations: A Queensland World Heritage case study', *Journal of Vacation Marketing* (in press)

King, L., Shick, H. and Brattstrom, T. (2008) 'Lava Tube Cave Tourism on the Big Island of Hawai'i: A low Impact Tour Model', in Dowling, R. and Newsome, D. (eds), *Inaugural Global Geotourism Conference Proceedings*, Promaco Conventions, Fremantle, WA, pp225–230

Mitchie, N. (2004) 'Tourist Caves: Airborne Debris', in Gunn, J. (ed) *Encyclopedia of Caves and Karst Science*, Fitzroy Dearborn, London, pp731–733

Shick, H. (2008) *Understanding Lava Tubes and Lava Caves*, Trafford Publishing, Bloomington, IN

Stone, F. and Howarth, F. (1994) 'Annotated list of the terrestrial cave fauna occurring in Hawai'i Volcanoes National Park', in *Hawai'i Volcanoes National Park, Cave Management Plan*, Hawai'i Volcanoes National Park, Honolulu

Stone, F. and Howarth, F. (2005) 'Hawaiian cave biology: Status of conservation and management, *Proceedings of the National Cave and Karst Management Symposium*, vol 19, Albany, New York

Stone, F., Howarth, F. and Nakamura, J. (2005) 'Lava cave management in Hawai'i Volcanoes National Park', *Proceedings of the National Cave and Karst Management Symposium*, vol 19 pp155–163, Albany, New York

United States Geological Survey (USGS) (1998) 'Kohala: Hawai'i's oldest volcano', www.hvo.usgs.gov/volcanoes/kohala, accessed 15 January 2008

USGS (1999) 'Explosive eruptions at Kilauea volcano, Hawai'i?', www.pubs.usgs.gov/fs/fs132-98/, accessed 4 November 2008

USGS (2001) 'Hualalai: Hawai'i's third active volcano', www.hvo.wr.usgs.gov/volcanoes/hualalai, accessed 3 November 2008

USGS (2002) 'Mauna Kea: Hawai'i's tallest volcano', www.hvo.wr.usgs.gov/volcanoes/maunakea/, accessed 3 November 2008

USGS (2006) 'Mauna Loa: Earth's largest volcano', www.hvo.wr.usgu.gov/maunaloa/, accessed 7 November 2008

USGS (2008) 'Kīlauea: Summary of the Pu'u 'Ō'ō-Kupaianaha eruption, 1983–present', www.hvo.wr.usgs.gov/kilauea/summary, accessed 3 November 2008

USGS (2009) 'Kilauea: Perhaps the world's most active volcano', www.hvo.wr.usgs.gov/kilauea, accessed 14 December 2008

University of Hawai'i Institute of Astronomy (2009) 'About Mauna Kea Observatories', www.ifa.Hawai'i.edu/mko/about_maunakea, accessed 9 November 2008

Watson, J., Hamilton-Smith, E., Gillieson, D. and Kiernan, K. (eds) (1997) *Guidelines for Cave and Karst Protection*, IUCN, Gland, Switzerland, and Cambridge, UK

Webb, R. (2004) 'Recreational Caving', in Gunn, J. (ed) *Encyclopedia of Caves and Karst Science*, Fitzroy Dearborn, London, pp621–622

5

Geotourism and Public Safety in Volcanic Environments[1]

Travis W. Heggie

Introduction

Geotourism is a relatively new concept that has emerged as a rapidly growing form of tourism (Turner, 2006). In response to the need for a more encompassing concept than ecotourism or sustainable tourism, the concept of geotourism was introduced by the Travel Industry of America and *National Geographic Traveler Magazine* in 2002 (Lew, 2002; Buckley, 2003; Kim et al, 2008). Through this introduction, geotourism was defined as tourism that sustains or enhances the geographical character of a place, its environment, culture, aesthetics, heritage and the well being of its residents (Lew, 2002). Moreover, much like ecotourism, geotourism incorporates the concept of sustainable tourism in that destinations should remain unspoiled for future generations (Lew, 2002). It also embraces the principle that tourism revenue should promote conservation while allowing for ways to protect a tourist destinations character (Lew, 2002).

Volcano tourism and travel to geothermal destinations figure prominently under the umbrella of geotourism. In 2008 1.2 million tourists visited the active volcanic features in Hawai'i Volcanoes National Park, 1.1 million visited Hawai'i's Haleakala volcano, 3 million visited the geysers and hot springs of Yellowstone National Park, 1.2 million visited Hot Springs National Park in Arkansas, and 415,000 visited Oregon's Crater Lake National Park (United States National Park Service Public Use Statistics Office, 2008). The geothermal and volcanic activity at Rotorua, New Zealand, Mt Etna in Italy, Japan's Mt Fuji, Mt Tungurahua in Ecuador, Villarrica volcano in Chile, and Iceland's active volcanoes are other popular destinations for volcano tourists (Lane et al, 2003; Ortiz et al, 2003; Behnke, 2009). However, as popular as these and other volcano destinations are the potential health hazards associated with them cannot be ignored. In fact, if volcano tourism is to be a successful tourism sector, the potential health hazards facing tourists at volcanic destinations must be recognized and mitigated. Thus, the purpose of this chapter is to review the health hazards associated with volcanoes and geothermal destinations with the intent of creating awareness amongst the tourism industry and practitioners of travel medicine.

Volcanic hazards

Many tourist destinations in hazardous locations are popular because of their high scenic value (Waller and Brink, 1987; Murphy and Bailey, 1989; Lane et al, 2003; Meheux and Parker, 2006). In fact, volcanoes in particular have been described as a powerful tourist attraction because of their aesthetic value (Dominey-Howes and Minos-Minopoulos, 2004). From a geologic perspective, volcanoes are generally described as being explosive or effusive with the quantity and behaviour of volatiles contained in their magma being a key determinant on the eruption style of a volcano (Bower and Woods, 1997; Huppert and

Woods, 2002; Hansell et al, 2006). For example, effusive volcanoes such as those in the Hawaiian Islands are known for their hot, less viscous magmas that allow gas to separate more efficiently. This in turn limits the explosiveness of eruptions (Garcia et al, 2000; Hansell et al, 2006). In contrast, more explosive volcanoes such as those in Indonesia have cooler, more viscous magmas that are more likely to fragment in an explosive eruption. It is important to note, however, that regardless of their eruption style volcanoes pose a range of health hazards for tourists during and between eruptions. These hazards range from acid rain to tephra and ash falls, earthquakes, volcanic gas emissions, landslides and mudflows, lava flows and volcanic laze (Table 5.1).

Volcanic gases

Volcanoes and geothermal areas are regularly associated with a variety of gas emissions. These gases include carbon dioxide (CO_2), sulfur dioxide (SO_2), hydrogen chloride (HCl), hydrogen sulphide (H_2S), hydrogen fluoride (HF), carbon monoxide (CO), nitrogen (N_2), hydrogen (H_2), helium (He), methane (CH_4), radon (Rn) and heavy metals such as lead and mercury (Bernstein et al, 1986; Hansell and Oppenheimer, 2004; Cantrell and Young, 2009).

Carbon dioxide

Carbon dioxide (CO_2) is abundant in volcanic gases and is particularly dangerous because it is odourless, denser than air and emitted during volcanic eruptions and in geothermal areas (Beaubien et al, 2003; Hansell and Oppenheimer, 2004). Like most gases, CO_2 poses the risk of asphyxiation. Lower to moderate concentrations of CO_2 (7–10 per cent) cause vomiting, dizziness, visual disturbances, headaches, sweating, rapid breathing, tachycardia, mental depression and tremors (Beaubien et al, 2003; Cantrell and Young, 2009). Moreover, exposure to CO_2 concentrations >100,000ppm (or concentrations of 10–30 per cent) can rapidly produce

Table 5.1 Potential hazards threatening volcano tourists

Hazard	Potential health effects
Acid rain	Irritant to eyes and skin. Also a potential threat to safe drinking water. Forms when rain falls through volcanic gas and acid particle emissions. Also forms where lava enters ocean water.
Earthquakes	Impact injuries from damage to tourist facilities and other structures. Earthquakes are common with volcanic activity. A tsunami may occur if water is displaced by underwater volcanoes.
Lava flows	Thermal injuries. Methane explosions can occur as active lava flows over vegetation. Lacerations, scrapes and abrasions, muscle strains and sprains, and other fall injuries when inactive lava flows used for recreational purposes.
Landslides/mudflows	Burial, drowning and impact injuries. May create a localized tsunami if either flow into an ocean or lake.
Laze	Irritant to eyes, skin, mucous membranes and throat. Exposure to high concentrations can cause laryngeal spasms and pulmonary edema.
Pyroclastic density	Thermal and impact injuries. Forms when a mixture of hot currents, ash, rocks and gas is pulled down a volcano by gravity.
Tephra and ash	Impact injuries, skin and eye abrasions, and respiratory irritation. Long term exposure can result in silicosis and chronic obstructive pulmonary disease. Hazardous to aircraft and the structural capability of tourist facilities. Lightning is common in ash clouds.
Volcanic gases	Asphyxiation, vomiting, headache, dizziness, visual disturbances, bronchopneumonia, eye irritation and throat irritation.

Source: Adapted from Table 1, Hansell et al, 2006

unconsciousness in 1–10 min and may result in seizures followed by death (Manning et al, 1981; Ikeda et al, 1989; Stupfel and Le Guern, 1989; Hansell and Oppenheimer, 2004; Cantrell and Young, 2009). Exposure to CO_2 in volcanic areas is generally the result of exposure to CO_2 clouds or CO_2 accumulations in low-lying topographic areas where the denser CO_2 concentrations accumulate below the air (Beaubien et al, 2003; Hansell and Oppenheimer, 2004). Such exposure often occurs near preferential pathways such as faults and fractures along which concentrations of CO_2 are able to migrate towards the surface (Hansell and Oppenheimer, 2004). Hence, the threat from CO_2 is most acute in locations such as health spas/thermal springs, near surface areas, poorly vented vacation homes or hotels in high seepage areas, or poorly ventilated vacation homes or hotels with ground-floor bedrooms, basement suites and wooden or cracked floors that permit high seepage (Baxter et al, 1999; Dibben and Chester, 1999). Small children may be particularly vulnerable because of their limited height and near surface patterns of play (Dibben and Chester, 1999). Likewise, those sleeping or lying near the floor may be vulnerable (Dibben and Chester, 1999). CO_2 related deaths in volcanic environments have been well documented. However, literature documenting CO_2 concerns directly effecting tourists have only been identified for tourists visiting Vulcano, a popular volcanic island off Sicily, tourists owning vacation homes in the Azores, tourists visiting Hawai'i Volcanoes National Park and tourists visiting Mammoth Mountain, a dormant volcano and popular recreation destination in the United States (Baxter et al, 1990; Sorey et al, 1998; Baxter et al, 1999; Dibben and Chester, 1999; Heggie and Heggie, 2004; Heggie, 2005; Cantrell and Young, 2009).

Hydrogen sulphide

In addition to CO_2, hydrogen sulphide (H_2S) is historically associated with volcanic emissions and degassing events. Hydrogen sulphide is a colourless gas with a sewer or rotten egg smell that is primarily found in destinations with high geothermal activity (Hansell and Oppenheimer, 2004; USGS Volcano Hazards Program, 2009a). At low concentrations, H_2S can irritate eyes and act as a depressant. At higher concentrations, H_2S can cause upper respiratory irritation and pulmonary edema (USGS, 2009a). Hydrogen sulphide is known to have resulted in tourist fatalities in various parts of Japan and at the geothermal field in Rotorua, New Zealand. Moreover, it is calculated that exposure to 500ppm of H_2S for 30 minutes can result in headache, dizziness, an unsteady gait and diarrhoea (USGS, 2009a). It can also be followed by the development of bronchitis and bronchopneumonia (USGS, 2009a). Acute exposures to >700ppm of H_2S can result in unconsciousness within a matter of minutes and eventual death from H_2S poisoning (Beaubien et al, 2003; Costigan, 2003; Hansell and Oppenheimer, 2004).

Sulphur dioxide

Following water and carbon dioxide, SO_2 is one of the more common gases in volcanic emissions and is a hazard to humans as a gas or a sulphate aerosol (International Volcanic Health Hazard Network, 2009). SO_2 is irritating to the eyes, throat and respiratory tract and induces coughing, burning of the eyes and difficulty breathing (International Volcanic Health Hazard Network, 2009). While these reactions are considered relatively short-term effects, tourists with pre-existing asthmatic conditions can be sensitive to SO_2 at low concentrations and suffer more severe consequences (Baxter et al, 1999; Hansell and Oppenheimer, 2004). In fact, SO_2 is known to have played a significant role in the death of several tourists at Aso, Japan, and in Hawai'i Volcanoes National Park. In these situations, half of the fatalities involved asthmatic tourists (Heggie, 2005; International Volcanic Health Hazard Network, 2009). The World Health Organization (WHO) air quality guidelines have set a maximum exposure limit for SO_2 at 175 ppb for ten minutes and 44ppb over a single day (World Health Organization, 2000). In contrast, the USGS Volcanic Hazards Program notes that a concentration of 6–12ppm of SO_2 can result in the immediate irritation of the nose and throat, 20ppm can cause immediate eye irritation and 10,000ppm will irritate moist skin within minutes (USGS, 2009a).

Hydrogen chloride/hydrochloric acid

Another volcanic gas posing potential health hazards for tourists is chlorine. Chlorine gas is emitted from volcanoes in the form of hydrogen chloride and hydrochloric acid (HCl) (USGS, 2009a). Exposure to HCl can irritate eyes, mucous membranes and the skin. It can further induce coughing, burning of the throat and a choking sensation (Stephenson et al, 1991). Exposure to concentrations over 35ppm will irritate the nose, throat and larynx after short exposure. However, exposure to concentrations >100ppm can result in acute laryngeal spasm or pulmonary edema (Stephenson et al, 1991). Recently it has been noted that when active lava in coastal regions flows into seawater, the results produce a dense HCl mist that is referred to as volcanic laze (Heggie et al, 2009). This process occurs when the lava entering the ocean rapidly boils, vaporizes seawater, and produces a white plume containing a mixture of HCl and concentrated seawater that is a brine with a salinity about 2.3 times that of seawater and a pH of 1.5–2.0 (Heggie et al, 2009). Table 5.2 displays the seawater chloride reactions that produce HCl. Exposure to this dense volcanic laze is known to have caused the death of tourists in Hawai'i (Heggie et al, 2009).

Tephra and ash

Tephra is a general term describing fragments of volcanic rock and lava that are blasted into the air by explosions or carried upward by hot gases and lava fountains (USGS Volcano Hazards Program, 2009a). Tephra fragments are classified by size with fragments <2mm in diameter labelled as ash. Tephra fragments that are between 2 and 64mm in diameter are called volcanic cinders or lapilli, and when >64mm in diameter are called volcanic bombs or volcanic blocks. Tourist fatalities resulting

from tephra have been documented on Mt Semeru in Indonesia and on Galeras volcano in Colombia (Baxter and Gresham, 1993; Thouret et al, 2007). In the incident on Galeras, three tourists and six volcanologists were killed while visiting the caldera of the volcano when a small eruption occurred without warning. The victims were pelted with volcanic bombs >1m in diameter for approximately 15 minutes and sustained devastating head and chest injuries along with other impact injuries (Baxter and Gresham, 1993). Volcanic bombs from this small eruption were found 1km beyond the rim of the caldera (Baxter and Gresham, 1993).

Aside from impact injuries, tephra can cause health problems through inhalation and contact with the skin and eyes. For example, newly fallen volcanic ash can have acid coatings and be very abrasive to the skin (Hansell et al, 2006). If inhaled, fine ash particles can cause respiratory irritation and chest discomfort as well as corneal abrasions and conjunctivitis.

Moreover, acute short-term conditions such as nasal irritation and dry coughing can occur. For tourists with asthma or other respiratory conditions, ash can cause the lining of the airways to produce more secretions which can easily result in more severe concerns. The severity of any such incident will naturally be influenced by duration of exposure and the presence of crystalline silica and any volcanic gases mixed with the ash. Long-term exposure to crystalline silica can result in silicosis and conditions such as chronic obstructive pulmonary disease (COPD) (Hansell et al, 2006).

Heavy or frequent amounts of volcanic ash pose an additional threat to the structural capabilities of tourist facilities such as hotels and ski lodges. Such conditions from volcanoes like Japan's Mt Usu have had considerable impact on the hot-spring resort town of Toyako-Onsen on the island of Hokkaido (Hirose, 1982). Moreover, another major concern about volcanic ash is the threat it poses to aviation and tourist transport operations. For example, visibility is greatly reduced during ash falls, and roads, highways and airport runways become slippery or impassable when ground ash becomes wet.

Moreover, volcanic ash particles can remain in the atmosphere for years and be spread globally by

---

Table 5.2 Seawater chloride reactions that produce HCl

$MgCl_2$ (sea salt) + H_2O (steam) = MgO (periclase) + 2 HCl (HCl gas)

2 NaCl (sea salt) + H_2O (steam) = Na_2O (sodium oxide) + 2 HCl

$CaCl_2$ (sea salt) + H_2O (steam) = CaO (lime) + 2 HCL (HCl gas)

Source: USGS Volcano Hazards Program, 2009

Figure 5.1 Hawai'i Volcanoes National Park: German tourists beyond boundary line to see lava flows from up close

high-altitude winds. More than 80 commercial aircraft have unexpectedly encountered volcanic ash during flight and at airports over the past 15 years causing considerable damage to jet engines and infiltrating the air-filter systems of plane cabins (Casadevall, 1994; USGS, 2009b). Incidentally, even volcanic fumes with the absence of tephra and ash are known to be immediately corrosive to the engines of tour helicopters and aircraft in Hawai'i, resulting in a restriction of engine air intake and a high number of crashes and emergency landings (Heggie, 2005).

Lava flows

Lava flows consist of molten rock expelled by volcanoes (Figure 5.1). Lava flows are extremely hot (700–1200°C when first expelled) and can flow long distances before cooling. Lava flows also destroy everything in their path (Kervyn et al, 2008; Chirico et al, 2009). For example, lava flows are known to have destroyed or caused serious damage to international airports and tourist facilities in Africa and Italy (Behnke and Neri, 2003; Clocchiatti et al, 2004; Kervyn et al, 2008).

Deaths caused directly by lava flows are uncommon because most lava flows move slowly. However, tourist fatalities from direct contact with lava flows have been recorded in Hawai'i (Heggie and Heggie, 2004; Heggie, 2005). Most of these fatalities were the result of tourists falling into active lava and falling on cooling lava (Heggie, 2005).

Another threat related to lava flows exists when cooled lava flows are utilized for recreational purposes such as hiking or when tourists trek over cooled lava flows in an attempt to view active lava flows. Severe burns, lacerations, scrapes and abrasions, and muscle strains and sprains from hiking the difficult terrain have been documented (Heggie and Heggie, 2004; Hawaiian Volcano Observatory, 2003).

Volcanic landslides and mudflows

Volcanic landslides, mudflows and pyroclastic flows are among some of the most potentially hazardous volcanic processes threatening tourists. A volcanic landslide, also called a debris avalanche, refers to the rapid down-slope movement of rock, snow or ice. Volcanic landslides are often caused by the gravitational collapse of volcanic features on the slopes and near summit areas of volcanoes (Behnke et al, 2003). However, it is important to note that rainfall or earthquakes can also trigger landslides. Moreover, volcanic landslides often evolve into mudflows (Hansell et al, 2006). Mudflows, also known as lahars, describe a hot or cold mixture of water and rock fragments flowing down the slopes of a volcano that can travel in excess of 60km at speeds over 30km per hour (Hansell et al, 2006).

Mudflows form in a number of ways such as the rapid melting of snow and ice by volcanic events, rainfall on loose volcanic deposits, and the breakout of crater lakes (Hansell et al, 2006; Marutani et al, 2007). Physical injuries related to burial, penetrating wounds and fractures, and eye lesions are documented results of landslides and mudflows (Hansell et al, 2006). Destinations such as the ski hills of Mt Ruapehu in New Zealand and the recreational areas on and around Mt Rainier in the United States are thought to pose the greatest hazards to tourists (Johnston et al, 2000).

Conclusion

Volcano tourism and tourism to geothermal destinations is becoming increasingly popular in many regions of the world. It is hoped that the present study has brought attention to the possible health hazards associated with tourism to volcanoes and geothermal fields. Geotourism and volcano tourism dictates that tourists will place themselves at some degree of risk by visiting volcanoes and geothermal areas. While it is recognized that the dynamics of these locations are not necessarily seasonal or periodic, if geotourism is to be an important source of income tourists must be made fully aware of the potential health hazards facing them. It is strongly recommended that future research efforts strive to quantify the health risks facing volcano tourists. This will help develop evidence-based tourism policy and improve emergency medical planning.

Note

1   This chapter was modified from Heggie, T. W. (2009) 'Geotourism and volcanoes:

Health hazards facing tourists at volcanic and geothermal destinations', *Travel Medicine and Infectious Disease*, vol 7, pp257–261.

References

Baxter, P. J. and Gresham, A. (1997) 'Deaths and injuries in the eruption of Galeras volcano, Colombia, 14 January 1993', *J. Volcanol Geotherm Res*, vol 77, pp325–338

Baxter, P. J., Baubron, J. C. and Coutinho, R. (1999) 'Health hazards and disaster potential of ground gas emissions at Furnas volcano, Sao Miguel, Azores', *J. Volcanol Geotherm Res*, vol 92, pp95–106

Baxter, P. J., Tedesco, D., Miele, G., Baubron, J. C. and Cliff, K. (1990) 'Health hazards of volcanic gases', *Lancet*, vol 336, p176

Beaubien, S. E., Ciotoli, G. and Lombardi, S. (2003) 'Carbon dioxide and radon gas hazard in the Alban Hills area (central Italy)', *J. Volcanol Geotherm Res*, vol 123, pp63–80

Behncke, B. (2009) 'Hazards from pyroclastic density currents at Mt. Etna (Italy)', *J. Volcanol Geotherm Res*, vol 180, pp148–160

Behncke, B., and Neri, M. (2003) 'The July and August 2001 Eruption of Mt. Etna (Sicily)'. *Bull Volcanol*, vol 65, pp461–476.

Behncke, B., Neri, M. and Carniel, R. (1999) 'An exceptional case of endogenous lava dome growth spawning pyroclastic avalanches: The 1999 Bocca Nuova eruption of Mt. Etna (Italy)', *J. Volcanol Geotherm Res*, vol 124, pp115–128

Bernstein, R. S., Baxter, P. J. and Buist, A. S. (1986) 'Introduction to the epidemiological aspects of explosive volcanism', *Am J. Public Health*, vol 76 (suppl.), pp3–9

Bower, S. M. and Woods, A. W. (1997) 'Control of magma volatile content and chamber depth on the mass erupted during explosive volcanic eruptions', *J. Geophysical Res*, vol 102, pp10273–10290

Buckley, R. (2003) 'Environmental inputs and outputs in ecotourism: Geotourism with a positive triple bottom line?', *J. Ecotourism*, vol 2, pp76–82

Cantrell, L. and Young, M. (2009) 'Fatal fall into a volcanic fumarole', *Wilderness Environ Med*, vol 20, pp77–79

Casadevall, T. J. (1994) 'The 1989–1990 eruption of Redoubt volcano, Alaska: Impacts on aircraft operations', *J. Volcanol Geotherm Res*, vol 62, pp301–316

Chirico, G. D., Favalli, M., Papale, P., Boschi, E., Pareschi, M. T. and Mamou-Mani, A. (2009) 'Lava flow hazards at Nyiragongo volcano, DRC. 2', *Bull Volcanol*, vol 71, no 4, pp375–387

Clocchiatti, R., Condomines, M., Guenot, N. and Tanguy, J. C. (2004) 'Magma changes at Mount

Etna: The 2001 and 2002-2003 eruptions', *Earth Planet Sci Lett*, vol 226, pp397–414

Costigan, M. G. (2003) 'Hydrogen sulphide: UK occupations exposure limits', *Occup Environ Med*, vol 60, pp308–312

Dibben, C. and Chester, D. K. (1999) 'Human vulnerability in volcanic environments: The case of Furnas, Sao Miguel, Azores', *J. Volcanol Geotherm Res*, vol 92, pp133–150

Dominey-Howes, D. and Minos-Minopoulos, D. (2004) 'Perceptions of hazard and risk on Santorini', *J. Volcanol Geotherm Res*, vol 137, pp285–310

Garcia, M. O., Pietruszka, A. J., Rhodes, J. M. and Swanson, K. (2000) 'Magmatic processes during the prolonged Pu'u 'O'o eruption of Kilauea volcano, Hawai'i', *J. Petrology*, vol 41, pp967–990

Hansell, A. L., Horwell, C. J. and Oppenheimer, C. (2006) 'Health hazards of volcanoes and geothermal areas', *Occup Environ Med*, vol 63, pp149–156

Hansell, A. L. and Oppenheimer, C. (2004) 'Health hazards from volcanic gases: A systematic literature review', *Arch Environ Health*, vol 59, pp628–639

Hawaiian Volcano Observatory (2003) 'Volcano watch: Viewing Hawai'i's lava safely – a reminder', www.hvo.wr.usgs.gov/volcanowatch/2003/ 03_03_13. html, accessed 1 June 2009

Heggie, T. W. (2005) 'Reported fatal and non-fatal incidents involving tourists in Hawai'i Volcanoes National Park, 1992–2002', *Travel Med Infectious Disease*, vol 3, pp23–31

Heggie, T. W. and Heggie, T. M. (2004) 'Viewing lava safely: An epidemiology of hiker injury and illness in Hawai'i Volcanoes National Park', *Wilderness Environ Med*, vol 2, pp77–81

Heggie, T. W, Heggie, T. M. and Heggie, T. J. (2009) 'Death by volcanic laze', *Wilderness Environ Med*, vol 20, pp101–103

Hirose, H. (1982) 'Volcanic eruption in northern Japan', *Disasters*, vol 6, pp89–91

Huppert, H. E. and Woods, A. W. (2002) 'The role of volatiles in magma chamber dynamics', *Nature*, vol 420, pp493–495

Ikeda, N., Takahasi, H., Umetasu, K. and Suzuki, T. (1989) 'The course of respiration and circulation in death by carbon dioxide poisoning', *Forensic Sci Int*, vol 41, pp93–99

International Volcanic Health Hazard Network (2009) 'Gas and aerosol guidelines', www.dur.ac.uk/claire. horwell/ivhhn/guidelines/gas/h2s.html, accessed 29 May 2009

Johnston, D. M., Houghton, B. F., Neall, V. E., Ronan, K. R. and Paton, D. (2000) 'Impacts of the 1945 and 1995–1996 Ruapehu eruptions, New Zealand: An example of increasing societal vulnerability', *Amer Geog Soc Bull*, vol 112, pp720–726

Kervyn, M., Ernst, G. G. J., Klaudius, J., Keller, J., Kervyn, F. and Mattsson, H. B. (2008) 'Voluminous lava flows at Oldoinyo Lengai in 2006: Chronology of events and insights into the shallow magmatic system', *Bull Volcanol*, vol 70, pp1069–1086

Kim, S., Kim, M., Park, J. and Guo, Y. (2008) 'Cave tourism: Tourists' characteristics, motivations to visit, and the segmentation of their behavior', *Asia Pac J Tourism Res*, vol 13, pp299–318

Lane, L. R., Tobin, G. A. and Whiteford, L. M. (2003) 'Volcanic hazard or economic destitution: Hard choices in Banos, Ecuador', *Environ Hazards*, vol 5, pp23–34

Lew, A. A. (2002) 'Geotourism and what geographers do', *Tourism Geographies*, vol 4, pp347–348

Manning, T. J., Ziminski, K., Hyman, A., Figueroa, G. and Lukash, L. (1981) 'Methane deaths? Was it the cause?', *Am J Forensic Med Pathol*, vol 2, pp333–336

Marutani, T., Yamada, Y., Kimura, M., Maita, H., Manville, V. and Leonad, G. (2007) 'Ruapehu Crater Lake break-out lahar, North Island, New Zealand', *J. Jpn Soc Eros Cont Eng*, vol 60, pp59–65

Meheux, K. and Parker, E. (2006) 'Tourist sector perceptions of natural hazards in Vanuatu and the implications for a small island developing state', *Tourism Management*, vol 27, pp69–85

Murphy, P. E. and Bayley, R. (1989) 'Tourism and disaster planning', *Geographical Rev*, vol 79, pp36–46

Ortiz, R., Moreno, H., Garcia, A., Fuentealb, G., Astiz, M. and Pena, P. (2003) 'Villarrica volcano (Chile): Characteristics of the volcanic tremor and forecasting of small explosions by means of a material failure method', *J. Volcanol Geotherm Res*, vol 28, pp247–259

Sorey, M. L., Evans, W. C., Kennedy, B. M., Farrar, C. D., Hainsworth, L. J. and Hausback, B. (1998) 'Carbon dioxide and helium emissions from a reservoir of magmatic gas beneath Mammoth Mountain, California', *J. Geophys Res*, vol 103, no 15, pp303–323

Stephenson, R., Burr, G., Kawamoto, M. and Hills, B. (1991) 'Exposures to volcanic emissions from the Hawaiian volcanoes: A NIOSH health hazard evaluation', *Appl Occup Environ Hyg*, vol 6, pp408–410

Stupfel, M. and Le Guern, F. (1989) 'Are there biomedical criteria to assess an acute carbon dioxide intoxications by a volcanic emission?', *J Volcanol Geotherm Res*, vol 39, pp247–264

Thouret, J. C., Lavigne, F., Suwa, H. and Sukatja, B. (2007) 'Volcanic hazards at Mount Semeru, East Java (Indonesia), with emphasis on lahars', *Bull Volcanol*, vol 70, pp221–244

Turner, S. (2006) 'Promoting UNESCO global geoparks for sustainable development in the Australian-Pacific region', *Alcheringa*, vol 31, pp351–365

USGS (United States Geological Survey) Volcano Hazards Program (2009a) 'Volcanic gases and their effects', www.volcanoes.usgs.gov/hazards/gas/index.php, accessed 6 January 2009

USGS Volcano Hazards Program (2009b) 'Danger to aircraft from volcanic eruption clouds and volcanic ash', www.volcanoes.usgs.gov/hazards/tephra/ashandaircraft.php, accessed 25 May 2009

United States National Park Service Public Use Statistics Office (n.d) www.nature.ps.gov/stats/viewReport.cfm, accessed 29 May 2009

Waller, J. A. and Brink, S. (1987) 'Trauma in tourist towns' *J. Rural Health*, vol 3, pp35–46

World Health Organization (2000) *WHO air quality guidelines for Europe*, 2nd edn, WHO, Geneva

6

On the Economics and Social Typology of Volcano Tourism with Special Reference to Montserrat, West Indies

Nick Petford, John Fletcher and Yegani Morakabati

Introduction

Type volcano tourism into Google and there are more than one million results, many of the early hits offering package tours or trips to volcanoes for sightseeing and exploration. Volcanic activity can cause major losses to human life, together with considerable financial cost arising from destruction of property and infrastructure. On other occasions volcanic activity happens in remote sparsely populated areas where there is little risk to humans or their properties. The economic damage of volcanic activity can range from the temporary loss of output as production is halted through the activities of the volcano to the destruction of airports, roads, houses and agricultural land. The 18 May 1980 eruption of Mt St Helens is a good example – the economic damage of the eruption is estimated at 1.1 billion USD in direct costs, or approximately 3300 USD for every second of peak eruptive activity.

To date, in spite of much research into the role of natural attractions in tourism development there has been little research into the scope and scale of volcano tourism, or the underlying social and economic factors that drive this activity (Sigurdsson and Lopez-Gautier, 2002). Anecdotal evidence, including data from the top volcano destinations (Table 6.1) provides some clues about the nature of this type of tourist activity. Presently, volcano tourism is niche market, high-end and exclusive. The unique selling point of volcano tourism may well be a mix of danger and thrill seeking, combined with scientific or educational curiosity, but this remains speculative. However, comparative analyses of this niche element of tourism imply it is growing faster than other forms of special interest tourism including visits to sites of other Earth science-related natural disasters (tsunamis, hurricanes or earthquakes). For example, Pompeii (Italy), the town destroyed famously in the AD79 eruption of Vesuvius, enjoys 2.5 million visitors per annum, but when the site was compromised tourism to the area as a whole fell by 20 per cent (Hooper, 2008). This fact alone elevates the study of volcano tourism above the purely speculative and points to these sites of natural interest as regionally important economic drivers.

In this brief paper we explore the literature in an attempt to discover those circumstances that facilitate tourism development, and how successful

Table 6.1 Top five world destinations for volcano tourists

Country	Volcano(es)
1. Indonesia	Mt Bromo, Merapi, Krakatoa, Gede, Papandayan
2. Italy	Etna, Vulcano, Stromboli
3. Tanzania	Kilimanjaro, Oldoinyo Lengai, Meru
4. Vanuatu	Yasur, Lopevi, Gaua, East Epi, Karua
5. USA	Hawai'i (Kilauea, Mauna Loa) Washington State (Mt St Helens)

they have been in offsetting the damage and economic costs caused by the volcanic activity. We use the Caribbean island of Montserrat as a case study to look at the loss of infrastructure and property caused by a recent eruption and how such losses may impede the development of tourism as a means to economic recovery. Briefly we will also examine wider issues relating to volcano tourism including the risks to tourists, the limitations of this form of tourist activity and ask how soon after a disaster, where lives have been lost, is it acceptable to reintroduce tourism. This final point links volcano tourism to that of dark tourism (Stone, 2006), and we examine how dark tourism may become lighter with the passage of time.

Tourism and the Earth sciences (geotourism)

Tourism occurs in a variety of guises from the mass-tourism that has dominated travel for more than half a century to the unusual or niche types of tourism activity that manifests in people travelling to the polar regions or to active volcanoes. The nature of tourism together with the motivations of the travellers has spawned various typologies of tourism. For instance, Cohen (1972, 1974) categorized tourists into four distinct groups:

- organized mass tourism;
- individual mass tourism;
- explorers; and
- drifters.

Applying this typology to volcano tourism, the 'explorer' provides the best fit although it is not a perfect description, with gaps to be filled partly through the development of technology and early warning systems that provide some assurance to tourists, thereby reducing the risk elements, and partly through the fact that many of the visitors to volcanoes are of a professional background with specific interests in the geology. Others such as Smith (1989) used typologies to examine the likely impact of tourism on the host communities by tourists with differing motivations to travel. Plog (1974) focused his attention more on the nature of the destination and the type of tourists that it will attract rather than on hosts at the destination and the adaptability of tourists to the local norm. In Plog's world volcano tourism would reflect the allocentric tourists who travel to destinations rarely visited, in pursuit of adventure and new experiences. Allocentric tourists tend to be independent, confident tourists that need little in the way of tourist infrastructure and superstructure. In summary, there are a number of different typologies that have been assigned to explain tourist behaviour and choice, and many of them are overlapping and point to similar conclusions (for example, see Fletcher in Cooper et al, 2008 p195).

All forms of travel contain an element of risk and tourists have different propensities to be risk averse. Often, as in the case of mass tourism, the perceived risk is relatively small and does not deter tourist activity. However, events, such as 9/11 and other serious incidents can severely disrupt tourism flows causing tourists to seek alternative destinations. However, volcano tourism may work counter to this general tendency by making the destination even more attractive to the visitor if there is recent volcanic activity.

Geotourism also overlaps with and shares many characteristics with ecotourism and may even be regarded a subset of it (Burek and Prosser, 2008). Distinct from volcanology, the wider Earth sciences, defined broadly to include coastal and marine environments and sites of scientific interest related to geology, are fairly numerous. For example, the coastline of southern England (December 2001) has been designated a world heritage site by the United Nations in recognition of its unique rock formations and fossil locations, and similar designations have been bestowed on regions of exceptional natural beauty the world over. Some of these, such as the national parks of Yellowstone in the USA and Hawai'i, are volcanic in origin. Indeed, in a fact not lost on most practicing geologists, many of the most popular and/or exclusive tourist resorts on Earth, including the Caribbean and Canary Islands and inland chains in the South Pacific are entirely volcanic in origin, making a direct link between their physical origin and geotourism inevitable. Indeed, something of a trend is developing in the wider geosciences community where the economic and social benefits of these precious natural resources are being recognized. For example, at the recent 33rd Geological Congress in Oslo, a research session was devoted to proposals for geoparks, UNESCO-approved areas of significant Earth science interest. The idea is that geoparks will provide a means of generating additional tourist income to countries that may be off the beaten track as far as mainstream tourism is concerned (Forty, 2008). On a more directly relevant theme, 2002 saw the opening in France of Vulcania, Parc European du Volcanism in the Puy de Dome, Auvergne, famous for its (now extinct) volcanic activity (see Chapter 17). These and other sites look set to continue a trend linking active or former sites of volcanic activity to theme parks with a strong educational component.

Tourism and the curse of natural resources

From an economic perspective, tourism has product characteristics that make it an attractive option. These include its role as a fast foreign exchange earner, its labour intensive nature, the opportunity to set prices without the need to invoke protectionism, a flexible supply system that can respond rapidly to fluctuations in market demand, and its role in creating and sustaining economic diversity. However, does a natural resource (that is, in the context of tourism a marketable feature that could include a volcano) automatically translate into economic growth for the host country? The answer may well be no: see Sachs and Warner (2001), who show in their analysis of post World War II economic output that those countries blessed with abundant natural resources have economies that have grown more slowly than resource-poor ones (Figure 6.1). The reason for this is still not entirely clear but may be due to the fact that resource-abundant countries have high-price economies and may have missed out on export-led growth. Assuming that this is indeed true, then an interesting corollary can be made with the tourism trade such that countries blessed with abundant environmental resources (sun, sea, sand, beautiful location and exotic attractions), may not grow rich from such activities, in fact the reverse.

A compelling example of this could be called a tale of two islands – Jamaica and Singapore. One (Jamaica) is formed from volcanic activity and a notable tourist destination, so in this sense is endowed with environmental resources, yet as an economic power it pales against Singapore which has one of the highest post-war GDP growth rates per capita, yet rates lowly as a tourist destination and lacks any substantial natural resource (e.g. oil). While by no means definitive, this correlation points to factors such as an over reliance on a single source of income (e.g. tourism) may act as a 'trap' or be considered a curse to those in a low wage, low innovation economy. Where development funds are available they are channelled into the front-line tourism industry hindering the development of other forms of production and, ironically, limiting the ability of destinations to hold on to the foreign exchange that follows the tourists. Clearly any such 'curse' would have implications for developing countries or regions trying to improve GDP by relying dominantly on, for example, volcano or ecotourism as the major or single source of economic growth.

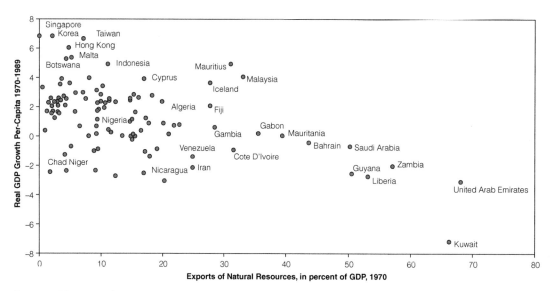

Figure 6.1 The curse of natural resources: Exports versus GDP growth for selected countries over the period 1970–1989

Source: Sachs and Warner, 2001

Montserrat case study

By way of example we turn to the Caribbean island of Montserrat as a case study in how a catastrophic volcanic eruption can have disastrous consequences for the local economy, but may yet provide some respite through volcano-related tourism (the natural resources curse notwithstanding). Montserrat is a British protectorate and the volcanic activity on which this paper focuses was centred around the Soufriere Hills in the south of the island, beginning in May 1995 after recording seismic activity since 1992. On 18 July 1995 the volcano erupted (Montserrat Volcanic Observatory, 2009).

The ongoing volcanic crisis of 1995–1997 destroyed much of the social and economic fabric of the island (Druitt and Kokelaar, 2002 and references therein). Effects included a substantial human exodus (the population fell from a pre-eruption figure of 11,500 to about 4000, the majority living predominantly in the middle and north of the island. GDP fell from £38.7M (1994) to £24.2M (1998) and tourism, which accounted for approximately 25 per cent of GDP before 1995 fell to 16.67 per cent of a falling GDP in 1995. Ongoing financial support from the UK (via DFID) had reached £200M by 2004.

The economy of Montserrat is dominated by tourism and agriculture both of which suffered enormously as a result of the volcanic activity and most commentators now accept there is an urgent need for the island to become self-sustaining, to some extent by repositioning Montserrat as a tourism destination and as a mechanism to attract *new* inward investment (to look at the perception of volcanic eruptions as an agent of change see Dove, 2008). Indeed, this seems to be a UK government priority, which has made available £1.5M over three years to assist the Montserrat Tourism Board to develop a long-term strategy. However, before any of this can realistically happen two fundamental issues need to be addressed: (1) risk management and risk perception relating to present and on-going volcanic activity; and (2) Island transport and infrastructure (Cardona 1997).

Living with ongoing volcanic activity

Over half the population fled the island in 1995 and many have yet to return. Indeed many living only a short distance away on Antigua (currently the only primary route onto Montserrat) are fearful of returning and may consider it so dangerous that they may never return. Coping with the volcano and volcanic risk, combined with a resignation that it is here to stay for the foreseeable future are essential psychological factors that both islanders and potential tourists alike need to face. Since 1995 a scientific team of international experts, set up to advise the governing body on Montserrat, have been monitoring the volcano and assessing the risk to the local population of future eruptions or other kinds of potential non-eruptive hazards including mudflows and dust inhalation. Their conclusions (as of 2009) are that there is an 80 per cent chance the current eruptive phase will last for the next five years, and a 50 per cent chance the volcano will be active for the next 33 years. It may of course erupt at any time.

A key development in monitoring volcanic activity was the setting up of the Montserrat Volcano Observatory (MVO), beginning its life as the Soufrière Hills Volcano Observatory in July 1995, and changing its name to the MVO when it moved to a rented villa in Olde Town in October of that year. The role of the observatory as originally formulated was to gather geophysical and geological data on the state of the volcano and make available that data to the risk assessors. Early in the eruption cycle this made sense, and while the primary remit of the MVO must remain the safety of the islanders, we argue here that it can and should be used to play a wider role in tourism development focused explicitly on the volcano.

The risks surrounding volcano tourism relate directly to the style of volcanic activity. Basically there are two kinds of volcano, ones that erupt mostly lava such as the shield volcanoes of Hawai'i and the Galapagos Islands, and those that erupt explosively and catastrophically (e.g. Pinatubo, Mt St Helens). The latter are by far the more dangerous and account for the majority of lives lost during eruptions. Montserrat falls into the latter category, meaning the risk of injury to the casual visitor is much higher. However, it is important to note that even on Montserrat itself the risk is variable, meaning that the northern part of the island is low risk even though the volcano is on a high state of alert (Figure 6.2). This accurate but nonetheless confusing state of affairs needs very clear and careful external communication to potential visitors. A sophisticated mechanism for doing this is at present lacking.

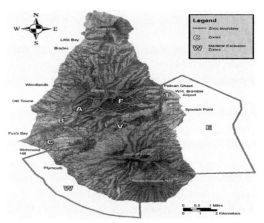

Figure 6.2   Hazard Map of Montserrat. The island is divided into six land zones and two maritime exclusion zones

Note: Even if the risk level is deemed high in the south, the region north of the zone boundary crossing the Centre Hills has unrestricted visitor access

Source: Montserrat Volcano Observatory

Transport and infrastructure

Prior to 1995 Montserrat had an international airport and jetty allowing passengers to disembark by ferry or from cruise liners that circuit the Lesser Antilles in abundance. Both were destroyed in the 1995 eruption. The airport WH Bramble (Blackburne) in the north-east is now completely unusable and the capital, Plymouth, was destroyed by a succession of devastating mudflows (see Figure 6.3b). At present there is no way onto the island by ferry. In 2005 a new airport, 'Gerald's Airport', was built on the north side of the island at a cost of £28M, but it is smaller than the old one and flights arrive from Antigua via two Twin Otter aircraft each with a seat capacity of only 18. So, passengers from cruise liners cannot disembark and inbound flights are volume constrained. Helicopter tours run from Antigua that allow sightseers to view the volcano but do not land. Presently no charge is made by the island for use of its air space.

Clearly much more needs to be done before the tourist trade can pick up substantially. The bare minimum would be a new jetty, but because of current hazard restrictions this would need to be on the north of the island. A potential site has been identified on the north-west coast (Little

Bay) but building work has yet to begin. One relatively straightforward and quick option might be to build a floating jetty away from any marine hazard zones. Several possible locations exist on the western side of the island.

The role of the MVO

One quick-win option for the island is to make better use of the MVO as a potential tourist attraction/visitor centre. Similar centres exist on other active volcanoes (Hawai'i is a prime example) and dormant ones also (e.g. Vesuvius), that are popular destinations and would help to generate much needed revenue and local employment via sales and catering. Provided of course people can get to the island in sufficient volume in the first place (see above). It seems to us that the physical presence of the observatory on Montserrat provides competitive advantage that could be put to good use as a base for the visiting public.

Would they come?

The discussion above assumes that provided access is made available, tourists would want to visit the island. The simple answer (although not explicitly researched for the case in hand) is yes – a glance at Table 6.1 shows that volcanoes are indeed significant tourist attractions, even those that are currently erupting.

Figure 6.3a Dark tourism?

Note: Visitors to Pompeii (destroyed in the AD79 eruption of Vesuvius) may be attracted by more than just the heritage and educational aspects of the site. Pompeii as an authentic site of death and suffering fulfils those characteristics defining the darkest end of the dark tourism spectrum of Stone (2006).

Source: Photo courtesy of FreeDigitalPhotos.net

Volcanoes as sites of 'dark' tourism

Dark tourism refers to products and places that draw visitors interested in disasters, sites of atrocities and other macabre events (Seaton, 1996; Stone, 2006). Recent examples broadly include sightseeing in New Orleans post Hurricane Katrina and visits to Aceh, Indonesia, site of the devastating Boxing Day tsunami. It is undeniable that certain aspects of volcano tourism involve visits to sites of disaster and death. Pompeii is a prime example of this, where visitors can photograph former residents in their death throws (Figure 6.3a). Compare this with a more recent site of destruction but one that did not result in loss of life (Figure 6.3b).

Dark tourism, although first recorded as being attributable to D. Dunlap (McFedries, 2007) in 1982 in the *New York Times* when he referred to 'a dark tourist attraction', and was first cited in 1997 by James Hall of *Scotland on Sunday*, 10 August 1997 (McFedries, 2007), when referring to JFK as a tourist attraction, is more recently attributed to Stone (2006) when he suggested that there are different shades of darkness according to the nature of the event and argued that other factors such as entertainment versus education, and heritage versus history, all help explain the level of darkness involved. The passage of time, although included in Stone's analysis as an element, is possibly one of the most significant determinants of just how dark an incident/event is in many cases. For instance, if the agonizing death

Figure 6.3b Plymouth, former capital of Montserrat destroyed in the 1995 eruption

Note: The former town is currently within the exclusion zone (Zone W, Figure 6.2) but is in effect a modern-day Pompeii minus human casualties. In Stone's (2006) dark spectrum classification, the site is authentic, likely to become history concentric (conservation/commemorative), but while spectacular, is not a site of death and suffering.

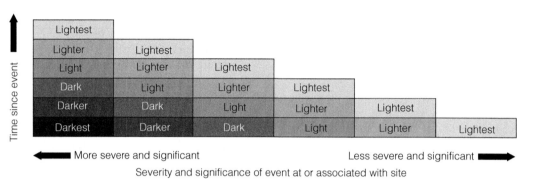

Figure 6.4 The relationship between dark tourism sites and time

Note: Here the added dimension of time acts to lighten the darkness of the original event, implying that after a critical (yet unquantified) threshold period, a site of mass destruction and death (e.g. the AD79 eruption of Vesuvius that destroyed Pompeii) becomes socially acceptable as a tourist destination.

Source: Based on Stone, 2006, p151

experienced by the residents of Pompeii had happened last year there would be a much higher level of unacceptability associated with visiting the site as a tourist; it would be considered very dark. The fact that Mt Vesuvius erupted 1930 years ago makes it more fascinating than macabre to view the remains of those that perished. There will always be exceptions to such 'rules' and some types of attraction, such as, say, Auschwitz–Birkenau maintain a dark shade for long periods of time because the horrors that took place were of such unimaginable magnitude and human cruelty. On the other hand, other events such as 9/11 have quickly become major tourist attractions complete with the customary T-shirts and guided tours.

Using the factors that Stone included it can be suggested that volcanoes are both heritage and educational sites. To what extent does this type of activity fit in with the broader spectrum of dark tourism? Figure 6.4 shows the dark tourism spectrum as proposed by Stone (2006), where the controlling dimension ranges from light (sites associated with death and suffering) to darkest (sites of death and suffering). It is probably fair to conclude that explosive volcanic eruptions (e.g.

Krakatoa in 1883 and Mt Pelee, 1902, that between them killed over 60,000 people) place them at the darker end. Viewing volcano tourism through a dark spectrum lens raises some interesting and ethical questions. For example, how soon after a major eruption is it acceptable to put on display the remnants of a disaster that has caused loss of life? In the case of Pompeii, several millennia have passed since the deaths of the town's inhabitants and any ethical or moral outrage at treating those deaths as spectacle has passed by. Similar behaviour at the site of a very recent disaster would be considered ghoulish at best, but no doubt would attract some tourists. Furthermore, a post eruption society will be under severe stress and opening up to tourism would undoubtedly add to this stress and may even hinder, if not physical at least psychological, recovery.

Summary

Volcano tourism provides a bridge between the natural sciences and economics. In this sense it could be considered a branch of *applied* volcanology analogous to hazard and risk management. Some outstanding issues relating to volcano tourism include whether tourists should be encouraged to visit an active volcano, especially one that is known to behave explosively, and how best should we manage risk of personal injury or even death (legally and financially). Questions arise as to how volcano tourism links with ecotourism (is it the same or something different?), and can the dark tourism spectrum help explain our fascination with the aftermath of volcanic activity, and other kinds of natural hazards?

References

Burek, C.V. and Prosser, C. D. (eds) (2008) *The History of Geoconservation* No. 300, Special Publication, Geological Society Publishing House, Bath

Cardona, O. D. (1997) 'Management of the volcanic cruises of Galeras volcano: Social, economic and institutional aspects', *Journal of Volcanology and Geothermal Research*, vol 77, pp314–324

Cohen, E. (1972) 'Towards a sociology of international tourism', *Social Research*, vol 39, pp164–182

Cohen, E. (1974) 'Who is a tourist? A conceptual clarification', *Sociological Review*, vol 22, pp527–555

Cooper, C., Fletcher, J., Fyall, A., Gilbert, D. and Wanhill, S. (2008) *Tourism Principles and Practice*, Pearson Education Limited, Edinburgh

Dove, M. R. (2008) 'Perception of volcanic eruption as agent of change on Merapi volcano, Central Java', *Journal of Volcanology and Geothermal Research*, vol 172, pp329–337

Druitt, T. H. and Kokelaar, B. P. (2002) 'The eruption of Soufriere Hills volcano, Montserrat from 1995 to 1999', *Memoirs*, vol 21, Geological Society, London

Forty, R. (2008) 'Geopark of the giant trilobites', *Geoscientist*, vol 18, pp22–24

Hooper, J. (2008) 'Italy declares Pompeii a state of emergency', *The Guardian*, Saturday, 5 July, www. guardian.co.uk/world/2008/jul/05/italy, accessed 27 September 2009

Maynard, R. (2008) 'The legacy of Krakatoa', *The Independent*, 24 August

McFedries, P. (2007) 'Dark tourism', *Word Spy*, www. wordspy.com/words/darktourism.asp, accessed 22 September 2009

Montserrat Volcano Observatory (2009) 'Chronology of the current eruption', www.montserrat volcanoobservatory.info/index.php? option=com_c ontent&view=article&id=242%3Ahistory-of-mvo&catid=50%3Ahistory-of-mvo& Itemid=101&lang=en, accessed 27 September 2009

Nield, T. (2002) 'Puy in the sky?', *Geoscientist*, vol 10, pp5–6

Plog, S. (1974) 'Why destination areas rise and fall in popularity', *Cornell Hotel and Restaurant Administration Quarterly*, vol 14, pp55–58

Sachs, J. D. and Warner, A. M. (2001) 'The curse of natural resources', *European Economic Review*, vol 45, pp827–839

Seaton, A.V. (1996) Guided by the Dark: From thanatopsis to thanatourism. *Journal of Heritage Studies*, Vol 2(4): 234-244.

Sigurdsson, H. and Lopez-Gautier, R. (2002) 'Volcanoes and tourism', *Encyclopaedia of Volcanoes*, 1283, Academic Press, New York

Smith, V. (1989) *Hosts and Guests: The Anthropology of Tourism*, University of Pennsylvania Press, Philadelphia, PA

Somarriba-Chang, M., Garnier, M. and Laguna, V. (2006) 'Estimation of the tourist carrying capacity of the Natural Reserve Mombacho Volcano, Granada, and the Natural Reserve Datanli-El Diablo, Jinotega, Nicaragua', *Sustainable Tourism II*, pp341–351

Stone, P. R. (2006) 'A dark tourism spectrum: Towards a typology of death and macabre related tourist sites, attractions and exhibitions', *Tourism*, vol 54, pp145–160

7

Volcano Tourism – Central and South American Examples

Henry Gaudru

Introduction: Tourism in volcano national parks

The main focus in the protection of natural areas around the Earth has been in the context of preserving landscape beauty, natural heritage, unique biological habitat or recreation. More recently, geology and volcanology has emerged at the forefront of interest for many protected areas (Eder and Patzak, 2004). This approach of crediting a park's existence to its geologic-volcanologic landscape seems intuitive, since many of the volcanic parks in the world exist because of their particular geological features. In this sense, their main purpose is to preserve geological heritage for future generations, educate and teach the public about issues in the geological sciences and environmental approach, and ensure sustainable tourism for many countries in the world. These parks are also a pedagogical tool for environmental education, training and inter-disciplinary research related to geoscientific disciplines, the understanding of broader environmental issues, and for sustainable development.

The implementation of a national park or a preserved area allows tourism to have an immediate positive impact upon an area by improving living conditions of the rural environment, strengthening identification of the population within their area, and triggering a cultural renaissance. The geologic patrimony constitutes a repaid investment in tourism terms;

that fact is amply demonstrated by the millions of visitors from all over the world who visit each year the great and small geologic and volcanic parks and their associated museums.

Volcanoes of Central America

Central America makes up a part of 'The Pacific Ring of Fire'. This extends all the way to New Zealand, along the eastern edge of Asia, Japan, then north across Kamchatka, the Aleutian Islands of Alaska, North America, Central and South America (Chapter 1). In the Americas five tectonic plates interact: the North America, Cocos, Caraïbes, Nazca and South American plates. Most active volcanoes in Central America occur in belts produced by subduction of the small Cocos Plate beneath the North American and the western edge of the Caribbean Plate, and trend parallel to the strike of the subducting Cocos Plate. The volcanic front in Central America is a chain, made of right-stepping linear segments, 100 to 300km in length. Volcanoes cluster into centres, whose spacing is random but averages about 27km. Large andesitic strat-ovolcanoes and silicic caldera are found in this region and also many basaltic fields, particularly in the Central Valley of Mexico and along the Guatemala–El Salvador border. Volcanism has an important impact on the region as was learned with the recent and violent eruption of the El Chichon volcano in 1982 in Mexico, but can also be seen in the numerous volcanic national parks of the region (Table 7.1).

Table 7.1 Main volcano national parks in Central and South America

Volcanic national park	Country	Description
Nevado De Colima National Park	Mexico	Two volcanoes are located within the boundaries of this 55,500-acre park. The dormant 4335m Nevado de Colima is visited frequently by European mountaineers. The foothills of this volcano are covered with pine, fir and oak forests inhabited by falcons, hummingbirds and many species of reptiles. A second volcano with active vents, Volcán de Fuego (3600m) is also located within the park.
Pico De Tancítaro National Park	Mexico	The Tancítaro volcano is the main attraction in this 73,290-acre park. Forests of pine and fir situated on steep slopes offer beautiful scenery and ample opportunities exist to hike or rock climb.
Pacaya Volcano National Park	Guatemala	In June 2001 the Pacaya volcano was made a national park. Located 50km to the south-west of Guatemala City, it is close enough for a daytrip yet far enough for a wild natural adventure. It has four peaks: Cerro Chiquito, Cerro de Agua, Cerro Chino and Pico Mackenney. The active crater is at the top of Pico Mackenney and is always throwing ash, water vapour and lapilli (small stones) up into the sky, and at least once a year it pours out lava. Since the volcano was included into the Pacaya National Park a trail to the summit has been opened, with rest areas, direction signs and trash bins along the way. Park rangers are employed, meaning that it is becoming ever more safe for climbers without guides.
Masaya Volcano National Park	Nicaragua	Masaya is a large basaltic volcanic caldera located 20km south of Managua, the capital of Nicaragua. It is Nicaragua's first and largest national park (1979), and one of 78 protected areas in the country. The park has an area of 54km² and includes two volcanoes and five craters. The park consists of a complex volcano with three craters that have formed one larger boiler. These are in constant activity and present lava outflows at different times. The park area contains various species in danger of extinction and is a representative sample of a Tropical Dry Forest.
Arenal Volcano National Park	Costa Rica	Arenal volcano is the most spectacularly active one in Costa Rica. Many people visit this park at night to watch the lava flows and red hot boulders ejected from the volcano glow in the darkness. Although eruptions are the main attraction, visitors should be aware that even in the dry season the clouds sometimes obscure the top of the volcano, and the chances of seeing a pyroclastic display are lessened in the rainy season.
Irazú Volcano National Park	Costa Rica	The park that includes the Irazu volcano covers 2309ha, its highest point being 3432 metres above sea level. The park is remarkable because of its surreal lunar landscape. There are two main craters, one is called the 'Diego de la Haya' and contains a strangely coloured lake (some days it's light green and others it's red) and the other is 300 metres deep. Irazú has erupted frequently in historical times — at least 23 times since its first well-recorded eruption in 1723. Its most famous recent eruption began in 1963 and continued until 1965. It is easily visited from the capital San José, with a road leading right up to the summit craters and a weekly bus service to the top. It is thus a popular tourist spot.
Poás Volcano National Park (Figure 7.1)	Costa Rica	The park covers 5600ha, and the Poás basaltic volcano stands at an altitude of 2708m above sea level. It is one of the few volcanoes that people can drive almost all the way to the rim – within 300m of the edge of one of the world's largest active craters (1.5km wide). The viewing terrace gives a bird's-eye view 320m down into the volcano, with its greenish sulphuric pool. The volcano has had a long history of eruptions, going back as much as 11 million years. On 25 January 1910, it ejected 640,000 tons of ash, and in the period 1952–1954 it bombarded nearby areas with ash and rocks. Since then, Poás has maintained a low profile, but in 1989 the park was closed because of dangerous sulphurous gas emissions. Its geyser-like eruptions of muddy water and steam have also given it the reputation as the world's largest geyser.
Rincón De La Vieja National Park	Costa Rica	Rincón de la Vieja (1895m), an active volcano in a period of relative calm, is the largest of five that make up the Cordillera de Guanacaste. It is composed of nine separate but contiguous craters, with dormant Santa María (1916m) the tallest and most easterly. Its crater harbours a forest-rimmed lake popular with quetzals, linnets and tapirs. The main crater, Von Seebach, sometimes called the Rincón de la Vieja crater, still steams. Lake Los Jilgueros lies between the two craters. The last serious eruption was in 1983 though lava and acid gases were ejected on 8 May 1991, causing destructive lahars.

Table 7.1 continued

Volcanic national park	Country	Description
Tenorio Volcano National Park and Vicinity	Costa Rica	One km north of the Río Corobicí, a well-paved road leads north-east 58km to Upala in the northern lowlands via the low-lying saddle of Tenorio and Miravalles dormant volcanoes.
Los Nevados National Park	Colombia	The Parque Nacional de Los Nevados (583km²) was created in 1974. It is home to the Volcano of Nevado Ruiz and other paramounts Santa Isabel and Tolima. The Paramounts Park is inside the Coffee Region 'Eje Cafetero'. To get to the park the best is to head for Manizales first and enter the park from there. A four-wheel-drive rental vehicle is a good idea for exploring the park, as is a guide: Colombians are getting serious about protecting what is left of their environment and it is difficult to acquire camping permits from the park entrance station without hiring a local escort. The high altitude volcano vegetation, the lakes and the active volcanoes are absolutely worth visiting.
Cotopaxi National Park	Ecuador	The Cotopaxi Volcano National Park, created in 1979, is the second biggest national park in Ecuador and the second most visited after the Galapagos National Park. In 1970 the Refuge named Jose Rivas located at 4800m above sea level was built. The park is located south of Quito, and includes the volcanoes Cotopaxi (5897m) and Sincholagua (4893m).
Sangay National Park	Ecuador	The Sangay National Park (271,000ha) was founded in 1979 and covers parts of the provinces of Chimborazo, Morona Santiago and Tungurahua. Within its borders three volcanoes can be found, two of them are still active. Tungurahua (5016m) which has showed increasing activity during 2008 represents a breathtaking spectacle. Sangay (5230m) is situated at the edge of the rainforest and is one of the most active volcanoes in the world. There is also the Altar volcano (5320m), which has been extinct for a long time.
Parque Nacional Lauca	Chile	Near Putre in the Parinacota Province. Covering 138,000ha it contains a third of all the bird life in Chile. Extremely high (4500m), this is the 'Altiplano' of Chile. Snow-covered volcanoes Parinacota (6342m), Pomerape (6282m), Guallarite (6060m) and Acotango (6050m) make for an impressive sky line. The park administration is located at Putre, a small village about 46km from the park itself.
Parque Nacional Volcan Isluga	Chile	About 228km north-east of Iquique. The park covers an area of almost 175,000ha, and a short distance from the park entrance are hot springs and within the park are various types of vegetation, flamingos and other birds.
Parque Nacional Llullaillaco	Chile	About 275km south-east of Antofagasta. This park covers an area of 268,000ha and contains the Llullaillaco volcano, the second highest peak in Chile at 6739m. This is good climbing country.
Lake Region of Chile	Chile	Conguillo National Park (Llaima volcano), located about 148km north-east of Temuco. Conguillo National Park is one of the most beautiful parks of Chile. 'Conguillio' in the Araucanian language, means 'water with feathers'. Among its greatest attractions is the 'Llaima' volcano at an altitude of 3125m, lakes and lagoons of volcanic origin, and ancient forests, many of which are unexplored. This park is also known as 'the umbrellas' due to its ancient araucaria forests.
Parque National Villarica	Chile	About 120km west of Temuco and 5km east of Pucón, this park covers an area of 63,000ha and includes the active, snow-covered Villarrica volcano that rises to a height of 2847m and forests that include the famous 'Araucaria' trees (Monkey Puzzle Tree).
Lanin Volcano National Park (Neuquen)	Argentina	This park was created in 1937 to preserve a good sample of the northern patagonian woods and forests, including here some species not found elsewhere. It comprises an area of 379,000ha; 194,600ha belong to the park and the remaining 184,000 belong to three reservations. Within this park is Lanin volcano (3776m), with its almost perfect conical form. Its mountaineous relief is rich in lakes. There is a trail to the shelter on the south face of Lanin volcano at 2300m above sea level. The ascent is regulated by the management of Argentine National Parks and the Argentine National Gendarmerie, and is relatively simple, but many deaths have occurred due to a lack of responsibility and caution on the part of the climbers. The nearest town, usually employed as a base for climbers, is Junín de los Andes.

Costa Rica

Costa Rica was the first country in Central America and the Caribbean to implement environmental actions at the ministry level (Hopkins, 1995). More than 25 per cent of Costa Rica's territory has been designated either as national park land or some kind of biological reserve, wildlife refuge or wildlife corridor. There are several volcano national parks and among them is the famous Arenal National Park based on an active volcano. The national parks and wildlife refuges of Costa Rica are managed by the Ministerio de Ambiental y Energia (MINAE). Eleven conservation areas were established by this Ministry in 1998 to oversee and manage the public lands of Costa Rica. These conservation areas are known as the Sistema Nacional de Areas de Conservacion, or SINAC. Costa Rica has attracted an average of 1.6 million tourists every year from 2003 to 2008, and of these 60 per cent said that they have visited at least one of the volcanoes in the country.

Because most tourism in Costa Rica is based on national parks, the tourism industry helps to support these parks and to encourage wise use and conservation. Future concerns for the national parks of Costa Rica include the economic situation, conservation education, the need to demonstrate the monetary value of conservation, population growth, the need for citizen involvement and the need for effective environmental legislation.

There are over 100 volcanoes in Costa Rica; ten of them show some type of activity such as solfataras, fumaroles and eruptive activity. The best known are Arenal, Poas, Irazu Turrialba and Rincon de la Vieja. Costa Rica's volcanoes are formed by subduction of the eastward-moving Caribbean Plate. They form part of the 'ring of fire' (see Chapter 1), the long belt of active volcanoes all around the Pacific Ocean. All of the active volcanoes noted above have been designated as Costa Rican national parks. One of them, the Arenal Volcano National Park allows visitors to observe an eruptive activity from the foot of the volcano.

Figure 7.1 Poas volcano is one of the few volcanoes where people can drive almost all the way to the rim

Note: The viewing terrace gives a bird's-eye view 320m down into the volcano and is visited by tourists from a variety of backgrounds.

Arenal National Park

Arenal Volcano National Park, was created by Executive Decree 20791 (MIRENEM, 1991) of 6 November 1991. It has an area of 12,124 hectares. The Parque Nacional Volcán Arenal lies within the larger (204,000 ha) Arenal Conservation Area, protecting 8 of Costa Rica's 12 life zones and 16 protected reserves in the region between the Guanacaste and Tilarán mountain ranges, including Lake Arenal. A joint project involving the Canadian International Development Agency and World Wildlife Fund Canada is helping local communities protect buffer zones where the land is under development pressure by drawing them into ecotourism. The symmetrical Arenal volcano (1657m) is the youngest stratovolcano in Costa Rica and one of its most active: the oldest known Arenal rocks are only 2900 years old. Rapid growth of the cone diverted local drainage and formed Arenal Lake. Before 1968 this volcano was considered extinct and it was even thought that it was not a volcano. It was known as the Hill Arenal and lies only three hours drive from San José in the central valley of Costa Rica. La Fortuna, a town with a population of only 6000, is the main starting place for tourists who want to go to the Arenal Volcano Park (in excess of 250,000 per year).

The volcano initiated its current active period on 29 July 1968, opening three craters towards the west flank. Crater A at 1000m caused the explosion, emanating a pyroclastic flow that devastated 12 square kilometres, destroying the little towns of Pueblo Nuevo and Tabacón and causing the death of approximately 87 people. In the month of September of the same year the volcano began to emit lava from crater A and this vent remained active until 1973, when the activity migrated towards Crater C, at a height of 1450m. This crater remains active until the present; it is characterized by permanent lava taps of andesite basaltic composition, explosions of pyroclastic materials and constant gas emission.

At the present time the population density in the area of this volcano is 40 people/km². The Arenal volcano offers an exceptional volcano tourism experience and practically the entire economy of the nearby town of La Fortuna is based on tourism. There are hotels, lodges, restaurants, tours, hikes and activities of every description that cater to people who make the long drive to the area for one reason: to hear the rumble and catch a glimpse of spewing smoke, ash and lava from Arenal. In addition to including in the national park system what is currently one of the world's most active volcanoes, the area now under park service protection encompasses the watersheds of several rivers and streams that flow into Lake Arenal, the country's most important source of hydroelectric power.

For observing violent activity Arenal is one of the best places in the world, its periodic eruptions of ash and molten rock, accompanied by sonic blasts, are an unforgettable experience anytime but become extremely spectacular after dark. At night the glowing red igneous rocks ejected with each eruption trace spectacular arches in the night sky before crashing down on the steep slopes and finally extinguishing themselves. Columns of lava also push their way down the sides of the volcano, and pieces of the advancing sections continually break off under the weight of new flows bearing down from above. At night, these falling pieces are visible as chunks of rolling red rocks, adding to the natural fireworks display between the frequent eruptions. Climbing Arenal is however forbidden for tourists due to the risk of damage to the environment and possible changes in the eruptive activity. For some time Arenal has been showing signs of reduced activity but continues to be very dangerous and has killed people in recent years. Park ranger signs mention: Do NOT climb the cone, do NOT enter closed areas, and take heed of ALL warning signs (Figure 7.2).

From the 600m elevation where visitors are allowed to approach atop a lava flow from the 1968 eruption, Arenal rises another 1000m to its 1633m summit, and although the peak is still three kilometres away, it seems very close. Short trails (3.4km and 2km) go through some young secondary forests and old lava from previous eruptions. The park rangers keep a sharp eye on the volcanic activity and determine which trails should be opened or not and will not hesitate to evacuate the park if they feel it's unsafe for visitors. MINAE's Comisión Nacional de Emergencías recently set up four 'safety zones' around the volcano and is now regulating commercial

Figure 7.2 Arenal volcano, Costa Rica: National Park access limit

Note: The sign behind the fence reads: Zona de Peligro, No Pase – Danger Zone, Keep Out.

development. It's a highly arbitrary zoning plan, however, and any particularly large eruption would devastate the entire area.

There is little vegetation or wildlife to be seen in the immediate area of the main viewing site since the effects of the major eruption of 1968 are only slowly being overcome. Nevertheless, this area offers an interesting opportunity to witness the early stages of lava flow colonization by a handful of plant species adapted to the task. Farther away, there are other areas that escaped direct damage and provide better wildlife viewing in the forested sections. The park also contains a second volcano, Chato, whose crater contains a lagoon. This is also called Cerro Chato (literally Mount Chato) as it has been inactive for around 3500 years – coinciding with the creation and

growth of Arenal itself. An interpretive centre has been under construction for several years about 2km south-west of the ranger station (but had yet to open at my last visit). This will feature a museum with exhibits on volcanology and local ecology, an auditorium for slide shows, a cafe and souvenir store. Meanwhile, the Arenal Observatory Lodge has a small but interesting Museum of Volcanology.

According to a recent study (Barquero and Melson, 2005, p3) the calculation of the probability of future fatalities at Arenal volcano involves two independent considerations: the probability at any time interval of eruptions with potentially fatal consequences, and the probability of someone being in a hazardous zone at the time of such an eruption. A near-crater ejected block killed a tourist in 1987 and in 2000 a pyroclastic flow killed a tourist and guide who were hiking in a dangerous area on an active flank of the volcano. Although these events are rare, as long as Arenal remains active they will continue to happen. Eruptions that lead to pyroclastic flows and hot avalanches normally come without a geophysical warning. They travel at speeds of 80–90km/hour, which do not allow time to escape if caught in its path. As a result of this tragedy at Arenal local volcanologists have provided information to the travel industry to establish safety guidelines for travellers because it was important to restrict access to the slopes and streams that drain the summit.

The creation of the Arenal National Park has also helped control access to the south-west slopes of the volcano. Between 1987 and 1994, Earthwatch and Smithsonian volunteers recorded 8067 pyroclastic eruptions over 189 days of continuous observations in 15 two-week time slices. Of these, 3246 explosions ejected blocks over a few hundred metres (common) up to 2000m (rare) from the summit crater(s), at an average of 17 explosions/day. Over the past 18 years, the frequency of pyroclastic events has decreased, punctuated by a few periods of increased frequency. Over the past 37 years, there have been two fatal pyroclastic flows, giving an average rate of .05 fatalities/yr. However data from 1994 to the present from seismic and acoustic automatic data acquisition system (ADAS) 2.8km south of the summit at the Arenal Observatory Lodge revealed no detected precursors to the 23 August 2000 fatal pyroclastic flow. Growing summit pyroclastic cones now pose additional risk through collapse that can produce hot avalanches. Pyroclastic event counts versus magnitude from field observations and ADAS reveal linear trends on log–log plots that are indicative of self-organized critical systems.

Guatemala

Guatemala is the westernmost country of Central America. It is bounded on the west and north by Mexico, on the east by Belize and the Caribbean Sea, on the south-east by Honduras and El Salvador, and on the south by the Pacific Ocean. Guatemala's highlands lie along the Motagua Fault, part of the boundary between the Caribbean and North American tectonic plates. In this region the Middle America Trench, a major subduction zone, lies off the Pacific coast and the Cocos Plate is sinking beneath the Caribbean Plate, producing volcanic activity inland of the coast. Guatemala has 37 volcanoes, 4 of which are currently active: Pacaya, Santiaguito, Fuego and Tacaná. The Guatemalan government has also protected more than 15 per cent of its land in national parks and other reserves. Tourism officially became Guatemala's second most important source of foreign exchange earnings, behind coffee, in 1993.

Pacaya volcano

Pacaya is the active vent in the Cerro Grande–Pacaya–Cerro Chino volcanic complex (Figure 7.3). It sits at the south end of the Guatemala City graben, a down-dropped fault block that forms the north–south valley in which Guatemala City lies.

Figure 7.3 Pacaya volcano in Guatemala is the active vent in the Cerro Grande–Pacaya–Cerro Chino volcanic complex

Pacaya (2552m) is a complex basaltic volcano constructed just outside the southern topographic rim of the 14 × 16km Pleistocene Amatitlán caldera. A cluster of dacitic lava domes occupies the southern caldera floor. The post-caldera Pacaya massif includes the Cerro Grande lava dome and a younger volcano to the south-west. A collapse of Pacaya volcano about 1100 years ago produced a debris-avalanche deposit that extends 25km onto the Pacific coastal plain and left an arcuate somma rim inside which the modern Pacaya volcano (MacKenney cone) grew. A subsidiary crater, Cerro Chino, was constructed on the north-west somma rim and was last active in the 19th century. Pacaya's current active phase began in 1965, and the volcano has been almost constantly in eruption since then. Eruptive activity ranges from minor gaseous emissions and quiet steam eruptions, to explosions powerful enough sometimes to hurl bombs up to 12km and necessitate the evacuation of numerous villages on the flanks of the volcano. Eruptions also include strombolian activity, vulcanian explosions, minor flows from the crater and larger flows emitted as flank eruptions.

Highly active Pacaya volcano is also the most frequently climbed volcano in Guatemala. It is relatively accessible and commonly puts on a good show for volcano enthusiasts. Pacaya lies approximately 25–30km south of Guatemala City, is easily accessible from Antigua and Guatemala and from Guatemala City itself. For tourists, the easiest and most secure way to visit Pacaya is to go with a licensed tour operator, of which there are numerous in Antigua taking groups to visit Pacaya every day. In case tourists are not travelling with an organized tour, it's better to hire a local guide. The easy trail, followed by most of the tour groups from Antigua, starts at San Francisco de Sales. That is the official entrance to the park, and the tourist needs to pay admission. The trail is well maintained and is patrolled by local rangers.

The second trail starts from the complex of radio towers on the flank of Cerro Chino; it is a bit tougher, but more rewarding for geology and photogenic views. Before taking this trail tourists should still check in at the park headquarters in San Francisco de Sales and pay admission. This trail starts from the base of the steep climb up to the radio towers. The trail continues to the left

along this rim, gradually climbing and circling around to the base of the Pacaya cone. Just before reaching the summit, the trail turns back to the left towards the old summit. To the right is the currently active vent. If there is any explosive activity it is best to continue to the old peak first. After observing the activity from the old peak for a while a judgement can be made as to whether or not it's possible to approach the active vent. However, that is dangerous because in addition to the possibility of being hit by a falling bomb during explosive eruptions, visitors to the rim must also be cautious about volcanic gases. Yellow sulphur sublimates on the rim trail attest to the sulphurous gases pouring over the crater rim. When the volcano is in a phase of strombolian eruptions or active flows, night-time views become very spectacular.

Volcanoes of South America
Chile

The Andean Arc covers the countries of Chile, Peru, Ecuador and Columbia and includes 200 potentially active volcanoes (Table 7.1). This area is seismically active due to the subduction of the Antarctic and Nazca plates below the South America plate. Where the angle of subduction is steep, that's where the active volcanoes are occurring. According to Corporation Nacional Forestal (CONAF), Chile's Forestry and Parks Department, Chile has 94 national properties ranging from the Atacama Desert to Patagonian icebergs: 31 national parks, 48 national reserves and 15 national monuments. CONAF oversees, maintains and protects approximately 14 million hectares, equivalent to 19 per cent of Chile's territory.

Chile has the region's largest number of historically active volcanoes, with 36 (ranking it fifth among nations, behind Russia's 52 and ahead of Iceland's 18). Chile is a country of startling contrasts and extreme beauty, with attractions ranging from the towering volcanic peaks of the Andes to the ancient forests of the Lake District. There are many volcano parks here, and plenty of opportunities for adventure travel. Chile stretches over 4300km along the south-western coast of South America. All along its length Chile is marked by a narrow depression between the mountains and the sea. To the north the land rises and becomes more arid, until one reaches the forbidding Atacama Desert, one of the most inhospitable regions on Earth. To the south just the opposite transformation takes place: the land falls away, and the region between mountains and ocean fades into the baffling archipelagic maze that terminates in Chilean Patagonia. As with many other countries on the Pacific Ocean coastline Chile has large geographical faults and a high geothermal activity, which explains the existence of numerous sources of thermal waters. One of the most famous geothermal fields in Chile is El Tatio.

El Tatio geology

The geothermal geyser field at El Tatio (Figure 7.4) is located near the Chile–Bolivia border in the northern Antofagasta province. The field is geologically associated with the Altiplano–Puna volcanic complex in the north–south trending Tatio Graben, bounded on the east by the Serrania de Tucle–Loma Lucero horst and on the west by El Tatio volcanics (Lahsen and Trujillo, 1976; de Silva and Francis, 1991). The geothermal field at elevations from 4200 to 4600m covers approximately 30km^2, but the majority of the thermal features are found within 10km^2, in three distinct basins (upper, middle and lower basin). From here, several small colourful streams coalesce to form the Rio Salado which drains westward through a narrow valley in the horst block forming the margin of the graben. Most of the springs are near boiling (86°C) at a neutral pH. Siliceous sinter deposits are found throughout the field, sometimes as large cones at geyser vents or as terraces at springs. Runoff from El Tatio forms the headwaters of the Calama Basin, where recharge is dominantly from mountain snowmelt.

Tourism and risk management at El Tatio

The Geysers del Tatio are located approximately 80km from the oasis town of San Pedro de Atacama in northern Chile. El Tatio geysers are in a remote, high altitude site (>4300m), in a largely uninhabited

Figure 7.4 The Tatio Geyser field near the Chile–Bolivia border is home to approximately 80 geysers

portion of northern Chile in the Atacama Desert. Precipitation in this desert is limited by the rain-shadow along the Andes Mountains, cold ocean current upwelling, and atmospheric subsidence (Hartley and Chong, 2002). The high altitude and climatic conditions make El Tatio one of the most extreme environments on Earth, and it is also one of the world's largest geyser fields. The valley is home to approximately 80 geysers at present. The salient feature of these geysers is that the average height of their eruptions is very low (the tallest eruptions are about six metres).

Geothermal tourism provides local employment and brings tourism money into this area of Chile. Geothermal tourism also promotes public awareness and support for preserving such natural areas. In the geyser area of the Tatio steam spurts arise from more than 70 smokers, forming about 60 pools of boiling water. Those have soft edges formed by mineral salts. The area is unrestricted and people can walk anywhere they like and visitors can even take a warm bath in thermal water pools. There are few safeguards at El Tatio, and there are no friendly park rangers to keep people from wading in the boiling pools which apparently tourists do with alarming frequency. However, to walk around the geothermal zone requires precaution and tourists are invited to stay on the pedestrian signposted footpaths and respect protection barriers. The associated boiling mud can cause serious burns, a reason why it is very dangerous to approach these steam spurts up close. People who desire to camp at El Tatio are asked to stay near the station, and there is a small kitchen for campers. The station is managed by locals from nearby villages.

The nearest medical facilities to El Taito are located ~150km away in Calama. To adjust to working at high elevation, main tour operators stay either in Chiu Chiu (about 1.5 hours drive from El Tatio, at 3000m elevation), or at San Pedro de Atacama (about two hours drive from El Tatio, but at a lower elevation). This makes accident management extremely difficult in the more active areas of the park and is something that visitors should take into account. In practice, however, tourists can drive up on their own, or they can join one of the many eco-adventure groups out of San Pedro de Atacama. Marginally

safer given their networks and resources, the tour groups leave in the early morning when it is still dark, and arrive at El Tatio at sunrise when the geysers are spectacular.

Tourism climbing on active volcanoes: Villarica National Park (Chile)

Situated on a lateral branch of the Andes mountain range, this park is characterized by its volcanoes, forests, caves, rivers and lagoons. Dominating the landscape, the Villarrica volcano is its major attraction (Figure 7.5). At an altitude of 2847m above sea level, and with the reputation of being one of the most active volcanoes in South America, this volcano is the centre of tourist activity in this area. The volcano also boasts a ski centre and volcanic caves worth exploring. Tourists can also climb up to the crater of the volcano to admire not only the boiling lava in the interior but also the view from above of the surrounding lakes, lagoons and other nearby volcanoes. The park has an area of 63,000 hectares (138,600 acres), with extensive forests of araucarias and lenga in the higher parts, and raulí, long-leafed mañío and coigüe in the lower parts.

Villarrica volcano is located in the recent volcanic chain of the Southern Andes Volcanic Zone at 39°30′S. It forms a north-west–south-east volcanic chain, with the Pleistocene-Holocene Quetrupillán and Lanín stratovolcanoes oblique to the recent volcanic arc and to the main structure located in the region, the Liquiñe–Ofqui Fault Zone. Villarrica volcano is the most active volcano of the southern Andes, with more than 54 recorded eruptions in the last 450 years (when the first Spanish conquerors arrived in the area). It is a large stratovolcano, located in a lake district that has evolved in three stages, from Pleistocene to recent times. During its postglacial eruptive history (the last 14,000 years) it has produced a series of explosive eruptions with the emission of large- and small-volume pyroclastic flows and surges, as well as lava flows and lahars. The volcano's most recent historic eruptions, in 1948, 1963, 1964, 1971 and 1984, have produced basaltic andesite lava flows and tephra fallout, as well as a series of lahars, which have travelled down the main river valleys of the volcano. Some of the latter have caused serious damage to villages, roads and bridges, and killed about 100 people. Villarrica has

Figure 7.5 With an altitude of 2847m Villarica volcano dominates the landscape

Note: Villarica volcano also has the reputation of being one of the most active volcanoes in South America.

maintained an active lava lake at its summit for over 20 years and has shown persistent strombolian activity from this lake situated at the bottom of the summit crater. This lava lake could not have survived for so long without sustained supply of heat by magma convection in the conduit.

The volcano's most recent notable eruptive episode began in August 2004 and ended around Christmas 2007 (during 29 March to 3 April 2005 strombolian explosions occurred from the lava lake and some gas explosions were observed). More recently, two significant phreatomagmatic explosions occurred on 26 October 2008 that deposited a layer of pyroclastic material several kilometres long on the eastern flank of the volcano. During this eruptive phase visitors were banned from climbing the volcano. The main

hazards therefore expected from future eruptions are those that derive from lava flows and pyroclastics fallout, together with those induced by them, such as lahars and river floods. Indeed, the existence of a large glacier together with seasonal snow makes the Villarica volcano a lahar generator durings its eruptions. Moreover, the lahars, generated by the ice and snow melts together with high lava effusion rates ($100m^3/s$), have been, as mentioned above, the worst and most destructive hazard during recent times. Today, the main potential volcanic hazards for the town of Pucón located at the foot of the volcano remain lahar flows descending the Urbio-Pedregoso and Zanjon Seco River systems. Summer tourism in the area increases the population by about 200 per cent and is an additional factor of risk.

The Villarica volcano is in the touristic Chilean Lake District about 400 miles south of Santiago. The volcano is the main tourist attraction to the town of Pucón located on the edge of Lake Villarica. The lake has black sandy beaches from the lava previously spewed from the volcano and Pucón is a focus of adventure tourism in Chile, but the smoking volcano less than eight miles away is a constant reminder that the next major eruption could obliterate the town. Pucón is like a Swiss Alpine town and the economy depends on outdoor activities such as skiing, climbing, white water rafting and mountain biking.

Pucón is a centennial tourist destination, created with the support of European settlers, particularly Germans, who started arriving at the end of the 19th century and the beginning of the 20th century. It was initially established as an army outpost to protect the borders and contribute to the pacification of Araucanía. A fort was thus erected on 27 February 1883 by the Chilean army, similar to the ones in Paillin (known today as Palguín) and Maichi. The successful coexistence between natives and settlers allowed cattle ranching and exploitation of the forests to fructify and become the main economic activities during the initial years. Tourist development did not begin in earnest until the 1930s, with the construction of the Gran Hotel Pucón. Today, the area around Villarrica volcano is a popular tourist resort with a summertime (December–February) population of up to 160,000 within a 25km radius of the crater.

Dominating the landscape, the Villarrica volcano is the major attraction. This volcano is the centre of tourist activity in the area. The volcano boasts a ski centre; in the winter (July–September) skiing is practiced on the northern slopes of Villarrica). Guided hikes to the crater are offered from the town of Pucón, which can be suspended in periods of seismic or increased volcanic activity. Helicopter sightseeing services offer flights over the crater as well. Due to its accessibility and non-technical nature, Villarrica is climbed by thousands of people, Chilenos and non-Chilenos alike, annually. Climbers are also drawn to Villarrica to experience the volcano's active crater. Villarrica's standard route is non-technical. Its level of difficulty, in terms of altitude, steepness and duration, is similar to that of Mt St Helens in Washington State in the USA. Crevasse danger on the standard route is not really existent; however, climbers should carry an ice axe and bring crampons in case of icy conditions, as the hazard of uncontrolled slides onto rocks is a concern. Experienced mountaineers climb it in two or three hours, while beginners complete it in approximately five hours. The crater of Villarrica is 100 metres deep and it is advisable not to get too close to the mouth of the volcano. Fluctuations in the level ($\pm$80m) of the 'lava lake' occur regularly and degassing can be a hazard. In particular, higher SO_2 emissions appeared to be related to higher levels of the lava lake, stronger bubble bursting activity and changes in the morphology and texture of the crater floor (Witter and Delmelle, 2004).

Conclusions

Although climbing Villarrica (and other volcanoes in Central and South America) is not that hard it is necessary to be in good physical condition and to have the authorization of Chile's National Forest Corporation (CONAF) in order to do so. Tourists need to be accompanied by a professional guide. Thousands of people make the climb each year, most of them in January and February, taking in the spectacular views of Llaima, Choshuenco, Quetrupillán, Lanin and Lonquimay on the horizon. Crampons, ice axe and/or trekking poles and warm windproof clothing are essential equipment year round. The ascent to the summit of Villarrica, towering menacingly over Pucón, is an adventure positively fizzing with excitement for tourists, but not without danger. At the summit the rim of the crater is very brittle, and changes shape according to changing temperatures, water content and all those little earthquakes the volcano is causing all the time. Walking here requires care, and this advice applies to all the volcano treks that are becoming increasingly popular for tourists.

References

Barquero, J. and Melson, W. G. (2005) *Uncertainties in Probability Calculations of Future Fatal Eruptions at Arenal Volcano, Costa Rica, a Favorite Tourist Destination*, Agu Abstract, San Jose

de Silva, S. L. and Francis, P. W. (1991) *Volcanoes of the Central Andes*, Springer-Verlag, New York

Eder, W. and Patzak, M. (2004) 'Geoparks – geological attractions: A tool for public education, recreation and sustainable economic development', Episodes, vol 27, no 3, pp162–164

Hartley, A. J. and Chong, G. (2002) 'A late Pliocene age for the Atacama Desert: Implications for the desertification of western South America', *Geology*, vol 30, pp43–46

Hopkins, J. W. (1995) *Policymaking for Conservation in Latin America: National Parks, Reserves, and the Environment*, Praeger Publishers, Westport, CT

Lahsen, A. and Trujillo, P. (1975) 'The geothermal field of El Tatio, Chile', *Proceedings, 2nd UN Symposium on the Development and Use of Geothermal Resources*, San Francisco, pp157–177

MIRENEM (1991) *Consolidation of the National System of Conservation Areas*, Ministerio de Recursos Naturales, Energía y Minas, San Jose

Witter, J. B. and Delmelle, P. (2004) 'Acid gas hazards in the crater of Villarrica volcano (Chile)', *Revista Geológica de Chile*, vol 31, no 2, pp273–277

Case Study 4

The Cascades

Connecting Canada and the United States

Malcolm Cooper

Introduction

The Cascades are a 700+km long group of volcanoes as well as non-volcanic origin mountains that stretch along the west coast of North America, from Northern California, USA into British Columbia, Canada (Hill, 2004; Dzurisin et al, 2008; Figure CS4.1). At its southern end the range is about 50 to 80km wide and 1370 to 1520m high. At its northern end at Lytton Mountain (2049m) in Canada, near the confluence of the Fraser and Thompson Rivers, the range is only 16km wide. The tallest volcanoes of the Cascades are known as the High Cascades and include the 4392m high Mt Rainier. Overall the North Cascades and south-western Canadian Cascades are extremely rugged, with many of the lesser peaks steep and glaciated, but the majority of the volcanoes lie in Washington, Oregon and northern California.

In addition to their latent and active volcanism the Cascades are a watershed range that has played a key role in human settlement in the Pacific Northwest of the USA and Canada. Heavy rainfall and forest environments produced rivers and lakes as well as good agricultural land and timber for industry. As a consequence the mountains support numerous population centres and are heavily used for recreation.

Geophysical aspects and history of activity

The Cascades form part of the Pacific Rim volcanic zone and result from the Pacific Plate and its smaller companion the Juan de Fuca Plate being subducted under the North American Plate (Hill, 2004, pp4–7). This 960km long area lies between 96 and 240km offshore, but produces its tectonic effects in the Cascade range. These effects are eruptions and earthquakes, all of which are extreme events. Most of the major peaks are stratovolcanoes made up of layers of lava and other volcanic debris, and many are quite young (e.g. Mt St Helens), although some such as Mt Rainier are thought to be considerably older. However, almost all the major volcanoes shown in Figure CS4.1 have erupted in the past 4000 years, with 7 being active within the past 250 years (Dzurisin et al, 2008). All are presently classed as active and can be expected to erupt in the future.

This history of activity is also reflected in local myth and legend, as is common with geothermal areas (Cooper-Erfurt and Cooper, 2009). Indigenous peoples have inhabited the area for thousands of years and developed their own beliefs concerning the origin and nature of the Cascades (Cashman and Cronin, 2008). According to some of these tales the mountains Baker, Jefferson and Shasta were used as refuges from a great flood. Other stories, such as the *Bridge of the Gods* tale, had

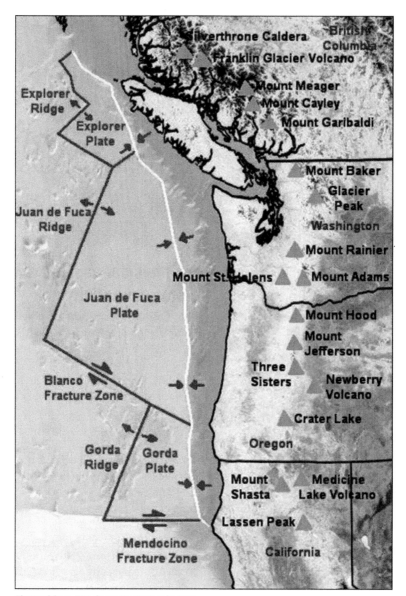

Figure CS4.1 The Cascade 'Volcanic Arc'

Source: Wikimedia Commons, 2009a

various High Cascade mountains such as Hood and Adams make war by throwing fire and stone at each other, and Mt St Helens was described as a beautiful maiden over whom Mts Hood and Adams feuded (Harris, 2005).

Risk factors

The risk factors for tourism associated with the volcanoes of the Cascades include earthquakes, explosive eruptions, lava flows, lahars, pyroclastic surges and flows, volcanic ash plumes, melt-water from the snowfields on many of the larger ones and acid rain. These volcanoes have produced more than 100 eruptions in the past 4000 years where pyroclastic events, lava flows, lahars and landslides have affected areas over 80km from the particular volcano. The eruption of Mt St Helens on 18 May 1980 was just the latest of these. The eruption itself was very small compared with those from Krakatoa or Taupo, for example, (Case Study 11 and Chapter 19 in this book), at only 0.42km³ of ejecta, but 57 people were killed and the damage bill exceeded USD1billion from the associated pyroclastic flows and lahars. This eruption followed that of Lassen Peak (1910s), Mt Baker (mid 1800s), and the frequent eruptions of Glacier Peak, Mt Rainier (most recently 1895), Mt Hood, Medicine Lake (the largest volcano in the Cascades), and Mt Shasta (every 300 years, last about 1786). The Three Sisters volcanic crater in Central Oregon has since 1997 developed a lava dome that is being watched closely for signs of an imminent eruption.

Tourism

Notwithstanding the implied risk associated with these known and still-active volcanoes (some research suggests perhaps because of this) the number of visitors has been steady since the 1980s except for that to the North Cascades area (Table CS4.1). Mt Rainier hosts over one million visitors yearly, while Mt St Helens also attracts over one million (Schmincke, 2006, pp282–283). In Oregon, the Mt Hood area receives around four million visitors and the Crater Lake National Park over 400,000 per year. While not all tourists are attracted to the geothermal resources, they are all visiting because of the topography, climate and biodiversity of the Cascades region, and many

would be *affected* should any of the volcanoes once again erupt.

Risk management

While risk management associated with the Cascades volcanic threat is now quite sophisticated, the myths and legends surrounding the volcanoes are a documentation of what to expect and how to behave that still have currency today. As a result of this cultural and natural history four national parks have been created over the Cascades area in the USA alone – Lassen Volcanic National Park in 1916, while the Lassen volcano was actually erupting. Mt St Helens is now within a 445km² National Volcanic Monument that has been set-aside for research, recreation and education. Inside the monument, the environment is left to respond naturally to the disturbance from the 1980s eruption. From the summer of 1983 visitors have been able to drive to Windy Ridge, only 6.4km north-east of the crater. From this vantage point tourists can see first-hand not only the evidence of a volcano's destructive power, but also the recovery of the land as revegetation proceeds and wildlife returns. Mountain climbing to the summit of the volcano has been allowed since 1986.

The eruption of Mt St Helens was the catalyst for the establishment of a volcano observatory for the Cascades. While it is not economically feasible to fully monitor all the Cascade volcanoes (Dzurisin et al, 2008), portable instrumentation

Table CS4.1 Visitors to the Cascades

Year	Crater Lakes NP	Mt Rainier NP	Olympic NP	North Cascades NP/Ross Lake NRA/Lake Chelan NRA	Lassen NP/Lava Beds National Monument
1980	455,143	1,268,256	2,032,418	796,079	482,418
1985	390,604	1,165,640	2,532,145	629,234	519,751
1990	384,941	1,327,101	2,794,903	456,444	533,487
1995	496,041	1,344,833	3,658,615	455,935	472,510
2000	426,883	1,173,897	3,327,722	351,225	489,248
2005	447,240	1,173,897	3,142,774	328,050	473,010
2008	415,686	1,163,227	3,081,451	296,197	497,437

Source: Various, compiled by author

can be rapidly deployed if unusual seismic activity is detected. Hazard warning mapping has been carried out and remote sensing is also used as an early-detection tool. Long-term hazard assessment is ongoing. All these activities have meant that emergency response planning by local communities in the Cascades region has as firm a foundation in science as possible given the nature of volcanoes; however, whether this preparation will reduce the risk to communities and tourism in this area or not from a major eruption only time will tell, since at least 80,000 people live in the Mt Rainier lahar hazard zones alone (Driedger and Scott, 2008). Having noted this, it must be recognized that the small eruptions of 1986 and 2004 at Mt St Helens were accurately predicted and communities and their visitors were warned in time to reduce the hazards that resulted.

References

Cashman, K.V. and Cronin, S. J. (2008) 'Welcoming a monster to the world: Myths, oral tradition, and modern response to volcanic disasters', *Journal of Volcanology and Geothermal Research*, vol 176, pp407–418

Cooper-Erfurt, P. and Cooper, M. (2009) *Health & Wellness Spa Tourism*, Aspects of Tourism Series, Channel View Press, London

Driedger, C. L. and Scott, W. E. (2008) *Mt. Rainier – Living Safely With a Volcano in Your Backyard*, USGS Fact Sheet 2008-3062, United States Geological Survey, Washington DC

Dzurisin, D., Stauffer, P. H. and Hendley, J. W. II. (2008) *Living With Volcanic Risk in the Cascades*, USGS Fact Sheet 165–97, United States Geological Survey, Washington DC

Harris, S. L. (2005) *Fire Mountains of the West: The Cascade and Mono Lake Volcanoes* (3rd edn), Mountain Press Publishing Company, Missoula, MT

Hill, R. L. (2004) *Volcanoes of the Cascades*, Globe Piquot Press, Guilford, CT

Schmincke, H.-U. (2006) *Volcanism*, Springer, New York

Wikimedia Commons (2009) 'Cascade volcanic arc', www.en.wikipedia.org/wiki/File:Cascade_Volcanic_Arc.jpg, accessed 20 July 2009

Case Study 5

Yellowstone National Park, Wyoming

Malcolm Cooper

Introduction

Established in 1872, Yellowstone National Park was America's first national park. Located in the states of Wyoming, Montana and Idaho, it is home to a large variety of wildlife and to the world's greatest output of geothermal water (Figure CS5.1). The park covers an area of nearly 9065km² in the north-west of Wyoming and contains the largest concentration of geothermal features in the world (Rhinehart, 1980), with around 100 different hot springs groups totalling over 10,000 individual thermal features (Bryan, 1986). The distribution of its thermal features is controlled by regional fault systems and the Yellowstone Caldera (Eaton et al, 1975; White et al, 1988). The terraced Mammoth hot springs are an example of the travertine hot spring type, with over 100 hot springs cascading over a number of travertine terraces (Bargar and Muffler, 1975) and are one of the most popular tourist attractions in the park.

Geophysical aspects and history of activity

The Yellowstone National Park comprises primarily high, forested, volcanic plateaus that have been eroded by glaciation and stream flows, and that are flanked on the north, east and south by mountains. Its elevation averages 2400m, ranging from 1600m in the north, where the Gardner River drains from the park, to 4000m in the east at the summit of Eagle Peak in the Absaroka range. The Washburn range is made of debris flows preserved in the north flank of an old dissected volcano. This volcano and

the Red Mountains, about 60km to the south, are joined by the volcanic arc of the Absaroka mountains east of Yellowstone Lake. The age of the rocks forming this complex ranges from 70,000 years or less to two million years old. The main landscape-forming events were a series of three caldera producing eruptions dating from 2.1 million years to 600,000 years ago that produced about 6669km³ of rhyolite (in comparison Mt St Helens produced about 1.04km³). Since then three further eruptive pulses about 150,000, 110,000 and 70,000 years ago produced about 1000km³ of rhyolite (Decker and Decker, 2007; Yellowstone National Park, n.d).

The geothermal activity that produced this landscape is today expressed in the form of hot springs, geysers, boiling mud pools and travertine terraces, although the volcanic caldera remains on the active list since earthquake and other geologic data indicate that magma is close to the surface in this area (the Yellowstone 'Hot Spot'; Decker and Decker, 2007, pp197–198). Yellowstone National Park contains an estimated 10,000 thermal features. Of these 3 per cent are geysers, and the rest are steaming pools, hissing fumaroles, bubbling mud pots or warm seeps. Most of Yellowstone's geysers are small but six erupt 30m or higher on a predictable daily basis. Old Faithful, the most famous of these, erupts approximately every 45 to 90 minutes.

Risk factors

While there may be little risk from an actual eruption at Yellowstone at present there remain many risky elements to visiting this park. First and foremost are of course the hot springs and mud pools themselves. At temperatures over boiling point they are of course not to be entered. There is also the risk to the formations of travertine and

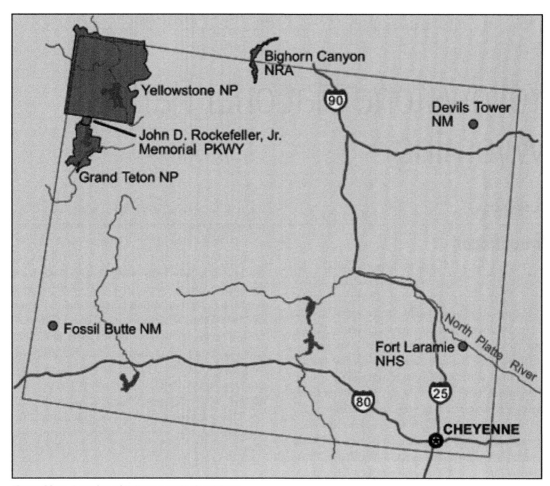

Figure CS5.1 Location of Yellowstone National Park

Source: Wikimedia Commons, 2009a

other materials associated with the geothermal activity from tourists – boardwalks are necessary. Nevertheless, each year some of the visitors who wander off a boardwalk or trail in thermal areas receive serious burns, occasionally resulting in death. Wading in thermal pools is illegal, but that does not stop some visitors from ignoring any warnings. Trees that fall as a result of natural causes or human disturbance also pose a risk to human safety and property, as do some of the animals inhabiting the national park. Park regulations prohibit approaching within 100 yards of bears or 25 yards of other wildlife. However, elk and bison are often closer than that to roads and sidewalks in developed areas and such easy proximity tends to create an illusion of safety. The major cause of

injury by wildlife occurs when visitors seek too close an encounter. Rangers spend significant time educating visitors about how to avoid harassing and being injured by animals.

While park managers hope that Yellowstone provides a respite from urban crowds, the vast majority of visitors arrive in the same six-week period between early July and mid-August each year – and most want to see the same highlights during their two-day visit. Combined with natural distractions and deteriorating road conditions, this heavy traffic makes for hazardous travelling for the unwary driver. While most park visitors leave Yellowstone after a safe visit, some may fall victim to offences against property, and rangers are occasionally called upon to search for missing visitors in conditions that range from desert-like in summer, to winter blizzards with 'white-out' visibility. In this respect Yellowstone's isolation from advanced medical facilities, as well as technological advancement and liability issues have increased the need to have highly trained park staff and equipment on hand to perform emergency extrication and life-support.

Tourism

Over three million visitors are attracted to Yellowstone National Park every year (Table CS5.1). When the park was first established in 1872 no tourist services of any kind existed, but by 1910 five major hotels had been built and in the 21st century overnight accommodation is provided at six locations throughout the park. Tourism in the park is outsourced to private concessionaires, as are emergency medical services (though the park rangers also provide emergency medical services and rescue, and in the past handled nature walks, field trips, etc., Figure CS5.2), retail outlets, fuel, and food and beverage outlets. Concessionaires are required to maintain and improve the facilities that they use and this has directly benefitted the park authorities.

Risk management

The recognition of areas like Yellowstone National Park as the core of a greater ecosystem is perhaps the most important shift in public perception since the first national parks were established for

Figure CS5.2 Poster for Yellowstone National Park, Wyoming/Montana, USA – 1938

Source; Wikimedia Commons, 2009b

recreation and protection of wildlife and scenery in the late 1800s. A park cannot be isolated from the complicated political and environmental pressures that surround it but it can be managed within those pressures. The Yellowstone Park Master Plan consolidates visitor accommodation

Table CS5.1 Visitor statistics Yellowstone National Park

Year	Total visitors	Lodges & hotels	Camping	Total visitor days	Total overnight stays
1980	1,986,870	577,171	642,775	4,820,547	1,219,946
1985	2,259,770	601,849	668,543	6,621,057	1,270,392
1990	2,870,621	604,603	704,541	8,199,885	1,345,144
1995	4,089,359	567,415	683,132	5,628,657	1,250,547
2000	3,804,467	572,069	619,292	5,232,452	1,191,361
2005	3,771,249	526,462	663,211	5,216,620	1,189,673
2008	3,979,371	570,673	623,564	5,456,995	1,194,187

Source: National Park Service, US Department of the Interior, 2009

and services, and the primary responsibility for law enforcement and visitor protection in the park lies with the Division of Resource Management Operations and Visitor Protection.

This park is an area of exclusive federal jurisdiction and the park's law enforcement rangers are authorized by Congress to enforce all applicable Federal and State laws. District rangers oversee visitor and resource protection in 13 sub-districts and five entrance areas. Each of these has a ranger station that issues permits, provides information to visitors and conducts daily patrols to check for safety hazards, resource impacts and violations, and opportunities to inform and educate visitors. Educating visitors about low-impact ways to enjoy park resources without danger to themselves or the park is the preferred and often the most successful law enforcement technique although access to law enforcement agencies is available should a wilful violation of law occur. Visitors are also reminded of the range of hazards and their management through the park's official newspaper, *Yellowstone Today*, which is handed out to visitors at entrance stations. Finally, the park encourages all permanent field rangers to be certified as emergency medical technicians (EMTs), which requires 120 hours of initial training plus continuing education and a 24-hour biennial refresher class. All park rangers must at a minimum be trained to serve as 'first-responders' and have received cardio-pulmonary resuscitation (CPR) training and certification. An emergency medical services coordinator arranges or teaches classes for rangers and other employees, and local citizens who wish to receive the training.

References

Bargar, M. L. and Muffler, L. J. P. (1975) 'Geologic map of the travertine deposits, Mammoth Hot Springs, Yellowstone National Park, Wyoming', *Geological Survey Miscellaneous Field Studies Map MF-659 1:48000 and 1:2400 scale*, USGS, Washington DC

Bryan, T. S. (1986) *The Geysers of Yellowstone*, Colorado Associated University Press, Boulder, CO

Decker, R. and Decker, B. (2007) *Volcanoes in America's National Parks*, Odyssey Books & Guides, Hong Kong

Eaton, G. P., Christiansen, R. L., Iyer, H. M., Pitt, A. M., Mabey, D. R., Blank, H. R. Jr., Zietz, I. and Gettings, M. E. (1975) 'Magma beneath Yellowstone National Park', *Science*, vol 188, pp787–796

National Parks service, US Department of the Interior (2009) Yellowstone, Online Document: www.nps.gov/state/WY/index.htm#, accessed 7 January 2010

Rhinehart, J. S. (1980) *Geysers and Geothermal Energy*, Springer-Verlag, New York

White, D. E., Hutchinson, R. A. and Keith, T. E. C. (1988) 'The geology and remarkable thermal activity of Norris Geyser Basin, Yellowstone National Park, Wyoming', *U.S. Geological Survey Professional Paper 1456*, USGS, Washington DC

Wikimedia Commons (2009a) 'Map Wyoming NPS sites USA', www.en.wikipedia.org/wiki/File:Map_Wyoming_NPS_sites_USA.gif, accessed 20 July 2009

Wikimedia Commons (2009b) 'Poster for Yellowstone National Park, Wyoming/Montana, USA – 1938', www.en.wikipedia.org/wiki/File:Yellowstone_Natl_Park_poster_1938.jpg, accessed 20 July 2009

Yellowstone National Park (n.d.) www.yellowstonenationalpark.com/calderas.htm, accessed 4 August 2009

Case Study 6

The Galapagos Islands

Volcanoes and Wildlife

Malcolm Cooper

Introduction

The Galapagos Islands are located in the Pacific Ocean 972km off the coast of Ecuador. The isolation of the islands has permitted life forms to evolve into species found only here, amongst the volcanic landscapes. Today the Galapagos Islands are a national park and wildlife sanctuary world heritage site. The Galapagos Archipelago consists of 7880km² of land spread over 45,000km² of ocean in 13 main islands, 6 smaller islands and 107 rocks and islets. The largest of the islands, Isabela measures 4640km² and makes up half of the total land area of the Galapagos. Wolf volcano on Isabela is the highest point with an elevation of 1707m above sea level.

Geophysical aspects and history of activity

The major volcanic islands of the archipelago are: Genovesa (lava fields); Bartolomé (lava); Isabela (five active volcanoes); Fernandina (recent volcanism); Santiago (basalt lava shoreline); Santa Cruz (lava tubes and the Charles Darwin Research Centre); San Christobal (cinder cone, island capital Puerto Baquerizo Moreno); Floreana (small volcanic cones). Initially formed between three million and five million years ago, the Galapagos Islands are located over a *hotspot* in the East Pacific Ocean responsible for the creation of the Islands as well as three major aseismic ridge systems,

Carnegie, Cocos and Malpelso, which are on two tectonic plates (Harpp et al, 2004). The hotspot is located near the Equator on the Nazca Plate near its boundary with the Cocos Plate. The tectonic setting of this hotspot is complicated by the Galapagos Triple Junction of the Nazca and Cocos plates with the Pacific Plate (Hey et al, 1972). The movement of these plates over the hotspot is therefore determined not solely by the spreading along the ridge but also by the relative motion between the Pacific Plate and the Cocos and Nazca plates (Harpp et al, 2002).

Generally, the individual islands have formed from single shield volcano eruptions. However, the largest island Isabela is made up of six volcanoes which have flowed into each other, filling the gaps between them. The islands have continuously erupted during the last 200 years, with the last eruption being in 2009 on Fernandina.

Risk factors

The Galapagos volcanoes remain fairly isolated, but are increasingly the target of migration from the mainland. While active (Wolf volcano has erupted ten times since 1797) they are less of a threat to visitors, who can stay away while still experiencing the unique flora and fauna of the islands. Absolute risk factors for tourism are the six active volcanoes themselves, the nature of the resulting land surface (lava flows, few points of easy access), overpopulation from approved and illegal migrants (the 'permanent' population has

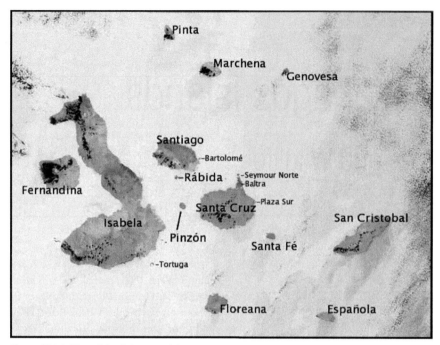

Figure CS6.1 Map of the Galapagos Islands

Source: Modified by P. Erfurt-Cooper based on the public domain NASA satellite map (Wikimedia Commons, 2009)

doubled in ten years to 30,000 and the number of tourists to 170,000 in 2007 (Kraul, 2009)), and the isolation of the islands. Risk factors associated with tourism itself are travel (airlines, cruise ships), low service standards, and tourist impact on the fragile ecosystem of the islands.

Tourism

Tourism to the Galapagos threatens to overwhelm the local ecosystem (invasive alien species, discharges from boats, untreated sewage), and as a result of this and the attraction of more permanent population in order to further develop tourism the islands were placed on UNESCO's World Heritage in Danger list in 2007 (UNESCO, 2009). Although it was the private sector that gave tourism its first big push in the late 1960s (hotels, cruise ships), the National Tourism Board (DITURIS, established in 1974) has a mandate to develop the country's tourism industry. In 1984 a Master Development Program for Tourism was drafted, which included the Galapagos. The resulting programme of investment has greatly

increased the number of people and money flowing into the islands. Unfortunately, the two have not consistently complemented one another.

The impact of increased tourism on the Galapagos Islands is twofold: economic and environmental. The changes in tourism are demonstrated by the increase in available beds from 1928 in 1991 to 3473 in 2006, the increase in passenger-days in boats and ships, which has increased by 150 per cent from 145,408 in 1991 to 363,226 in 2006, and a rise in the number of visitors to Galapagos from 40,000 in 1990 to over 170,000 in 2007 (Epler, 2007). In 2006 Galapagos tourism generated USD418million for Ecuador, of which an estimated USD63million enters the local economy (Watkins and Cruz, 2007). In the last 20 years, debt-ridden Ecuador has moved swiftly to take short-term economic advantage of the Galapagos. The financial flows from tourism promote unregulated growth in local small enterprises, which, in turn, contributes to increased migration to the islands. As jobs and public services are provided, they create a higher standard of living, in turn making the islands more attractive to immigrants. In this way the growth of tourism and the population stimulate the arrival of more flights and more cargo ships, decreasing the isolation of the archipelago and thereby increasing the arrival of invasive species – the greatest threat to local biodiversity. In 1987 the government imposed a 25,000 level restriction on the number of tourists allowed to visit but that limit has not since been enforced.

Risk management

Sustainable development on the Galapagos is complicated by the same factors that affect the development of islands all over the world. The islands are resource-poor, have few marketable products, and have high transportation costs to external markets. Production costs are high because of the absence of economies of scale, and because most raw materials must be brought from the mainland. In addition, there is a shortage of trained human resources because the resident population size is usually small and training is costly. As a result, risk management on the Galapagos Islands relates mainly to the archipelago's wildlife sanctuary status and the size of the 'permanent' population, not to its volcanism. In 1959, the centenary of *The Origin of Species*, the Ecuadorian government declared 97.5 per cent of the archipelago's land area a national park. The Charles Darwin Foundation (CDF), an NGO located in Belgium, was founded the same year with a core responsibility to conduct research for the Government of Ecuador on the effective management of the islands. In 1986 70,000km² of ocean surrounding the islands was declared a marine reserve and in 1990 the archipelago became a whale sanctuary. In 1978 UNESCO recognized the islands as a world heritage site and in 1985 as a biosphere reserve. This was later extended in December 2001 to include the marine reserve.

Tourism on the islands has begun to shift away from nature-oriented and Darwin-linked tourism, and illegal migrants are being removed. Adventure tourism, larger cruise ships (up to 500 passengers), low-budget hotels and activity-based tourism (sport fishing, beach camping, biking, kayaking and parachuting) are being promoted. And it is only a matter of time before such activities begin to incorporate the volcanoes on the islands. At that point the national park will need to establish more comprehensive regulations if the risk associated with volcanism is to be managed effectively.

References

Epler, B. (2007) *Tourism, the Economy and Population Growth and Conservation in Galapagos*, Fundación Charles Darwin, Puerto Ayora

Harpp, K. S., Wirth, K. R. and Korich, D. J. (2002) 'Northern Galápagos Province: Hotspot-induced, near-ridge volcanism at Genovesa Island', *Geology*, vol 30, no 5, pp399–402

Harpp, K. S., Wanless, V. D., Otto, R. H., Hoernle, K. and Werner, R. (2004) 'The Cocos and Carnegie aseismic ridges: A trace element record of long-term plume–spreading center interaction', *Journal of Petrology*, vol 46, no 1, pp109–133

Hey, R. N., Deffeyes, K. S., Johnson, G. L. and Lowrie, A. (1972) 'The Galapagos triple junction and plate motions in the east Pacific', *Nature*, vol 237, pp20–22

Kraul, C. (2009) 'Galapagos boots Ecuadorians as tourism booms', *Japan Times*, World/Classified Section 1, Tokyo

UNESCO World Heritage Centre (2009) *List of World Heritage in Danger*, UNESCO, Paris

Watkins, G. and Cruz, F. (2007) *Galapagos at Risk: A Socioeconomic Analysis of the Situation in the Archipelago*, Fundación Charles Darwin, Puerto Ayora

Wikimedia Commons (2009) 'Galapagos Islands map', www.en.wikipedia.org/wiki/File:Galapagos-satellite-esislandnames.jpg, accessed 20 July 2009

Case Study 7

Death by Volcanic Laze[1]

Travis W. Heggie, Tracey M. Heggie and
Tanner J. Heggie

Introduction

Despite the potential risk to human life, active
volcanoes have become popular attractions for
tourists and others interested in adventure
recreation pursuits. One such example is the
ongoing eruption of Kilauea volcano and the Puʻu
Oʻo vent in Hawaiʻi Volcanoes National Park,
where tourists and other spectators regularly
gather to hike to active lava flows and view lava
flowing into the ocean. In November 2000,
authorities at Hawaiʻi Volcanoes National Park
received a report of two bodies found near the
ocean entry in an area of the park referred to as the
Eruption Site. Both bodies (one Caucasian male;
one Caucasian female) were located approximately
91m directly inland from the ocean entry and were
located on the eastern side of active lava flows. The
bodies were located approximately 12m apart from
each other. In addition, the male victim had a
backpack that was found 6m west of his body. An
expert geologist at the scene with considerable
experience in the park reported seeing no sign of
volcanic spatter and no evidence of a recent
explosion in the area.

The aftermath

The bodies were removed via a sling load attached
to a Hawaiʻi County rescue helicopter. Two days
later autopsies of the victims were conducted by a
medical examiner for the County of Honolulu.
Dental records identified the victims as a 43-year-
old male and a 42-year old female. Examination of
the female victim found no obvious burns on her
clothing. However, her state of decomposition was
extremely advanced for the estimated time of
death (maximum 48 hours prior to body recovery)
and in comparison to the male victim. According
to the medical examiner, the female had
perimortem first- and second-degree burns to her
head, neck, shoulders and upper chest area, and to
all limbs. She also had perimortem wounds to the
head, face and limbs that were superficial in
nature. Examination of the male victim also found
no obvious burns to his clothing. Moreover,
abrasions and lacerations to his body were also
perimortem and superficial in nature. However,
there were very obvious perimortem first- and
second-degree burns to his head, neck, limbs and
areas of his trunk.

During the autopsies, no evidence was found
indicating that lightning or violence could have
been factors in the deaths. The medical examiner
did report, however, that the burns were consistent
with those caused by a hot gas or vapour rather
than contact with hot liquid, contact with a hot
object, or radiant heat. This was based on the
findings of undamaged clothing and the regions of
the bodies that were burnt. For example, both
victims sustained burns to areas that were
unprotected or protected by a single layer of
clothing. No burns were indicated or obvious
where there were three layers of clothing. In areas
where there were two layers of clothing there
were some burns indicated and observed where
the clothing may have been penetrated or tucked
up. The final cause of death determined by the
medical examiner was death as a result of
pulmonary edema caused by inhalation of volcanic
laze, sustained when the victims were exposed to
the plume near the ocean entry.

This incident highlights a potential hazard
when entering areas of volcanic activity. What

Figure CS7.1 Volcanic laze at an ocean entry in Hawai'i Volcanoes National Park

makes this a case of interest, however, is that it was the first known incident of its nature in Hawai'i and that it specifically highlights a potential global hazard present in locations where lava enters ocean waters (Figure CS7.1). Conditions near the ocean entry typically involve exposure to volcanic laze, a dense hydrochloric acid (HCl) mist that is formed when hot lava enters the ocean (Stephenson et al, 1991; Hansell and Oppenheimer, 2004; Hansell et al, 2006). This laze is often mistakenly referred to as a steam plume. Heat from the lava entering the ocean rapidly boils and vaporizes seawater, producing a large white plume. This plume contains a mixture of HCl and concentrated seawater that is a brine with a salinity about 2.3 times that of seawater and a pH of 1.5 to 2.0 (USGS, 2008). Moreover, dense laze plumes are known to contain as much as 10 to 15ppm of HCl (USGS, 2008). The density of the plume decreases as it moves away from the ocean entry, but acid rain commonly precipitates on individuals and land near the plume's proximity (USGS, 2008). Hence, following the inhalation of the laze, the bodies of the victims were exposed to extreme heat and acidic conditions during the maximum 48 hours they were at the ocean entry.

Lessons

In addition to the loss of life, the final cost of this incident included US$3025 for aircraft assistance and US$9507 for personnel costs. Volcanic hazards at the Eruption Site and in the vicinity of the ocean entry are not always recognized, and access to the area is not restricted. However, warning signs and safety messages should be strongly heeded by all visitors.

Note

1   This chapter was modified from Heggie, T. W., Heggie, T. M. and Heggie, T. J. (2009) 'Death by Volcanic Laze', *Wilderness and Environmental Medicine*, vol 20, pp101–103.

References

Hansell, A. and Oppenheimer, C. (2004) 'Health hazards from volcanic gases: A systematic literature review', *Arch Environ Health*, vol 59, pp628–639

Hansell, A. L., Horwell, C. J. and Oppenheimer, C. (2006) 'The health hazards of volcanoes and geothermal areas', *Occup Environ Med*, vol 63, pp149–156

Stephenson, R., Burr, G., Kawamoto, M. and Hills, B. (1991) 'Exposures to volcanic emissions from the Hawaiian volcanoes: A NIOSH health hazard evaluation', *Appl Occup Environ Hyg*, vol 6, pp408–410

United States Geological Survey (USGS) (2008) 'Volcano Hazards Program. When lava meets the sea: lava haze or laze air pollution', volcanoes.usgs. gov/Hazards/What/VolGas/Laze.html, accessed 5 August 2008

Case Study 8

Alaska's Volcanoes

The Aleutian Arc and Wilderness

Malcolm Cooper

Location

The most northerly state of the USA, Alaska is home to two groups of volcanoes – some 44 along the Aleutian Arc, and another 50+ on the mainland (Wood and Kienle, 1990, pp9–15; Figure CS8.1). These volcanoes are catalogued on the Alaska Volcano Observatory website www.avo.alaska. edu/volcanoes/ and in Wood and Kienle (1990). Many of these volcanoes have been active within the last 10,000 years (and might be expected to erupt again), and around 44 on the Aleutian Arc have been active within historical time (since about 1741; Wood and Kienle, 1990, p10). The

volcanoes in Alaska make up well over three-quarters of US volcanoes that have erupted in the last 200 years. The most frequently encountered volcano types are stratovolcanoes and calderas, and the dominant activity is explosive (strombolian, vulcanian, plinian) (Miller et al, 1998; Rosi et al, 2003).

In terms of their attraction as tourist destinations it must be understood that access is generally difficult and visitation therefore requires specific expeditions to be formed (Wood and Kienle, 1990, p10), especially to the islands. Permission to visit must be obtained from National Wildlife Refuge authorities or local communities where they exist, but may also be restricted.

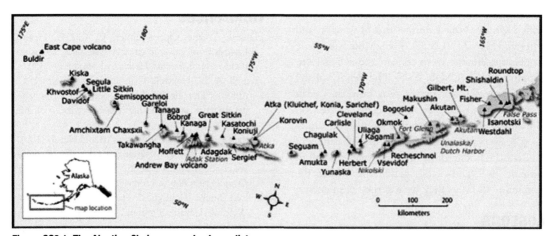

Figure CS8.1 The Aleutian Chain map and volcano list

Source: Alaska Volcano Observatory, 2009

Geophysical aspects and history of activity

Alaska's volcanoes and volcanic fields with an active past are mostly found in the Aleutian Arc extending over 2500km out into the north Pacific Ocean towards Kamchatka and enclosing the Bering Sea, or on the mainland. Aleutian Arc volcanism is the result of active subduction of the Pacific Plate beneath the North American Plate, and since 1741 $\cong$ 44 Alaskan volcanoes have had more than 230 confirmed eruptions. For the past 40 years – a period in which there are fairly good records – Alaska has averaged more than two eruptions per year. However, while the frequency of reports of eruptions is higher now than in the past, and was increasing during the 20th century, the increases from 1880 to the present day are probably the result of increased population, communications and travel, rather than an actual increase in the frequency of eruptions (Rosi et al, 2003).

This case study looks at the most important of the major volcanoes of Alaska in order to illustrate their impact on tourism and on surrounding communities. The first of these, Novarupta (Alaska peninsula) is the least topographically prominent volcano in the Katmai area and was formed during a major eruption in 1912. This eruption was the world's largest during the 20th century and produced a large amount of tephra and the renowned Valley of Ten Thousand Smokes (VTTS) ash flow (Rosi et al, 2003, pp218–219). Ash from Novarupta spread worldwide and locally roofs in Kodiak City collapsed due to the weight of the ash; six villages close to Katmai and Novarupta were permanently abandoned. Novarupta is accessible on foot and is uninhabited wilderness.

The 1989–1990 eruptions from Mt Redoubt on the other hand, were the second most costly in the history of the United States, and had significant impact on the aviation and oil industries as well as the people of the Kenai peninsula where, during periods of continuous ash fallout, schools were closed and some individuals experienced respiratory problems. At the Drift River oil terminal, lahars and lahar run-out flows threatened the facility and partially inundated the terminal on 2 January 1990 (Dorava and Meyer, 1994). The Redoubt eruption also damaged five commercial jetliners, and caused several days worth of airport closures and airline cancellations in Anchorage and on the Kenai peninsula (Casadevall, 1994). Drifting ash clouds disrupted air traffic as far away as Texas. Mt Redoubt is within Lake Clark National Park and Preserve and is accessible by small aircraft to the glaciers and the Drift River gravel banks.

The three eruptions of Mt Spurr's crater peak (125km west of Anchorage and only accessible by small charter aircraft) in 1992 deposited ash on Anchorage and surrounding communities, closed airports, made ground transportation difficult and disrupted air traffic as far east as Cleveland, Ohio. Mt Augustine is a stratovolcano on Augustine Island in south-western Cook Inlet 80km south-west of Anchorage. This volcano last erupted in 2006 and is especially dangerous for its debris avalanche activity, which can cause tsunamis in Cook Inlet.

Mt Iliamna is a glacier-carved stratovolcano located approximately 215km south-west of Anchorage on the west side of the lower Cook Inlet. Holocene eruptive activity from Iliamna is indicated, all before the European settlement of Alaska. However, fumaroles located at about 2740m elevation on the eastern flank produce nearly constant plumes of condensate and minor amounts of sulphurous gases. These plumes are quite vigorous and have resulted in numerous pilot reports and early historical accounts of 'eruptions' at Iliamna volcano, which last erupted during 1876 (Schafer and Nye, 2008).

Risk factors

The Global Volcanism Program database for the volcanoes of Alaska currently contains 92 Holocene volcanoes and one Pleistocene volcano with thermal activity, and most of these are located along the 2500km long Aleutian Arc, which extends westward to Kamchatka and forms the northern portion of the Pacific 'ring of fire'. Other volcanoes that have been active in the last few thousand years exist in south-eastern Alaska (such as Mt Edgecumbe) and in the Wrangell Mountains. Smaller volcanoes, some active within the last 10,000 years, are found in interior Alaska and in western Alaska as far north as the Seward peninsula.

Alaska's volcanoes are potentially hazardous to passenger and freight aircraft as jet engines sometimes fail after ingesting volcanic ash. On 15 December 1989, a Boeing 747 flying 240km north-east of Anchorage encountered an ash cloud erupted from Redoubt volcano and lost power in all four jet engines (Rosi et al, 2003; Casadevall, 1994). The plane, with 231 passengers aboard, lost more than 3000m of elevation before the flight crew was able to restart the engines. After landing, it was determined the airplane had suffered about $80 million in damage (Brantley, 1990). It is estimated, based on information provided by the US Federal Aviation Administration that more than 80,000 large aircraft per year, and 30,000 people per day are in the skies over and potentially downwind of Aleutian volcanoes, mostly on the heavily travelled great-circle routes between Europe, North America and Asia. Volcanic eruptions from the Cook Inlet volcanoes (Spurr, Redoubt, Iliamna and Augustine) can also have severe impacts on local communities and the state's tourist trade, as these volcanoes are close to Anchorage, the state's largest population centre.

Tourism

Tourism marketing efforts emphasize Alaska's outstanding scenery, wildlife, parks, museums and dining opportunities, as well as the ability to travel independently. Nearly all visitors perceive Alaska as an excellent place to see wildlife in its natural habitat and see Alaska's natural beauty and scenery. Katmai and Lake Clark National Parks (6000 and 5500 visitors per year respectively) are two of those favoured destinations. The 19,122 km² Katmai Park and Preserve was established on 2 December 1980 on the Alaska peninsula south-west of Anchorage. Originally, the area was designated a national monument on 24 September 1918, to protect the area around the 1912 eruption of Novarupta, which formed the Valley of Ten Thousand Smokes, a 100km² in area, 100–700 foot deep pyroclastic flow.

Activities at Katmai include hiking, back-packing, camping, cross-country skiing, fishing, kayaking, boat tours and interpretive programmes. There are at least 14 active volcanoes within the national park, including the Fourpeaked volcano, which became active on 17 September 2006 after more than 10,000 years of being dormant. The park also contains many archaeological sites, which indicate a long history of human occupation, and is well known for brown bears and salmon, which attract some 6000+ people (Miller et al, 1998). Katmai contains the world's largest protected brown bear population, estimated to number in excess of 2000. Bears are especially likely to congregate at the Brooks Falls viewing platform when the salmon are spawning, and many well known photographs of brown bears have been taken there. The vast majority of Katmai visitors come to Brooks Camp, one of the only developed areas of the park, and few venture further than the bear viewing platforms. Rangers at the park are extremely careful not to allow bears to obtain human food or get into confrontations with humans. As a result, bears in Katmai Park are uniquely unafraid of and uninterested in humans, and will allow people to approach (and photograph) much more closely than bears elsewhere (Miller et al, 1998).

Risk management

Risk management in these circumstances involves a mixture of requirements relating to the volcanoes as well as to wildlife. Redoubt volcano, for example, is located within a few hundred kilometres of more than half of the population of Alaska. This volcano has erupted explosively at least six times since historical observations began in 1778, the latest being in 2009 (Dorava and Meyer, 1994). Based on new information gained from studies of the 1989–90 eruption, an updated assessment of the principal volcanic hazards is now possible. Volcanic hazards from a future eruption of Redoubt and the other volcanoes of Alaska require public awareness training and logistics planning so that risks to life and property are reduced as much as possible (Dorava and Meyer, 1994).

In 1996 the National Park Service (NPS) completed a Development Concept Plan (DCP) and Environmental Impact Statement (EIS) for the Brooks River area of the Katmai National Park. The DCP presented six alternatives for the management, use and development of the area. The proposed action called for a reorientation of management and use to more adequately preserve and interpret the area's globally significant Alaskan brown bear viewing opportunities and prime brown bear habitat, and to manage these elements as integral parts of an evolving environment that also contains nationally significant cultural resources, scenic values, active volcanism and world-class sport fishing opportunities. Major features of the proposed action included removal of all NPS and concession facilities north of Brooks River, designation of the north side of the river as a 'people free' zone, construction of new visitor facilities (ranger station, orientation centre, lodge, campground, employee housing and maintenance facility) on the Beaver Pond terrace south of the river, establishment of day use limits for the Brooks River area, recommendation of temporary closures on reaches of Brooks River during times of intense bear use, and improvement of the area's wildlife and volcanism interpretive programme (Dorava and Meyer, 1994).

Conclusion

Alaska hosts within its major volcanic centres volcanoes that have erupted during the Holocene period (<10,000 years) and before to the present day (Kienle and Wood, 1990). These volcanic centres have been the source for more than 230 eruptions reported from Alaskan volcanoes (Rosi, 2003). Risk management for mass geotourism would be difficult owing to the difficulty of access; the individuals and small groups that make up the present tourist market are generally more experienced mountaineers at least, and may be expected to understand, factor in and act upon risk information in their movements.

References

Alaska Volcano Observatory (2009) 'Aleutian chain map and volcano list', www.avo.alaska.edu/volcanoes/aleutians.php, accessed 20 July 2009

Brantley, S. R. (ed) (1990) 'The eruption of Redoubt volcano, Alaska, December 14, 1989–August 31, 1990', *US Geological Survey Circular C 1061*, Washington DC

Casadevall, T. J. (ed) (1994) 'Volcanic ash and aviation safety: Proceedings of the first international symposium, Seattle, Washington, July 1991', *US Geological Survey Bulletin, B 2047*, Washington DC

Dorava, J. M. and Meyer, D. F. (1994) 'Hydrologic hazards in the lower Drift River basin associated with the 1989–1990 eruptions of Redoubt volcano, Alaska', in Miller, T. P. and Chouet, B. A. (eds) 'The 1989–1990 Eruptions of Redoubt Volcano, Alaska', *Journal of Volcanology and Geothermal Research*, vol 62, no 1, pp387–407

Miller, T. P., McGimsey, R. G., Richter, D. H., Riehle, J. R., Nye, C. J., Yount, M. E. and Dumoulin, J. A. (1998) Catalog of the historically active volcanoes of Alaska', *US Geological Survey Open-File Report OF 98-0582*, Washington DC

Rosi, M., Papale, P., Lupi, L. and Stoppato, M. (2003) *Volcanoes*, Firefly Books, Buffalo, New York

Schaefer, J. R. and Nye, C. (2008) 'The Alaska Volcano Observatory: 20 years of volcano research, monitoring, and eruption response', *Alaska GeoSurvey News*, vol 11, no 1, pp1–9

Wood, C. A. and Kienle, J. (1990) *Volcanoes of North America*, Cambridge University Press, Cambridge

Case Study 9

Active Volcanoes in Mexico as Tourist Destinations

Malcolm Cooper

Location

The Mexican volcanoes generally lie south of Mexico City (Secor, 2005). The Trans-Mexican Volcanic Belt *(Eje Volcánico Transversal)* also known locally as the Sierra Nevada extends 900km from west to east across central-southern Mexico (Figure CS9.1). The highest point, also the highest point in Mexico, is Pico de Orizaba (5636m) also known as Citlaltépetl; other notable volcanoes in the range include (from west to east) Nevado de Colima (4339m), Parícutin (2774m), Nevado de Toluca (4577m), Popocatépetl (5452m), Iztaccíhuatl (5286m), Matlalcueitl (4461m), Cofre de Perote (4282m) and Sierra Negra, a companion of Pico de Orizaba (4580m).

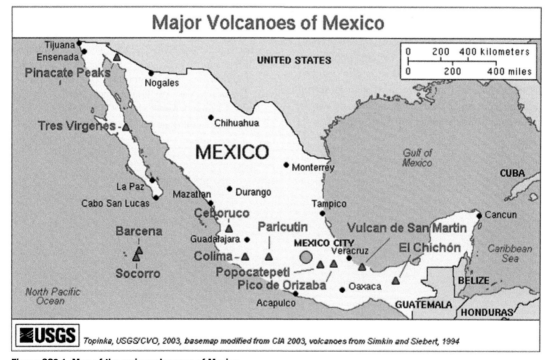

Figure CS9.1 Map of the major volcanoes of Mexico

Source: Wikimedia Commons, 2009

Mexico is currently 8th on the United Nations World Tourism Organization (UNWTO) list of major tourism markets, with some 22 million visitor arrivals every year and a corresponding level of domestic tourism (UNWTO, Tourism Barometer, 2009). Several major volcanoes within the country are well-known outside it (Popocatépetl, Colima, Parícutin), but nevertheless it does not appear that volcano tourism is particularly important to Mexico (it is not possible to obtain accurate statistics so comments are at best speculative), although this may change in the near future (see below).

Geophysical aspects and history of activity

The major volcanoes potentially of interest to tourists and their most recent activity are given in Table CS9.1. Perhaps the most famous, Popocatépetl last erupted in 2006, while the 200,000 residents of the City of Colima are at present threatened by the 2009 eruption of the Colima volcano. Parícutin is a cinder cone volcano in the State of Michoacán, close to a lava-covered village of the same name. It appears in many versions of the Seven Natural Wonders of the World (CNN, 1997). It is part of the Michoacán–Guanajuato Volcanic Field, which covers much of west central Mexico and began as a fissure in a cornfield on 20 **February 1943**. Local farmers all witnessed the initial eruption of ash and stones first-hand as they ploughed their fields. The volcano grew quickly during its first year, while it was still in the explosive pyroclastic phase. The nearby villages of Parícutin (after which the volcano was named) and San Juan Parangaricutiro were both buried in lava and ash; the residents relocated to vacant land nearby. In 1952 the eruption ended and Parícutin went quiet, having gained a final height of 424m above the cornfield and a total elevation of 3170m above sea level. The volcano has been quiet since, and like most cinder cones it is a monogenetic volcano, which means that it will never erupt again (Siebert et al, 2003).

El Chichón is located in north-western Chiapas State. Its only recorded eruptive activity was between 29 March and 4 April 1982, when it produced a 1km wide caldera that then filled with an acidic crater lake (Robock, 2002). The eruption killed 2000 people who lived near the volcano. El Chichón is part of a geologic zone known as the Chiapanecan Volcanic Arc, thought to be the result of the subduction of the Tehuantepec Ridge, an undersea ridge which lies on the Cocos Plate off the Pacific coast of Mexico (Manea and Manea, 2005).

Table CS9.1 Major volcanoes of Mexico

Volcano	Type	Elevation (metres)	Last eruption
Parícutin	Cinder cone	3170	1952
El Chichon	Lava dome	1060	1982
Colima	Stratovolcano	4330	2009
Pico de Orizaba	Stratovolcano	5700	1687
Ceboruco		2280	1885
Jorullo/Michacan-Guanajuato	Cinder cone field	3860	1952
Popocatépetl	Stratovolcano	5426	2006
San Martin Tuxtla	Shield	1650	1796
Socorro/Barcena	Shield	1050	1993
Tacana	Stratovolcano	4060	1986
Tres Virgenes		1940	1857

Source: Siebert et al, 2003

El Jorullo (began erupting 29 September 1759) is one of two known volcanoes to have developed in Mexico in recent history. The second, born about 183 years later, was Parícutin, about 80km north-west of El Jorullo. Once the volcano started erupting, it continued for 15 years eventually ending in 1774, and grew approximately 820 feet (250 metres) from the ground in the first six weeks. The eruptions from El Jorullo were primarily phreatic and phreatomagmatic, covering the surrounding area with sticky mud flows, water flows and ash falls.

Popocatépetl is one of the most active and famous volcanoes in Mexico, having had more than 20 major eruptions since the arrival of the Spanish in 1519. Major eruptions occurred in 1947, 1994, 2000 and 2006. Popocatépetl is linked to the Iztaccíhuatl volcano to the north by the high saddle known as the Paso de Cortés, and lies in the eastern half of the Trans-Mexican volcanic belt. Popocatépetl is only 70km (44 miles) to the south-east of Mexico City, from where it can be seen regularly, depending on atmospheric conditions. The volcano is also one of the three in Mexico to support glaciers, with the others being Iztaccíhuatl and Pico de Orizaba. Magma erupted from Popocatépetl is a mixture of dacite and basaltic andesite. The early 16th-century monasteries on the slopes of the mountain are a world heritage site.

Finally, the Sierra de Los Tuxtlas are a volcanic belt along the south-eastern Veracruz Gulf coast in south central Mexico. Peaks in this range include Volcano Santa Marta and Volcano San Martín Tuxtla, both rising above 1700m. San Martín Tuxtla is the only recently active volcano in the belt, erupting in 1664 and again in May 1793. It is a broad alkaline shield volcano with a 1km wide summit. Hundreds of smaller cinder cones are prevalent throughout the Sierra Biosphere Reserve.

Risk factors

The risk factors relating to Mexican volcanoes are the same as for any other group: lava flows destroying towns (Parícutin in the 1940s and 50s); ash eruptions and pyroclastic flows affecting both air transport and human settlements (El Chichón, 1982); extreme weather conditions and glacial environments (Pico de Orizaba, Popocatépetl); and the hazards generally associated with mountainous terrain (altitude sickness, unstable terrain, hypothermia). Risk factors for the mountains and the traveller come from litter and other waste products. Should any of these problems occur each of the major volcanoes has a climber registration facility (Secor, 2005), and the national parks and local communities have rangers and visitor centres for assistance.

Tourism

Tourism is the third most important economic sector for Mexico, contributing almost 9 per cent of GDP and two million jobs to the national economy in 2007. Nearly 22 million overseas visitors are attracted to the country each year, 96 per cent from North America, but they are mainly visiting for 'sun, sea and sand' and/or cultural tourism. However, the vision of what the industry and government expect of tourism in the long run is somewhat different as can be seen from the National Tourism Policy Review of Mexico, which states:

> By 2025 Mexico will be a leading country in tourism, since it will have diversified its markets, products and destinations, and its firms will be competitive at the domestic and international level. Tourism will be recognized as playing a key role in economic development and it will have grown with full respect for the natural, cultural and social environment, contributing all the while to enhancing national identity. (OECD, 2001)

In the wake of the worldwide success and popularity of ecotourism, official Mexican advertising has begun to shift focus from pure 'sun and sand' attractions to cultural, historic and environmental topics (OECD, 2001). However this is at best tentative and while Mexico is a multi-destination country, when looking at total tourist arrivals (domestic plus international tourists) it is apparent that the six busiest destinations account for 52 per cent of all arrivals. These include the three largest cities in the country (Mexico City 20.6 per cent of arrivals in 2000, Guadalajara 4.9 per cent, and Monterrey 3.3 per cent), two traditional beach destinations, Acapulco and Veracruz, and Cancun, an integrally planned coastal resort centre. Seven other destinations, which include smaller cities, border cities and beach destinations, account for between 2.1 and 3.1 per cent of all tourist arrivals, and push the share of the top 13 destinations to just over 70 per cent of arrivals. The remaining

30 per cent is shared by 42 destinations spread all over the country (OECD, 2001).

Thus, despite the new rhetoric, government strategies still seem to continue following the path chosen in the 1960s. Efforts to develop tourism are increasing in intensity but remain focused on mainstream (resort) tourism. This a pity, because Mexico's tourism industry is already highly developed and too large to only rely on one or two types of tourism. Alternative forms of tourism such as ecotourism and cultural/archaeological/ethnic tourism can and should be more emphasized. For many visitors of mainstream tourism sites and resorts, alternative tourism such as the volcanoes could at least be an 'add-on option' offering day trips into natural areas (there are excellent mountain tours available and Socorro Island is a popular scuba diving destination) and maybe creating some environmental awareness and limited income for local people and natural parks. In other areas, however (like Chiapas State, Oaxaca and some parts of the Yucatán), alternative tourism developments should not just be an 'add-on', but should be given the highest priority considering the natural infrastructure and the socio-cultural attributes of these areas (OECD, 2001).

Risk management

The management of risk has always posed a challenge for populations living in the shadow of volcanoes. In primitive societies, volcano risk was managed simply but effectively through avoidance – living near the summit of an active volcano was a religious taboo. In the 21st century, however, the fertile slopes of active volcanoes are often densely populated because of their agricultural abundance, and are often great visitor attractions as well. Therefore, volcano risk management procedures need to involve an economically and sociologically realistic assessment of risk. Prudent volcano risk management therefore dictates that well before any volcano crisis develops visitors and host communities should familiarize themselves with available hazard maps. Although it is not usually possible to predict when a dormant volcano will become active, once it does make this transition monitoring will allow the tracking of the probability of an eruption. And once an eruption occurs, which might last for months, years or even decades, higher priority risk management levels can be implemented.

Mexico's national parks system has this requirement under notice, and hazard mapping is progressing (Secor, 2005).

Conclusion

Mexico's range of active and dormant volcanoes are a well-known national tourism asset, and are progressively being upgraded for visitors. While Popocatépetl and Colima are closed at the time of writing owing to eruptions and threats of eruptions, the others enjoy a limited number of visitors, controlled by national park regulations and/or access difficulties. Risk management is as found in other national park systems around the world, and is primarily based on environmental conditions and environmental damage protection, rather than on the nature of the volcanoes, unless these are erupting or in danger of erupting.

References

CNN Destinations (1997) *The Seven Natural Wonders of the World*, Cable News Network, New York

Manea, V. C. and Manea, M. (2005) 'The origin of the modern Chiapanecan volcanic arc in southern Mexico inferred from thermal models', GSA Special Paper, *Natural Hazards in Central America*, Seismological Laboratory 252–21, CalTech, Pasadena, CA

OECD (2001) 'National Tourism Policy Review of Mexico', Directorate for Science, Technology and Industry, OECD, Paris

Robock, A. (2002) 'Volcanic Eruption, El Chichón', in MacCracken, M. C. and Perry, J. S. (eds) 'The Earth System: Physical and Chemical Dimensions of Global Environmental Change', *Encyclopedia of Global Environmental Change*, vol 1, pp736–737, John Wiley & Sons, Chichester

Secor, R. J. (2005) *Mexico's Volcanoes*, The Mountaineers Books, Seattle, WA

Sigurdsson, H. (2000) *Encyclopedia of Volcanoes*, Academic Press, San Diego, CA

Siebert, L., Calvin, C., Kimberly, P., Luhr, J. F. and Kysar, G. (2003) *Volcanoes of México*, vol 1.0, Smithsonian Institute, Global Volcanism Program, Digital Information Series, GVP-6, Smithsonian, Washington DC

UNTWO Tourism Barometer (2009) Online Document: www.pub.unwto.org/epages/Store.sf/?ObjectPath=/Shops/Infoshop/Products/1324/SubProducts/1324–1, accessed 7 January 2010

Wikimedia Commons (2009) 'Major volcanoes of Mexico', www.en.wikipedia.org/wiki/File:Map_mexico_volcanoes.gif, accessed 20 July 2009

Part IV

Asia

Introduction

Volcano tourism in Asia includes the opportunity to visit highly active and potentially dangerous volcanic and related geothermal landforms within the close vicinity of active volcanoes. The chapters and case studies in this section allow for a deeper insight into a tourism sector that to date has not been researched and described in greater depth for this region. Visitors to these particular volcanic areas include not only international volcano lovers, scientists and geotourists, but also local residents who, like in many other highly active regions, have a very close cultural and spiritual connection to their local fire mountains. Special appeasement festivals and events are connected with religious pilgrimages to active mountains at times of imminent danger of eruption, and sacrificial offerings are still common in countries where human settlements are close to volcanic activity.

8

The Need for a Planning Framework to Preserve the Wilderness Values of Sibayak Volcano, North Sumatra, Indonesia

David Newsome

Introduction

Indonesia has more volcanoes than any other country, with 130 active volcanoes and 76 significant eruptions recorded during historical times. Marapi volcano in Sumatra is the most active and has erupted about 50 times since its first recorded eruption in 1770. Merapi volcano, located in Central Java and which last erupted in 2007, was active throughout the Holocene. This frequent and widespread volcanic activity results from the subduction of the Indian Ocean crust underneath the Asian Tectonic Plate. The resultant island arc extends some 3000km from north-west Sumatra eastwards to the Banda Sea.

Over time many of these volcanoes have become a focus of attention for the cultural activities of local people, sites of international tourist visitation and areas where local and domestic tourists recreate. Many volcanoes in Indonesia have a long history of human interest and visitation, for example, Bromo, Merapi, Krakatau, Gede and Tangkuban Parahu, with the latter receiving around

1000 visitors a day. Indonesian volcanoes are included on global volcano visit agendas and several are listed in the top ten in the world to visit (see *Travellers Digest*, 2009).

According to Vaisutis et al (2007) the top volcanoes to visit in Java are Bromo, Merapi (last eruption in 2007) and Krakatau (last ash eruption in 2009), and in Sumatra Sibayak, Marapi and Kerinci. The focus of this chapter is on Sibayak (Figure 8.1) because it is a widely promoted site to visit on the north Sumatra tourism circuit, is one of the most accessible volcanoes in Indonesia and is popular with day-trippers from Medan. The issues surrounding visitation to Sibayak are explored from the perspective of site access, observation of visitor attitudes towards the volcano, and how the volcano is presented to the visitor as a geotourism destination. At present there is no suitable planning framework in place that is able to adequately assess, predict and manage uncontrolled recreation and tourism at Sibayak. Attention is therefore given as to how sustainable geotourism might be conducted through the application of a tourism-planning framework.

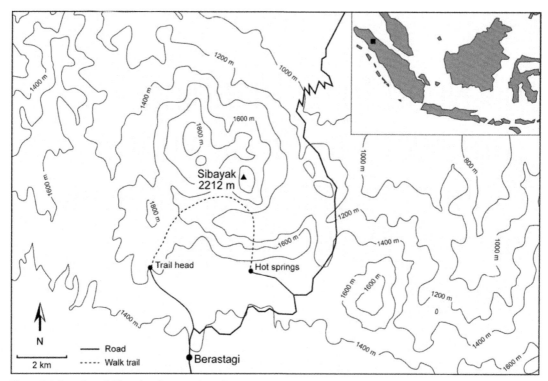

Figure 8.1 Location of Sibayak volcano and tourism access

Tourism at Sibayak volcano

Volcano tourism in Indonesia involves free independent travellers, who sometimes use local guides, and organized tour trekking. Some volcanoes are easier to access than others and organized tours (treks range from 5 to 12 days) focus on the higher and less accessible volcanoes like Semuru (3676m) in Java. Sibayak (2212m) is probably one the easiest volcanoes to climb in Indonesia. Visitation statistics are difficult to acquire but up to 100 people a day may visit the summit area. Preliminary observations suggest that the visitor profile comprises international tourists, day, weekend visitors from Medan (population two million) and locally sourced youth groups such as scouts and school groups. The summit area can be reached in two to three hours and some visitors climb the volcano at night so that they can watch the sunrise from the summit at daybreak. Overall visitation tends to peak during public holidays and festivals when groups of visitors from Medan hike in the park.

Sibayak is a stratovolcano that last erupted in 1881. Fumeroles occur in the vicinity of the crater and are constantly discharging steam, and sulphur deposits have accumulated around their vents. The crater is 900m wide and is backed by a rock wall (see Figures 8.3 and 8.4). The floor of the crater is stable allowing visitor access. Hot springs are also present on the lower slopes of the mountain.

Impacts of tourism on the volcano

Even though it might be expected that a natural feature such as a dynamic and potentially destructive volcano is difficult to spoil as a result of visitation, the environment and particularly the summit area is showing clear signs of degradation. Degradation of Sibayak can be examined from several visitor management perspectives namely

Figure 8.2 Broken and poorly maintained concrete steps on the descending trail

the condition of access trails, modification of the crater floor, graffiti, littering and the lack of environmental interpretation.

Access to Sibayak is initially via a sealed road and then a natural surfaced single trail that ascends the summit from the south side (Figure 8.1). Steeper sections of the trail have concrete steps but many are in a state of disrepair. There is no clear signage especially at the summit area and this has led to trail bifurcation and the development of many secondary trails as people have explored the summit area and also tried to locate the trail that descends on the eastern side of the volcano. The bifurcating trail network and frequent low cloud can pose a visitor safety issue with visitors getting lost around the summit area. Steep sections of the descending trail have been managed via the construction of stone steps. Due to lack of maintenance many are broken and eroded to upstanding bars due to loss of soil from the sections of trail between the steps (Figure 8.2). Overall many sections of the trail (and especially the descending trail) are muddy and slippery making trail use difficult. Eroding conditions, the

lack of signage and the presence of a loose boulder-strewn surface at the upper levels have resulted in trail bifurcation and widening, and pose risks to the unwary visitor.

Activities at the summit include sightseeing, filming fumerole activity, photography, some camping and exploring the crater area. Often these activities are conducted in a random fashion along user created trails and access points which has led to informal trail proliferation and dispersed erosion scaring of the landscape. There is a lack of on-site management, such as signage that relates to keeping people on walk trails and out of the crater area. Some graffiti and littering is also present in the summit area. The crater floor has been modified in the form of lines of stones that have been arranged into names and words (Figure 8.3). The geometric arrangement of stones constitutes a visual impact that is likely to impoverish natural values of the most significant part of the viewing experience for some visitors.

There is no interpretation in place to enrich the Sibayak volcano experience or point to the risks involved. Interpretation in tourism serves to enhance visitor experience, inform the public about and therefore mitigate impact problems and explain management strategies (Newsome et al, 2002). This lack of interpretation translates to a lack of opportunity to learn about the volcano and encourage appropriate behaviour and activity. There are no pamphlets to orientate and guide the visitor. There is an absence of interpretation panels, which can be used to show walk trail maps, inform the visitor about codes of conduct and provide information about the volcano.

The presence of informal trail networks, trail erosion, graffiti, littering and modification of the crater coupled with a complete lack of inter-pretation reduces the quality of the Sibayak volcano experience by taking away the wilderness value of the volcano and reducing the sense of wonder for those visitors seeking natural experiences. Erfurt-Cooper (2008) notes that international visitors to the volcano are likely to be seeking an experience that is based on unspoilt nature; any visitor dissatisfaction with current issues therefore constitutes a management problem that has the potential to compromise the sustainability of Sibayak as a quality volcano tourism experience.

Figure 8.3 Sibayak crater

Note: Visitors have uncontrolled access to the crater floor where over time people have arranged rocks and stones into names, words and various patterns

Planning for the management of protected areas and natural attractions is essential to adequately conserve a resource while at the same time making provision for appropriate uses (Worboys et al, 2005). Cochrane (1996) reported that there are organizational and cultural barriers to effective visitor management in Indonesian national parks and natural areas. Such barriers are primarily related to an absence of management planning, a lack of resourcing, complex bureaucratic dealings and inefficiency and the lack of skilled staff on the ground. The application of a tourism-planning framework would go a long way in resolving the issues identified at Sibayak. A planning framework can be used to guide tourism management, foster sustainable tourism and preserve the natural attributes of Sibayak.

The use of tourism planning frameworks in geotourism

Planning frameworks are designed to maximize the quality of visitor experience and protect the natural environment in order to ensure future visitor satisfaction. Various planning frameworks have been developed in order to plan and manage visitor activity in natural areas (Newsome et al, 2002). All are designed to protect the environment while providing opportunities for visitor use. The planning process involves establishing goals and objectives, defining actions and implementing and reviewing those actions. Planning frameworks commonly include several key factors. Each process involves: identification of how visitors use a natural area; where given uses take place within the area; an inventory of natural assets; identification of possible or existing impacts and establishment of standards and indicators. Some frameworks have additional components that include identification of the cause of impacts and appropriate management action to reduce impacts. The ultimate objective is to accommodate demand for certain activities within a park while ensuring conservation of important natural systems.

Whatever specific planning framework, or combination of frameworks, is selected, the key to successful implementation is in the quality of data gathered. Without information about biophysical features and ecological processes of a park, who uses it, how it is used and exactly what impacts take place over a given period, a planning framework cannot be effectively applied. This relates both to comprehensive baseline data and consistent collection of data on an ongoing basis as part of the management process.

A one-off inventory of what a park contains and how it is used may be sufficient to provide a foundation from which a planning framework can be devised. However, the ongoing implementation of a planning framework relies on consistent and accurate monitoring both of indicators and management practices. Monitoring is the central plank of any planning framework without which it is ineffectual. That is, a planning framework relies on a management structure with the capabilities to gather and analyse information over a long time period. In addition, systems must be in place to evaluate management of the framework to ensure appropriate and effective implementation.

Issues associated with applying a tourism-planning framework to Sibayak

The current lack of a coordinated approach to visitor and park management (using a planning framework) means that uncontrolled recreation/ tourism is degrading the Sibayak volcano experience. Unfortunately, the extent of the threat has not been accurately determined because the lack of a planning framework has resulted in an absence of monitoring procedures. This also makes it difficult to gauge exactly how people

react to the damage or the risks and creates the difficulty of effectively conducting sustainable management practices for the park. Clearly there is a need for the collection of baseline data on tourist activity, preferences and biophysical data in order to provide a basis for monitoring change and assessing recreational impacts on the volcano. Such data then need to be fed into a comprehensive and adequately funded visitor management strategy. From this, the source and extent of the threats to Sibayak can be identified and addressed.

Because of the likely increasing number of domestic visitors to Sibayak, socio-cultural issues may then shape the choice of a visitor management system. Cochrane (1996) noted that Indonesians generally have a preference for crowds rather than small group or solitary experiences of natural areas. In the past, Indonesians have generally not placed much emphasis on nature observation and appreciation when visiting natural areas. This may stem from a dominance or history of subsistence lifestyles that have been prevalent in Indonesia, where people view nature as a resource for survival more than a place for reflection and aesthetic appreciation – although this attitude may be changing as a greater middle class emerges in Indonesia. Thus, any planning framework applied to Sibayak may need to take into account the strong emphasis domestic visitors have on socialization rather than on aesthetic appreciation in natural areas.

One approach for Sibayak may be a system to determine the level of acceptable impact on the environment through a combination of the Limits of Acceptable Change (LAC) and Visitor Impact Management (VIM) planning frameworks (Newsome et al, 2002). The contribution that could be made by these frameworks is that of providing a means for determining what environmental and social conditions are acceptable and by assisting in identifying appropriate management actions to achieve defined end-state conditions. The reasons for such a choice are that VIM and LAC rely on minimum to moderate stakeholder input (McArthur, 2000) and that tourism planners in Indonesia have stated that government should make decisions for the benefit of society at large (Timothy, 1999). Moreover, 'stakeholders' in the developing world do not expect to participate in the environmental planning process.

This planning approach would involve defining park areas in relation to intensity of use, identifying indicators to monitor key environmental and social conditions, conducting a survey of current conditions within the park and setting standards to establish the limits of acceptable change. The VIM aspect involves steps to identify the probable cause(s) of an identified impact and the appropriate management actions required (Newsome et al, 2002). Such a framework could take into account the heavy use of the area while also aiding in the identification of key sources of impact and required actions. Of course this system, as with any style of management, will only be as successful as the quality of the resources and personnel assigned to implement it.

The problem with applying such a planning framework to Sibayak is in accounting for the strong emphasis on socialization and general lack of interest in conserving or aesthetically appreciating the environment. This situation is problematic because the area might be just a backdrop to social activities rather than the focus of attention itself. This must mean that higher levels of disturbance and degradation will be acceptable to visitors (than say in Australian protected areas) but these higher levels at the same time are detrimental to the ecological, aesthetic and geo-heritage integrity of the park. A situation where domestic visitors apparently don't care whether their geological heritage is maintained or not but just to have somewhere to go and socialize away from the city implies that a framework looking at 'acceptable change' from the visitors or park use point of view will not work to conserve ecological processes. So a balance must somehow be achieved between allowing park use as a social venue and restricting impacts to preserve its geological attributes. In addition to this there is the key issue of adequate funding, as at present it appears that Sibayak Park does not have the staff and resources to properly implement a framework. Implementation will also rely on suitably informed and motivated park management. In such a case the setting of standards and indicators could be

entirely management driven along with a wider stakeholder education programme that fosters interest, respect and other appropriate attitudes towards the environment.

What can be done to build the Sibayak volcano experience as a sustainable international geotourism attraction?
Understanding tourism activities

The management of natural areas is dependent on knowledge of visitor use and activities (Buckley and Pannell, 1990; Newsome et al, 2002). The nature and degree of environmental impacts will vary according to the specific type of activities, numbers of visitors and temporal/spatial aspects of visitation. It is therefore important to collect visitor information in the form of surveys, interviews or by direct observation of visitor activities.

The significance of collecting visitor information lies in the data being able to inform a management plan. Watson (2008), who reported on visitor surveys conducted in Nambung National Park, Western Australia, found that 53 per cent of visitors were on a day trip from Perth and that 80 per cent were from interstate or overseas and 61 per cent were on a tour. He also found that geological formations, scenery, the opportunity to learn and the unspoilt nature of the Pinnacles Desert in Nambung National Park were key attracting features. Such information about visitor interests is able to inform management about the application of site infrastructure, the management of peak visitor loads and educational activities that could be implemented to enhance the visitor experience.

Visitor surveys conducted in Bako National Park, Sarawak by Chin et al (2000) found that 76 per cent enjoyed hiking, 72 per cent engaged in sightseeing and 61 per cent took photographs. Respondents also indicated that enjoying nature (78 per cent), learning about nature (70 per cent) and viewing scenery rated to be very to extremely important. Chin et al (2000) maintain that such visitor preferences are strongly dependent on the quality of the natural environment. Perceptions of visitor-related environmental impacts reported in the visitor survey include soil erosion along walk trails (62 per cent), damage to vegetation (57 per cent), hiking off trails and the presence of litter (69 per cent). Litter is reported to be a significant impact because it is being increasingly perceived as spoiling natural values, especially from a Western cultural perspective. When visitors were asked (support/strongly support) about potential management strategies there was support for visitor education (79 per cent), additional maps and directional signage (61 per cent), restriction of hiking in some areas (58 per cent) and a desire for more staff (49 per cent).

A survey at Mt Bromo in Java carried out by Cochrane (2006) involved a combination of questionnaires, interviews and participant observations. Indonesian visitors completed 72 and foreigners completed 101 questionnaires. The Indonesian visitor data set provides some insights into the nature of domestic tourism in recent years. Group sizes averaged around 15.5 as compared to 2.2 for non-Asians. Western tourists showed a preference for hiking, had come to view the volcano and demonstrated environmental awareness. They were interested in naturalness, authenticity and tranquility. A significant proportion (37 per cent) found commercial development, litter, crowding and the lack of information to detract from their experience of the volcano. From a Western perspective these detracting components negatively impact on the tourism experience at Mt Bromo. Indonesian visitors by contrast had a more recreation focus to their trip consisting of hiking and satisfying the challenge of getting to the top. Once at the top picnicking, socializing and viewing the scenery was preferred over the nature experience approach that Westerners desired. This view is reflected by comments (40 per cent of respondents) relating to a lack of facilities around the summit area. In direct contrast to other visitors only 3 per cent of Indonesians would have preferred more information about the park. Cochrane (2006) however is of the view that the Indonesian perspective is changing with Indonesians travelling in smaller groups and showing a preference for more natural experiences and knowledge about the place they are visiting. This latter observation

by Cochrane (2006) and the push for Indonesia to recover and expand its international markets provides a sound rationale for the proposed interpretation strategy discussed below.

Sustainable trail management

Trail systems are important in providing access to valued natural attractions while at the same time offering a directional route for visitors to follow so that trampling of vegetation and substrates can be avoided. If trails are not planned and managed, degradation generally occurs in the form of soil erosion, trail widening and visitor-created trail proliferation. An LAC framework can be applied to existing trail systems as in the case of Sibayak. The use of indicators and desired standards can set the scene for a monitoring programme that evaluates management success and implementation of responses (Anderson et al, 1998). The existing trail network at Sibayak needs to be assessed and if found to be unsustainable may require improvement maintenance, reconstruction or in places re-routing. A problem-based assessment process may be the most useful approach as this technique assesses the frequency, extent and location of problems encountered along the entire trail (Leung and Marion, 1999). Documentation of impacts along the trial provides a basis for targeted management actions such as the replacement/reconstruction of steps, trail surface water control measures, trail hardening, directional signage and the closure and rehabilitation of visitor created trails (Newsome et al, 2002; Marion and Leung, 2004). Ongoing monitoring and maintenance then needs to be employed in order to maintain sustainable conditions (Mende and Newsome, 2006).

Managed access programme and crater floor rehabilitation

In addition to adequate trail directional signage, areas around the summit need to be protected from uncontrolled access and trampling. This can be achieved through the use of on-site interpretation panels that can guide the visitor to planned viewing areas while at the same time advising visitors, with reasons, not to access the crater area (Figures 8.4 and 8.5).

Figure 8.4 Tourist viewing of fumaroles from the rim of Sibayak Crater

Note: The area shows evidence of erosion at and beyond the site due to uncontrolled access. The area depicted could be selected as a formal viewing area. The site may need hardening to control erosion and needs to be supported with an interpretive panel.

Interpretive panelling can be used to orientate visitors to the crater area and indicate where people are allowed to go. It can also point out safety issues and explain why access is restricted in the crater area (Figure 8.5).

The crater floor itself (Figure 8.3) needs rehabilitation work to remove stone lines, names and other features that spoil natural values.

Developing a geosite interpretation plan

Interpretation is a very important aspect of natural area tourism and serves to increase visitor satisfaction, raise awareness of environmental issues and aid in visitor management. It is guided by a suite of principles originally developed by Tilden (1957) that state: interpretation should be based on a theme and associated messages; provide

opportunities for first-hand experiences and active involvement; maximize the use of all senses; foster self discovery and provide emotional meaning for visitors. These principles imply that interpretation is potentially an expensive and complex strategy ranging from fairly simple information sheets and panels through to active tour guiding and the use of built facilities. Although educational materials for geotourism have been produced in Indonesia (Dowling and Newsome, 2006) much remains to be done to develop a comprehensive interpretation strategy for volcano tourism in Sumatra. In the first instance at Sibayak interpretive pamphlets and panels can be used to achieve some of the objectives indicated above.

A geosite interpretation plan for Sibayak needs to cover the following aspects in English and

Welcome to Hawks Head

Hawks Head Walk
200 m return

Follow the path to a lookout over an evocative rock formation. Marvel at the extensive view of the mighty Murchison River. Find out about some of the creatures that inhabit the natural communities of the river and gorge. Learn about the impact of feral pigs and goats and the efforts being made to restore the natural system here in Kalbarri National Park.

Gorge Risk Area

Beware of:

❖ undercut cliff edges

❖ loose rocks and unstable surfaces

For your safety:

❖ keep to the path and lookout

❖ do not venture onto the Hawks Head formation

River access is not available here. The easiest place in the Park to access the river is at Ross Graham, 5 km south by road.

Kalbarri is a special place for the Nanda Aboriginal people, as it has been for thousands of years. Today, the Nanda people welcome visitors who respect the cultural and natural heritage of Kalbarri National Park.

Figure 8.5 Interpretive panel at the Hawks Head Lookout in Kalbarri National Park, Western Australia

Note: Panels such as the one depicted provide examples of what may be employed at Sibayak

Indonesian: site orientation (Figure 8.6); explanation of volcano etiquette and appropriate visitor behaviour and thus protecting natural attributes; aspects of the origin of the volcano such as tectonics, friction melting of rock and the rise of magma through zones of weakness in the Earth's crust. In addition to this it is important to focus on specific aspects of Sibayak itself such as eruption history, rock types and fumerole activity.

The key to protecting Sibayak is interpretation because if visitors learn about a place and understand its geological, ecological and social significance they will pay more attention to being environmentally sensitive and the incidence of damage will be reduced. Chin et al (2000) found in their survey that 90 per cent of respondents were interested in learning about nature as part of their experience in Bako National Park. Data such

as these suggest that investing in an interpretation strategy for Sibayak is a viable option in fostering sustainable tourism. Interpretation however needs to be planned and delivered with Tilden's principles in mind. Interpretive panels are somewhat restricted in delivering active involvement, maximum use of the senses and fostering self-discovery, as in this case it will depend on the visitor reading the panel and engaging with its content. These aspects can be more effectively delivered via a tour guide but good guiding is in turn dependent upon the guide understanding the site and its geology, gauging individual differences within the tour group and being passionate about protecting the volcano as a wild and interesting tourism resource. A longer-term component of the Sibayak interpretation plan should be to create trained, officially recognized and good guiding services.

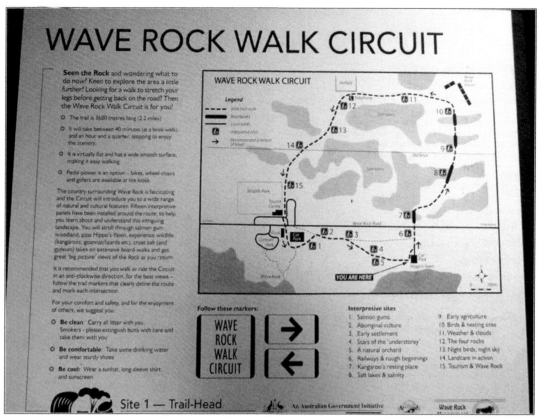

Figure 8.6 Route plan for the Wave Rock Walk Trail in Western Australia

Note: The panel orientates visitors to the site, provides an indication of what may be seen and highlights the location of stopping points where interpretive panels explain the geology and landscape.

Conclusion

Sibayak is a significant geotourism resource with no management support and urgently in need of funding to manage tourism sustainably. Important attributes of the volcano are landscape views, fumeroles and the crater walls and floor. Current visitation and tourism activity is degrading the natural features and authenticity of Sibayak. Identified impacts are trail degradation, user created trail proliferation, unrestricted access resulting in erosion scars, modification of the crater floor, litter and graffiti. There is no ranger presence, no trail maintenance, poor signage and a lack of interpretation. The long-term sustainability of tourism is dependent on sustainable trail management (track repair and maintenance; additional signage), removal of graffiti, restoration of the crater floor and on-site interpretation.

Sustainable tourism can be achieved through the application of a suitably crafted tourism-planning framework. The planning process involves establishing goals and objectives, defining actions and implementing and reviewing those actions. Planning frameworks commonly include several key factors. Each process involves: identification of how visitors use a natural area; where given uses take place within the area; an inventory of 'natural assets'; identification of possible or existing impacts and establishment of standards and indicators for future monitoring of visitor activity and impacts, and the assessment of management effectiveness.

Obtaining reasons for tourists visiting a site, gauging visitor motivations and preferences, and soliciting views on management provides essential data for the development of a planning framework.

At the outset the plan can be informed by what people are attracted to, which in turn has implications for access and potential management actions. The examples of visitor surveys provided here also demonstrate visitor concerns about the environment and support for potential management actions with a strong interest in visitor education, hence the call for a geosite interpretation plan.

While certainly not a panacea, the establishment of a planning framework is an important step toward addressing many issues. A tourism-planning framework provides structure for strategic, and more effective, allocation of often meagre management resources. The key to successful implementation of a tourism-planning framework is possession of reliable tourism (human use) and biophysical impact data. In Sumatra this type of information is very often patchy or non-existent owing to a lack of skills or resources to gather and analyse data. Because of the absence of evaluation and monitoring data it is often difficult to come up with accurate figures on the extent of recreation and tourism in natural and protected areas. However, because of the need to protect Indonesia's remaining natural areas, and a rising interest in human visitation to volcanoes and other natural environments, recreation/tourism specific management strategies will need to be employed.

References

Anderson, D. H., Lime, D. W. and Wang, T. L. (1998) *Maintaining the Quality of Park Resources and Visitor Experiences* (Report No. TC-777), Cooperative Parks Studies Unit Department of Forest Resources University of Minnesota, St Paul, MN

Buckley, R. and Pannell, J. (1990) 'Environmental impacts of tourism and recreation in national parks and conservation reserves', *Journal of Tourism Studies*, vol 1, no1, pp24–32

Chin, C. L. M., Moore, S. A., Dowling, R. K. and Wallington, T. J. (2000) 'Ecotourism in Bako National Park, Borneo: Visitors' perceptions on environmental impacts and their management', *Journal of Sustainable Tourism*, vol 8, pp20–35

Cochrane, J. (1996) 'The Sustainability of Ecotourism in Indonesia: Fact or Fiction', in M. J. G. Parnwell and R. L. Bryant (eds) *Environmental Change in South-East Asia: People, Politics and Sustainable Development*, Routledge, London and New York

Cochrane, J. (2006) 'Indonesian national parks: Understanding leisure users', *Annals of Tourism Research*, vol 33, no 4, pp979–997

Dowling, R. and Newsome, D. (eds) (2006) *Geotourism*, Elsevier/Heinemann Publishers, Oxford

Erfurt-Cooper, P. (2008) Geotourism: Active Geothermal and Volcanic Environments as Tourist Destinations, in Dowling, R. and Newsome, D. (eds) *Conference Proceedings, Inaugural Global Geotourism Conference*, 17–20 August 2008, Perth, Western Australia, pp165–174

Leung, Y.-F. and Marion, J. L. (1999) 'Assessing trail conditions in protected areas: Application of a problem assessment method in Great Smoky Mountains National Park, USA', *Environmental Conservation*, vol 26, no 4, pp270–279

McArthur, S. (2000) 'Visitor management in action: An analysis of the development and implementation of visitor management models at Jenolan Caves and Kangaroo Island', PhD Thesis, University of Canberra, Canberra, ACT

Marion, J. and Leung, Y.-F. (2004) 'Environmentally Sustainable Trail Management', in Buckley, R. (ed) *Environmental Impacts of Ecotourism*, CABI Publishing, Wallingford

Mende, P. and Newsome, D. (2006) 'The assessment, monitoring and management of hiking trails: A case study from the Stirling Range National Park, Western Australia', *Conservation Science Western Australia*, vol 5, no 3, pp27–37

Newsome, D., Moore, S. and Dowling, R. (2002) *Natural Area Tourism: Ecology Impacts and Management*, Channel View Publications, ClevelandTilden, F. (1957) *Interpreting Our Heritage*, Chapel Hill, NC: University of North Carolina Press.Travellers Digest (2009) www.travellersdigest.com/best_volcanoes.htm, accessed 5 September 2009

Timothy, D. J. (1999) 'Participatory planning: A view of tourism in Indonesia', *Annals of Tourism Research*, vol 26, no 2, pp371–391

Vaisutis, J., Elliot, N., Ray, N., Stewart, I., Ver Berkmoes, R., Williams, C., Witton, P. and Yanagihara, W. (2007) *Lonely Planet Guide to Indonesia*, Lonely Planet Publications, London

Watson, G. (2008) 'Pinnacles Desert Discovery: Maintaining the Magic of a Western Australian Tourism Icon', in Dowling, R. and Newsome, D. (eds) *Conference Proceedings, Inaugural Global Geotourism Conference*, 17–20 August 2008, Perth, Western Australia, pp. 377–382

Worboys, G., Lockwood, M. and De Lacy, T. (2005) *Protected Area Management*, Oxford University Press, Melbourne, Australia

9

Volcano and Geothermal Tourism in Kyushu, Japan

Patricia Erfurt-Cooper

Introduction

In Japan volcano tourism and geotourism are part of many tourists' trip agendas, although as yet not under these specific categories. Most people who visit volcanic environments in Japan do so under the guise of nature-based hot spring tourism or *onsen* tourism which benefits from the geophysical attributes especially on the island of Kyushu. The number of national parks in Kyushu offers a broad range of recreational opportunities; moreover, most of them with access to volcanic and geothermal areas. To give a quick indication of the destinations discussed in this chapter a map of Kyushu (Figure 9.1) has been modified to indicate where the major volcanoes are located.

Mt Unzen and Mt Sakurajima were also classed as 'decade volcanoes' several years ago, which made them objects of special studies and monitoring through the IAVCEI (International Association of Volcanology and Chemistry of the Earth's Interior). A sub-commission of the IAVCEI was appointed for the Decade Volcanoes Project with the aim to 'direct attention to a small number of selected, active volcanoes worldwide and to encourage the establishment of a range of research and public-awareness activities aimed at enhancing an understanding of the volcanoes and the hazards posed by them' (USGS, n.d.).

Classifications of individual tourism sectors such as geotourism and volcano tourism are slowly being integrated into the marketing of

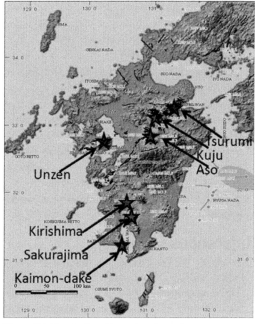

Figure 9.1 Kyushu's active volcanic centres

Note: All the volcanic centres are located within a national park with visitor facilities, accommodation, hot spring spas, theme parks and many other attractions for visitors.

Source: Map modified by author

individual regions, for example, the 'Shimabara Volcanic Area', which includes the notorious Mt Unzen, has become officially recognized as a global geopark. The most important features for this geopark are its volcanic and geothermal attractions, several volcano museums and a village buried by lahars, as well as the natural environment linked to these features. Several regions in Japan became UNESCO Global Geoparks in 2009, all of them including volcanic and/or geothermal landforms. Mt Usu in Hokkaido, part of the Shikotsu-Toya National Park, is another example (UNESCO Global Geoparks Network, 2008; Chapter 10). Volcanic features are amongst the greater draw cards in Japanese national and prefectural parks, considering that at least two thirds of the parks can offer more or less active volcanic landforms.

In Japan over 100 volcanoes are currently classed as active. The Japan Meteorological Agency (JMA) defines volcanoes that erupted during the last 10,000 years, or which have fumarolic activity as active volcanoes. To indicate the degree of volcanic activity the JMA started in November 2003 to apply alert levels (0–5; Table 9.1) to some active volcanoes, which are continuously monitored. The JMA issues volcano information to the disaster prevention authorities and to the public to initiate and take relevant disaster reduction measures.

The island of Kyushu is the third largest island of Japan and is located in the south-west of the Japanese island arc. Like Honshu and Hokkaido, Kyushu has a number of active volcanoes (seven), some of which are constantly erupting, but generally maintain a low level of activity. All of

Table 9.1 Volcanic Activity Level classification

Level	General activity (Detailed activity is described for each volcano)
5	**Very large eruption** Danger over wide areas
4	**Large eruption** Danger also in areas apart from the crater
3	**Eruption** Small eruption or precursor of eruptions. Danger near the crater
2	**Active** Seismic swarm, tremor or slight eruption. Preliminary stage for eruptive period
1	**Calm** Small seismic activity, fumarolic activity but no signs of eruption
0	**Dormant** No fumarolic activity, No seismic activity for a long time

Source: Japan Meteorological Agency, 2009

these seven volcanoes and volcanic complexes are tourist destinations, are surrounded by national or prefectural parklands, and have more or less developed facilities for access and accommodation in close proximity to the volcanic mountains. All of these active volcanoes are also located close to large cities and have a rather recent eruption history as Table 9.2 shows.

Table 9.2 Seven active volcanic areas in Kyushu with close proximity to large cities

Volcano	Elevation	Last erupted	Nearby cities
Mount Aso Aso-Kuju National Park	1529m	2005 AD	Kumamoto (670,000 inhabitants) and many small villages in and around the caldera
Mount Kuju Aso-Kuju National Park	1788m	1996 AD	Beppu (130,000) and Kumamoto
Tsurumi lava dome complex	1584m	867 AD	Beppu
Unzen stratovolcano complex	1500m	1996 AD	Shimabara (50,000), Nagasaki (446,000) and Kumamoto
Sakurajima	1117m	ongoing	Kagoshima (605,000)
Kirishima shield volcano	1700m	2008 AD	Kagoshima
Kaimon-dake Ibusuki volcanic field	922m	885 AD	Kagoshima

Source: Various, compiled by author

Mount Aso

Most tourism sectors in Kyushu are linked to volcanic activity, usually through the Japanese passion for *onsen* (hot spring) bathing, which is a great attraction for visitors from other areas without hot springs. One of the popular onsen areas is near Mt Aso which is located in the centre of Kyushu and is part of the Aso-Kuju National Park. Mt Aso draws large crowds on any day with reasonable weather and favourable winds to keep the toxic gas emissions from the crater away from the visitors. This volcano is unique as it is not just classed as one of the most dangerous volcanoes in the world, but it also has access to the summit via a toll road as well as a ropeway to cater for the mass tourism that takes place here on a regular basis.

A number of other attractions such as hot spring resorts are linked to the volcano and recreational activities are combined with visits to the crater, for example, horse riding, hiking, trekking and bird watching. Souvenir shops, restaurants and the Aso Volcano Museum are located at a short distance from the volcano and can be accessed even if the summit is closed. The volcano itself is located within one of the largest calderas in the world with a circumference of over 120km (24km diameter). The summit crater of Naka-dake, the only currently active peak, is accessible by toll road and cable car and is one of Kyushu's most popular tourist destinations (Global Volcanism Program, 2009). People visit the crater with their friends and families, often several times in a year, as the landscape changes with the colours of the four seasons. In May, for example, the lower flanks of the volcano are covered in mountain azaleas in all shades of pink and in winter the snow adds another attraction to the volcanic landscape.

A survey on the risk perception of visitors was carried out by the author and students on Mt Aso in July 2008, and the reasons for visiting active volcanoes, as well as any possible concerns about the potential dangers while visiting, were investigated. A short summary (Table 9.3) of the results indicates that the Japanese rather enjoy their active volcanoes for a number of reasons. The survey findings suggest that all respondents were aware that Mt Aso is classed as an active volcano

Table 9.3 A brief overview of what is important for volcano tourists in Japan while visiting Mt Aso in Kyushu

	Reasons for visiting Mt Aso-Kuju National Park		
	Very important	Important	Not important
Volcanic activity	50%	38%	12%
Volcanic landscape	68%	30%	2%
Volcanic national park	27%	59%	14%
Volcanic museum	20%	29%	31%
Hot springs	38%	43%	19%
Holiday	46%	31%	23%
Hiking, walking	14%	39%	47%
Volcano photography	38%	51%	11%
Natural environment	54%	42%	4%
Volcanic history	20%	57%	23%

Source: Survey from 2008 carried out by the author and a class of research students from Ritsumeikan Asia Pacific University

and Table 9.3 demonstrates how important volcanic activity is as a reason for visiting. Only 12 per cent of the respondents considered volcanic activity as not important. Most people (75 per cent) had no concerns that Mt Aso could suddenly erupt, because they trusted the relevant authorities to evacuate everybody in time. A number of concrete bunkers (Figure 9.2) are available on the viewing platforms near the crater rim in case an unscheduled eruption takes place, although it is not clear how several hundred tourists (Figure 9.3) should fit into the half a dozen concrete shells and be sheltered from larger sized ballistic ejecta (Figure 9.4) as well as from toxic fumes out of the crater. This is a hazard which could make a visit during an eruption a very unpleasant experience.

The Aso Volcano Disaster Prevention Council maintains a website in English which contains valuable information for tourists not familiar with Mt Aso and the immediate surroundings. Maps and other useful information are also made available in English for the increasing numbers of

Figure 9.2 Concrete bunkers near the viewing area at the crater of Mt Aso

Note: After a few years the bunkers need replacing as the sulphur in the air eats into the concrete, exposing the aggregate and the steel structure making the shelter unsafe.

Figure 9.3 Volcano tourists at the crater rim of Mt Aso taking photos

Figure 9.4 Large sized volcanic bombs are scattered over the barren landscape of the summit of Mt Aso

foreign visitors to Kyushu. The most commendable advice on this website is the real-time updated crater status as well as a live webcam. Every volcano visited by tourists should have a website like this to provide useful information for visitors *before* they arrive at their destination. From a safety point of view the audibility of the PA system at the crater is very good while the volcano is quiet, and evacuations happen swiftly as soon as the wind direction changes and toxic fumes from the crater are blown towards the viewing areas and the walkways (pers. observation).

There have been fatal accidents in the past caused by emissions of sulphur dioxide (SO_2), not eruptive activity. This is a colourless gas with a pungent odour that irritates skin and eyes and can affect the respiratory system. Six fatalities occurred over a period of nine years between 1989 and 1997 and autopsies suggested that they each had a health condition which put them at a higher risk of death by volcanic gas inhalation (Ng'walali, 1999).

To avoid accidents visitors on the summit of Mt Aso have to listen for announcements, which

are constantly repeated in four languages (Japanese, Korean, English and Chinese). At the entrance to the crater there are sign boards and warning signs (Figure 9.5) as well as colour-coded light signals as a safety measure to provide information on the density of the volcanic gases, reminding visitors to be watchful and stay alert. Gas recognition and safety measures have been implemented for tourists, with automated measuring equipment now installed at six locations near the crater. As soon as they detect a gas density above a specified level, access to the crater is restricted (Aso Volcano Disaster Prevention Council, 2008).

All the boardwalks are maintained well and kept very clean. People take their whole families including children from a very young age (Figure 9.6) for a day out on the volcano, as the walkways are wheelchair and stroller friendly. While walking around there are opportunities to buy a block of sulphur or some volcanic rocks as a souvenir from one of the small stall holders who have their tables covered with volcanic memorabilia as well as batteries for cameras. The only thing that

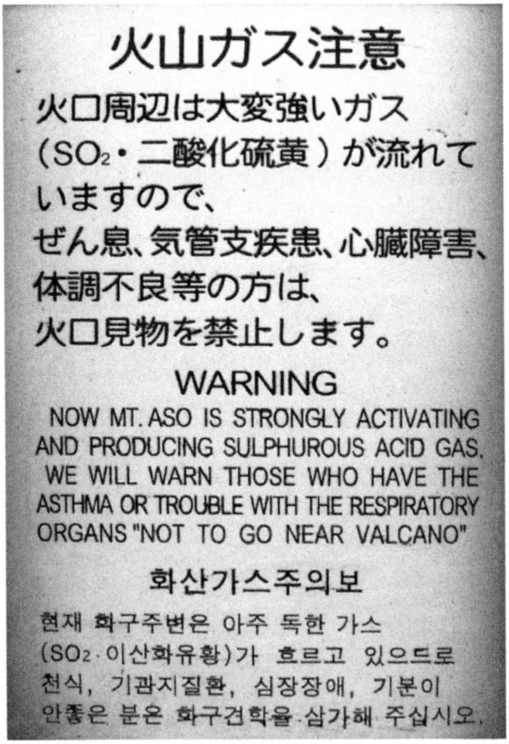

Figure 9.5 One of the warning signs at the crater entrance of Mt Aso

may be worth considering upgrading is the low open fence around the crater rim, which would not stop a small person from falling towards one of the craters.

Volcano photography is another important reason to visit active mountains; only 11 per cent of the visitors questioned were not interested in taking photos. For the majority it is a little ritual in Japan to have their photo taken with the steaming crater behind them. The stall holders on the summit offer step ladders to stand on for a better photographic angle, as the crater is currently rather deep and the photos must include the crater lake.

Risk perception and visitor satisfaction

The overall risk perception of visitors to Mt Aso was noted as low (25 per cent), which is countered by a relatively high awareness of the potential danger of active volcanic environments (88 per cent). Due to obvious warning signs and constant PA announcements, flashing warning lights with

easy recognizable colour coding, security guards in the car parks and more recently on the viewing platforms at the crater rim, people feel that in case of an emergency there will be enough time to retreat safely and with dignity.

Visitor satisfaction is high at Mt Aso; 92.5 per cent said the visit to the crater met their expectations and 98.5 per cent said they would recommend a visit to Mt Aso to other people. The best experience was being able to look into the crater and all respondents thought that volcano tourism is a great idea with 48 per cent of the respondents having visited other volcanic areas elsewhere. Special safety guidelines over and above the safety measures available at Mt Aso were expected by 53 per cent of the visitors. The proportion of repeat visitors was calculated at 11 per cent, with a number of people coming on a regular basis as they live in Kyushu and spend weekends at the numerous hot spring *Ryokan* (hotels, inns) around Mt Aso.

The Kuju volcano complex

The Kuju volcano complex is also part of the Aso-Kuju National Park and consists of 20 lava domes and cones, located in the central part of Kyushu Island, and includes Iwoyama, one of the most active geothermal fields where sulphur used to be mined (Nabakoh et al, 2003). A phreatic eruption occurred at Kuju volcano in October 1995 (Sudo and Matsumoto, 1998) and Mt Kuju does not share the easy access to the higher elevations found at Mt Aso. However, many hot springs and hydrothermal fields are located at the Kuju complex with the town of Kokonoe in the foothills a popular place for weekend houses or country side retreats. People come from all over Japan to the area around Mt Kuju and Mt Aso to enjoy a different lifestyle for either a few days or weeks or as a second home to retire. An active volcano is no deterrent at all; the many volcanic hot springs with their waters so rich in beneficial minerals hold an enormous attraction for Japanese people. The Ryokan owners often use one of the nearby volcanoes in the background of their hot spring inn or resort advertising material and to verify the quality of the local onsen water. Artificial heating or cooling of hot springs by

Figure 9.6 Volcano tourism on Mt Aso involves family members of any age group

Note: The long walkways are user friendly for wheelchairs and strollers

mixing with 'normal' water is rejected as is any adulteration of natural hot spring water with chemicals which is condemned by the Japanese onsen connoisseur. This goes for all natural (volcanic) hot springs in Japan.

Mt Sakurajima

Sakurajima, one of Japan's most active volcanoes, is an island opposite the city of Kagoshima in the south of Kyushu, but during the great *Taisho* eruption in 1914 the island was connected to the mainland by extensive lava flows and is now considered a peninsula within the Aira caldera which includes Kagoshima (*Kinko*) Bay. Sakurajima is erupting currently on a daily basis and attracts many visitors to the island and the surrounding mainland with striking displays of rising ash columns and rumbling noises. Sakurajima is part of the Kirishima-Yaku National Park and can be

reached from Kagoshima by ferry within half an hour. Not far from the ferry terminal on Sakurajima Island is a visitor information centre with access to a lava trail (3km long) through lava extrusions from the Taisho eruption. Directly at the waterfront is a new outdoor foot spa fed by hot springs, which is unusual due to its extraordinary length – hard to estimate afterwards from photos and memory, but as it is not in a straight line it may be at least 60m or even longer.

The visitor centre itself is a reinforced concrete structure, built to withstand at least the average eruptions of Sakurajima, and offers a good selection of information for tourists about the volcanic history of the mountain, the local ecology and disaster prevention measures. Many sightseeing spots can be found all over the island and can be easily accessed by following the ring road. Concrete shelters are found along the roads, most of them

Figure 9.7 Public phone on Sakurajima Island with a concrete roof to protect against ashfall and more serious eruption fallout

looking like heavy duty bus stops and constructed of reinforced cement walls with rounded roofs, all facing away from the volcano. Even public phones are surrounded by concrete to protect this important lifeline for emergencies (Figure 9.7). Most residents who live on the flanks of Sakurajima have their own concrete fallout shelters in their gardens close to their houses, and on the slopes diversion channels leading lahars and mudflows to the ocean are constantly undergoing either upgrading or maintenance.

Despite the ongoing activity of Mt Sakurajima volcano tourism is booming, starting on the mainland with hotels offering rooms with volcano views across Kagoshima Bay. Near the Kagoshima ferry terminal the 'Dolphin Port', a large boardwalk type facility, hosts a considerable number of restaurants and shops, all facing Mt Sakurajima with viewing terraces for outdoor dining. To reach the actual volcano, however, is not something tourists should attempt, as it is too dangerous due to the almost daily eruptions, and climbing Sakurajima past the fourth stage at the Yunohira Observatory is not allowed anymore (Kagoshima Visitor's Guide, 2009).

To the north of Sakurajima lies Kirishima, a large group of more than 20 quaternary volcanoes located in the Kirishima-Yaku National Park. Their crater-pocked peaks are described by Sutherland and Britton (1995) as partly lunar landscape and partly covered in lush vegetation. No research by the author has been undertaken in this area as yet.

Mt Unzen

Mount Unzen is one of the decade volcanoes and is part of the Unzen-Yamakusa National Park. Since August 2009 it has also been recognized by UNESCO as the Unzen Global Geopark. It is known as a dangerous volcano which erupted during 1990–95 after nearly 200 years of lying dormant when a lava dome formed at the summit

Figure 9.8 Mass tourism at one of the disaster zones in Shimabara

Note: The roof of one of the many houses buried by lahar flows is visible in the centre of the picture. This is a tourist attraction and one of the must-see stops when busloads of visitors come to Shimabara.

Figure 9.9 The local communities are very involved in disaster prevention and share their experiences of Mt Unzen's eruption period

and subsequently collapsed, resulting in thousands of pyroclastic flows (9432 according to a sign at the buried village in Shimabara). These pyroclastic flows caused 43 fatalities and damaged populated areas near Shimabara City (Global Volcanism Program, 2009), creating large disaster zones in the city of Shimabara.

However, some of the disaster zones were later developed into major tourist attractions. The 'Buried Village', for example, is part of a suburb of Shimabara and is a constant reminder of the dangers of living close to active volcanoes. This area was located in the flow path of the lahars which followed the pyroclastic flows; monsoonal rains caused large mudflows destroying over 2500 houses. Every day busloads of tourists start arriving in the morning and keep coming throughout the day, bringing domestic and international visitors to view the destruction caused and take the opportunity to talk to local residents about their ordeals during that time (Figures 9.8 and 9.9).

The same busloads with the same tourists also go to other disaster sites like the primary school that was severely damaged by a pyroclastic flow and was subsequently turned into a tourist attraction with Mt Unzen looming in the background. Next to the destroyed school a volcano observatory was built which also includes a commemorative information centre, a museum and a volcano viewing platform for visitors. Another sightseeing location popular for viewing Mt Unzen is from a lookout at Nita Pass, again frequented by busloads of visitors who can't get close enough to an active volcano, especially one with a bad reputation. To see the most chilling evidence of the Unzen eruptions, the Disaster Memorial Hall in Shimabara has many exhibits, including a camera found in the pyroclastic debris which (Figure 9.10) still had a few seconds of footage that could be saved, showing the pyroclastic cloud approaching the people waiting to take photos and video documentaries. Forty-three

Figure 9.10 One of the cameras found after the eruption of Mt Unzen, containing a few seconds of footage before the pyroclastic flow engulfed the 43 people that died on that day in their effort to report from close up to the action

Note: Watching these last moments is a sobering experience.

people died in this pyroclastic flow (see Chapter 1). However, this has not stopped volcano tourists from visiting the city of Shimabara to benefit from the many hot springs in the area and to drive up to Mt Unzen for walks and picnics on the mountain.

With the final seal of approval by UNESCO the new Unzen Volcanic Geopark has now an added status, which ranks high when it comes to marketing strategies and will attract even more visitors to the area surrounding this potentially dangerous mountain. However, volcanic sites in Japan are very closely monitored and the Japanese are trained to cope with disasters from an early age. School children practise safe behaviour in case of a volcanic crisis and the visitor information and sign boards are usually in at least four different languages. Hazard maps and leaflets with essential information are generally available for every active volcano and can be found on the local council or local government websites. These websites usually also have English translations for foreign residents and visitors.

The Tsurumi dome complex

The city of Beppu is known as the hot springs capital of Japan and is located on the flanks of the Tsurumi dome complex, with over 2200 active hot springs (Erfurt-Cooper and Cooper, 2009). However, the figures vary greatly according to the data source with Beppu City (2009) listing 2832 hot springs and other sources suggesting 3800 to 4000 hot springs. The confusion may arise over the actual source of the hot spring water, which is then distributed to a number of users such as hotels, Ryokan, public bathhouses and domestic residences from each source.

Nearly 12 million visitors come to Beppu every year to enjoy the eight different hot spring districts in town, each of them with a specific type of water, courtesy of the volcanoes surrounding the town. In addition to Beppu's hot springs the neighbouring small town of Yufuin has 859 hot springs (Beppu City, 2009), which supply a number of hot spring resorts which are designed as cosy getaways rather than catering for tour groups and conventions (Seki and Heilman

Brooke, 2005). Apart from enjoying the many onsen facilities in Beppu the majority of visitors also engage in different types of volcano tourism by visiting Mt *Tsurumi*, Mt *Yufu* (Yufudake) and Mt *Garan* (Garandake). The only volcano currently showing outward signs of activity is Mt Garan, classed as rather insignificant by the local experts (pers. communication with a scientist from the Aso Volcano Observatory, 2007), but nevertheless is popular with tourists, and although not considered as dangerous, Mt Garan has active fumaroles on the flanks of the crater and a boiling mud pool (which has recently dried out and at the time of writing was sporting a hissing steam vent instead) and attracts increasing numbers of visitors. Over the last two years a small entrance fee of ¥200 is required to use the newly established concrete walkways to the crater. Before this upgrade a short but steep climb on an undeveloped path through shrubs and trees was required to reach the crater. The road leading to the car park for crater visitors and hot spring patrons has been slightly upgraded as well, indicating that tourist numbers are increasing. The locals however prefer the small onsen at the entrance to the crater for its special geothermal water quality which rises from below the volcanic complex of Tsurumi and Garandake.

Beppu has some unique geothermal attractions in the middle of the city; ten *Jigoku* (Japanese for 'hell') with geothermal springs at extreme temperatures have been developed into small, independent geoparks with boiling lakes of different colours, steam vents, boiling mud pools and geysers. Some of the Jigoku have hot spring spas (onsen) onsite for visitors who want to combine the visual with their favourite pastime (Erfurt-Cooper and Cooper, 2009). Tour groups usually arrive by the busload at the Jigoku, often covering more than one of the ten Jigoku between breakfast and lunch. Sometimes it only takes 15 to 20 minutes and the tour group has moved on, but not without having their photo taken in front of one of the boiling and hissing geothermal features. Due to the large tourist volumes some of the Jigoku have in recent years undergone renovations (e.g. enlargement of foot spas and retail outlets),

Figure 9.11 At the Kamado Jigoku (Oven Hell) the hot spring fed foot spas are popular with visitors, especially during the cooler months

Note: The 'speciality of the house' are onsen tamago, which are eggs cooked for 24 hours over a steam vent until they acquire a brown colour and a unique flavour, and are eaten with salt and soy sauce either on site or as a 'take away' snack.

reconstruction (Chino-ike Jigoku) or added features (steam inhalation, foot treatments and mineral water drinking stations) to their existing attractions (e.g. Kamado Jigoku, Figure 9.11). It can be safely assumed that most of the hot spring tourists coming to Beppu will visit at least some of these geothermal curiosities, which are a reminder of the volcanic activity that is still ongoing underground.

The Tsurumi dome complex which surrounds the city of Beppu and is part of the Aso-Kuju National Park is used by the residents as well as visitors for recreational purposes all year round. Activities such as hiking, climbing and taking the ropeway to the summit to enjoy the views over Beppu Bay are independent of the time of the year. The four seasons are actually one of the attractions of these volcanoes, as they change their scenery several times throughout the year and thus encourage repeat visits.

Conclusion

Despite the continuous activity of Kyushu's volcanoes all of them are main attractions for visitors. The attractions and activities of volcanic areas in Japan are very similar to those in other parts of the world, with the difference that for millions of Japanese people natural hot springs play a large role in their everyday life. The tourism infrastructure in active volcanic areas generally includes typical Onsen Ryokan or hot spring resorts as well as historical sites, shrines and temples and restaurants.

As Chapter 10 notes, Japan is very well organized when it comes to safety issues in public places including national parks and from now on, global geoparks. However, with the growing numbers of foreign tourists in rural areas as well as the big cities more volcanic areas need to include signage in languages other than Japanese to warn visitors of any potential danger.

References

Aso Volcano Disaster Prevention Council (2008) 'Council activities', www.aso.ne.jp/~volcano/eng/html/conference.html, accessed 12 June 2009

Beppu City (2009) 'Hot spring data', www.city.beppu.oita.jp/01onsen/english/03hyakka/data.html, accessed 12 June 2009

Erfurt-Cooper, P. and Cooper, M. (2009) *Health and Wellness Tourism: Spas and Hot Springs*, Channel View Press, London

Global Volcanism Program (2009) 'Tsurumi', www.volcano.si.edu/world/volcano.cfm?vnum=0802-13=, accessed 7 June 2009

Japan Meteorological Agency (JMA) (2009) 'Active volcanoes in Japan', homepage3.nifty.com/hyamasat/jmaobs.html, accessed 7 June 2009

Nakaboh, M., Ono, H., Sako, M., Sudo, Y., Hashimoto, T. and Hurst, A. W. (2003) 'Continuing deflation by fumaroles at Kuju volcano, Japan', *Geophysical Research Letters*, vol 30, no 7, pp49.1–49.4

Ng'walali, P. M. (1999) 'Fatalities by inhalation of volcanic gas at Mt. Aso crater in Kumamoto, Japan, *Legal Medicine*, vol 1, issue 3, pp180–184

Kagoshima Visitor Guide. (2009) 'Sakurajima information – Climbing Sakurajima?' www.synapse.ne.jp/update/whatup/back/sakurajima-e.html, accessed 7 June 2009

Seki, A. and Heilman Brooke, E. (2005) The Japanese Spa: *A Guide to Japan's finest Ryokan and Onsen*, Tuttle Publishing, Tokyo, Japan

Sudo, Y. and Matsumoto, Y. (1998) 'Three-dimensional P-wave velocity structure in the upper crust beneath Kuju volcano, central Kyushu, Japan', *Bulletin of Volcanology*, vol 60, no 3, pp147–159

Sutherland, M. and Britton, D. (1995) *National Parks of Japan*, Kodansha International, Tokyo

UNESCO Global Geoparks Network (2008) 'Geopark candidate sites: Unzen and Usu volcanic area, Japan', www.globalgeopark.org/publish/portal1/tab128/info2378.htm , accessed 7 June 2009

USGS (n.d) 'Decade volcanoes', vulcan.wr.usgs.gov/Volcanoes/DecadeVolcanoes/framework.html, accessed 7 June 2009

10

Volcano and Geothermal Tourism in Japan – Examples from Honshu and Hokkaido

Malcolm Cooper

Introduction

Hokkaido is the most northerly of Japan's main islands and is the country's wild frontier, a volcanic tourism destination that contains the newly listed world heritage Shiretoko Peninsula (complete with thermal waterfalls), many hot springs and active volcanoes, and a developing domestic and international geotourism. As a whole, there are 108 active volcanoes in Japan, and Hokkaido is host to 19 of these. The Japan Meteorological Agency (JMA) defines active volcanoes as those that have erupted in the past 10,000 years or currently have fumarolic activity, and is continuously monitoring the activities of 20 of these using seismic and visual observations. These more active volcanoes are listed in Tables 10.1 and 10.2 below, and include Meakandake, Tokachidake, Tarumae, Usu, Hokkaido-Komagatake, Azuma, Adatara, Bandai, Nasu, Kusatsu-Shirame, Asama, Ontake, Izu-Tobu, Izu-Oshima, Miyakejima, Kuju, Aso, Unzen, Kirishima and Sakurajima. The other volcanoes are surveyed regularly but not continuously by the JMA. If some abnormal phenomena are detected, temporal observation stations are installed and the data are continuously monitored by the JMA. Temporal observation is also carried out at Iwatesan, Akita-Komagadake, Fuji, Satsuma-Iwojima, Kuchinoerabujima and Suwanosejima volcanoes, in recognition that even those volcanoes in Japan that have not shown signs of activity in the recent past are merely dormant and local communities and their visitors require protection should a major event occur.

The Global Volcanism Program database built by the Smithsonian Institute for Honshu, Kyushu and Hokkaido confirms that there are currently 46 volcanoes with thermal activity on Honshu (Siebert and Simkin, 2002). This chapter documents the impact of these volcanoes on the pattern and nature of volcanic tourism on both islands while Chapter 9 looks at Kyushu, home to decade volcanoes Unzen and Sakurajima. In doing so, it examines volcano tourism's main characteristics, and looks closely at the way in which the inherent risks of this active volcanic environment for tourists are dealt with by hosts and visitors. The chapter makes an important practical contribution to the debate on risk management in extreme environments through its analysis of geotourism on Honshu and Hokkaido.

Geological background

There are around 1300 active volcanoes in the world at the present time, and the Japanese archipelago has nearly 10 per cent of them. Volcanic and other mountainous areas in Japan make up around 67 per cent of the country. The

Table 10.1 Major volcanoes in Honshu

Volcano	Type	Location on Honshu	Last known eruption
Abu	Shield volcanoes	Japan Sea Coast	1450BCE
Sanbe	Stratovolcano	Japan Sea Coast	650CE
Oki-Dogo	Shield volcano	Islands in Japan Sea	Unknown
Izu-Tobu	Pyroclastic cones	Izu Peninsula	1989
Hakone	Complex volcano	SW Tokyo*	1170CE
Fuji-san	Stratovolcano	SW Tokyo*	1708
Kita Yatsuga-Take	Stratovolcanoes	Nth Japan Alps	1200CE
On-Take	Complex volcano	Nth Japan Alps	1980
Haku-san	Stratovolcano	Nth Japan Alps	1659
Norikura	Stratovolcanoes	Nth Japan Alps	50BCE
Yakedake	Stratovolcanoes	Kamikochi Resort*	1995
Washiba-Kumonotaira	Shield volcanoes	Chubu Sangaku NP*	10,000BCE?
Tateyama	Stratovolcano	Nth Japan Alps	1839
Niigata-Yake-Yama	Lava dome	Niigata*	1998
Myoko	Stratovolcano	Nagano	750BCE
Asama	Complex volcano	Karuizawa Resort*	2009
Kusatsu-Shirane	Stratovolcanoes	Kusatsu (Onsen City)*	1983
Shiga	Shield volcanoes	Shiga-Kogen Ski Area*	10,000BCE?
Haruna	Stratovolcano	Honshu	550
Akagi	Stratovolcano	Kanto	1938?
Hiuchi	Stratovolcano	Nikko National Park*	1544
Nikko-Shirane	Shield volcano	Nikko National Park*	1952
Nantai	Stratovolcano	Nikko National Park*	Unknown
Omanago Group	Lava domes	Nikko National Park*	3050BCE
Takahara	Stratovolcano	Utsunomiya City	4570BCE
Nasu	Stratovolcanoes	Kanto Plain	1963
Numazama	Shield volcano	Fukushima	3400BCE
Bandai	Stratovolcano	Lake Inawashiro*	1888
Adatara	Stratovolcanoes	Fukushima City	1996
Azuma	Stratovolcanoes	Fukushima City*	1977
Zao	Complex volcano	Northern Honshu	1940

Volcano	Type	Location on Honshu	Last known eruption
Hijiori	Caldera	Northern Honshu	Unknown
Narugo	Caldera	Sendai	837CE
Onikobe	Caldera	Akita*	300CE
Kurikoma	Stratovolcano	Akita	1950
Chokai	Stratovolcanoes	NE Honshu	1974
Akita-Komaga-Take	Stratovolcanoes	NW Honshu	1971
Iwate	Complex volcano	Iwate*	1919
Hachimantai	Stratovolcano	NW Honshu	5350BCE
Akita-Yake-Yama	Stratovolcano	NW Honshu	1997
Megata	Maars	Oga Peninsula	2050BCE
Iwaki	Stratovolcano	Tsugaru	1863
Towada	Caldera	Lake Towada	915CE
Hakkoda Group	Stratovolcanoes	Mutsu Bay	1550
Osore-Yama	Stratovolcano	Shimokita Peninsula	1787
Mutsu-Hiuchi-Dake	Stratovolcano	Shimokita Peninsula, North Honshu	Current fumaroles

Note: * Popular tourist attractions.

Source: Siebert and Simkin, 2002

reason for this is that the country sits on top of the meeting point of four tectonic plates (Eurasian Plate, Philippine Sea Plate, Pacific Plate and North American Plate), which means that the country is prone to volcanic eruptions and earthquakes as a result of their shifting boundaries and subduction zones. Volcanoes in Japan are distributed in a west Japan volcanic belt and an east Japan volcanic belt. The west belt runs from Kyushu to Chugoku, and the east belt from Tohoku to Hokkaido (Figure 10.1). There is a gap of some 150km between the two. The Eastern Japan Volcanic Belt includes the Kuril Arc, Hokkaido and north-east Honshu and out along the Izu-Bonin Arc, and the Western Japan Volcanic Belt includes south-west Honshu and Kyushu, and along the Tokara Islands.

Two main classes of volcano are identified in Japan. One is the polygenetic type where eruptions

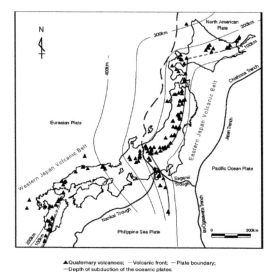

▲Quaternary volcanoes; —Volcanic front; —Plate boundary;
—Depth of subduction of the oceanic plates

Figure 10.1 The volcanic belts of Japan

Source: www.numo.or.jp/en/publications/pdf/Level3_SF_Final-09.pdf

Table 10.2 Major volcanoes in Hokkaido

Volcano	Type	Location on Hokkaido	Last known eruption
Oshima-Oshima	Stratovolcano	Japan Sea Island	1790
E-san	Stratovolcano	Oshima Peninsula	1874
Komaga-Take	Stratovolcano	Oshima Peninsula	2000
Nigorigawa	Hydrothermal Field	Uchiura Bay	Pleistocene
Usu	Stratovolcano	Muroran*	2001
Niseko	Stratovolcanoes	Niseko City	4900BCE
Yotei	Stratovolcano	Oshima Peninsula	1050BCE
Kuttara	Stratovolcanoes	Toya*	1820
Shikotsu	Caldera	Nthn Island	1981
Rishiri	Stratovolcano	Nthn Japan Alps	5830BCE
Tokachi	Stratovolcanoes	Central Hokkaido	2004
Daisetsu	Stratovolcanoes	Daisetsu*	1739
Nipesotsu-Maruyama	Stratovolcanoes	Nukabira Lake	1898
Shikaribetsu Group	Lava domes	Shikaribetsu	Unknown
Akan	Caldera	Lake Akan*	2008
Kutcharo	Caldera	NE Hokkaido	1320
Mashu	Caldera	Lake Mashu*	970CE
Rausu	Stratovolcano	Shiretoko Peninsula	1800
Shiretoko-Iwi-Zan	Stratovolcano	Shiretoko Peninsula	1936

Note: * Major tourist attraction with resort, ropeway.

Source: Siebert and Simkin, 2002

repeat within the same centre, and these comprise most of the Eastern Japan Volcanic Belt and the major part of the Western Japan Volcanic Belt from north-east Kyushu to the Tokara Islands. The other type is monogenetic, formed by a single eruptive episode, and these are mainly located in south-west Honshu to north-west Kyushu. These two types, polygenetic and monogenetic, have different tectonic origins in terms of their relationship to subduction and melting processes (NUMO, 2009). Polygenetic volcanoes are predominantly andesitic, associated with magma generation in the mantle wedge above the descending oceanic plate at depths of around 100km, controlled by decompression melting and slab dehydration. Monogenetic volcanoes are generally associated with alkali basalt extrusion, a product of deeper melting where magma generation is controlled by up-welling and decompression of mantle material and not directly related to the subducting slab (NUMO, 2009).

Located on the boundary of the eastern belt is Mt Fuji, Japan's highest and most noted volcano and also its most frequented tourist attraction. This modern postglacial stratovolcano is constructed above a group of overlapping earlier volcanoes, remnants of which form irregularities on Fuji's profile. Growth of the younger Mt Fuji began with a period of voluminous lava flows from 11,000 to 8000 years ago, which account for four-fifths of the volume of the present Mt Fuji. Minor explosive eruptions dominated activity from 8000 to 4500 years ago, with another period of major lava flows occurring from 4500 to 3000 years ago. Subsequently, intermittent major explosive eruptions occurred, with subordinate lava flows and small pyroclastic flows. Summit eruptions dominated from 3000 to 2000 years ago, after which flank vents were active. The extensive lava flows from the summit and some of the more than 100 flank cones and vents blocked drainage routes around the mountain, forming the Fuji Five Lakes. The last eruption of this dominantly basaltic volcano occurred in 1707 and formed a large new crater on the east flank. The view of vulcanologists (Hoshizumi and Nakano, 2009) is that there may be some minor volcanic activity at Mt Fuji in the next few years.

The cultural and historical significance of the Japanese volcanic environment for tourism

In Japan the use of volcano environments for leisure and recreation and of volcanically derived water for bathing is an important part of life. The country is blessed with an abundance of these resources that are of historical significance, having been utilized for many centuries (Erfurt-Cooper and Cooper, 2009). The volcanoes and the tourism that they support have been incorporated in the national and quasi (prefectural) national park system (Table 10.3; Ministry of the Environment, 2002; Southerland and Britton, 1995), while the Japanese hot springs (onsen) maintain a traditional atmosphere even if they are found in a modernized bath-house. This situation comes about as a result of there being a definite cultural preference for authentic hot spring water and the shared experiences of volcanic eruptions and related natural phenomena in Japan. The ambience of the natural environment is carefully guarded and preserved in national parks especially around hot spring resources and the water is considered to have a good 'feel' due to certain minerals, which

are highly valued for their beneficial properties. Of equal importance is the fact that friendly socializing on equal terms in relaxing surroundings is central to Japanese society, be that in a mountain hut on a volcano or in a hot spring.

Although it is not clear whether the earliest communities in Japan used these resources during the Jomon period of settlement (from c. 10,000 years ago to 600BC; Habu, 2004), considering the the extent of the resources and their physical presence (active volcanoes and hot springs), the climate and human nature it seems more than likely that the earliest communities made use of geothermal activity wherever it was available. As in most countries, however, the ancient people of Japan did not concern themselves with recording the origin and development of thermal resources and attractions, except where they were of use for military, medical or imperial family purposes.

There is some indication that the Japanese did have a tradition of ritual hot spring bathing using local geothermal resources by the end of the subsequent Yayoi period around AD297 as mentioned in the History of the Kingdom of Wei (Clark, 1999; Erfurt-Cooper and Cooper, 2009), but it is not clear if this refers to the use of natural hot springs or the general use of water for purification purposes. Sekioka and Yoshii (2000) suggest that hot spring bathing may have been practised as early as 6000 years ago on the eastern side of Lake Suwa (Nagano Prefecture) where ruins of ancient settlements have been found. At this site stones with [mineral] encrustations were discovered at a depth of approximately six metres and it is thought that these stones could have been used to frame hot spring pools used for geothermal bathing. Whatever the truth of this, many traditional hot springs in Japan date back several centuries and the custom of hot spring bathing based directly on geothermal resources derived from volcanism has a special place in Japanese culture, and continues to be maintained by the majority of the population.

Patterns of volcano tourism in Honshu and Hokkaido

Noboribetsu in south-western Hokkaido is the location of the Noboribetsu-onsen, Karurusu-onsen

Table 10.3 The major national parks with volcanic tourism resources

Name	Island	Characteristics
Shiretoko National Park	Hokkaido	Established 1964, UNESCO world heritage site, hot springs waterfall
Akan National Park	Hokkaido	Established 1934, craters, caldera, boiling mud and hot springs
Kushiro Shitsugen National Park	Hokkaido	Established 1987, wetlands ecosystems
Daisetsuzan National Park	Hokkaido	Established 1934, largest national park in Japan, 16 peaks over 2000 metres in three volcano groups, includes the hot spring resorts of Asahidake Onsen, Fukiage Onsen, Sounkyo Onsen and Tenninkyo Onsen. **6 million visitors per year**
Shikotsu-Toya National Park	Hokkaido	Established 1949, named after the volcanic caldera lakes of Lake Shikotsu and Lake Tōya. The popular hot spring resort of Noboribetsu is in the park
Towada-Hachimantai National Park	North Honshu	Established 1936, includes Towada caldera and Lake Towada. Hachimantai plateau is an area of ancient volcanic activity, with boiling mud pools, steam and smoke vents and hot springs
Bandai-Asahi National Park	Tohoku, Honshu	Established 1950, includes Mt Bandai (noted for its eruptions), the Azuma volcanic group, important religious sites (Mt Dewa-Sanzan); snow covers these into the summer making hiking, camping and skiing very popular there
Nikkō National Park	Kanto, Honshu	Established 1934, includes the Nikko-Shirane shield volcano that last erupted 1952, Lake Chuzenji
Fuji-Hakone-Izu National Park	Honshu	Established 1936, includes the most famous of all the Japanese volcanoes, Mt Fuji and its associated tourist attractions. Approx **150 million people** visit the area every year. The park is actually a collection of dispersed tourist sites rather than a discrete location
Chūbu-Sangaku National Park	Honshu	Established 1934, this park is popularly known as the Japan Alps National Park and includes more than 100 peaks some over 3000m. Ravines and lava plateaus branch out from these mountains. Many hot springs are available at the foot of the mountains
Hakusan National Park	Honshu	Established 1962, this park forms the backbone of the Hokuriku area and is noted for its heavy snowfall. Hakusan (2702m) is a tholoide style volcano with eight craters near the summit and is regarded as one of the three most noted mountains in Japan together with Mt Fuji and Mt Tateyama
Daisen-Oki National Park	Honshu	Established 1936, this park includes Mt Daisen, the highest mountain (1729m) in the Chugoku region, and a tholoide style volcano. The best season to visit this park is from spring to autumn, there are many spas in and around the park such as Kaike, Tamatsukuri and Sanbe

Source: Ministry of the Environment, 2002

and Noboritbetsu-rinkai-onsen hot springs, and has a rich variety of scenery including forests, lakes and marshes. It has been designated a part of Shikotsu-Toya National Park, and is a preferred domestic tourism destination despite its relative isolation. The Noboribetsu-onsen is one of Hokkaido's best-known hot springs, and is surrounded by virgin forest 200 metres above sea level. It has over ten different kinds of water containing minerals such as hydrogen sulphide, salt and iron. The quality of these minerals results in the spa being ranked among the world's most exceptional hot springs. Apart from this the most impressive scene at the hot spring is the jigoku valley (hell valley), where yellowy grey volcanic gas seeps from the rocks. This makes the whole place smell strongly of sulphur. The valley is in fact a

Table 10.4 Visitors to geothermal onsen, by Prefecture

Prefecture	1998	2000	2004	2005
Hokkaido	16,672,271	14,747,469	13,673,989	14,288,625
Aomori	1,813,377	1,867,734	1,906,229	1,771,060
Iwate	3,374,891	3,430,093	2,640,879	2,656,189
Miyagi	3,336,463	3,020,195	3,092,964	3,374,637
Akita	2,588,467	2,772,071	2,823,211	2,771,174
Yamagata	4,769,089	4,513,143	4,237,515	3,947,504
Fukushima	6,208,028	7,514,749	6,272,245	6,253,964
Ibaraki	565,265	615,763	1,394,278	727,358
Tochigi	8,401,787	7,665,321	6,827,274	6,732,735
Gunma	7,464,352	7,418,184	6,703,286	6,820,062
Saitama	136,270	350,538	313,925	390,741
Chiba	1,326,958	1,466,344	1,946,805	2,318,857
Tokyo	251,046	173,998	205,230	221,057
Kanagawa	6,478,756	6,160,111	6,077,129	5,961,606
Niigata	5,876,842	6,114,971	4,674,371	5,093,743
Toyama	1,402,387	1,671,793	1,520,123	1,498,594
Ishikawa	4,741,178	4,731,476	4,155,579	3,833,843
Fukui	1,674,061	1,359,458	1,296,409	1,241,920
Yamanashi	2,932,317	2,953,362	4,081,016	4,092,550
Nagano	10,149,303	10,304,344	9,988,594	9,964,165
Gifu	4,592,319	4,428,346	4,143,268	3,634,321
Shizuoka	11,481,307	11,044,942	12,395,482	12,486,502
Aichi	954,586	1,498,223	1,874,496	1,847,515
Mie	1,954,068	1,801,791	3,036,952	3,963,208
Shiga	954,710	1,031,153	1,084,390	1,136,445
Kyoto	906,564	1,419,572	1,414,199	1,091,031
Osaka	400,111	907,033	905,327	918,268
Hyogo	3,893,516	3,473,937	3,781,871	4,248,442
Nara	461,987	412,421	462,067	440,864
Wakayama	4,169,348	4,073,028	3,743,492	3,641,382
Tottori	1,724,540	1,640,253	1,542,460	1,449,648
Shimane	1,278,844	1,269,646	1,175,422	1,085,337
Okayama	1,150,206	1,256,447	1,261,442	1,150,147

Table 10.4 continued

Prefecture	1998	2000	2004	2005
Hiroshima	563,992	574,028	650,518	669,603
Yamaguchi	2,076,631	1,994,187	2,192,505	2,161,455
Tokushima	249,886	286,242	453,190	523,863
Kagawa	1,114,070	852,541	974,839	880,495
Ehime	1,736,482	1,696,599	1,737,506	1,719,635
Kochi	398,590	592,179	471,995	501,422
Fukuoka	821,396	1,007,346	812,955	877,878
Saga	1,377,282	1,307,186	981,082	1,107,118
Nagasaki	2,883,988	2,973,241	2,217,963	2,325,045
Kumamoto	4,146,508	3,777,658	3,715,798	3,631,277
Oita (mainly Beppu City)	8,267,125	10,131,485	11,141,122	11,113,174
Miyazaki	540,397	835,922	953,990	986,806
Kagoshima	4,130,880	3,498,813	3,399,942	3,160,473
Okinawa	425,518	491,414	618,075	634,688
Total	152,817,959	153,126,750	150,973,399	151,346,426

Source: Beppu City Tourism Office, 2007

450m-diameter mouth of a volcano, which produces 3000 litres of hot water a day, and the forests in this area have been designated as a natural monument.

Similar destinations exist across both the eastern and western volcanic arcs, and cannot all be described here, but given that onsen are (along with earthquakes, lahars and pyroclastic flows) one of the major products of volcanism in Japan it is possible to obtain some kind of estimate of how important this feature of the Japanese landscape is to domestic tourism at least. Table 10.4 outlines the patronage of onsen locations in Japan to 2005.

Near the hot spring city of Toya the active volcano Mt Usu and its smaller neighbour the lava dome Showa-Shinzan (a parasitic volcano), are tourist magnets and attract busloads of visitors on a daily basis. Trips to the crater of Mt Usu by ropeway are popular (Figure 10.2) despite the fact that Mt Usu is known as a dangerous volcano with a recent eruption history. Crater visits are

Figure 10.2 The ropeway leading up to Mt Usu

Note: In the background Showa-Shinzan, a young lava dome which started growing on the flanks of Mt Usu in the year 1944 after strong earthquakes in the area. Today Mt Usu and Showa-Shinzan are important tourist attractions not just as part of the Shikotsu-Toya National Park in Hokkaido, Japan, but also as a new UNESCO global geopark.

Source: Photo courtesy of Patricia Erfurt-Cooper

Figure 10.3 The viewing platform on Mt Usu offers not only extensive views across Uchiura Bay (Volcano Bay) but also offers access to a walking trail around the crater rim, which can sometimes be closed off depending on activity levels or gas emissions

Source: Photo courtesy of Patricia Erfurt-Cooper

independent of the seasons and walking trails around the crater area are used at times of low level activity (Figure 10.3).

Risk management in volcano tourism

Japan is particularly vulnerable to natural disasters because of its climate, tectonic vulnerability and topography (Cooper and Erfurt, 2007), and level of development (www.infojapan.org/policy/disaster/21st/2.html). Earthquakes are the most common natural disaster; the country experiences more than 5000 per year, but they are by no means the only destructive force. The others range from volcanic eruptions, through tsunamis and typhoons to heavy pollution of the natural environment from inadequate waste management. A number of physical factors contribute to the high incidence of natural disasters in Japan – these being extreme climatic variations, rugged topography prone to disturbance, and its location on the circum-pacific 'ring of fire' in which most of the world's volcanoes are located and where the Pacific Plate subduction zone is at its most active (Aramaki and Ui, 1982). Furthermore, the fact that many earthquakes are combined with tsunamis adds another aspect to the complexity of disaster risk management. In Japan, volcanoes which have erupted in the past 10,000 years are defined as active, and they are considered to have the

potential to erupt again in the future. As noted earlier there are 108 active volcanoes recognized by the JMA, and regardless of their scenic beauty and associated hot springs that attract sightseers and climbers, most of the recognized volcanoes, once reactivated, may cause serious destruction to themselves and surrounding areas.

Data collected by the JMA on the patterns and scales of past eruptions are used as basic material to establish hazard maps (charts of expected damage due to an eruption) by local administrations.

Earthquakes and volcanism

Sorensen (2002, pp125–127) notes that the Great Kanto (Tokyo-Yokohama) earthquake (M8.3) of 1923 is recognized as perhaps the most devastating to hit a developed country in the past 100 years. The earthquake caused extensive damage in the cities of the region, destroying or damaging several hundred thousand homes and buildings, and the fires that followed caused more damage. The death toll is estimated to have been greater than 140,000 and over 44 per cent of the urban area of Tokyo was destroyed by fire, with some 74 per cent of all households affected (Watanabe, 1993). This damage was comparable to the human and infrastructural damage caused by the later World War II bombing in the same area, and required a similar reconstruction effort. Legislation was brought in to control redevelopment (the Ad Hoc Town Planning Act 1924) which had at its core a system of 'land readjustment' where all land was pooled in specific project areas and public purposes land (roads, parks – typically about 30 per cent of the total) abstracted before individual building plots were reinstated (Cooper and Erfurt, 2007). This system allowed reconstruction of road and other public services before housing, and therefore aided rationalization of the often chaotic building patterns of earlier periods.

In terms of the implications of disaster and its management for activities like tourism, the Kanto earthquake established two important precedents for Japan's ability to deal with such events. The first was the system of land readjustment described above, and the second was the creation of the forerunner of an important class of public organization, the Mutual Prosperity Association

(Dojunkai Foundation). The original public organization was formed in 1924 with the aim of supplying both housing and work for earthquake victims, but rapidly became known for innovations in self-help (upgrading of slum areas) and community approaches to new forms of housing (of greater strength to withstand new earthquakes). As is discussed below, such self-help organizations are an essential part of the Japanese local response to natural disasters, and their openness to including visitors (especially foreign tourists) needs to be examined in any analysis of how tourism may be affected by such events in Japan.

The Tokyo earthquake was followed by the massive Kobe (Great Hanshin) earthquake of 17 January 1995. Lasting for only about 20 seconds (M6.8) the Kobe earthquake nevertheless extensively damaged infrastructure, left 300,000 homeless and killed in excess of 6400 people. The newly constructed port of Kobe was devastated by widespread and severe liquefaction of the subsoil and permanent ground deformation, which destroyed over 90 per cent of the port infrastructure. Over 350 fires contributed to the damage bill, mainly caused by ruptured gas mains. The total damage from this earthquake was estimated to be up to 140 billion US dollars (www.dragonstrike. com/mrk/disaster.htm). Noticeably, despite the earlier Tokyo reconstruction experience, buildings constructed before 1981 (largely concrete frame or wood) performed very poorly in the Kobe disaster. However, post-1981 buildings constructed with strong concrete shear walls performed well, and this indicates that the revised building codes progressively introduced after the enactment of the Disaster Countermeasures Basic Act 1961 have contributed to the protection of lives and property from this form of disaster.

Compared with the earthquakes that are a product of the same tectonic movements, actual volcanic eruptions in Japan are a much lesser form of hazard. However, Japan has a long record of documented eruptions, starting with the eruption of Mt Aso (central Kyushu, see Chapter 9) in AD710. Mt Aso is the country's most active volcano with more than 165 eruptions. Japan's largest eruption in historic times was the Towada caldera (Honshu) collapse in AD915, and in 1792 the collapse of the Mayuyama lava dome (Kyushu)

created an avalanche and tsunami that killed an estimated 14,524 people (Simkin and Siebert, 1994). Japan in fact leads the world's volcanic regions on this measure of natural disaster risk with 1274 dated eruptions from 94 volcanoes (Simkin and Siebert, 1994). Japan also leads the world with 41 large explosive eruptions in the last 10,000 years. Pyroclastic flows, one of the deadliest volcanic hazards, have occurred at 28 per cent of Japan's eruptions (Siebert and Simkin, 1994). Other episodes of historical volcano activity are also known to have generated tsunamis, including:

- landslides from Komagatake volcano on Hokkaido which killed 700 people in 1640;
- a landslide on Oshima-Oshima volcano (Hokkaido) which killed 1474 people on Hokkaido and northern Honshu in 1741–42; and
- a landslide on Augustine volcano, Alaska, in 1883 that triggered a tsunami that swept across Cook Inlet onto the Kenai peninsula in Japan but apparently caused no damage (www. volcano.und.nodak.edu/vwdocs/volc_ images/img_unzen2.html).

Japan's response to natural disasters

Even when significant problems exist in society there is often no close correlation between these and appropriate policy responses from government (Reich, 1984; Healy, 1989; Murphy and Bayley, 1989; Hall et al, 2004; Prideaux, 2004). Such has been the case in Japan with respect to many environmental problems (Smith, 1975), although never with respect to natural disasters. A problem becomes an issue for government through two basic mechanisms (Faulkner, 2001): 1) where communities and private organizations/individuals are faced with a problem and force public recognition by government (outside initiatives); and 2) where issues that arise in government discussions are given official sanction and are then expanded to include public support (the internal initiative – Hecko, 1974). The second of these mechanisms was how Japan first developed natural disaster legislation through the pollution inspired Health Damage Compensation Law 1973, but which has attracted significant international interest for its coverage of natural disaster compensation based on the destruction of human life (Gresser, 1975; Foster, 1980) rather than that of property. The definition of critical environmental problems in this way meant that the environmental movement could count on significant political support for the realization of the democratic rights of unrepresented and injured citizens, while the government could respond more rapidly to actual natural disasters (Takabatake, 1975; Reich, 1984).

Relief programmes (including disaster planning and research)

Countermeasures against disasters in Japan fall into the following categories:

1 Research into the scientific and technical aspects of disaster prevention.
2 Reinforcement of the disaster prevention system (facilities and equipment).
3 Construction projects designed to enhance the country's ability to defend against disasters.
4 Emergency measures and recovery operations.
5 Improvement of information and communications systems.

Japan has in fact a long history of public relief programmes for the victims of natural disasters extending back into the Edo and early Meiji periods (Kase, 2004). After the Great Kanto (Tokyo–Yokohama) earthquake in September 1923, for example, many thousands of workers from Korea and other parts of Japan were employed on relief construction works. These were in two phases: immediate construction (requiring non-skilled labour – until autumn 1924); and urban planning reconstruction (requiring more skilled workers – 1925 on). In August 1925 the national government's Agency for Social Affairs began an ongoing policy of public construction works as part of general social welfare provision in Japan, which has survived and been extended to the present day. In addition, some big cities (Kobe, Osaka) introduced mutual aid systems to supplement public reconstruction as a social safety-net, while in recent years these provisions have been extended into all big population centres and many smaller cities (Cooper and Erfurt, 2007).

As might be expected from these reactions, much research has been undertaken on natural disasters in Japan. This has ranged from research on long-term changes of the hydrologic cycle due to global warming and their social impacts, through real-time analysis of the source process of large earthquakes, to greater understanding of hazard mechanisms caused by earthquakes, volcanic eruptions, landslides and floods, and the development of disaster mitigation technologies through observations, experiments and field surveys. A three-dimensional full-scale earthquake testing facility (E-Defence) is under construction in Miki City, north of the Kansai (Kobe–Osaka–Kyoto) area. When completed E-Defence will be able to precisely reproduce the three-dimensional ground motion recorded during the Kobe earthquake in 1995 on a test table (www.infojapan. org/policy/disaster/21st/2.html). When coupled with data in real-time currently available from the nationwide networks of seismometers, strainmeters and tiltmeters, this facility will provide building code information and standards that will allow much more precise volcanic and related disaster mitigation regulations to be implemented.

Seismic and volcanic activity forecast mapping, as well as hazard maps compiled by local governments serve as the foundation of national and local disaster-prevention plans (Chapter 1 this volume; Sorensen, 2002, p269). Hazard maps indicate the scale of damage that might be caused by a predicted event based on estimates from specific data for each district in an area, such as the strength or weakness of the ground, the concentration of buildings, the deterioration of housing, and so on. However, although a seismic activity forecast map gives a kind of bird's-eye view of the whole, it is the hazard map that is important in actually helping to minimize damage and casualties. Local governments must draw up hazard maps, inform residents of them and encourage communitywide efforts to increase the earthquake resistance of buildings and formulate evacuation plans. In particular, it is essential that local governments prepare evacuation plans based on tsunami, lahar and pyroclastic hazard maps.

All this attention means that Japan can be said to be in one of the highest states of natural disaster readiness of any modern country. This is also reflected in the availability of insurance and insurance underwriting for natural disasters in Japan. At the time of the Great Kanto earthquake in 1923 businesses had to write off quake inflicted losses (Sawai, 1999). Today, adequate earthquake insurance is available although it is very expensive because of high inner city land costs. This is illustrated by the 2004 earthquakes in Niigata Prefecture which caused catastrophic landslides and destroyed buildings. According to insurance specialists (*Japan Times*, 2004a) these events will not greatly damage non-life insurance firm balance sheets because of their high statutory reserves and the nation's financial safety net that protects them. Under this earthquake insurance system, established in 1966, the greater the damage, the more the government pays. If total damage is assessed at 75 billion yen or lower, insurance companies have to bear the full cost of payments. But if damage reaches between 75 billion yen and one trillion yen, the government will split the cost with insurers, while damage beyond this amount will be covered by the government up to 95 per cent of the difference.

The likely impact of natural disasters on inbound and domestic tourism

What then has been the effect of such natural disasters on tourism in and to Japan? Although there is very little published information on this question, several observations can be made. At a forum held to discuss Japan's difficulty in attracting foreign visitors and analyse what is needed to make the 2003 Yokoso Japan! (Welcome Japan!) campaign a success, it was suggested that high prices were not the sole reason for Japan's reputation as an unsuitable holiday destination (*Japan Times*, 2004b). Long lines at immigration counters, a lack of information in English and other languages, restrictive banking hours (and very poor inter-bank connectivity/lack of internet banking), a lack of shops that accept credit cards and difficulties for foreigners in using highways because of poorly displayed signs have also harmed Japan's tourist potential. Participants to the forum also commentated on factors ranging from the reserve of the Japanese towards foreigners to the

question of safety in natural events such as earthquakes, eruptions, typhoons and the like (*Japan Times*, 2004b).

While none of the above-mentioned problems are beyond solving (and some don't even really exist at all – like concerns over how the foreigner might react in a natural disaster, if appropriate measures are in place to avoid them), the perception is growing that visitors may not receive the same assistance in a disaster situation as locals. Eyewitness accounts of the Kobe disaster report that the Japanese self-defence forces preferentially rescued Japanese citizens rather than foreigners in some cases, while a quarantine period was imposed on rescue dogs from Switzerland with the clear implication that this was a deliberate ploy to exclude foreign help in clean-up operations (www.dragonstrike.com/mrk/disaster.htm).

That such anti-foreigner attitudes are not held by all Japanese may be evidenced by the fact that in the aftermath of the 2004 Niigata earthquakes the Kyoto City International Foundation began raising money to help offer counselling services assistance to foreign residents and visitors affected by the earthquakes. The Foundation uses the cash raised to provide foreigners in the area with psychological care, as many of them have been left shell-shocked by the seemingly non-stop temblors that rocked the region during the last months of 2004. Some foreign workers even lost their jobs because of damage to workplaces and business operations after the earthquakes (*Japan Times*, 2004b).

However, the existence of a difficult language barrier in these situations was recently acknowledged in a report that local governments and radio and television stations might broadcast disaster warnings and information using children's-level Japanese so that foreigners could understand them (*Japan Times*, 2005a). The announcements have been printed in a manual that will be distributed mainly to the disaster preparedness departments of Prefectural governments and broadcasters. The manual, written in a level of Japanese which would otherwise be suitable for elementary school second- and third-graders, was compiled by a group led by a Professor of Sociolinguistics. Tsunami warnings, for example, will be broadcast as: *Tsunami wa totemo takai nami desu. Umi no chikaku wa abunai desu* ('Tsunamis are very high waves. It is dangerous near the sea'). And instead of *hinansho* (shelter), the term *nigeru basho* (place to flee to) will be used. Why national and local authorities cannot provide translations of disaster warning and advice documentation in all the main languages currently used in Japan as a matter of course (or even in Japanese and English as is now standard on most public transport) remains a mystery, nevertheless attempts have been made in some areas by providing English and Korean translations for hazard maps and local information brochures.

Conclusions

The consensus in the academic literature is that it is difficult to predict the likely impact of natural disasters on tourism, as tourists go by sentiment as much as by perceived realities (Drabek, 1992, 1994). If a tourist likes a destination then it is entirely possible that he or she will discount the potential for natural disasters to affect travel to it (Cooper, 2005). Conversely, if not, then the potential for disasters could assume a higher order of negative importance for the tourist than is warranted by actual experience (Carter, 1998). For a destination it is of course possible to exercise a considerable degree of hindsight in describing the actual impact of any disasters that have occurred there in the past, and also to overemphasize preparedness for the next disaster. Nevertheless, for any destination, even if natural hazards cannot be avoided their dramatic consequences can be reduced through appropriate preparations and risk reduction measures (Cassedy, 1991). In this regard, as an offset to such measures of vulnerability the Japanese volcanic eruption, earthquake, typhoon and tsunami observation and defence networks have been considerably upgraded over the last decade. There is no doubt that the country is one of the safest to be in during a major disaster in terms of its readiness and ability to respond to such events, but the fact that typhoons, earthquakes and volcanism still manage to impact on the country and on its tourism just indicates how difficult it is to guard against all possible eventualities.

While Japan has not suffered many major eruptions in recent years the country did experience a record ten landed typhoons in 2004, breaking the earlier record of six, plus a series of strong earthquakes, prompting Salvano Briceno, Director of the International Strategy for Disaster Reduction (ISDR) to make the following statement: 'The tragic series of natural hazards that has recently hit Japan reminds us that all countries, rich or poor, are subject to increasing threats from social vulnerability and natural hazards' (UNISDR, 2004). The impact on tourists is less easy to ascertain, though they do not appear to be overly concerned with the implications of such reports as *Megacities–Megarisks* published in January 2005 (Munich Re Group, 2005), in which the Tokyo–Yokohama conurbation is calculated to have a natural hazards risk index rating of 710 (including an eruption of Mt Fuji), away ahead of the next most vulnerable large cities, San Francisco (167), Los Angeles (100) and Kobe–Osaka–Kyoto (92). A score of this magnitude is a reflection of when, not if, a natural disaster will occur in the Tokyo Metropolitan Area, but again it is not as real a measure of impact to the tourist as the prices they may have to pay for goods and services in Tokyo and/or in Japan as a whole, and therefore does not influence travel decision making quite as directly as the cost of travel itself (Santana, 2004).

On the other hand the attraction of volcanoes in Japan for tourists can be appreciated from the fact that they are major elements in 18 of Japan's 28 national parks. Many popular ski parks utilize the slopes of volcanoes. Furthermore, volcanoes provide spring water at the foot of the mountains. The last major eruptions of volcanoes in Hokkaido or Honshu were in 1986 (Uzu-Oshima) and in 2000 (Usu lava dome – no casualties, 234 houses destroyed), while the most dangerous were in Kyushu in 1991–1995 (Mt Unzen – pyroclastic flows killed 43 people), and offshore on Miyakejima from 2000 (gas emissions resulted in the evacuation of all residents). Although volcanic activities themselves are natural phenomena, they cause disasters and damage both to human life and industrial activities. The first step in developing disaster prevention measures starts from fully understanding volcanoes. It is then necessary for individuals, experts, communities, governing bodies and nations to take measures from each of their respective standpoints to reduce those impacts through quick circulation of information, cooperation of agencies, hazard mapping and safety training for all. Volcanoes let us feel the 'living earth' as tourists and they greatly excite our curiosity. And, while volcanoes bring life-threatening eruptions and landslide disasters, they can also enrich our lives with hot springs and geothermal and mineral resources. Coexistence with volcanoes is an eternal theme for those who live on and tour the Japanese archipelago.

Postscript: In a major boost to geotourism and its recognition in Japan it was reported in the *Japan Times* on 24 August 2009 that three Japanese sites, including Lake Toya on Hokkaido, have been added to the UNESCO-sponsored global geoparks list of nature parks with particular importance in terms of geological features, education and risk management. Geoparks are nationally protected parks that are considered Earth heritage sites for their geological, environmental, cultural and social values, and are perfect candidates for the task of sustainably developing tourism to volcanic environments. The other sites in Japan are the Itoi river in Niigata Prefecture (Honshu), and the Shimabara peninsula in Nagasaki Prefecture on Kyushu (Chapter 9), both with major volcanic tourism implications.

References

Aramaki, S. and Ui, Y. (1982) 'Japan', in Thorpe, R. S. (ed) *Andesites*, John Wiley and Sons, New York, pp259–292

Carter, S. (1998) 'Tourists and traveller's social construction of Africa and Asia as risky locations', *Tourism Management*, vol 19, pp349–358

Cassedy, K. (1991) *Crisis Management Planning in the Travel and Tourism Industry: A Study of Three Destinations and a Crisis Management Planning Manual*, PATA, San Francisco

Clark, S. (1999) *Japan, A View from the Bath*, University of Hawai'i Press, Honolulu

Cooper, M. J. (2005) 'Japanese Outbound Tourism and the SARS Epidemic of 2003', in Prideaux, B. and Laws, E. (eds) *Crisis Management in Tourism: A Special Issue of the Journal of Travel and Tourism Management*, vol 19, nos 2/3, pp119–133

Cooper, M. J. and Erfurt, P. (2007) 'Tsunamis, Earthquakes, Volcanism and Other Problems: Disasters, Responses and Japanese Tourism', in Laws, E., Prideaux, B. and Chon, K. (eds), *Crisis Management and Tourism*, CABI, Wallingford, pp234–251

Drabek, I. E. (1992) 'Variations in disaster evacuation behaviour: Public response versus private sector executive decision-making', *Disasters*, vol 16, no 2, pp105–118

Drabek, I. E. (1994) 'Risk perceptions of tourist business managers', *The Environment Professional*, vol 16, pp327–341

Erfurt-Cooper, P., and Cooper, M. (2009) *Health and Wellness Tourism: Spas and Hot Springs*, Channel View, Bristol

Faulkner, W. (2001) 'Towards a framework for tourism disaster management', *Tourism Management*, vol 22, pp135–147

Foster, H. D. (1980) *Disaster Planning: The Preservation of Life and Property*, Springer-Verlag, New York

Gresser, J. (1975) 'The 1973 Japanese law for the compensation of pollution-related health damage: An introductory statement', *Law in Japan: An Annual*, vol 8, pp91–135

Habu, J. (2004) *Ancient Jomon of Japan*, Cambridge University Press, Cambridge

Hall, C. M., Timothy, D. J. and Duval, D. T. (2004) 'Security and Tourism: Towards a New Understanding?', in Hall, C. M., Timothy, D. J. and Duval, D. T. (eds) *Safety and Security in Tourism*, The Haworth Hospitality Press, Binghamton, NY, pp1–18

Healy, R. J. (1989) *Emergency and Disaster Planning*, John Wiley & Sons, New York

Hecko, H. (1974) *Modern Social Politics in Britain and Sweden: From Belief to Income Maintenance*, Yale University Press, New Haven, CT

Hoshizumi, H. and Nakano, S. (2009) 'Active volcanoes and volcanic disasters', National Institute of Advanced Industrial Science and Technology, Japan, www.aist.go.jp/aist_e/aist_today/2005_16/feature/feature_04.html, accessed 15 July 2009

Japan Times (2004a) 'Deadly quakes unlikely to devastate insurers', *Japan Times*, Saturday, 29 October

Japan Times (2004b) 'The foreign angle', *Japan Times*, Wednesday, 16 November

Japan Times (2005a) 'Disaster alerts to be in "easy" Japanese', *Japan Times*, Sunday, 15 January

Japan Times (2009) 'Lake Toya makes U.N. "geopark" list', *Japan Times*, Monday, 24 August

Kase, K. (2004) 'Unemployment policy in prewar Japan: How progressive was Japanese social policy?', *Social Sciences Japan Journal*, vol 7, no 2, pp199–221

Ministry of the Environment (2002) *National Parks of Japan*, National Parks Division, Nature

Conservation Bureau, Ministry of the Environment, Tokyo

Munich Re Group (2005) *Megacities-Megarisks* Munich Re Group, Berlin

Murphy, P. and Bayley, R. (1989) 'Tourism and Disaster Planning', *Geographical Review*, vol 79, no 1, pp36–46

NUMO (2009) 'Evaluating site suitability for a HLW repository: Scientific background and application of NUMOs siting factors', *Report of NUMO TR-04-04*, Nuclear Waste Management Organization of Japan, Tokyo

Prideaux, B. (2004) 'The Need to Use Disaster Planning Frameworks to Respond to Major Tourism Disasters: Analysis of Australia's Response to Tourism Disasters in 2001', in Hall, C. M., Timothy, D. J. and Duval, D. T. (eds) *Safety and Security in Tourism*, The Haworth Hospitality Press, Binghamton, NY, pp281–298

Reich, M. R. (1984) 'Mobilizing for environmental policy in Italy and Japan', *Comparative Politics*, vol 16, no 4, pp379–402

Santana, G. (2004) 'Crisis Management and Tourism: Beyond the Rhetoric', in Hall, C. M., Timothy, D. J. and Duval, D.T. (eds) *Safety and Security in Tourism*, The Haworth Hospitality Press, Binghamton, NY, pp299–321

Sawai, M. (1999) 'Noda Shoichi and Roku-Roku Shoten, a machine tool manufacturer', *Social Sciences Japan Journal*, vol 2, no 1, pp107–122

Sekioka, M. and Yoshii, M. (2000) 'Country update: Report of geothermal direct uses in Japan', Proceedings of the World Geothermal Congress 2000, Kyushu-Tohoku, 28 May to 10 June, pp433–437

Simkin, T. and Siebert, L. (1994) *Volcanoes of the World*, Geoscience Press, Tucson, AZ

Siebert. L. and Simkin, T. (2002) *Volcanoes of the World: An Illustrated Catalogue of Holocene Volcanoes and their Eruptions*, Smithsonian Institute, Global Volcanism Program Digital Information Series, GVP-3, www.volcano.si.edu/world/, accessed 10 May 2009

Smith, E. (1975) *Minamata*, Holt, Rinehart, and Winston, New York

Sorensen, A. (2002) *The Making of Urban Japan*, Routledge, London

Southerland, M. and Britton, D. (1995) *The National Parks of Japan*, Kodansha International, Tokyo

Takabatake, M. (1975) 'Citizens movements: A new model for creating citizen movements in Japan', *Japan Interpreter*, vol 9, Winter, pp315–323

UNISDR (2004) 'Natural disasters: Rich countries also pay their toll', UN/International Strategy for Disaster Reduction press release, New York, 24 October

Watanabe, S. (1993) *The Birth of 'Urban Planning' – Japan's Modern Urban Planning in International Comparison*, Kashwashobo, Tokyo

Internet sites consulted

www.dragonstrike.com/mrk/disaster.htm, 15 July 2009

www.infojapan.org/policy/disaster/21st/2.html, 15 July 2009

www.volcano.si.edu/world/volcano.cfm?vnum=080329-A, 15 July 2009

www.volcano.und.nodak.edu/vwdocs/volc_images/img_unzen2.htm, 15 July 2009

www.infojapan.org/policy/disaster/21st/2.html, 15 July 2009

11

Jeju: South Korea's Premier Island Geotourism Destination

Kyung Sik Woo, Young Kwan Sohn and Lisa M. King

Introduction

Koreans have been attracted to mountains, rivers, hot springs and coastlines for spiritual rejuvenation and the provision of material needs for hundreds of generations (Huh et al, 2008). With a population of about 48.5 million people (OECD, 2009), natural places to relax, recreate and emotionally revive are becoming ever more important to Koreans. Today, one of the most highly sought-after holiday destinations in the country is Jeju Island, located off the southernmost tip of the Republic of Korea (Figure 11.1). Jeju holds a very special place in the minds of most Koreans as an idyllic island paradise famous for its natural features, favourable climate, citrus fruit, woman divers, and its cultural and historical sites. In addition to its well known natural attractions, tourists can shop, visit museums, botanical gardens, aquariums and bonsai parks or enjoy a variety of recreational activities including water sports, golf courses and festivals (Khan and Su, 2003) – all on and around a shield volcano.

This chapter describes the volcanic origins of Jeju Island and its principal geotourism attractions – Mt Hallasan, Seongsan Ilchulbong tuff cone, Sangumburi crater, Sanbangsan lava dome, Yongmeori coast, and Manjang Cave (belonging to the Geomunoreum lava tube system). It then introduces the reader to tourism on the island and reflects on the current status and future of geotourism to Jeju Island.

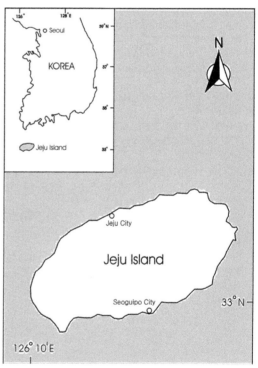

Figure 11.1 Location of Jeju Island

Volcanic origins

Jeju Island, also known as Cheju, is one of the few shield volcanoes in the world created over a hot spot on a stationary continental plate. The island has the typical shield volcano morphology characterized by an overall gentle topography and an elliptical shape (Figure 11.2; Park et al, 2000). Dark-coloured (basaltic) to light-coloured

Figure 11.2 Digital elevation model of Jeju Island, showing the overall shield morphology of the island with a central peak (Mt Hallasan) and numerous volcanic cones

Source: Courtesy of Dr K. H. Park

(trachytic) lavas occur extensively on the island together with diverse volcanic landforms, including Mt Hallasan which rises 1950m above sea level at the centre of the island. Numerous tuff rings and tuff cones are scattered around the island and were produced by repetitive explosive hydrovolcanic activity and intervening volcaniclastic sedimentary deposits as it rose above the waters of the continental shelf of the Yellow Sea some two million years ago and continued to historic times (Sohn and Park, 2004; Sohn et al, 2008). After the last glacial maximum 18,000 years ago explosive hydrovolcanic eruptions occurred at several places along the present shoreline. These eruptions resulted in several tuff rings and tuff cones with fresh morphology, including Songaksand, Seongsan, Ilchulbong and Udo tuff rings/cones (Sohn and Chough, 1989, 1992, 1993; Chough and Sohn, 1990). There are also historical records of minor eruptions at about one thousand years ago, although it is uncertain where these eruptions occurred. Today, these volcanic features create splendid natural landscapes enjoyed by the millions of visitors to Jeju Island every year.

Tourism on Jeju

Though the records left by those living on Jeju centuries ago praise the spectacular natural landscapes, tourism did not develop on the island until after Japanese colonization (from 1910 to 1945) and the Korean War (1950–1953) (Suh and Hunter, 2006). Foreigners began to visit Korea as tourists in 1958 and over the past several decades the Jeju tourism industry has flourished. Roughly 5.8 million visitors came to the island in 2008 (*Joongang Daily*, 2009) with the overwhelming majority of visitors being domestic travelers (Suh and Hunter, 2006). The Jeju Island government has wisely diversified its tourism products to include such niche markets as business and conference tourism, sports tourism, cultural tourism, ecotourism and experiential tourism with the overwhelming majority of visitors being domestic tourists (Suh and Hunter, 2006). Nevertheless, the fact that tourists cannot visit Jeju Island without taking time to visit several 'must-see' geotourism destinations is in no small part due to the recent and widely publicized UNESCO World Heritage listing of several prominent volcanic-related features.

The volcanic geotourism attractions of Jeju Island

Jeju Island's volcanic features attract visitors from around the world. The following section introduces some of the major geotourism features of the island.

Mt Hallasan

Often shrouded in clouds, Mt Hallasan is a shield volcano, standing in the middle of Jeju Island and the highest peak in South Korea, reaching 1950m above sea level (IUCN, 2007). Formed from approximately two million years of volcanic activity, the mountain is composed mainly of dark-coloured to light grey (basaltic to trachytic) volcanic lavas and a variety of fragmented volcanic deposits with a small crater lake at its center (IUCN, 2007). The flanks of Mt Hallasan are dotted with numerous volcanic cones and are carved by several deep gorges. The most famous topographic feature formed by erosion of the volcano is the *Yeongsilgiam,* where a series of strangely shaped rock formations are exposed along a deep valley wall.

In recognition of its outstanding flora, fauna and geologic features, Mt Hallasan was designated as a Natural Monument in 1966, a National Park in 1970 and a UNESCO Biosphere Reserve in 2002 (IUCN, 2006). In 2007, Mt Hallasan, along with the two other sites on Jeju received the prestigious natural World Heritage designation (UNESCO, 2009). The strenuous but rewarding hike to the top of Mt Hallasan and back can be completed in one day with an early start. Those visitors who decide to take on the rigorous adventure are rewarded with magnificent scenery along the trail and expansive views from the summit. Hundreds of thousands of people visit this sacred mountain every year (UNDP-WCMC, 2007).

Figure 11.3 Aerial view of the Ilchulbong tuff cone and the eastern coastal area of Jeju Island

Note: Mt Hallasan, the central peak of Jeju Island is visible in the background.

Seongsan Ilchulbong tuff cone

Seongsan Ilchulbong Tuff Cone (Seongsan), also known as 'Sunrise Peak', is one of the best known volcanic cones on Jeju Island. Unlike the other volcanic cones found on Jeju, Seongsan formed by the explosive interaction of hot magma and seawater upon a shallow seabed about five thousand years ago (Sohn and Chough, 1992). The hydro-magmatic eruption, similar to that of Surtsey in Iceland in 1963 (Thorarinsson, 1967), produced a steep-sided cone of tephra, a pile of air-fall material thrown into the air by a volcanic eruption and called a 'tuff cone'. This 182m high tuff cone dominates the eastern seaboard of Jeju Island like a huge ancient castle (Figure 11.3), with its bowl-like crater and excellent geological exposures, thus revealing the birth and growth history of an emergent volcano erupted from a shallow seabed (Sohn and Chough, 1992). Seongsan is probably the best example of hydromagmatic volcanoes that has the typical morphology of a tuff cone, shows diverse internal structures along the sea cliff exposures, and boasts outstanding beauty (IUCN, 2007). It is a cherished landmark which attracts numerous tourists to view it at dawn and dusk as it catches sunrise and sunset light from its rim. Seongsan is the most heavily visited geotourism sites on Jeju Island (UNDP-WCMC, 2007).

Sangumburi crater

Sangumburi, meaning 'hole-in-the-ground', is a peculiar volcanic crater distinguished from the other volcanic cones and craters of Jeju Island. The crater rim of Sangumburi is 31m higher than the surroundings; the rim-to-rim width is 635m; the diameter of the crater floor is about 300m; the height from the crater floor to the rim is 132m. The crater is a pit crater formed by sinking or collapse of the surface surrounding a vent that exuded lava flows. Sangumburi may have been a small shield volcano before the collapse. Sangumburi is a geotourism landmark containing a variety of visitor infrastructure including rest rooms, souvenir shops, information centre, a modest food kiosk and well developed pathways and overlooks. In autumn, the crater is also surrounded by pampas grass, creating photogenic landscapes.

Sanbangsan lava dome

Sanbangsan is a gigantic lava dome formed by the slow effusion of highly viscous lava. It is located in the south-western margin of Jeju Island, rising 395m above sea level (Figure 11.4). A lava dome results from the slow effusion of felsic, commonly very viscous lava from a volcanic vent. The viscosity of the lava prevents it from flowing far from the vent, causing it to solidify quickly and creating a circular dome-like shape. The lava dome is one of the oldest rock formations on Jeju Island, being about 800,000 years old (Won et al, 1986). Vertical columnar joints, about 2m in width and more than 100m in height are well exposed on the southern cliff wall of the lava dome. Beneath the jointed lava occurs a thick layer of volcanic breccia composed of angular fragments of lava. The breccia suggests that the dome experienced explosive eruptions or dome collapse during its growth due to build-up of gas pressure. The dome-forming lava and breccia overlies the basaltic tuff of Yongmeori, the oldest rock formation on Jeju Island (Sohn, 1995) and indicates that it was the site of the first lava eruption. A roadcut between the lava dome and Yongmeori shows clearly the relationship between these two rock formations.

Sanbangsan contains the Sanbang Cave Buddhist Temple on the middle of its southern slope which is a tourist destination in itself. The steep but well maintained steps allow visitors to reach the cave where Buddhist monks still worship. Visitor infra-structure includes eating opportunities, souvenir shops, rest rooms and parking. Large numbers of visitors experience this site.

Yongmeori coast

Yongmeori, meaning 'dragonhead', forms a small promontory to the south of the Sanbangsan lava dome. The overall geologic structures suggest Yongmeori is a remnant of a tuff ring, which is a kind of hydromagmatic volcano with a relatively large crater compared with its height, deposited mostly from pyroclastic surges and debris flows that were generated by either remobilization of wet tephra or by expulsion of wet vent-filling slurry of tephra (Sohn, 1995). A recent study suggests that the tuff ring has a rather complex

Figure 11.4 The 395m-high Sanbangsan trachyte dome with vertical columnar joints

growth history compared to its small size (Sohn and Park, 2005).

Yongmeori was built on unconsolidated 'U Formation' shelf sediment. The path of magma supply was probably diverted in some cases after collapse, giving rise to migration of the active vent. The resultant volcanic edifice thus became non-circular or irregular. Yongmeori is also an historic site where a Dutch merchant ship was shipwrecked in 1653. One of the sailors on that ship introduced Korea to the Western world for the first time when he published a book on Korea after his 13-year-long detention in the country.

The Geomunoreum lava tube system

The Geomunoreum lava tube system consists of a number of lava tubes and is a significant tourism draw card. There is a wide variety of visitor facilities on site including information centres, souvenir shops, restaurants, rest rooms and ample parking for both cars and large tour buses. Three caves within the system are discussed below,

Manjang cave and Yongcheon and Dangcheomul caves.

Manjang cave

Manjang cave (Manjanggul in Korean) is a well known tourist attraction on Jeju with hundreds of thousands of visitors annually (Huh et al, 2008). Manjang measures up to 23m across and 30m in height (Figure 11.5), and stretches about 7.4km in length, making it amongst the 15 longest lava tubes in the world (IUCN, 2006). A large, single-passage lava tube, Manjang has approximately a kilometre of 'show cave' open for tourism since 1967 (Woo, 2005). Manjang cave is self-guided and interpretation is generally provided at the beginning of the cave with fairly comprehensive signage in Korean and English throughout the 'show cave' section (Huh et al, 2008). The lava tube cave is accessed by two sets of wide, cement stairs down to the floor of the cave. The show cave section of the lava tube is generally well-lit with level walking. Occasional signage in the cave

Figure 11.5 The main passage of the Manjang cave showing beautifully preserved internal morphologies

identifies features of particular visitor interest (Huh et al, 2008). Guided tour programmes are currently being prepared. Despite the age of its formations, about 300,000–200,000 years old (IUCN, 2006), Manjang still retains perfectly preserved internal morphology and structure. Visitors may view a variety of lava features including lava stalactites, lava stalagmites, benches, shelves, lava helictites and ropy lavas. Manjang cave also contains a 7.6m-high lava column (IUCN, 2006), the largest known in the world (Hyunchul, 2008).

Yongcheon and Dangcheomul caves

Yongcheon lava tube cave (*Yongcheondonggul* in Korean) was accidentally discovered when the Jeju Island power company was erecting an electric power pole in 2005. Dangcheomul lava tube cave (*Dangcheomuldonggul* in Korean) was also accidentally discovered in 1995 by a local farmer when heavy earth-moving equipment broke through the roof of the cave. The ceiling, wall and floor of both dark-coloured lava tube caves are

spectacularly adorned with various secondary white-coloured speleotherms such as stalactites, stalagmites, soda straws, columns, cave corals, flowstone, draperies, cave pearls and rimstones, which is one of the best displays of this type in the world (Figures 11.6 and 11.7). Calcium and carbonate ions responsible for the formation of white carbonate speleothems were supplied by percolating rainwater from overlying carbonate sand dunes. The secondary speleothems and the presence of opalescent carbonate mineral deposits in Yongcheon and Dangcheomul, peculiar to only those lava tube caves, create an amazing caving experience. Their aesthetic value in the cave world is unequalled. Instantly recognizing their unique attributes, Yongcheon was designated as a National Monument in 2006 and was included in the World Heritage designation in 2007 (UNESCO, 2009). Currently, the lava tubes are not open to public visitation. There is some discussion of potentially opening one of the caves to limited tourism after the installation of appropriate infrastructure.

Figure 11.6 Beautiful carbonate speleothems in Yongcheon cave

Figure 11.7 Stalactites and columns in Dangcheomul cave

Columnar-jointed lava at Daepodong

Volcanic rocks formed by cooling of hot lavas commonly have cooling joints, which are typically expressed as vertical columnar jointing. The best exposures of columnar-jointed lavas in Jeju Island are found along the coast of Daepodong where dark grey trachybasalt lava crops out for about 2km (Figure 11.8). The joint systems in this area are mostly six-sided, but there are also some four-sided to seven-sided joints (Koh et al, 2005). The site is well-fitted for tourism with parking, rest rooms, paved walkways, boardwalks and a small food kiosk. Visitors come to not only admire the striking honeycomb-like columnar joints, but also the outstanding coastal views from the wooden boardwalks and pathways. Unusual outdoor sculpture provides unique photo-taking opportunities. Guided tours are available upon request.

The current status of geotourism on Jeju

In its current form, geotourism is a type of mass tourism on Jeju Island. A number of tour companies off-load tourists to favoured geotourism sites regularly throughout the day. Such high numbers of visitors come to see the sites that the paved walkways are atypically wide by Western standards and site entrances often park-like in their immaculate landscaping and maintenance.

With the 2007 listing of the Jeju Volcanic Island and Lava Tubes as Korea's first natural area inscribed onto UNESCO's World Heritage list, awareness about Jeju's unique geologic features, and subsequently its geotourism, has increased significantly. While the growth rate in the number of tourists to the island is holding relatively

Figure 11.8 Columnar-jointed trachybasalt lava at Daepodong, showing well-developed colonnade (lava columns) in the lower part overlain by entablature (chaotic upper part)

steady at 6–7 per cent, the number of travellers to the three sites included in the World Heritage listing – Mt Hallasan, Seongsan Ilchulbong tuff cone, and the Geomunoreum lava tube system – has risen by 13–30 per cent (Chosun, 2008) with the most heavily visited site being the Seongsan Ilchulbong Tuff Cone (UNEP-WCMC, 2007). With the publicity associated with the World Heritage listing, the number of foreign travellers also rose – by 52.5 per cent, from 81,779 in May 2007 to 124,770 in May 2008 (Chosun, 2008).

Geologic interpretive signage varies greatly across these sites. However, new signage helping visitors understand the World Heritage values of the listed sites greatly enhances visitor understanding of the volcanic processes that formed the island (Huh et al, 2008). In a bold step towards educating the public about the superlative values of Yongcheon and Dangcheomul, the Jeju National Museum created a reproduction of a short segment of one of the lava tubes for visitors to walk through, view videos and read interpretive signage to learn about these unique caves.

The future for geotourism on Jeju

The big three UNESCO protected area brand categories are World Heritage, Biosphere Reserve and Global Geopark. In 2002, both Mt Hallasan and the Seogwipo coastal area were designated as UNESCO Biosphere Reserves. In 2007, Mt Hallasan, the Seongsan Ilchulbong Tuff Cone and the Geomunoreum Lava Tube System were combined and listed as the first natural World Heritage area in the Republic of Korea (South Korea). The South Korean government is now aiming to include parts of Jeju's geological heritage under the Global Geoparks Network (Chosun, 2008). The Jeju Special Self-governing Province government has already formed a task force to select appropriate areas to be included in the nomination (Chosun, 2008).

Despite the presence of numerous geotourism sites and high visitation numbers, the educational aspects of geotourism have yet to be fully realized. With the new world heritage listing of Jeju Island

and Lava Tubes and the active pursuit of Global Geopark status, this important facet of geotourism should increase across the island in the next few years. Other lesser known geotourism sites on Jeju, such as the Columnar Joint Seashore along the southern coast including the Jeongbang waterfall, three islands off Seoguipo (Seopseom, Munseon and Beomsum) and the lava tube caves at Hallim Park will no doubt contribute more substantially to a yet more fully realized geotourism potential of Jeju (Huh et el, 2008).

Conclusion

A picturesque holiday destination, Jeju is filled with geotourism opportunities for visitors to view the volcanic origins of the island. Geotourism is intricately linked to Korean cultural values and aesthetics. The appreciation of the need to protect these landscapes in a sustainable manner while incorporating tourism is spreading across Korea (Huh et al, 2008). The World Heritage listing of some of Jeju's volcanic features and the designation of Mt Hallasan as a UNESCO Biosphere Reserve clearly proves that Jeju sites display outstanding geologic values and aesthetic beauty. Unfortunately, the educational aspects of geotourism are not yet fully realized and mass tourism is prevailing in the most popular tourist sites. However, geotourism will grow rapidly in the future as Jeju works towards joining the Global Geoparks Network (Seo et al, 2009). The variety of volcanic landforms, excellent geologic exposures, favourable climate, ready accessibility and beautiful scenery will continue to make Jeju an exceptional place for volcano tourism and geological field excursions in the near future, while the environmental awareness of tourists will be enhanced by geotourism concepts and practices.

References

Chosun Ilbo (2008) 'Jeju rejoices in UNESCO World Heritage listing', www.english.chosun.com/site/sata/html_dir/2008/06/27/2008062761014.html, accessed 10 June 2009

Chough, S. K. and Sohn, Y. K. (1990) 'Depositional mechanics and sequences of base surges, Songaksan tuff ring, Cheju Island, Korea', *Sedimentology*, vol 37, pp1115–1135

Huh, M., Woo, K. S. and Spate, A. (2008) 'Aspects of geotourism in South Korea', presented to the

Plate 1 Photo opportunity close to the crater rim of Mt Etna, Italy. At many volcanoes safety considerations are left to the individual visitor. Photo courtesy of Henry Gaudru

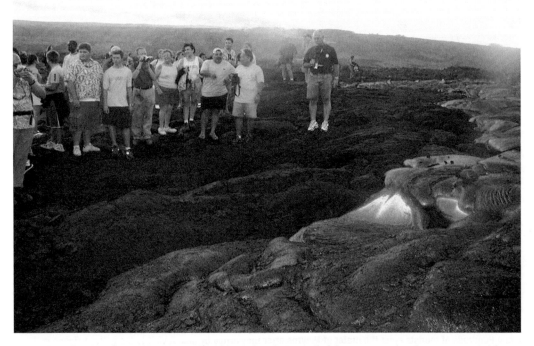

Plate 2 Hawaiian lava flows are very popular with tourists, but not all visitors are wearing the recommended foot protection while taking a closer look. Lava crusts are brittle and cause severe cuts when people lose their balance while taking photos. Photo courtesy of Travis Heggie

Plate 3 Mt Vesuvius with Naples in the background facing north. Some volcano tourists are rather casual when it comes to wearing suitable shoes for the hike up the mountain (see insert). Photo courtesy of Jonathan Karkut

Plate 4 Hundreds of tourists enter the crater of Nisyros after they arrive by bus. A visit to the active volcano is treated more like a family outing and the steep climb to the bottom of the crater does not appear to deter any of the visitors (CS15). Although classed as active, no interpretive signs or information boards are posted. The only instructions regarding safety are given by the bus drivers who tell the tourists to be 'very, very careful' because the thermal springs in the crater are 'very, very hot'. Photo courtesy of Patricia Erfurt-Cooper

Plate 5 Active volcanoes attract a wide variety of visitors. A group of nuns are looking into the crater of Poas volcano in Costa Rica. The fence has more a symbolic than protective function, especially for small children. Photo courtesy of Henry Gaudru

Plate 6 The use of helicopters to access remote volcanic destinations is not uncommon. Arrival on Erta Ale in 2002 with a MI-8 military helicopter. Photo courtesy of Jens Edelmann

Plate 7 The Erta Ale pit crater in 2002 with few signs of activity and the lava lake in the crater at a low level. Photo courtesy of Jens Edelmann

Plate 8 Note the significant rise of the lava lake's level in 2009 compared to the much lower level in 2002. Photo courtesy of Hans-Jürgen Knoblauch

Plate 9 The sinter terraces of Pamukkale in Turkey draw large crowds on a daily basis, adding up to millions of visitors each year. Tourism as such appears to be sustainable, but whether the environment can be sustained under such visitor pressure is a different question. The majority of tourists at this geothermal attraction are cruise ship passengers from Russia, and a visit to the hot spring terraces usually includes the ruins of the ancient city of Hierapolis, which are located at the top of the terraces. To maintain the 'pristine' look of the hot spring pools as best as possible the water flow is alternated constantly with sections of the pools empty in the morning and full in the afternoon. Photo courtesy of Patricia Erfurt-Cooper

Plate 10 The Mt Unzen Volcanic Area was recently (August 2009) officially recognized as a UNESCO Global Geopark and attracts busloads of visitors while the conditions are favourable. Viewing platforms allow large numbers of volcano tourists to have a close look at this volcano. Photo courtesy of Patricia Erfurt-Cooper

Plate 11 Volcano tourists at the summit of Mt Aso on the Japanese island of Kyushu are using the crater on the left as a backdrop for pictures of friends and family. Despite being classed as an active and potentially dangerous volcano Mt Aso is a very popular destination for visitors and residents of the region. Photo courtesy of Patricia Erfurt-Cooper

Plate 12 Mt Sakurajima is located in the south of the Japanese island of Kyushu, opposite the city of Kagoshima and often erupts 'while you wait' (Chapter 9). The full moon gives the scenery a special appeal. Sakurajima Island's population numbers approximately 7000 people and has a ring road with access to a volcano information centre and several volcano viewing areas. Photo courtesy of Patricia Erfurt-Cooper

Plate 13 Mt Fuji seen from above. Aircraft pilots usually let the passengers know when the visibility is good enough to take a look out of the window while flying over Fuji-san. It is a very impressive mountain and does not always allow for a view in its entirety. The chances are in fact better from the air than from the ground. Photo courtesy of Malcolm Cooper

Plate 14 Crowds are watching the Lady Knox Geyser eruption which is induced with soap, Wai-O-Tapu Geothermal Area. Photo courtesy of Richard Roscoe

Plate 15 The 40 metre high cliff face shows the remains of a basalt lava flow from the Nandewar Volcano, Mt Kaputar National Park in New South Wales, Australia. These beautiful basalt columns are locally known as 'Sawn Rocks' for their distinctive columnar jointing. Photo courtesy of Brian Brogan, Scotland

Plate 16 The Glasshouse Mountains are a chain of ancient volcanoes in south east Queensland, Australia. People use the 'Mary Cairncross Lookout' for a view of the eroded plugs in the distance. Although dormant, these mountains attract many visitors for a wide range of recreational activities. Photo courtesy of Patricia Erfurt-Cooper

Inaugural Global Geotourism Conference 2008, Fremantle, Western Australia, pp355–359

Hyun-chul, S. (2008) 'Manjanggul lava tube caves', *The Korea Times*, 7 October, www.koreatimes.cokr/www/news/art/2009/05/153_27375.html, accessed 7 October 2008

IUCN (2007) 'World heritage nomination – IUCN technical evaluation: Jeju volcanic island and lava tubes (Republic of Korea) – ID No. 1264'. http:whc/unesco.org/archive/advisory_body_evaluation/1264.pdf, accessed 10 June 2009

Joongang Daily (2009) 'Local tourism bites back', 20 February, English version www.joongangdaily.joins.com/article/view.asp?aid=2901269, accessed 10 June 2009

Khan, M. and Su, K.-D. (2003) 'Service quality expectations of travellers visiting Cheju Island in Korea', *Journal of Ecotourism*, vol 2, no 2, pp114–125

Koh, J. S., Yun, S. H. and Hong, H. C. (2005) 'Morphology and petrology of Jisagae columnar joint on the Daepodong basalt in Jeju Island, Korea', *Journal of Petrological Society of Korea,* vol 14, pp212–225

Lee, M. W. (1982) 'Petrology and geochemistry of Jeju volcanic Island, Korea', *Science Reports of the Tohoku University*, vol 15, pp177–256

Lee, M. W., Won, C. K., Lee, D. Y. and Park, G. H. (1994) 'Stratigraphy and petrology of volcanic rocks in southern Cheju Island, Korea', *Journal of Geological Society of Korea*, vol 30, pp521–541

Organisation for Economic Co-operation and Development (OECD) (2009) *OECD Stat Extracts*, www.stats.oecd.org/wbos/viewhtml.aspx?queryname=1816&querytype=view&lang=en, accessed 10 June 2009

Park, K. H., Lee, B. J., Kim, J. C., Cho, D. L., Lee, S. R., Choi, H. I., Park, D. W., Lee, S. R., Choi, Y. S., Yang, D. Y., Kim, J. Y., Seo, J. Y. and Sin, H. M. (2000) 'Explanatory note of the Jeju (Baekado, Jinnampo) sheet (1:250,000), Korea Institute of Geoscience and Mineral Resources, Taejon

Seo, J.-H., Park, S.-Y. and Yu, L. (2009) 'The analysis of the relationships of Korean outbound tourism demand: Jeju island and three international destinations', *Tourism Management*, vol 30, no 4, pp530–543

Sohn, Y. K. (1995) 'Structures and sequences of the Yongmeori tuff ring, Cheju Island, Korea: Sequential deposition from shifting vents', *Journal of the Geological Society of Korea*, vol 31, pp57–71

Sohn, Y. K. and Chough, S. K. (1989) 'Depositional processes of the Suwolbong tuff ring, Cheju Island (Korea)', *Sedimentology*, vol 36, pp837–855

Sohn, Y. K. and Chough, S. K. (1992) 'The Ilchulbong tuff cone, Cheju Island, South Korea: Depositional processes and evolution of an emergent, Surtseyan-type tuff cone', *Sedimentology*, vol 39, pp523–544

Sohn, Y. K. and Chough, S. K. (1993) 'The Udo tuff cone, Cheju Island, South Korea: Transformation of pyroclastic fall into debris fall and grain flow on a steep volcanic cone slope', *Sedimentology*, vol 40, pp769–786

Sohn, Y. K. and Park, K. H. (2004) 'Early-stage volcanism and sedimentation of Jeju Island revealed by the Sagye borehole, SW Jeju Island, Korea', *Geosciences Journal*, vol 8, pp73–84

Sohn, Y. K. and Park, K. H. (2005) 'Composite tuff ring/cone complexes in Jeju Island, Korea: Possible consequences of substrate collapse and vent migration', *Journal of Volcanology and Geothermal Research*, vol 141, pp157-175

Sohn, Y. K., Park, K. H. and Yoon, S. H. (2008) 'Primary versus secondary and subaerial versus submarine hydrovolcanic deposits in the subsurface of Jeju Island, Korea', *Sedimentology*, vol 55, pp899–924

Suh, Y.-K. and Hunter, W. (2006) *Tourism, in Jeju Island: History and Lives, Tourism and Citrus, Plants and Animals, Jeju, S. Korea*, Educational Science Research Institute, Cheju National University, pp99–129

Thorarinsson, S. (1967) *Surtsey: The New Island in the North Atlantic*, The Viking Press, Inc., New York, p47

UNEP-WCMC (2007) 'Jeju volcanic island & lava tubes, South Korea', www.unep-wcmw.org/sites/wh/pdf/JEJU KOREA.pdf, accessed 12 June 2009

UNESCO (2009) 'Jeju volcanic island and lava tubes', whc.unesco.org/en/list/1264, accessed 10 June 2009

Won, J. K., Matsuda, J., Nagao, K., Kim, K. H. and Lee, M. W. (1986) 'Paleomagnetism and radiometric age of trachytes in Jeju Island, Korea', *Journal of Korean Institute of Mining Geology*, vol 19, pp25–33

Woo, K. S. (2005) *Caves: A Wonderful Underground*, Hollym, Seoul, p229

12

Volcano Tourism in Iran: Mt Damavand, the Highest Peak in the Middle East

Kazem Vafadari

Introduction

Mt Damavand is the second highest volcano in Asia after Kunlun in Tibet and the highest volcano in the Middle East. Damavand is also the name of an area (Damavand county) in the north-east of Tehran, the capital of Iran. Mt Damavand the volcano is located in the Alborz mountain range in the north of Iran, which form a natural barrier between the south part of the Caspian Sea and the central plateau of Iran (Figure 12.1). This mountain range is more than 1500km long and its width varies from 30 to 130km (Esham, 1972; Guest, 2004). The length of this mountain range determines the nature of the 'Caspian Mild' climate in the northern part of Iran, which is significantly different to the desert and semi-desert climate of the central plateau of Iran.

Summer and winter are the two major seasons of Mt Damavand, spring and autumn are usually too short and not significant. The short spring is however very attractive at Damavand especially because of its natural red poppy fields that start blooming at the beginning of May in the lower parts and gradually cover the upper parts in June. The minimum temperature at high altitudes in Damavand is −60°C and the highest is −2°C in summer. There are strong winds which exceed 150

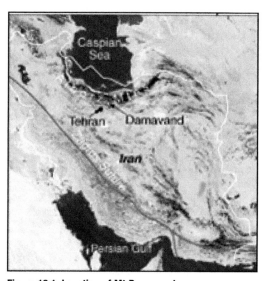

Figure 12.1 Location of Mt Damavand

kilometres per hour some times and the direction is from the north and north-west to the east.

Mt Damavand is also important in the history of Iran, and was registered as a national heritage site in 2009. Damavand in Iranian mythology is the very heart and centre of Persia where the Iranian people reside (Mansour, 2002). Damavand is also the symbol of Iranian resistance against foreign rule in Persian poetry and literature. The mountain is said to hold magical powers in the 'Shahnameh', which means 'the book of kings' in

Figure 12.2 The Alborz range, Mt Damavand in the centre foreground, Caspian Sea to the right and Tehran to the left

Source: Photos @ Views of the Earth

the Persian language, written by the Iranian poet Ferdowsi around 1000 CE, and the national epic of the Persian speaking world. One of the best examples of Persian literature that shows the place of Mt Damavand in the national psyche is the poem 'Damavand' by Mohammad Tagi Bahar, the famous Iranian poet. The poem starts with:

> *Oh white demon with feet in chains*
> *Oh terrestrial dome, Oh Mount Damavand...*
> (Mansour, 2002)

The Alborz mountain range

The Alborz mountains are located along the northern border of Iran with Tehran lying on their southern central slopes (Esham, 1972; Guest, 2004). Their height increases from west to east. There are several peaks above 4000m along the mountain range, with 5671m Mt Damavand as the highest peak. The average height is 3000m. Among the other mountains in the same region are Mt Golzard (3693m) and Mt Gharedagh (4076m), the most important peaks in Damavand county (Guest, 2004). For those who visit Damavand, Mt Firuzkooh is also important and attractive, and Mt Poldar (2689m), Mt Navas (2829m) and Mt Tappemorad (3219m) are the most attractive destinations for mountain climbing activities.

Damavand summit: Geological background

Mt Damavand is located in Amol county of Mazandaran province 66km to the north-east of the capital and 70km south of the Caspian Sea; the summit is visible in good weather from Tehran. The volcano is surrounded by three rivers: Tine River in the north, Haraz River to the east /south and Delichai River in the west. The stratovolcano contains a volume of 400 cubic km and overlies the active fold and trust base of the Alborz mountains. There are about 70 craters in Mt Damavand and the biggest one (400m in diameter) is the main site known as Damavand volcano (Davidson et al, 2004).

The slopes of Damavand comprise trachyandesite lava flows and the youngest activity consisted of the eruption of a series of lava flows from the summit vent that cover the western side of the volcano (Allenbach, 1966). Two periods of eruptive activity have been identified in the Holocene (approximately 38,500 years ago). One significant ignimbrite has been identified, however pyroclastic eruptions have been small and infrequent. No historical eruptions are known from Damavand, but hot springs are located on the volcano's flanks, and fumaroles are found at the summit crater

Figure 12.3 View of Mt Damavand's west face during Summer

occasionally. The summit crater contains a small lake. The eruptive style has remained the same throughout the volcano's 1.8 million year history despite one or more sector collapse events and the formation of a second cone overlying the old eroded cone (Figure 12.3).

Mt Damavand as a volcano tourist destination

The significance of the geothermal environment of Damavand has for years attracted not only geologists but also ordinary people with an interest in nature and volcano tourism. The history of travel to and climbing Damavand summit is long and well documented (Mansour, 2002; Tourudi, 2002). Ancient stone reliefs found in the area contain tales of the travels of Persian kings to the volcano for climbing, for stay as a summer resort, and for hunting (Shahosini, 2003).

Mt Damavand has also had a symbolic role in representing Iranian nationality and it was used in the national symbol of the country during the rule of the Pahlavi dynasty. Damavand hosts both international and domestic tourists at present, but the incidence of acute mountain sickness in climbers who attempt Mt Damavand is 60 per cent (Shahosini, 2003).

Routes to the summit

There are four routes to reach the summit: The south route, the north route, the north-east route and the south-west route. The Haraz road, which connects Tehran to Amol city, is the only route to Mt Damavand and runs around the volcano, and all roads and access to Damavand end in Haraz. The south route is the oldest and easiest way of climbing Mt Damavand and the most difficult one is the north route.

The south face: Favourite route for Damavand visitors

The most popular route to climb Mt Damavand is the south route, which takes about eight hours from the base camp to the summit. It in fact starts from Tehran and also it's the easiest way to reach the peak. It takes about 1.5 hours by car from Tehran to Polour, which is the first camp in south route, and belongs to the Iranian Mountain Climbing Federation. The second camp is Goosfandsara and it is about an hour away from the first camp (Polour) by an off road car. This is the base camp (3040m) where the journey to Mt Damavand usually starts on foot. Visitors walk the distance between the base camp and the next one called Bargah-E Sevvom for about three to four hours and stay overnight there at 4150m to get ready for climbing up to the peak early next morning (Figure 12.4).

It takes five to seven hours slow and steady walk to reach the summit of Mt Damavand at 5671m from the Bargah-E Sevvom camp. There is no shelter or camp at the peak and nowhere to spend a long time in shelter. Visitors are recommended to return back to Bargah-E Sevvom camp quickly due to the high risk of quick weather changes once they have reached the top. The second most popular route to the summit is the south-west route, which takes about seven hours to reach the summit. This route also starts at Polour village in the south face of Mt Damavand and there is Camp Simorgh at 4159m altitude in this route to support climbers (Figure 12.5). The other routes to the summit are the north and north-east routes, which are longer and not as popular as the routes in the south face of the volcano. These routes attract repeat visitors to Damavand, those who have tried southern routes and are seeking a different experience.

Figure 12.4 Bargahe-E Sevvom camp, Mt Damavand 4150m, south route

Figure 12.5 Simorgh camp, Mt Damavand 4150m, south-west route

Mt Damavand as a natural world heritage site

Mt Damavand was placed on the tentative list of Iran's world heritage sites submitted by the Iranian government to UNESCO in 2008. The site is described as an inactive volcanic mountain and the highest elevation in Iran with numerous thermal springs and rich flora and fauna. Among the universal values are the numerous endemic plant species mentioned by the Iranian specialists who introduced Damavand as a world heritage site. The volcano that was first activated in the Quaternary period is one of the world's highest elevations with rich flora including endangered species that should be protected.

Water sources of the volcano: Hot springs, rivers, waterfalls and lakes in Damavand

There are numerous hot springs and rivers at Mt Damavand that attract tourists to the volcano, and tourist facilities are located on the riversides. Usually the direction of river flow is from north to south in Damavand, the rainfalls and permanent snowcap on the peak being the source of water. The main rivers of Damavand are the Lar and the Hablehrood. The Lar River is also one of the sources of Tehran's drinking water and Lar Dam which is built on the river attracts many tourists in summer time to enjoy the cool weather and tourist activities including fishing. Damavand icefall is one of the most famous tourist attractions. This is 12m high, 3m in diameter and is found at 5100m altitude near the southern climbing route. The icefall is almost a permanent one and only in a very hot summer might it collapse. The icefall has an important place in the advertisement literature of Damavand volcano tourism. It is one of the reasons that makes the south route more popular than other routes to the summit and attracts many visitors during summer, especially those coming from the hot climates of central Iran and international tourists from the Middle East (Figure 12.6).

Figure 12.6 The icefall at 5100m altitude, Mt Damavand south route

Mineral water springs in Damavand are the main source of revenue that attracts investment into the region. Cheshme-Aala, Polour and Abali are the most famous and the bottled mineral water from these springs is found in other countries in the Middle East as well as in domestic Iran. The most important thermal springs are Ask and Larijan with therapeutic applications. Larijan or 'Abe Garm-e Larijan' is in a village with the same name in the district of Larijan in the Lar valley. There are public baths with relatively small pools for tourists who visit the village mainly for hot spring tourism. Visitors believe that the water in Larijan hot spring is useful for treatment of chronic wounds and skin diseases.

National parks and protected areas of Mt Damavand

The flora and fauna of the Damavand region, with more than 2000 endemic plant species have attracted people for many centuries. The wildlife on the slopes of the volcano have been used as a royal hunting ground for Iranian kings. The Lar and Haraz rivers were declared protected areas in 1951 to protect the environment and natural resources of the region. Later, in 1975, the surrounding area of the two rivers (73,500 hectares) on the slopes of the volcano became a national park and hunting is forbidden to the present time in this area.

Risk management of volcano tourism on Mt Damavand

As is usual in high altitudes, changes in weather patterns are one of the main sources of risk in volcano tourism to Mt Damavand. It can change quickly to disaster in winter, with strong winds above 150km/h and freezing temperatures below −60°C. Rescue and medical facilities are not available in case of injury and emergency. The main cause of casualties are bad weather and foggy conditions in a region called 'Danger Zone' in the south route that is located between the fake summit at 5400m and the peak at 5670m. Some novice and even famous Iranian climbers have lost their way and accordingly their life in this place; however at other times it is a mild climbing slope without rocks. The average tourist must therefore be advised not to attempt the mountain during bad weather.

Tour guides and emergency services

There are several travel agencies and other associations such as the Iranian Mountain Climbing Federation that offer travel services and organize volcano tourism events with professional guides. Full-guided winter ascents, which usually take a week, are also available for people who have previous experience of winter mountaineering or ski touring at altitude in unstable weather conditions. February and March is the best time to visit Damavand and view the volcano, with numerous night campers, mountain huts and tourists who stay also in local houses nearby.

Safety guidelines for visitors to Mt Damavand

Volcano tourism to Mt Damavand, as one of the world's highest volcano peaks, is not mass tourism and the visitors are usually those with experience of climbing in high altitudes. The volcano is not currently active and there is almost no risk of poisoning by sulphuric or other volcanic gases as may happen frequently in other volcanic areas. Safety guidelines for Mt Damavand are therefore mainly concerned with weather conditions, timing and how to reduce the risk of getting lost at high altitudes. Never climbing in danger zones (over 5400m) or staying overnight at the summit is

emphasized by almost all guidelines and instructions or experienced guides. Visiting Damavand summit in winter should be well planned with equipment and an experienced local guide. Going higher than the fake summit is dangerous and a hand held GPS unit or a compass is necessary especially during bad weather conditions.

References

Allenbach, P. (1966) 'Geologie und Petrographie des Damavand und seiner Umgebung (Zentral-Elburz)', Iran, *Abhandlung zur Erlangung der Würde eines Doktors der Naturwissenschaften der Eidgenössischen Technischen Hochschule, Zürich*, pp1–145

Davidson, J., Hassanzadeh, J., Berzins, R., Stockli, D. F., Bashukooh, B., Turrin, B. and Pandamouz, A. (2004) 'The geology of Damavand volcano, Alborz mountains, northern Iran', *Geological Society of America Bulletin*, New York, vol 116, nos 1/2, pp16–29

Esham, E. C. (1972) *Damavand: Geological Map of the Central Alborz / Geological Survey of Iran*, Offset Press, Tehran

Guest, B. (2004) 'The thermal, sedimentological and structural evolution of the central Alborz mountains of northern Iran: Implications for the Arabia–Eurasia continent–continent collision and collisional processes in general', thesis dissertation, unpublished

Mansour, N. (2002) *Damavand khstgahe asatiri- e Iran* (Damavand the origin of Iranian myth), Feiz-e Kasani, Tehran

Shahosini, Y. (2003) *Negin-e Alborz Jazebehaye Gardeshgari-e Damavand va Firuzkuh* (the signet of Alborz: Tourist attractions of Damavand and Firuzkuh), Naghshe Bayan, Tehran

Tourudi, N. P. (2002) *Asar-e tarikhi-e Damavand: Joghrafiya-e tarikhi va moaferi-e mohavatehaye bastani va banahaye tarikhi farhangi* (Damavand's historical sites: An Introduction to Historical areas and Buildings of Damavand), Iran Cultural Heritage Organization, Tehran

13

Volcano Tourism in the Philippines

Jens Edelmann

Introduction

A look at a map of the Philippines shows an archipelagic country. Its 7100 islands cover a land area of 299,764km², spread over an area of two million km² of sea, grouped into three regions: Luzon, the Visayas and Mindanao with the capital city of Manila. The Philippines has some 90 million inhabitants with many affinities to the outside world, derived mainly from the cultures of Spain, Latin America and the United States. Partly as a result, tourists play an important role in the Philippine economy; in the year 2008, net tourism income in the Philippines totalled 3.6 billion US dollars (www.traveldocs.com/ph/economy.htm). Most visitors come from the United States, Japan, South Korea and Hong Kong. But there are also tourists from Taiwan, Australia, Canada, Singapore, Great Britain, Switzerland and Germany. Though Philippine tourism started to flourish in the 1970s and 1980s, the country has remained fairly 'non-touristic' compared to other regions in south-east Asia. Nevertheless, one objective of the Philippine government is to boost the so called ecotourism, and this is supported by the authorities and Philippine laws.

Geological setting

The Philippines is built on a vast array of fractured tectonic plates belonging to the western part of the circum-Pacific 'Ring of Fire' (Chapter 1). This belt, that runs from the north of Japan, through the Philippines to New Zealand is an area with continuously moving tectonic plates, floating on the Earth's liquid magma. These movements reveal themselves outwardly in numerous earthquakes and other volcanic activity. The formation of the archipelago into several big and a greater number of smaller islands results from the collision of two major lithospheric plates, the south-east Asian and the Philippine Sea plates. No less than six major subduction zones appear on these complex volcanic arcs, and three of them are related to active volcanism in historic times: the Manila Trench (to Pinatubo and Taal), the Negros Trench (to Kanlaon) and the Philippines Trench (to Mayon and Bulusan). The other subduction zones include the Central Mindanao Arc, the East Luzon Trough and the Cotobato Trench. The latter lack – with some exceptions – volcanism and/or well developed seismic zones. The last major trench is the Sulu Trench with an extinct arc system (Datuin, 1982). Thus the archipelago is surrounded by active subduction zones giving rise to frequent tectonic earthquakes, volcanic eruptions and mass earth movements.

Volcanic hazards and volcano monitoring in the Philippines

The eruptions of Hibok-Hibok on Camiguin Island in the years 1948–53 and of Taal in Batangas province 28–30 September 1965 brought to the fore the importance of volcanological studies in the Philippines and the need for surveillance of its active and potentially active volcanoes (Alcaraz, 1966). In the wake of the ravaging Hibok-Hibok eruption in December 1951, when 600 people

Table 13.1 The active volcanoes of the Philippines

Name	Location	Number of historical eruptions
Mayon	Legaspi City, Albay	45
Taal	Talisay, Batangas	33
Kanalaon	Negros Oriental	25
Bulusan	Sorsogon	12
Ragang	Cotobato	9
Smith	Babuyan Island	8
Hibok-Hibok	Camiguin Island	6
Didicas	Babuyan Island Group	5
Babuyan Claro	Babuyan Island	4
Carmiguin de Babuyanes	Babuyan Island Group	1
Cagua	Cagayan	2
Banahaw	Laguna / Quezon	Unknown
Calayo	Valencia, Bukidnon	3
Iraya	Batanes	1
Pinatubo	Zambales	1
Iriga	Iriga, Camarines Sur	2
Biliran	Biliran	1
Bud Dajo	Jolo Island	1
Matutum	Cotobato	1
Kalatungan	Bukidnon	Unknown
Makaturing	Lanao, Mindanao	10
Parker	South Cotobato	3

Source: Modified after Sigurdsson et al, 2000

lost their lives, the government created the Commission on Volcanology, which was the predecessor of the current Philippine Institute of Volcanology and Seismology (PHIVOLCS). Another important impetus to the further scientific investigation and monitoring of Philippine volcanoes was the plinian eruption of Mt Pinatubo in June 1991 (Newhall et al, 1996). PHIVOLCS runs a programme of surveillance of all active volcanoes in the archipelago that includes the most modern observation techniques and methods. This survillance is geophysically based on seismic monitoring, on geodetic methods (electronic distance measurement, precise levelling and tilt measurements), and on the analysis of volcanic gases and visual observations.

There are 22 active and 88 currently inactive volcanoes in the Philippines at the present count. The currently active volcanoes of the Philippines are shown in Table 13.1.

Active volcanoes can, once erupting, heavily affect people, buildings, agricultural areas and infrastructral settings. The influence of several cataclysmic historical eruptions on the world's climate and the desire to observe an eruption is well-proven. Despite the fascination derived from volcanism, volcano tourists should always consider that both active and 'sleeping' volcanoes may be more than a 'beast of beauty' but in fact a danger to life.

Volcano tourism to volcanic active areas that are related to the 'Ring of Fire' subduction zone mechanisms is primarily endangered by:

- eruptions from craters and vents;
- hot and toxic volcanic gases;
- ash and pumice fall;
- hot pyroclastic fallout from plinian eruption columns;
- surges and blasts;
- pyroclastic flows;
- acidic crater lakes;
- lava domes; and
- lahars.

Secondary dangers that should not be underestimated are:

- heavy rainfall;
- typhoons and thunderstorms;
- slippery trails;
- straying from marked tracks; and
- carelessness.

Though lava flows are universally considered to be dangerous, in the subduction zones lava eruptions are mostly much less physically devastating than other volcanic dangers (such as pyroclastic flows) due to their mineralogical content and structure and their cooler temperatures compared to the hot basaltic magmas produced in the rift zones (Chapters 2 and 3 this volume) and their resulting slow speed of advance when travelling down slopes.

Volcano tourism in the Philippines

Volcano tourism in the Philippines covers a variety of different activities, such as:

- climbing active and potentially active volcanoes;

- monitoring of volcanoes: crater activity, fumaroles, solfataras, eruptions, lahars, pyroclastic flows, lava flows;
- walks and treks on the slopes for monitoring and determination of animals and plants;
- sampling of volcanic rocks and minerals;
- bathing in hot spots and mud pools; and
- photography and painting.

Volcano tourism is part of ecotourism, a trend in tourism that has been developed worldwide since the 1990s. Almost the whole of the Philippines, as well as some of its volcanoes are potentially to be seen as a focus for ecotourism and its replacement discussed elsewhere in this book, geotourism (Dowling and Newsome, 2006). The Philippines is regarded as one of the top 25 biodiversity hotspots in the world in view of its high percentage of endemic plants and animals which are threatened by extinction. On Mt Mayon (Albay province, Bicol region), for example, the Mayon Volcano Ecotourism Project was established at the beginning of the 21st century. Recognizing the diverse natural and cultural resources of the country, Executive Order No. 111 was issued on 17 June 1999 to establish the guidelines for ecotourism development in relation to the Philippines volcanoes and the national park system.

Seen from a touristic point of view, the volcanoes of the Philippines can be divided into two categories:

1 popular and easily accessible volcanoes; and
2 volcanoes for the more adventurous.

While the first category includes such well known volcanoes as Mt Pinatubo, Taal, Hibok-Hibok and Mt Apo, the second comprises more remote and harder to access fire mountains, such as Mts Mayon, Kanlaon, Bulusan, Isarog, Parker and Kalatungan. This classification obviously differs from a serious scientific classification but is descriptive of tourist behaviour and motivations. The following short descriptions of some active volcanoes in the Philippines should help to make the access to this fiery matter easier and safer.

Taal

Taal volcano is a stratovolcano in Batangas province on the island of Luzon. Sometimes nicknamed 'the world's smallest volcano', Taal is part of a chain of volcanoes along the western side of the island of Luzon, which were formed by the subduction of the Eurasian Plate underneath the Philippine Mobile Belt. Taal produces lavas originated from a mantle wedge metasomatized by aqueous fluid dehydrated from the subducted basaltic crust, and melt plus fluid derived from subducted terrigenous sediment (Castillo and Newhall, 2004) and – if erupting – a very dangerous and turbulent, water-rich mixture of exploded bits of lava and steam. These eruptions, first observed at Taal volcano in 1965 are the origin of base surges resembling those created by the underwater detonation of atomic bombs at Bikini Atoll in the 1950s.

The volcano itself consists of an island in Lake Taal (Figure 13.1), which is situated within a caldera formed by an earlier, very powerful eruption, which probably took place around 3580BC. Taal is located about 50km (31 miles) from the capital of Manila and is also to be seen as 'a volcano inside a volcano'. The volcanic island of Taal covers an area of about 23km², and consists of overlapping cones and craters; 47 different cones and craters have been identified here.

Taal has erupted 34 times in the last 400 years, causing loss of life in the populated areas surrounding the lake, the current death toll standing at around 5000–6000. The greatest recorded eruptions in historical times were in 1754 and in 1965. Although the volcano has been quiet since 1977, it has shown signs of unrest since 1991 with strong seismic activity and ground fracturing events, as well as the formation of small mud pots and mud geysers on parts of the island. Because of its proximity to populated areas and its eruptive history, the International Association of Volcanology and Chemistry of the Earth's Interior (IAVCEI) has designated Taal a 'decade volcano'

Figure 13.1 Taal volcano

Source: Photo courtesy of Christoph Weber (Vulkanexpeditionen International (VEI), Germany)

worthy of close study to prevent future natural disasters (Hargrove, 1991).

Taal can be visited easily on a daytrip from Manila or (better) from San Nicolas and Talisay, where a boat can be hired for the crossing. Bathing in the lake might be dangerous due to water snakes, as reported by locals. A walk on Taal Island gives a good impression what it really means to stay on a volcano: ground and air forming a unique torrid zone, caused by solar radiation *and* the geothermal energy below the soles (Figure 13.2). To contact the volcano observatory based in Talisay before trying to climb this outstanding volcano is not a mistake. The Volcanic Explosivity Index (VEI) of Taal has changed from 6 (3580BC ± 200 years) to 4 (28 September 1965). The younger eruptions of Taal had a VEI of 1–2 (Smithsonian Global Volcanism Program).

Pinatubo

Before 2 April 1991 volcanologists knew Mt Pinatubo as an inconspicuous stratovolcano, active within the past millennium, and the site of an aborted geothermal development. Geologically Mt Pinatubo is flanked on the west (and partly underlain) by the Zambales Ophiolite Complex, an easterly-dipping slab of Eocene ocean crust uplifted during the Oligocene (Villones, 1980). The oldest references to volcanic rocks from Mt Pinatubo are accounts of the 19th century, describing the mineralogy and texture of pumice in tuffs in the vicinity of Porac, Magalang and the O'Donnell River. Mt Pinatubo seems to show a general trend from tholeiitic rocks on the west to slightly alkaline rocks on the east, with calcalkalaline rocks dominating the main volcanic belt (Newhall et al, 1996, pp165–166).

The first geologic commentary about Mt Pinatubo itself was by Smith (1909) who, after describing the Aglao Valley (Marella River valley) as once filled to a depth of 120 to 150m with loose sand and boulders, then described Mt Pinatubo as 'devoid of volcanic ash (and) any of the usual indications of volcanic activity'. Smith

Figure 13.2 A hike on the rim of the main crater of Taal, Philippines

Source: Photo courtesy of Christoph Weber (Vulkanexpeditionen International (VEI), Germany)

Figure 13.3 Oblique aerial view of the crater of Mt Pinatubo, Philippines

Source: Photo courtesy of Christoph Weber (Vulkanexpeditionen International (VEI), Germany)

concluded that 'Mount Pinatubo is not a volcano and we saw no signs of it ever having been one, although the rock constituting it is porphyric' (Smith, 1909). On 15 June 1991 we finally knew better when about 5.5 cubic kilometres of pyroclastic-flow deposits were ejected during the climatic eruption of the volcano, which, combined with plinian pumice-fall deposits, distinguishes the event as one of the five greatest eruptions of the 20th century. Pyroclastic flows travelled as much as 12 to 16 kilometres from the vent, impacted directly an area of almost 400km², and profoundly altered the landscape (Scott et al, 1996). A flight over the summit caldera of Mt Pinatubo (Figure 13.3) gives an astonishing view of the revegetated landscape after the devastation and the crater lake of this volcano and is very much recommended. The VEI of Pinatubo concerning the great eruption of June 1991 is set at 6 (Smithsonian Global Volcanism Program). Due to the danger of getting lost in the pyroclastic flow canyons on the flanks of Mt Pinatubo it is wise to

hire a guide before climbing the volcano. The tourist office in Angeles City will recommend them.

Mayon

Mayon (2421m, circular base radius of about 48 kilometres) is a highly active stratovolcano that belongs to the Bicol Arc on the east margin of southern Luzon (Figure 13.4). Geologically the activity of Mt Mayon is associated with the Philippine Trench where the Philippine Sea Plate, with a modest cover of pelagic sediment, is being subducted toward the west. These volcanic centres belong to the east Philippine arc system and are grouped regionally into the Bicol Arc at the northern end of the Philippine Trench (Newhall, 1979, Knittel and Defant, 1988), volcanoes on Leyte Island in the centre (Sajona et al, 1994), and into the East Mindanao Arc at the southern end (Sajona et al, 1997). The Bicol Arc is underlain by Tertiary–Quaternary sedimentary and volcanic rocks and pre-Tertiary schists, gneisses and

Figure 13.4 Mt Mayon in Bikol Province, Philippines is one of the most symmetrical volcanoes currently known

ultramafics. Petrographic and major element data indicate that Mayon has produced a basaltic to andesitic lava series by fractional crystallization and magma mixing. Trace element data indicate that the parental basalts came from a heterogeneous mantle source. The unmodified composition of the mantle wedge is similar to that beneath the Indian Ocean. To this mantle was added a subduction component consisting of melt from subducted pelagic sediment and aqueous fluid dehydrated from the subducted basaltic crust (Castillo and Newhall, 2004).

Although its first recorded activity was in AD1616, Mayon has probably been erupting since the Pliocene and has continued to erupt intermittently up to the present. A heavy volcanic eruption with pyroclastic flows occurred in February 1814, caused severe destruction, bringing the town of Cagsawa to complete ruin and submersing it in mud, boulders and ash. Another

destructive eruption occurred in 1897 and the latest was in June 2001. During an eruption in 1993 77 people were killed by Mayon's pyroclastic flows. In spite of these facts Mt Mayon is still loved by the Albayanos who regard it as their fountain of strength and persistence.

Every year in May the 'On to Mayon' conquest expedition is undertaken and sponsored by the Department of Tourism (DOT). Reaching the summit will take two days and one night with a stop over at different designated camp sites. As a result, the climb to Mt Mayon is in turn famous among local and foreign mountaineers. Since it is very tricky to find the right gully for the access to Mt Mayon, it is recommended to hire a guide for this trip. The area around Mayon is abundant with varieties of rare and endangered flora, some of which were listed in the Convention of International Trade of Endangered Species. To preserve this variety of fauna and flora is one of the main targets of the recently founded Mayon Volcano Natural Park Ecotourism Project. The VEI of Mayon mostly ranges between 1 and 3. The great eruption of 1 February 1814 has been estimated at a VEI of 4 (Smithsonian Global Volcanism Program).

Kanlaon

Mt Kanlaon is the highest mountain of the Central Philippines. Kanlaon is a stratovolcano situated in the province Negros Occidental. Its summit has an elevation of 2465 metres. Kanlaon is one of the 13 most active volcanoes in the country. Its volcanic activity during the last 125 years has been nearly exclusively restricted to phreatic eruptions and permanent fumarolic emissions. In 1993 a climber was reported to have died close to the crater rim when hit by rocks which were surprisingly thrown out of the crater. Based on 52 samples of the Negros region volcanics von Biedersee and Pichler (1995) stated that the bulk of those rocks are typical calc-alkaline andesites and basaltic andesites, which belong to the high K-calc-alkaline series with tendencies to shoshonites. Compared with other Cenozoic Philippine volcanics, that is from the Bicol and Central Luzon Belts and from Hibok-Hibok volcano, the Negros suite differs significantly by its higher ratios of K_2O. The Negros volcanics correspond to typically continental or microcontinental associations like those developed in the central Andes or on the North Island of New Zealand (von Biedersee and Pichler, 1995).

The volcanic massif of Mt Kanlaon is part of the Mt Kanlaon National Park, an undisturbed natural and historical refuge on the 'Sugar-island' of Negros. Climbing enthusiasts, tackling the mountain range feel it a demanding endeavour because of its size and natural geophysical features – deep ravines and crevices plus massive vertical rock walls that can become slippery from the irregular mountain water drainage. The best time to climb is during the dry season which is between February and May. Because it rains all year round even during the dry season, it is always good to prepare for poor weather. Group tours should be led by the experienced tour guides based in Dumaguete City or Bacolod. There are many routes up to the mountain's summit. The Mambucal

Trail from the north-west is said to be the longest but most beautiful trek which may take in all three days. It is advised to assess personal physical condition, equipment and supplies before taking on the ascent. The hot springs of Mambucal are very worth visiting for relaxing after the ascent. The VEI of Kanloan ranges between 1 and 2 (Smithsonian Global Volcanism Program).

Hibok-Hibok

Mt Hibok-Hibok or Catarman is the most prominent member of a group of seven volcanoes towering over the lush island of Camiguin in the southern Visayas. The peak elevation of this very interesting compound volcano, consisting of a stratovolcano and dome complex, is 1332m. It has a base diameter of 10km and several craters at or near its summit, some representing shallow lakes or water holes. The present crater area at the north-east slope facing Mambajao was mined for sulphur before the volcano's activity in 1948.

The tectonic setting of Hibok-Hibok is related to the Central Mindanao Arc. Its main rock type is Hornblende andesite and dacite. Hibok-Hibok has created five historical eruptions, the most destructive eruption series lasted from September 1948 to July 1953. In December of 1951 Hibok-Hibok had a major eruption of the rare pelean type that killed 600 people. During this eruptive cycle dome building with smaller nueé ardentes was observed at Hibok-Hibok. While the site of the 1948 initial eruption was Kanangkaan crater, the eruption series of 1949 and 1950–52 resulted from Itum crater and Ilihan crater respectively. The VEI of Hibok-Hibok ranges between 2 and 3 (PHIVOLCS/ Smithsonian Global Volcanism Program).

The island of Camiguin is accessible by ferry from Cebu City and from Jagna (Bohol). The summit of Hibok-Hibok is accessible by trail from Mambajao/Ardent hot springs. The ascent takes about four to five hours. Since it might be difficult to find the right trail it could be wise to hire a guide for the ascent. Once on the way it is worth visiting the Quiboro Volcano Observatory, 4.7km north-east of the summit. Another tourist attraction are the hot springs at Mambajao (Ardent Spring), Tangob, Bugong, Tagdo and Nassag.

Conclusions

This chapter has briefly outlined the origins and major types of volcanism in the Philippines context. Reference to tourism and to the types of risks involved in volcano tourism has been made, but perhaps the most telling observation is that the risks and their management are well-known and planned for in this country, with adequate information and assistance, yet deaths and injuries still occur. As with other examples in this book this situation makes it even more imperative to understand volcanism, *and* the motivations and behaviours of tourists to these most dangerous areas of the Earth's surface.

References

Alcaraz, A. (1966) 'Surveillance of Taal volcano: The eruption of *Taal volcano* in Batangas Province, Philippines on September 28–30', *Jour. Geol. Soc. Philippines*, vol 20, no 1, pp1–3

Castillo, P. R. and Newhall, C. G. (2004) 'Geochemical constrains on possible subduction components in lavas of Mayon and Taal volcanoes, southern Luzon, Philippines', *Journal of Petrology*, vol 45, no 6, pp1089–1108

Datuin, R. (1982) 'An insight on Quarternary volcanoes and volcanic rocks of the Philippines', *Journal of the Geological Society of the Philippines*, vol 36, pp1–11

Dowling, R. K. and Newsome, D. (2006) *Geotourism*, Elsevier, London

Hargrove, T. R. (1991) *The Mysteries of Taal. A Philippine Volcano and Lake, Her Sea Life and Lost Towns*, Bookmark Publishing, Manila

Knittel, U. and Defant, M. J. (1988) 'Sr isotopic and trace element variations in the Oligocene to Recent igneous rocks from the Philippine island arc: Evidence for Recent enrichment in the sub-Philippine mantle', *Earth Planet. Sci. Lett*, vol 87, pp87–99

Newhall, G., Daag, A. S., Delfin Jr, F. G., Hoblitt, R. P., McGeehin, J., Pallister, J. S., Regalado, T. M., Rubin, M., Tubianosa, B. S., Tamayo Jr, R. A. and Umbal, J. V. (1996) 'Eruptive History of Mount Pinatubo', in Newhall, G. and Punongbayan, R. S. (eds) *Fire and Mud. Eruptions and Lahars of Mount Pinatubo, Philippines*, Philippine Institute of Volcanology and Seismology, Quezon City and University of Washington Press, Seattle and London, pp165–195

Sajona, F. G., Bellon, H., Maury, R. C., Pubellier, M., Cotten, J. and Rangin, C. (1994) 'Magmatic response to abrupt changes in geodynamic settings: Pliocene–Quaternary calc-alkaline and Nb-enriched lavas from Mindanao (Philippines) ', *Tectonophysics*, vol 237, pp47–72

Sajona, F. G., Bellon, H., Maury, R. C., Pubellier, M., Quebral, R. D., Cotten, J., Bayon, F. E., Pagado, E. and Pamatian, P. (1997) 'Tertiary and Quaternary magmatism in Mindanao and Leyte (Philippines): Geochronology, geochemistry and tectonic setting', *Journal of Asian Earth Science*, vol 15, pp121–153

Sigurdsson, H. (ed) (2000) *Encyclopedia of Volcanoes*, Academic Press, San Diego/London

Scott, W. E., Hoblitt, R. P., Torres, R. C., Self, S., Martinez, M. L. and Nillos, T., Jr (1996) 'Pyroclastic Flows of the June 15, 1991, Climatic Eruption of Mount Pinatubo', in Newhall, G. and Punongbayan, R. S. (eds) *Fire and Mud. Eruptions and Lahars of Mount Pinatubo, Philippines*, Philippine Institute of Volcanology and Seismology, Quezon City and University of Washington Press, Seattle and London, p545

Smith, H. D. (1909) 'Contributions to the physiography of the Philippine Islands: IV. The country between Subig and Mount Pinatubo', *Philippine Journal of Science*, vol 4(A), pp19–25

von Biedersee, H. and Pichler, H. (1995) 'Volcanism in South East Asia', *Journal of Southeast Asian Earth Sciences*, vol 11, issue 2, pp111–123

Villones, R. (1980) The Aksitero Formation: Its Implications and Relationship with Respect to the Zambales Ophiolite', *Philippine Bureau of Mines and Geosciences, Technical Information Series*, No. 16-80, 21pp

Case Study 10

Challenging Destinations

The World Heritage Listed Volcanoes of Kamchatka

Henry Gaudru

Introduction

Kamchatka is the name for a peninsula located on the far east of Russia; it is one of the largest in the world and famous for its wildlife and volcanic activity. The 700km-long volcanic belt that makes up the peninsula is the surface expression of the north-westerly subduction by 8–10cm a year of the Pacific Ocean Plate under the Eurasian Plate, and exhibits the complete range of vulcanism characteristic of the Pacific Ring of Fire. Since 1690 some 200 eruptions have been recorded. The peninsula has some 300 volcanoes of which 33 are currently active – most of these of explosive character and many of perfect pyramidal form. Of these, 34 in total and the 13 most active volcanoes on Kamchatka occur in heritage areas. Most of these are basaltic composite stratocones and andesite stratovolcanoes, but some are shield volcanoes. There are also calderas, scoria cones, lava streams, cinder fields, over 160 thermal and mineral springs, geysers, solfataras, mud pots and many other volcanic features. The volcanoes of Kamchatka are protected areas and are included in the United Nations world heritage list.

Tourism

Tourism activities have largely developed over the last 15 years. Travelling to this distant part of Russia's wilderness can be done, though not easily. Transportation is scarce and roads are even scarcer, but one can land in Petropavlovsk-Kamchatsky, the capital, by way of a Mi-8 helicopter, which must be chartered (Figure CS10.1). The main geological and volcanological trips offered include trekking/hiking in volcanic and geothermal areas with climbing on volcanoes, ski tourism and descents from volcanoes with the use of helicopters (heli-skiing), ski trekking, downhill skiing, flights over the Komandorsky and Kurile islands, and flights over active volcanoes. In past years the infrastructure of tourism in this area has seen development in the most picturesque places, such as the Valley of Geysers, Nalichevsky Natural Park, Lake Kuril, Malkinsky hot springs and along the rivers Zhupanova and Opala. Approximately 15,000 tourists visited Kamchatka in 1995, 4000 of them foreign.

Kronotskiy Nature Park is the only site in Russia with large geysers that enhance its tourist potential. Approximately 2000 tourists visit the Valley of the Geysers each year where a helipad and boardwalk have been built and some measures taken to protect it from overuse by tourists (Krever et al 1994). There are ecological education centres in both Kronotskiy Reserve and Nalychevo Park. Helicopter access to tourist cabins within Nalychevo and Southern Kamchatka Nature Reserves is available. Between 1993 and 1999 the Klyuchevskaya group averaged about 250–300 visitors a summer, 100 being foreigners, but it does not yet cater for many tourists. Projects to promote ecotourism are now underway, partly to supplement reduced government funding. The reserves are normally reached by helicopter.

Figure CS10.1 Transport to the volcanoes of Kamchatka by helicopter

The Kronotsky State Biosphere Preserve has the highest designation of all the protected areas in the UNESCO world heritage site 'Volcanoes of Kamchatka'. It is also one of the most dynamic, geologically active protected areas in the world. One of the oldest protected areas in Russia (gazetted 1939), Kronotsky is located in the south-eastern part of the Kamchatka peninsula, backed by the Vostochniy mountain range. This is Russia's largest preservation area; Kronotsky is a multi-faceted place covering 1,007,134ha of land and a 5km zone of 243km of shoreline. Nestled in a part of the Kronotsky Preserve is the Valley of Geysers. The valley is named for its multitude of geysers, situated between boiling mud pots, steam vents and warm to hot rivers. While there are other important areas of the world that feature large geysers, such as Iceland and Yellowstone National Park in the US, Kronotsky sets itself apart by its remoteness, true wilderness quality, and high concentration of geysers in one place (Kamchatka Explorer, 2009).

The Geyser Valley (Figure CS10.2) is a unique and world-famous natural feature situated on the east of Kamchatka peninsula, about 200km north-east of Petropavlovsk. It was discovered in 1941 by the Russian geologist Ustinova (Rianovosti, 2007). She found many geysers, hot springs, boiling mud, vapour springs and geothermal fields close to the River Shumnaya. Scientists of different disciplines started exploring and studying this area in the 1940s to explain why these geysers and hot springs appear, how they operate and to discover their influence on the surrounding areas. Within the steep canyon valley approximately 200 geysers exist, with many more hot springs and perpetual spouters. The geysers of this particular valley are special as many of them erupt at angles and few have the geyser cones that exist in many other geyser fields.

Geysers are natural hot springs with a permanent rhythmical activity and are quite rare. The cycle of geyser activity consists of several phases. During the initial phase, water fills an underground basin and then a pool located at ground level. On its way up to the surface the superheated water depressurizes and starts boiling. The water converts into vapour and increases its volume very rapidly, so the geyser starts exploding. These eruptions are very loud. The fountains of hot

Figure CS10.2 The Valley of the Geysers, Kamchatka

water may be vertical, for example, geysers Velikan ('The Giant') and Bolshoi ('The Great'), or inclined, as with geysers Triple and Pioneer. The fountain of Velikan geyser is 2m in diameter and reaches up to 30m. Other geysers are not so huge, although they are also very impressive. After eruption comes the phase of evaporation, and when the vapour disappears it leaves the drying empty mouth of the geyser. At the same time under the ground the water starts filling for the next eruption. The duration of a full cycle varies from geyser to geyser; Velikan, for example, erupts every three hours, the Triple geyser erupts once in two-and-a-half hours and Smaller geyser erupts every 30 minutes.

Pulsating hot springs differ from geysers as they are continuously erupting with very short calm periods. For example, Sakharnyi ('Sugar') hot spring has eruptions every four to five minutes, with a duration of about two minutes. The small pools of these hot springs are always full of boiling water pouring over the edges and forming small streams. Some of the pulsating hot springs have been geysers in the past, but changed their character for natural reasons (mainly micro relief changes) or because of human activity (EWP Ecotourism, 2009).

Every second there are about 250–300 litres of thermal water pouring out in the Geyser Valley. The various hydrothermal phenomena of Geyser Valley influence their local environment, such as rock, relief, air, soil, flora and fauna. The air has a permanent chemical laboratory smell as water vapours produced by geysers and fumaroles are associated with hydrogen sulphide, methane and other gases. Thermal grounds also do not get a permanent snow cover during the winter as the intense geothermal activity of this area has a great effect on the surrounding environment, and in spring, trees and grasses come to life long before they do in other regions. River banks are commonly overgrown with warmth-loving plants, the vegetation bursts into bud earlier in spring, birds start making nests, insects and brown bears wake up earlier too. The varied mineral compositions and temperatures of natural springs has resulted in some of them having associated health and medical resorts (EWP Ecotourism, 2009).

The 2007 event

On 3 June 2007, a devastating mudflow virtually obliterated this natural wonder, forcing the emergency evacuation of visitors and national park personnel (Rianovosti, 2007). A mound covered by snow collapsed 'within seconds' and caused a huge landslide engulfing two-thirds of the valley park. Millions of cubic metres of mud and stones were dumped in the landslide's path, destroying most of the geysers and springs. The Far East's main tourist attraction, Geyser Valley reopened for tourists on 1 July 2008, over a year after the series of devastating landslides which severely damaged the site. Enquiries from tourists wanting to visit the region rose sharply after the two mudslides buried nearly two-thirds of the valley on 3 June 2007. The mudslide dammed the Geysernaya River at the bottom of the valley, creating a thermal lake. However, despite fears that the site would never be restored to its former grandeur, the region is beginning to recover with some 30 geysers surviving intact, while only 10 have been lost forever. And although the rest are underwater, they are expected to recover as flood waters gradually subside. In addition, all the bears who left the area following the disaster have returned to the valley, which features some 200 thermal pools and 90 erupting geysers across a 6.5km² area (Kamchatka.name, 2008).

Risk management

Since the site was opened to the public in 1991, about 3000 visitors a year have visited the remote geyser field, one of only five in the world where the spectacular eruptions of steam and boiling water can be observed. And despite its relative inaccessibility, there have always been more than enough people willing to pay up to USD600 for a four-hour visit (Kamchatka.name, 2008). As the Valley of Geysers is a state guarded area included in Kronotsky State National Park, it can be accessed by organized tourists only – such travellers can follow a special route equipped with footpaths and wooden coverings. The Valley of Geysers can be dangerous; even a small event may cause scalded limbs as the most dangerous areas in the valley are covered with harmless looking grass. A person utterly unaware of the scalding slush hidden under the attractive grass blanket can hardly imagine that legs may simply be sucked down by the hot springs.

Because Kronotsky is not really a *national* park, access for the general public is limited. The special status of the reserve places the value of its wilderness and its preservation and research as its highest priority, above public use. The reserve does, however, have designated recreational zones allowing limited human use. Tourism management is focused on using ecotourism practices. It is required that one of the preserve's inspectors accompanies each tourism group to point out important conservation efforts and to provide safety and security in case of encounters with bears (Kamchatka Explorer, 2009).

Conclusions

Of highest interest in the reserve's management is joint scientific research as well as working with volunteers who have expertise in protected area management or in the field of natural resources available in the reserve. Scientists also are interested in the geothermal features in Kamchatka because they differ from other geothermal areas like those in Yellowstone National Park. The pristine nature of Kamchatka gives scientists access to a variety of recently formed and untouched geothermal features. In addition, Kamchatka's hot springs are at a relatively low elevation, unlike the hot springs of Yellowstone. This allows the water in the hot springs to reach a higher temperature before boiling, and just this few degrees more can make a significant difference in particular microbiological studies.

References

EWP Ecotourism (2009) 'Geyser Valley – Kamchatka', www.ewpnet.co.uk/kamchatka/geyser.htm, accessed 6 May 2009

Kamchatka Explorer (2009) 'Kronotsky State Biosphere Preserve', www.kamchatkatourism.com/protected-kronotsky.htm, accessed 6 May 2009

Kamchatka.name (2008) 'Kamchatka's Geyser Valley reopens for tourists', www.kamchatka.name/content/view/46/32/, accessed 6 May 2009

Krever, V., Dinerstein, E., Olson, D. and Williams, L. (1994) *Conserving Russia's Biodiversity: An Analytical Framework and Initial Investment Portfolio*, World Wide Fund for Nature, Washington, DC, p207

Rianovosti (2007) 'Mudflow destroys unique Geyser Valley on Kamchatka', www.en.rian.ru/russia/20070604/66619912.html, accessed 6 May 2009

Case Study 11

Krakatau, Indonesia

A Volcano with a History

Malcolm Cooper

Introduction

Krakatau is a stratovolcano in the Sunda Strait between the islands of Java and Sumatra in Indonesia (Thornton, 1997; Figure CS11.1). The name is used for the island group, the main island (also called Rakata) and the volcano as a whole. Indonesia has over 130 active volcanoes along the axis of the Indonesian island arc system, which are produced by north-eastward subduction of the Indo-Australian Plate. Krakatau is located directly above the subduction zone of the Eurasian Plate and the Indo-Australian Plate where the plate boundaries make a sharp change of direction, possibly resulting in an unusually weak crust in the region. The best-known eruption of Krakatau culminated in a series of massive explosions on 26–27 August 1883, which was among the most violent volcanic events in modern recorded history and contributed to the island's attraction for tourists.

Geophysical aspects and history of activity

The first massive explosion from the Krakatau volcano in 1883 (others were in AD535 and the Holocene) with a VEI of 6, ejected approximately 21km³ of rock, ash and pumice (Simkin and Fiske, 1983). The explosion was distinctly heard as far away as Perth in Western Australia (3110km, Furneaux, 1965). In the vicinity of Krakatau 165 villages and towns were destroyed and 132 seriously damaged. At least 36,417 (official toll) people died, and many thousands were injured by

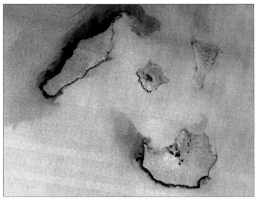

Figure CS11.1 NASA Earth Observatory Landsat picture of Krakatau Island area 18 May 1992

Source: www.en.wikipedia.org/wiki/File:Landsat_krakatau_18may92_cropped.jpg

the eruption or from the tsunamis that followed the explosion, according to official records. The eruption destroyed two-thirds of the island of Krakatau. In the year following the eruption, average global temperatures fell by as much as 1.2 degrees Celsius, and weather patterns continued to be inconsistent for years, with temperatures not returning to more normal levels until 1888.

Eruptions at the volcano since 1927 have built a new island in the same location, named Anak Krakatau ('Child of Krakatau'). This island currently has a radius of roughly 2km and a high point of 300m above sea level, and is growing by 5m each year. According to some reports (SVE Volcano News, 2009) the explosive activity at Krakatau has resumed from 22 August 2009 with strong vulcanian-type eruptions from the growing lava dome in the new crater.

Risk factors and risk management

Pumice mining was undertaken on the island until 1916 but after this ceased the western half of Rakata and Verlaten Island were designated a national monument in July 1919. The eastern half was added in 1925, and the islands were included in the Ujung Kulon Nature Reserve, which had been established in 1921. In 1982, Ujung Kulon was made a national park. This led to a political problem since the Krakatau Islands were politically controlled by the Lampung province of Sumatra, but were part of a Java-based park. This paradox was resolved in 1990, when Krakatau was made a separate nature reserve. Park rangers have a station on Sertung Island, from which they patrol the island group.

Anak Krakatau is active and does emit 'bombs' and ash. This makes it dangerous to approach at all times, so visitors are advised to remain off-shore at a distance of 3–5km in order to be relatively safe. On 6 May 2009 the Volcanological Survey of Indonesia raised the eruption alert status of Anak Krakatau to Level Orange (intermediate danger of a major eruption level).

Tourism

Krakatau occupies the same position in the tourist image of adventure and volcanoes as do Santorini or Vesuvius. It is a known powerful volcano associated with a recorded major disaster and tourists wish to see this in action if at all possible. A unique location in the middle of the Sunda Strait adds to this attraction. Krakatau can be reached from either Sumatra or Java in approximately two hours by speedboat or three-and-a-half hours by slow diesel boat. There are three islands surrounding Anak Krakatau, all of which are remnants from Krakatau before the eruption of 1883. Besides the volcano, fishing is very attractive in this location because the lagoons created by the eruption are home to giant trevally, red snapper, grouper and many other reef fish.

Wednesday 23 August each year is the anniversary of the 1883 eruption and locals and tourists have an opportunity to remember the disaster when they visit Anak during the annual Krakatau Festival – not exactly a celebration, more of a cultural memorial dedicated to one of recent history's most momentous natural disasters. While Anak Krakatau is one of the most dangerous volcanoes in the Pacific 'Ring of Fire', visitors who have their morning coffee in a boat in the shadow of the volcano in the Sunda Strait's choppy waters about a one-and-a-half-hour ride from the mainland say they feel safe (Supriyatin, 2007). Scientists monitoring the volcano say Anak Krakatau is not especially dangerous and will continue to rumble for some time, but warn people to stay out of a 3km zone around the mountain. The tourists have mixed feelings: 'We are a little worried sometimes when we heard the big boom and we see rocks that fall, I don't know, half kilometre from the hole', said one of a group of eight tourists who spent the night in a boat in the ocean to watch the volcano, 'sometimes we see the splash inside the ocean. That's a little scary but no, I think it might be stupid but I feel safe'; 'It's spectacular, it's just amazing to be here', said a tourist from New Haven in the United States, 'I feel incredibly lucky to be able to see it' (Supriyatin, 2007).

Conclusions

Krakatau then for tourism is a reminder of how dangerous a volcano can be, but also an opportunity to have a 'controlled' extreme tourism adventure. Risk management is continuous and effective through exclusion zones with respect to the volcano itself, though nothing is known about the tour boat operators or the associated fishing opportunities.

References

Furneaux, R. (1965) *Krakatoa*, Martin Secker and Warburg, London

NASA Earth Observatory Landsat picture of Krakatau island area (1992) www.en.wikipedia.org/wiki/File:Landsat_krakatau_18may92_cropped.jpg. This file is in the public domain because it was created by NASA. NASA copyright policy states that 'NASA material is not protected by copyright unless noted'. (NASA copyright policy page or JPL Image Use Policy)

Simkin, T. and Fiske, R. S. (eds) (1983) *Krakatau, 1883 – The Volcanic Eruption and Its Effects*, Smithsonian Institute Press, Washington DC

Supriyatin (2007) 'Indonesia's Krakatau roars, dazzles with fireworks', *Thomson Reuters*, Sunday, 11 November

SVE Volcano News (2009) 'Indonesia volcanoes activity VSI – CVGDM reports: Recent events in 2008–2009: Anak Krakatau (Sunda Strait)', www.sveurop.org/gb/news/news.htm, accessed 25 September 2009

Thornton, I. W. B. (1997) *Krakatau: The Destruction and Reassembly of an Island Ecosystem*, Harvard University Press, Boston, MA

Case Study 12

Geothermal Attractions and Active Volcanoes in China

Malcolm Cooper

Introduction

The most recent volcanoes of China are distributed generally in the north and west of the country (Jilin, Heilongjiang Provinces, Nei Mongolia, Tibet) or the south west (Hainan, Qiongzhou Strait, Tengchong). It is possible to find representatives of almost all types of former volcanic activity in these areas, from basaltic magmatic eruptions and phreatomagmatic explosions, strato and shield volcanoes, lava cones, pyroclastic cones (spatter cones, cinder cones), lava tubes and maars. An interesting feature of Chinese volcanoes is that they are designated as biosphere reserves, national parks or, increasingly, national or provincial geoparks. Several have also been designated Global Geoparks (Table CS12.1). As a consequence they are important tourism resources in educational and scenic terms, as well as for their current and/or past geothermal activity.

Geophysical aspects and history of activity

There are a number of very large volcanic fields in China; the *Hainan Dong* on Hainan Island, for example, covers 4100km². Another example is the Kunlun Volcanic Group that stretches some 1000km in Tibet. The underlying geological reason for this group structure is the Kunlun strike-slip fault that bounds the north side of Tibet. Left-lateral motion along the 1500km length of

the Kunlun Group has occurred uniformly for the last 40,000 years at a rate of 1.1cm/yr, giving a cumulative offset of more than 400m, with resulting periodic massive earthquakes and volcanic events (70 pyroclastic cones; Seach, 2009).

A newly discovered field is that of Arshan (Arxan) in Inner Mongolia, 70km from the border with Mongolia. The field includes cinder cones, pyroclastic sheets and lava flows, with more than 40 cinder cones in the group. The most recent eruptions occurred at Yanshan cone (local relief 362m), and Gaoshan crater (140m deep) in approximately 100 AD. Basaltic lava flows also occurred, creating six lava-dam lakes that are now tourist attractions.

On a world-wide basis mud volcanoes are remarkably uncommon, found in only about 20 countries around the world, and they are highly unpredictable. 'Erupting' at intervals and oozing streams of thick, sticky mud and flammable gas, mud volcanoes are a fascinating variant in our catalogue of volcano-based tourism, and one exists in Taiwan in the Southern-most county of Pingtung. This particular volcano erupts several times a year, opening up a fresh crater in a new position each time. Mud volcanoes are very common in Azerbaijan and it is believed that nearly half of the world's approximately 700 mud volcanoes are located in this country (Gallagher, 2003).

On a more traditional note, the Tengchong area in Yunnan is a large volcanic field located on the border of the Europe-Asia continental plate, and since 1500 AD there have been over 70 earthquakes in the area measuring 5 and over on

Table CS12.1 Volcanoes of China

Location	Type	Height (Metres)	Global geopark	Last erupted
Changbaishan (Baekdu), Jilin Province	Stratovolcano	2773		1702, 1994?
Honggeertu, Nie Mongolia	20 Cinder Cones	1700		Holocene
Jingbo, Heilongjiang Province	Volcanic Field	500	Yes	520BC
Keluo, Heilongjiang Province	14 Pyroclastic Cones	670		Holocene
Kunlun Group, Tibet	70 Pyroclastic Cones	5608		1951
Leizhou Bandao Group, 480km SW of Hong Kong, northern part of Leiqiong global geopark	Volcanic Field (Cenozoic basalts)	259	Yes	Holocene
Longgang, Jilin Province	150 Cinder Cones	1000		350
Tengchong (Myanmar border area)	97 Pyroclastic Cones (Burma Arc Microplate) and Rehai Geothermal Field	2865		1609 (Hydrothermal eruptions post 1993)
Tianshan, 440km W of Urumchi	Volcanic Field	–		650
Turfan, 168km W of Urumchi	Cone	–		1120
Unnamed, NW Tibet	Volcanic Field	5400		Holocene
Wudalianchi, Heilongjiang Province	14 Pyroclastic Cones	597	Yes	1776
Luishan Mud Volcano, Taiwan	Mud & Gas Volcano	–		2009
Tatun Volcanic Group, 15km N of Taipei, Taiwan	Hydrothermal	1120		Constant, last major volcanic event Holocene
Arshan, Nei Mongolia	40+ Cinder Cones	362		100
Datong, 265km W of Beijing	6 Cinder Cones	1422		450
Hainan Dong, N Hainan Island	30+ Pyroclastic Cones, continuation of Leiqiong volcanic field global geopark	–	Yes	1933

Source: after Siebert & Simkin, 2002; Seach, 2009, revised to include Taiwan.

the Richter scale (China Yunnan Travel Information, 2009). Tengchong has the best well-preserved volcano groups from the Cenozoic Era in China, but more importantly for tourism over 80 geothermal springs are scattered around the volcanoes, making this the second largest hydrothermal field in China. Yihong Hot Lake is one of the biggest geothermal lakes in China, covering a total area of 10km². The natural hot springs are also popular with visitors because of their medicinal effects on the human body.

Risk factors

As the volcanoes listed in Table 12.1 are not presently active in terms of eruptions, the risk factors associated with them are generally those of thermal burns from boiling water. Tengchong's *Dagungou* (Big Boiling Pot) hot spring is 6.1m in diameter and 1.5m deep and has a surface water temperature of 87.7°C (Liu et al, 2000) to 96.6°C (Wu, 2003). Tengchong's volcanoes are described by Wu (2003) as although they 'have been sleeping for centuries, people can hear their snore and feel their breath while they visit the hot springs scattered around Tengchong'. Earthquakes, rockslides (Changbaishan), and other risks common to extreme environments are present as well as those relating to visitor activity and tourism's impact on the environment.

Tourism

China is currently the world's fourth largest inbound tourism market (55 million visitors and foreign exchange income of USD41.9 billion in 2007) and is ranked fifth in terms of total outbound expenditure (UNWTO, 2008). In 2007 the number of domestic tourists reached 1.61 billion, distributing 777 billion Yuan to domestic destinations. By 2020, according to the UNWTO, China will become the top ranked tourist country in the world. This is a long way from the situation in the late 1970s when only 230,000 foreign visitors were allowed to enter, or for domestic tourism before local travel restrictions were lifted in the early 1980s. The volcanoes of China feature strongly in both inbound and domestic tourism, Changbaishan is, for example, listed as a 'famous natural site' as well as an important home to the rare Siberian Tiger, and Hainan is referred to as the 'Hawai'i of the Orient', complete with volcano, but this is mainly due to the existence of hot springs and spectacular scenery rather than the potential for more dangerous activity on the part of the volcanoes.

Risk management

Risk management in the Chinese volcano tourism context is, accordingly, more about conserving biodiversity through Geopark, World Heritage and National Park status. Changbaishan Biosphere Reserve (designated 1979) is a case in point, where vegetation diversity and the fauna generate management issues, mapping, planning and zoning measures and the *fact* of the volcano is limited to preserving visual amenity from the lookouts, preserving the biological status of the caldera lake, and preserving/utilizing the hot springs found within the river beds that flank the mountains. Since joining the *International Convention Concerning the Protection of World Cultural and Natural Heritage* in 1985, China has had 38 world heritage sites listed to date; of these 27 are cultural heritage sites,

seven are natural heritage sites, and four are cultural and natural (mixed) sites. There are 28 biosphere reserves and 44 Geoparks (of which 20 are on UNESCO's world Geopark list).

For a Geopark to qualify as a global Geopark it needs to have:

- a management plan designed to foster socio-economic development that is sustainable (most likely to be based on agritourism and geotourism);
- demonstrate methods for conserving and enhancing geological heritage and provide means for teaching geoscientific disciplines and broader environmental issues; and
- joint proposals submitted by public authorities, local communities and private interests acting together, which demonstrate the best practices with respect to Earth heritage conservation and its integration into sustainable development strategies.

Thus the risk management associated with this form of tourist attraction is similar to that practised in relation to biosphere reserves and world heritage sites, and the forms of extreme tourism that do occur are those relating in the main to mountain climbing. Nevertheless, these areas are volcanic in origin and remain prone to earthquakes, as well as having hot springs and other activities that need to be managed for their risk. For example, as noted above, in the Tongcheng (Rehai geothermal area) volcano field the main attraction is Dagunguo (Big Boiling Bowl), a large spring that reaches a temperature of 97°C (China Culture Center, 2008). Locals offer visitors eggs cooked in the spring's heat, and hot water is ejected intermittently into the nearby streams. Among the numerous smaller springs and geysers, the park also has cooler springs suitable for bathing, including the Frog Mouth, Lion Head, Pearl and Drum-beat Springs. All these assets are included in and controlled by the Park Management Plan.

Risk management is also enhanced by the conversion of nature parks into fully fledged geoparks. A further two parks in China, Qinling Geopark in Shannxi Province and Aixa Geopark in Inner Mongolia were designated during August

2009 as this book was being compiled. China now has 22 geoparks, which aim to promote the goals of developing sustainable environments, educating in the earth sciences at large, and fostering sustainable local economic development (Xinhua News Agency, August 23, 2009).

References

China Culture Center (2008) 'Tengchong', www. chinaculturecenter.org/chinaguide/regions/ yunnan/tengchong/, accessed 4 August, 2009

Gallagher, R. (2003) 'Mud volcanoes – mysterious phenomena fascinate scientists and tourists', http:// azer.com/aiweb/categories/magazine/ai112_ folder/112_articles/112_mud_volcano.html, accessed 20 July 2009

Liu, Z., Yuan, D., He, S., Zhang, M. and Zhang, J. (2000) 'Geochemical features of the geothermal CO_2-watercarbonate rock system and analysis on its CO_2 sources', *Science in China (Series D)*, vol 43, no 6, pp571–576

Siebert. L. and Simkin, T. (2002) *Volcanoes of the World: an Illustrated Catalog of Holocene Volcanoes and their Eruptions*, Smithsonian Global Volcanism Program Digital Information Series, GVP-3, Smithsonian, Washington, DC

Seach, J. (2009) 'Volcanoes of the world', www. volcanolive.com/world.html, accessed 4 August, 2009

UNESCO (2009) 'Global network of National Geoparks', www.unesco.org/science/earth/geoparks.html, accessed 4 August, 2009

UNWTO (2008) *Travel Barometer*, UNWTO, Madrid

Wu, S. (2002) 'Hometown of volcano jade and hot springs', http://edu.sina.com.cn/en/2002-06-30/4022.html, accessed 25 July 2009

Xinhua News Agency (2009) 'Five geoparks newly approved as global geoparks network members, Xinhua News Agency, August 23, 2009

Part V

Europe

Introduction

Europe has both dormant as well as very active volcanic regions and volcano tourism has been practised for several centuries with increasing ease of access as well as growing visitor numbers. Travellers to Italy include visits to Vesuvius and Etna in their trip agendas. In Spain it is often Mt Teide on the Canary Islands which draws over three million visitors annually and in Greece the islands of Santorini and Nisyros are popular for their volcanic heritage. Turkey's bizarre landscapes of Cappadocia are also of volcanic origin; so is the Vulkaneifel in Germany and the Auvergne in France. Iceland, located in the far north of the Atlantic, offers volcano and geothermal tourism all over the country due to its unique landforms and spectacular scenery which offers insights into the geologic processes continuing to this day. Several volcanic regions of Europe are presented here as an important sector integrated within mainstream tourism. Additional short case studies cover areas well known for their volcanic and geothermal activity, including world heritage listed sites.

14

Emerging Volcano and Geothermal Related Tourism in Iceland

Ross Dowling

Introduction

Iceland is located in the North Atlantic Ocean just south of the Arctic Circle. At 103,000km² in size, it is the world's 18th largest island, and Europe's second largest island following Great Britain. It is considered to be a part of Europe, not North America, though geologically the island belongs to both continents. Due to its cultural, economic and linguistic similarities, in some contexts Iceland is also included in Scandinavia. It is reasonably remote with its nearest neighbours being Greenland (287km) and the Faroe Islands (420km). The population is 316,000, and its capital city Reykjavik is the world's northernmost one. The majority of the people live in coastal areas near the capital with other major towns scattered around the coast. Only a quarter of the country is vegetated and much of the remainder is lakes, glaciers or lava-covered wasteland.

Geology and volcanism

Sitting astride the Mid-Atlantic Ridge, Iceland's geology is a work in progress as it is the youngest country in Europe (Einarsson, 2006). It has 22 active volcanoes, 250 geothermal areas, 780 hot springs, and the world's third largest ice-cap. It is one of the world's most active hot-spots with one-third of all the lava to surface on Earth in the last 1000 years being of Icelandic origin.

Nowhere on Earth is such a showcase of volcanic features found (Harlow, 2008) and on average there are eruptions occurring every four to five years (Guðmundsson, 2007). The volcanoes include Hekla, Eldgjá and Eldfell and the eruption of Laki in 1783–1784 caused dust clouds and haze to appear over most of Europe and parts of Asia and Africa for months after the eruption. Recent eruptions have included the new island of Surtsey, which rose above the ocean in a series of volcanic eruptions between 1963 and 1968. A second occurred on the island of Heimaey in 1973 which produced the new red cinder cone Eldfell, and a third is Hekla which produced a series of powerful earthquakes which shook the country in 2000.

Iceland has a high concentration of active volcanoes due to unique geological conditions (Wikipedia, 2009a). The island has about 130 volcanic mountains, of which 18 have erupted since the settlement of Iceland. Over the past 500 years, Iceland's volcanoes have erupted a third of the total global lava output. Although the Laki eruption in 1783 had the largest eruption of lava in the last 500 years, the Eldgjá eruption of 934AD and other Holocene eruptions were even larger. Geologists explain this high concentration of volcanic activity as being due to a combination of the island's position on the Mid-Atlantic Ridge and a volcanic hotspot underneath the island (Thordurson and Hoskuldsson, 2002; Jonasson, 2007). The island sits astride the boundary between the Eurasian and North American Plates, and most volcanic activity is concentrated along the plate boundary, which runs across the island from the south-west to the north-east of the island. Some volcanic activity occurs offshore, especially off the southern coast. This includes wholly submerged submarine volcanoes and even newly formed volcanic islands such as Surtsey and Jólnir.

Iceland's other landform features include geysers such as Geysir, from which the English word is derived. The word geyser simply means 'one that erupts with vigour' (Guðmundsson, 2007). This is now inactive but the nearby geyser of Strokkur is a major tourist drawcard. The geysers lie in the geothermal area of the Haukadalur Valley.

Iceland is composed primarily of basalt, similar to the islands of Hawai'i, but it also has various kinds of volcanoes, many of which produce more evolved lavas such as rhyolite and andesite. Glaciers cover one-ninth of Iceland's land surface and Vatnajökull in the south-east covers almost 13 per cent of the country, and is the largest glacier in Europe. Iceland also has a number of spectacular waterfalls, of which Dettifoss, located in north-eastern Iceland, is the most powerful in Europe.

Sea-floor spreading continues today and Iceland is still growing in size. Volcanic eruptions occur on average every three to five years, with some occurring under the extensive ice-caps. Added to the volcanoes and earthquakes are the constant erosive forces of frost, wind and sea, sculpting its already youthful landforms even further.

Tourism

Tourism is growing in Iceland. Over the past decade the number of travellers to Iceland has grown at an average annual rate of 11 per cent, and in 2007 Iceland had more than 530,000 international visitors, mostly from Europe and North America (Icelandic Tourist Board, 2005; Rannsoknir and Radgj of Ferdapjonustunnar, 2008). The tourism sector is expanding, with the recent trends incorporating ecotourism, including bird watching and whale watching, as well as

adventure tourism, including cycling, glacier exploration and snowmobiling.

Iceland offers a great variety of tours, some covering large parts of the country, others small areas at a time. Nature tours focus on the striking landscapes, young lava fields, roaring waterfalls and majestic glacial ice-caps. In addition, there are organized day tours, and weekend and holiday tours all year round with Icelandic touring clubs where the emphasis is on hiking. Travelling into the uninhabited interior of Iceland is limited to the months of July and August, except for some specially organized winter tours. Winter tours in Iceland include skiing, glacier tours on snowmobile or snowcats, and ice-fishing.

Iceland has four national parks – Þingvellir, Snæfellsjökull, Jökulsárgljúfur and Skaftafell. Þingvellir, the country's oldest national park and 'Symbol of Icelandic Consciousness', is famous for its scenic 84km² lake and the geologically significant Almannagjá rift valley separating the American and European continental plates. Snaefellsjökull National Park in west Iceland extends from the mountains to the sea protecting the Snaefellsjökull glacier and surrounding lava fields and coast. Jökulsárgljúfur National Park in north-east Iceland has been formed by torrents gushing down from the Vatnajökull glacier and it contains Dettifoss, the largest waterfall in Europe. Skaftafell National Park in south-east Iceland is a beautiful wilderness area and includes much of the Vatnajökull glacier.

Whereas ecotourism and adventure tourism are well established in Iceland, geological tourism, or more simply geotourism, is in its infancy (Dowling, 2008). The most popular tour in Iceland is 'The Golden Circle' which includes some of the best known geological attractions in the country (Guðmundsson, 2007). They are Þingvellir, Gullfoss and Geysir. These sites make up Iceland's major tourist destinations offering visitors the opportunity to see its most important historical area, a major waterfall and an area of hot springs. At Þingvellir the Vikings established the world's first democratic parliament, the Althing, in AD930. Þingvellir became a national park in 1928 due to its historical importance, as well as the special tectonic and volcanic environment. Evidence of continental drift can be seen in the cracks or faults which cross the region, the biggest one, Almannagjá, being a large canyon. Here the plates of the Earth's crust are moving apart causing earthquakes in the area.

Þingvellir is situated on the northern shore of Þingvallavatn (assembly plains lake), the largest natural lake of Iceland. The Öxará River traverses the national park and forms a waterfall at the Almannagjá, called Öxarárfoss. Þingvellir was designated a UNESCO world heritage site in 2004. Gullfoss (Golden Falls) is a waterfall located in the canyon of Hvítá River in south-west Iceland. It is one of the most popular tourist attractions in the country. The falls plunge in two stages (11m and 21m) into a crevice 32m deep. The average amount of water running over this waterfall is 140 cubic metres/second. Near to the falls is a visitor centre explaining the geology of the falls as well as their history, which at one point included being considered for use for hydroelectric power generation.

Volcanic and geothermal related tourism

There are a number of volcanoes and geothermal areas in Iceland but the greatest concentration is in the southern part of the island in 'The Golden Circle', the Reykjanes peninsula, and off the coast in the Vestmannaeyjar Islands.

The Golden Circle

The Golden Circle comprises the three areas of Þingvellir, Gullfoss and Geysir. Together they make up Iceland's major tourism destination. Þingvellir is an area renowned for its natural beauty and historic significance and was first established as a national park in 1928 and as a world heritage region in 2004 (Parnell and O'Carroll, 2007). Gullfoss is the country's most famous waterfall which drops 32m in a spectacular two tier cascade (Figure 14.1) and Geysir is one of Iceland's most famous tourist

Figure 14.1 Gullfoss (Golden Falls) waterfall, part of Iceland's 'Golden Circle' tourist route

attractions, as the original geyser after which all others around the world are named.

Historically Geysir is Iceland's most famous tourist attraction. It is the original hot water spout from which all others are named. It has had a history of intermittent eruptions and in recent times earthquakes have tended to revive its activity. Changes in the activity of the Geysir and the surrounding geysers are strongly related to earthquake activity. In records dated 1630 the geysers erupted so violently that the valley around them trembled.

The neighbouring geyser Strokkur erupts to heights of up to 30m approximately every five minutes. Both Geysir and Strokkur are surrounded by 30 much smaller geysers and hot pools in the area, including one called Litli Geysir (Little Geysir). At the geyser site there is a tourist complex which contains a Geoscience Centre housing an audiovisual exhibition on geysers and volcanoes with an earthquake simulator (Figure 14.2).

Also in this region is the explosion crater Kerið. It is a cinder cone considered to have erupted 5000–6000 years ago. Today much red earth is visible on the inside of the crater, caused by oxidation of iron in the magma (Guðmundsson, 2007). The bottom of the crater is below the groundwater table so it is often covered in water. As with many geological features in Iceland, the geo-attraction is well interpreted with full signage explaining its formation (Figure 14.3).

The Reykjanes peninsula

Nowhere on Earth is the junction between the American and European tectonic plates in the Earth's crust as clear as on the Reykjanes peninsula in the south-west. Here the plates diverge by as much as 2cm per year but the gap is constantly being filled, as volcanoes have been erupting regularly throughout Iceland's history (Visit Iceland, 2009). The Reykjanes peninsula is an area of dramatic lava landscapes, geothermal activity

Figure 14.2 Geysisstofa: An audiovisual exhibition on geysers and volcanoes

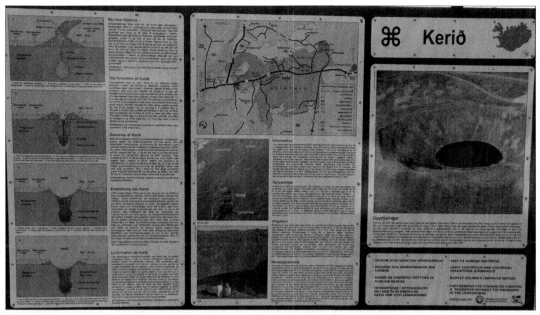

Figure 14.3 Geological interpretive sign on the rim of the Kerið explosion crater

and a striking coastline. Its tourism marketing is 'Reykjanes Peninsula: Crossing Continents' (Hlooversson and Nielsen, 2008; Figure 14.4). The region sits astride the Mid-Atlantic Ridge and includes virtually every volcanic feature in Iceland (Harlow, 2008). Activity during the Ice Age produced tuff ridges which run its length, while post-glacial lavas and craters are also found.

Several high-temperature geothermal areas are found on the Reykjanes peninsula, two of which have been harnessed to generate electricity, at Svartsengi and Hengill. A further two geothermal power stations are currently under construction: Hellisheiði Power Station and Reykjanes Power Station. At Svartsengi, the Gjáin visitor centre explains geological history, and nearby is the Blue Lagoon spa, whose mineral-rich waters are internationally known for their curative powers (Erfurt-Cooper and Cooper, 2009). In many geothermal areas villages have sprung up growing fruits and vegetables in greenhouses heated by the hot springs.

The Blue Lagoon

On the peninsula is the Blue Lagoon, one of Iceland's major tourist attractions (Figure 14.5). The geothermal spa is located in a lava field in Grindavík on the peninsula and is one of the most visited attractions in Iceland. The water temperature in the lagoon averages 40°C and the waters are rich in minerals like silica and sulphur. The lagoon is fed by the water output of the nearby geothermal power plant Svartsengi (Wikipedia, 2009b). Superheated water is vented from the ground near a lava flow and used to run turbines that generate electricity. After going through the turbines, the steam and hot water pass through a heat exchanger to provide heat for the Keflavik municipal hot water heating system, then the water is fed into the lagoon for recreational and medicinal users to bathe in.

The super-heated seawater is rich in blue-green algae, mineral salts and fine silica mud giving it a bright blue colour. The waters are surrounded by black lava with the steam rising from the geothermal plant adding to the surreal setting. While more of a spa setting than a geotourism one, nevertheless the fabulous geological setting provides tourists with an incredible geologically inspired experience enhanced by its Lava Restaurant built into the cliff and featuring a natural lava wall.

Nearby in Gjáin (The Rift) is a dramatic exhibition of Icelandic geology. It comprises an

Figure 14.4 Reykjanes Peninsula 'Crossing Continents' brochure

Figure 14.5 The Blue Lagoon, Iceland's leading tourism attraction, is a milky-blue spa fed by geothermal waters set in a tortured black lava field

Figure 14.6 Midpoint interpretive signage

exhibition of geology, geothermal heat and energy conservation and is brought to life through multimedia displays. Also close by, in the former NATO military base a comprehensive centre of scientific, academic and economic knowledge is being built up in the area of Vallarheidi. The centre's aim is to expand international education in the field of geosciences, tourism and sustainable development.

The 'Bridge between Two Continents'

Also on the Reykjanes peninsula lies the 'Bridge between Two Continents', a remarkable and dedicated geotourism attraction. It is situated on the lava-scarred peninsula where two of the Earth's tectonic plates split. The 'bridge' spans the two continents and is situated in the Alfagja rift valley, a chasm marking the boundary of the North American and Eurasian continental tectonic plates. Crossing the bridge takes you from North

America to Europe with the midpoint marked by a sign (Figure 14.6).

Vestmannaeyjar

Vestmannaeyjar (The Westmen Isles) is a small archipelago off the south coast of Iceland. It comprises 16 islands, the largest of which is Heimaey (13.4km²) which has a population of 4000 (Ruriksson, 1995). The islands are named after the Irish from the Old Norse word Vestmenn (Wikipedia, 2009c). The region is volcanically active with two major eruptions in recent times. They are the creation of the island of Surtsey in 1963 and the eruption of Eldfell on the island of Heimaey a decade later.

The miracle of Surtsey

The island of Surtsey was created by an undersea volcanic eruption in 1963 (Figure 14.7). It was first seen by the crew of a fishing boat, *Ísleifí II*

Figure 14.7 Surtsey World Heritage Region

Source: Oscar Friðriksson

from Vestmannaeyjar early on the morning of 14 November 1963. They had laid their fishing lines 7km west of Geirfuglaskeri, which at that time was the southern-most island in the Vestmannaeyjar archipelago and consequently the southern-most point of Iceland. They described what they saw as though the sea was 'on fire'. Over the next four years the island grew in size due to continuous eruptions, which only stopped for short periods.

By April 1964 the island had grown to about one square kilometre and now the lava began to run from the crater in a similar fashion to that of eruptions on land. Streams of lava exploded 50 to 100 metres into the air and rivers of hot molten lava streamed down into the sea. In this way formations of rock were created from the thin layers of lava. The lava ran out over the edge of the crater and also through long tunnels into the ocean. These tunnels of streaming lava made the many caves that exist on Surtsey today. When the Surtsey eruption ceased in June 1967, the volcano had produced 1.1km^3 of material, 70 per cent of

which was tuff and 30 per cent lava. Only 9 per cent was above sea level but formed a 2.8km^2 island.

The Surtsey eruption is one of the best documented submarine eruptions of all time. Because of erosion, the island has now been reduced to 1.5km^2. Vegetation was found on the island quite soon after the eruption with the first plant being discovered there in 1965. By 1990 over 20 different types of plants had been found and five species of birds have also established their homes on the island. Surtsey is a protected area and travel to the island is only allowed for scientific reasons and with special permission. Because the island is an area where the natural evolutionary processes have been able to act without any kind of human impact, scientists have been able to gather invaluable information in this unusual natural 'science laboratory'.

As a result of this unique situation, the island was added to UNESCO's world heritage list in 2008 for its major role in studies of succession and colonization. It has been the site of one of the few long-term studies worldwide on primary succession, providing a unique scientific record of the process of colonization of land by plants, animals and marine organisms. Not only is it geographically isolated, but it has been legally protected from its birth, providing the world with a pristine natural laboratory, free from human interference. Above all, because of its continuing protection, Surtsey will continue to provide invaluable data on biological colonization long into the future, since the degree to which the island remains undisturbed is outstanding. Apart from a small helicopter platform and a cabin for research work, the island is undisturbed. While there is no tourism on the island, visitors to Vestmannaeyjar often visit the area by taking flights over it or boat trips to view it from the sea.

The volcanoes of Heimaey

Heimaey is the only inhabited island in Vestmannaeyjar. The most prominent feature on Heimaey before 1973 was Helgafell, a 200m high volcanic cone formed in an eruption about 5000 years ago. However, on 23 January 1973 a volcanic eruption began without warning on the island just outside the town. This eventually led to the formation of a new volcanic cone Eldfell (Fire Mountain), which is 220m high.

During the initial eruption a fissure opened up on the eastern side of the island, barely a kilometre away from the centre of the town of Heimaey (Bárðarson and Jónasdóttir, 2003). The fissure rapidly extended from 300m to a length of 2km, crossing the island from one shore to the other. Submarine activity also occurred just offshore at the northern and southern ends of the fissure. Spectacular lava fountaining 50 to 150 metres high occurred along the whole fissure, which reached a maximum length of about 3km during the first few hours of the eruption, but activity soon became concentrated on one vent, about 0.8km north of the old volcanic cone of Helgafell and just outside the eastern edge of the town.

In total, the volume of lava and tephra emitted during the five-month eruption was estimated to be about 0.25km³. About 2.5km² of new land was added to the island, increasing its pre-eruption

area by some 20 per cent. In the end, the harbour entrance was narrowed considerably but not closed off, and the new lava flow acted as a breakwater, actually improving the shelter afforded by the harbour. Flakkarinn rafted several hundred metres towards the harbour along the top of the lava flow, but came to a halt well away from the water's edge.

By the end of the eruption, Eldfell stood about 220 metres above sea level. Since then, its height has dropped by 18 to 20 metres due to slumping and compacting of the unconsolidated gravelly tephra as well as to wind erosion. The islanders have planted grass around the lower slopes of the otherwise bare hill, to stabilize it against further erosion, and eventually it is expected that most of the volcano will be covered by grass, as neighbouring Helgafell is.

Tourism in Vestmannaeyjar

The islands are famed in Iceland for their yearly festival which attracts a large portion of the nation's youth (Ruriksson, 1995). The festival was originally held in 1874 concurrent with Iceland's celebration commemorating the 1000th anniversary of the inhabitation of Iceland. Vestmannaeyjar residents had been prevented by weather from sailing to the mainland for the festivities and thus celebrated locally. Over the last century, the festival has grown to become the largest festival in Iceland, with an annual attendance of 10,000, with up to 7000 travelling from mainland Iceland.

On the main island of Heimaey, the 1973 eruption of Eldfell created a 1.5km fissure which split the eastern side of the island. The eruption area formed a new mountain and the island increased in size by 2.3km². One third of the town on the island was buried beneath the lava flow and today the resulting cinder cone is a major tourist drawcard (Figure 14.8). The marketing of Vestmannaeyjar for tourists is now focused on its volcanic heritage with its latest brochure entitled 'Vestmannaeyjar: Volcanic World' (Figure 14.9). It has given rise to the local tourist attraction of a volcanic film show which focuses on the eruption as well as the new Volcanic World tourist attraction based on excavations of some of the islanders' houses buried by the Eldfell eruption.

Figure 14.8 English school students on an Icelandic study tour, climbing Eldfell, July 2008

Figure 14.9 Vestmannaeyjar 'Volcanic World' marketing brochure, 2009

Eldheimar – 'The Pompei of the North' tourist attraction

Currently the local council is developing an exciting geotourism attraction called 'Eldheimar – the Pompei of the North'. This is based on the 1973 eruption, which occurred 5000 years after the preceding one, causing its 5000 inhabitants to flee to the mainland. The eruption continued for five months engulfing 400 houses in lava and tephra. The proposed attraction aims to excavate 14 of the former houses which were buried in tephra by the eruption. Inside the houses are all of their contents which were buried four days after the eruption commenced.

The excavations so far have revealed much that is well preserved over the past 35 years, and it is hoped that some of the home's former residents will be able to recover some of their treasured possessions that they thought were lost forever. At present excavations have commenced and the tops of some houses are exposed. Interpretive signs have been erected and it is already attracting many visitors. When completed it is hoped to have excavated seven to ten houses so that in time a small village will be on display so that tourists and visitors will be able to more easily comprehend the extent of the devastation that the volcanic eruption caused.

The future of geotourism in Iceland

Iceland is a country of geological superlatives. It has a sound tourism industry, emerging geotourism attractions, and the base to establish a number of geoparks. The future for geotourism in this country is bright and could be enhanced if it embraced the concept of geoparks. A geopark is a nationally protected area containing a number of geological heritage sites of particular importance, rarity or aesthetic appeal (UNESCO, 2006). They are part of an integrated concept of protection, education and sustainable development and geoparks achieve their goals through conservation, education and geotourism.

The country has two world heritage regions, four national parks and 80 nature reserves, but as yet has no geoparks. Yet Iceland is a geotourist's dream destination and with appropriate development and smart marketing it could capture this emerging market. Thus this presentation makes the case for Iceland to become a geopark and capitalize on the rising interest of geotourism in general, and geoparks in particular. In essence, the whole of Iceland could be proposed as a global geopark. It is a geologist's paradise and a magnificent attraction for geotourists. It has been described as 'a living showcase of nature' and 'probably nowhere else on earth exhibits such a variety of volcanic activity' (Jonasson, 2007). However, three places naturally lend themselves to immediate geopark development. They are the Reykjanes peninsula, the Vestmannaeyjar islands and Þingvellir.

The Reykjanes peninsula is the first place in Iceland that may form the basis of a geopark. A group led by Landvernd, the Icelandic Environment Association, is currently pursuing this possibility. The peninsula is the site of Keflavik International Airport, where most international visitors arrive in the country. Such a geopark would probably focus on Mid Atlantic Ridge passing through it with its Bridge between Two Continents, Svartsengi geothermal plant, the Blue Lagoon tourist attraction, and the Vallarheidi with its focus on international education in geosciences, tourism and sustainable development.

Another ideal geopark site is the Vestmannaeyjar islands focusing on the only inhabited island Heimaey, with its twin volcanic cones of Helgafell and Eldfell provide easy access for geotourists wishing to get up close to recent volcanoes. The film show of the 1973 Eldfell eruption is an excellent geotourism attraction but the emerging 'Pompei of the North' buried village attraction currently being developed, provides one of the most exciting geotourism developments in the country and with a state-of-the-art visitor centre, the attraction could form the centre piece of a global geopark.

Finally, the region of Þingvellir has been a nature reserve for over 80 years. It is the country's spiritual heartland, a national park, and a world heritage site. Lying in the path of the Mid Atlantic Ridge, it is an area of exceptional geological interest where one can view the tectonic forces which have shaped, and are continuing to shape, the landscape. The land is an area of exceptional beauty and together with Gullfoss and Geysir, these combined geological attractions make Þingvellir a remarkable set of attributes from which a geopark could be formed.

A five-year tourism development plan is currently being undertaken in north-east Iceland based on geotourism (Hull et al, 2008). The planning and development of tourism in this region will require public–private partnerships which help to maintain the tourism industry businesses over the long term (Hull, in press). Such tourism should be small-scale and sustainable, fostering conservation of geological features at the same time as delivering economic and social benefits to host communities. In time, this is what is needed for all other regions of Iceland – then the promise of volcano and geothermal related tourism will deliver benefits to all Icelandic people.

Acknowledgements

Much of the information in this chapter was derived from field work in Iceland conducted in mid 2008. Whilst there I was generously hosted by

Elias Fridriksson and Kolbrim Kristjansdótter. I also wish to thank the following for their assistance and advice whilst in the country: Ellioi Vignisson, Mayor, Vestmannaeyjar; Ms Guðríður Þorvarðardóttir, Divisional Manager, Department for Legal and Administrative Affairs, Environment Agency of Iceland; Mr Bergur Sigurdsson, Managing Director, Landvernd, Icelandic Environment Association; and Ms Katrin Anna Lund and Dr Anna Karlsdóttir, Department of Geography and Tourism Studies, University of Iceland. Finally I wish to thank the Perth Convention Bureau for awarding me the 2007 Perth Airport Tourism and Aviation Scholarship, part of the proceeds of which assisted me with the costs incurred in this research.

References

Bárðarson, H. and Jónasdótter, M. (2003) 'When the earth split open: 30 years from the Heimaey eruption', *Icelandic Geographic*, vol 2, pp28–34

Dowling, R. K. (2008) 'Geotourism in Iceland', in Dowling, R. and Newsome, D. (eds) *Geotourism*, Proceedings of the Inaugural Global Geotourism Conference 'Discover the Earth Beneath our Feet', Fremantle, Western Australia, 17–20 August, Promaco Conventions Pty Ltd, pp151–157

Einarsson, þorleifur (2006) *The Geology of Iceland: Rocks and Landscape*, Mál og Menning, Reykjavik, Iceland

Erfurt-Cooper, P. and Cooper, M. (2009) Health and Wellness Tourism: Spas and Hot Springs, Channel View Publications, Bristol, UK

Guðmundsson, H. (2007) *The Golden Circle*, JPV Publishers, Reykjavik, Iceland

Harlow, C. (2008) *Iceland*, Landmark Publishing, Ashbourne

Hlooversson, V. and Nielsen, B. (eds) (2008) *Reykjanes Peninsula: Crossing Continent*, The Icelandic Tourism Association, Reykjanes, Iceland

Hull, J. (in press) 'Promoting Geotourism in the Land of Fire and Ice: A Case Study from Northeast Iceland', in Dowling, R. and Newsome, D. (eds) *Geotourism: The Tourism of Geology and Landscape*, Goodfellow Publishers, Oxford

Hull, J., Patterson, C., Huijbens, E. and Milne, S. (2008) *The State of Affairs of Tourism in Northeast Iceland, Report #*, Althing, Husavik, Iceland, forthcoming

Icelandic Tourist Board (2005) *Tourism in Iceland: In Figures*, Icelandic Tourism Board, Reykjavik

Jonasson, B. (ed) (2007) *The Geology of Iceland*, JPV Publishers, Reykjavik, Iceland

Parnell, F. and O'Carroll, E. (2007) *Iceland*, Lonely Planet Publications, Footscray, Australia

Rannsoknir and Radgj of Ferdapjonustunnar (2008) *Ferðamenn í Þingeyjarsýslum 2001–2007*, Reykjavik

Ruriksson, B. (1994) *The Westman Islands*, Geoscan Publishing, Seltjarnarnes, Iceland

Thordarson, T. and Hoskuldsson, A. (2002) *Classic Geology in Europe: Iceland*, Terra Publishing, Hertfordshire, UK

UNESCO (2006) *Global Geoparks Network*, United Nations Educational, Scientific and Cultural Organization, Paris

Visit Iceland (2009) 'Iceland regions: South and southwest Iceland', www.visiticeland.com, accessed 1 August 2009

Wikipedia (2009a) 'Volcanism of Iceland', www.en.wikipedia.org /wiki/Volcanism_in_Iceland, accessed 1 August 2009

Wikipedia (2009b) 'Blue Lagoon (geothermal spa)', www.wikipedia.org/wiki/Blue_Lagoon_%28geothermal_spa, accessed 1 August 2009

Wikipedia (2009c) 'Vestmannaeyjar', www.en.wikipedia.org/wiki/Westman_Islands, accessed 1 August 2009

15

Volcano Tourism and its Influence on the Territory of Mt Etna (Italy) – Explored with Digressions to Stromboli (Italy)

Ariane Struck

Summary of important geographic and volcanic characteristics

Mt Etna is the highest active volcano in Europe. Due to its natural characteristics and frequent volcanic activity, it is one of the most famous volcanoes in the world. With a surface area of about 1200km² and a present summit height of aproximately 3310m Mt Etna is located in the eastern part of the island of Sicily (Italy), 25km north of the city of Catania. Placed at the southern edge of the Eurasian Plate, close to the collision zone with the African Plate, in a complex geodynamic setting, Etna is composed of overlapping products of different phases. Its historical volcanic origin began about 0.5 million years ago with small volume volcanism. About 0.2 million years ago the volcanism became more energetic resulting in the development of a series of overlapping central volcanoes (Behnke and Struck, 2005; Branca et al, 2004). The volcano as

we know it today has grown during the past 15,000 years, following a series of explosive eruptions that blew off the previous deposits and led to the collapse of a vast summit caldera (Behnke and Struck, 2005). During the past 15,000 years the volcanic character has been mildly explosive with voluminous lava ejections from the summit craters and flanks, discontinuously interrupted by more strongly explosive but short-lived eruptive episodes at the summit (Behnke and Struck, 2005; Coltelli et al, 2004). Volcanic products formed in explosive eruptions like ash, scoria and volcanic bombs appear in a comparatively small quantity. Only a few volcanoes of the world share this quality and have a low explosive index at the same time. This combination of qualities has supported the development of volcano tourism at Mt Etna and underpins its importance to the study of volcanism.

The island of Stromboli is part of the municipality of Lipari in the province of Messina. It has an area of 12.6km² with about 450 permanent inhabitants and belongs with its neighbouring islands to the Aeolian Islands in the

Tyrrhenian Sea, near the north-eastern coast of Sicily. The archipelago consists of seven major and numerous small islands and owes its name to the Greek god of the wind 'Aeolus'. The largest portion of the island is the volcano itself. At the beginning of the 20th century the island was depopulated by emigration to America and Australia after it was ravaged by big volcanic eruptions in 1919 and 1930. Stromboli is a stratovolcano and ranges from a depth of about 2000m to the summit, named Pizzo Sopra la Fossa, at 926m above sea level. Its historic record of activity goes back more than 2500 years before the present and there is evidence that its persistent activity has been going on for as long as 5000 years (Behnke, 2005). The majority of eruptions consist of small explosions with lava fragments, ash or both. Several explosions at irregular intervals, lasting from five minutes to more than one hour, occur each day, larger eruptions and lava flows are less frequent. When this type of eruption is observed at other volcanoes it is often referred to as a Strombolian eruption (Behnke, 2005). Part of the normal activity is characterized as well by the presence of active lava in one or more vents. Activity departing from normal is defined as prolonged Strombolian bursts or fountaining (more than one minute), strong explosions with block and bomb ejection onto the Pizzo sopra la Fossa or beyond, pyroclastic flows and emission of lava (Behnke, 2005).

Historical development of volcano tourism at Etna and Stromboli

The easily accessible volcanoes of Italy remain, next to the volcanoes of Hawai'i, probably the most popular volcano destinations in the world. Mt Etna on the Italian island of Sicily is one of the most frequently visited active volcanoes on Earth, the total number of visitors exceeding one million per year (Behnke and Struck, 2005). Worldwide tour operators include these volcanoes in their programmes and in addition numerous smaller local suppliers have established package deals for local and international demand and tourism has become a major source of income for the local population. Since the

second half of the 19th century, both areas have become regular tourist destinations for visitors. Between them, the grand tour and the needs of the artists of the 18th and 19th centuries for new and picturesque landscapes began a new phase of cultural history, where Etna became the subject of a literary and artistic myth. The views of the snow-capped volcano in the background of the ancient theatre in Taormina have appealed to many international tourists since that time, and the volcano's journey through historical time laid the foundation stone of tourism to the island. Compared to today however, Etna was infrequently visited by tourists until the first half of the 20th century. A change began during the 1960s when elite tourism evolved into mass tourism; as a result, the trip to Sicily and Etna is now no longer exclusively reserved for the affluent strata of society. Since the late 1950s mass tourism has experienced consistent growth, and tourist infrastructure such as access roads, restaurants, accommodation and ski lifts has been installed to cater for increased demand from international guests.

Post the 2002–2003 eruption tourism on Etna has been characterized by a lack of new investment. Primarily, this has meant that while the infrastructure destroyed at that time has been restored, little else has been provided. However, with the growth of an ecological consciousness in larger parts of the population since the middle of the 1980s the popular view on the Etna area has changed. The area was proclaimed a natural preserve in 1987, which led to a reappraisal of the Sicilian mountain-culture for tourism. Today the accessibility of Etna with four comfortable roads leading up to the two main tourist areas on the mountain, along with the common idea of Etna being an essentially non-explosive volcano, appeals to tourists of all ages. The presence of numerous tourist facilities, especially hotels, restaurants and souvenir shops on the south and north-east flank (Figure 15.1), serve to channel the tourist flow. Guides accompany tourists for excursions to higher points of the volcano and sites of particular interest. During the season (March–November) excursions are made in jeeps; on the south flank in combination with a cable car; both permit continuous visitor counts.

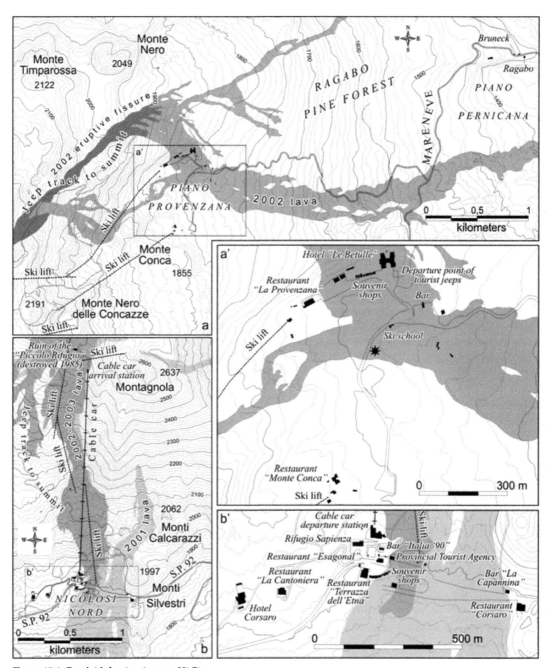

Figure 15.1 Tourist infrastructure on Mt Etna

Notes: The figure indicates the two main tourist areas on Etna: PP (a) and NN (b), showing the most important structures of the tourist industry and lava flows of the eruption 2001 and 2002–2003. More detail is shown in the enlarged maps in 'a' and 'b'. S.P. 92 in panel b stands for Strada Provinciale (Provincial Road) No. 92. The situation shown is based on a 1999 topographic map (contour interval is 10m) and thus pre-dates the 2001 and 2002–2003 eruptions, which destroyed Piano Provenzana and severely damaged the Nicolosi Nord station (Behnke and Struck, 2005).

Stromboli is also one of the most tourist friendly volcanoes in the world. It is the only permanently active volcano that tourists can climb up and watch eruptions from only 150m away. Stromboli gained worldwide fame in the year 1949 from the movie *Stromboli – God's Land*, directed by Roberto Rossellini and starring Ingrid Bergmann. The film aroused the interest of tourists in the early 1950s and has strongly influenced tourism on this island until today. Since 1950 there has been a considerable increase in the number of visitors – during the late 1960s and early 1970s, the island became attractive for hippies and dropouts. Since the late 1970s, however, the island has become one of the major tourist attractions of southern Italy and tourism the main source of economic activity in the region. The majority of visitors come especially to see the volcano. Usually, they arrive during the day by ship, climb to the summit, return to their holiday-homes or stay at the summit (which is dangerous and officially forbidden) and leave the island the next morning or a few days later. The dramatic influx of tourists especially during the high season (July–August) sometimes causes an almost complete breakdown of municipal organization. On the other hand, tourism is virtually the only economic resource of the island.

Assessment of the volcanic hazard potential and its impact on tourism

The fertility of the soil, the aesthetic value of the landscape, a fundamental development of infrastructure and the growth of tourist-offers in recent decades led to an increase in the flow of visitors and the population density on the slopes. Mt Etna is a mountainous and volcanic massif and this means that tourism to it is accompanied by certain risks not solely related to the volcano itself. For example, while lava flows represent the most typical hazard in the Etna area and can destroy entire population centres, adventure tourism based on climbing and other activities can impact far more on tourists unless an eruption occurs. In spite of these hazards and the frequent eruptions (summit activity occurs nearly continuously and the intervals between flank eruptions vary from a

few months to several years), nearly one million people live in the area exposed to the direct effects of eruptions. The lower southern and south-eastern flanks are among the most densely urbanized areas of southern Italy and therefore are highly vulnerable in case of major flank eruptions at low altitude (Behnke and Struck, 2005).

The summit region is not inhabited and is not used for agricultural purposes, therefore the long-term volcanic activity of the summit is not seen as a danger to the local population. Only tourists, photographers, scientists and other visitors to the immediate summit area take a moderate volcanic risk. The main danger of paroxysmal summit eruptions comes from strong tephra ejection (Behnke and Struck, 2005). Bombs and blocks provide an unpredictable threat to visitors in the summit region. Increased gas concentrations occur at the summit but visitors without breathing masks can leave in time. Also these subterminal eruptions are generally regarded as dangerous for visitors *outside* the summit area, although the visitor stations are not greatly exposed to explosive activity due to distance.

Lava flows in flank eruptions primarily cause infrastructural damage. Though Stromboli's activity is not of this type normally, the volcano has a significant hazard *potential*. Most of the activity is of a moderate size, consisting of short and small abrupt ejections of glowing lava fragments to heights of rarely more than 150m above the vents. However, there are periods of stronger, more continuous activity with fountaining lasting several hours, violent ejection of blocks and large bombs. Furthermore, the volcano is capable of larger and potentially disastrous eruptions. While these events with significant effects are restricted to the immediate summit area at the Sciara del Fuoco they occur about once per year (Behnke, 2005). Moreover, twice during the last century (in 1919 and 1930) there have been large eruptions that caused significant damage and killed visitors even at considerable distance from the craters.

Bigger eruptions occur every few decades and should be expected in the future at any time. When tourists climb to the summit, they expose themselves to the risk of being surprised by a 'larger-than-normal' explosion. Such eruptions may occur without any premonitory signs. Several explosions in the past few years have surprised groups of tourists in the summit area, causing various accidents as people began to run around in panic (Behnke, 2005). In contrast, the phenomenon of lava-flows is completely non-hazardous to nearly all accessible parts of the island. The worst-case scenario at Stromboli would be a sector collapse of the unstable Sciara del Fuoco flank. During its evolution sector collapses were repeated, most recently about 5000 years ago. Such a collapse would create calamitous tsunamis that might jeopardize the surrounding coasts (Behnke, 2005). Evidence for this is the minor collapse on the Sciara del Fuoco on 30 December 2002, which generated tremendous tsunamis several metres high on the coasts of Stromboli island and injured a few people. Areas below the main valleys also have avalanche risks with hot material sliding from the steep upper slopes of the volcano. These avalanches are able to reach the coast. Substantial secondary hazards also exist for tourists through the unsecured terrain. In addition, the risk of a surprising weather turnaround with all its consequences, such as fog or lightning, is always present. Particularly with regard to the descent, there is a widely unknown risk from rock falls that may lead to significant injury.

Tourism in the surrounding area of Etna and Stromboli

Analysis of the accommodation situation at Mount Etna and Stromboli

An analysis of the hotel structures of the province of Catania and the Etna Park communities can help to understand the current situation for tourism in the region. The most evident fact is the low number of hotels. According to the Azienda Autonoma Provinciale per l'Incremento Turistico (AAPIT) 2008, the province of Catania is the most densely populated province of Sicily with an area of 3553km^2 and 1.07 million inhabitants. Nevertheless, with only 108 hotels there is a big shortage of accommodation and initiatives for visitors. The situation in the municipalities of the Etna Park is even worse (24 hotels; 4-stars: 1; 3-stars: 13; 2-stars: 6; 1-star: 3; total 864 rooms and 2009 beds), compared with 73,977 arrivals.

Further, 7 holiday-rooms, 4 apartments, 4 campgrounds, 17 agritourism accommodations, 3 refugios and 1 hostel, with a total of 1227 rooms and 2490 beds (AAPIT, 2008) are available. The average stay in the hotels of the Etna Park is only one-fifth of the time of similar accommodation elsewhere in the region (AAPIT, 2005). Hotels are located in nearly each of the total 20 communes of the park, but comfort is by international comparison low and prices are on a high level. There is a lack of small modern hotels, which are able to offer beds at middle price levels.

While the accommodation situation in the larger area of Mt Etna is bad, that in Stromboli is good. Three small hotels are available during the high season (March until October). In addition, unregistered bed & breakfast guesthouses and simple private accommodation provide elemental services at a high price-level. All major hotels use small vehicles, hand-trucks or three-wheelers to pick up guests and baggage from the boat jetty at Scari. Taking cars to Stromboli is not allowed – to the main village or to Ginostra. Transport between the two villages (Stromboli and Ginostra) is possible by ship, hydrofoil or small boats. However, there is no campsite on Stromboli and casual camping is not permitted (Alean et al, 2009).

Analysis of tourism infrastructures and tourist facilities at Mt Etna and Stromboli

The presentation of spectacular nature as attractions is not enough to evoke a tourism demand in the area arround active volcanos. A series of elementary services are needed. Besides accommodation and attractions an area requires efficient road networks, basic urban services and hiking facilities as well as information services. The first few visitors that bothered to climb Etna in the beginning of the 19th century had to endure many hours of mule riding from Nicolosi at 800m to about 2000m and then hike the remaining 1300m to the summit. Things began to change in the 1930s with the building of tourism infrastructure, initally the construction of the first paved road on the south flank, from Nicolosi up to the Cantoniera mountain hut at 1930m elevation (Provincial Road 92; see Figure 15.1). Since the late1950s tourism at Mt Etna has experienced strong growth based on the construction of further access roads and the building of hotels and lodges, mountain huts, restaurants, souvenier shops and other tourist infrastructure concentrated essentially in two areas: Nicolosi Nord (NN) on the south flank and Piano Provenzana (PP) on the north-east flank (see Figure 15.1). Together they concentrate almost all visitors.

NN is also named the Rifugio Sapienza tourist area and is the better known of the two tourist stations on Etna. It is located on the south flank at about 1900m, in the northern part of the territory belonging to the commune of Nicolosi, next to the Cantoniera mountain hut, along the traditional access route from Nicolosi to the summit. The nucleus of NN occupies an area of approximately $0.17km^2$, immediately to the west of the impressive crater row of Monti Silvestri, formed during an eruption in 1892 (Figure 15.1; Behnke and Struck, 2005). It consists of eight major buildings and various small huts: the Rifugio Sapienza (mountain hut), two hotels (Corsaro, CAI), restaurants and bars (Cantoniera, Esagonal, Terrazza dell'Etna) and the departure station of the cable car. Some minor buildings include the Italia '90 and La Capannina bars, a shack for mountain guides, a big cluster of souvenir shops and various parking areas. A further building next to the Esagonal houses a sporadically staffed post of the Provincial Tourism Agency of Catania (APT) and the hut of a medical guard, staffed in high season. Most buildings are open from 9 a.m. till 5 p.m.; before and after the station is nearly deserted. Comsumption-orientated visitors to the mountain lack nothing. Hawkers from Africa and south-east Asia sell picture postcards, watches, sunglasses, spyglasses. Local mobile traders open their booths to sell honey, nuts, pasta, mustard, volcanic rocks and ashtrays made from the lava of past eruptions. Mobile barbeque grill huts offer sausages and steaks. With the hundreds of buses and countless cars, vendors, thousands of tourists and local visitors the station is completely overcrowded on weekends in season. However, tourists who are looking for serious information about the volcano are not easily able to find any.

Unlike in most other national parks, a visitor centre with survey maps, brochures about the park and its volcano, with some useful environmental codes of conduct wasn't established in the past. The high visitor demand manifested in historical times during the development of NN station, so it immediately evolved into a major mass tourism destination, not into a small-scale visitor centre.

The tourist station at PP is in contrast to the busy volcano-tourism business at the south flank. PP is significantly smaller and less known than NN. With a green mountain landscape and a quiet atmosphere it is located amidst a pine forest on Etna's north-east flank, contrasting with the dark colours of the recent lava flows and the bustling tourism business on the south flank. A small parking area, some individual tourists, a few overland-buses and rural surroundings show a completely different scene of the same volcano. The development of tourist facilities began in the 1960s after the construction of the access road Mareneve, which leads from Fornazzo on the east flank and Linguaglossa on the north-east flank to the isolated Rifugio Citelli (constructed in the 1930s) and to a few mountain huts (the 'Bruneck' and 'Ragabo'; Figure 15.1; Behnke and Struck, 2005). The PP tourist station stretches over an area of $2.5km^2$ and lies at 1800m on a broad plain, adjacent to the Northeast Rift – one of the most active systems of flank eruptive fissures on Etna (Behnke and Struck, 2005). This unstable sector is often accompanied by earthquakes and ground fracturing with structural damage like the recorded earthquakes in 1984, 1985, 1986 and 1988 (Behnke and Struck, 2005). In spite of potential hazards, through frequent seismicity PP grew to a remarkable tourist complex with two hotels (Le Betulle, La Provenzana), a few restaurants, a cluster of souvenir shops and an extensive skiing area with five ski runs. A jeep service (STAR) provided guided excursions to the summit area. From the beginning of tourism business in the late 1950s, however, the PP station was always disadvantaged, less known among foreign visitors and travel agencies. Some years before the completion of PP, the NN station was already finished. Tour operators responded to this offer and closed contracts at PP. Furthermore, PP was linked to the Mareneve road across the 'Ragabo' pine forest, but bus drivers preferred the more comfortable access roads to NN on the south flank (Behnke and Struck, 2005). That gave NN a competitive edge and the PP station was not able to reduce this advantage.

For many years the station was spared the damage caused by major eruptions. However, on the first day of the 2002–2003 eruption, which affected the south and north-east flanks, nearly all of its buildings were damaged by an earthquake and after this it was nearly completely overrun and buried by lava flows (Behnke and Struck, 2005). All buildings, like the hotels and restaurants, souvenir shops, a ski school and a large part of the access road disappeared under the lava. Although the eruption was short, the negative effects on tourism business were worse. The destruction was nearly complete and reconstruction started only slowly. The province distributed aid subsidies for reconstruction works late and sparsely. The access road was completed in the summer of 2004 and a few souvenir shops and provisional containers have opened, to run a tourism business in any way they can.

Besides these two main tourist locations there are some minor tourist structures in the area of Mt Etna: small hotels, a few restaurants, private bed & breakfast guesthouses, 'agriturismi' institutions and two tourist information bureaus in the periphery. Theoretically, it seems that the infrastucture and the tourist facilities of the Etna Park are similar to other national parks elsewhere in Europe, but in fact there are big differences. For example, the visitor centres are located in small villages far away from the hot-spots of tourist demand, and are only reachable by tourists with a car (and guide-books). Also, while information is available in Italian or French, the equipment and the scale of information is more that of a rural museum of local history of the post-war period rather than a visitor centre in one of the most famous volcanic regions on Earth. Altogether, the tourist structures in the Etna Park are far away from international standards, even behind the development of other Italian nature reserves like Trentino.

In contrast, Stromboli does not have a tourist station. The island has preserved its low-key historical style. A few shops and restaurants, a pharmacy, a bookshop, a post-office and one bakery provide tourists their services. Most shops open only during the season and generally it is rather difficult to buy everyday commodities. But unlike at Mt Etna, tourists do have the possibility to visit a small but highly informative visitor centre and a museum near Scari, if they are interested in the volcano, its geological evolution and activity.

Visitors' demand, profile, interest and activities at Mt Etna and Stromboli
Visitor demand

Tourist demand in the area of Mt Etna is difficult to assess and the investigation of tourist flows is neither in quantitative nor qualitative terms easy to implement. Only a few official statistics exist. Perhaps because Etna Park admission is free, currently no organizations are assigned with the task of data collection on tourism. The authorities of the park should provide this function, but during the last three decades no efforts have been made to do this. The only material available is some surveys about accommodation facilities in the municipalities of the park (Tables 15.1–15.3) and these statistics from the AAPIT illustrate amounts of international and national registered guests, based on provincial considerations.

The volcano tourism business on Etna is essentially an inbound tourism (AAPIT, 2005). The majority of all registered visitors are Italians (Table 15.2), especially inhabitants of Sicily. International visitors are mainly from Europe, in the first instance from France and Germany (Figure 15.2). Nevertheless, these official data are not reliable because hotel owners and other hirers hesitate to register a significant number of guests, in order to save taxes (Behnke and Struck, 2005).

The biggest problem in quantifying tourist flows at Etna is tabulating the numbers of day-visitors. A large number of domestic visitors spend a day trip at the volcano. So far, it is impossible to quantify how many tourists visit the volcano every year, because neither the cable car nor the jeep company STAR/SITAS can be consulted. Both are private enterprises that keep their data undisclosed. Therefore, the annual number of visitors has to be estimated, and is nearly one

Table 15.1 Total number of registered international visitors in all types of accommodation of the Etna Park

Year	1997	1998	1999	2000	2001	2002	2003	2004	2007
Arrivals	9010	10,600	15,300	16,775	19,398	23,033	24,329	28,611	31,681
Nights	24,074	32,551	39,644	44,361	56,687	60,048	65,120	71,819	98,235
Duration of stay	2.67	3.07	2.59	2.64	2.92	2.61	2.68	2.51	3.10

Source: AAPIT, 2005; APT, 2009 (also 15.2, 15.3 below)

Table 15.2 Total number of registered national visitors in all types of accommodation of the Etna Park

Year	1997	1998	1999	2000	2001	2002	2003	2004	2007
Arrivals	43,274	46,665	51,488	58,719	50,638	49,606	59,801	73,977	81,428
Nights	112,842	118,452	133,658	148,219	139,579	139,790	187,372	216,415	249,115
Duration of stay	2.61	2.54	2.60	2.52	2.76	2.82	3.13	2.93	3.05

Table 15.3 Total number of registered national and international visitors in all types of accommodation of the Etna Park

Year	1997	1998	1999	2000	2001	2002	2003	2004	2007
Arrivals	52,284	57,265	66,788	75,494	70,036	72,639	84,130	102,588	113,109
Nights	136,916	151,003	173,302	192,580	196,266	199,838	252,492	288,234	347,350
Duration of stay	2.62	2.64	2.59	2.55	2.80	2.75	3.00	2.81	3.07

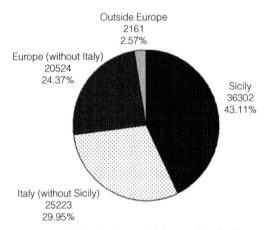

Outside Europe
2161
2.57%

Europe (without Italy)
20524
24.37%

Sicily
36302
43.11%

Italy (without Sicily)
25223
29.95%

Figure 15.2 Origin of registered visitors to Etna Park

million people (Behnke and Struck, 2005). A stereotypical tourist is a middle aged holiday-traveller on a round trip booked as a package tour, travelling in a group, arriving in an overland bus, accompanied by a tour guide and interested in history and culture. The main tourist-flow is from April to October, with a constant peak in August (AAPIT, 2005). Domestic visitors trigger this peak during the holiday period in Italy; foreign guests prefer a trip during spring and autumn (AAPIT, 2005). Visitors of foreign origin favour a half-day or single-day excursion organized by tour operators (frequently already contained as a part of a culture package tour round Sicily) or with a rented car, to get an impression of the important characteristics of the area, and the majority conclude their trip after visiting the biggest points of tourist interest. In addition, the increase of low-budget flights to Palermo and Catania as well as the expansion of both airports boosted tourism further. Moreover, Etna's short distance to Taormina (30km), as one of the most important centres for package-tourism in Sicily contributes a high emergence rate of visitors for one day

(Chester et al, 1985). On the other hand, the volcano is not always the main target; many tourists visit it casually for a few hours as an incidental programme-point during their holiday-trip. A study of 2011 international tourists (Struck, 2009) showed that only one third said that Mt Etna was a significant reason for their vacation to Sicily. Mt Etna has less importance as a pull factor for volcano tourism than Stromboli.

Only a few visitors take time for a trip lasting several hours or more (AAPIT, 2005). Those prefer to stay in the area to have easier access to the volcano, and rent cottages or stay in agro-tourist accommodation, mountain huts, on farms or campsites, and only a small proportion stay in a hotel. Local recreation/leisure visitors from the province of Catania and Messina organize their trip to the volcano almost individually on weekends, by car. This comes along with negative consequences like environmental pollution and a large traffic volume. Individual travellers depend primarily on a rental car due to a lack in the public transport system. Besides the Circumetnea railway, which transports visitors along the foot of Mt Etna from Catania (105km) to Giarre, only one public bus departs daily from Catania to NN (to PP it is not available). Currently, both are used by less than 1 per cent of all visitors (Struck, 2009).

Mainly individual travellers visit the island of Stromboli. In addition, some small tour-operators offer the island in their programme and provide special-interest tours like study-trips, hiking/trekking-tours and volcano-tours. The season lasts from March to October. Off-season, almost all tourist attractions and facilities are closed and arrival/departure by ferry is uncertain. In general, the journey is possible in different ways: to cruise by ferry from Milazzo to the northern coast of Sicily (six hours) or in a faster and twice as expensive way on a hydrofoil (three hours). Owing to the fact that the island of Stromboli can be reached only by boat, the total number of visitors is easier to quantify. According to AAPIT Lipari (2009), 17,024 tourists spent a total of 45,202 nights on the island in the year 2008, and mountain guides suggest that each year about 15,000 tourists climb the volcano. This indicates that nearly every visitor to the island climbs up the volcano.

The influence of volcano events on volcano tourism business

Volcano activity cycles generally have a certain influence on visitor flows. Depending on the size of the explosive events, one group might abandon their planned holiday, but others may visit consciously the volcano in connection with corresponding media-reports. Frequent eruptions during the past decades have made both Etna and Stromboli a famous subject in the media and have attracted more and more visitors. The number of tourists reached a maximum in 1999, at the time of a long, non-explosive and well-accessible eruption when mountain guides were able to accompany tourists right to the source vents of the eruption (Calvari et al, 2002; Behnke and Struck, 2005). One year later, the volcano tourism business became difficult when the south-east crater produced fire-fountaining and lava emission that resulted in heavy tephra fallout over many kilometeres around the crater. The combined effects of eruption-related damage of touristic infrastructure in 2001 and 2002–2003, the consequences following the 9/11 USA event, and tight access restrictions to the upper portions (>1950m) of Etna, brought a severe blow to volcano tourism for the following few years (Behnke et al, 2005). With the cable car out of action and the prohibition of visitors entering restricted areas, many tourists limited their Etna experience to a short visit of NN and the crater row of Monti Silvestri. Since 2004 tourism has grown again, as the cable car was reopened and access restrictions were lifted. Presumably, the effects of the current economic crisis will have an effect on tourism in the season of 2009/2010.

Volcanic events at Stromboli have only limited impact on local tourism businesses. Unusual patterns in the volcano's activity attract only a small number of additional visitors. A tsunami in the winter of 2002/03 was followed by a subsequent evacuation of the entire island that brought negative publicity for a few months, but while casual tourists may visit the island less, visitors with strong interests in volcanism are less affected by negative impacts.

Tourism in the protected area of Mt Etna and its ecological and economic impact

The 'Parco dell' Etna' (Parco Naturale Regionale dell'Etna) was the first park under the regional parks provision (DPR) of 17 March 1987, No. 73 in Sicily. Big parts of the volcano were put under protection to conserve the landscape and to prevent further damage. In the 19th century the environment was transformed by the extension of viticulture. Forest areas up to an elevation of 1000m were deforested, followed by the building of extensive terracing and the construction of country houses. However, these changes were negligible compared to the uncontrolled development of various buildings like vacation houses. This phenomenon originated from prosperous populations in Catania in the 19th century and culminated in the 1970s in vacation village tourism. From this time tourists came all year round, not only in summer. In response the inhabitants of the Etna region, who represented the largest group of private investors, began to build numerous small accommodation on a simple level with the purpose to rent it to national and international tourists. Simultaneously, they prevented the development of a strong hotel-structure. In addition, the implementation of ski slopes, the building of the road Mareneve and the deforestation of Mt San Leo for tourist interests had significant damaging impact and contributed to erosion. The tolerance of the local administration combined with their unhappy politics supported a considerable expansion of development in the 20th century. In order to prevent further damage, scientists and

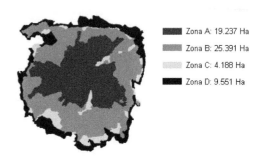

Figure 15.3 Areas of Mt Etna Park (Parco Naturale Regionale dell'Etna)

nature-conservation organizations strove to realize a nature reserve to counteract these patterns. The establishment of the park had to overcome numerous obstacles and lit conflicts between local interests and the needs and demands of conservation of the environment.

Ultimately, the Parco dell' Etna was established in 1987 with a total area of about 59,000ha over several climate and vegetation zones. It is divided into four zones with different levels of protection and restrictions, increasing with altitude, from zone D to zone A (Figure 15.3; Table 15.4). Areas A and B are located above the ring road and together cover about 45,000ha or 70 per cent of the total area of the park. All four areas allow access to the public. The tourist areas (NN and PP) have been designated as low-protection zones (C) to permit further expansion and to allow fast reconstructions in case of eruption-induced damage.

The following four main themes are the primary objectives of the park: protection of natural heritage; rehabilitation and upgrading of the buildings; protection of agricultural heritage; and protection of tourism. Administratively, it has

Table 15.4 Areas of Mt Etna Park (Parco Naturale Regionale dell'Etna 2009)

Zone A:	'Strict nature reserve' (19,237ha) without settlement structures. Any intervention by people is prohibited, except for the purpose of renewal and expansion of forest areas. Livestock farming is allowed, as long as the vegetation is not affected.
Zone B:	'General reserve' (25,391ha), populated since the ancient times. Intensive agriculture with industrial connotations is excluded. The practice of animal husbandry is for a maximum load of two livestock units per hectare. Traditional farming is permitted (e.g. wine, hazelnuts, pistachios), as are forestry activities and breeding.
Zone C:	Several isolated 'Protected areas' (4,188ha). The construction of tourist facilities (e.g. hotels, ski lifts) is allowed, when built in harmony with nature.
Zone D:	'Controlled area' (9,551ha) with restrictions on construction, pollution and the introduction of non-endemic flora and fauna.

not always been easy to realize these objectives – especially the last – in recent years, Despite the large variety of natural and environmental resources, most of them are undeveloped for tourist purposes. The majority of initiatives were structural interventions like the creation of footpaths and viewing platforms, signposting and the redevelopment of cottages. Today's official focus is the promotion of sustainable tourism to approve positive impacts on the socio-economic development and to afford a serious alternative for the migration-streams from rural areas. In reality, the park is still far away from its objectives. For sustainable tourism-management, the sporadic development of infrastructure, the offering of guided tours and the management of its own administrative structures are not enough. Volcano tourism should rather be planned and organized through an analysis of the current situation and the potential demand in the area – only then can a basis for revaluation and rescheduling tourist infrastructure systems, for adding to public services for tourism, as well as providing the activities to support tourist utilization be found. Furthermore, cooperation between the different official and economic stakeholders would be necessary to offer an integrative tourist concept for the region.

Conclusions

Mount Etna and Stromboli belong to the most popular volcano destinations of the world due to their frequent and moderate volcanic activity, their aesthetic landscapes, development of infrastructure and the growth of tourist attractions in recent decades. However, these volcano tourism destinations have their differences as the previous sections have shown – mainly in terms of visitor structures and numbers, visitor activities and travel incentives, tourism development, infrastructure and their individual hazard potential.

Mount Etna is primarily an excursion tourism destination for package tourists and domestic tourism has great significance. The distance from international markets and the absence of advertising and lack of transport systems causes a ratio of 1:3 between foreign and Italian visitors (AAPIT, 2005). Despite limited resources for tourism promotion, various projects have been initiated to expand international tourism demand, for example,

improvements in the road network, the development of shipping companies to provide further connections, modernization of the airport at Catania and preservation of structures of general interest. But there is a need for action to restructure the public transport network to Mt Etna, to modernize the hotel industry in both areas and to develop general volcano tourism services. In particular on Mt Etna, without central visitor information centres the public relations and the scale of information services for tourists is low. Actually, local authorities do not seem to have the intention to support these structures financially, notwithstanding that tourism is the most important economic resource on the island. In contrast, the tourist information system at Stromboli is much better with numerous signs, a tourist-information centre and a museum that gives visitors all the information they need.

Nevertheless, the lack of physical structures or projects is not the only reason for low international demand. It is rather a lack of attention from tourist operators as well as the inadequate presence of pages of private hirers and tour operators themselves on international booking sales channels like the Internet. The analysis of hotel structures also shows a big shortage of modern tourism accommodation and a clear lack of initiatives in this area. It is also visible through representation of the Etna and Stromboli region in travel catalogues. The focus is on commercial payoff without major reinvestments from the enjoyment aspect of volcanism. In consequence, existing structures become obsolete and prices continue to rise. A lack of professional marketing combined with a lack of information channels for interested visitors are responsible for the fact that little further international tourist demand has been generated in the past few years. The local political and tourism management system is disorganized and there is little meaningful use of public funds by local authorities. There are still shortcomings relating to organization and cooperation between different authorities like the park management, representatives from the commune and province, scientists and representatives of the tourism industry, and in the meantime the volcanoes continue to be active and a risky environment for tourists.

References

AAPIT (2005) 'Relazione ed analisi del movimento tustristico nella provinzia di Catania dal 1197 al 2004', VIII edizione, Catania, Italy, pp1–250, unpublished

AAPIT (2008) 'Movimenti turistici anno 2008', www.regione.sicilia.it/turismo, accessed 15 June 2009

AAPIT (2009) 'Dati statistici Stromboli 2008', Lipari, Italy, unpublished

APT Catania (2003) 'Movimiento turistico del parco dell'Etna dal 1999 al 2002', Catania, Italy, unpublished

APT Catania (2008) 'Relazione e analisi del movimento nella Provincia di Catania', periodo 1997–2006, Catania, Italy, unpublished

APT Catania (2008) 'Relazione e analisi del movimento turistico nella Provincia di Catania', periodo dal, 2006–2007, Catania, Italy, unpublished

APT Catania (2009) 'Riepilogo Comuni del Parco dell'Etna strutture alberghiere/extralberghiere anno 2007', Catania, Italy, unpublished

Alean, J., Carniel, R. and Fulle, M. (2009) 'Stromboli Online', www.swisseduc.ch/stromboli/index-de.html, accessed 26 May 2009

Bardintzeff, J.-M. (1999) *Vulkanologie*, Ferdinand Enke Verlag, Stuttgart

Behnke, B. and Neri, M. (2003) 'The July–August 2001 eruption of Mt. Etna (Sicily)', *Bull Volcanol*, vol 65, pp461–476

Behnke, B. (2005) 'Italy's volcanoes: The cradle of volcanolegy', www.boris.vulcanoEtna.it/STROMBOLI.html, accessed 26 May 2009

Behnke, B., Neri, M., Pecora, E. and Zanon, V. (2005) 'The exceptional activity and growth of Southeast Crater, Mount Etna, between 1996 and 2001', unpublished

Behnke, B. and Struck, A. (2005) 'Volcano tourism on Etna and Stromboli: A survey to Mount Etna (Italy)', unpublished

Bernard, S. (2004) 'Die Aktivitäten des Ätna und sein Einfluss auf die Bevölkerung: Nutzen und Gefahren des Vulkanismus', Universität Göttingen, Germany, unpublished

Branca, S., Coltelli, M. and Groppelli, G. (2004) 'Geological evolution of Etna volcano', in Bonaccorso, A., Calvari, S., Coltelli, M., Del Negro, C. and Falsaperla, S. (eds) 'Mt. Etna: Volcano Laboratory', Am Geophys Union, Geophys Monogr, vol 143, pp49–63

Calvari et al., 2002 S. Calvari, M. Neri and H. Pinkerton, 'Effusion rate estimations during the 1999 summit eruption on Mount Etna, and growth of two distinct lava flow fields' *J. Volcanol. Geotherm. Res.* 119 (2002), pp. 107–123

Chester, D. K., Duncan, A. M., Guest, J. B. and Kilburn, C. (1985) *Mount Etna, Anatomy of a Volcano*, Chapman Hall, London

Corsaro, R. A., Cristofolini, R. and Patanè, L. (1996) 'The 1669 eruption at Mount Etna: Chronology, Petrology and Geochemistry, with Inferences on the Magma Sources and Ascent Mechanisms', *Bull. Volcanol*, vol 58, pp348–358

Duncan, A., Chester, D. K. and Guest, J. E. (1981) 'Mount Etna volcano: Environmental impact and problems of volcanic prediction', *Geographical Journal*, vol 147, no 2, pp164–178

Gregg, C. E., Houghton, B. F., Johnston, D. M., Paton, D. and Swanson, D. A. (2004a) 'The perception of volcanic risk in Kona communities from Mauna Loa and Hualālai volcanoes, Hawai'i', *J. Volcanol Geotherm Res*, vol 130, pp179–196

Gregg, C. E., Houghton, B. F., Paton, D., Swanson, D. A. and Johnston, D. M. (2004) 'Community preparedness for lava flows from Mauna Loa and Hualālai volcanoes, Kona, Hawai'i', *Bull Volcanol*, vol 66, pp531–540

Forgione, G., Luongo, G. and Romano, R. (1989) 'Mt. Etna (Sicily): Volcanic Hazard Assessment', in Latter, J. H. (ed) IAVCEI Proc in Volcanology, vol 1, *Volcanic Hazards*, Springer-Verlag, Berlin, pp137–150

Parco Naturale Regionale dell'Etna (2009) 'Parco dell'Etna', www.parcoetna.it, accessed 26 May 2009

Patanè, G., La Delfa, S. and Tanguy, J.-C. (2004) *L'Etna e il Mondo dei Vulcani*, Giuseppe Maimone Editore, Catania

Raufmann, B. (2002) 'Mögliche Probleme und Risiken bei Vulkantouren auf aktive Vulkane', Fachhochschule Worms, Germany, unpublished

Rittmann, A. (1981) *Vulkane und ihre Tätigkeit*, 3rd edn, Enke, Stuttgart

Rother, K. and Tichy, F. (2000) *Italien*, Wissenschaftliche Buchgesellschaft, Darmstadt

Sigurdsson, H. and Lopes-Gautier, R. (2000) 'Volcanoes and Tourism', in Sigurdsson, H. (ed) *Encyclopedia of Volcanoes*, Academic Press, San Diego, CA, pp1283–1299

Struck, A. (2009) 'Wo bitte geht es hier zum Vulkan? (Natur)-Tourismus in (Schutzgebieten) Sizilien(s) und, sein Einfluss auf das Territorium untersucht am Beispiel des Ätna Naturparks unter besonderer Berücksichtigung der Wahrnehmung seiner Besucher', PhD thesis, Universität Duisburg-Essen, unpublished

16

Under the Volcano – Can Sustainable Tourism Development be Balanced with Risk Management?

Jonathan Karkut

Introduction

At a time when global population growth is exposing more and more communities to volcanic hazards, an expanding body of work is being dedicated to lessen the impacts of major eruptions. A trend has been identified that shows a shift away from pure Earth scientists simply attempting to understand how and when eruptions occur, towards a more integrated and applied approach of risk management involving volcanologists, social scientists, emergency planners, local communities and others (Aguirre and Ahearn, 2007). The catalyst for this shift was a series of significant eruptions in the final decades of the 20th century and a focusing of minds through the UN declaration in the 1990s of an International Decade for Natural Disaster Reduction (Chester et al, 2002).

Within this context, it would at first thought seem to be the greatest folly for destinations near to active volcanoes to propose expanding tourism development and thereby push further significant numbers of people into an already difficult situation. As a result, it is probably not surprising that insufficient consideration has been given as to where tourism fits in to the burgeoning set of volcanic risk management plans and strategies. However, the natural fascination with the dramatic landscapes and experiences around active volcanoes has ensured that tourism to these sites is already a major business, with arrivals to some locations expanding into millions of people annually. It consequently follows that input from a tourism perspective somehow has to be woven into any emergency policy and planning, otherwise a significant segment of the population at risk will be overlooked and a major social and economic stimulus underestimated in the resulting plan.

This chapter therefore considers how the essential balancing act between development and risk management might occur. A brief introduction presents the broader concerns currently occupying hazard management around volcanoes. Then drawing upon the example of Vesuvius and its surrounding municipalities in the Campania region of Italy, a description of the specific emergency plan for the Vesuvius area of Italy is given and consideration offered as to the implications of bringing tourism into such an equation.

Volcano hazard management

Over the latter decades of the 20th century there has been a growing interest and understanding regarding the risks that volcanoes pose for the populations around them. As the world population has grown, urban growth, particularly in developing countries, has led to a greater exposure to volcanic hazards (Chester et al, 2001). The recognition of this increasing danger has been refocused by the occurrence of numerous emergencies linked to volcanic activity and the subsequent attempts by civil authorities to lessen the impact of such eruptions. These efforts have had mixed success, from the disasters and major loss of life experienced around the 1982 eruption of El Chichon, Mexico or the 1985 eruption of Nevado del Ruiz, Colombia – to the relatively positive outcome of responses to eruptions such as 1980 Mt St Helens, USA or 1995–98 Soufrière Hills, Montserrat (Chester et al, 2002).

In response to this situation, the General Assembly of the United Nations reacted by declaring the 1990s the International Decade for Natural Disaster Reduction (IDNDR). Driven by this initiative, a whole range of studies were inspired to review how the risk to populations living in the vicinity of volcanic hazards could be significantly reduced (Chester et al, 2002). Up until this point, volcanology had addressed these issues primarily from an Earth sciences perspective by looking to establish the strength, nature and periodicity of major eruptive events. Through the concerted focus of the IDNDR, a shift in approach began to occur through a moving away from the pure science 'dominant' response to a more applied approach involving multidisciplinary teams of volcanologists, social scientists, emergency planners, local communities and others (Aguirre and Ahearn, 2007).

This more integrated and applied methodology represents an acknowledgement that hazard reduction is dependent not just upon understanding and recognizing the geological processes, but also on appreciating the impacts they may have on the socio-cultural and economic fabric of the effected communities and the broader physical environment. Hence, reactions or preparations for volcanic events should demonstrate sensitivity for the specific physical environment encountered and crucially be 'incultured' to the human environment (Degg, 1998). Most importantly, the key point taken by this approach is that it:

> … *emphasises the uniqueness of place: Hawai'i is not Etna and Iceland is not the Azores.*
> (Chester et al, 2002)

In practical terms it is critical for strong lines of communication to be established between the geoscientists and the emergency managers, and with contacts within the local communities themselves. As volcanic events are manifested in complex multiple cycles of raised and lessened activity followed by quiescence, one of the huge demands is for communications around known active volcanoes to remain ongoing and to motivate the populations at risk even when the public perception might be that there is no danger present (Perry and Godchaux, 2005). Through observation of case studies around the world, Perry and Godchaux (2005) identify six main guidelines to appreciate when constructing a public education strategy to communicate volcanic hazard management:

1 Stress should be placed not just on 'awareness', but the transmission of actions that will ensure a greater adoption of protective measures by the affected public.
2 Communications efforts must not just be concentrated in a single campaign or event, but be longitudinal and repeat the threats and safeguards required to mitigate those circumstances.
3 It is important to ensure education flows within an inter-organizational and inter-governmental framework. The local, regional and national levels should be aware of the messages each is presenting. A further factor is for the credibility of local agencies to be ensured by establishing links with other organizations that are perceived as having specialist knowledge for specific hazards.
4 Messages need to address attitudes towards the adjustments in behaviour or actions that need to be taken, rather than solely creating hazard awareness.
5 Recognition of the roles that the media can take. Again the emphasis is on long-term as

opposed to a campaign led process of dissemination. Such an active programme should approach the breadth of media channels that are now available: from newspapers, magazines, radio and TV, to the Internet and email. Specific audiences and sections of the community should also be identified so that specialist programmes reaching particular age, gender, ethnicity or socio-economic status may be targeted.

6   It should be appreciated that public education still has its limitations and is not a panacea. It is just one amongst a range of methods that can lead to improved protection for communities living in proximity to hazardous volcanoes; others include regulations, incentives etc. Even if a hugely effective campaign is run it must be appreciated that other factors can still impinge when the 'real' event occurs.

Considering that tourism, directly or indirectly is a significant social and economic activity around many active volcanic sites, the presence of large numbers of what effectively represent temporary populations is rarely acknowledged, least of all incorporated into the type of guidelines indicated above. Factors beyond the simple numerical pressures of further tourists that have the potential to disrupt or slow down the effectiveness of well laid plans include a lack of fluency in the local language, unfamiliarity with the local geography, infrastructure and the chain of command within agencies integral in implementing action on the ground during an emergency.

When the issues and principles described above are taken into account, the region around Vesuvius begins to look extremely vulnerable. This area represents one of the highest concentrations of predominantly urban population in Europe. Growth and rural to urban population flows followed government-funded schemes which were further fuelled by cheap but speculative, unplanned and often illegal building, which led to encroachments closer and closer to the volcano itself (Dobran, 2000). In addition, Vesuvius and the archaeological sites linked to its tempestuous history attract annual numbers of tourists far higher even than the permanent resident population. Set against this backdrop, it was

therefore recognized by the early 1990s that a comprehensive emergency plan for the Vesuvius area was long overdue.

The National Emergency Plan for the Vesuvian Area

The National Emergency Plan for the Vesuvian Area (NEPVA), was finally agreed and published in 1995 as the first comprehensive hazard evaluation and evacuation plan for the region (Dipartimento della Protezione Civile, 1995). It is structured around a model informed by the last major sub-Plinian eruption of 1631 and assisted by computer generated maps outlining the area of hazard vulnerable to pyroclastic flow and ash fallout (Barberi et al, 1990). The plan is based on an assumption that following the pattern of warning earthquakes felt for over a fortnight before the 1631 eruption, the 700,000 residents living in the danger zone would have the opportunity to be evacuated over a seven-day period. To support this premise, it is stated that the extensive spread of different monitoring devices across the region will allow a lag of around 20 days between the first signs of movement in the magma chamber and the commencement of the eruption.

The model created three zones of hazard (Figure 16.1):

1   An inner 'red zone' that is most immediately at danger from pyroclastic flows and lahars spreading out from the cone. In the red zone there are an estimated 550,000 residents, who would have to be evacuated from the area.

2   An outer far wider area called the 'yellow zone' is vulnerable to pyroclastic fallout. It is delineated based upon the spread of ash deposits laid down during former sub-Plinian eruptions (VEI of 4).

3   A further area of around 98km² called the 'blue zone', where it is anticipated major floods and lahars may occur.

As a result of the significant debate that arose from the presentation of the 1995 plan (Masood, 1995), there has been a further wave of information gathering and surveys to assess the volcanic risk

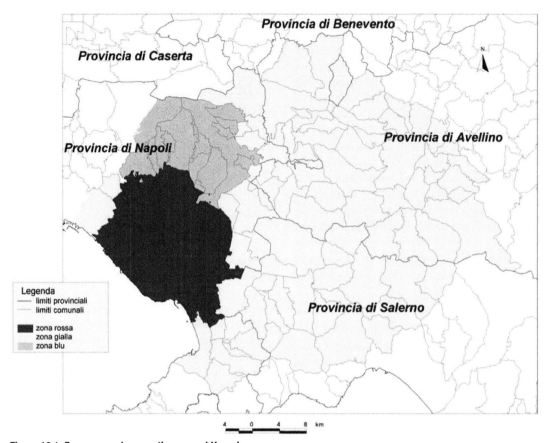

Figure 16.1 Emergency plan zonation around Vesuvius

Source: Dipartimento della Protezione Civile, 2008

perception of the local population. Amongst these studies, Barberi et al (2008) found that local communities have expressed a wish to be more intensively involved in consultation, particularly through public discussions relating to emergency planning and methods to ensure better individual preparedness. The results of the survey also indicate that there is still need for a major advance in the field of education and presentation of information. Particularly working through the Vesuvius Observatory, situated high up on the flank of the volcano, extensive educational programmes have consequently targeted local schools through classes, distribution of publications, and guided tours around exhibitions about the volcanic risks.

A further initiative was launched in 2003 by the regional government of Campania, through a programme called 'Vesuvia', which is targeting the reduction of risk around Vesuvius. Actions have included the banning of the construction of new houses in all of the municipalities located in the red zone. Combining a stick and carrot method, financial incentives of up to 30,000 Euros per family are also offered to those who are prepared to move permanently away from the red zone (Barberi et al, 2008).

Other surveys conducted by Solana et al (2008) and Carlino et al (2008) point to a conclusion that although groups such as the civil authorities and young people living around Vesuvius are now more aware of the volcanic risk, their understanding of the precise nature of volcanological hazards and which measures are appropriate in which circumstances is less complete. Nonetheless, across the recent wave of studies and surveys accessing the Vesuvius emergency plan, it is clear that many of the local stakeholder groups have now been consulted at some level. However, there is still little or no mention made of the significant numbers of visitors and tourists that make their way into the region and – most importantly for any emergency evacuation plans – place further burdens on the already overstretched infrastructure. This is a somewhat disturbing situation, as interviews with local municipalities, the national park and other authorities around Vesuvius have indicated that all are interested in creating a wider range of products for tourists in order to extend their stay and spend in the region. Various regional, national and EU programmes are being identified through which to attract support for further tourism development. The principle motivation behind these actions is the pressing need to improve the high levels of unemployment and poor levels of return received by the local communities from the tourism industry as it is currently structured.

Drawing tourism into the hazard management equation

Tourism to Vesuvius and its hinterland is not a recent phenomenon. In AD79 Pliny the Younger became the first person to fully chronicle a major volcanic eruption. In so doing, the disasters that overcame the towns of Pompeii and Herculaneum were permanently lodged in our collective memory and Vesuvius became the most (in)famous volcano on the planet. Today the spectacular archaeological sites attract up to 2.5 million visitors annually, while over a million people trek up the final hundred or so metres to the main crater or *Gran Cono* of Vesuvius (personal communication with Vesuvius National Park authorities). Additionally since 1995 an area of some 8482ha surrounding the volcano has been designated as a national park, with the following aims outlined in its statute:

• conservation of its fauna, flora and geomorphologic structures;
• application of administration and environmental protection programmes;
• promotion of educational, recreational and sustainable research activities;

• reconstitution and defence of hydraulic and hydrogeological balances in the area; and
• promotion of traditional cultural, agricultural and craftwork activities.

(Vesuvius National Park, 2008)

Hence, as well as geotourism per se there is recognized potential for a wide spread of other tourism niches to be catered for in the region around the volcano.

Set against this backdrop, one of the key questions that arises is this: when apprehension is rising regarding the state of awareness and preparedness for future eruptions, can a further growth in tourism arrivals be mitigated against such a growing risk? In order to explore this issue and identify current and future structures and plans for tourism around the volcano, the author conducted an initial phase of qualitative research around some of the relevant institutions linked to development in the areas adjacent to the Gran Cono. The research was conducted through face-to-face interviews, participant observation, literature reviews and personal communications with a Naples based company working on sustainable planning and development. In addition short semi-structured conversations were conducted with a range of international tourists during their visits to the volcano peak.

The strong opinion expressed by many of those interviewed was that tourism in the region continues to be poorly implemented. It was expressed on several occasions that a very small percentage of what should be major benefits ended up filtering through to the local economies and alleviating unemployment. Several interviewees expressed concern that governmental institutions, particularly at the local level, were either weak and poorly staffed or corrupt. This meant that speculative building, illegal clearing of land and illegal dumping of waste had continued unabated, with the principle driving force and only significant beneficiary being the Campanian organized crime clans, collectively known as the Camorra (personal communications with Vesuvius National Park, 2008 and Legambiente Campania Branch, 2008). The creation of the national park in 1995 was in part a response to this situation – the intention being that the protected area would act as a buffer zone to halt and reverse development in increasingly hazardous locations.

However, particularly in the early years after its creation, the national park authorities discovered that the touristic activities in and around Vesuvius were taken out of their control and managed entirely by one company, in some way linked to the agricultural ministry. For an annual contract thought to be around 15,000 euros, this company was allowed to collect all takings (personal communications with Vesuvius National Park, 2008). Entrance fees just to the Gran Cono are currently 6.5 euros for adults and 4.5 euros for under 18s and students (personal observation). With over a million visitors annually passing through this entry point, this adds up to a very substantial profit for the management company.

Perspectives on the current state of tourism around Vesuvius

In order to view directly how the volcano was being presented under this management scheme,

fieldwork was conducted at the site of the Gran Cono. Access to the site is via a narrow and poorly signposted road, that winds its way up through Ercolano municipality to a point around 1000m above sea level. At this location the track widens out to a car park where cars, coaches and taxis stop. After paying at the entrance gate visitors carry on by foot up a broad newly resurfaced path. No public transport goes up to this area and coaches tend to bring their own guides linked with the respective tours. Thus, very little contact and no commercial advantage is gained by the local community from the tourists passing through. From personal observations made during excursions in 2008 and 2009 around the Gran Cono, the input by the management company back into infrastructure around Vesuvius is also limited. Interpretation of the volcano and information concerning the geo-hazards plus details of the emergency plan were more or less non-existent. All that could be seen was a basic map showing the route of the path up to the crater rim; portable toilet units at the entrance gate; a café/souvenir shop at the entrance gate;

Figure 16.2 'Volcanological' guides offering tour guide services near Vesuvius crater rim

plus three further souvenir shops at points around the crater rim.

The souvenir shops offered just a few basic guide books and no further specific geological or volcanological information. It was unclear who regulated the contents and takings from these shops. At the first kiosk at the top of the crater rim itself, however, we were approached by a group of blue jacketed 'volcanological' guides who were hawking trade from the tourists (see Figure 16.2).

A brief conversation with one of them indicated that they were trained and validated by the Region of Campania authorities, but the nature and extent of their training was unclear. When being interviewed by the author, a small group of French, Dutch, Australian and American tourists who had taken one of these guides indicated that the fairly basic information the guide presented was probably pitched at the correct level for them as none had any specialist volcanological knowledge themselves, although most had been to other active volcanic sites before. Some minor concerns were raised by some of the tourists, about the lack of any guidelines regarding evacuation in the event of a volcanic eruption, even though it was indicated that the guide had told this group that an eruption of Vesuvius was now considered to be 'overdue'. But as a way of reassuring the group and staying concordant with the NEPVA, the guide had indicated that the advanced earthquake swarms linked to a rising magma chamber would provide a forewarning of around two weeks before such an eruption. Hence when the volcano did eventually erupt, no tourists would have been allowed near to the Gran Cono for several weeks.

Later interviews with the national park authorities indicated that the volcanological guide business was in the hidden economy and that future plans included making a new tender out for 'official' guiding services.

From personal observations at different times and at different points on the Gran Cono, it was apparent that many other tourists were interested in picking up and collecting souvenir rock samples from the volcano. However, no interpretation boards were present to help generate further interest and to assist identification during such fossicking. Equally, there was no guidance to describe the range of volcanological features visible inside and around the main cone of Vesuvius, which included active fumeroles and numerous lava flows representing a whole sequence of past eruptions with their associated experiences and stories (Figure 16.3).

When consulted about the future organization of the park and takings from tourism, the park officers indicated that their single greatest struggle is in levering away the influence of the Camorra and their extraction of revenues to the hidden economy. This has been dealt with in the political arena through lobbying to the federal parliament and in the past few years has achieved some success. For example, the management of the site is now jointly organized by the private company mentioned earlier and the national park authorities themselves. This means that the national park now receives approximately one euro from each of the entrance tickets sold (personal communication with Vesuvius National Park officers). With this income there are plans to stop more polluting transportation such as coaches coming all the way to the terrace at 1000m. The aim is for them to stop outside of the national park limits where passengers would then be transferred to a refurbished terrace through the use of electric shuttle buses.

Future plans are aimed at strengthening links between the national park and its surrounding municipalities, in order that tourism development might connect with agricultural outputs and traditions, along with other cultural practices. The prospects of transporting tourists to additional urban and rural locations are aided by the existence of a substantial infrastructure around the volcano. In particular, mobility is provided by a network of 96 stations and six lines that form the 'Circumvesuviana' narrow-gauge railway. This network joins up all the municipalities and main towns around Vesuvius with a service going into the centre of Naples (Circumvesuviana, 2008).

A wealth of traditions and experience are embedded in the communities that inhabit the land around the volcano, but these are not currently transmitted to the tourists arriving in the region, hence this channel for possible economic benefits is not exploited. Equally there is a very long-standing tradition of viticulture around Vesuvius:

Figure 16.3 Vesuvius crater rim with fumerole and souvenir stand

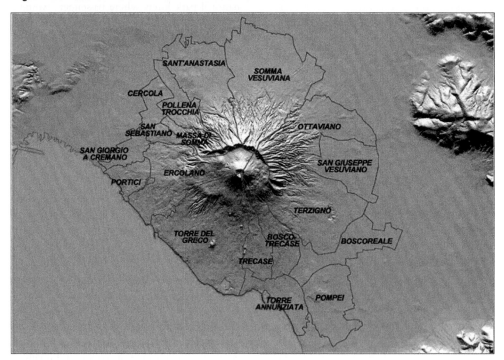

Figure 16.4 Municipalities in the 'red zone' around Vesuvius

Source: Dipartimento della Protezione Civile, 1995

The Greeks introduced viticulture to Campania, home of Mount Vesuvius and Pompeii, in the eighth century B.C. Grape growing spread throughout the peninsula, but flourished most notably in the volcanic soils of Campania. By the end of the first century B.C., the region was supplying wines to the entire Roman Empire. The writings of Horace, Virgil and Pliny the Elder attest to the fame of the region's wines. (Coopers Oak Wine of the Month Club, 2008)

Today the most renowned wine from the region is called Lacryma Christi (the tears of Christ), which is produced mainly in the municipality of Terzigno (see Figure 16.4). But again, this tradition and opportunities for activities such as wine tasting are not currently connected to the tourism product presented to visitors.

Breathing new life into Vesuvian tourism

In response to the situation outlined above, the national park authorities, local municipalities and NGOs are 'leading the way' in looking for ways to support such tourism developments and have been considering local and national funding, plus EU programmes that might support such interventions. After years of disconnection, this would appear to be an ideal opportunity to link and embed new tourism development proposals, which could be pursued for the benefit of many more parts of the local community. Such developments could then be used to provide alternative methods of communicating more clearly and more systematically, what the hazards of the volcano are, how they are manifested and what actions all sections of the population (including tourists) would need to take in the case of a major eruptive sequence.

It is acknowledged locally that approaches to these issues will need to incorporate more contemporary, dynamic and interactive ways of engaging with new audiences, as many attempts thus far have been static and unimaginative. Recent suggestions to improve this situation include:

- update and expand existing museum spaces in the region;
- create a wider and more mobile range of exhibitions and events, taking advantage of advances in 3-d computer simulations and computer generated images (CGI);
- improve guiding services, including geological/volcanological guides but also linking to guides with local cultural and environmental knowledge;
- increase the range and quality of interpretation and signage around Vesuvius;
- involve a wider spread of local stakeholders especially from those who can draw upon aspects of the intangible heritage of the region and present those features to touristic audiences; and
- ensure that local accommodation (B & Bs and hotels) are supported with further hospitality training and have access to other information on Vesuvius and to the emergency plan.

(From personal communication with Vesuvius National Park officers in 2008 and the Legambiente Campania branch, 2008 and 2009.)

A demonstration of a more creative and thoughtful style of heritage presentation has already emerged in the town of Ercolano. There, the ruins of Herculaneum continue to unveil stories from the AD79 eruption of Vesuvius. In an attempt to try and convey the extent and drama both of the eruption and the now 300 years of archaeological exploration of Herculaneum, a new 'virtual archaeological museum' or MAV (www.museomav.com) has opened a few hundred metres away from the site of the ruins. This museum in its own promotional language is:

… a contemporary look at the past (where) thanks to the opportunities provided by new technologies, the visitor can experience a multisensory and emotional visit to the archaeology of the Vesuvian area. Unlike traditional museums, the MAV is an immersive experience where the visitor isn't in contact with physical, crystallized, static objects – but lives a dynamic and atmospheric journey through virtual reconstructions and visual interfaces that recreate and reveal the reality of the past, before the Plinian eruption of AD 79.

(Museo Archeologico Virtuale Ercolano (MAV), 2009)

Similar approaches to the MAV have significant potential to be developed and used to engage and expand the levels of interest and understanding concerning the geological and volcanological processes that continue to have a major bearing on the livelihood of the whole Vesuvian region. However, local institutions including the Vesuvius National Park currently do not have immediate plans to directly consider the development or marketing of geo (geological) or volcano tourism. Although they have expressed that they would be open to learn more about the emerging recognition of the potential for this niche of tourism (personal communication with Vesuvius National Park).

Linking tourism to emergency plans

As well as having roles in the development of tourism around the volcano, the national park and the Vesuvius Observatory are integral organizations in education and awareness raising of the emergency plan for Vesuvius and ideally placed to form significant bridges between tourism and local geological and environmental information. However, in terms of the actual physical evacuation process in the case of an eruption, the national park authorities emphasized that as their staff were not trained for that task and there were also not sufficient numbers of them, they would defer those tasks to the national civil protection authorities (personal communication with Vesuvius National Park officers, 2008). Clearly then, if tourist numbers do rise in the future, awareness of the NEPVA must still be the responsibility, among other institutions, of the Vesuvius National Park. But equally those awareness materials will have to indicate that in the actual eventuality of an eruption, the national civil protection department is in charge of the evacuation procedures. This is just a small example of the type of complexities faced when attempting to balance further tourism development with effective risk management around Vesuvius.

Currently the national park headquarters are located in the municipality of San Sebastiano al Vesuvio. However, there are advanced plans to relocate to a historic building at the entrance to the national park near to Ottaviano (see Figure 16.4). In an expression of the problems facing the authorities, this building has only recently become available after being illegally occupied by the Camorra. Such complexities have

been commonplace all around the region and meant that huge amounts of funding for well considered developments have never been properly implemented or reached their intended recipient (personal communication with Vesuvius National Park). The aim is for the building in Ottaviano to become the principal visitor centre for the park and focus for the dissemination of information, including that regarding the NEPVA. In addition two other entrances to the park in the west and the south will have what are described as 'information points'.

The Vesuvius Observatory conversely has an historic building located 600m up on the western flank of the volcano. Originally completed in 1845, it has witnessed eight notable eruptions of the volcano, the last of which took place in 1944. With the need to house more extensive modern monitoring equipment, the site of the observatory institution was moved down to the city of Naples itself. The original building was then converted into a volcanological museum, which can be accessed during weekdays by schools and groups through advance bookings and on weekend mornings it is open to the general public (Vesuvius Observatory, 2008).

However, the limited access and capacity of the present museum leaves potential scope for expansion of their activities and the development of further museum spaces. For the conveyance of essential information to as wide a set of audiences as possible, the messages also need to find a more accessible form of language in order to both engage and interest people and not to 'blind them with science'. In terms of printed media, effective examples of this approach can be gathered from the Montserrat Volcanic Observatory (MVO, 2008). In collaboration with the British Geological Society, a series of educational pamphlets has been produced to explain the various volcanological phenomena. These can be downloaded from the observatory website and provide useful graphic illustrations rather than just dense scientific data (Figure 16.5).

Such printed media would only form one element of a wider, more sustained effort at educating and informing tourists and residents alike. In recognition that museums do not appeal or cannot be easily accessed by everyone, to reach

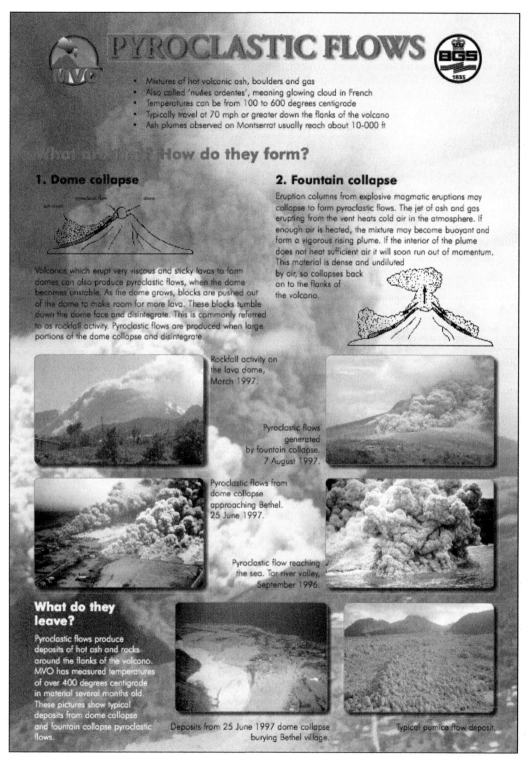

Figure 16.5 Information leaflet on volcanic hazard

Source: Montserrat Volcanic Observatory, 2008

the broadest spread of audiences an effective media strategy connecting to TV, Radio, Internet and public meetings additionally needs to be devised. This view is supported by results from a recent survey of residents living in the municipalities of the red and yellow emergency zones around Vesuvius. When asked about the sources from which they received the majority of their information about volcanic risks, residents of both zones indicated that television and newspapers were significantly the first and second most common sources of information, well ahead of sources such as the Vesuvius Observatory or local government (Barberi et al, 2008). However, as outlined in the disagreements within the scientific community that surrounded the publication of the emergency plan in 1995 it should be noted that;

> ...contradictory advice (based on differences of opinion among academics that are often emphasised by the media, at the expense of reporting on where opinions agree) can worsen a crisis and cause public confusion and antagonism against decision makers.
>
> (Solana et al, 2008)

In other words, links to the media have to be consistent and 'on message' for effective embedding of information in a population.

The information received by residents and that received by tourists, naturally have differences in detail as one audience is permanently exposed to volcanic hazards whilst the other is only temporarily at risk. Nonetheless, it is important that knowledge of what to do in case of an emergency is common and shared amongst all people. This was perfectly illustrated during the 1999 eruption of Mt Tungurahua in Ecuador, when scientists and government officials demanded that the residents of nearby towns should be evacuated for their own safety. But as the local economy was totally dependent on tourism, this message was opposed by community leaders who conducted an aggressive campaign countering the official information and argued to both locals and tourists that the volcanic activity was not a threat but an attraction (Lane et al, 2003). Although on that occasion major loss of life did not occur, if similar confusion reigned in connection with an eruption of Vesuvius, then much of the positive work surrounding the emergency plan might be undone.

One further initiative under consideration, aimed at broadening the tourism offer and at the same time assisting in the transmission of information regarding volcanic risk and the attempts to alleviate this, is the development of a new 'geopark' linking the three active volcanic sites around the Bay of Naples: Vesuvius, Campi Flegrei and Ischia (personal communication with Legambiente Campania Branch, 2008, 2009). Geoparks are a framework whereby:

> ...geological heritage and geological knowledge is shared with the broad public and linked with broader aspects of the natural and cultural environment, which are often closely related or determined to geology and landscape.
>
> (UNESCO, 2008)

A 'Volcanoes of Campania' geopark would not just present on the only active volcanoes in mainland Europe, but could also enable elements of tangible and intangible heritage plus a rich natural environment to be interwoven into the overall tourism product. In so doing, information about the volcanic landscape and how the people occupying that landscape relate to the volcanoes could be more continuously shared with domestic and international visitors. That process of generating further understanding and engaging with the local communities could then lead to self-efficacy and deeper engagement with the emergency plan. Both factors are identified as encouraging at-risk populations, not just to be aware of volcanic hazards, but also to be prepared and know how to act during a crisis (Barberi et al, 2008).

Conclusions

As documented across volcanic sites throughout the centuries, a very thin line exists between natural drama and disaster. Hence a burgeoning body of research has evolved, from the geological understanding of when and how eruptions occur, to risk management and prevention for the populations living around active volcanoes. More recently multi-disciplinary teams have emerged to create bridges between the volcanologists, social scientists, emergency managers and community representatives to ensure effective transferral of information alongside the construction and implementation of robust crisis plans. However, much of this work is understandably directed at the resident communities. Little has been written as to how destinations in volcanic regions can reconcile often much needed economic growth through sustainable tourism development with the demands required for effective risk management.

While conducting this research the author found that even in the case of the extensively analysed Vesuvius emergency plan there does not currently appear to be full acknowledgement that economic and cultural factors have the potential to override the best laid strategies, even if there is great awareness of the volcanic risk. Furthermore, the lack of benefits to the local communities from the existing tourism products and continued high unemployment is leading many local authorities and agencies around Vesuvius to consider new ways of developing tourism in their localities. Thus a collision course seems to be being steered between the emergency plan on one hand and social and economic necessities on the other. However, the sustainable tourism proposals suggested by agencies such as the Vesuvius National Park and environmental NGOs like Legambiente, by working to improve the chances of benefits filtering down to the local communities rather than increasing the risk to populations in an emergency situation, might actually offer additional pathways to ensure that both awareness and preparedness for the next eruption of Vesuvius are engrained in both residents' and tourists' minds. But for such benefits to occur and strategies such as the NEPVA not to be compromised, geological tourism with its potential to both attract and educate tourists, has to play a central and linked role in any tourism growth.

Additionally if a modified tourism is to succeed in playing an effective supporting role in the transfer of volcanic risk information and link more closely with local communities, then new ways of communicating with tourists and permanent residents alike will have to be applied to revitalize the situation around the volcano. Examples of some more contemporary and engaging methods have already started to become apparent. In particular these have addressed the ways in which archaeological discoveries and interpretations are presented to the public in

museums and other attractions, such as those in and around the ruins at Ercolano.

However, when considering the efforts required to interlink the Vesuvius emergency plan with existing and future sustainable tourism developments around the volcano there still appears to be few initiatives that focus directly on the nature and relevance of the geological and volcanological forces that created and continue to reshape these dramatic landscapes in the first place. The only model that did have the potential to bridge this gap was the possible 'Volcanoes of Campania' geopark. Although at a very early stage in its development, by providing a different management configuration outside of current political structures, the geopark approach might offer at least one alternative route in the very long-term struggle to avoid the grip of the Camorra. For that to become a viable option though it has been stressed on more than one occasion by local stakeholders that there would have to be considerably more dialogue, cooperation and understanding of respective roles between the participating institutions than currently exists. Furthermore, the general public in the locality would have to be actively involved in the creation and running of the geopark in order for them to feel connected with it and understand the impacts it could make on local employment opportunities or more fully comprehend the implications of living 'under the volcano'.

Transferring from a micro-scale examination of the specific set of circumstances around Vesuvius, to the macro scale of more global projections for volcano tourism, it is important to recognize that each active volcanic site around the world is set in its own culture-specific setting and exposed to differing levels and opportunities for tourism development to take place. Thus when considering the opening question of this chapter, 'whether sustainable tourism can be developed around an active volcanic risk?', the evidence points to a situation where case-by-case studies should be undertaken if this is to occur. However, based on the preliminary research around Vesuvius, if one significant generality could be found it is this: that as long as development is integrated with ongoing risk management plans, no matter where the volcano is located, certain forms of tourism which focus in on the volcanological and geological phenomena may actually be able to assist in the spread of educational initiatives and the dissemination of information about the hazards posed to residents and tourists alike.

References

Aguirre, J. A. and Ahearn, M. (2007) 'Tourism, volcanic eruptions, and information: Lessons for crisis management in national parks, Costa Rica, 2006', *PASOS, Revista de Turismo y Patrimonio Cultural*, vol 5, no 2, pp175–191

Barberi, F., Macedonio, C., Pareschi, M. T. and Santacroce, R. (1990) 'Mapping the tephra fallout risk: An example from Vesuvius (Italy)', *Nature*, vol 344, pp142–144

Barberi, F., Davis, M. S., Isaia, R., Nave, R. and Ricci, T. (2008) 'Volcanic risk perception in the Vesuvius population', *J. Volcanol Geotherm Res*, vol 172, pp244–258

Carlino, S., Somma, R. and Mayberry, G. C. (2008) 'Volcanic risk perception of young people in the urban areas of Vesuvius: Comparisons with other volcanic areas and implications for emergency management', *J. Volcanol Geotherm Res*, vol 172, pp229–243

Chester, D. K., Degg, M., Duncan, A. M. and Guest, J. E. (2001) 'The increasing exposure of cities to the effects of volcanic eruptions: A global survey', *Environmental Hazards*, vol 2, pp89–103

Chester, D. K., Dibben, C. J. L. and Duncan, A. M. (2002) 'Volcanic hazard assessment in Western Europe', *J. Volcanol Geotherm Res*, vol 115, pp411–435

Circumvesuviana (2008) 'Rete e Orari', www.vesuviana.it, accessed 12 June 2008

Coopers Oak Wine of the Month Club (2008) March Newsletter, www.coopersoak.com/marchnewsletter.htm, accessed 11 June 2008

Degg, M. (1998) 'Natural Hazards in the Urban Environment: The Need for a More Sustainable Approach to Mitigation', in Maund, D. R. and Eddleston, M. (eds) *Geohazards in Engineering Geology*, Geological Society, London, Eng. Geol. Spec. Publ. 15, pp329–337

Dipartimento della Protezione Civile (1995) 'Rischio vulcanico – Vesuvio', www.protezionecivile.it/minisite/index.php?dir_pk=250andcms_pk=1440, accessed 8 July 2008

Dobran, F. (2000) 'Mitigation of volcanic disasters in densely populated areas', www.westnet.com/~dobran/publ.html, accessed 30 June 2008

Lane, R. L., Tobin, G. A. and Whiteford, L. M. (2003) 'Volcanic hazard or economic destitution: Hard choice in Baãos, Ecuador', Environmental Hazards: Human and Policy Dimensions, *Global Environmental Change*, Part B v5, pp23–34

Masood, E. (1995) 'Row erupts over evacuation plans for Mount Vesuvius', *Nature*, vol 377, p471

Montserrat Volcanic Observatory (2008) 'Education: Illustrated explanation of pyroclastic flows', www.mvo.ms, accessed 8 July 2008

Museo Archeologico Virtuale Ercolano (2009) 'Visiting MAV', www.museomav.com, accessed 15 May 2009

Perry, R. W. and Godchaux, J. D. (2005) 'Volcano hazard management strategies: Fitting policy to patterned human responses', *Volcano Hazard Management*, vol 14, no 2, pp183–195

Solana, M. C., Kilburn, C. R. J. and Rolandi, G. (2008) 'Communicating eruption and hazard forecasts on Vesuvius, southern Italy', *J. Volcanol Geotherm Res*, vol 172, pp308–314

UNESCO (2008) 'Global Network of National Geoparks', www.unesco.org/science/earth/geoparks.shtml, accessed 14 July 2008

Vesuvius National Park (2008) 'The Park', www.parconazionaledelvesuvio.it/grancono/index.asp#parco, accessed 10 July 2008

Vesuvius Observatory. (2008) 'The Vesuvius Observatory exhibition – Vesuvius: 2000 years of observation', www.ov.ingv.it/index_en.html, accessed 12 July 2008.

17

The Auvergne – Centre of Volcanic Tourism in France

Malcolm Cooper and Jeremy Eades

Introduction

Even though France is not known for active volcanoes there are a number of dormant volcanoes and a number of active geothermal sites, especially in the Massif Central of the country. Here, the remnant volcanic landscape has been exploited for geotourism in two main ways. The first is the establishment of the Auvergne Volcanoes Regional Park, the largest natural park in France, and a major centre for health and wellness spa tourism, geotourism and adventure tourism. Second, there are two educational theme parks in this area devoted to volcanoes: Vulcania, a series of displays and exhibitions built into the cone of a dormant volcano, and Lemptégy, where visitors can descend into an actual crater. This chapter explores the geological background, cultural and historic uses, and management of the Auvergne and other sites (Cap d'Agde in the south of the Languedoc, for example), and the development and management of the attractions based on them and the ways in which the surrounding regions attempt to link them in with other forms of regional tourism (food and wine, heritage and culture, etc.), through joint publicity and marketing, and through tour suggestions.

France is the most visited country in the world in the 21st century (Table 17.1; UNWTO, 2008). Eighty-two million visitors were recorded in 2007 (Direction du Tourisme, 2008), 68 million (83 per cent) of which had France as their primary destination and 14 million (17 per cent) were transiting. Of the 68 million, 72 per cent were tourists and 11 per cent business travellers; 48 per cent stayed between one and three nights and 54 per cent more than four nights. Some of the 14 million transit passengers stayed one night while waiting for onward flights. The country's tourism shows a distinct spike April to September, whereas business flows are constant all year round. Of these, tourists sightseeing opportunities attracted 83 per cent, cultural tourism 29 per cent, shopping 16 per cent, and sporting activities and theme parks attracted 7 per cent of all visitors each. Of the countries of origin the Germans, Japanese and Italians favoured cultural tourism and shopping, while the British (the largest group), Belgians and Americans favoured sporting activities (UNWTO, 2008).

Table 17.1 lists the top ten countries on arrivals as determined by UNWTO (2008), but shows that these rankings are not necessarily correlated with the level of inbound receipts, and can be considerably different from rank on outbound expenditure. On these additional measures France ranks third in receipts from inbound tourism despite its first placing in terms of arrivals, suggesting that there is less revenue gained from the 14 million transit passengers, and fourth in outbound expenditure, resulting in a net benefit from tourism of 17 billion USD in 2007. Germans on the other hand spent more than double the amount overseas than that country gained from inbound tourism in 2007, as did those from the UK and Japan, which continued to rate very low on inbound tourism in 2007 but was

Table 17.1 World tourism flows, 2007

Rank	Country	Arrivals (millions)	Receipts billion USD	Rank on receipts	Outbound expenditure billion USD	Rank on expenditure
1	France	81.9	54.2	3	36.7	4
2	Spain	59.2	57.8	2	19.7	11
3	USA	56.0	96.7	1	76.2	2
4	China	54.7	41.9	5	29.8	5
5	Italy	43.7	42.7	4	27.3	6
6	UK	30.7	37.6	6	72.3	3
7	Germany	24.4	36.0	7	82.9	1
8	Ukraine	23.1	4.6	45	3.3	44
9	Turkey	22.2	18.5	10	3.3	45
10	Malaysia	22.1	14.0	14	5.6	30
28	Japan	8.3	9.3	26	26.5	7

Source: UNWTO World Tourism Barometer, 2008

Table 17.2 Evidence of the distribution of volcanic activity in France

Region	Basic geology	Relief	Notes
Vosges-Ardennes	Sedimentary granites	Very rounded, faintly undulating	Extends into Belgium and Germany
Bassin Parisien	Sedimentary	Flat	Extends into UK
Alpes-Jura	Sedimentary granites (centre) Metamorphic rocks	Mountainous	Extends into Switzerland and Italy
Plaine Saone-Rhone	Sedimentary	Flat	
Maures-Esterel-Corse	Metamorphic rocks Ancient volcanics	Uneven, hilly	
Massif Central	Metamorphic rocks Granites Recent Volcanics	Rolling to steep in places, dissected by rivers	Recent volcanism overlays earlier metamorphic and sedimentary rocks
Pyrenees-Languedoc	Metamorphic rocks Granites (centre) Sedimentary (north & south)	Very uneven, hilly	Volcanic outliers in the Cap d'Agde area
Bassin Acquitaine	Sedimentary	Hilly	
Massif Armoricain	Metamorphic Rocks Granites Sedimentary	Rounded hills	

Source: after Bril, 1998

seventh in terms of overall tourism expenditure offshore. For the French volcano tourism attractions there is therefore a large potential market, and this chapter seeks to determine whether this potential has been turned into reality.

Geological background

Table 17.2 outlines the general regional pattern of the geology of France and places the main centres of volcanism within this. The evidence of volcanism lies mainly in the Massif Central (Figure 17.1); in Armorica and Brittany, in the Pyrenees-Languedoc bordering Spain and the Mediterranean, Corsica, and in isolated areas of the east and north of the country there are areas of granites and other metamorphic rocks that had their origins in volcanism but this was in extremely ancient times (Precambrian/Cambrian to Permian (295 million years ago); Bril, 1998). The rocks of the Massif Central and parts of Languedoc and the Jura are comparatively recent, being of Tertiary origin

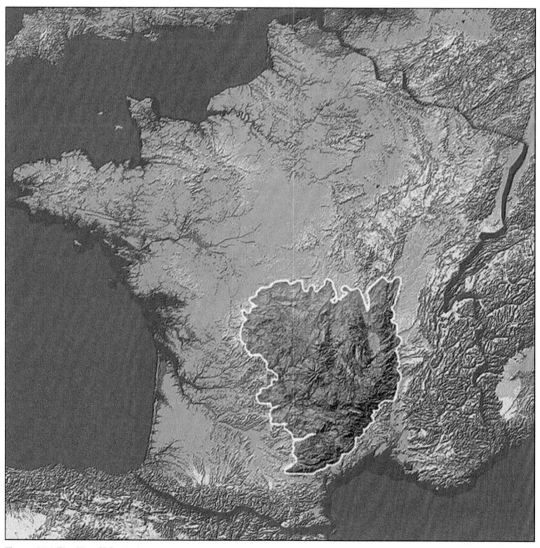

Figure 17.1 The Massif Central

Source: Wikipedia, 2009 (Permission is granted under the terms of the GNU Free Documentation Licence, Version 1.2)

Figure 17.2 Puy de Dôme (left) and Puy de Côme

Source: Malcolm Cooper

(24 to 65 million years), and the volcanism that formed the most visited areas of France in terms of volcano geotourism, the area of the Chaîne des Puys near Clermont Ferrand, is just 5–10,000 years old.

The Chaîne des Puys, prominent in the development of volcanology as an Earth science (Brule-peyronne and Lecuyer, 1998; Cattermole, 2001), are a north–south oriented chain of basaltic and trachytic cinder cones, basaltic maars and trachytic lava domes in France's Massif Central that has been active into the Holocene period (Global Volcanism Program, 2010), and are the major subject of this chapter. The chain is about 40km long, and the identified volcanic features include 48 cinder cones, 8 lava domes and 15 maars and explosion craters. Its highest point is the lava dome of Puy-de-Dôme (Figure 17.2), which is located near the middle of the chain and about 10km from the regional centre of Clermont Ferrand. Development of the present-day Chaîne des Puys began about 68,000BCE, and was largely completed by the beginning of the Holocene (12,000BCE). Holocene eruptions constructed lava domes such as the Puy de Dôme, whose growth was accompanied by pyroclastic flows, cinder cones, lava flows, and maars (Bril, 1998, p121–125). The latest documented activity took

place about 4000BCE near Besse-en-Chandesse and included the powerful explosions that formed the Lac Pavin maar.

In the Massif Central as a whole there are approximately 450 extinct volcanoes (Scarth and Tanguy, 2001); the major ones in the Auvergne region are listed in Table 17.3.

The Puy-de-Dôme is a large lava dome at 1464m and one of the youngest volcanoes in the Chaîne des Puys region of the Massif Central (approximately 10,000 years old), whose last eruption has been dated at approximately 5760BCE. The Puy-de-Dôme département (local government area) is named after the volcano, which itself has recently been listed as one of just six 'Grand Sites of France'. There is a roman temple, an observatory and other buildings on the summit. The entire region is famous in the history of volcanology (Brule-peyronne and Lecuyer, 1998; Cattermole, 2001), as it was the subject of the pioneering research of English geologist George Scrope starting in the 1820s. In 1827 he published *Memoir on the Geology of Central France, Including the Volcanic Formations of Auvergne, the Velay and the Vivarais*, which was later republished in a revised form in *The Geology and Extinct Volcanoes of Central France* (Scrope, 1858). These books were the first widely

Table 17.3 Major mountains of the Auvergne

Range	Mountain	Height (m)
Chaîne des Puys	Puy de Dôme	1464
	Puy de Pariou	1210
	Puy de Lassolas	1187
	Puy de la Vache	1167
Monts-Dores	Puy de Sancy	1886
Le Cantal	Plomb du Cantal	1855
	Puy Mary	1787
Forez	Pierre-sur-Haute	1634
Cevennes	Mont Lozère	1702 (not volcanic)
	Mont Aigoual	1567

Source: Graveline, 1999, p6

published descriptions of the Chaîne des Puys, and Scrope's analysis of their geology laid the foundation for many of the basic principles of the present-day science of volcanology.

Cultural and historical significance of the volcanic environment

A regional natural park (parc naturel régional (PNR)) is a public park established and operated in partnership by local authorities and the French government and covering a rural area of outstanding beauty, created in order to protect scenery and heritage as well as allowing for sustainable economic development in the area. The authority for the creation of PNRs was established by a central government decree on 1 March 1967, and the territory covered by each PNR is decided by the Prime Minister's Office and reviewed every ten years. The Parc Naturel Régional des Volcans d'Auvergne (created 25 October 1977) was one of the earliest and covers 395,000 hectares at an altitude of between 400 and 1886 metres above sea level. It is 120km long, contains 153 communes within its boundaries, and is home to 88,000 inhabitants.

The park is divided into subregions; in the north is the Monts Dômes area, which is characterized by an alignment of 80 young volcanoes of diverse form and origin and the Monts Dore Massif, a complex ensemble of volcanoes culminating in Puy de Sancy (1885m). In this area there are also remnant glaciated valleys (Vallée de Chaudefour, Fontaine Salée) containing a number of lakes such as Lac du Pavin and Guéry ou Chambon. The center is occupied by the Cézallier volcanic plateau massif, and in the south is the Monts du Cantal, the largest volcano in Europe, with a diameter of 70km and an area of 2500km². The Puy Mary, Plomb du Cantal and the Puy Griou form the centre of this southern area, and they are surrounded by deep valleys such as the Mandailles ou Brezons. Also in the south is the subregion of l'Artense, which is an area that is not the result of recent volcanic activity but is a very old granite plateau.

In this area use policies have to strike a balance between fauna and flora protection, heritage protection and renovation, tourism, and the needs of the communities within and adjacent to the park. For the preservation of environmental and cultural heritage the park's charter and mission is five-fold, to:

- protect the richness and to perennialize the biodiversity of the natural inheritance;
- control the evolution of the landscapes and to improve the framework of life;
- preserve the environmental resources (especially water quality) and raw materials;
- develop and add value to the products and activities specific to the region; and
- enhance and protect the views of the park.

In order to achieve these objectives there are three basic policy actions in operation, the second of which is key to our discussion of tourism in this context:

- develop the actions of dialogue and partnership amongst stakeholders;
- inform and sensitize visitors to the park on the richness and fragility of the area; and
- develop and support economic, social and technical studies of the environment of the area.

For the realization of these tasks the park has a technical and administrative team whose members are in general territorial public servants, although the scientific team may include outside experts from time to time. Importantly, these resources are significantly boosted by partnerships with the private tourism attractions such as Vulcania and the Lemptégy Volcanic Theme Park.

Patterns of tourism
The background

We have seen that France remains dominant in terms of tourist arrivals in the early 21st century (see Table 17.1). While the country's share has been dropping in recent years under competition from China and the rest of the Asia Pacific region, it remains the single most visited country in the world. So much so that even preliminary UNWTO figures for the first months of 2009 that indicate a continuation of the negative growth already experienced in the second half of 2008 do not indicate a change in ranking on inbound tourism (UNWTO, 2009). Nevertheless, destinations all around the world have suffered from a decrease in demand in major source markets, with the exception of Africa and both Central and South America, who all posted positive results in the range of 3–5 per cent. So far northern, southern and Mediterranean Europe, north-east Asia, south Asia and the Middle East are amongst the most affected subregions (UNWTO, 2009). In this context, UNWTO expects tourism to France to decline between 2 per cent and 3 per cent in 2009.

The Auvergne Volcanic Regional Park

As one of the attractions of France the Massif Central, a large, rugged plateau of ancient granite and hardened lava punctuated by volcanic peaks and deep river gorges lies in the centre of the country, located midway between Paris and the Mediterranean. On the western side of the Massif in the national regional park of the Volcans d'Auvergne is the Puy de Sancy, the highest point (1886m) in the Massif Central. To the east, the regional park of Livradois Forez covers an area of woodland and the regional capital of Clermont-Ferrand is 32km north of Issoire and the departments of the Cantal and Haute-Loire are to the south.

The region has been inhabited since prehistoric times. Today, the Auvergne is the location of some of France's most important Romanesque churches, medieval castles, cave paintings and Renaissance palaces, as well as the volcanic landscapes. The first cathedral to be built in present-day Clermont-Ferrand was erected by St Namace around AD450, and rebuilt in the Gothic style at the beginning of the 13th century. In the medieval town of Montpeyroux as well as in many of the smaller villages continuing artisanal traditions can be found, while gastronomic traditions include cheeses, pastry and wine.

A major natural attraction in the Auvergne is the Puy de Dôme, an extinct volcano that rises 1465m and provides views of the rest of the Puy mountain chain and the intermontane landscape (Graveline, 1999, p29). Tourists may drive up to the peak, where remains of a Roman Temple to Mercury can still be seen. On this site in 1648 Blaise Pascal performed his famous experiment on the weight of air (Davidson, 1983). While a wide cross-section of France's cultural history can be found in the villages, churches, pilgrim sites and châteaux the area is also home to important outdoor activities, including skiing, bird watching, rafting, biking, golfing, hiking and hang-gliding. Lakes Guéry, Aydat, Pavin and Chambon provide facilities for water sports such as canoeing, fishing, swimming and sailing. The Auvergne Volcanic Regional Park thus offers to sports, family and extreme tourists opportunities for snow sports, forest trekking, fishing and other activities in the rivers and volcanic lakes, hiking in the valleys and mountains, and for horse riding on the tracks of the Domes-Sancy and the Cézallier-Silt. The latter make it possible to ride more than 300km of the park on public trails.

While the park is a protected environment for exceptional flora and fauna, its mountains also provide three classified downhill ski resorts, cross-country skiing, and protect an agricultural landscape that produces a wide range of wines and cheeses, amongst other products. Its ancient volcanoes have in addition ten associated thermal spa areas, five of which are among the leading thermal resorts in France (these include Vichy, Royat, Mont Dore, Saint Nectaire and Volvic), as well as mineral water springs, caves and rivers supporting rafting and canoeing.

Vulcania

One of the major attractions in the park and of great significance to our discussion of volcano tourism in France is the theme park Vulcania, located about 15 kilometres from the centre of Clermont-Ferrand. It was created to inform visitors about volcanoes throughout the world, based on the volcanic history of the Auvergne area. There is also the Puy de Lemptégy close by Vulcania where visitors can get an alternative guided trip through the remains of a 'real' volcano (a heavily mined small cinder cone in reality), part of which is by train and sometimes made more interesting by pyrotechnic displays (see Figure 17.3). Vulcania is also a major site for the diffusion of scientific information on the geology of the Earth and the Universe, and espouses the following objectives of a scientific and tourism nature:

- The Vulcania Theme Park will assume an educational role by diffusing information about Earth sciences, which will include the majority of the current environmental debates.
- The Vulcania Theme Park will be a mediator between specialists in Earth sciences and the public, with the assistance and the guarantee of a scientific council made up of European specialists validating its contents.
- The Vulcania Theme Park will position itself at the same time on a regional, national and European scale.
- The Vulcania Theme Park will put in place diversified tools allowing visitors to make discovery of the Earth an activity, in accordance with the principle 'of learning while recreating'.
- The Vulcania Theme Park will regularly develop and bring up to date its attractions and information, by conceiving new animations adapted to different publics.
- The Vulcania Theme Park will promote the regional natural environment and its use.
- The Vulcania Theme Park will create a place for experiments and scientific discussions of subjects of topicality in Earth sciences.
- The Vulcania Theme Park will take part in reflection on volcanic landscape evolution (design/installation of scenographic innovations and new communications media).

- The Vulcania Theme Park will reinforce scientific direction at the same time as diversifying the media of presentation.
- The Vulcania Theme Park will optimize networks and partnerships at various scales.
- The Vulcania Theme Park will be a centre of documentary resources on sets of Earth science themes.

In addition, in order to preserve the natural beauty of the site most of the park facilities are underground, with one major exception being the 28-metre cone at the centre that is shaped like a volcano. Vulcania is therefore largely concealed in the volcanic subsoil of a former lava flow and its deepest point is 20 metres under the surface. Volcanic stone from the local region was used in the construction of the buildings, enhancing the harmony between the park and its environment. A 35-metre deep crater, caldera and lava tunnel are some of the architectural features inspired by the surrounding vulcanism. The theme park offers major multimedia attractions in the Adventure of Planet Earth and Planets and Volcanoes (the changing history of volcanoes from the Solar System to Planet Earth), scientific discovery trails, scale models of the Auvergne volcanoes, associated geothermal activity and other interesting geotourism features of the region, information on the fauna and flora of the region's natural heritage, scientific information on the development of volcanology and risk management in relation to this extreme environment (Man and Volcanoes exhibit), the Rumbling Chamber, dug out of 30,000-year-old lava flows and incorporating volcanic sound effects and films, The Planisphere (updated information on the 1300+ active volcanoes on the planet, either dormant, on alert or erupting), and a Volcanic Garden portraying the volcanic environments of other countries such as New Zealand.

Special tourist facilities at Vulcania

The park is not only an attraction for day trippers and longer-stay visitors in the Massif Central region:

1 It has from the start welcomed disabled visitors, individually and in groups. The theme

park has been awarded French National Accessibility Charter status and in 2003, the Tourism and Disabled Persons quality label for its capacity to welcome physically and mentally disabled visitors. In 2006 the site was also awarded this label for hearing and visually-impaired persons. Disabled visitors (15 maximum) are met and escorted on tours of up to five hours maximum (excluding lunch).

2   It conducts educational tours (in partnership with the Clermont-Ferrand Education Authority and Volcan Terre d'Eveil Association), for both disabled and able bodied school-age visitors. These complement self-guided tours and are supervised by a guide specialized in Earth sciences. They also allow for a more interactive approach to the theme park and can be adapted to each school level (duration 75 minutes); however, there is a charge for this service and it is accessible by reservation only and subject to availability. The Experiments Area is also available for families during weekends and school holidays.

3   The safety and navigation of the site is enhanced by the VolcanBul, an electric vehicle guided by GPS. This is completely silent and environmentally friendly internal transport for the park complex.

Lemptégy

Located across the main road in the middle of the Chaîne de Puys from Vulcania, the Lemptégy Volcanic Theme Park has been constructed out of the excavated remains of a small scoria cone. This park allows tourists to discover history through a landscape not normally found, that of the inside of a volcano, including volcanic bombs, chimneys and lava flows. This opportunity came about as a result of the post Second World War extraction of materials from the Lemptégy volcano for the rebuilding of the towns of Normandy and in particular of the town of Rouen. The removal of scoria made it possible to view the anatomy of the region as expressed in its volcanoes. During a 1.5 hour tour visitors are able to discover two volcanic chimneys (approximately 30,000 years old), stone dykes, lava flows, faults, fumerolic deposits, carbonized remains of forests (approximately 9500

years old) and volcanic bombs (rocks thrown from a volcano).

Lemptégy is a unique site in France and even in Europe; it is an open air display which has the primary objective of informing general and scientific tourists of the morphology of an actual volcano. It is a place of interest with a teaching goal which attracts 120,000 people per annum. During the summer months it is also open at night, adding pyrotechnic displays to the daytime experience. One of the reasons why this park is of interest and can compete with the much larger and very close Vulcania is precisely that it exposes the anatomy of an elementary volcano of scoria cone type for visitors to discover. And the reason that this is important lies in the fact that geological structure usually has to be either inferred from landforms or carried out in a landscape often mainly covered with vegetation, which means that the points of direct observation can be rare.

Before its excavation the Puy de Lemptégy was present in the form of a small Strombolian cone of 50m in height at an altitude of 1019m above sea level, built on previous volcanic landforms. In spite of these modest dimensions examination of the walls of the crater reveals a complex structure. Two eruptions followed one another here approximately 30,000 years ago: the first was begun, built up and subsided in the Chaîne de Puys environment at the same time as it was covered in debris by an eruption of its immediate neighbor, the Puy de Gouttes. The second was in its turn partially buried under the products emitted successively by two others of its close relatives: initially, on the southern side, by the Puy de Côme (for more than 11,500 years) during a period of icy climate which affected the development of any vegetation; then, on the northern side by the Puy Chopine (for 9500 years), when climate change had allowed the reinstatement of forest cover. In all, the discovered history of five eruptions informs the route of a visit to this Open Sky Theme Park.

On the floor of the crater visitors can observe the products of an initial Strombolian episode (Lemptégy 1), whose composition is basalts and trachybasalts. The site of the first chimney is a resistant base of lava and welded tuff (spatter-cone) culminating in two enormous volcanic bombs of

Figure 17.3 The 'chimneys' of Lemptégy 1

Source: Malcolm Cooper

which the bulkiest is $24m^3$ and weighs 60 tons (Figure 17.3). In the walls north of this area, projections of Lemptégy 1 are separated from the deposits of Lemptégy 2 by deposits from Puy de Gouttes. The colour of these lapilli (pyroclastic material; Ritchie and Gates, 2001, p128) is normally black, but here their colour is red close to their base. This implies that they fell on still hot Lemptégy 1 material and this suggests synchronous activity of both Lemptégy 1 and Puy de Gouttes from the same volcanic system. Their lava is chemically and mineralogically identical. This initial building of the Puy de Lemptégy was recently dated at approximately 60,000 years by thermoluminescence from the quartz that abounds in its substance (Graveline, 1999, pp22–23). This is also the age of the Puy de Gouttes.

A Strombolian trachyandesitic second eruption, Lemptégy 2, occurred about 30,000 years ago. The magma is different to Lemptégy 1 being trachyandesite (Bril, 1998, p124) and similar to that found in the Volvic area (Graveline, 1999). The chimney of this eruption, characterized by the welding of materials together, was preserved by the excavation of scoria. Subsidiary 'escapes' of liquid lava subsequent to the formation of this chimney gave seams of rock that are locally known as dykes. These are south-west trending, which led to their discovery during the excavations for Vulcania, and they are quite similar to the outflow from the more famous Puy de Côme. In fact the latter volcano more recently covered Lemptégy 2 with wind-borne deposits of lapilli (Ritchie and

Gates, 2001) and finely grey ash up to 3m thick (approximately 16,000 years ago). Similarly, products of the even more recent eruption of Puy Chopine form at the top of the Lemptégy excavation a 50cm to 3m thick layer resulting from a pyroclastic flow of about 9500 years ago. Puy Chopine is classically described as a trachytic protrusion resulting from a violent explosive phase which opened a vast crater in the pre-existing Strombolian cone of Puy de Gouttes.

The tourism to this site is characterized by the operators as 'Instant Nature' inside a volcano. Family groups are especially catered for and the point is, like Vulcania, that the anatomy of a volcano over time is laid out for all to see. Travel is made easier by the train, there is an attached restaurant and playground, and impact is assured by the 'Mine Explosive' or fireworks display at night. Having said this, the intention is not merely to entertain; there is a serious information flow occurring during the two-and-a-half hour tour, and the nature and risks of volcano tourism are emphasized. Study workshops and other community values are also provided.

Associated geotourism phenomena

Throughout central and southern France there exist thermal springs, some of which have been in continuous use for thousands of years. Some two millennia after the Romans built their thermal baths at Aix en Provence, for example, tourists are still seeking out the therapeutic waters from the underground springs (Erfurt-Cooper and Cooper, 2009). In the 21st century Thermes Sextius supplies the resort, a vast modern spa built on top of the Roman Baths (still visible through glass panels in the lobby). Similar resources are found associated with the volcanoes of the Massif Central, and include the world famous Vichy and Volvic springs from which bottled water is exported all over the world.

Other volcanic areas of France
Metropolitan France

Other areas of volcanism in metropolitan France do not have as much direct influence on tourist flows; they are more in the nature of background scenery or constitute the physical makeup of

Figure 17.4 La Grande Conque, Cap d'Agde

Source: Malcolm Cooper

mountainous areas suitable for hiking and skiing (often without the visitor realizing that they have a volcanic origin). One exception is the Cap d'Agde in the Languedoc region of southern France. Cap d'Agde is one of the largest leisure ports on the French Mediterranean. Development as a tourist resort started in the 1970s when the only buildings at the Cape were small houses typically used for weekends by local people, and Brescou fort and farm buildings built on the remains of volcanoes dating from around 700,000 years ago (Renault, 2001). The cliffs of the Cape and the cove of La Grande Conque with its black sand beach are the results of a series of submarine volcanic eruptions that occurred at the southern end of the Auvergne volcanic chain (Figure 17.4) at this time. The resulting coast of black rocks is a unique site in the Languedoc-Roussillon, and for tourism purposes has been developed as a 'sentier des falaises' (cliff path), but also as an underwater trail close to the shoreline.

In fact the Cap d'Agde is the seaside resort of the town of Agde on the Hérault River, which started life as a 5th century BCE Greek colony settled by Phocaeans from Massilia. The symbol of the city, the bronze Ephebe of Agde (4th century BCE) was recovered from the Hérault river bed. Agde is also known for the distinctive black volcanic basalt used in the local architecture, for example, in the Cathedral of Saint Stephen, built in the 12th century, and in the surviving Greek and Roman remains.

With respect to tourism, however, it is not the volcanism that attracts tourists to Cap d'Agde but the beaches, in particular the naturist enclave. In 1968 the French government and Agde council signed an agreement with SEBLI (Société d'Equipement du Biterrois et de son Littoral) to design and build, market and finance the construction of a major tourist resort at the Cape (Renault, 2001). Work began in 1969 on the concept which was inspired by the typical character of villages in Languedoc-Roussillon, and paid particular attention to architectural unity, diversity, colour harmony and alternating busy and quiet areas. The resort gradually grew around the marina, international golf course, aquarium, casino and shopping malls, but also includes a thriving naturist village. The naturist village is entirely autonomous and offers a wide range of services and facilities: marina, restaurants, boutiques and shopping centres, banks and medical services. Today, Agde ranks as the number one French tourist resort in terms of the number of people it can accommodate at any one time, around 175,000.

Other former volcanic areas exist in Metropolitan France, in Armorica and Brittany, in the Pyrenees-Languedoc bordering Spain and the Mediterranean, in Corsica and in isolated areas of the east and north of the country (Alpes-Jura) where there are areas of granites and other metamorphic rocks that had their origins in volcanism in extremely ancient times (Bril, 1998). In most cases these are no longer easily identifiable as volcanoes by tourists, who tend to use them for their mountainous or hilly nature in hiking, river rafting, skiing and similar outdoor pursuits, or as a source of spring water, rather than for their geothermal origins. As was seen in Table 17.2, the ages of many of these volcanic areas are in the

100s of millions of years (Cambrian, Precambrian: Jersey, Cotentin, Bolazec in Brittany, Ste Marie in the Jura) or are from the Permian (10s of millions of years old: Pyrenees, Alpes-Jura, Brabant).

French overseas territories

Not strictly part of the discussion in this chapter, the active volcanoes on French soil actually lie in the French overseas territories of French Polynesia (Tahiti, Moorea, etc.), Guadeloupe (Soufriere), Reunion (Piton de Fournaise – last erupted 2008), Martinique (Mt Pelee – last erupted in 1902 and has the title of the most destructive volcano of the 20th century) and Teahitia (submarine volcano near Tahiti). These volcanic areas are the subject of other case studies in this book.

Risk management

Apart from those risks relating to the active volcanoes in French overseas territories, tourism risk management with respect to French volcanoes is not concerned with vulcanism and related geothermal events as such, but more with tourist activities. Extreme weather, for example, can disrupt tourism in all areas of the country; when this is combined with the volcanic terrain problems can occur. Ordinary everyday risks can also impact tourism, such as accidents, crime, financial problems and the like. On Mont Dore, for example, a cable car link was built to one of the needles just below the summit. In December 1965 an accident injured ten passengers and killed seven others (Graveline, 1999). Additionally, water-based activity on the numerous maar lakes formed by volcanism is itself dangerous to the unwary or untrained.

Countermeasures against natural and man-made disasters in France fall into the following categories (as they do in most other countries):

- research into the scientific and technical aspects of disaster prevention;
- reinforcement of disaster prevention systems (facilities and equipment);
- construction projects designed to enhance the country's ability to defend against disasters;
- emergency measures and recovery operations; and
- improvement of information and communications systems.

Countermeasures concerning 'ordinary' accidents and crimes against or by tourists are also quite similar wherever they occur:

- prevention through education and regulations on risky environments or substandard technology (cars);
- insurance cover;
- rescue and police services funding and training for the range of events that might occur;
- restitution or rehabilitation; or
- criminal and civil sanctions where appropriate after the event.

The consensus in the literature (Prideaux, 2004; Santana, 2004; Cooper and Erfurt, 2007) is that it is difficult to predict the likely impact of natural disasters, accidents and/or crimes on tourism, as tourists go by sentiment as much as by perceived realities. If a tourist likes a destination then it is entirely possible that he or she will discount the potential for such problems to affect travel to it. Conversely, if not, then the potential for problems could assume a higher order of negative importance for the tourist than is warranted by actual experience. For a destination it is of course possible to exercise a considerable degree of hindsight in describing the actual impact of any problems that have occurred there in the past, and also to overemphasize preparedness for the next set. Nevertheless, for any destination, even if natural and man-made hazards cannot be avoided their dramatic consequences can be reduced through appropriate preparations and risk reduction measures. France, like Japan and other developed countries, is in fact one of the most prepared nations in the world in this respect. That accidents, extreme natural events and crime still manage to impact on the country and on its tourism just indicates how difficult it is to guard against all possible risks.

Conclusions

In terms of an active–passive continuum model of volcanic geotourism, the Massif Central volcanoes and the other areas of volcanic origin in France are not active (though perhaps not extinct) and therefore do not attract visitors seeking active volcanic experiences. In other words, observing various types of eruption as they are happening is not possible at this end of the possible spectrum of experiences in volcanic geotourism but nevertheless the landforms concerned are attractions in their own right as volcanoes (size, geological composition, shape and as a record of past volcanic activity), and are also important as sites for other forms of tourist activity. Also, the fact that they are of volcanic origin is what supports and legitimates the positioning and activities of the Vulcania and Lemptégy tourist parks.

Visitors to these areas experience instead:

- striking geomorphological structures – the domes, cones and maars (often filled by lakes);
- associated geothermal facilities and products (hot springs, spas, bottled water);
- mountainous terrain suitable for climbing and hiking, and skiing when there is snow;
- distinctive cultures and architectures – legends, myths and black stone (roman baths, temples and cathedrals in Clermont and Agde); and
- educational tours and information about volcanoes and vulcanism.

For the purposes of this book this suggests a development pattern typical of volcanic areas over time: activity (formation and continuation) through to quiescence (dormancy until the next volcano erupts and becomes active) and the cycle starts all over again. The tourism patterns associated with each of these broad phases is also different, involving observation of eruptions and direct risk from the activity of the volcano in its formative stages, through increasingly diversified tourist activity in the volcanic landscape which is less and less directly related to the fact of volcanism, to the creation of theme parks designed to inform about the nature of volcanoes from a position of authenticity (this area was once volcanic) but with no actual possibility or risk of real volcanic activity.

References

Bril, H. (1998) *Volcans de France*, Loubatieres, Portet-sur-Garonne

Brule-peyronne, M. and Lecuyer, F. (1998) *Massif du Sancy & Monts Dore*, Miroir Nature, Clermont-Ferrand

Cattermole, P. (2001) *Auvergne (Classic Geology in Europe 2)*, Terra Publishing, London

Cooper, M. and Erfurt, P. (2007) 'Tsunamis, Earthquakes, Volcanism and Other Problems: Disasters, Responses and Japanese Tourism', in Laws, E., Prideaux, B. and Chon, K. (eds) *Crisis Management and Tourism*, CABI, Wallingford, pp234–251

Davidson, H. M. (1983) *Blaise Pascal*, Twayne Publishers, Boston, MA

Direction du Tourisme. (2008) *Tourisme des Français – Saison Estivale 2007*, Ministère de L'Économie, des Finances et de L'Emploi, Paris

Erfurt-Cooper, P. and Cooper, M. (2009) *Health and Wellness Tourism: Spas and Hot Springs*, Channel View Publications, Bristol, UK

Global Volcanism Program (2010) 'Chaîne des Puys' Online Document: www.volcano.si.edu/world/volcano.cfm?vnum=0100-02-, accessed 8 January 2010

Graveline, N. (1999) *Known and Little Known Volcanoes of the Massif Central*, Editions Debaisieux, Beaumont, France

Prideaux, B. (2004) 'The Need to Use Disaster Planning Frameworks to Respond to Major Tourism Disasters: Analysis of Australia's Response to Tourism Disasters in 2001', in Hall, C. M., Timothy, D. J. and Duval, D. T. (eds) *Safety and Security in Tourism*, The Haworth Hospitality Press, Binghamton, NY, pp281–298

Renault, G. (2001) *Cap d'Agde 1970–2000*, Impresiones Graficas, Barcelona

Ritchie, D. and Gates, A. E. (2001) *Encyclopedia of Earthquakes and Volcanoes*, Checkmark Books, New York

Santana, G. (2004) 'Crisis Management and Tourism: Beyond the Rhetoric', in Hall, C. M., Timothy, D. J. and Duval, D. T. (eds) *Safety and Security in Tourism*, The Haworth Hospitality Press, Binghamton, NY, pp299–321

Scarth, A. and Tanguy, J.-C. (2001) *Volcanoes of Europe*, Oxford University Press, Oxford

Scrope, G. P. (1858) *The Geology and Extinct Volcanoes of Central France*, J. Murray, London (reprinted in 1978 by Arno Press)

UNWTO (2008) *World Tourism Barometer*, vol 6, no 2, UNWTO, Madrid

UNWTO (2009) *World Tourism Barometer*, vol 7, no 1, UNWTO, Madrid

18

Volcanic Geotourism in West Coast Scotland

Thomas A. Hose

An introduction to Scotland's 'west coast' volcanic tourism

This chapter examines volcanic tourism as an aspect of 'geotourism' (Hose, 1995, 2000) on Scotland's west coast (Figure 18.1). This area includes parts of two discrete geographical and tourism regions: Ayrshire and Arran in the south and the Highlands in the north and extends some 50km inland. It includes the area encompassed by the Lochaber Geopark and that delineated by the British Geological Survey (BGS) as the 'Palaeogene

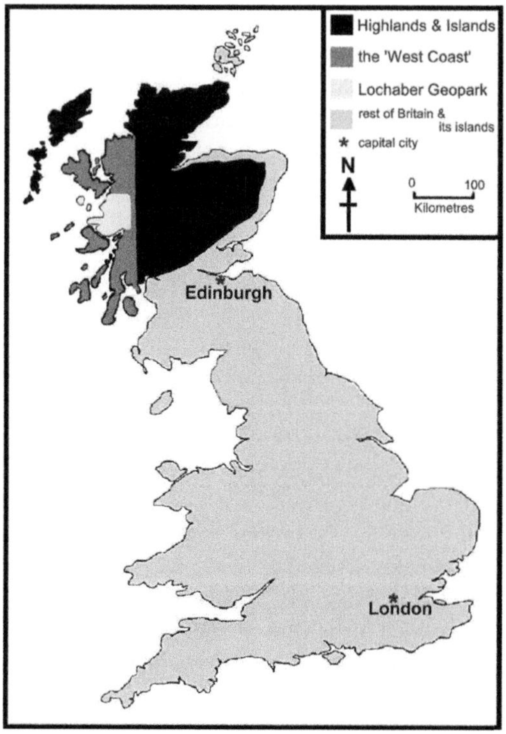

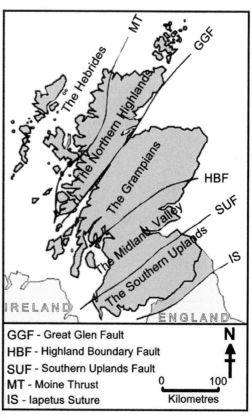

Figure 18.1 West coast Scotland location map

Figure 18.2 The major landscapes of Scotland map

volcanic districts of Scotland' (Emeleus and Bell, 2005), the handbook for which notes that its boundaries 'are not easy to define, either geographically or geologically' (Emeleus and Bell, 2005, pix). Geologically it encompasses sections of the major tectonic features of Scotland and parts of its principal uplands (Figure 18.2).

Overall in Scotland's 14 tourism regions around 80 per cent of the workforce is engaged in the service sector, accounting for more than two thirds of GDP which is worth around £90 billion a year. Tourism in Scotland accounts for some 8 per cent of the country's workforce, providing some 193,000 jobs. In 2007, domestic tourists to Ayrshire and Arran (around 40 per cent from Scotland and 60 per cent from England) took 740,000 trips, stayed for 2.28 million bed nights and spent £117 million; international visitors contributed 160,000 trips, stayed 0.98 million bed nights and spent £50 million (Visit Scotland, 2008a). In 2007, domestic tourists took 2.08 million trips to the Highlands, stayed for 8.83 million bed nights and spent £497 million; international visitors took 550,000 trips, stayed for 2.72 million bed nights and spent £161 million (Visit Scotland, 2008b). In Ayrshire and Arran some 11 per cent of the workforce is engaged in tourism while in the Highlands and Islands it is around 15 per cent. Of course, it is difficult to separate out from the various tourism statistics the exact significance of tourism to just the west coast of Scotland and volcanic tourism specifically, but they do indicate the overall significance and potential of tourism in the area. Indeed, in Scotland tourism employs more people than the oil, gas and whisky industries combined; it contributes around £4 billion a year to its economy.

Scotland's west coast traditional industries are farming, fishing, forestry, mining (especially for coal) and associated processing activities together with ship-building. Since the mid-19th century tourism has supplemented the traditional industries and began to replace some of them from the 1980s. Undergraduate geology students have been introduced to the geology of the Isle of Arran since the early 20th century. For tourists the area offers, apart from some mass tourism activities and visiting country houses and other cultural heritage sites, niche activities such as angling, cycling, golf,

hiking, climbing, sailing and windsurfing. It is particularly visited by American and German tourists. By the early 1990s the need for new and more sustainable forms of tourism (see Edwards and Priestley, 1996) in Scotland was recognized especially to replace traditional coastal tourism that was then in decline; alternative tourist attractions and experiences such as geotourism were developed; its development required a major shift in landscape recognition and tourism exploitation, the antecedents of which were the aesthetic movements of a century or two ago that promoted 'wild' landscapes as safe and worth visiting.

The aesthetic landscape movements

European travellers have from the late 17th century explored new and different experiences with landscapes as a core element. Travel writers' texts and artists' original paintings and their reproductions were a major 18th-century influence on where they went and what they expected to see. From the early 19th century, commercial tourist literature generated specific expectations of landscapes. Landscapes are social and cultural constructs with tourists' perceptions and their values ascribed to them an admixture of direct observation and cultural interpretation (Figure 18.3).

Edmund Burke's *A Philosophical Enquiry into the Origin of Our Ideas of the Sublime and Beautiful* (1857) likened the Sublime Movement to astonishment, fear, pain, roughness and obscurity. The succeeding Picturesque Movement conversely focused on the softer effects resulting from nature's subsequent (mainly geomorphological) operations that produced the variegation and harmony expressed by the meandering curves or rivers and lake shores, the grouping of their flanking trees, the interplay of natural light and shade over these features and the subtle colour gradations that bounded the scene being major foci of interest; such a topographical approach was adopted from the late 18th century by the pioneering travellers, and the artists who accompanied them, who picture-framed landscapes from scenic 'stations' or viewpoints. The later Romantic Movement focused on the tumultuous chaos of mountains with precipitous rock faces and deeply gouged valleys backed by rolling foothills;

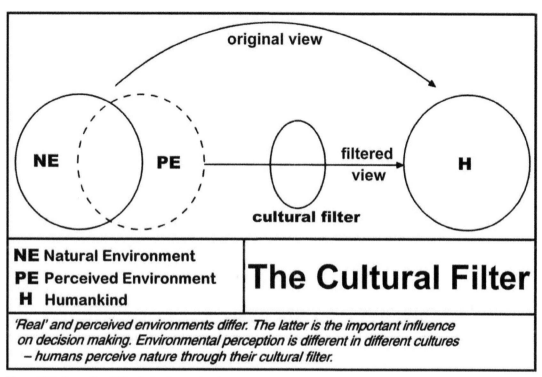

original view

NE | PE | filtered view | H

cultural filter

NE Natural Environment
PE Perceived Environment
H Humankind

The Cultural Filter

'Real' and perceived environments differ. The latter is the important influence on decision making. Environmental perception is different in different cultures – humans perceive nature through their cultural filter.

Figure 18.3 The cultural filter in landscape tourism

their wildness and ruggedness solicited viewers' awe and wonder. William Wordsworth suggested it was 'the result of Nature's first great dealings with the superficies of the earth' (Wordsworth, 1835, p35). It was an all-embracing movement, influential from around 1780 to 1850, involving viewers' emotional reflections on landscapes and their evocation and visualization by artists and writers. The three movements reflected interrelated elements:

- travellers' nature and purpose;
- meanings ascribed to, and understandings of, natural phenomena; and
- the shift from a rural agrarian to an urban industrial society and the concomitant rise of the middle-classes in numbers, education and influence.

An initial limiting factor in promoting tourism into wild landscapes was the physical difficulty of access. Up to the late 19th century leisure travel over any distance was restricted to the social elite who had the available time, financial resources (to cover the cost of the available but rather limited transport and accommodation) and requisite education. It was only with the arrival of the passenger railways that opportunities for, especially coastal, excursions opened up the countryside for the majority of the by then largely urban-based population; until then, they had to just accept the published second-hand observations and accounts.

For much of the early development of landscape appreciation the dominant representations were provided by artists trained in Europe's major cultural centres working in pencil and ink, oils and watercolour. Their originals were initially viewed by the social elite in commercial galleries and somewhat later in the emerging public art galleries by the middle classes in London, Edinburgh and the major provincial centres; lithography's 19th-century developments enabled the mass printing of good-quality copies to be seen by those unable by geography or social class to view the originals. Photography was increasingly used as a recording medium from the late 19th century onwards and by the close of the century it was the basis of many guidebook illustrations. Thus for tourists lacking first-hand experiences of actual landscapes their impressions and expectations were markedly influenced by artistic and photographic visualizations, some of which appeared in guidebooks.

The curiosity and aesthetic worth that inspired travellers and tourists, before scientific value, as motivators for travel was partly evoked by such visualizations. Of course, guidebooks have always attempted to satisfy the curious and promote newly recognized attractions. Geology's increasing popularity, especially amongst the leisured classes and in schools, in the 19th century encouraged field excursions, and field-guides evolved to support them; the Scottish geosites identified in them are the mainstay of present-day geotourism provision whose origin lies with the reportage of somewhat earlier travellers. A national schools' geology syllabus had been published by the British Association in 1890 but was not implemented. Again, despite geology's early development in the United Kingdom it was not a major subject in its universities until the 1960s; indeed, in the 1930s there were only some 30 geology undergraduates per year (Hamilton, 1976, p105). However, 'By 1956 Geology had an important role in scientific education in schools in Britain. Experiments in integrated sciences, field sciences, rural and environmental studies developed in the non-examination secondary schools' (Hamilton, 1976, p110).

From the late 1960s to the late 1980s university geology underwent a major expansion (Hamilton, 1976); this was probably encouraged by the discipline's popularization as a result of plate tectonics and its fieldwork requirement when environmental education was widely promoted in schools. Many of the graduates who studied geology during the boom years are now in teaching and management positions in a variety of academic, public sector and commercial environmental service sector organizations and able to influence opinion at a variety of levels; however, these potential geology ambassadors are not being replaced and new means of promoting geology need to be explored to continue geotourism's expansion in the future.

Scotland's west coast volcanoes

The west coast is geologically noteworthy for its Paleogene (some 24 to 65 million years ago) Igneous Province (see Emeleus and Bell, 2005), the principal but not sole focus of the country's volcanic geotourism. The Province has one mainland (Ardnamurchan) and five island (Arran, Eigg, Mull, Rum and Skye) volcanic centres. Ardnamurchan is one of the real gems of Scotland's volcanic tourism although it is not fully exploited as such; it was an active volcano some 60 million years ago. The principal volcanic island centre of Rum lies about 25 kilometres off Ardnamurchan; it was declared a national nature reserve in 1957 for its flora and fauna rather than its geology, which has been studied for well over a century from the gentlemen geologists of the late 19th century to today's academic geologists.

Both Ardnamurchan and Rum were included in the designation of the Lochaber (European) Geopark in 2007. Scotland's west coast volcanoes were the end result of the pooling of a huge volume of magma below northern Britain around 61 million years ago when the north Atlantic Ocean had not opened and western Europe was attached to Greenland and North America. This magma plume eventually split the continental plates prior to their drifting as it enabled molten rock to migrate upwards through the crust and, where it was fractured, reach the surface to form the volcanoes of Ardnamurchan, Arran (Figure 18.4), Mull, Rum and Skye (Figure 18.5). This magmatic activity domed the crust bringing up ancient rocks from great depth and producing a series of volcanic cones (with their associated lavas and ash deposits to mark their approximate location) and calderas with their associated ring dykes; subsequent erosion, especially during the last Ice Age has picked out these features in the landscape to create dramatic and aesthetically attractive scenery.

All of the volcanoes were involved in major geological and rather catastrophic events. For example, on Rum around 60.5 million years ago the roof of a large magma chamber collapsed, leaving a 12×7km caldera, that released (judging from the thick and extensive tuff deposits now found) huge

Figure 18.4 Aran, Goat's Fell and the northern granite outcrop viewed from the ferry on its way to Portree

Note: The amphitheatre-like nature of the upland outcrop is evident as is the low cloud that all too often obscures summit views in the traditional Autumn and Easter university field excursion seasons.

Figure 18.5 Skye, the Black Cuillin

Note: The spectacularly eroded, during the last Ice Age, gabbroic remnants of a major volcano are revealed in the precipitous slopes much explored by hill walkers and climbers despite the all too frequent low cloud evident in this August view.

quantities of incandescent ash over a 20km radius; the event was similar to, but around ten times larger than, the 1980 Mt St Helens, USA eruption. Successive cataclysmic eruptions piled up great thicknesses of lavas and ash deposits over the caldera as a new magma chamber consumed the lower reaches of the old caldera. While Rum's volcano would have towered a thousand or more metres above the surrounding landscape it was rapidly eroded (estimated at 3–4mm per year, around twice as fast as that of the Himalayas today) when it became extinct as the crustal plate carried it away from the mantle plume. Rum has comparatively few visitors, and most go to see the birdlife, because of its protected status and difficulty and cost of access. Skye is the other great volcanic destination, and much more visited due to its accessibility especially since it was linked to the mainland by a road bridge in 1995. The island's volcanic centre and its Cuillin Hills (made of gabbro from a magma chamber that supplied a volcano that erupted around 50 million years ago) have been a major mountain tourist attraction and latterly a mountain climbing centre since the late 19th century.

Much further to the south of Ardnamurchan and great island volcanic centres of Rum and Skye is the Isle of Arran volcanic centre, much visited by geology students for the past 150 years since Hutton's seminal text. Its geology is dominated by two exposed volcanic rock associations, the northern granite pluton and the central ring complex. The former, which forms the highest and most spectacular scenery of the island, is the unroofed remains of a major but strictly non-volcanic diapiric intrusion and the latter the remains of a volcanic caldera complex noteworthy for its inclusion of incorporated blocks of fossiliferous Jurassic and Cretaceous limestones that provide the only evidence of the former northern extent in Britain of such deposits. However, the discovery of the region's geology required the opening up of the area to travellers, the precursors of modern geotourists.

Geotourism in the Highlands and Islands
Early travellers

Before the 1760s, the Highlands and Islands were an exotic destination (and a real journey into the wild, dangerous and unknown) for English travellers; indeed until the arrival of the few railways from the mid-1850s journeys into and around the region were slow and accommodation unreliable. The final volume of Englishman Daniel Defoe's three-volume *A Tour Thro' the whole Island of Great Britain* of 1724 to 1727 covered Scotland and became *the* Scottish guidebook – based on his 1706 to 1708 and 1712 travels although it seems that the accounts of the Highlands and Islands were not based on his actual first-hand observations. New military roads, laid from the 1720s onwards, improved access to the region. Thomas Gray, a pioneer of the Romantic, was one of the earliest Highlands travellers, in 1764 and 1765, to admire their natural beauty. In 1789 William Gilpin published his *Observations, Relative Chiefly To Picturesque Beauty, Particularly the High-Lands of Scotland* following his tours across Britain in the 1760s and 1770s. His 1776 Highlands tour introduced its scenic beauty to a wide audience when it was published in 1789, making them a desired destination for generations of landscape painters; his textual descriptions and landscape and nature aquatints created a new style of travel writing.

Surprisingly, even the new military roads were reluctantly trodden by Scottish artists. Even the founder of Scottish landscape painting Alexander Nasmyth rarely ventured outside his comfortable Edinburgh studio in the early 1800s for long despite his commissions to paint large houses and castles in their landscapes; *Lugar Water* (1775–1799) is typical of his highly romantic stylized classical approach. His painting *A View in Glen Coe, Argyllshire* (1814) captures the grandeur of the scene with some redolence to contemporary visualizations of the European Alps, and his circa 1820 painting *Portencross, at the Mouth of the Clyde* is a romanticized dramatic coastal scene in which the geology of the cliffs is most accurately depicted.

Nasmyth's youngest daughter, Charlotte, painted atmospheric landscapes, amongst the finest of which is *Mountainous Landscape with a Sailing Boat on the Lake*. Nasmyth's worthy successor was Aberdeen based James Giles; Queen Victoria commissioned him to paint the 1849 watercolour *Lochnagar: The loch in the corrie of the mountain*, on the Balmoral estate which had been leased a year earlier after Prince Albert had seen the artist's watercolours of the area. Despite doing the initial sketches in early October driving wind, rain, sleet and snow Giles depicted the mountain and loch in mellow sunlight as he had visualized it. As a studio painter his *Isle of Handa*, requiring a short Hebridean sea voyage, benefited from similar post-visit visualization.

Early naturalists

The same roads were traversed and sea voyages undertaken by several significant scientific and literary travellers. John Ray, the distinguished English naturalist, is one of the earliest recorded; in August 1661 he rode from Berwick to Edinburgh, thence to Stirling and Glasgow, before returning via western Scotland, but his route missed the volcanic areas. The distinguished Welsh naturalist Thomas Pennant undertook two Scottish tours. His first Highlands tour was on horseback in 1769 through Perthshire and Aberdeenshire thence along the coast to Caithness, returning west along Glen Mor and through Argyllshire to the Lowlands; overall it missed the volcanic area. The tour's account, *A Tour In Scotland* (1771), was a major publishing success and numerous editions followed; encouraged by its success, he undertook a second sailing tour of Scotland centred on the western seaboard and its islands, from June to August 1772 when he was accompanied by the botanist John Lightfoot (who had published the 1777 *Flora Scotica* on Scotland's native plants) and Moses Griffith, a Welsh servant whom he had trained to draw sketches for his travelogues. Voyaging along Scotland's west coast and Inner Hebrides, he visited Arran, Gigha, Jura, Islay, Oronsay, Colonsay, Iona, Canna, Rhum, Skye and Mull and thus visited some of the key volcanic sites. The voyage's account, *A Voyage to the Hebrides* illustrated by Griffith's sketches was published in two parts in 1774 and 1776. Pennant was crucial to the discovery of the Highlands and Islands in the 18th century's second half because he published both their first scientific travel accounts and proved they could be safely visited despite the period's bitter political feuding; his accounts were widely read as guidebooks up to the opening of the 19th century.

The distinguished and influential naturalist Joseph Banks undertook a voyage to Iceland via the Hebrides in 1772 and stopped off at the islands of Islay, Jura, Oronsay, Mull and Iona. Having heard about the basaltic pillars on Staffa and deciding to view them, he returned via the Orkney Isles. His account of Staffa and drawings of Fingal's Cave were included in the first part of Pennant's 1774 *Tour in Scotland, and Voyage to the Hebrides* making it a magnet for scientists from across Europe. The French geologist Faujas St-Fond visited (and published in 1799 *Travels in England, Scotland and the Hebrides*), with William Thornton as official artist, Staffa in 1799 and noted it was 'erect basaltic columns, on the broken tops of which one must step with considerable dexterity, at the risk of falling into the sea' (Burton and Burton, 1978, p48). Later, the Scottish geologist Hugh Miller recorded in his 1897 *The Cruise of the Betsey a* voyage to the Hebrides and wrote on Eigg: 'We found it composed of various beds, each of which would make a Giant's Causeway entire' (Miller, 1897, p33).

James Boswell and Samuel Johnson, whose separately published accounts established the region as one worth well visiting by those interested in scenic landscapes, are probably the best-known of the 18th century's travellers to the region. In late-summer 1773 they met in Edinburgh for a three-month tour visiting Skye, Raasay, Coll, Mull and Iona travelling by coach on the east coast to Inverness, continuing on horseback to Bernera on the west coast, and journeying on foot through the islands. In 1775, Johnson published A *Journey to the Western Islands of Scotland*; his unfavourable opinions of the Scots and distaste for Gaelic culture aroused considerable protest in Scotland but his journal inspired subsequent generations to follow the route. Boswell published *The Journal of a Tour to the Hebrides, with Samuel Johnson, LL.D* in 1786, ten years after Johnson's account and a year after his death. It was a great success because it covered their journey and also gave an intimate portrait of Johnson; it includes several geological references.

Sir John Stoddart, an English journalist, whilst residing in Edinburgh in 1799 and 1800 made several journeys through Scotland, often accompanied by the watercolourist John Claude

Nattes; his perception of the Highlands was heavily influenced by the Romantic Movement, evident in his 1801 *Remarks on Local Scenery & Manners in Scotland*. Sarah Murray, the English authoress, is one of the region's earliest recorded solo women travellers. In 1796 she travelled, mainly by carriage, through Argyllshire and the central Highlands. In 1800, she visited Mull, Staffa and Iona. She continued her Hebridean tour in 1802, visiting Mull, Ulva, Coll, Eigg, Rhum, Skye and Scalpay. She published in 1799 *A Companion, and Useful Guide to the Beauties of Scotland: To the Lakes of Westmoreland, Cumberland, and Lancashire*, and *A Companion and Useful Guide to the Beauties in the Western Highlands of Scotland* in 1805. Both included practical advice for travellers and were widely plagiarized in later guidebooks.

Dorothy Wordsworth's 1874 *Recollections of a Tour Made in Scotland A.D. 1803* was published long after her death in 1855, even though it was her only journal actually intended (unlike the better known *Grasmere Journals*) for publication. In December 1799, Dorothy and her brother William moved to Dove Cottage in Grasmere from where in 1803 she, William and the poet Samuel Taylor Coleridge started a six-week tour of Scotland. William had already visited Scotland in 1801, but it was a first visit for Dorothy and Coleridge. They travelled on a horse and cart through Dumfriesshire and Lanarkshire to Glasgow, thence onto Loch Lomond where Coleridge left due to illness. Dorothy and William journeyed on through Argyllshire and returned via Glen Coe to the route of the small Highland tour; on their way back they visited the Trossachs, returning via Edinburgh to England. Dorothy Wordsworth returned to Scotland in 1822. The Scottish doctor John Macculloch published Scotland's earliest scientific account, a *Description of the Western Isles of Scotland*, in 1819 and a detailed map in 1836.

Promoting geotourism to the west coast volcanoes

The country's earliest geology map was included in Ami Boue's *Essai Geologique sur l'Ecosse* of circa 1820. Official Geological Survey Scottish fieldwork began in 1854 in the Lothians, but the Highlands had to wait until 1882. Publications on Scotland's

volcanic geology date from the late 18th century. Amongst the first of these were observations by James Hutton, arguably the founder of modern geology, who between 1785 and 1788 undertook fieldwork across Scotland seeking the evidence in the rocks to support his theories. He was often accompanied by Sir John Clerk of Penicuick whose seventh son, Sir John Clerk of Eldin, accompanied Hutton on his 1787 Arran trip, during which Clerk was inspired enough by the geology and related scenery to prepare several superb cross-sections of the island. Hutton observed on Newton Shore that layers of sedimentary rock were tilted up vertically and overlain by other sediments of a different age and at a different angle; he concluded that lower layers of rock had been deposited eons before, then later upturned and covered by newer layers of rock. In these 'unconformities' between rock layers, Hutton saw evidence of vast expanses of time in Earth history. This and related observations and critical thinking led to Hutton's main ideas: the processes that shape the Earth are slow, continuous and cyclical and the driving force is volcanism, as published in his seminal and eventual three-volume, *Theory of the Earth*.

Almost a century later, John Wesley Judd commenced fieldwork and scientific publication on the Province's volcanoes (Judd, 1889). Modern accounts of Scotland's geodiversity are widely available in both technical and populist formats – a measure of its interest to both dedicated and casual geotourists and its significance in the development of an understanding of volcanic activity; for both, the publications of the BGS provide a sound geological underpinning and Scottish Natural Heritage (SNH), particularly for Arran, Skye and Rum, provide a good background on landscape evolution.

Modern Scottish geotourism
Geotourism and geoparks

Modern geotourism was recognized and defined in the early 1990s (Hose, 2008); its original definition (Hose, 1995, p17) along with some of its associated concepts was incorporated within the UNESCO 2000 Geoparks Programme Feasibility Study (See Patzack and Eder, 1998), as were the essential elements of its subsequent redefinition:

The provision of interpretative facilities and services to promote the value and societal benefit of geological and geomorphological sites and their materials, and to ensure their conservation, for the use of students, tourists and other casual recreationalists.

(Hose, 2003)

It is a form of 'special interest' or 'niche' (Hose, 2005) tourism whose participants are motivated by specific interests for which they express some dedication. Geotourism is a geology-focused, and visitor-centred sustainable development of 'environmental interpretation'; 'a range of activities carried out by managers of countryside and heritage sites. It can be defined as: "the art of explaining the meaning and significance of sites visited by the public"' (Badman, 1994, p429) that evolved from developments in the USA where, from the 1920s, sport-based wildlife recreation and interpretation was much promoted by the national parks service.

Modern UK environmental interpretation dates from the mid-1960s (Barrow, 1993). The first temporary nature trails were established in 1964 during 'National Nature Week'; the first permanent nature trail was only established in 1966 in the Forestry Commission's Grizedale in the Lake District. During the 1980s the United Kingdom saw a considerable increase in the number and range of heritage sites and products; the boom's antecedents were in the transport and associated industrial preservation movement of the early 1960s resulting from attempts to save the rapidly disappearing railway branch lines following rationalization of the British Railway network. By the beginning of the 1990s, there were some 500 museums with industrial history collections, and that figure excludes the various industrial heritage attractions based on mining and quarrying, with approximately one-third established since 1970. The development of many of these attractions was a consequence of the decline in employment in traditional heavy industries and mining and the subsequent need to find new employment opportunities, coupled with the economic repositioning of many ex-industrial areas; some of these had geotourism potential the realization of which requires:

- continuing geological research and publication (if the creation of a 'legacy geology' is to be avoided);
- identifying, protecting, conserving and monitoring (that is 'geoconservation') of geosites and geocollections;
- a knowledge and understanding of geotourists (that is 'visitor studies'); and
- the development and promotion of competent interpretative provision (See Hose, 1998; Hose, 2006).

Further, two major categories of geotourist with different needs can be recognized:

- 'Dedicated geotourists' who purposefully select to visit geosites for the purpose of personal educational or intellectual improvement and enjoyment; and
- 'Casual geotourists' who occasionally visit geosites mainly for recreation, pleasure and some limited intellectual stimulation.

Provision for the former as field-guides and journal papers is longstanding. Provision for the latter as populist guides, trails and visitor centres is relatively recent. The locations visited by the two categories can overlap, although their usages and understandings are often very different. Two major geosite categories can be recognized:

- 'Primary geosites' with geological and/or geomorphological features, either natural or artificial and generally permanently exposed, within a delimited area and of some significance for their scientific, educational or interpretative value. They range from quarries and natural cliffs to mines and caves requiring husbandry rather than strict preservation for much of their value lies in the access they provide to *in-situ* rocks and their fossils and minerals.
- 'Secondary geosites' with some feature(s) and/or item(s), inside or on a structure or delimited area, of at least local significance to the history, development, presentation or interpretation of geology or geomorphology. Museum and library collections, heritage/visitor centres, geologists' residences, memorials along with commemorative plaques and monuments can be included.

Both geosite types have tourism development potential with appropriate interpretative and informational provision to explain their meaning and significance. The development of geoparks within Europe has seen these requirements come under considerable scrutiny. While UNESCO recognition has been available for globally significant geosites since 1972, the most significant being world heritage list citation, not all significant geosites can meet the 'outstanding universal value' criterion required by the World Heritage Convention. An alternative recognition was clearly required and the 1990 UNESCO geoparks programme was developed to promote landscapes on a holistic rather than purely geological basis. Ideally, the geological interest is allied with archaeological, cultural, historical or ecological interests. A UNESCO geopark is territory with:

> well-defined limits that has a large enough surface area for it to serve local economic development. The Geopark comprises a number of geological heritage sites of special scientific importance, rarity or beauty; it may not be solely of geological significance but also of archaeological, ecological, historical or cultural value.
>
> (UNESCO, 2000, p43)

European geoparks are territories that combine geoconservation and geoheritage promotion with sustainable local development underpinned by:

- geodiversity sufficient to provide enough geosites of sufficient quality (in terms of their science, rarity, aesthetics and educational value) to generate tourism interest;
- a formal agreement between the relevant local authorities on a sound economically underpinned promotion and management strategy with clearly defined boundaries establishing an area large enough to be economically viable and with access to some European Union financial support; and
- linkage to the geoparks network and benefiting from protection and management measures that oblige and enforce geoconservation – consequently, the sale of geological materials from within or without them is banned.

They must provide educational facilities and promote research, meeting the needs of both geotourist types. They must also actively participate in the economic development of their own and adjacent territory by working with locally based small- and medium-sized enterprises to develop and promote new products and services, ranging from interpretative provision to souvenir manufacture; equally, more general leisure, rather than purely education, related activities should be encouraged so that the geopark's inhabitants recognize and appreciate their geoheritage and are actively involved in its cultural and economic regeneration. The Lochaber Geopark exemplifies these various issues.

The Lochaber Geopark

The Lochaber Geopark stretches from Rannoch Moor in the south to Glen Garry in the north, and from Loch Laggan in the east to the Small Isles of Eigg, Muck, Rum and Canna in the west. Its inception was in a public meeting, held in Fort William in January 2004, at which representatives of the European Geoparks Network gave a presentation outlining the requirements for European geopark status and a local geologist gave an account of the area's geodiversity. Subsequently, a working group was established to undertake the task of preparing the application. The initial application in 2005 narrowly failed because it lacked sufficient evidence of a formal management structure and a project officer to promote the geopark; subsequently, a community based company, Lochaber Geopark Association (LGA), was established in February 2006 to drive the process forward and a project officer was appointed in October 2006. In April 2007 Lochaber was awarded European and global geopark status, the second such in Scotland after the North West Highlands Geopark was designated in October 2004.

The geopark's geodiversity includes Ben Nevis, Britain's highest mountain and 'The Parallel Roads of Glen Roy' created by the staged draining of a glacially dammed lake in the last Ice Age, as well as the volcanic centres of Ardnamurchan and Rum. The geopark is unique among European geoparks because its geological record includes not only the creation of a huge mountain chain

Figure 18.6 The Glen Coe area viewed south-east from Pap of Glencoe – the extensive outcrop of a deeply eroded volcanic caldera

Note: Most recently the action of ice which melted some 11,000 years ago has had an obvious impact on the spectacular mountain landscape much explored by hill walkers and climbers

from the collision of giant tectonic plates, but also the dramatic volcanic activity associated with the much later plate rifting when Greenland and Europe drifted apart. The igneous rocks formed when the Caledonian mountains were created include several calderas; these were actually first recognized and described from Glen Coe, in the early years of the 20th century, where the road runs right across a deeply eroded ancient example (see Figure 18.6).

The geology of the Glen Coe caldera volcano has recently been resurveyed and a new map and handbook (Kokelaar and Moore, 2005) published; the latter notes that it is now interpreted as a new form of 'probably the world's best exposed, tectonically controlled, multi-subsidence, piecemeal caldera volcano' (Kokelaar and Moore, 2005, p30). Again, the rocks forming the summit of Ben Nevis collapsed more than 600 metres to form a similar caldera around 400 million years ago. Rum is noteworthy for its layered ultrabasic complex, probably the remnant of a Hawai'ian style shield volcano; as such it is a major research location in the understanding of basaltic volcanism. The calderas were the inspiration for the geopark's logo.

Setting aside the geology, the mountainous scenery of the geopark is spectacular and it requires some agility to explore many of the key volcanic outcrops. In the 18th century, lead ore was mined near Strontian from where a new mineral was discovered which the chemist Adair Crawford named strontianite after the village. It was from strontianite that the element strontium was first isolated by Sir Humphrey Davy around 1807. The LGA has published several promotional leaflets and trails suitable for casual geotourists; it has also promoted numerous tourism events. Meanwhile SNH has published several in its 'Landscape Fashioned by Geology' series booklets on both Lochaber's and the west coast of Scotland's geology.

Paying for geoparks

The LGA is funded by SNH, The Highland Council, Highlands and Islands Enterprise Lochaber, Leader Plus, The Heritage Lottery Fund and The Robertson Trust; it also works with a broad spectrum of local, regional and national organizations, including the John Muir Trust, The Association of Lochaber Community Councils, the Nevis Partnership, Outdoor Capital of the UK, the British Geological Survey, the Forestry Commission, the National Trust for Scotland and Visit Scotland. There have been attempts to licence and charge a fee for the right to collect from geosites in Scotland and elsewhere; the most notable was on the Isle of Arran (Robinson, 1990) where the landowner, whose land accounted for four-fifths of the localities in the island's main field guide, proposed to make a per capita weekly charge (initially £10 but subsequently reduced to £4) for geology parties. Opinions were mixed amongst both the broad geological and the local island's hotelier community. Overall, it was an unwelcome if plausible option to generate legitimate income propounded in terms of new approaches to land and estate resource management; however, a drawback was that it implied that the land agent was responsible and liable for the health and safety of anyone paying fees and this might well have led to the withdrawal of the proposal. Arran was the base for two-day geotourism courses run by SNH in 2004 and 2005 (MacFadyen, 2006). This was an initiative prompted by the island's hoteliers and bed and breakfast owners, who approached SNH. The subsequent initial course (run in conjunction with Destination Arran, The National Trust for Scotland and the Royal Society for the Protection of Birds) involved a day of sessions on the significance of biodiversity and geodiversity and how these can be marketed locally and nationally, with a brief field excursion. The second day was a whole-day field excursion with lectures and briefings on Arran's geology. Presently, on Arran and elsewhere some income can obviously be generated from charges to visit visitor and heritage centres, as well as from the sale of publications.

Some concluding remarks

The area examined in this chapter has the geotourism advantage that its rocks were important in the development of scientific geology and they have significant geohistorical significance. However, even geotourism's early development had negative impacts which have some modern counterparts; for example, in 1844: 'On Staffa travelers carved their names into the basaltic pillars and fired shots inside Fingal's Cave to hear the echo' (Rackwitz, 2007, p219). The former activity is not unknown today, although paint aerosols sometimes substitute for chisels! Fortunately, modern geotourism provision depends upon geoconservation and such 19th-century practices are now actively discouraged. However, the issue of responsible collecting of geological material is something that still needs addressing at some key localities, especially for rocks and minerals since the launch of SNH's Scottish Fossil Code in 2007.

Overall, the region exemplifies the significance of opening up safe and reliable access together with the popularization of aesthetic landscapes, in illustrated accounts, in the development of early geotourism by elite travellers; as these improved in quality and quantity so it increased its mass appeal. Geoparks such as Lochaber are a natural evolution from 19th century approaches to landscape promotion and late 20th century approaches to environmental interpretation. They encourage cooperation between landowners and agents, tourism operators and the geological community to promote geology and landscape to tourists (See Zouros, 2006). Additionally they can link quite diverse, in terms of age and geological interest, primary and secondary geosites through trails and associated publications. Geotourism has a clear role in extending the timing and nature of tourism provision in the Highlands and Islands. Increasingly, the tourism industry is promoting active, participative outdoor and adventure activities involving the individual in a greater knowledge and understanding of the host environment. Recreational geology promoted through geotourism should find a place in such future developments and continue the 200-year popularity of the region for tourists interested in landscapes underpinned by volcanic features.

References

Badman, T. (1994) 'Interpreting Earth Science Sites for the Public', in O'Halloran, D., Green, C., Harley, M., Stanley, M. and Knill, J. (eds) *Geological and Landscape Conservation*, The Geological Society, London, pp429–432

Barrow, G. (1993) 'Environmental Interpretation and Conservation in Britain' in Goldsmith, F. B. and Warren, A. (eds) *Conservation in Progress*, Wiley, London, pp271–279

Burton, A. & Burton, P. (1978) The Green Bag Travellers: Britain's First Tourists. London: Andre Deutsch, London.

Edwards, J. A. and Priestley, G. K. (1996) 'European Perspectives on Sustainable Tourism', in Priestly, G. K., Edwards, J. A. and Coccossis, H. (eds) *Sustainable Tourism? European Experiences*, CAB International, Wallingford, pp189–198

Emeleus, C. H. and Bell, B. R. (2005) *The Palaeogene Volcanic Districts of Scotland* (4th edn), British Geological Survey, Keyworth

Hamilton, B. M. (1976) 'The changing place of geology in science education in England', *Journal of Geological Education*, vol 24, no 1, pp105–110

Hose, T. A. (1995) 'Selling the story of Britain's stone', *Environmental Interpretation*, vol 10, no2, pp16–17

Hose, T. A. (1998) 'Mountains of fire from the present to the past: Effectively communicating the wonder of geology to visitors, *Geologica Balcania*, vol 28, nos 3–4, pp77–85

Hose, T. A. (2000) 'Geological Interpretation and Geoconservation Promotion for Tourists', in Barretino, D., Wimbledon, W. A. P. and Gallego, E. (eds) *Geological Heritage: Its Conservation and Management*, Madrid: Sociedad Geologica de Espana/Instituto Technologico GeoMinero de Espana/ProGEO, pp127–146

Hose, T. A. (2003) 'Geotourism in England: A two-region case study analysis', unpublished PhD thesis, Department of Ancient History and Archaeology, University of Birmingham, UK

Hose, T. A. (2005) 'Geo-Tourism – Appreciating the Deep Side of Landscapes', in Novelli, M. (ed) *Niche Tourism: Contemporary Issues, Trends and Cases*, Elsevier, Oxford, pp27–37

Hose, T. A. (2006) 'Leading the Field: A Contextual Analysis of the Field-Excursion and the Field-Guide in England', in Wickens, E., Hose, T. A. and Humberstone, B. (eds) *Critical Issues in Leisure and Tourism Education*, Leisure and Tourism Education Research Centre, Buckinghamshire Chilterns University College, High Wycombe, pp115–132

Hose, T. A. (2008) 'Towards a History of Geotourism: Definitions, Antecedents and the Future', in Burek, C. V. and Prosser, C. D (eds) *The History of Geoconservation*, The Geological Society, London, pp37–60

Judd, J. W. (1889) 'The Tertiary volcanoes of the western isles of Scotland', *Quarterly Journal of the Geological Society*, vol 45, nos 1–4, pp187–219

Kokelaar, B. P. and Moore, I. D. (2005) *Classical Areas of British Geology: Glencoe Caldera Volcano, Scotland*, British Geological Survey, Keyworth, Nottingham

MacFadyen, C. (2006) 'Training helps travel trade boost geotourism', *Earth Heritage*, vol 26, p29

Miller, H. (1897) *The Cruise of the Betsey* (facsimile reprint of 1858 edition with introduction and additional notes by Michael Taylor and preface by T. C. Smout), National Museums of Scotland, Edinburgh, 2003

Patzak, M. and Eder, W. (1998) 'UNESCO GEOPARK, a new programme – A new UNESCO label', *Geologica Balcania*, vol 28, nos 3–4, pp33–35

Rackwitz, M. (2007) *Travels to Terra Iccognita: The Scottish Highlands and Hebrides in Early Modern Travellers' Accounts c.1600 to 1800*, Waxmann, Munster

Robinson, E. (1990) 'Arran 1999 – A watershed?', *Geology Today*, vol 6, no 3, pp74–75

UNESCO (2000) *UNESCO Geoparks Programme Feasibility Study*, UNESCO, Paris

Visit Scotland (2008a) *Tourism in Ayrshire & Arran 2007*, Visit Scotland, Edinburgh

Visit Scotland (2008b) *Tourism in Highlands of Scotland 2007*, Visit Scotland, Edinburgh

Wordsworth, W. (1835) *A Guide Through the District of the Lakes of Northern England with a Description of the Scenery, &c., for the use of Tourists and Residents* (5th edn), Longman, Hurst, Rees, Orme and Brown, London

Zouros, N. (2006) 'The European Geopark Network: Geological Heritage Protection and Local Development – A Tool For Geotourism Development in Europe', in Fassoulas, C., Skoula, Z. and Pattakos, D. (eds) *4th European Geoparks Meeting – Proceedings Volume*, pp15–24

Case Study 13

The Azores

Volcanic Islands in the Atlantic

Henry Gaudru

Introduction

The nine volcanic islands of the Azores are located in the Atlantic Ocean about two hours flying time and 1500km from Lisbon (Portugal), and about five hours flying time or 3900km from the eastern coast of North America (Azores.com, 2009a). The Azores have a total area of 355km², sit on top of the Mid-Atlantic Ridge, where mountains sometimes reach above sea level (*Encyclopaedia Britannica*, 2009), thus forming islands of volcanic origin. The Azores have been created by outpourings of lava from the ocean floor, due to the high level of activity in the area which is a result of three major tectonic plates meeting at this point (Siebert and Simkin, 2002). The North American Plate to the north-west of the Azores is gradually drifting west, the Eurasian Plate to the north-east is drifting east and south and finally the African Plate is drifting east and north. The small Azores Microplate, which is drifting westwards, further complicates the picture. The last volcano to erupt in the archipelago was the Capelinhos volcano (Vulcão dos Capelinhos) in 1957, in the western part of Faial Island, increasing the size of that island by 2.4km.

Pico Volcano Natural Reserve

Pico Island is the furthest south of the central cluster of the Azores and is the second largest in the archipelago (around 46km long and 15km wide). The main settlements are the capital Madalena, São Roque do Pico and Lajes do Pico; the total population is around 15,000 inhabitants. Tourism is the main industry in Pico Island, but it does not seem very crowded as yet. Pico is the most mountainous island in the Azores and contains the most dramatically beautiful landscapes, including Pico Alto, Portugal's prominent stratovolcano, which at 2352m is the highest peak (Global Volcanism Program, 2009) and can be seen from all over the island and from peaks on the other Azores islands (Figure CS13.1).

Pico volcano overlies an older linear volcano with a number of flank cones making up most of the 48km long island. The volcano rises 3500m above the surrounding ocean floor and has a subaerial volume of 97km³ as compared with the total subaerial volume of Pico Island of 207km³. The conical Pico volcano is dominantly basaltic and developed above the Montanha volcanic complex on the eastern side of Pico Island with a 500m wide summit crater and a small steep sided cone (Global Volcanism Program, 2009). Historical eruptions have been limited to the sides of Pico volcano as well as to the south-east-trending rift zone, the São Roque Piedade volcanic complex, which is covered with pyroclastic cones. During 1562–64 an eruption from the south-east rift zone formed lava flows that reached the northern coast. An erupting nearby vent produced lava flows that moved into the sea on the south side of

Figure CS13.1 Pico, the highest mountain of the Azores, Portugal

the island. A flank eruption from Pico in 1718 created lava flows that reached both coasts (Global Volcanism Program, 2009). The last eruption on the island was in 1963, with a small submarine eruption off the north-west coast (Frysinger, 2009). Available data shows that 14 eruptions have taken place on Pico Island over the last 1000 years with more than 35 eruptions in the last 2000 years. Repose times on the Planalto da Achada were longer than on Pico volcano with average repose time for the whole island according to recent carbon dating of 130 years (Nunes et al, 2006).

Pico volcano has been classified a protected natural reserve since 1972. It is an interesting geologic place and tourists can view the lava fields and black lava rocks around the volcano. To the east the Planalto da Achada also contains numerous volcanic cones and crater lakes as well as volcanic caves and stunning rock formations at Arcos (*iknow* Portugal, 2009). Pico volcano dominates this island and many visitors do climb to the crater peak via a guided walking tour or they climb individually. In winter the peak is covered in snow.

Dozens of small volcanic cones and craters on the plateau area at 800 metres are covered by basaltic slag and are dominated by Pico do Topo with a height of 1007m (Azores.com, 2009b). Car parking space is located on the west side of the mountain at 1200m altitude. A series of secondary craters, called furnas, at an altitude of about 1500m are on the cone of Pico, and people usually spend the night when they climb this volcano (Azores.com, 2009b). The climb is technically easy but people have to be in good shape to climb, because it's an 1150m high hike. Climbing starts from the parking area at 1200m and it takes about three-and-a-half hours to reach the summit at 2351m. Up to around 1500m around the mountain, thick forests carpet the plateau. Moving higher, the landscape changes to shrubs, then to lava fields. The crater of Pico Alto itself measures about 700m across and reaches a depth of 30m. At the edge of the crater lies the volcanic cone Piquinho or Pico Pequeno with fumaroles at its base. At a height of about 70m this small peak constitutes the summit of the mountain (Azores.com, 2009b).

The Azorean government has produced a number of useful pamphlets describing various routes for tourists, safety precautions and maps of the different hikes on Pico Island. Additionally, it is compulsory for hikers on Pico to hire a guide as well as registering at the local fire station. The Civil Protection Service is involved in rescues (Burbank, 2008) and requires such information to ensure that this function can be carried out.

References

Azores.com (2009a) 'The practical site of Azores', www.azores.com/azores/azores.php, accessed 10 August 2009

Azores.com (2009b) 'Volcanic curiosities', www.azores.com/azores/pico.php?attribute=11,accessed 8 January 2010

Burbank, R. (2008) 'Portugal's highest peak mirrors Mt.Washington', www.newhampshire.com/article.aspx?headline=Portugal%E2%80%99s+highest+peak+mirrors+Mt.+Washington&articleid=1538, accessed 25 August 2009

Encyclopaedia Britannica (2009) 'Mid-Atlantic Ridge', www.britannica.com/EBchecked/topic/380800/Mid-Atlantic-Ridge, accessed 25 July 2009

Frysinger, G. R. (2009) 'Pico Island', www.galenfrysinger.com/azores_pico_island.htm, accessed 25 August 2009

Global Volcanism Program (2009) 'Volcanoes of the world: Pico', www.volcano.si.edu/world/volcano.cfm?vnum=1802-02=, accessed 24 August 2009

iknow Portugal (2009) 'Madeira & Azores Tourism Guide – Do Pico Island', www.iknow-portugal.co.uk/tourist_information/madeira_azores/azores/pico_island_azores.htm, accessed 25 August 2009

Nunes, J. C., Camacho, A., França, Z., Montesinos, F. G., Alves, M., Vieira, R., Velez, E. and Ortiz, E. (2006) 'Volcanic geology of the Azores Islands: Gravity anomalies and crustal signature of volcano-tectonic structures of Pico Island (Azores)', *Journal of Volcanology and Geothermal Research*, vol 156, issues 1–2, pp55–70

Siebert, L. and Simkin, T. (2002) 'Volcanoes of the world: An illustrated catalogue of Holocene volcanoes and their eruptions', Smithsonian Institute, *Global Volcanism Program Digital Information Series, GVP-3*, www.volcano.si.edu/world/, accessed 10 May 2009

Case Study 14

Canary Islands

Volcanic World Heritage of Spain

Malcolm Cooper

Location

The Canary Islands are an autonomous Spanish archipelago of 7447km², which is located 100km off the north-west coast of mainland Africa, west of Morocco, and supports a total population of two million. There are seven major islands, one minor island and several small islets. The major islands are Tenerife, Gran Canaria, Lanzarote, Fuerteventura, La Palma, La Gomera and El Hierro (Figure CS14.1).

Geophysical aspects and history of activity

The islands were formed by the Canary *hot spot*, which first appeared about 60 million years ago (Holik et al, 1991; although see Cruz, 2001). The Teide volcano (Figure CS14.2) on Tenerife is the highest mountain in Spain (3718m), and the third largest volcano on Earth on an ocean island. All the islands except La Gomera have been active in the last million years; four of them (Lanzarote, Tenerife, La Palma and El Hierro) have historical records of eruptions since European discovery. In

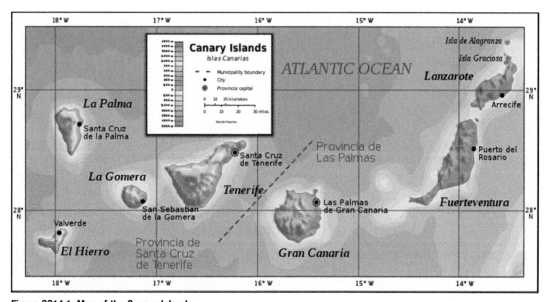

Figure CS14.1 Map of the Canary Islands

Source: Wikimedia Commons, 2009

Figure CS14.2 Tourists exploring the crater of Mt Teide

Source: Photo courtesy of Henry Gaudru

recent times documented major activity has been concentrated on Tenerife (1704–1706, 1798, 1909), Lanzarote (1730, 1824) and La Palma (1585, 1646, 1678, 1712, 1949, 1971). Four of Spain's 13 national parks are located in the Canary Islands and are based on existing dormant or active volcanoes (Parque Nacional de la Caldera de Taburiente, La Palma; Garajonay National Park, La Gomera; Teide National Park, Tenerife; Timanfaya National Park, Lanzarote). La Palma is in its entirety a biosphere reserve.

Risk factors

The standard risk factors relating to volcanic activity are present but as the archipelago is a volcanic hot spot there are many safeguards in place. Nevertheless, the United Nations Committee for Disaster Mitigation (in conjunction with the IAVCEI) has designated Teide (on Tenerife) as a Decade Volcano (16 major volcanoes worldwide; Newhall, 1996) because of its history of destructive eruptions and its proximity to several large towns, of which the closest are Garachico, Icod de los Vinos and Puerto de la Cruz.

Tourism

Tourism contributes 32 per cent of the GDP of the islands and there are about ten million tourists a year. Economic growth on the islands has been fuelled mainly by huge foreign investment in tourism real estate and by EU funding. To this investment the volcanoes provide an attractive visual setting, influence the climate and physically have contributed to tourism resources of sand, mountains and hot springs. They also contributed to the world heritage listing of Mt Teide National Park, which reflects the significance of volcanic environments as tourist destinations.

Risk management

Risk management in the Canary Islands context is overseen by WOVO, the World Organization of Volcanic Observatories, and the National Parks. The Spanish Scientific Volcanic Evaluation and Monitor Committee, a national commission that evaluates volcanic activity in the country, and the IGN (National Geographic Institute), a public organization responsible for the observation, surveillance and communication of volcanic activity, also assist the authorities responsible for civil protection on the island. Tourists are included in the plans for risk management should one or more of the volcanoes show signs of increased activity, and this information will be distributed by local councils, tourism organizations and hotels.

References

Cruz, C. M. G. (2001) *The Origin of the Canary Islands: A Chronology of Ideas and Related Concepts, from Antiquity to the End of the 20th Century*, INHIGEO (International Commission on the History of Geological Sciences, Sydney, October

Holik, J. S., Rabinowitz, P. D. and Austin, J. A. (1991) 'Effects of Canary hotspot volcanism on the structure of the oceanic crust off Morocco', *Journal of Geophysical Research*, vol 96, no B7, pp12039–12067

Newhall, C. (1996) 'IAVCEI/International Council of Scientific Unions' Decade Volcano Projects: Reducing Volcanic Disaster', *Status Report*, USGS, Washington DC

Wikimedia Commons (2009) 'Map of the Canary Islands', www.en.wikipedia.org/wiki/File:Map_of_the_Canary_Islands.svg, accessed 20 July 2009

Case Study 15

Greece

How Dormant Are the Islands?

Malcolm Cooper and Patricia Erfurt-Cooper

Introduction

The Greek volcanoes are part of the Aegean Volcanic Arc, which is caused by the subduction of the African tectonic plate under the Eurasian plate (Siebert and Simkin, 2002). These are Santorini (shield volcano), Methana (lava dome complex), Milos (stratovolcano), Nisyros (stratovolcano), Yali (lava domes) and Kos (fumaroles). The most recent volcanic eruption in Greece was on Santorini in 1950. Greece also has 752 geothermal springs which are popular tourist destinations.

Geophysical aspects and history of activity

The most famous Greek volcano is Santorini, which last erupted in 1950. Its most devastating recorded eruption was in 1600BC and buried the city of Akroteri, possibly giving rise to the legend of Atlantis. Three islands remained after this eruption – Thera, Therasia and Aspronisi. The Santorini caldera has a diameter of 11km north–south and 7.5km east–west, with a depth of 390m in the north. The 1950 eruption produced a lava dome, lava flow and explosive activity, while activity was also recorded in 1939–41, 1925–28, 1866–70, 1707–11, 1650, 1570–73, 726, AD46–47 and 197BC (Seach, 2009). Methana, on the Methana Peninsula of the Peloponnese is made up of a series of lava domes, which last erupted in

Figure CS15.1 Location of the Greek volcanoes

Source: USGS, 2003

258BC although some activity was recorded in 1922. The island of Milos is currently quiet, with activity confined to solfatara, fumaroles and hot springs (Figure CS15.1).

The island of Nisyros, located at the eastern end of the Hellenic island arc, 340km south-east of Athens is part of the Kos-Yali-Nisyros Volcanic Field in the south-eastern Aegean Sea. The Hellenic Volcanic Arc has been formed by the active north-east directed subduction of the African Plate beneath the Aegean Plate. The volcano contains a 3.8km-wide caldera and its historical activity has

Figure CS15.2 Hundreds of tourists climb down the crater walls of Nisyros after their arrival by bus

Note: A visit to the active volcano is more like a family outing and the steep climb does not appear to deter any of the visitors.

Source: Photo courtesy of P. Erfurt-Cooper

produced phreatic eruptions. Currently fumarolic activity occurs in the caldera, and hot springs are found on the coast. The volcano has erupted at least 13 times during recorded history. A volcano-seismic crisis on Nisyros occurred between 1995 and 1998, and was accompanied by 14cm of ground uplift on the island. More than 1600 seismic events were located within the Kos–Nisyros–Tilos area. Several shallow tectonic earthquakes at depths up to 10km with larger magnitudes up to 5.5 occurred along the fault system between Tilos and Kos. And in January 2003 the crater was declared off limits due to increasing temperatures and growing surface cracks. The temperatures in the hydrothermal system increased from 210°C to 315°C.

Minor activity is noted on Kos, with fumarolic activity found at Kos volcano and emissions of hydrogen sulphide and hot springs along the coast. Yali is a small island located between Kos and Nisyros and has no recent recordings of activity.

Risk factors

As has been noted elsewhere in this book, in relation to many volcanoes the risk factors for tourism deriving from the Greek volcanoes are latent at present. The most dangerous situation is considered to be Santorini, which has been labelled a decade volcano in order to be closely monitored and researched. However, as stated above, the activity of Nisyros volcano is evident by many hydrothermal vents or fumaroles as well as small boiling springs at the bottom of the crater and this activity attracts the attention of hundreds of visitors daily during the tourist season (Figure CS15.2). Transport to the volcano is usually by organized bus tours, with the approach of the narrow, windy road into the caldera only possible in one direction according to agreed times. Once inside the caldera the crater itself can be accessed via a steep, but potentially unsafe climb downhill, which is made even more difficult

Figure CS15.3 Children are playing among steam vents and boiling springs while others take photos of the unique thermal features

Source: Photo courtesy of P. Erfurt-Cooper

by its narrowness. It is surprising that not a single warning sign can be seen; neither at the top of the crater nor at the bottom where the geothermal activity draws people close to hissing steam vents and boiling springs.

Apart from a low fence at the crater rim the whole area is completely open and accessible without any indication for inexperienced tourists that they are entering an active volcanic area. Many people undertake a climb into the crater as a recreational activity with the whole family including small children who play around the thermal features (Figure CS15.3). Taking photos also lures people very close to everything that steams and bubbles and some interpretive signs would certainly raise the awareness of the geothermal environment of Nisyros, which is without doubt very interesting. It is not clear what measures are in place in case of an emergency which does not necessarily have to originate in volcanic activity. Thermal burns or a broken leg at

the bottom of the crater in the heat of the summer could make for an unpleasant holiday memory.

Tourism

Greece is a popular holiday destination and tourism receipts for this country totalled USD15.7 billion in 2008, from around 18 million visitors (including 1.2 million cruise ship passengers). While there are no specific data on volcano tourism in Greece, Santorini features as one of the travel agency Abercrombie and Kent's locations for extreme tourism, a reference to its volcanic past and present, and the southern Aegean islands have all recorded healthy tourism flows in the recent past (National Statistical Service of Greece, 2009). Tour operators who have specialized in volcano tourism offer 'geologic study and walking tours' on Santorini during spring, autumn and winter (Volcano Discovery, 2008).

Risk management

Disaster risk management is carried out in the context of EU regulations. The natural environment must be protected and there is a national land-use plan to control the spread of activities like tourism. Other than these constraints there appear to be few specific measures in relation to tourism in volcanic areas, with the island of Nisyros as an example.

References

National Statistical Service of Greece (2009) 'Arrivals and nights spent at collective accommodation establishments, year 2008', press release, The National Statistical Service of Greece, Pireaus

Seach, J. (2009) 'Volcano live', www.volcanolive.com/kos.html, accessed 31 July 2009

Siebert, L. and Simkin, T. (2002) 'Volcanoes of the world: An illustrated catalogue of Holocene volcanoes and their eruptions', Smithsonian Institute, *Global Volcanism Program Digital Information Series, GVP-3*, www.volcano.si.edu/world/, accessed 10 May 2009

USGS (2003) 'Location of the Greek volcanoes', United States Geological Survey, Washington DC

Volcano Discovery (2008) 'Geologic tours on Santorini, Greece – Study and walking tour programs', www.decadevolcano.net/santorini_tours.htm, accessed 20 August 2009

Case Study 16

The Vulkaneifel in Germany

A Destination for Geotourism

Patricia Erfurt-Cooper

Introduction

With geotourism as an expression of a growing trend towards the natural as well as cultural landscape (Pforr and Megerle, 2006) geoparks appear to hold the future for tourism in designated areas on a global scale. One of these geoparks is the Vulkaneifel which covers approximately 2000km² in the German State of Rhineland-Palatinate bordering on Belgium and Luxembourg in the west and on the Rhine in the east (Figures CS16.1 and CS16.2). In 2004 the Vulkaneifel European Geopark was officially recognized as a UNESCO global geopark, which is a significant step up from the original regional geopark designation as the guidelines and criteria defined by UNESCO are quite stringent and are evaluated by an international team of experts (UNESCO, 2006a). Below is a definition of geoparks by UNESCO:

> *A Geopark is a nationally protected area containing a number of geological heritage sites of particular importance, rarity or aesthetic appeal. These Earth*

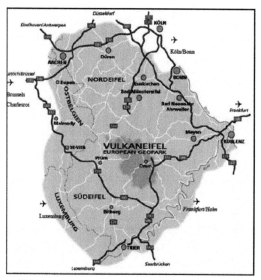

Figures CS16.1 and CS16.2 Maps showing the area of the Vulkaneifel

Source: Locator Map Vulkaneifel, 2010; Vulkaneifel European Geopark, 2010a; modified by author

heritage sites are part of an integrated concept of protection, education and sustainable development. A Geopark achieves its goals through a three-pronged approach: conservation, education and geotourism.

(UNESCO, 2006a)

In the literature the Vulkaneifel is generally attributed with a unique geology and therefore holding a special attraction for visitors (Spielmann, 2003; Schmincke, 2009). The region has long been a popular holiday destination with easy access, good infrastructure for transport and accommodation combined with attractive volcanic landscapes including 70 maars, of which 8 are still filled with water.

History of tourism in the Eifel

The Vulkaneifel and especially the area around the Laacher See was over a century ago described as a major tourist attraction of the volcanic kind by Rudolph Blenke (1879), who declared that it would be difficult to find another equally interesting region anywhere else in Germany. In his opinion the Laacher See and its surroundings held a range of attractions for people with an interest in geology and mineralogy, but also offered ecosystems with rare types of vegetation growing in the volcanic environment and, moreover, the unique landforms were also catering for the connoisseur of scenic beauty.

A few years later Johann Baumgarten (1884, 1888) published two books which included several chapters about the Eifel and its volcanic attractions for tourists with detailed advice how to get to the different places of interest including timetables for trains. His publications were very similar to the contemporary Lonely Planet guidebooks, although without illustrations. Baumgarten also refers to the numerous hot and mineral springs as having their origin in past volcanic activity, which has been confirmed by a variety of authors as an attraction of the Vulkaneifel (e.g. Meyer et al, 2007).

Past volcanic activity

The European Cenozoic Volcanic Province (ECVP) comprises several small volcanic areas with the Eifel volcanism being part of this ECVP (Meyer et al, 2007). The geological heritage of the

Vulkaneifel consists of approximately 270 eruption centres (Vulkaneifel European Geopark, 2010b) which dominate the landscape. Volcanic maars and diatremes, remnant volcanoes and scoria cones, calderas (Laacher See) and mineral springs, lava and tephra layers, pumice deposits, tuff rings and columnar jointing are common volcanic features and although some of the older volcanoes have nearly eroded away, many of them are still visible. The origin of the volcanic activity in this region is suspected to be possibly related to hot spot activity, although the opinions differ. Due to the fact that some of the volcanic landforms have been dated as being of more recent times this has given rise to the assumption that the Vulkaneifel may not be as dormant as previously thought.

Although the eruption which caused the collapse of a magma chamber creating the Laacher See was seen as one of the last events (Baales et al, 2002; Meyer et al, 2007), and one of the most powerful late Quaternary eruptions in central Europe (Schmincke, 2004, 2009; Park and Schmincke, 2009), future eruptions are taken into consideration and seen as possible by geoscientists (Bojanowski, 2007; Meyer et al, 2007), with smaller earthquakes on a regular basis indicating ongoing seismic activity, a situation which is very similar to the younger volcanic centres in the south of Australia and in Queensland.

The Laacher See may well be the main attraction in the Vulkaneifel with two million visitors every year, athough according to Spielmann (2003) the whole region is one of the most diverse mountain landscapes in Germany with many remnants of its fiery past.

Tourism in the Vulkaneifel

Germany has a longstanding history of marketing the dormant volcanic region of the Vulkaneifel as a key tourist destination. The Vulkaneifel was one of the first European geoparks and offers everything related to 'geo' such as geo-destinations, geo-adventure, geo-knowledge, geo-conservation, as well as interpretation and communication within the geo-environment. Healing hot springs, already appreciated by the Romans 2000 years ago are among the many attractions; so is a 28 metre high 'Volcano-Info-Platform' with views over the region, and volcano museums with interactive

Figure CS16.3 The Vulkangarten (Volcano garden) in Steffeln is popular with interpretive walking tours starting at the community hall in Steffeln and leading through the rural landscape with views of the dry Laacher Maar into the Vulkangarten

Note: An old quarry has been opened to the public with walkways and signage for people who are not on a guided tour.

Figure CS16.4 Tuff layers from former eruptions of the Steffelnkopf are one of the attractions in the Vulkangarten

exhibitions and open-air classical concerts are all set against the backdrop of an ancient volcanic landscape.

The Vulkaneifel is one of the major holiday destinations in Germany and appears to be one of the most successful. The Eifel maars (*Augen der Eifel* – Eyes of the Eifel) are probably the best known landscape feature having first been used as unique selling points (USP) for tourism marketing in 1975 (Schüller, 2007), and are commonly known for their attraction as leisure and recreation destinations. They present a wide range of recreational attractions and activities and many people choose the Vulkaneifel for their holidays to enjoy the 'maar atmosphere' while camping,

swimming, fishing or enjoying other water sports (Rieder, 1998). According to a survey mentioned by Schüller (2007) 29 per cent of visitors are on the second and third visit, 24 per cent are frequent visitors and 47 per cent, less than half, are on their first visit.

The Vulkaneifel draws many visitors to the volcanic landscape either with maars or with remnants of volcanoes such in the 'Vulkangarten' near Steffeln (Figures CS16.3 and CS16.4), which was created to revitalize the former quarries near the Steffelnkopf volcano (Frey et al, 2006), where interpretive walking tours are offered by volunteers from the local community. Other interesting volcanic heritage sites are found throughout the Eifel with many of them described by Schmincke (2009) in his latest book. A tourist programme has been developed for the Vulkaneifel Geopark to raise awareness of geological heritage for residents and visitors through interpretation, excursions and visits to a number of geo-museum facilities, for example, Eifel-Volcano Museum Daun, Maar-Museum Manderscheid and Vulkanhaus Strohn (Vulkaneifel European Geopark, 2006; Schüller, 2007). Mountain biking activities around the volcanoes such as 'VulkanBike Eifel Marathon', 'VulkanBike Cross-country' and 'Vulkan Bike TrailPark' (VulkanBike, 2009) and other sports events such as the 'Five-Maar-Run' are part of the recreational offers in this dormant volcanic environment. Geology and classical music is a combination here that is used in other parts of the world as well, for example, in Australia in the Undara Volcanic National Park, where annual opera and theatre events take place (see Chapter 21).

Guided interpretive hiking and walking tours with a touch of adventure (Vulkaneifel European Geopark, 2007) are promoted for visitors to get in touch with the surrounding landscape. The local media (Eifel Gäste Journal, 2010) provide information about all current events of interest for visitors, with most of them linked to the geological heritage of the region. Special magazines report about what is happening at the geo-museums and let the public know about upcoming events such as presentations by volcanologists who talk about the Vulkaneifel.

Among the interesting geophysical features of the Vulkaneifel are over 180 volcanic cones and remnant volcanic plugs, shield volcanoes, maars and crater lakes, lava pits with tuff layers, lava flows and basalt columns, cinder cones and ancient volcanic crater walls, colourful ash layers, columnar jointing, hot and mineral springs, volcano museums as well as historic architecture using volcanic rocks as building material. However, the Eifel region is also marketing a vast variety of recreational attractions to cater for every taste and every budget. All activities commonly refer to the volcanic past of the Eifel and often include some form of educational experience or guided tours with visits to interpretive centres where tourists can learn about the history, the geology, culture and architecture while sampling the local cuisine, tasting Vulkanpark butter or trying a beer from the Vulkan Brewery (Bell GmbH, 2004).

Commercial use of volcanic landforms

The thick basalt layers common to the region have been used as quarries for building material and have been used since historical times to cut millstones (Meyer et al, 2007; Schmincke, 2009; Vulkan Brauerei und Brauhaus, 2009). The Vulkan Brewery in Mayen was built on a lava flow, which was used as a storage facility after excavation with a constant temperature of 6–8°C (Meyer et al, 2007; Vulkan Brauerei Mendig, 2009) and is included as a tourist attraction with guided tours through the extensive lava caves. Not just the basalt layers were exploited; pumice deposits in the area of the Neuwieder Becken were mined as well (Vulkan Brauerei und Brauhaus, 2009). However, of late former quarries have been returned to nature and the establishment of special ecosystems and biotopes has been encouraged (Schmincke, 2009) to offer visitors an insight into former volcanic activity and how nature is kind to the scarred landscape by existing next to where man has exploited the volcanic deposits.

Conclusion

The Vulkaneifel has a long history of volcano tourism, even if this may go rather unnoticed by many visitors. However, the landscape with its geological heritage is tightly interwoven with most attractions and activities in this region. Whether it is the cultural aspect including the architecture from volcanic building materials or the recreational activities on or near the maars and the mountains, the volcanic past is a major draw card of the Vulkaneifel and offers holiday destinations for every kind of visitor. Many people are repeat visitors who have made the Eifel their annual holiday destination for years, which is not uncommon in Germany. Tourism marketing generally includes the volcanic environment, and many sports activities are carried out in close proximity to anything volcanic, as the dormant state of the Vulkaneifel allows for a completely different planning and infrastructure than those near active volcanoes.

References

Baales, M., Jöris, O., Street, M., Weninger, B. and Wiethold, J. (2002) 'Impact of the late glacial eruption of the Laacher See volcano, Central Rhineland, Germany', *Quaternary Research*, vol 58, pp273–288

Baumgarten, J. (1884) *Coblenz nebst Ausflügen und Rundreisen am Rhein, an Lahn und Mosel, sowie in der Eifel, Führer für Einheimische und Fremde, Mit einem Plane der Stadt und vier Spezitalkärtchen*, Wilhelm Groos Hofbuchhandlung, Coblenz, Germany

Baumgarten, J. (1888) *Mittelrhein: Mosel, Lahn, Eifel, Taunus und Westerwald*, vierte Auflage, W. Groos, Hofbuchhandlung (Kindt and Meinardus), Germany

Bell GmbH (2004) 'Burgfestspiele – Vulkane und Wohlfühlen', www.reisebuero-bell.de/servlet/de. blueorange.xred.util.GetFile/?db=bell&tbl=int_xr edfile&key=id&keyval=801&imgcol=xred_file, accessed 10 August 2009

Blenke, R. (1879) *Der Laacher See und seine vulkanische Umgebung*, Strüder'sche Buchdruckerei and Buchhandlung in Neuwied, Germany

Bojanowski, A. (2007) 'Forscher warnen vor Vulkangefahr in der Eifel', *Spiegel Online*, 13 February 2007, www. spiegel.de/wissenschaft/natur/0,1518,466051,00. html, accessed 20 June 2009

Eifel Gästejournal (2010) Online Document: www. eifel.de/go/gaestejournal/842.html, accessed 8 January 2010

Frey, M. L., Schäfer, K., Büchel, G. and Patzak, M. (2006) Geoparks – A Regional European and Global Policy, in Dowling, R. and Newsome, D. (eds) *Geotourism*, Elsevier Butterworth Heinemann Oxford, pp95–117

Locator Map Vulkaneifel (2010) Locator map of Landkreis Vulkaneifel in Rhineland-Palatinate,

Germany, available under Wiki GNU Free Documentation License, Online Document: www.commons.wikimedia.org/wiki/File:Locator_map_DAU_in_Germany.svg, accessed 2010

Meyer, R., Hertogen, J. and Thein, J. (2007) *Volcanism of the Eifel, Germany*, Guide d'excursion 1/2007, Association Géologique du Luxembourg, www.geology.lu/agl/2007/AGL_Eifel_guide.pdf, accessed 26 July 2009

Park, C. and Schmincke, H. U. (2009) Apokalypse im Rheintal, *Spektrum der Wissenschaft*, www.spektrum.de/artikel/977241&_z=798888, accessed 26 July 2009

Pforr, C. and Megerle, A. (2006) Geotourism: a perspective from southwest Germany, in Dowling, R., Newsome, D. (eds), *Geotourism*, Elsevier Butterworth Heineman, Oxford, UK, pp117–139

Rieder, E. (1998) *GEO-Begleiter Vulkaneifel*, Vulkaneifel Touristik & Werbung GmbH, Daun, Germany

Schmincke, H. U. (2004) *Volcanism*, Springer Verlag, Berlin

Schmincke, H. U. (2009) *Vulkane der Eifel: Aufbau, Entstehung und heutige Bedeutung*, Spektrum Akademischer Verlag, Heidelberg, Germany

Schüller, A. (2007) 'Setting up a tourist program with local community and enterprises', PowerPoint Presentation Natur- und Geopark Vulkaneifel GmbH, www.taiex.ec.europa.eu/Seminar%20Organisation/tools/presentations/25176/AndreasSch%C3%BCller.pdf, accessed 5 August 2009

Spielmann, W. (2003) *Geologische Streifzüge durch die Eifel*, Rhein-Mosel-Verlag, Germany

UNESCO (2006) 'Global Geoparks Network', www.unesdoc.unesco.org/images/0015/001500/150007e.pdf, accessed 17 July 2009

VulkanBike (2009) 'Mountainbiken im Herzen der Vulkaneifel, www.vulkanbike.de/, accessed 5 August 2009

Vulkan Brauerei Mendig (2009) 'Vulkan Brauerei Mendig GmbH', www.bierspot.de/brauereien/vulkan_brauerei_307.html, accessed 5 August 2009

Vulkan Brauerei und Brauhaus (2009) 'Felsenkeller, die tiefsten Lager- und Gärkeller der Welt', www.vulkan-brauerei.de/brauerei/1/2/, accessed 5 August 2009

Vulkaneifel European Geopark (2006) *Vulkaneifel Magazin: Unterwegs im Land der Maare und Vulkane*, Natur- and Geopark GmbH Vulkaneifel

Vulkaneifel European Geopark (2007) *Erlebniswanderungen*, Gerolsteiner Land, Germany

Vulkaneifel European Geopark (2010a) 'Übersichtskarte', Online Document: www.geopark-vulkaneifel.de/ngpve/maps/pu-geoparkuebersicht.htm, accessed 8 January 2010

Vulkaneifel European Geopark (2010b) 'Willkommen auf den Internetseiten des Vulkaneifel European Geopark', Online Document: www.geopark-vulkaneifel.de/ngpve/index.php, accessed 8 January 2010

Part VI

Oceania

Introduction

This part of the world has some of the most active volcanic and geothermal areas and is attracting a growing number of tourists who have the desire to come face to face with powerful displays of nature at work. Not all destinations in this region offer active volcanism, but many volcano connoisseurs appreciate dormant landscapes as well as active environments. Visitor statistics, however, are difficult to research because not every volcanic national park has a fixed entry point. The general lack of information about visitor numbers for particular tourism sectors indicates that more research is required. Due to the fact that there are significant gaps in the literature concerning volcanic and geothermal tourism, especially with a focus on risk management as well as international safety guidelines for visitors, no valid statistics are available other than those researched for this book.

19

Volcanic Landscapes of New Zealand

Malcolm Cooper

Introduction

Tectonically, Aotearoa-New Zealand lies on the rim of the Pacific Plate which meets the Indo-Australian Plate at this point on the Earth's surface. Similar geological processes occur here as with Japan, the west coast of the United States and the rest of the Pacific Rim. However those at work in the North Island of New Zealand are a result of the Pacific Plate sliding under the Indo-Australian Plate, while those of the South Island are a result of the two plates directly meeting each other. This latter collision has created the Southern Alps mountain range. In the North Island, the result of the geological process is volcanic activity and this is centred in Rotorua and the Central Plateau area of the Island, collectively known as the Taupo Volcanic Zone (TVZ). Mt Tongariro, which gives its name to the national park that is the primary focus of this chapter, Mt Ngauruhoe and Mt Ruapehu are the three main volcanoes at the Central Plateau end of the TVZ. These volcanoes are active – Mt Ruapehu as recently as 1995 and 1996 and Mt Ngauruhoe in 1972 – and it is this fact that both creates and constrains the patterns of tourism found in this area.

To the west of the Central Plateau lies Mt Taranaki, an almost cone-shaped volcano near the coast which last erupted in 1755. Further to the north in the Rotorua area is Mt Tarawera. In 1886 this volcano sent 2km³ of lava and rock onto the surrounding countryside, killing many people, and

in that process it destroyed New Zealand's most spectacular natural tourist attraction of the time, the world famous Pink and White Terraces (Figure 19.1). North of Mt Tarawera and three hours by boat off shore is the White Island volcano, at the northern end of the TVZ. This volcano is usually on alert level 1 while continually releasing pressure, and future eruptions cannot be excluded. Nevertheless, tourists are visiting this volcano on a daily basis, weather permitting, either by boat or by helicopter (Erfurt-Cooper and Cooper, 2009).

The biggest and most dangerous volcano in Aotearoa-New Zealand and the world is actually Taupo, which presently has the country's largest lake in its caldera and is in the Rotorua–Central Plateau area of the North Island (Froggatt, n.d.). This volcano, which has been in existence for more than 65,000 years last erupted in the year AD186, and erupts approximately once every 2000 years. The AD186 eruption was over 50 times the magnitude of the recent Mt St Helens eruption in the USA (Mt St Helens removed 3km³ of earth, and Krakatoa (the biggest eruption in recent times) in Indonesia moved 8km³ in 1887, but Taupo removed 110km³ in AD186). This eruption is regarded by volcanologists as the largest of the last 5000 years, and was recorded by Chinese and Roman chroniclers (e.g. Herodian of Antioch, 1961) The Chinese apparently actually heard the eruption and made a record of the brilliant sunsets that lasted for approximately six months (Wilson et al, 1980). Prior to this eruption, about 22,000 years ago Taupo experienced the

Figure 19.1 Artist's view of the White Terraces at Lake Rotomahana before they were destroyed in 1886

Source: Blomfield, 1888

world's biggest and most destructive eruption ever (the Oranui eruption produced 1170km³ of tephra). That event dwarfed the AD186 eruption. Still active, the Rotorua–Central Plateau area contains many thermal reserves with examples of boiling mud pools, hot springs, geysers, thermal rivers, boiling lakes, steam vents (fumaroles) and volcanic terraces. It is these that attract tourists to the region, and it is these along with the active volcanoes themselves that pose the extreme hazards for those tourists and their host communities that are the subject of this book.

Geological background

Simkin and Siebert (1994) credit the North Island of New Zealand as containing the world's largest concentration of youthful rhyolitic andesite volcanoes. However, like Japan the volcanoes here are not randomly scattered but are grouped into

areas of more intensive and long-lived activity, whose position (and the composition of the lavas erupted) can be related geologically to the large-scale movement (subduction) of the Indo-Australian and Pacific tectonic plates. Most New Zealand volcanism in the last 1.6 million years has occurred in the TVZ. This is an elongated area that extends from White Island to Mt Ruapehu (Figure 19.2) – a 250km-long zone of intense volcanism that marks the boundary of the Australian and Pacific tectonic plates. The TVZ is extremely active on a world scale: it includes three frequently active polygenetic volcanoes (Ruapehu, Tongariro/Ngauruhoe, White Island), and two major calderas (Okataina and Taupo). In a continuation of this chain of volcanic activity out to the north, much of the seabed is made up of seamounts and small islands, including 16 submarine volcanoes.

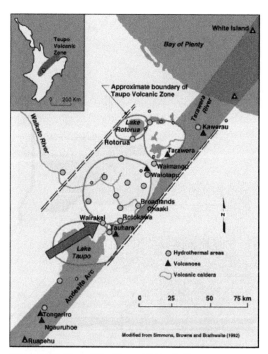

Figure 19.2 Map of the Taupo Volcanic Zone

Mt Ruapehu (2797m) lies at the southern end of the zone and is one of the most active volcanoes in the world (Keys and Green, 2004). It began erupting at least 250,000 years ago, and in recent recorded history *major* eruptions have been about 50 years apart (1895, 1945 and 1995–1996). Minor eruptions are much more frequent, with at least 60 since 1945. Some of the minor eruptions in the 1970s generated small ash falls and lahars (mudflows) that damaged skifields and disrupted other forms of outdoor recreation. Between major eruptions a warm acidic crater lake forms, fed by melting snow. Where a major eruption has deposited a tephra dam across the lake's outlet this may collapse after the lake has refilled and risen above its normal outlet level, and the outrush of water can cause a large lahar. In 2000, an early warning system (ERLAWS) was installed on the mountain to detect such a collapse and alert the relevant authorities.

Volcanic processes can be seen in action in this region and studied as a 'natural laboratory'. The Ruapehu Crater Lake is one of two such lakes (together with Kelut in Java) that are regarded as classic case studies of the interaction

between magmatic fluids and lake water that often produces lahars. The Crater Lake is located over the actual vent of the volcano and is especially important. Twice last century Crater Lake was completely emptied during eruptive episodes. On both occasions, in 1945 and 1995, bridges were destroyed and damaged. When the lake also partially emptied on 24 December 1953 the resulting lahar washed away a rail bridge at Tangiwai killing 151 of the 285 passengers and crew aboard a passing express train. This was one of New Zealand's worst tragedies, and preventing a recurrence of it has been a major focus of government agencies since that time.

The Tongariro andesitic volcanic complex (which includes Ngauruhoe) first erupted about 270,000 years ago (Smithsonian Institute, 2010). Eruptions from the 12 or more composite cones making up the complex have continued intermittently since. The youngest vent on the Tongariro volcano is Mt Ngauruhoe (Figure 19.3), which first erupted about 2500 years ago and last century was the most active volcano in New Zealand, with frequent eruptions no more than nine years apart although its last eruption was in 1975. Other than from the Ngauruhoe vent, Mt Tongariro's last eruption was in 1896 from the active Te Maari crater. Mt Ngauruhoe is a composite or stratovolcano composed of layered lava flows and volcanic ash and debris. Some others, such as Mt Tarawera (near Rotorua), are dome-shaped and composed largely of viscous lava which does not flow readily. Another readily identifiable landform resulting from extreme volcanism shape is the collapsed volcanic centre known as a caldera (see Chapter 1). These are often filled by lakes such as Lake Taupo and Lake Rotorua. Ketetahi Springs, on the side of Mt Tongariro, is a collection of hot mineral springs and steam vents (fumeroles) and there are more of these throughout the Central Plateau region. Further fumerolic activity is responsible for the tiny steam plume sometimes visible above Mt Ngauruhoe and for the activity near the Red Crater.

To the west is Mt Taranaki/Egmont. Formerly known as Mt Egmont, this stratovolcano last erupted about 200 years ago at the end of an eight-eruption cycle that had occurred over the

Figure 19.3 Mt Ngauruhoe, the tallest peak of the Tongariro complex on the North Island of New Zealand

Source: Photo courtesy of Don Swanson

preceding 300 years. Deposits around the base record intermittent activity at this site over the last 130,000 years, and while these eruptions have not occurred at regular intervals there has been a moderate or major sized eruption on average every 340 years, with numerous smaller events at more frequent intervals. There is therefore no evidence to suggest Mt Taranaki has finally ceased erupting – rather it must be regarded as an active volcano in a state of quiescence and is one of a number of volcanoes in New Zealand where future eruptions are to be expected (Newhall and Dzurisin, 1988).

The Rotorua caldera lies near the western margin of the TVZ. This formed as a result of the eruption of 200km³ (dense-rock equivalent) of Mamaku ignimbrite from a lava dome collapse over 10,000 years ago. Subsequent lava dome eruptions in the caldera, from one to ten cubic kilometres in volume, have not been dated, but have formed several crater lakes that are now tourist attractions. No eruptions (other than hydrothermal explosions) are known from the past

10,000 years, but the Rotorua–Whakarawarewa area is internationally recognized for the hot springs, geysers and other geothermal features that support a significant tourist industry.

White Island-Whakaari, the northernmost active volcano in the TVZ, is the summit of a large (16 by 18km) submarine volcano which has grown up from the sea floor at between 300 and 400 metres depth. Only half the height and a very small proportion of the volume of this volcano are above sea level. Sitting 48km offshore, the island has been built up by continuous volcanic activity over the past 150,000 years. The island has a history of long periods of continuous hydrothermal activity and steam release, punctuated by small-to-medium eruptions (White Island Tours, 2010). Between 1976 and 1993 White Island was more active than at any time in the past few hundred years, and ash from its 1998 eruptions was recorded as far inland as Rotorua. The volcano's activity is often visible to people in Bay of Plenty with gas and ash plumes rising as high as ten kilometres on clear, still days. Craters and fumaroles on the island continually emit gases at rates of several hundred to several thousand tonnes per day. The gases are mostly steam, carbon dioxide and sulphur dioxide, with small quantities of chlorine and fluorine. Acid gases combine with water in the steam to form acid droplets that can sting the eyes and skin, and can affect breathing, and can also damage cameras, electronic equipment and clothes.

In spite of its hostile environment, White Island is host to a number of bird species including a gannet colony, and has had human settlement in the form of sulphur mining. The sulphur mining venture on the island stopped abruptly in 1914 when part of the crater wall collapsed and a landslide destroyed the mine and village with 12 lives lost. Mining resumed again in the 1920s and the remains of buildings from that era are a tourist attraction. The sulphur was used to make fertiliser, for export as sulphur ore, and for the manufacture of sulphuric acid (Robinson, 2006).

Tongariro National Park

The volcanoes of the Tongariro National Park and Mt Ruapehu in particular are one of the major areas of outdoor recreation in New Zealand. Past volcanic activity has created a varied alpine landscape, with Rotorua the largest such area close to the major population centre of Auckland and therefore to the majority of international tourist flows through Auckland airport. The Ruapehu Crater Lake is second only to the hiking trail known as the Tongariro Crossing in the park as a focus of visitation to active volcanic landscapes. Visitation is not however limited to volcanic features; Ruapehu and the other volcanoes are internationally known skifields so domestic and international skiers, snow boarders, climbers, hikers, sightseers and others also enjoy this park for a much wider range of attractions. Nevertheless, the active volcanic nature clearly adds to the attraction for many of the people who come to the park.

Tongariro is New Zealand's oldest national park and the fourth oldest park in the world (Keys and Green, 2004). It was established in 1887 when Horonuku Te Heuheu Tukino, the paramount chief of the Ngati Tuwharetoa Confederation of tribes gifted the central portion of the park to the

nation. The outstanding natural values of Tongariro were officially recognized in 1990 when it was awarded world heritage status. The area's important Maori cultural associations were also accorded the same status in 1993, making the park one of the few with double world heritage status. The park is currently managed by the Department of Conservation.

As a national park, the Tongariro National Park Management Plan documents the objectives of its management and outlines the way the park, including natural hazards from volcanism and human impacts from tourism are managed. In a national park it is essential that significant areas receive a very high degree of protection from human intervention. This is reinforced by the world heritage cultural and landscape status of the park that in turn creates global obligations for protection and monitoring of its environmental values. On Mt Ruapehu the area above 2250m except within the ski area boundaries (up to 2320m) is designated a Pristine Area under the Resource Management Act (1991) to avoid human intervention or development and to offset more intensive development in the Amenity designated areas around the skifields below. This reinforces the original Gift Area, and is essential for retaining and enhancing the pervading aspects of wildness, quietness and outstanding visual features in the vicinity of the Crater Lake plus the park's very significant cultural, historical and conservation values.

Patterns of tourism

Forer and Pearce noted in 1984 that the Tongariro National Park, Rotorua, Auckland and White Island were essential components of one of New Zealand's longest and most favoured tourism circuits. This is of course primarily due to the mountains created by volcanism, although Maori culture also plays a part (Forer and Pearce, 1984). The park was created to protect the land encompassed by the three volcanoes of Tongariro, Ngauruhoe and Ruapehu. On Tongariro current volcanic activity is limited to geothermal features such as warm ground, steam and gas emissions, and hot springs. The most active area is Ketetahi hot springs on the flanks of the volcano. This area can be approached easily by a two hour walk (one way); however visitors are asked to maintain the springs' *tapu* or sacredness by not visiting them; good views can be enjoyed from the track. The other active geothermal area on Tongariro is Red Crater, with some steam release. The access to Red Crater, although not difficult, involves a three hour walk (one way) over mountain terrain (Williams, 1998), and the visitor information on risk suggests that walkers should be suitably experienced and equipped parties only and obtain up-to-date environmental information from the local ski-village visitor centre before beginning their walk.

Thanks to its spectacular volcanic background, to a diversity of landscapes and ecological units, to good tracks and an excellent network of huts, the park therefore offers superb yet relatively easy walking for tourists. The Tongariro Northern Circuit is one of New Zealand's Great Walks (Department of Conservation, 2009), and attracted over 5000 hikers in 2008. A shorter version of it, the Tongariro Crossing, has been described as 'New Zealand's finest day walk'. When done in clear weather both offer spectacular views of the volcanic landscape traversed, as well as of the surrounding country, plateau, ranges and lakes. A longer walk of up to six days, the Round the Mountain circuit leads the visitor through the diversity of landscapes that stretch down the sides of Ruapehu: from wet rainforest and extensive bogs dominated by lofty lava cliffs and waterfalls in the south-western quarter, through the desolate fields of volcanic ashes and scoria of the Rangipo Desert in the east, and into shrub lands and tussock lands further north.

Among the most significant one-day walks are the walks to the summits of the three large volcanoes. Other forms of tourism are found in the three skifields constructed on the sides of Ruapehu, which offer the best downhill skiing in the North Island, white-water rafting on the Tongariro River, mountain biking on Ruapehu, licensed fishing spots, and hunting (deer, pigs and goats). When the conditions are right, usually in late winter and spring, the park also offers good opportunities for ski-touring, on Ruapehu as well as Ngauruhoe.

Overall, Aotearoa-New Zealand's tourism industry contributed some 8 billion dollars or

Table 19.1 The value of the New Zealand tourism industry in 2007 and 2009

Indicator	2007	2009
Inbound	2.5 million	2.4 million
Outbound	1.9 million	1.9 million
Domestic tourism (nights)	N/A	18.9 million
International guest nights	N/A	13.3 million
Total guest nights	32.2 million	32.2 million
Domestic tourism expenditure	11.3 billion NZD	–
International tourism expenditure*	8.8 billion NZD	–
Total tourism expenditure	20.1 billion NZD	–
Contribution to GDP	7.9 billion (5.1%)	–
Indirect value added	6.2 billion NZD	–
Full-time employee equivalents	108,100	–
International tourism as % of total exports	18.3%	–

Note: *Includes spending by foreign students.

Source: Tourism Satellite Account, 2007; Statistics New Zealand, 2008

Table 19.2 Tourism value by region 2009

Region	% Total visitor nights	% Domestic visitor nights	% International visitor nights
Auckland	17	16	19
Christchurch	13	12	16
Wellington	6	7	5
Queenstown	10	6	14
Rotorua	5	5	6
Dunedin	3	3	3
Taupo	3	4	2
Nelson	3	4	3
Other Regions	40	43	32

Source: Destination Rotorua, 2009

Table 19.3 Visitor patterns by national parks in New Zealand

Calendar year	Abel Tasman	Fiordland	Westland	Aoraki/Mt Cook	Tongariro	Paparoa
1997	28,800	196,100	205,500	154,300	32,100	11,700
1998	31,100	234,500	207,300	147,100	41,900	30,100
1999	31,700	205,100	233,900	135,500	45,500	33,400
2000	54,400	250,300	278,900	158,400	48,600	40,500
2001	48,200	239,300	271,500	143,100	51,800	40,500
2002	57,900	273,000	280,900	158,100	55,100	44,400
2003	93,000	308,400	342,300	157,700	80,800	71,200
2004	94,400	393,700	362,400	209,900	96,700	87,700
2005	95,800	409,700	386,000	201,000	100,300	98,300
2006	96,700	438,000	372,800	192,200	95,000	116,700
2007	110,700	439,900	376,700	172,700	97,800	97,400
2008	119,300	441,200	379,300	201,800	83,200	121,200

Source: International Visitor Survey, Ministry of Tourism, various

5.1 per cent to the country's gross domestic product from 20.1 billion dollars of tourist expenditure in 2007 (Table 19.1), and made up 18 per cent of total exports. The number of inbound tourists has remained fairly constant in the early part of the 21st century; in 2009 2.4 million international tourists contributed 13.3 million bed nights to the accommodation industry, while in the same year domestic tourists contributed 18.9 million bed nights. In New Zealand inbound and domestic tourism contribute roughly in the order of 43–57 per cent of accommodation activity respectively.

The Taupo region, which includes the Tongariro National Park contributes around 4 per cent of total visitor nights to total national tourist activity (Table 19.2). The whole volcanic region including Rotorua and White Island contributes around 10 per cent, with the Rotorua region making up most of this. There is a seasonal pattern to visitor nights spent in both regions with peaks occurring in the summer season and troughs in the winter, although the Taupo region attracts proportionally more in winter due to the skifields. Table 19.3 shows the level of international visitors to the national parks

of New Zealand; these data indicate that Tongariro National Park has been losing ground relative to the others in both the North and South Islands, having peaked in 2005. However, the Ministry of Tourism states that the proportion of international visitors visiting at least one national park during their visit is about 30 per cent and has varied little over time so there may be a reversal of this trend in the future. Within the park, Mt Ruapehu is also home to New Zealand's two largest ski areas with over 1800 hectares of useable slopes, and the trend in recent years has been for an increase in visitors of about 6 per cent per year overall to the mountains because of this fact.

Risk management

The Tongariro National Park's world heritage status, popularity, environmental and tourist values, dynamic volcanic nature, and destructive potential including the 1953 Tangiwai lahar and other disasters all help to focus public, media and political attention on the issue of risk management. In terms of theories of natural hazard risk management and tourism (Foster, 1980; Murphy and Bayley, 1989; Cassedy, 1991; Faulkner, 2001;

Hall et al, 2004; Prideaux, 2004) the situation in regard to the Tongariro volcanoes is unusual for two main reasons (Keys and Green, 2004):

- It is predictable well in advance of the significant risks it raises.
- The 1953 disaster and its aftermath created action precedents, some of which conflict with strongly held environmental and cultural values.

The Minister of Conservation is responsible for the management of national parks in New Zealand and the Department of Conservation has produced a number of plans including an 'Environmental and Risk Assessment for mitigation of the hazard from Ruapehu Crater Lake' in April 1999. This followed the development of a draft Assessment of Environmental Effects (AEE) in October 1998 that presented 24 options for risk management within the following 6 categories:

- allow a lahar to occur, but develop alarm and response systems, improve land use planning but implement no specific engineering intervention at the crater or in lahar flood zones;
- allow a lahar to occur but intervene in lahar flood zones to reduce its size and/or confine it;
- prevent or reduce lahars by hardening or perforating the tephra barrier at the crater;
- prevent or reduce lahars by excavating a trench through the 1995-1996 tephra barrier at the crater;
- prevent lahar and reduce lake volume by excavating trenches into underlying lava at the outlet; and
- defer, prevent or reduce lahars by other options, e.g. siphoning or barrier trusses.

These options were subsequently incorporated into the early warning systems now set up on Mt Ruapehu as outlined in the next section. The more massive impact from eruptions has also been discussed and programmes implemented. Following the 1995 and 1996 eruptions of Mt Ruapehu the psychological aspects of community vulnerability were also studied and the results suggest that self-efficacy and problem-focused coping reduce

vulnerability. In other words communities must take responsibility for their own protection. While there are differential implications of physical and economic hazard consequences for community vulnerability, resilient communities (and resilient visitors) result from education and training in the nature and likelihood of disaster and adequate information about how to cope in the event of one (Munro and Parkin, 1999).

Mitigation: EDS, ERLAWS and planned responses

The Department of Conservation manages two early warning systems for the Tongariro National Park – an eruption detection system (EDS) and the Eastern Ruapehu Lahar and Warning System (ERLAWS) (Department of Conservation, 2008). For the intending visitor, updates on volcanic activity are available from these systems at www.geonet.org. nz. In May 2000 the Government formalized emergency management response and contingency plans, and following discussions with stakeholders and a technical design review, ERLAWS was installed during 2001/2002. ERLAWS consists of three types of sensors at three sites in the upper Whangaehu River Valley (the crater-lake outlet stream):

- Site 1 (Crater Lake outlet) – three geophones to detect the vibration from the collapse of the tephra dam and from lahars, a buried tripwire to detect collapse of the dam and water level sensors to detect a sudden drop in Lake level.
- Site 2 (NZ Alpine Club hut in the upper valley) – two geophones to detect the vibration from passing lahars.
- Site 3 (near Tukino skifield) – two geophones to detect the vibration from passing lahars.

When incoming data exceed pre-set thresholds an alarm will automatically be sent to police, local government offices, transport operators and duty scientists who will then respond following predetermined plans. This should be up to two hours before the lahar reaches Tangiwai. In December 2000 the Ministry of Conservation also requested that the Tongariro National Park Management Plan be amended to permit the construction of a 'bund' or embankment to prevent overflow from the Whangaehu River into the Tongariro catchment (and from there into Lake Taupo). This embankment is located just inside the national park boundary near the head of the Whangaehu outwash fan and the primary aim of the bund is to increase public safety by reducing risks to people using State Highway 1 as well as to protect public safety in the Tongariro River. Its secondary purpose is to protect the aquatic environment of the Tongariro River and Lake Taupo. Prior to this a volcano risk mitigation plan was developed by Environment Waikato (Munro and Parkin, 1999), the responsible regional council.

Protecting infrastructure and other assets against future lahars and eruptions is clearly a key to keeping communities and tourism resilient in the face of severe and ongoing hazards. However, a fundamental question the ministry had to address was whether interference with the natural, cultural and scientific values of a world heritage site should proceed simply because there are risks to communities and their visitors. The risk to life is low because of the warning and response system plus the construction of a bund, but cannot be absolutely removed. Nevertheless, carrying out engineering work at Crater Lake would also not be without risk due to the high altitude alpine volcanic nature of the site. Such work would also create precedents for further direct interference with other volcanic risks in the national park as well as more common natural hazards elsewhere. In such a situation a more appropriate risk management action is to use knowledge of the likely range of events in order to be prepared for such hazards and where necessary place infrastructure such as roads, rail and power lines at sites less likely to be at risk or to design them in ways to make them safe. This is a more sustainable course of action and in concert with warning and response systems for tourists and the host communities this will reduce risks to a low level, even for the larger hazards that the recent geological record suggests will no doubt occur sometime in the future.

In addition to the physical dangers of volcanism there are those that occur in adventure tourism (slips, trips and falls; Bentley et al, 2007) and these must also be mitigated. Recreationalists engaged in unguided, independent adventure activities, notably skiing and mountaineering were amongst the most frequently injured or killed as a result of their activities on the volcanoes (Bentley et al, 2007, pp4–5). This suggests the need for improved safety messages and other information for these visitors, preferably on location or at accommodation sites. Also, the level of claims for injuries during commercially organized and run activities appears to be high in New Zealand, a situation that raises questions about the risk management standards of operators (Bentley et al, 2007, pp13–14).

Visitor safety recommendations

Visitor safety is a priority for all who live and work in the Tongariro National Park and other adventure tourism locations (Bentley and Page, 2008). The following is a summary of the range of information provided to assist visitors to the park:

- While a key attraction of the Tongariro National Park is its wilderness and spectacular beauty, visitors embarking on any trip without the assistance of experienced local guides must be prepared to carry adequate clothing, food, water, camping and first aid equipment. Guided tours are essential for the inexperienced overnight visitor on the walking trails.
- Visitors should always seek and heed advice about weather, clothing and levels of fitness. In particular they should note that weather changes can be rapid in alpine environments and clothing for all conditions should be carried regardless of the season. Most importantly they should also make sure that someone knows their plans and is advised on return.
- Visitors are strongly advised to stay on the marked tracks and to carry out all rubbish so as to help maintain the pristine environment. Toilet facilities are limited and visitors should note locations before setting out each day.
- Skifields are a special case because of alpine conditions, the potential for avalanches and for eruptions and the advice given by lodges, instructors and security personnel must be taken into account and/or adhered to.

As a supplement to this is the volcanic risk mitigation plan by Environment Waikato (Munro and Parkin, 1999) that has been written:

- to achieve the natural hazards risk management objectives of the Waikato Regional Policy Statement;
- in response to Environment Waikato's volcanic risk management responsibilities under the general provisions of the Resource Management Act 1991 and the Civil Defence National Plan;
- to achieve Environment Waikato's responsibilities under the Civil Defence Act 1983, which are to prevent loss of life, to help the injured, and to relieve personal suffering and distress;
- to meet the International Decade for Natural Disaster Reduction requirements, including the provision of mitigation plans involving long term prevention, preparedness and community awareness; and

- to integrate Environment Waikato's activities with other organizations, and assist them to achieve their organization and professional responsibilities.

In the plan there is an emphasis on working in partnership with local government and communities to find acceptable solutions to volcanic hazard issues. The first section of the plan outlines the roles and responsibilities of local government in implementing volcanic risk avoidance and mitigation measures, the second section outlines pre-event information sources and techniques for understanding alert levels, and the third section outlines mitigation techniques that could be used during an eruption or lahar

Figure 19.4 This was the only warning sign in 2006, and is not necessarily seen when landing on the island, as everybody wants to have a look at the crater lake

Note: There are no safety rails around the crater or the active fumaroles and visitors have to be very careful how close they want to go to any of the volcanic features.

Source: Photo courtesy of Patricia Erfurt-Cooper

event. Thus it can be said that risk factors and management requirements at the sites of Aotearoa-New Zealand's premier volcanic attractions have been adequately interpreted and will be enforced at the local community level, and that this in theory includes the interests of visitors.

Indeed, the recent experience of tourism at White Island can be seen to conform with this intention. Up until the 1990s anyone could land there and walk around, but in the 21st century the New Zealand Institute of Geological and Nuclear Sciences now monitors the island continuously as it does for the Tongariro area. Alert-level data is constantly made available to potential visitors by the local tour operators and through web-based information services (on a scale of 0–5, where 0 is dormant, 3 erupting and 5 is a national disaster). While White Island-Whakaari last erupted in 2000; it has been at level 1 continuously since then and tour operators now take great care in advising their clients of the dangers and their risk management procedures in the event of a change in level of activity (the author, personal experience, 2006). However, the main risk prevention measures are the advice to stay away from the rim of the crater lake, to wear a hard hat as well as having a very basic face mask handy 'just in case'. Tourists generally do not know what danger signs they should look out for and follow their group while taking photos. Unless there have been changes over the last three years no warning signs or interpretation boards are on White Island apart from one (Figure 19.4).

Conclusions

The tephra dam at the Mt Ruapehu Crater Lake most recently collapsed on 18 March 2007 and as a result a moderate to large sized lahar passed down the Whangaehu River. The emergency response 'worked like clockwork' (Department of Conservation, 2008) and the lahar passed down the river channel with minimal damage to infrastructure in its path and disruption to the travelling public. This was despite the fact that the lahar had a flow rate of about 1000 cubic metres per second at Tangiwai, which was about twice as large as that of the disastrous 1953 event. Just what happens when the TVZ complex of volcanoes erupts again is of course unknown, but we can be

relatively confident that if tourists and local communities have obtained and absorbed the information about risk management that is available the resulting impact on their lives and property will be minimized as much as possible, especially in the Tongariro National Park.

The New Zealand community and its visitors have learnt a great deal about risk management since the 1886 eruption of Mt Tarawera in the TVZ that killed 150 people and produced an eruption cloud that spread over 15,000km^2 at the same time as it destroyed the then eighth wonder of the world, the Pink and White Terraces (Robinson, 2006, p121). The associated geothermal resources are still used for domestic and international tourism, going in one case by the name of Hells Gate in order to increase the excitement felt by tourists, but nevertheless there is a healthy local regard for the consequences of increased activity and recognition that such events are in fact commonplace in the TVZ. Nevertheless, the average tourist to the centres of Rotorua and Lake Taupo who does not go into the Tongariro National Park as a walker or just experiences the hot spring spas in every motel will not really understand the true nature of volcanism until the next major eruption, and there appears to be very little that can or perhaps needs to be done about this situation even in such an active area. Nevertheless, there may be a need for some level of regulatory intervention with the aim of improving risk management practices among tourism operators (Northey, 2003).

Postscript

While not at the time of writing being considered for the TVZ, the 2005 Cabinet direction to the Ministry of Civil Defence & Emergency Management (MCDEM) to conduct national disaster exercises to test New Zealand's all-of-nation preparedness for a major disaster is indicative of the importance of volcanic risk management in New Zealand. The first of these, Exercise Capital Quake, took place in November 2006 and tested response to a Wellington earthquake. The second of these exercises, Exercise Ruaumoko, commenced in November 2007 (it took place mainly in March 2008), and tested preparedness for a volcanic eruption somewhere in the Auckland Volcanic Field.

Exercise Ruaumoko was a Tier 4 (national-level) exercise in accordance with the National Exercise Program. Planning for the exercise was led by the Department of the Prime Minister and Cabinet, the MCDEM, and the Auckland Civil Defence Emergency Management (CDEM) Group. The exercise was supported by the Northland, Waikato and Bay of Plenty CDEM Groups (responsible for the TVZ), central government departments, emergency services, lifeline utilities, and other agencies and organizations, as appropriate.

The three core objectives in these exercises are:

- Roles: understand, develop and practice the respective roles of agencies in response;
- Arrangements: embed the national CDEM plan arrangements in standard processes for all participating agencies; and
- Connections: confirm the connections between local, regional, national and international agencies.

The four supporting objectives of Exercise Ruaumoko were:

- planning for the evacuation of affected communities;
- planning for the continuance of essential services, including local government, lifeline utilities, emergency services, and government agencies;
- management of potential economic impacts; and
- coordination of science aspects; and management of public information and education.

While the existence of many tourists was not referred to explicitly in this simulation exercise, the evacuation of Auckland did include recognition of the need to cover hotels and backpacker hostels so presumably this means that the tourist would be included in the event of a real risk management situation arising.

References

Bentley, T. A. and Page, S. J. (2008) 'A decade of injury monitoring in the New Zealand adventure tourism sector: A summary risk analysis', *Tourism Management*, vol 29, pp857–869

Bentley, T. A., Page, S. J. and Macky, K. A. (2007) 'Adventure tourism and adventure sports injury: The New Zealand experience', *Applied Ergonomics*, vol 38, no 6, pp791–796

Blomfield, C. (1888) 'Painting of the White Terraces, near Rotorua, New Zealand', www.en.wikipedia.org/wiki/Image: White_Terraces,_Blomfield.jpg., accessed 25 July 2009

Cassedy, K. (1991) *Crisis Management Planning in the Travel and Tourism Industry: A Study of Three Destinations and a Crisis Management Planning Manual*, PATA, San Francisco, CA

Department of Conservation (2008) 'Crater Lake status report – 26 April 2008', Department of Conservation, Wellington

Department of Conservation (2009) 'New Zealand's Great Walks', www.doc.govt.nz/parks-and-recreation/tracks-and-walks/great-walks/, accessed 4 August, 2009

Erfurt-Cooper, P. and Cooper, M. (2009) *Health & Wellness Spa Tourism*, Aspects of Tourism Series, Channel View Press, London

Faulkner, W. (2001) 'Towards a framework for tourism disaster management', *Tourism Management*, vol 22, pp135–147

Forer, P.C. & Pearce, D.G. (1984) Spatial patterns of package tourism in New Zealand, *New Zealand Geographer*, 40(1): 34–42

Foster, H. D. (1980) *Disaster Planning: The Preservation of Life and Property*, Springer Verlag, New York

Frogatt, P. (n.d.) 'New Zealands volcanoes: The Taupo volcanic centre - Volcanic Hazards at Taupo Volcanic Centre', Online Document: www.gns.cri.nz/what/earthact/volcanoes/nzvolcanoes/taupoprint.htm, accessed 7 January 2010

Hall, C. M., Timothy, D. J. and Duval, D. T. (2004) 'Security and Tourism: Towards a New Understanding?', in Hall, C. M., Timothy, D. J. and Duval, D. T. (eds) *Safety and Security in Tourism*, The Haworth Hospitality Press, Binghamton, NY, pp1–18

Herodian of Antioch (1961) Translated from the Greek by Edward C. Echols, *History of the Roman Empire*, University Of California Press, Berkeley and Los Angeles, Online Document: www.ccel.org/ccel/pearse/morefathers/files/herodian_00_intro.htm, accessed 7 January 2010

Keys, H. and Green, P. (2004) *Mt Ruapehu Crater Lake Lahar Threat Response: Crater Lake Issue – A Management Dilemma*, Department of Conservation, Wellington

Munro, A. and Parkin, D. (1999) *Volcanic Risk Mitigation Plan*, Environment Waikato, Environmental Waikato Policy Series 1999/10, Hamilton East

Murphy, P. and Bayley, R. (1989) 'Tourism and disaster planning', *Geographical Review*, vol 79, no1, pp36–46

Newhall, C. G. and Dzurisin, D. (1988) *Historical Unrest at Large Calderas of the World*, US Geological Service, USGS Bulletin 1855, Washington DC

Northey, G. (2003) 'Equestrian injuries in New Zealand, 1993–2001: Knowledge and experience', *The New Zealand Medical Journal*, vol 116, pp1–8

Prideaux, B. (2004) 'The Need to Use Disaster Planning Frameworks to Respond to Major Tourism Disasters: Analysis of Australia's Response to Tourism Disasters in 2001', in Hall, C. M., Timothy, D. J. and Duval, D. T. (eds) *Safety and Security in Tourism*, The Haworth Hospitality Press, Binghamton, NY, pp281–298

Robinson, R. (2006) 'Volcano Legends of New Zealand', Online Document: www.volcano. oregonstate.edu/legends/newz/newzealand.html, accessed 7 January 2010

Simkin, T. and Siebert, L. (1994) *Volcanoes of the World*, Geoscience Press, Tucson, AZ

Smithsonian Institute (2010) 'Tongariro', Online Document:www.volcano.si.edu/world/volcano. cfm?vnum=0401-08=, accessed 7 January 2010

Statistics New Zealand (2008) Online Document: www.stats.govt.nz/, accessed 7 January 2010

White Island Tours (2010) 'The Volcano – White Island (Whakaari)', Online Document: www.whiteisland. co.nz/white_island.html, accessed 7 January 2010

Williams, K. (1998) 'Volcanoes of the South Wind: Fieldguide to the Volcanoes of Tongariro National Park', Tongariro Natural History Society.

Wilson, C.J.N., Ambraseys, N.N., Bradley, J. and Walker, G.P.L. (1980) A new date for the Taupo eruption, New Zealand, *Nature* London 288:252-253

20

Volcano Tourism in the New Kanawinka Global Geopark of Victoria and SE South Australia

Bernie Joyce

Introduction

Landforms due to volcanism have been constructed during all phases of the Earth's history, and subjected through time to erosional processes which have modified the original landforms. Volcanic features are in large part constructional but sit on earlier landscapes which have often influenced cone-building, ash deposits and lava flows; for example, existing valleys may often control lava flows.

There is an increasing tendency to include volcanoes in both natural protection areas, and in tourism, wherever they exist in significant numbers or as measured by activity. The actual mechanism to achieve this is increasingly a variant of the national parks that are found in virtually all countries across the Globe. Australia's first geopark is on the broad Western Plains of Victoria and the adjacent part of south-eastern South Australia in the south of the country, and this includes some 100 well-studied volcanoes ranging in age from five million years to just a few thousand years old.

Classifying volcanic landforms

A system of classification of landforms due to volcanic processes provides a necessary starting point for any discussion of volcanic features, and

this should also be followed by a further classification of the effects of erosional processes through time. Volcanic landforms are mainly *constructional*, produced by processes, which have built up deposits on pre-existing landscapes. Some are *destructional*, for example, maar craters formed by phreatomagmatic explosions often extend below the original ground surface, and may expose underlying rock in their inner walls. Calderas are generally destructional, collapsing over subsurface spaces formerly occupied by ascending magma. Erosional processes are responsible for post-eruption landform changes, and a sequence of changes over time (a chronosequence) in landforms, weathering, soils and drainage development can be used to estimate the time which has passed since volcanic activity occurred and so help in estimating the possibility of future eruption (Joyce, 2005).

A further level of classification of volcanoes and their deposits is provided by the chemical composition of the ascending magma, which directly influences the violence of eruption, and thus the landforms constructed. Magma compositions may range from basalt (basic magma), giving mild eruptions with generally small volcanoes and extensive mobile flows, to rhyolite and andesite (acid magma), giving violent eruptions and over long periods of time constructing large volcanoes, with little lava flow but possibly extensive ash deposits including ignimbrite sheets, and at the eruption points perhaps large collapse calderas.

Two classifications of types of eruptions and related landforms, based on several textbooks, are given in Tables 20.1 and 20.2.

It can be argued that detailed classifications such as these are not the best way to approach the study and description of volcanic features, when the audience may include mostly non-geologists. A simple geological and geomorphological scheme of classification may be better, leaving more scope for discussions of non-geological cultural heritage, including historic, artistic, aesthetic and other values, which may be of equal or greater interest to many of the visitors to volcanic areas.

The classification into eight types of eruptions (Table 20.1) can be simplified into just two main groupings of *small* and *large* volcanoes – that is, based on the size of the landform constructed at the eruption point. Small and large volcanoes

often have other differences, which can be characterized by the amounts and types of lava and ash produced, which are in turn related to their chemical composition. The discussion which follows deals with small volcanoes, which are more directly relevant to geoparks.

Small (monogenetic) volcanoes

Numerous small scoria (cinder) cones, characterized by Strombolian/Hawaiian activity, broad but low elevation lava shields, explosive maar craters, and associated and often long basaltic flows, 65km or longer, following pre-existing slopes and river valleys, are characteristic of monogenetic (single episode of activity) volcanoes. A single magma type, generally basalt, predominates in the activity, which may continue over millions of years, with many short-lived individual volcanoes scattered with a high density across a broad area; the volcanism is often termed 'areal' or 'polyorifice' to describe the regional distribution.

Table 20.1 A classification of volcanic activity and landforms

Type	Magma	Flows and explosivity	Landforms
Icelandic	Basic, low viscosity	Thick extensive flows from fissures, weak explosivity	Lava shields and lava plains, with cones along fissures
Hawaiian	Basic, low viscosity	Thin extensive flows from central vents, weak explosivity, but sometimes water-generated phreatic explosions	Broad lava domes and shields, and long lava flows, fed by internal lava tubes, sometimes scattered scoria cones, spatter cones, maar craters and tuff rings, built up by lava fountains, i.e. areal volcanic activity
Strombolian	Moderate viscosity; mixed basic and acid	Flows often absent, weak to violent explosivity	Cinder (scoria) cones with shallow craters and short flows; sometimes more extensive lava flows, scattered scoria cones, spatter cones, maar craters and tuff rings, built up by lava fountains, i.e. areal volcanic activity
Vulcanian	Acid, viscous	Flows often absent, moderate to violent explosivity	Ash cones, explosion craters
Vesuvian	Acid, viscous	Flows often absent, moderate to violent explosivity	Large cones built up of alternating ash and lava, i.e. stratovolcanoes, extensive ash fall, explosion craters and large collapse calderas
Plinian	Acid, viscous	Flows may be absent, very violent explosivity	Widespread pumice and ash deposits
Pelean	Acid, viscous	Domes and/or short very thick flows, nuées ardentes, moderate explosivity	Domes, spines, ash and pumice cones, ash flows forming ignimbrite plains and plateaus
Krakataun	Acid, viscous	No flows, cataclysmic explosivity	Large explosion caldera

Source: Based on Ollier, 1969 and Gray, 2004; from Joyce, 2009

Table 20.2 Four types of volcanic landforms

Types of landforms	Landforms and morphogenesis	Examples

Constructional volcanic landforms	• volcanic cones, shields, domes and spines
	  • central, fissure or areal in extent
	  • with or without craters and calderas
	• large to small in height, and in crater diameter and depth
	• single or multiple landforms; nested or parasitic
	• characterised by their shape and slope angle
		Paricutín in Mexico, with several cones and craters, steep scoria (cinder) slopes; airfall ash deposits and extensive blocky to aa lava flows.

Original constructional volcanic landforms affected by subsequent erosion	• erosion by water, wind and ice • mass movement including landslides, and mudflows (lahars) • development of radial drainage, and perhaps parasol ribbing and planezes • wind erosion forming yardangs	Exposure of volcanic necks (Le Puy-en-Velay in France), dykes (Ship Rock, New Mexico), dyke swarms (Iceland) and sills (the Whin Sill of Northern England).
Lava flows	• original flow surfaces including pahoehoe and aa flow surfaces; (the names come from Hawai'i) • flow ridges and tumuli due to flow pressure, as well as flow collapses • formation of lava channels and lava caves (lava tubes) • tree moulds • pillow lavas when flows enter water or travel over wet ground • flows channelled down valleys • burial of alluvial sediments – buried alluvium deposits containing gold, tin or other minerals are known as deep lead or placer deposits • littoral cones and lava deltas built where flows enter seas and lakes • plateau surfaces formed as streams lateral to flow edges erode valleys, causing inversion of relief • waterfalls at plateau edges, often showing exposures of columnar jointing • extensive and often thick piles of basaltic lava formed from flood basalts, apparently rapidly and catastrophically emplaced • flow landforms, like cones, can be degraded by later weathering and erosion	Lava flows of Hawai'i, lava deltas of Taveuni Island in Fiji, flood basalts of the Deccan Traps of India. Plateaus, waterfalls, columnar jointing of the Newer Volcanic Province of South-eastern Australia.
Ash falls and ash flows	• airfall mantle bedding • phreatomagmatic base surge deposits • ash flows (nuée ardente) • ignimbrite plains and plateaus	

Source: Joyce, 2009

Such monogenetic, areal basaltic fields are widely distributed across the world, largely as intraplate volcanism (i.e. volcanism away from plate boundaries). Well-studied examples include the Auckland region of New Zealand, the Eifel area in Germany, the Newer Volcanic Province of south-eastern Australia, the Auvergne region of south-eastern France, and the Rift valleys of East Africa and Ethiopia. Other areas include China, Korea, Mexico, south-west United States, north-eastern Spain, Armenia, western Hungary and southern Slovakia. Similar examples of monogenetic volcanic activity can often be found superimposed on areas of current large-scale volcanism, such as Hawai'i and Iceland.

Geoparks and volcanic regions

Some 48 geoparks are currently listed by UNESCO but of these so far only 4 are volcanic, and are mostly based on small monogenetic volcanoes. The numbers of nominations for geopark status is growing rapidly, and given UNESCO's recent indication of increasingly limited potential for further inscriptions of volcanic sites on the world heritage list, volcanic sites will probably be important in any future geopark nominations. In this regard, six new volcanic geoparks have been listed in China, including Wudalianchi, last active in 1721 (Dowling and Newsome, 2006, p150). Other recently listed or proposed global geoparks with volcanic values include the Giant's Causeway (Ireland), and the Vulkaneifel in Germany (Frey et al, 2006).

In Australia the new Kanawinka Global Geopark is part of the extensive Newer Volcanic Province of south-east Australia. Significant geological features and sites have been documented over many years in the Newer Volcanic Province, including the internationally significant lava caves (Joyce and Webb, 1993), and a review of the main eruption points has been documented (Rosengren, 1994), sponsored jointly by the Geological Society of Australia and the National Trust (Victoria). Equally, the Llancanelo and Payun Matrú Volcanic Field together with about 800 small mafic volcanoes near Malargüe, Mendoza (Argentina) is one of the volcanic fields on Earth that have the highest density of volcanoes. This field is suggested as a potential candidate for a UNESCO geopark,

and would be one of the first in South America (Risso et al, 2006).

Geoparks, with their allowable large extent, and associated human and cultural values, fit well with the features of small (monogenetic) volcanic fields. In contrast large (strato) volcanoes are often more localized, and often sparsely settled, and may already be part of a park or reserve, and so fit best with world heritage requirements. Any analysis of possible world heritage volcanoes, and possible global geopark volcanoes, would probably suggest that this division between large and small volcanoes is a good approach in planning future volcanic heritage reserves.

The young volcanoes of south-eastern Australia

Extensive volcanic areas, both old and young, are features of the Australian landscape, with Quaternary monogenetic (single short-lived eruption) scoria cones, lava shields and flows, and maar craters with ash deposits, found in south-eastern Australia (Figure 20.1) and also in north-east Queensland. The young volcanic regions of south-eastern Australia, known as the Newer Volcanic Province, occupy broad coastal plains, and an elevated upland to the north of the plains. Beginning about 6–7Ma ago, but mainly since 5Ma, a new volcanic province was formed, and nearly 400 small, monogenetic scoria cones, maars and lava shields were built up by Strombolian/Hawaiian eruptions (Nicholls and Joyce, 1989).

In 1866 the large maar volcanic crater of Tower Hill in western Victoria was set aside as a public park, and in 1892 state legislation was passed which made the Tower Hill volcano Victoria's first national park. Significant geological features and sites in the Newer Volcanic Province were first discussed in Joyce and King (1980). A review of the main eruption points, sponsored jointly by the Geological Society of Australia and the National Trust (Victoria) was published in 1994 (Rosengren, 1994). Some of the other National Trust classified landscapes in western Victoria include Mt Elephant, Tower Hill, Mt Leura, Lake Purrumbete, Lake Gnotuk and Lake Bullen Merri (Figure 20.2), Lake Keilambete, and the Stony Rises and Mt Porndon. Other landscapes

Figure 20.1 Mt Napier lava shield, south of Hamilton, looking down on the well preserved young stony surfaces of the Byaduk valley flow from Mt Napier lava shield, in the Kanawinka Geopark, Western Victoria. The youthful flow surface was damaged by rock crushing, rolling and stone raking in 2004 to allow more productive farming

Note: The flow is on the Register of the National Estate.

Figure 20.2 Lake Bullen Merri maar crater, near Camperdown, Kanawinka Geopark, Western Victoria

Source: Painting by von Guerard 1857

of interest include the Western Plains Grassland, Lake Condah and the Floating Islands, and coastal areas such as the Port Campbell National Park and the Bay of Islands Coastal Park, and Bridgewater Bay.

Nomination of the volcanic areas of western Victoria and south-east South Australia as the Kanawinka Global Geopark

Australia's first geopark is on the broad Western Plains of Victoria and the adjacent part of south-eastern South Australia, with some 100 well-studied volcanoes ranging in age from five million years to just a few thousand years. Within the area of the new Kanawinka Geopark are many important volcanic features including lava caves of international significance, open volcanic vents, major tumuli groups, and springs and waterfalls. Coastal features include limestone cliffs, calcareous dunes, basalt headlands and cliffs, drowned lava flows and a large offshore volcanic island. Extensive karst plains and limestone caves are found in the west, and in the east Quaternary, often saline, lake/lunette systems are major Ramsar sites. Cultural features include indigenous heritage such as stone

Figure 20.3 Reconstruction of a stone house on the Tyrendarra stony rise flow

Note: The Tyrendarra Indigenous Protected Area, demonstrated by Darryl Rose of the Gunditjmara people, in the Budj Bim National Heritage Landscape, was declared by the Australian government in July 2004 for its outstanding values as part of Australia's national heritage.

Source: Photo courtesy of Chris Pavich

houses and fish and eel traps, and also post-contact basalt stone walls and historic buildings (Figure 20.3). An active art and history movement is part of the cultural heritage of the local people.

For these reasons, the area was recognized as the Kanawinka Global Geopark in June 2008, and in the following 12 months the geotourism of the area has been under development, with programmes to assemble further information, and develop new material for use by geotourists, geotourism operators and local government bodies. The accuracy and usefulness of the volcanic information must be based on the extensive past scientific studies of the volcanoes and other geological and cultural features of the area, but will also make use of the new approach of the 'Geomorphosites and Volcanism' chapter in *Geomorphosites* (Joyce, 2009).

The Kanawinka Geopark of south-east Australia as an example of volcano tourism

The young volcanic areas of the Western Plains of Victoria and adjacent South Australia have more than 100 small scoria cones, maars and lava shields, built up by Strombolian/Hawaiian eruptions over the past five million years. Fluid basalt flows spread laterally around vents, often for many tens of kilometres down river valleys. Where the lava flows blocked drainage, lakes and swamps were formed. Phreatic eruptions deposited ash and left deep maar craters, often now with lakes. The youngest dated eruption is that of Mt Gambier in south-eastern South Australia, at 4000–4300BC. The highest volcano is Mt Elephant, near the centre of the plains. It rises nearly 200m above the plains to an elevation above sea level of 393m, with a crater 90m deep, and is similar in size to Mt Kooroocheang, the highest volcano in the Western Uplands. First identified as a volcanic region nearly 170 years ago the Newer Volcanic Province of south-eastern Australia is now one of the best studied of the world's many young basaltic monogenetic lava fields.

Both the European cultural history of the plains, and the first recognition of its volcanic geology go back to the explorer Major T. L. Mitchell, who in 1836 was the first person to identify volcanoes and flows on the plains, and he also provided the first written description of the

Western Plains – 'We now travelled over a country quite open, slightly undulating and well-covered with grass … vast plains, fringed with forests and embellished with lakes … the open plains extended as far as the eye could reach' (Mitchell, 1838).

In the 1840s and 1850s several books and scientific journal articles made the area widely known, at a time when popular interest in volcanoes was growing. James Bonwick, an inspector of schools, recorded his observations of western Victoria and many of its geological features in a book published in 1858, and in 1866 he compared the volcanic rocks and features of Victoria with those of the area around Rome, in a scientific paper in the Proceedings of the recently founded Royal Society of Victoria. The Reverend Julian Tenison Woods, working across the border in South Australia, published a book in 1862 which described the volcanic features of Mt Gambier and Mt Schank in detail, and he also gave a public lecture series in Portland in 1865 on the volcanic features of the plains. One of many later workers was E. D. Gill, from the Museum of Victoria, who helped start a new phase of study of the volcanoes in the 1960s, and was the first to make use of the newly invented radiocarbon dating technique to determine the ages of young volcanoes such as Tower Hill.

The geology of the geopark, which stretches from near Colac in western Victoria, to Mt Gambier and beyond in South Australia, is based on scientific study going back over 150 years, and the area is one of the best studied of the world's young basaltic lava fields. Equally important to the success of the application have been the studies of local history, plants and animals, and indigenous features, as well as cultural aspects including art and architecture (Joyce, 2007).

The indigenous heritage of the plains includes a complex of Aboriginal fish and eel traps, and remains of stone houses, in the stony rise flow landscapes of the Mt Eccles volcano. Historic 'bluestone' (basalt) houses, bridges, churches, other town buildings and the many striking stone walls help record European post-contact settlement. These cultural features, supported by a detailed geological and geomorphological story, made the area an ideal candidate for nomination as a geopark.

Parks and reserves include Tower Hill, the Mt Eccles volcano, flows and lava caves, and the Mt

Figure 20.4 Old 'bluestone' (basalt) Volcano Discovery Centre at Penshurst, with Kanawinka Geopark Director Joanne McKnight (left)

Source: Photo courtesy of Chris Pavich

Napier volcano and its flows and lava caves. New reserves have recently been developed at Mt Elephant and Mt Rouse volcanoes, there have been improvements to interpretation at other sites, and across much of the volcanic plains of Victoria and South Australia the Volcanoes Discovery Trail has been set up (Figure 20.4). A National Trust landscape study of Stony Rise lava flows, and the establishment of the Penshurst Volcanoes Discovery Centre (Figure 20.4), near the Mt Rouse volcano, are also promising developments. In the future the integration of volcanic research, local history study, and heritage interpretation could be the key to developing a greater awareness, not just of heritage values, but also of volcanic hazard and risk concepts, a research area of growing interest to volcanologists working in this geologically youthful and potentially active volcanic area.

Sustainability is one of the suggested attributes of an area which is to become a geopark. Fortunately volcanic areas often provide 'rugged' geomorphological sites – that is, resistent to human damage. In the Kanawinka Geopark several large areas have been set aside as national parks (Mt Eccles, Mt Napier), under full state government protection and management. Other areas are under the control of local government (Bullen Merri and Gnotuk craters), community groups (Mt Leura, Mt Elephant), or enlightened private owners (Mt Noorat), all of whom are anxious to provide sustainable geotourism activities.

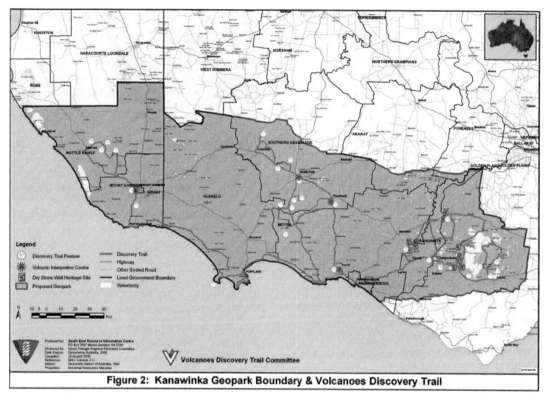

Figure 2: **Kanawinka Geopark Boundary & Volcanoes Discovery Trail**

Figure 20.5 Map of the Kanawinka Global Geopark area

After four years of work by local people, UNESCO approved the proposed Kanawinka Global Geopark in western Victoria and south-east South Australia on Monday, 23 June 2008 at a meeting in Germany (Figure 20.5). It is Australia's first geopark, and one of only a few in the southern hemisphere.

Conserving geological sites in the Kanawinka Geopark

A small number of volcanic landforms in western Victoria have been set aside as reserves. Mt Eccles and Mt Napier are national parks, and Tower Hill is a state game reserve. Mt Leura cone is a reserve run by the local shire, and a part of the rim, Mt Sugarloaf, is owned by the National Trust. Much of the Leura volcanic complex is private land, and includes a large active scoria quarry, with further areas under threat. Similarly, Red Rock and Mt Rouse volcanoes have access roads and viewpoints, but are essentially private land, with some quarries, mostly not in current operation. Mt Elephant is

owned by the Trust for Nature and the local Derrinallum community, with access and information available. Mt Noorat is private land, but the local shire oversees access, and information is provided. Lake Gnotuk and Lake BullenMerri maar craters have road access, but are private farmland, a golf course, and a recreation reserve and boat access areas.

These volcanic landforms have been classified by the National Trust, and also by the Geological Society of Victoria. Most of these volcanic landforms are on the Australian government's Register of the National Estate, but not on the state Heritage Register, or, with the exception of parts of the Mt Eccles lava flows, on the new National Heritage Register.

Threats to the volcanic landforms in the Kanawinka Geopark

The following are the major threats to the Kanawinka Geopark:

- Quarrying: although with increasing rationalization and control by the Geological Survey of Victoria and the Mines Department, the number of active quarries is decreasing, but at the same time becoming more extensive.
- Excessive planting of vegetation: often following clearing of past, often exotic vegetation, but with the new planting likely to provide future problems with visibility of landforms, and views from the landform to the surrounding landscape. Both the Geological Society of Australia and the National Trust Landscape Committee have developed guidelines and policies on this problem.
- Covering over and landscape degradation by building of houses and other structures: especially in the suburban sprawl near Melbourne, for example, at Mt Aitken, Mt Ridley and Mt Cottrell north of Melbourne, but also inside the crater of Lake Gnotuk at Camperdown, and most recently as threats to the outer slopes of Tower Hill.
- Rock crushing, rolling and stone raking of young stony flow surfaces to allow more productive farming: for example, on the Register of the National Estate-listed Byaduk valley flow of Mt Napier, south of Hamilton, in 2004, and most recently in the National Trust-classified Stony Rises of Mt Porndon.

Conclusions

Recent threats to the volcanic heritage of western Victoria, which includes many landforms of national and international significance have included quarrying of cones, housing development on cones and inside craters, and landform destruction of stony rises. New reserves have however been developed at Mt Elephant and Mt Rouse volcanoes, there have been recent improvements to interpretation at other sites, and across much of western Victoria a Volcanoes Discovery Trail has been developed, with maps, leaflets, signboards and a web site.

The western Victorian portion of the Newer Volcanic Province also has a strong cultural heritage, with its complex Aboriginal and early European settlement history, its historic 'bluestone'

Figure 20.6 Group of geotourists inside Tunnel Cave, Mt Eccles volcano

Source: Photo courtesy of Chris Pavich

(basalt) houses, bridges, churches, other town buildings, monuments and stone walls. These, together with its detailed and well-studied geological and geomorphological story, have helped make it Australia's first geopark.

Both scientific and cultural values are being used to plan the management of the Kanawinka Geopark. Management must be based on continuing scientific studies, including the results of recent assessments of the possibility of further volcanic activity (Joyce, 2005). The story must be communicated to those involved in managing the geopark, and to those who live and work in the area, as much as to those who come as geotourists to see its scientific and cultural features (Figure 20.6).

References

Dowling, R. K. and Newsome, D. (eds) (2006) *Geotourism*, Elsevier, Amsterdam

Frey, M. L., Schafer, K., Buchel, G. and Patzak, M. (2006) 'Geoparks: A Regional, European and Global Policy', in Dowling, R. K. and Newsome, D. (eds) *Geotourism*, Elsevier, Amsterdam, pp95–117

Gray, M. (2004) *Geodiversity, Valuing and Conserving Abiotic Nature*, Wiley, Chichester

Joyce, B. (2005) 'How can eruption risk be assessed in young monogenetic areal basalt fields? An example from southeastern Australia', *Zeitschrift fur Geomorphologie N.F,* suppl.-vol 140, pp195–207

Joyce, B. (2007) 'Geotourism, Geosites and Geoparks: Working together in Australia', *Special Report, The Australian Geologist,* Newsletter No 144, September, pp26–29

Joyce, B. (2009) 'Geomorphosites and Volcanism', in Reynard, E., Coratza, P. and Regolini-Bissig, G. (eds) *Geomorphosites*, Verlag Dr. Friedrich Pfeil, Munchen, pp175–188

Joyce, E. B. and King, R. L. (1980) *Geological Features of the National Estate in Victoria*, An inventory compiled for the Australian Heritage Commission, Victorian Division, Geological Society of Australia, Melbourne

Joyce, E. B. and Webb, J. A. (1993) 'Conservation of Lava Caves: Examples from Australia', in Halliday, W. R. (ed) *Proceedings of the Third International Symposium on Vulcanospeleology*, Bend, Oregon, June 1982, International Speleological Foundation, Seattle, pp121–123

Mitchell, T. L. (1838) *Three Expeditions into the Interior of Eastern Australia*, T. and W. Boone, London, 2 vols

Nicholls, I. A. and Joyce E. B. (1989) 'Newer Volcanics, Victoria and South Australia, East Australian Volcanic Geology', in Johnson, R. W. (ed) *Intraplate Volcanism in Eastern Australia and New Zealand*, Cambridge University Press, Cambridge, pp137–143

Ollier, C. D. (1969) *Volcanoes*, Australian National University Press, Canberra

Risso, C., Nemeth, K. and Martin, U. (2006) 'Proposed geosites on Pliocene to recent pyroclastic cone fields in Mendoza, Argentina', *Zeitschrift der Deutschen Gesellschaft für Geowissenschaften*, vol 57, pp477–490

Rosengren, N. J. (1994) 'The Newer Volcanic Province of Victoria, Australia: The use of an inventory of scientific significance in the management of scoria and tuff quarrying', in O'Halloran, D., Green, C., Harley, M., Stanley, M. and Knill, J. (eds) *Geological and Landscape Conservation*, Geological Society, London, pp105–110

21

Volcanic Landforms as Tourist Attractions in Australian National Parks and Other Protected Areas

Patricia Erfurt-Cooper

Introduction

The Australian east coast has a large diversity of geological features including inactive remnants of volcanoes, many of them located in national parks or conservation areas. These areas of dormant or extinct volcanism offer an abundance of tourist destinations. In the north of Queensland large parts of the landscape are shaped by volcanic activity with over 60 remnant volcanoes in the Atherton Tablelands alone. The 'far north' offers various volcanic features including lava tubes, columnar joints, cinder cones and maars. In south-east Queensland the Glasshouse Mountains are a well known landmark surrounded by a national park. On the New South Wales – Queensland border the Mt Warning caldera in the Tweed Valley is an impressive reminder of a volcanic past and further south the Warrumbungle National Park offers old vents at Crater Bluff, nature trails, lookouts and lava domes from Split Rock to the Breadknife and Belougery Spire.

In the south of Australia Mt Gambier, a volcanic complex of maar volcanoes including the Blue Lake and the Valley Lake is set in a unique landscape formed by rather recent volcanism

(c2500BC). Volcano parks in areas of extinct or dormant volcanism are advertised as family friendly environments, educational and cater for all age groups. Activities range from trekking, hiking, climbing, abseiling, skiing, bushwalking and camping on or around volcanoes to water sports (canoeing, water skiing and fishing) on crater lakes. This chapter is a further example of the variety of volcanic landforms and features worldwide, and outlines the major volcanic environments of Australia that are either part of the overall tourist attraction of individual regions or are marketed as the main drawcard for visitors interested in geological heritage. The significance of Australia's geological heritage and the dimensions of its potential for tourism are clearly demonstrated through the diversity of tourist attractions related directly to landscapes created by volcanic activity in the past.

Tourism in Australia

Australia has a long history of using its natural environment as a tourist attraction, mainly due to the fact that the country has variously promoted the 'Outback', the 'Wet Tropics' and the 'Great Barrier Reef' as major destinations for nature-based tourism. These images have included ecotourism and marine tourism, but also volcano tourism, even if this is not obvious initially. As volcano tourism has not received much attention as an individual tourism category there is an apparent lack of research into its nature and extent, despite the fact that an increasing number of people are shifting their focus towards the physical landscape, including our geological heritage of which volcanoes are a part. Volcanoes do not have to be active to represent interesting and unique landscape features and are being progressively put to use to attract visitors to even the remotest areas to benefit from the tourist dollar.

Australia's volcanic past has been included in many areas, often in national parks, as a unique landscape attraction offering visitors the opportunity to learn more about the geological history of certain regions including accounts of volcanic activity, remnants of which can be found along the eastern seaboard and in the south-east of Australia (Figure 21.1).

The eastern part of Australia, extending from far north Queensland to the south-east of South Australia, including Tasmania, is subdivided into individual volcanic provinces dominated by numerous volcanoes and extensive lava fields (Johnson et al, 1989). At first glance Australia does not look as if its remnant volcanoes could represent a significant attraction for nature-based tourism; however, when participating in guided tours along

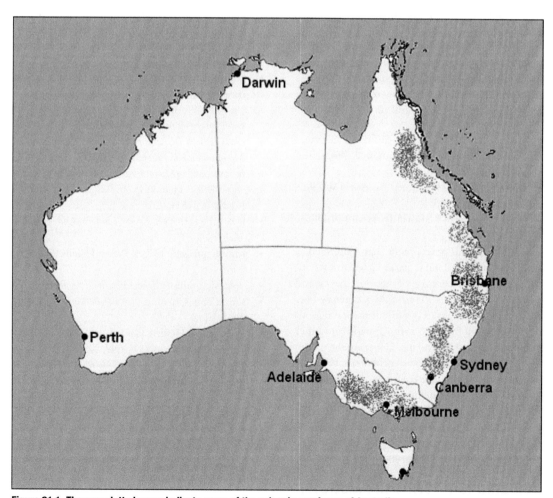

Figure 21.1 The grey dotted areas indicate some of the volcanic provinces of Australia

Note: Map modified by author.

the east coast and in the south-east of Australia it soon becomes apparent that there has been considerable volcanic activity in some areas in the not so distant past. Australian *geosites* and *geotopes* as they are increasingly called, are natural areas of geological significance and in some cases are of world heritage status, which represents an additional drawcard for visitors. Although in many protected areas volcanic landforms are not the main attraction or obvious to everybody, this chapter highlights the fact, that many national parks and other protected regions are based in part on its volcanic heritage. National parks and geoparks are areas which have been set aside and designated for preservation and are made available for purposes of recreation and culture for the public. These areas of countryside are usually protected for their scenic value, geological heritage, their biodiversity and overall environmental significance and are kept in their natural state by special national park legislations and national park acts. In Australia national parks are administered by their respective state governments under the control of:

- Queensland Parks and Wildlife Services (QPWS) and the Environmental Protection Agency (EPA);
- New South Wales National Parks and Wildlife;
- Parks Victoria; and
- South Australian National Parks and Wildlife.

The Queensland government has published a guide to Queensland's parks and forests to commemorate a century of national parks and protected areas from 1908 to 2008. Currently over eight million hectares of important natural regions are protected in over 900 national parks and other protected areas (Queensland Government, 2008) including five magnificent world heritage areas. When looking at the number of Australian national parks that include volcanic features, it becomes clear that volcanism, whether active or dormant, has a special attraction for many people, although the actual volcanic past may not be immediately obvious to everybody.

Volcanic landforms in Australia

Volcanic landforms are not always recognized as such in Australian national parks, although many

protected sites along the east coast and down south in the border region of South Australia and Victoria openly promote their volcanic landforms as tourist attractions. To present an overview of 'what's on offer' some of the Australian volcanic landscapes are discussed here to illustrate the dimensions of this type of nature-based tourism. The prerequisites for volcano tourism are features such as volcanic landforms, rock formations and other phenomena, preferably in an area with easy road access and other necessary service infrastructure. The following list presents a number of volcanic features as examples of dormant or extinct volcanic environments in Australia that are actively promoted for tourism:

- crater lakes, maars and diatremes *(Tower Hill National Park, south-west Victoria; Lake Eacham, Lake Barrine, Hypipamee Crater, Crater Lakes National Park, Qld)*;
- columnar jointing, tessellated pavements or basalt columns *(e.g. Organ Pipes NP, Melbourne; Sawn Rock, Mt Kaputar NP, Central NSW; Mt Canabolas Volcanic Complex, NSW)*;
- entablatures *(Rosette Rock, Organ Pipes NP, Vic; Monaro Volcanic Province, NSW)*;
- pillow basalt *(Monaro Volcanic Province)*;
- lava flows, channels, shields, ridges, domes *(Qld, Vic, NSW)*;
- lava tubes, tunnels, caves *(Undara, Qld, Byaduk, Vic)*;
- tumuli, pressure ridges *(Newer Volcanic Provinces, Vic)*;
- volcanic bombs *(Monaro Volcanic Province, NSW)*;
- scoria cones, spatter cones *(Mt Scoria, Qld; Red Rock, Vic)*;
- stony rises *(Western Plains, Vic)*;
- volcanic provinces *(Vic, Qld, NSW)*;
- central volcanoes *(Nandewar, Warrumbungle, Peak Range, Springsure, Main Range and Tweed)*.

The list of activities and attractions related to such volcanic landforms is quite extensive. Depending on their location and nature, any of the following attractions, activities and information centres may be offered to the tourist:

- hiking and trekking;
- biodiversity;

- bird watching;
- native history;
- photography;
- picnic and BBQ areas;
- bus tours;
- camping grounds;
- climbing and abseiling;
- geological heritage;
- golf course;
- guided activities;
- parks;
- information centres;
- interpretive visitor centres;
- mountain biking;
- unique rock formations;
- viewing platforms;
- visitor facilities, shops, car parks;
- volcanic landforms;
- walking trails;
- waterfall and caves;
- water sports on crater lakes.

In the tropical north of Queensland the Atherton Tablelands (Atherton Province) contain 52 known eruption centres with a variety of volcano types from lava shields and cinder cones to maars and one diatreme (Johnson et al, 1989). Of interest for the geotourist are the '... contrasts in erosion from remnant plugs ... to volcanoes that have craters and associated lava fields in excellent preservation' (Johnson et al, 1989, p89). One of the most remarkable volcanic regions of the Far North is the Undara Volcanic National Park where opera and theatre in the relative isolation of the Outback are part of the 'Undara Experience'. They may be rather unusual events, but for nine years the annual Undara Opera has drawn visitors to combine the volcanic heritage with a touch of culture.

The Undara lava tubes are described as the oldest in Australia and with the longest tunnel up to 160km long they could well be the longest in the world. Over the years weaker sections of the lava tubes collapsed forming today's line of depressions and caves with the collapsed sections of the lava tubes being marked by rainforest growth and clearly visible from the air. Undara Volcanic National Park is one of Queensland's conservation areas with the potential to attract increasing numbers of visitors to north-western

Queensland. However, due to the sensitivity of the ecology of the area the Queensland's Department of Environment and Heritage (DEH) currently allows only supervised public access with a set quota of 200 visitors a day to see the lava tubes, which adds up to around 20,000 people going on a tour of the lava tubes each year during the dry season. Despite an entrance fee being charged these lava tubes are the region's main attraction (Undara Experience, 2009).

The volcanic history of the Atherton Tablelands is protected in several sites such as conservation parks and national parks, which include attractions of the region's more recent volcanic past like Lake Barrine and Lake Eacham that are promoted as major tourism attractions due to their scenic beauty. Both lakes are maar craters and formed when super-heated groundwater exploded. Lake Eacham was gazetted a national park in 1934 and was included within the Wet Tropics World Heritage Area in 1988. By the year 1994 Lake Eacham joined with Lake Barrine under the name Crater Lakes National Park (Queensland Government, 2009a). Another unique volcanic feature of the Crater Lakes National Park is Mt Hypipamee, a small diatreme about 82m deep and filled with water, which attracts around 40,000 visitors per year (pers. communication with park ranger, 2008). Other volcanic craters dating back to a similar time period are the Mobo Creek crater and Lake Eumaroo located in the Danbulla National Park. Other major volcanic features of the Atherton Tablelands are the Seven Sisters and Mt Quincan. The Seven Sisters are a series of seven volcanic mounds, some of which have been cleared for dairying. Neither the Seven Sisters nor Mt Quincan have been developed as tourism sites as they do not have national park status and several of the ancient volcanic cones remain in private ownership, but people go for a drive to see the Seven Sisters in the distance or view them from Mt Halloran (Figure 21.2).

The volcanic chains which extend from the north of Queensland to the area around Mt Macedon (Hanging Rock) in Victoria include the following volcanoes:

- Cape Hillsborough volcano (north of Mackay);

Figure 21.2 The Seven Sisters are volcanic cones which can be seen from the road across the cane fields

Note: These are private property with no access for tourists. Some of the volcanic cones are used as orchards for olives (see insert) or have been quarried in the past.

- Glasshouse Mountains (north of Brisbane);
- Warrumbungles (100km north of Dubbo near Coonabarabran); and
- Canabolas (near Orange).

The Cape Hillsborough National Park contains the Cape Hillsborough volcanics – a diversity of landforms which were created by volcanic activity and attract visitors with their geologic heritage. Rhyolite boulders, layers of lava and the volcanic plug 'Pinnacle Rock' are part of this national park in Central Queensland. In southern Queensland basalt occurrences extend in an almost continuous line including Bundaberg (The Hummock), Bunya Mountains, Kingaroy and Toowoomba all the way to the New South Wales border (Johnson, 2004, p170).

Central Queensland has extended areas of volcanic origin, including the Whitsunday Volcanic Province, Nebo volcano, Springsure, Peak Range, Monto, Bauhinia, Buckland Volcanic Province (Johnson et al, 1989), some of which are part of national parks or other preserved sites such as Mt Scoria. The sharp peak of Mt Scoria rises 150m (Willmott, 2006; Queensland Government, 2008) above the otherwise flat landscape near the town of Biloela. One of the attractions of this small volcanic cone is the basalt columns which cover the mountain slopes. Mt Scoria is not a scoria cone as the name suggests as only small amounts of scoria are found (Queensland Government, 2009a). In order to stay safe around Mt Scoria the park management offers some guidelines for conduct specifically for this conservation park:

> *While Mount Scoria Conservation Park provides the opportunity to encounter the region's diverse wildlife and striking geology, it can also present some hidden dangers. Follow the tips below for a safe and enjoyable visit:*

- *Stay on the track. You may get lost if you leave the walking track. Follow markers and signs carefully and let someone responsible know your plans in case you get lost.*
- *Avoid bites, stings and scratches. Wear protective clothing and insect repellent to protect yourself from stings, scratches and insect bites, especially bites from ticks. Detour around snakes; never provoke them.*

> *Be sun-smart. Wear a hat, shirt and sunscreen, even on overcast days, to avoid sunburn. Drink frequently to avoid dehydration.*

(Queensland Government, 2009b)

This example indicates a commitment of the authorities in charge towards visitor safety in designated natural public recreation areas, whether there are active volcanoes or not. Basic safety rules should be considered by everyone when entering unfamiliar territory.

Volcanic features in Queensland are too numerous to discuss in one chapter although not all of them have been integrated in the tourism sector as yet; for example, Mt Walsh National Park or Coalstoun Lakes National Park near Biggenden have the potential to develop into real tourist attractions once some facilities could be added to attract visitors. Further down the coast in south-east Queensland the Glasshouse Mountains are a distinctive landmark (Figure 21.3) and attract visitors to the Glasshouse Mountains National Park to view at least a dozen volcanic plugs, some of them showing well developed columnar jointing (e.g. Mt Beerwah). The region around the Glasshouse Mountains, which were sighted and named by Captain James Cook in 1770 (Australian Museum Online, 2004), caters for geotourists, both domestic and international, often backpackers. The shape of the mountains reminded Captain Cook of the glass furnaces of his hometown in England as he wrote in his journal on 17 May

Figure 21.3 Some of the volcanic remnants of the Glasshouse Mountains

1770, where he made the following comment: 'they [Glasshouse Mountains] are remarkable for the singular form of their elevation, which very much resembles a glass house and for this reason I called them the Glass Houses' (Queensland Government, 2009c).

Although the volcanoes (eroded cores of central volcanoes) which form the Glasshouse Mountains are extinct (or at least presently dormant) their distinctive silhouettes in the distance viewed from one of the lookouts tell an impressive story of immense volcanic activity. The Glasshouse Mountains area offers a vast range of activities for visitors, incorporating many smaller communities in the loop of attractive tourist destinations. Lookouts, walkways and other facilities in the Glasshouse Mountains National Park offer wheelchair access and ranger guided summit hikes are offered at certain days (Queensland EPA, 2007).

Extreme sports are one of the attractions supported by the volcanic terrain in this area. The 100 Mile Run is an event that attracts athletes from around the world. Abseiling the steep cliffs of the mountains, mountain biking and mountain running are some of the more demanding sports carried out using the volcanic landscape as a challenge (The Official Glasshouse Mountains Tourism Website, n.d). However, the mountains **are** dangerous and it is now illegal to climb Mt Coonowrin as several deaths have occurred here. Some climbs are still possible, but should only be undertaken by experienced climbers (Sunshine Coast Queensland, 2006). But many visitors to the region and the national park itself are happy to enjoy the scenic drives with lookouts offering stunning views over the landscape and great photo opportunities. Because of the variety of recreational activities around the Glasshouse Mountains this area is one of the major tourist attractions in the hinterland of south-east Queensland.

The world heritage listed Gondwana Rainforests of Australia are described as having 'outstanding geological features displayed around shield volcanic craters' combined with a 'high number of rare and threatened rainforest species … of international significance for science and conservation' (UNESCO, 2009). This world heritage site is 'composed of a series of eight distinct groupings of parks and reserves distributed between Newcastle and Brisbane' (Department of the Environment, Water, Heritage and the Arts (2008); Big Volcano Tourism, 2009). As mentioned earlier, it takes more than one book chapter to do justice to the numerous volcanic landforms of Australia, especially when more are being discovered, protected and developed for tourism.

Volcanic environments of New South Wales

South of the border from Queensland in northern New South Wales inland from Tweed Heads lies another volcanic region. Mt Warning (the Aboriginal name is Wollumbin, meaning 'fighting chief of the mountains'), was named by Captain Cook during the same voyage in May 1770 along the east coast of Australia. The name was actually intended to warn future mariners of the offshore reefs Captain Cook encountered on his trip in this area (Mt Warning National Park, 2001). Mt Warning is a world heritage listed national park (2210ha) with the mountain itself the central core of the southern hemisphere's largest extinct shield volcano (over 4000km^2 in extent) and the first place on Australia's mainland to be touched by the morning sun. The New South Wales government website explains the geological and cultural importance of world heritage listed Mt Warning (Wollumbin), which is not only the remnant central plug of an ancient volcano, but also a sacred place of great significance to the people of the Bundjalung Nation as a traditional place of cultural lore, initiation and spiritual education. To respect their law and culture, the Bundjalung ask that people consider choosing **not** to climb the mountain because under Bundjalung law, only specifically chosen people are allowed to climb Wollumbin (New South Wales Government, 2009). However, some tour operators do recommend climbing to the summit for the adventurous to watch the sunrise, which is common at many volcanoes worldwide and is considered as a special and often spiritual experience (compare Mt Fuji, Japan; Haleakala, Hawai'i; Mt Bromo, Indonesia; Mt Teide, Spain;

Gunung Batur, Bali; Telíca volcano, Nicaragua; Cotopaxi, Ecuador; Ngauruhoe, New Zealand).

Mountain retreats and spa cottages around Mt Warning cater for the more relaxed tourist, who prefers rainforest walks and viewing the mountain from a distance instead of attempting to climb the ancient volcano. The eroded caldera is today known as the Tweed Valley. In the year 1928 Mt Warning was reserved for public recreation and in 1966 was dedicated as a national park. Thousands of visitors enjoy the summit views every year; however, the impact of the visitor numbers on a small area such as the top of the volcano has meant a ban on camping on the summit (Tweed Shire, 2009). Bird watching, rainforest safaris and scenic flights are just a few examples of other activities in the volcanic environment of Mt Warning National Park.

Further south in central New South Wales is the Warrumbungle National Park (Figure 21.4) which has for over 70 years attracted rock climbers and bushwalkers to an important habitat with a rich biodiversity of Australian native flora and fauna and was included in the National Heritage List in 2006 (Australian Government, 2008). Driving through the Warrumbungles is an

awe-inspiring experience due to the atmosphere of a natural environment with a long volcanic history, especially when no other cars or people are in sight. The views of the old volcanic plugs are remarkable, even for visitors who are not too interested in natural landforms. The geological heritage of the Warrumbungles as well as the local biodiversity is well explained on many sign boards throughout the park – a learning experience even without a guide. Camping, day walks, rocky spires, and sunsets in the peaceful environment (Australian Tourism Net, 2006) of a national park that was shaped by volcanic activity are recommended and give an insight into a landscape that has eroded over time and created the distinctively rugged features of the Warrumbungles.

Not far from the Warrumbungle National Park, some 120km to the north is the Nandewar Range (Duggan and Knutson, 1993) with Mt Kaputar National Park, of which more than 80 per cent has been declared a wilderness area (Fox, 1994). This park is a popular destination for rock climbers who like the challenge of the volcanic landforms. A series of volcanic eruptions and years of erosion have created the area known today as

Figure 21.4 Warrumbungle National Park in New South Wales

the Mt Kaputar National Park. The rugged wilderness rises high above the surrounding plains in a dramatic landscape of volcanic plugs, lava terraces and ring dykes with the peak of Mt Kaputar reaching 1510m and offering great views from the top of the range. One of the most spectacular reminders of the volcanic past is Sawn Rock, an excellent example of columnar jointing and classed as one of the best in Australia (Mt Kaputar National Park, 2008). The volcanoes we see today are only small compared to their original size; however, they are still quite impressive and the landscape features include deep narrow valleys, lava terraces, steep ridges and cliffs – in many places eroded to flat remnants of the original volcanoes (Mt Kaputar National Park, 2008).

Close to the border between South Australia and Victoria lie more examples of the country's volcanic past. These are the crater lakes of Mt Gambier, the Blue Lake and the Green Lake. This area is estimated to have been active quite recently in geological terms, with the last eruption from this volcano occurring approximately 4500 to 5000 years ago. In fact, the rising incidence of earthquakes in Australia in recent years has raised the suspicions of some scientists (Joyce, 2005) that these could be linked to ancient volcanoes (Australian Associated Press, 2003). With respect to tourism to these locations, however, information on visitor numbers at individual locations must presently be researched through surveys and requests for information where available, as there are no statistical data collected to date. Volcano tourism in Australia has not yet been widely accepted as an individual branch of nature-based tourism.

Conclusion

The real extent of geotourism in volcanic environments is uncertain without reliable visitor statistics. To recognize volcanic landforms in Australia requires some initial interest in the geology of a particular region that is well-supported in many nature parks by interpretive signage and visitor centres. For people interested in visiting sites with remnant volcanic landforms, a large geological heritage is available which is usually combined with outdoor activities offered in protected environments. Compared to active

volcanic environments elsewhere in the world one of the positive factors in Australia is the relative safety without the potential dangers of eruptions, toxic gas emissions and other hazards related to active volcanoes, although that is often what people want – excitement.

In Australian natural environments like the geological and especially volcanic heritage often takes second place after attractions such as the unique biodiversity of reefs and rainforests; although with the geotourism movement visitors to natural sites will become more and more aware of the country's rich geological heritage. Actual volcanic activity is not necessarily an important aspect for the less extreme side of nature-based tourism. However, even in presently non-active volcanic areas there is always the risk of a variety of potentially dangerous situations. As these tourism attractions are mostly located in vast natural reserves people can get lost, or suffer from exposure or dehydration, and there is of course no limit to personal accidents. Therefore, in the case of an emergency situation it is paramount that visitors or tourists have sufficient information on how to deal with extreme situations should these arise.

This chapter has described a number of the remnant volcanic features and given an overview of some of the volcanic landscapes used for tourism in Australia within the national or conservation park system. Future research will further identify their actual attraction for visitors and their function as essential landscapes in a network of geoparks across the country.

References

Australian Associated Press (AAP) (2003) 'Australian quakes linked to dormant volcanoes', www.smh.com.au/articles/2003/01/26/1043533958092.html, accessed 10 June 2009

Australian Government (2008) 'National Heritage – Warrumbungle National Park, New South Wales', www.environment.gov.au/heritage/places/national/warrumbungle/index.html, accessed 20 June 2008

Australian Museum Online (2004) 'Glass House Mountains', www.amonline.net.au/geoscience/earth/glass_house.htm, accessed 1 July 2008

Australian Tourism Net (2006) 'North West National Parks New South Wales – Warrumbungle National

Park', www.atn.com.au/nsw/west/parks-b.htm, accessed 20 June 2008

Big Volcano Tourism (2009) 'The properties of the Gondwana Rainforests of Australia

CERRA – Central eastern rainforest reserves of Australia', www.bigvolcano.com.au/natural/cera. htm, accessed 20 July 2009

Department of the Environment, Water, Heritage and the Arts (2008) 'Gondwana Rainforests of Australia, MAP', www.environment.gov.au/heritage/places/world/gondwana/pubs/gondwana-map.pdf, accessed 22 July 2009

Duggan, M. B. and Knutson, J. (1993) *The Warrumbungle Volcano – A Geological Guide to the Warrumbungle National Park*, Australian Geological Survey Organisation, Sydney

Fox, P. (1994) *Mount Kaputar National Park Guidebook*, NSW National Parks and Wildlife Service, Sydney

Johnson, D. (2004) *The Geology of Australia*, Cambridge University Press, Melbourne

Johnson, W., Knutson, J. and Taylor, S. R. (eds) (1989) *Intraplate Volcanism in Eastern Australia and New Zealand*, Cambridge University Press, Cambridge

Joyce, B. (2005) 'How can eruption risk be assessed in young monogenetic areal basalt fields? An example from southeastern Australia', special issue on volcanic geomorphology, *Zeitschrift für Geomorphologie NF*, suppl.-vol 140, pp195–207

Mt Kaputar National Park (2008) 'Geology & landscape', New South Wales Government Department of Environment and Climate Change, Sydney, www2.nationalparks.nsw.gov.au/parks.nsf/ParkContent/N0038?OpenDocument&ParkKey=N0038&Type=Xj, accessed 14 June 2009

Mt Warning National Park (2001) www.tropicalnsw.com.au/nationalparks/warning.html, accessed 20 June 2008

New South Wales Government (2009) 'Mount Warning National Park', Department of Environment, Climate Change and Water, www.environment.nsw.gov.au/NationalParks/parkHome.aspx?id=N0024#, accessed 24 July 2009

Queensland Government (2008) 'Guide to Queensland's parks and forests, available free of charge from park information centres and accredited visitor information centres across Queensland', www.epa.qld.gov.au/parks_and_forests/new_free_guide_to_queenslands_parks_and_forests.html, accessed 24 June 2009

Queensland Government (2009a) 'Lake Barrine, Crater Lakes National Park – Nature, culture and history', Environment and Resource Management, www.epa.qld.gov.au/parks_and_forests/find_a_park_or_forest/lake_barrine_crater_lakes_national_park/lake_barrine_crater_lakes_national_park__nature_culture_and_history/, accessed 20 July 2009

Queensland Government (2009b) 'Lake Eacham, Crater Lakes National Park', Environment and Resource Management, www.epa.qld.gov.au/parks_and_forests/safety_in_parks_and_forests.html, accessed 25 July 2009

Queensland Government (2009c) 'Glass House Mountains and surrounds – Nature, culture and history', www.epa.qld.gov.au/parks_and_forests/find_a_park_or_forest/glass_house_mountains_and_surrounds/glass_house_mountains_and_surrounds__nature_culture_and_history.html, accessed 23 July 2009

Queensland EPA (2007) 'Glasshouse Mountains and surrounds', www.epa.qld.gov.au/parks_and_forests/find_a_park_or_forest/glass_house_mountains_and_surrounds/#things_to_do, accessed 1 July 2008

Sunshine Coast Queensland (2006) 'The Glasshouse Mountains', sunshinecoast.platypus.net.au/glasshouse.htm, accessed 24 June 2009

The Official Glasshouse Mountains Tourism Website (n.d.) 'Extreme sports', www.glasshousemountains.com.au/sports.htm, accessed 1 July 2008

Tweed Shire (2009) 'Mount Warning in the Tweed Coast hinterland: Australia's "Green Cauldron"', www.mtwarning.com/, accessed 20 June 2008

Undara Experience (2009) 'Tunnels to a wildlife underworld', undara.com.au/lava-tubes/tunnels-to-a-wildlife-underworld/, accessed 23 July 2009

UNESCO World Heritage (2009) 'Gondwana Rainforests of Australia', whc.unesco.org/en/list/368, accessed 23 July 2009

Willmott, W. (2006) *Rocks and Landscapes of the National Parks of Central Queensland*, Geological Society of Australia, Queensland Division, Brisbane

Case Study 17

Vanuatu

Active Volcanism in the Pacific

Henry Gaudru

Introduction

Vanuatu (formerly called the New Hebrides Islands) is a line of volcanic islands and submarine volcanoes 2,300km east of north-east Australia. There are 13 main islands, 9 of which are home to active volcanoes. Present day volcanism is related to the north-eastward directed subduction of the Australian Plate beneath the edge of the Pacific Plate. The two plates converge at a rate of about 9cm/year. A divergent plate boundary (called a spreading centre or spreading axis) is east of Vanuatu (Monzier et al, 1997). The main active volcanoes are: Yasur volcano, one of the world's most active with Strombolian eruptions occurring many times per hour; Lopevi volcano, a perfect volcanic cone located in a beautiful South Pacific setting; Amrbym volcano, with a large caldera including two cones with lava lake; and Gaua volcano, with one of the world's most colourful and scenic multi-coloured summits and a crater lake which creates an unforgettable landscape. Ambae volcano erupted in December 2005 after being dormant for 120 years (Seach, 2009).

Yasur volcano

Yasur volcano on Tanna Island is an active cone, 365m in elevation, with a base about 1.5km wide. This is the youngest of several small volcanoes which occupy the Siwi area. Yasur is one of the most famous volcanoes in the Oceania region,

simply because it is so easy to reach. Each year the Yasur volcano attracts near 3000 visitors. Tour operators make a good business in volcano tours although it's easy to visit independently. Tourists can travel up this volcano in a four-wheel drive from Lenakel to just near the top and then walk to the edge of the crater and peer down at the seething mass of bubbling magma. Although Yasur is active year round, it is unusual for it to be too active to approach so it has become an extremely popular tourist attraction. Yasur usually has at least 50 people or more on top during most evenings in the high season (June to September). When Captain Cook first sighted Yasur in 1774, he likened it to Stromboli in the Mediterranean because of its constant glow at night, like a beacon. In fact, Yasur often erupts with Strombolian type eruption, throwing out incandescent ejecta or lava fountains from a central crater, but also can sometimes show a Vulcanian type of eruption. In this case large blocks and glowing fragments of new, viscous lava are thrown out and this is what most people see when they stand on the edge of the Yasur and look in.

Generally, the blocks are not thrown too high so it is not dangerous. For those living on the island, it is common knowledge that Yasur seems most active around late February to April. This time of year is the wet season. A lot of rain means a higher groundwater table, possibly allowing water to come into contact with hot rocks around the magma chamber. Explosive phreatic eruptions are known to occur sometimes, but whether this has anything to do with the wet season is only speculation. However, it is a fact that this time of year is the most spectacular and the volcano is generally very quiet at the end of the dry season (Vanuatu Tourism Office, 2009).

Tour guides are employed on Yasur to prevent visitors from putting themselves in danger. Even though the access rules are clearly defined, your guide may let you go closer than allowed and although a safer distance is still beautiful some tourists are seeking an adrenalin rush. As a result several tourists have been killed by hits from lava bombs in the past (Wantok Environment Centre, 2009), which is not good for the tourism industry. Admittedly this was during the wet season and Yasur was more active than usual, but sadly those who died had gone to areas at the edge of the vent that tourist guides normally keep people away from, knowing these areas are potentially dangerous. In the first incident, a Tannese ni-Vanuatu from another part of the island had gone to the volcano alone, was hit in the leg by a piece of lava and instead of going to a doctor, went to seek 'bush medicine' treatment; he eventually bled to death. In the second incident, both a guide and tourist were killed because the tourist had insisted on going to a dangerous area and the guide accompanied her. Both were hit by erupting pieces of lava and died instantly. Thereafter the upper rim of the volcano was closed until activity quietened down some weeks later. However, the lesson here is, stay on the path in dangerous places (Vanuatu Tourism Office, 2009).

Conclusions

Active volcanoes, such as Yasur are NOT theme parks. they are nature at its most awesome – dangerous and unpredictable. To ensure security and safety on Yasur, public education and awareness measures were set up near the volcano. These include several posters and documents, including a map with viewing points related to the Yasur intensity of explosions with an explanation describing the different alert levels.

Activity levels and access rules

There are five levels of volcanic activity: Level 0: Low activity, access to the crater allowed. Level 1: Normal activity, access to the crater allowed. Level 2: Moderate to high activity, lava bombs may land beyond the crater rim, access to the crater is closed. Level 3: Severe activity with loud explosions, lava bombs ejected up to hundreds of metres outside the crater and large plumes of smoke and ash, access to the summit zone is closed. Level 4: Major eruption affecting large areas around the volcano and possibly other parts of Tanna and even neighbouring islands, all access closed.

References

Monzier, M., Robin, C., Eissen, J. P. and Cotton, J. (1997) 'Geochemistry vs. seismo-tectonics along the volcanic New Hebrides Central Chain (Southwest Pacific)', *Journal of Volcanology and Geothermal Research*, vol 78, pp1–29

Seach, J. (2009) 'Vanuatu Volcano Travel', www.volcanolive.com/vanuatutravel.html, accessed 10 July 2009

Vanuatu Tourism Office (2009) 'Vanuatu Islands – Tanna Yasur Volcano', www.vanuatu.travel/vanuatu/volcanoes/tann-yasur-volcano.html, accessed 10 July 2009

Wantok Environment Centre (2009) 'Visiting the Mount Yasur Volcano, Tanna', www.positiveearth.org/bungalows/TAFEA/yasur.htm, accessed 10 July 2009

Case Study 18

Geothermal Parks in New Zealand

Richard Roscoe

Introduction

Since the advent of affordable long-haul air travel, New Zealand has developed into a popular tourist destination for international travellers, with over 1.1 million foreign visitors entering the country for the purpose of tourism in 2008 (NZ Ministry of Tourism, 2009). Further, over 17 million domestic tourism trips were recorded. The popularity of New Zealand can be largely attributed to the diversity of its landscapes, including the spectacular volcanic landscapes of the North Island as well as the alpine landscapes and dramatic coastlines of the South Island with their diverse wildlife. A large proportion of international visitors visit the geothermal areas in and around Rotorua, where the local economy receives one third of its income from the 1.5 million visitors it receives annually (one third each from forestry and agriculture makes up the rest; Rotorua District Council, 2008). For NZ as a whole, tourism represents about 9.2 per cent of gross domestic product (GDP), and accounts for 9.7 per cent of total employment (NZ Ministry of Tourism, 2009).

Geological background and activity

New Zealand is located at a plate boundary where subduction of the Pacific Plate under the Indian-Australasian Plate is occurring. Present-day volcanic activity is restricted to the Taupo Volcanic Zone (Cole, 1990). This includes the Ruapehu and Tongariro volcanoes near its southern end and the prominent offshore White Island volcano towards its north-eastern end. Eruptions have been recorded at each of these in the last 50 years. In between lie several large calderas such as Taupo, Maroa, Okataina, Reporoa and Rotorua, together harbouring the main geothermal sites. White Island (Figure CS18.1) and the mainland geothermal sites at Rotorua, nearby Waimangu Valley and Wai-O-Tapu are the focus of this case study.

All sites have some form of protected status. White Island is a designated private scenic reserve, with access only by permit since 1995. Tourists must use the authorized helicopter or boat operators to visit the island. Rotorua's main geothermal field, Whakarewarewa, is in a fenced enclosure together with the adjacent New Zealand Maori Arts and Crafts Institute. The latter pays tribute to the fact that Rotorua remains a major Maori settlement. Wai-O-Tapu and Waimangu Valley are both enclosed areas designated scenic reserves which affords them protection from development.

Historical aspects

Small-scale touristic exploitation of New Zealand's geothermal areas started in the late 19th century. Rotorua rapidly developed as a spa resort for European visitors after a passenger rail service to Auckland was established in 1894 (Cooper-Erfurt and Cooper, 2009). The beautiful Tudor-style Government Bath House building, which was

Figure CS18.1 Aerial View of White Island, New Zealand

erected in 1908, is a relic of the spa era and today houses the Rotorua Museum. Even before these times, tourists visited the area in particular to see the stunning Pink and White sinter terraces on the shores of Lake Rotomahana in the Okataina Volcanic Complex, about 25km from Rotorua. Guests were accommodated at the small Rotomahana Hotel in the Maori village of Te Wairoa, and were ferried by canoe to the terraces. However, the 1886 Plinian eruption of nearby Mt Tarawera completely reshaped the surrounding landscape, leading to a ten-fold increase in the size of Lake Rotomahana and complete destruction of the terraces. The eruption was one of the largest eruptions witnessed by man in this area. In less than five hours, one to two cubic kilometres of basaltic lava were erupted from a fissure which bisected the pre-existing rhyolite dome complex over a length of 8km, and extended a further 9km to the south-west through the lake and into Waimangu Valley (Sable et al, 2006). The loss of the terraces resulted in a shift of tourism away from the area towards nearby Wai-O-Tapu, which

lies at the northern perimeter of the Reporoa caldera, where the largest remaining sinter terraces were located. However, these bear no comparison with the Rotomahana terraces, which were comparable to terraces found today at Pamukkale in Turkey or at Mammoth Springs, Yellowstone National Park, USA.

Tourism briefly returned to the Waimangu Valley when in 1900 the largest geyser ever recorded became active at Echo crater (Figure CS18.2). This erupted dark sediment-rich water up to a maximum height of several hundred metres, and led to a guesthouse and several viewpoints being established in the area. Unfortunately, the geyser stopped erupting in 1904 (Keam, n.d.).

Tourism at White Island existed as early as the 1860s, when locals or day trippers from passing Northern Star Company cruise ships occasionally visited the island by boat. The island was also the site of several small-scale sulphur mining operations between 1883 and 1933. Remnants of the sulphur-processing infrastructure can be seen today (Pee Jay White Island Tours, n.d.).

Figure CS18.2 The site of the Waimangu geyser

Current focus

Today, geothermal tourism is largely centred around the city of Rotorua which lies on the shore of a large lake of the same name. The town, which provides a wide variety of accommodation, also has a lakeside base for floatplanes and helicopters, which provide scenic flights. In particular it is possible to fly by helicopter to White Island volcano, or to view the impressive fissure formed during the 1886 Tarawera eruption. White Island, which is also accessible by boat leaving from Whakatane, is an extremely interesting site. The crater floor harbours a number of geothermal features, such as fumaroles, boiling pools or mud-pots, along with the main crater-lake which is hot and acidic. The temperature and level of the lake fluctuate gradually, and this is taken as an indicator of the underlying volcanic activity.

Rotorua itself has several freely accessible geothermal areas, including an area by the lakeside with numerous hot pools. However, the main attraction is Whakarewarewa geothermal area, which has several geysers, bubbling mud pools and other hot pools and steaming vents. In this area the main attraction is the Pohutu geyser which erupts frequently and sprays water and steam up to about 20m high. It is perched together with several other geysers on a high sinter platform from which water cascades downwards during eruptions. The site is highly frequented at peak times. The 'Quality Hotel Geyserland' has been built overlooking the site, allowing a balcony view of Pohutu geyser for those who don't mind the sulphurous odours.

Waimangu Valley is a less frequented area with good walking opportunities to various geothermal features (note: bus is also available). Some of the craters along the 1886 eruption fissure can be visited, as can the former site of Waimangu geyser at Frying Pan Flats. Numerous hot pools and sinter terraces can also be seen. Boat trips on Lake Rotomahana are possible (Keam, n.d.).

Wai-O-Tapu is the most colourful of New Zealand's geothermal attractions (Wai-O-Tapu

Figure CS18.3 Lady Knox geyser, Wai-O-Tapu geothermal area

Geothermal Wonderland, n.d.). The main site, accessible via the visitor centre has 3km of paths taking the visitor past a large number of geothermal features. Most notable is the multicoloured Artist's Palette and adjoining Primrose Sinter Terrace which is fed with water from the large Champagne Pool. This hot pool gains its name from the carbon dioxide bubbles that constantly rise to the surface. The small but photogenic Lady Knox geyser is located a short drive away and is artificially induced to erupt every morning using soap powder, so that the tourists can view it from the wooden stands nearby (Figure CS18.3). Tickets must be obtained from the visitor centre before driving to the geyser. Slightly further towards the main road is an impressive bubbling mud pool.

Risk factors/management

In order to reduce the risk of serious injury or fatality at New Zealand's mainland geothermal sites much effort has been spent on providing walkways for tourists and fencing off any potentially hazardous areas. These areas include the mud pools and geysers, and also places where the ground may be unstable due to underlying geothermal activity. These management practices, which are somewhat comparable to that at Yellowstone National Park in the United States, not only protect the tourists but also the fine crystalline deposits that form around many hot springs and provide much of their attraction.

Violent hydrothermal explosions may occur at geothermal sites. Over 90 such events have been recorded around Rotorua City since 1845, yet none have caused fatalities (Scott and Cody, 2000). Such events seem to correlate to disturbances in the geothermal systems, yet to what extent they can be predicted is unclear. A massive 1915 hydrothermal explosion occurred at Echo crater in the Waimangu Valley geothermal area in 1915 (Keam, n.d). While this was preceded by a series of smaller eruptions the magnitude of the main eruption, which blew the roof off the nearby accommodation house and showered it with boiling water and rocks, took everyone by surprise. Two inhabitants of the house died of their injuries. Nevertheless, such incidents are extremely rare.

The situation at White Island is slightly different. Guides accompany tourists at all times and seismic activity is continuously monitored. Hence, it is unlikely that tourists would be allowed on the island if a major eruption was considered imminent. Nevertheless, small phreatic eruptions may occur with little warning (Cole, Nairn and Houghton, n.d.). Further, crater wall instability may present a hazard. In 1914, a landslide occurred inside the crater, which displaced the crater-lake and resulted in the burial of the small mine settlement together with 11 workers in a torrent of warm mud and rocks (Pee Jay White Island Tours, n.d.). The trigger for this event is unknown.

Potential conflict between geothermal power and touristic exploitation

Much time has passed since the Maoris first exploited geothermally heated waters to cook their food. More recently, Rotorua landowners bored small holes to benefit on a small scale from the hot waters underneath. This had a noticeable negative impact on the geothermal features at Whakarewarewa. Rising public concern then led to a bore closure programme in 1987–88 involving the cementing shut of 106 wells. This and other legislative measures led to a recovery of geothermal activity (Scott and Cody, 2000). However, exploitation on a larger scale is occurring about 80km south of Rotorua. Driving towards Taupo, a visitor passes the Wairakei Geothermal Power Station, which is the oldest of several geothermal plants in the area. Since 1958 it has been providing an average annual generation of 1250GWh (New Zealand Geothermal Association, n.d.). Within a few years of its operation, about 70 geysers and 240 alkaline hot springs became inactive in the Wairakei Geothermal Valley, once a popular tourist attraction (Scott and Cody, 2000). Hence, there is clearly a conflict between the use of geothermal resources for power generation or for drawing tourists. Unfortunately, due to increasing demand for power and a poor record of protection of geysers, it is likely that only a few core tourism sites will ultimately remain.

References

Cole, J. W. (1990) 'Structural control and origin of volcanism in the Taupo Volcanic Zone, New Zealand', *Bull. Volcanol.*, vol 52, pp445–459

Cole, Nairn and Houghton (n.d.) 'Volcanic Hazards at White Island', in *Volcanic Hazards Working Group of the Civil Defence Scientific Advisory Committee – Booklet No.3*, Civil Defence Scientific Advisory Committee, Wellington

Cooper-Erfurt, P. and Cooper, M. (2009) *Health & Wellness Spa Tourism*, Aspects of Tourism Series, Channel View Press, London

Keam, R. F. (n.d.) 'Eruption Chronicles, Waimangu Volcanic Valley', www.waimangu.co.nz/, accessed 5 June 2009

New Zealand Geothermal Association (n.d.) www.nzgeothermal.org.nz, accessed 5 June 2009

NZ Ministry of Tourism (2009) 'Key Tourism Statistics', www.tourismresearch.govt.nz, accessed 5 June 2009

Pee Jay White Island Tours (n.d.) www.whiteisland.co.nz/white_island.html, accessed 5 June 2009

Rotorua District Council (2008) 'Annual Report 2007–2008', www.rdc.govt.nz, accessed 5 June 2009

Sable, J. E., Houghton, B. F., Wilson, C. J. N. and Carey, R. J. (2006) 'Complex proximal sedimentation from Plinian plumes: The example of Tarawera 1886', *Bull. Volcanol.*, vol 69, pp89–103

Scott, B. J. and Cody, A. D. (2000) 'Response of the Rotorua geothermal system to exploitation and varying management regimes', *Geothermics*, vol 29, nos 4–5, pp573–592

Wai-O-Tapu Geothermal Wonderland (n.d.) www.geyserland.co.nz/, accessed 5 June 2009

Case Study 19

Deception Island

Hot Times on a Chilly Continent

Ted Brattstrom

Introduction

Located 110km north of the Antarctic Peninsula and 860km south-south-east of Cape Horn, South America, Deception Island is part of the South Shetland Islands group and one of only two active volcanoes in Antarctica (Antarctic Treaty Signatories, 2005). Deception's drowned caldera gives the island a roughly doughnut shaped appearance. The secret kept by the forbidding coastline is what gave Deception Island its name. If a captain navigated his ship to the proper position on the south-east side of the island and braved the narrow channel known as Neptune's Bellows, he would enter the large calm bay in the island's centre called Port Foster, a welcome respite from the fierce weather of the Furious Fifties.

Between 1967 and 1970 a series of volcanic eruptions occurred within Port Foster, on the right side of the bay known as Pendulum Cove. These eruptions destroyed the nearby Chilean research station and created a hydrothermal area within the Cove's shallow waters with temperatures occasionally exceeding 70°C (Antarctic Treaty Signatories, 2005). The unique opportunity to 'swim in Antarctica' quickly turned into a must do tourist activity and photo opportunity. Today, Deception Island is one of the most visited destinations along the Antarctic voyaging route and visitor numbers are increasing. During the 2004–05 voyaging season, about 12,000 visitors arrived on the island. Three years later, 25,668

visitors aboard IAATO (International Association of Antarctic Tour Operators) vessels landed. Between 2200 and 5000 of them landed at Pendulum Cove (IAATO, 2008).

A visit to Pendulum Cove

The typical 'swimming in Antarctica' activity begins with the expedition ship mooring in Port Foster. Visitors board zodiacs and are tendered to the thermally active area of Pendulum Cove. Non-swimmers visit the former Chilean base. As water temperatures vary, expedition guides carefully assess the beach area to determine the place with proper water temperature that day. When found, the swimmers switch from their Antarctic gear to regular swimsuits, an exciting proposition when the air temperature may be 0°C

Figure CS19.1 Volcanic hot springs rising through the sand make for a memorable experience on the Antarctic Island of Deception Bay

with a gentle 10–30km/h breeze blowing. Getting in and finding the best place to enjoy the thermal waters is easy, but expedition guides remind swimmers to pay close attention to the water temperature while soaking, as bursts of very hot water may rise through the sand. An occasional penguin may swim by. Non-swimmers clad in the typical full cold weather gear gleefully snap photos of those luxuriating in the warm water (Figure CS19.1). Some folks decide to take a proper swim by heading into deeper water and taking a few strokes. It stays shallow for a distance and while the water cools off, it doesn't get cold.

When the time comes to leave, bathers RUN to the lee of the zodiacs, dry off as best as they can and quickly don expedition clothing with as much decorum as possible under the chilly circumstances. Fortunately, the heat 'baked in'

during the soak allows sufficient time for the change of clothing without much discomfort. This entire experience is a memorable one, and unique in Antarctic travels. It forms the introduction for travel stories for years to come: 'I swam with penguins on Christmas morning in Antarctica', can it get much better than that?

References

Antarctic Treaty Signatories (2005) 'Management Plan for Antarctic Specially Managed Area No. 4, Deception Island, South Shetland Islands, Antarctica', www.deceptionisland.aq/documents/deception_island_management_package.pdf, accessed 18 January 2009

IAATO (International Association of Antarctica Tour Operators) (2008) '2008–2009 Statistic', www.iaato.org/tourism_stats.html, accessed 18 January 2009

Part VII

22

Conclusions and Recommendations

Patricia Erfurt-Cooper and Malcolm Cooper

Concluding remarks

The growing interest in natural processes as well as the geological heritage of interesting landforms with volcanic and geothermal features includes some high-risk areas as attractive tourist destinations. This interest has been fuelled by an increasing number of publications about volcanic and geothermal areas from the early 1990s, and another surge of these sources of information in the early 2000s. However, the majority of these are mainly guides to national parks (for example, in the USA, especially the western part of the country). The growing interest in volcanoes is more likely to have been triggered by the eruption of Mt St Helens in the early 1980s, as this was the first time that such a catastrophic event was broadcast worldwide in real time.

The subsequent re-establishment of the Mt St Helens recreational area as a 'safe' tourist destination also took advantage of the growing interest of the media in this form of disaster, with the onset of the 'worldwide web' further adding to the dissemination of information. Two years after the eruption the Mt St Helens National Volcanic Monument was established (1982) to encourage research, education, interpretation and recreation on the volcano and is administered by the Forest Service (Decker and Decker, 1993). The experience of the Mt St Helens disaster and its aftermath shows that, while it is not possible to prevent natural disasters such as volcanic eruptions, it is possible to reduce the risk and speed up recovery of tourism through education and therefore raising the awareness of the public when spending their holidays in a volcanic environment.

To mitigate the potential risks of volcano tourism, effective warning and rescue systems and community awareness-raising programmes need to be in place at every volcanic destination. Efficient cooperation and coordination between the authorities in charge and tourism organizations as well as with tour operators is important to ensure that every stakeholder is aware of the current state of a volcano, as far as that is possible. Community awareness is, however, different from visitor awareness; many affected areas have invested in educating the communities who live in close proximity to active volcanoes, because people who live near volcanoes multiply their exposure by 365 in contrast to tourists visiting for a day only. BUT, while the potential risk of living near an active volcano pertains to millions of local residents, it is mainly the tourists (their numbers are also in millions annually) who are going to see active craters and lava flows up close. Local residents do not visit their volcanoes every day; their exposure is not as imminent as that of the visitors, who want to look into active craters and view eruptive activity from as close as possible.

Volcano tourists, even if they are aware of the potential risk, often have the motive of 'wanting to see some action'. To verify this, the reader only has to go to *YouTube* on the internet to see hair raising examples of tourist behaviour close to volcanic and geothermal activity. Poking red hot lava flows with a stick is one of the more harmless 'recreational' pastimes that are posted on the internet. More seriously, as a consequence of the increasing interest in volcano tourism, the time has come for scientists and tourism operators to join ranks to achieve effective risk management and hazard reduction to avoid major disasters which could involve large numbers of tourists. With the large number of active volcanoes worldwide, many of them already key tourist destinations, it is imperative that the potential dangers of active volcanic and geothermal environments are not understated. Although the associated risks of volcanic and geothermal activity are the same attractions that promise a unique experience for a very diverse group of tourists, many volcanic environments worldwide can be classed as extreme environments – requiring the utmost care in their use for tourism.

It should be noted that the same cities that are located close to active volcanoes are attracting visitors not just for their volcanic landscapes, but for other reasons as well (e.g. culture, history, festivals, shopping, wildlife etc.). Nevertheless, although these visitors strictly speaking are not volcano tourists they also face the potential hazards of eruptive activity and they too are not catered for, as they are not permanent residents and therefore may not be familiar with any necessary emergency strategies. As a result, much of what is written about volcanic risk perception and people's behaviour associated with volcanic hazards and their adjustment to a volcanic environment is based on local residents only, and while risk reduction strategies have been developed for all major volcanic events, these generally do not include temporary visitors. This fact requires a separate approach to risk management for tourists, as significant danger issues as well as subsequent insurance issues could arise. Current research into risk management in volcanic and geothermal areas should be therefore reviewed to include temporary visitors and their potential exposure to volcanic hazards. Increased interest in volcano and geothermal tourism can also indicate a growing potential for accidents and injuries near these active environments, as has been noticed by Callander and Page (2003) with certain types of adventure tourism in New Zealand.

Continuous monitoring of all volcanoes is impossible due to logistical, financial and political restrictions; consequently, eruptions frequently occurring at poorly monitored volcanoes (Tilling, 1989) are not incorporated in risk reduction programmes. Even if constant monitoring would be feasible there are volcanoes that suddenly and unexpectedly erupt as did Chaitén in Chile in 2008. Because of the long time lapse since this volcano was last active, which is estimated at several thousand years, people were unaware that Chaitén could suddenly turn into a dangerous volcano. If Chaitén had been monitored though, early warning signs could have been detected indicating a reawakening of the volcano. With the United States Geological Survey (USGS) being at the forefront of information dissemination, other regions without risk strategies are well advised to follow their lead and work together to be able to include warnings and guidelines for all residents, as well as the transient population, in the future. While people's actions when facing natural disasters reflect that these are often beyond their control due to economic and social constraints (Wisner et al, 2004; Gaillard, 2008), this is not the case for temporary visitors who have the freedom to avoid potential disaster areas. Annual fatalities from volcanic eruptions, measured over the past three centuries are still at an average of nearly 1000 people (Marti and Ernst, 2005), with possible catastrophic events in the future.

Agencies in charge of disseminating information to tourists will gain more credibility if they cooperate with relevant authorities such as volcano observatories and emergency services, thus portraying the expertise necessary to reinforce the message. This strategy has been recommended by Perry and Godchaux (2005) to increase public awareness of residents in volcanic areas. However, it is good advice for the development of safety guidelines for volcano tourists as well.

What do the experts say?

A small survey carried out by the authors amongst a group of geoscientists and volcanologists in January 2009 (conference delegates at the Volcanic and Magmatic Studies Group (VMSG) meeting, a specialist group of the Geological Society of London in Bournemouth) provided information relating to risk and hazards for tourists on active volcanoes from an expert point of view. The general comments from the 20 respondents indicate that safety standards for tourists on volcanoes are not everywhere as they should be, and these opinions were reinforced by informal follow-up interviews with individual respondents.

Questioned as to whether irresponsible behaviour by tourists on active volcanoes had been observed, 71 per cent said yes, while 13 per cent said no and the remainder did not provide an answer. Most respondents also provided brief examples of their observations and offered remedial actions, but included some well-founded criticism of some of the foolish actions they had witnessed. In particular, several survey respondents who had worked in Hawai'i commented on 'tourists ignoring all advice on Kilauea' and one respondent's comments about their behaviour as observed while he worked at the volcano observatory there for six months shows that:

> *dangerous behaviour by tourists occurs on an almost daily basis. There was also one death and one severe burn accident while I was there. (pers. com)*

The concern of several of the scientists was that 'irresponsible people will not change and responsible people are doing the right thing anyway', with a number of the respondents putting the blame clearly on tourists who act carelessly, often endangering others as well, including potential rescue teams, which is unacceptable.

Personal observations and views of volcanologists and geoscientists

This survey also led to the development of a list of volcanoes in order of popularity as nominated by scientists and volcanologists who are familiar with them (Table 22.1). Five stars for Kilauea in Hawai'i are closely followed by Montserrat and Etna. The results may not be representative for the whole community of geoscientists or of the full range of geotourists, but certainly reflect the view of individual scientists who are talking from personal experience of working with these mountains. Another question asked was which volcanoes the respondents would consider as the most dangerous ones for tourists and why. The 'blacklisted'

Table 22.1 Responses to the question 'which volcanoes are your personal favourites?'

Volcanoes nominated by survey respondents as their preferred mountains

***** Kilauea, Hawai'i	* Fogo – Cap Verde
**** Montserrat, British overseas territory	* Lanzarote – Canary Islands
*** Etna, Italy	* Mauna Loa, Hawai'i
*** Santa Maria /Santiaguito, Guatemala	* Mt St Helens, USA
** Merapi, Indonesia	* Paricutin, Mexico
** Santorini, Greece	* Rainier, USA
** Stromboli, Italy	* Ruapehu, New Zealand
** Teide, Spain	* Rungwe Volcanic Province, Tanzania
** Vesuvius, Italy	* Shasta, USA
** Yellowstone, USA	* Tarawera, New Zealand
* Arenal, Costa Rica	* Tongariro, New Zealand
* Cotopaxi, Ecuador	* Yasur, Vanuatu
* The Chilean volcanoes	

Note: Five stars down to one star indicate the degree of popularity

Table 22.2 These volcanoes were considered to be the most dangerous for visiting tourists

Location	Evaluation by geoscientists (% of respondents)
Italian volcanoes (Etna, Vesuvius)	25
Hawai'i (Kilauea, Mauna Loa)	22
Merapi	12
Yellowstone	11
Santa Maria – Santiaguito	8
African volcanoes	7
Indonesian volcanoes	5
Montserrat	4
Tarawera	3
Yasur	3

volcanoes (Table 22.2) are all well-known tourist destinations, with the majority of them located within a national park.

When questioning why this group considered these volcanoes dangerous the results sometimes contradicted each other. Nevertheless some examples are presented below, as the comments were made by geoscientists who are working in a wide range of volcanic settings and therefore may have an equally wide range of experience/expertise and individual reasons for their opinions. To illustrate the scientific opinions on *why certain volcanoes are considered more dangerous than others* some of the comments made during the survey are reproduced here as direct quotes:

- [volcanoes] with unexpected explosive activity, even if small scale, e.g. dome collapse, phreatomagmatic explosions, lava delta collapses;
- [volcanoes] that suddenly erupt;
- unpredictable activity;
- volcanoes near cities;
- [volcanoes] open to public who are oblivious to dangers;
- [volcanoes] with frequent activity such as strombolian eruption can change quickly – attracting tourists to crater rims [with fireworks];
- volcanoes with continuous strombolian activity as they are most attractive, but lull people into a false sense of security as the level of activity can change without warning;
- [volcanoes] that are not 'famous' or regularly effusing – the hazards may not be obvious or signposted;
- volcanoes that are fairly easy to access for the general public as opposed to volcanoes in inaccessible locations;
- [volcanoes] in remote regions where there is a lack of tourist supervision and advice available;
- steep volcanoes with crater lakes;
- also crater lakes and gas pockets – as dangers are not obvious;
- [volcanoes] that are not currently active and tour guides are therefore not as active on safety promotion;
- persistently active systems characterized by small-medium explosion or dome building/collapse episodes;
- most of them.

Each comment was made by a different respondent and therefore this list reflects a broad range of views based on observation in the field. The resulting advice from geoscientists and volcanologists for tourists and tour organisers includes hazard maps with explanations of current volcanic activity, emergency contact details along with a list of fatal accidents and injuries for individual regions to make people understand that the danger is real. It was also suggested that signage with site-specific information has to be clear about the volcanic and/or geothermal hazards of a particular region. Signage should be visible when entering a volcanic area with an info box containing trail maps and leaflets with pictures or standard symbology which may have a better chance to be read and understood. The basic hazards at particular volcanoes, escape routes, emergency services locations, and precautions to take should be clearly illustrated and marked for everybody to understand.

These professional recommendations further include the suggestions that volcano tourists do need more information, should attend safety orientation prior to ascent, must obey current expert advice which should be provided clearly on site, and that tourists should use more common sense and accept responsibility for any injury they incur. Their suggestions of keeping to the paths, walking tracks or trails, together with paying attention to warnings and listening to local officials point towards the fact that *qualified tour guides* may also be required in potentially dangerous volcanic and geothermal environments.

The need to wear appropriate outdoor clothing, especially footwear (ankle-covered hiking boots) was emphasized repeatedly as well as the importance of carrying enough water on excursions to a volcanic area. Another measure that was suggested is exclusion zones that would prevent tourists from being able to get too close to dangerous spots (lava flows, fumaroles) with barriers that cannot be ignored. However, to enforce this form of control increased numbers of park rangers would be needed.

The provision of emergency radios was also suggested given that mobile phones are unreliable. Further recommendations included developing a general website about volcano tourism with

Figure 22.1 Volcano tourist at Mt Aso, Japan, trying to take a photo of the active crater by using the low barrier to get a better view

information on all volcanoes and advice for visiting tourists and residents. This would assist many volcano tourists by cutting down on the numbers of websites that have to be consulted to find necessary information. Several respondents made the point that there will always be people who do not listen, which unfortunately is true, but it is also necessary to provide more vital information to the majority who are looking for guidelines they can follow to minimize their personal risk.

The heightened awareness of danger often increases the interest in volcanic environments even more, and the excitement of watching a volcano erupt can cause people to lose focus on their personal safety. In many areas warning signs have been erected (Iceland, New Zealand, Japan etc.), but often the information is not understood by visitors due to language barriers. Even with the widespread use of the English language, not every tourist is confident enough to read signs which often use local expressions and are not translated and many volcanic destinations are in non-English speaking countries. As long as there are insufficient

translations into enough languages to cover the range of tourists who may frequent a site, interpretive or warning signs will fail to be effective. That is where visual images are a better option, as they are graphic and educational with many pictograms or symbols already being used and which are globally understood (e.g. the red sign for STOP).

Another problem is the often observed low guard rails around active sites. Many tourists ignore fencing if it is too low or incomplete as this does not imply serious danger (Figure 22.1). As this is a cost factor, active volcanic and geothermal areas should not be open to the public if safety standards are not met, or fees should be raised to allow redevelopment of the fences.

Recommendations for the development of safety guidelines for tourism in active volcanic environments

The following recommendations for safety guidelines were developed over a number of years by the authors while doing field research at volcanic destinations in several countries. A comprehensive review of existing literature as well as requests to authorities for updated safety guidelines which include temporary visitors produced no results, apart from responses by individual national parks that do what is possible to keep their visitors safe. However, as the previous section showed, this is not enough to give volcano tourists with language problems the information they need. The following recommendations are an option that could be used as a basis for an internationally applied code of conduct for visitor safety in active volcanic environments:

1   Visitors to volcanic environments need to be made aware of the potential and individual dangers relating to a particular area.

2   The accumulation of relevant (and agreed) basic information and knowledge should be encouraged for all visitors of active volcanic areas by the relevant authorities including governments, local governing bodies, tourism organizations, tour organizers and operators. Information dissemination could also be through hotel receptions, vehicle hire companies, tour booking agencies, etc.

3   Updated advice on destinations should be provided by all authorities, organizations and companies involved, and should be made available through appropriate media outlets, internet, etc.

4   Visitors must be made aware of the difference between an acceptable and an unacceptable risk.

5   Tour operators and tour guides, travel agents, tourist organizations and all information centres need to communicate very clearly any possible risk factors involved in the products they sell.

6   Tour guides need to be specially trained for emergencies and should have sufficient geological knowledge to be able to assess situations of imminent danger.

7   Guidelines and safety instructions must be available in ALL major languages appropriate to the visitor patterns at a site.

8   More signage is needed in more languages and more images for quick visual recognition.

9   Development of suitable factsheets with symbolic signage or pictograms should be undertaken, which should be handed out to all visitors of volcanic environments, active as well as dormant. Simple fact sheets following a generic template and containing essential information including emergency phone numbers, hazard map with danger zones, escape routes, shelter locations and collecting points, which could largely be based on pictograms for easy visual recognition (Erfurt-Cooper, 2007a,b; 2008a,b; 2009).

10   Fact sheets should be short and precise – no information overload.

11   Precise location maps – easy to interpret and to follow – handed out at entrance to volcanic environments. Multilingual editions should include copies of signage of the area and pictograms. Where that is not possible, sufficient signage must be provided.

12   Escape routes must be clearly marked – on printed maps and on sign posts in the field. Sign posts or guide posts could be colour coded to indicate whether the tourist is in a safe (green) zone or in a dangerous (yellow, orange, red) zone. It would also make rescue efforts easier if these guide posts were numbered (colour and numbers both have to be reflective to be useful after dark) and thus could be used as markers to identify a location. Tourists need to be aware of the zone they are in at all times.

13   More emergency shelters are needed and should contain posters with visual interpretation of signs for potential danger situations, emergency phones and possibly either webcams or CCTV surveillance in particularly dangerous places.

14   Communication services such as local telecom companies need to supply access (mobile phone reception) to remote areas if these are frequented by large numbers of tourists, as many rely on their mobile phones to contact emergency services.

15   First aid kits should be available at these points as well.

16   Emergency phones also need to be installed at certain distance intervals, again with visual explanation of how to use them in an

emergency (e.g. emergency phones along the motorways (*Autobahn*) in Germany) with arrows indicating in which direction the closest phone is located.

17 Helicopter rescue services should be available in every country for every volcanic environment that receives high volumes of tourism. The cost factor should be of little relevance as most countries can afford to maintain extensive defence forces (taxpayer funded) who would be delegated to assist in rescue situations on a standby basis. Defence forces could also assist with the logistics of communication and transport in an emergency. This is already common practice in several countries after a disaster has happened. In the case of disaster prevention it is important to enlist the help of all organizations that are trained for various disaster scenarios.

18 The access to active volcanic environments should be graded according to potential risk factors and up-to-date advice from experienced scientists (e.g. volcano observatories) who are monitoring not just volcanoes in action but also seismic activity in earthquake prone areas.

19 Excursion and expedition participants should undergo training for emergencies before embarking on their trip, in order to be able to deal with unexpected situations. Relying on the leader of any excursion group is not enough.

20 Insurance companies should provide information for travellers not just in risk prone areas, but also where visits to active volcanic environments are part of a general sightseeing itinerary, and encourage policy holders to seek detailed information about any potential risk beforehand and whether they are covered in the event of injury or death in a volcanic accident or disaster.

21 Although the responsibility to supply up-to-date information is distributed between multiple stakeholders it is up to the individual traveller to act upon advice. To encourage this, it must be clear that any cost incurred by careless and reckless action has to be covered by the person who caused it. This may encourage responsible behaviour.

22 To minimize the overall risk only vehicles suitable for access to volcanic environments should be permitted to be used. They need to contain first aid kits and necessary communication equipment in case of emergency. Strict policing is required.

23 In case of dangerous environments precise information is essential – logistics with no room for error are needed. In these areas visitors also need to wear safe footwear and protective clothing (closed heavy-duty shoes) or hard hats (helmets) and carry a gas mask.

24 Tourist organizations of countries with volcanic environments should DEMAND international safety guidelines to pass on to their clients.

Final comments

The above recommendations are the result of observation, interviews, surveys and literature reviews over a number of years. The results from the survey undertaken during the VMSG conference 2009, which was discussed at the beginning of this chapter, reinforce the need for safety guidelines by supporting a number of the suggestions from the research that we have carried out and which were subsequently included in this book, and will also be made available on the internet in due course.

It must be noted here that future research into visitor safety in active volcanic and geothermal environments is an important issue because of the growing number of people who travel further in their quest to experience unique landforms and unusual displays of volcanic and geothermal activity. Adventure destinations worldwide are using the trend 'back to nature' to attract visitors to stay longer in more interesting and sustainable nature-based environments with volcanic and geothermal phenomena as an important integration. Internet blogs from travellers, word-of-mouth, and increased marketing of destinations which promise time-out with a difference, contribute to the growing numbers of volcano tourists. Moreover, this particular tourist sector contributes to the economy in many countries and therefore all temporary visitors need to be included in the risk management strategies to help them to avoid risky situations that may result from potential hazards in active volcanic and geothermal environments.

References

Callander, M. and Page, S. J. (2003) 'Managing risk in adventure tourism operations in New Zealand: A review of the legal case history and potential for litigation', *Tourism Management*, vol 24, no 1, pp13–23

Decker, R. and Decker, B. (1993) 'Road guide to Mount St. Helens', www.dartmouth.edu/~volcano/texts/DekMtStHelen.html, accessed 20 July 2009

Erfurt-Cooper, P. (2007a) 'Volcanic environments: Tourism destinations with a risk factor?', presented as Poster to the *Cities on Volcanoes 5 Conference*, Shimabara, Japan, 19–23 November

Erfurt-Cooper, P. (2007b) 'Volcanic environments: Geothermal phenomena as tourist attractions', presented to the *ERE Conference*, James Cook University, Cairns, Australia, 1–3 December

Erfurt-Cooper, P. (2008a) 'Geotourism: Active geothermal and volcanic environments as tourist destinations', presented to *The Inaugural Global Geotourism Conference*, Perth, Australia, 17–20 August

Erfurt-Cooper, P. (2008b) 'Geotourism in volcanic environments: Destinations with a risk factor?', Poster presentation at *The Inaugural Global Geotourism Conference*, Perth, Australia, 17–20 August

Erfurt-Cooper, P. (2009a) 'Volcano tourism: A disaster waiting to happen?', Keynote presentation at *The VMSG Conference*, University of Bournemouth, Bournemouth, 4–6 January

Gaillard, J. C. (2008) 'Alternative paradigms of volcanic risk perception: The case of Mt. Pinatubo in the Philippines', *Journal of Volcanology and Geothermal Research*, vol 172, pp315–328

Marti, J. and Ernst, G. G. J. (eds) (2005) *Volcanoes and the Environment*, Cambridge University Press, Cambridge

Perry, R. W. and Godchaux, J. D. (2005) 'Volcano hazard management strategies: Fitting policy to patterned human responses', *Disaster Prevention and Management*, vol 14, no 2, pp183–195

Tilling, R. I. (1989) 'Volcanic hazards and their mitigation: Progress and problems', *Reviews of Geophysics*, vol 27, pp237–269

Wisner, B., Blaikie, P., Cannon, T. and Davis, I. (2004) *At Risk: Natural Hazards, People's Vulnerability, and Disasters*, 2nd edn, Routledge, London

Appendix 1

An Overview of Recent Volcanic Activity Worldwide

In order to provide a general overview of recent volcanic activity as a framework for the material in this book the following list was compiled from a number of sources. The baseline of previous activity was drawn at the Holocene as this period is increasingly used as the timeframe in an apparently quiet volcano's life where renewed activity at some point in the future cannot be excluded. Ninety-two (92) countries are listed in this table, many containing volcanoes with a potential for further eruptive activity. The 'real' number of eruptions worldwide during the Holocene is in all likelihood much higher, however, with only the first column of the table reflecting reasonably reliable records of volcanic

eruptions. Anything beyond that list cannot be complete as not every country has kept written records of eruptions over time and in many regions volcanic activity would have gone unnoticed due to the remote location of some active volcanoes. In fact, the combined activity of all known and unknown volcanoes dating back further than a few decades would result in much higher figures than those commonly available in academic texts or other public sources. Given the number of eruptions over the past decade recorded in this limited list (152) even a conservative increase to take this point into account would suggest a staggering amount of volcanic activity during the Holocene.

Country or region	Active: past decade	Active: past century	Active: past millennium	Active: past 5000 years	Active: Holocene
Antarctica	1	4	1	1	8
Argentina	1	3	3	–	15
Armenia	–	–	–	–	4
Ascension Island	–	–	–	–	1
Australia	3	1	1	8	5
Bolivia	–	2	1	?	23
Brazil	–	–	–	–	1
Cameroon	1	–	–	–	3
Cascades	1	1	8	9	10
Canada	–	–	5	4	49

Source: Patricia Erfurt-Cooper

Country or region	Active: past decade	Active: past century	Active: past millennium	Active: past 5000 years	Active: Holocene
Cap Verde	–	1	–	–	2
Chad	–	–	–	–	3
Chile	7	27	13	5	55
China	–	1	3	3	4
Colombia	2	6	2	2	2
Comoros	1	–	–	–	1
Costa Rica	3	2	1	1	6
Congo (DR)	2	1	–	–	1
Djibouti	–	1	–	–	?
Dominica	–	1	1	1	2
Ecuador	7	9	6	2	5
El Salvador	2	2	2	–	14
Equatorial Guinea	–	1	–	–	2
Eritrea	–	–	1	1	4
Ethiopia	3	6	3	–	34
Fiji	–	–	2	–	2
France	–	–	–	2	5
French Antarctic	–	1	1	–	5
Georgia (country)	–	–	–	1	3
Germany	–	–	–	–	4
Greece	–	1	1	2	1
Grenada	1	–	–	–	?
Guadeloupe	–	1	–	–	?
Guatemala	3	2	4	1	10
Honduras	–	–	–	–	4
Iceland	4	10	9	9	6
India	2	–	–	–	1
Indonesia	28	36	12	–	1
Iran	–	1	–	–	5
Italy	2	7	2	–	2
Japan	13	36	16	14	11

Country or region	Active: past decade	Active: past century	Active: past millennium	Active: past 5000 years	Active: Holocene
Kenya	–	2	4	–	11
Korea	–	1	1	–	2
Libya	–	–	–	1	1
Madagascar	–	–	–	–	5
Malaysia	–	–	–	–	1
Martinique	–	1	–	–	?
Mexico	2	6	8	1	11
Mongolia	–	–	–	1	4
Montserrat	1	2	–	–	?
Myanmar (Burma)	–	–	–	1	2
Netherlands Antilles	–	–	1	1	?
New Zealand	6	4	7	4	3
Nicaragua	5	2	1	1	10
Norway	–	1	–	–	?
Panama	–	–	2	–	1
Papua New Guinea	7	6	2	1	10
Peru	2	1	2	–	6
Philippines	3	13	9	1	9
Portugal	1	3	5	1	2
Réunion	1	–	–	–	?
Russia/Kamchatka	6	11	5	7	54
Russia/Kurils	3	20	6	–	9
Russia/Other	–	–	1	2	2
Rwanda	–	–	–	–	2
St Kitt & Nevis	–	–	–	1	1
St Lucia	–	–	1	–	?
St Vincent/ Grenadines	–	1	–	–	?
Sâo Tomé & Príncipe	–	–	–	–	1
Saudi Arabia	–	–	3	2	2
Solomon Islands	2	1	1	–	?

Country or region	Active: past decade	Active: past century	Active: past millennium	Active: past 5000 years	Active: Holocene
South Africa	–	–	1	–	?
South Sandwich Islands	2	5	1	–	?
Spain	1	2	2	1	1
Sudan	–	–	–	3	2
Syria	–	–	2	–	4
Taiwan	–	–	–	–	1
Tanzania	1	1	1	–	6
Tonga	3	8	1	–	2
Tristan da Cunha	1	–	–	–	?
Turkey	–	–	3	2	6
Uganda	–	–	–	–	7
USA Alaska	9	26	8	8	1
USA American Samoa	–	–	1	–	?
USA Hawai'i	2	1	2	1	1
USA Mariana Islands	1	2	2	–	?
USA (Other)	–	2	17	13	24
Vanuatu	5	6	2	–	2
Vietnam	–	1	–	–	4
Wallis Island	–	–	–	–	1
Western Samoa	–	1	–	–	1
Yemen	1	1	3	3	4
Total	152	294	203	122	530

1301 recorded volcanic eruptions

Appendix 2
Major Volcanoes Worldwide

This table was compiled with the intention to provide a general overview of the major volcanoes worldwide classed as active and as a quick reference with some examples of countries or regions with active and dormant volcanic areas. The table is by no means representing every single volcano known at the time of writing. The figures are subject to change; for example, future eruptions and resulting developments in scientific research. The intention is to show the reader some well known names of volcanoes and offer some indication how these are integrated in the leisure and recreational industries.

The majority of people who died (in parentheses after year of eruption and name of volcano) from volcanic activity in recent times were in South America (Armero, Colombia), Africa (Nyos, Cameroon) and in the Asia Pacific region (Philippines and Indonesia). However, accidents on a larger scale cannot be excluded around volcanoes with the potential for future eruptions, whether this may be, for example, Vesuvius, Mt Fuji, Arenal, Hekla, Mt Rainier or Ruapehu. These mountains all draw vast numbers of visitors for a range of recreational and cultural activities. Therefore it is important that these temporary visitors receive as much information in

the form of brochures or fact sheets to assist them in the case of an emergency. The number of deaths due to volcanic activity also includes fatalities caused by lahars/mudflows, which can be triggered many years after the actual eruption event.

The fact that less people perish on volcanoes or from volcanic activity than from a number of other natural hazards does not make them any safer for inexperienced visitors. Growing awareness certainly plays a key role in decreasing numbers of casualties among residents of volcanic areas. But while the local population is increasingly aware of the potential dangers near active volcanoes, temporary visitors, in growing numbers, are seeking close encounters with volcanic and geothermal activity, often without sufficient information about the area they are planning to explore.

This table can only give an overview of areas where information is available, although quite often the figures referring to the number of active volcanoes, the actual summit height, and the number of casualties at the most dangerous mountains differ depending on the source. The actual cause of the casualties is also rarely recorded – data that of course is difficult to collect in the case of volcanic disasters and in their aftermath.

Country or region	Number of volcanoes (examples)	Status (last active)	Protected area type*	Attractions and activities	Information about risk, safety aspects, accidents and number of deaths (in brackets)
AFRICA					
Cameroon *4 volcanoes*	**Mt Cameroon** *4040m stratovolcano*	2000	NP	Geotourism, ecotourism, wildlife, nature, culture, hiking, climbing, hunting, unique landscapes, lava flows, crater lakes	1984 – Lake Monoun (37) 1986 – Lake Nyos (1700+) 2001 – Mt Cameroon (23) CO_2 release from Lake Nyos crater is monitored
Cape Verde Islands *4 volcanoes*	**Fogo** *2829m stratovolcano and fissure vents*	1995	NP	Hiking, mountain climbing, geotourism	Alert level system: green - yellow - red
Congo, African West Rift *12+ volcanoes*	**Nyiragongo** *3470m stratovolcano Decade volcano* **Nyamulagira** *3058m shield volcano*	2002–ongoing lava lake 2006–ongoing	NP WHA (Virunga NP)	Expeditions to lava lake; volcano safaris; mountain gorillas in Virunga Park; wildlife viewing, ecotourism, geotourism, adventure tourism	1912 – Nyamuragira (20) 1977 – Nyiragongo (2000) 2007 – Nyiragongo, a tourist fell into the crater and died
Ethiopia *62 volcanoes*	**Erta Ale** *613m shield volcano* **Dabbahu** *1442m stratovolcano* **Dalaffilla** *613m stratovolcano*	2005–ongoing 2005 2008	-	Adventure tourism, geotourism, organized expeditions to permanent lava lake of Erta Ale, colourful hot springs at Dallol Mountain	It is advisable to travel in groups and have local tour guides who are familiar with the area and can negotiate when necessary. Tourism may be affected by the war-like clashes between Ethiopia and Eritrea. Old and new land mines in **Danakil** cause additional safety problems
Kenya *20+ volcanoes* **Tanzania** *10 volcanoes*	**Kilimanjaro** *5895m stratovolcano* **Mt Meru** *4566m stratovolcano* **Ol Doinyo Lengai** *2890m stratovolcano*	Holocene 1910 2007–ongoing	NP NP NP	Trekking, hiking, volcano expeditions, Lake Natron, guided night tours to summit to view the sunrise, wildlife safaris, adventure tourism	**Kilimanjaro** – altitude sickness problems may be caused during all activities due to the high elevation or when ascending toc fast. No risk management – even with authorized guides. Some information in the visitors centre (registration point) at Moshi. **Lengai** – temporarily it was very dangerous to camp in the crater due to Hornito activity and very fast flowing black lavas. Some people received severe burns

Region	Volcano / type	Date	Designation	Features / activities	Hazards / management
Reunion Comores Madagascar *8 volcanoes*	**Piton e la Fournaise** *2631m basalt shield volcano*	2007–ongoing	NP	Climbing to the crater, view Piton de Neige – highest peak in the Indian Ocean, view flowing lava channels, guided tours	1972 – Piton de la Fournaise (3) Hazard warnings by National Park Services and all national authorities
AMERICA North					
Alaska (USA) *92 volcanoes* Aleutians *Volcanic arc, over 150 islands, 1750km long*	**Mt Augustine** *1252m* **Mt Okmok** *1073m* **Mt Redoubt** *3108m* **Mt Shishaldin** *2857m*	2006 2008 2009 2004	NP	Northern Ring of Fire, glaciers, ice fields, geotourism, hiking, ecotourism, cruises between islands, flight-seeing, wildlife viewing, climbing, unique vegetation, geological heritage	Tsunami hazard for the entire Pacific because of eruptions Mosquitos can be a plague
Hawai'i (USA) *Volcanic island arc* *5 major volcanoes* *+submarine volcanoes*	**Kilauea** *122m shield volcano* **Mauna Loa** *4170m shield volcano* **Mauna Kea** *4206m shield volcano* **Haleakala** *3055m shield volcano*	2009–ongoing 1984 2500BC 1790	NP	Visitor centres, Kilauea lava lake, glowing lava flows, black, green and red sand beaches, volcano boarding, hiking, trekking, campsites, cabins	Signs throughout the national parks, but mainly in English, Rangers advising on potential dangers, educational videos, visitor centres Between 1992 and 2002 there were 65 fatal accidents at the eruption site in Hawai'i Volcanoes National Park – mainly through thermal burns
USA & Canadian Cascades *80+ volcanoes*	**Mt St Helens** *2550m stratovolcano* **Mt Rainier** *4392m stratovolcano* *Decade volcano* **Mt Hood** *3426m stratovolcano* **Mt Baker** *3285m stratovolcano* **Mt Shasta** *4317m stratovolcano* **Lassen Peak** *3189m stratovolcano* **Crater Lake** *2487m caldera*	1983, 2008 1894 1790, 1907? 1880, 1884? 1786 1917 Holocene	NP	Recreation areas, wildlife, skiing, Lava Beds Monument (Shasta), interpretive centres, hiking trails, mountain climbing, ice climbing, snowboarding, biking, water sports, crater lakes, scenic drives, camp grounds, glaciers, spectacular views, waterfalls, hot springs (developed and undeveloped), volcano air safaris especially to Mt St Helens crater area	**Mt St Helens** – Rangers advising on potential dangers, educational videos, visitor centre, warnings to stay away from crater rim **Mt Rainier** – Climbing permits needed above 3000m Ranger stations and visitor centres issue updated information as well as weather forecasts and keep track of the number of people on the mountain if they have registered
Mexico *42 volcanoes*	**Colima** *3850m stratovolcano* *Decade volcano* **El Chichón** *1060m lava domes* **Popocatépetl** *5426m stratovolcano* **Iztaccíhuatl** *5230m stratovolcano* **Los Azufres** *caldera* **Paricutin** *3170m (cinder cone itself is only 424m)*	2009 1982 2009–ongoing Dormant - 1952	WHA NP	Izta-Popo National Park is a popular family destination, mountaineering, hiking, trekking, skiing, volcanic fields, monasteries on the slopes of Popocatépetl, hot springs, glaciers, bushwalking, camping, 4WD tours, lava flows, cinder cones, maars, tuff rings, lava domes, volcanic vents, visitor centres	1982 – El Chichón (3500) 1996 – Popocatépetl (5) Rangers present at visitor centres, register for climbs with signing on return, skilled rescue group, closure of national parks at times of heightened activity

Country or region	Number of volcanoes (examples)	Status (last active)	Protected area type*	Attractions and activities	Information about risk, safety aspects, accidents and number of deaths (in brackets)
AMERICA Central American volcanoes have often been given national park status and offer organized tours (Adventure Travellers, 2000)					
Costa Rica *10 volcanoes*	Arenal *1633m stratovolcano* Rincon de la Vieja *1916m complex volcano* Poas *2708m stratovolcano* Irazu *3432m stratovolcano*	2009 1999 2008 1994	NP	Hiking, mountain climbing Rincon de la Vieja NP, wildlife, hot springs on Rincon volcano. Irazú is a nice drive-in volcano with a green crater lake.	Signage around all volcanoes Arenal – ascent is off limits – 1968 (78), 2000 (10) sightseeing plane crash Poás – descend to crater also off limits Compass is recommended when climbing through clouds, protective clothing
Guatemala *24 volcanoes*	Fuego *3763m stratovolcano* Pacaya *2552m complex volcano* Santa Maria *3772m stratovolcano* *Decade volcano*	2009 2009 2009	NP	Volcano tours (adventure tours, private tours), hot springs, trekking, geotourism, ecotourism	1902 – Santa Maria (6000) 1990 – Santa Maria (33) 1929 – Santiaguito (5000)
El Salvador *16 volcanoes*	Santa Ana *2365m stratovolcano* San Miguel *2130m stratovolcano*	2005 2002	-	Santa Ana erupted unexpectedly and two people died in landslides Hiking to the volcanoes is sometimes dangerous due to 'Banditos'	
Nicaragua *19 volcanoes*	San Christobal *1745m stratovolcano* Cerro Negro *675m cinder cones* Masaya *635m caldera*	2009 1999 2008	NP	Volcano boarding (Cerro Negro), abundance of hot springs, lakes, rainforest	1996 – Lahar near Maderas volcano (6) All volcanoes in Nicaragua are popular with climbers and most have access tracks
Lesser Antilles, Caribbean *13 volcanoes*	Soufrière Hills, Montserrat *915m stratovolcano* Soufrière, Guadeloupe *1467m stratovolcano* Mt Pelée,Martinique *1397m stratovolcano* Soufrière St Vincent *1220m stratovolcano* Qualibou *777m caldera* Kick 'em Jenny *(Grenada)*	2009 1977 1932 1979 1766 2001	NP	St Kitts and Nevis – volcano climbing, hiking, bushwalking, guided tours, adventure tourism Guadeloupe – hik ng to the summit of Soufrière volcano Historical sites	1902 – Mt Pelée, Martinique (29,000) 1902 Soufrière, St Vincent (1500) 1997 – Soufrière Hills, Montserrat (19) Montserrat is off limits
AMERICA South					
Argentina *34 volcanoes active and dormant*	Aracar *6082m stratovolcano* Tupungatito *6000m stratovolcano* Maipo *5264m caldera* San José *5856m stratovolcano* Viedama	1993 1986 1912 1960 1988	Protected nature reserves NP	Volcanoes are major tourist attractions in Argentina, snow capped mountain peaks, volcanic craters to explore, mountain resorts, skiing, hiking, hot springs, sunrise viewing Beware of land mines on the Chilean/Argentinean border	

Country	Volcano	Dates	Designation	Tourism	Notes
Chile *100+ volcanoes*	Copahue 2997m stratovolcano	2000	NP	Rapa Nui National Park, Easter Islands. Volcanoes are major tourist attractions in Chile, volcano route through three national parks, skiing, walking, hiking, horse riding, glaciers, boating on volcanic lagoons, Copahue crater lake, hot spring spas, rock climbing, El Tatio geysers	Climbing season is from December to March or April. Weather is a problem. Refuge huts
	Villarica 2847m stratovolcano	2008	WHA		
	Chaitén 962m caldera	2009			
	Nevados de Chillan 3212m stratovolcano	2009–ongoing			
	Llaima 3125m stratovolcano				
	Lascar 5592m stratovolcano	2009			
	El Tatio Geysers 4280m hydrothermal field	2007			
Colombia *15 volcanoes*	Galeras 4276m complex volcano Decade volcano	2009	NP	Glaciers, fumaroles, hot springs, summit craters, national parks, refuge huts, lava flows, glaciers	1993 – **Galeras** (9). 1985 – **Nevado del Ruiz** (25,000–28,000 – official figures vary). 1994 – **Nevado del Huila**, mudflows (1000+), 1994 (10)
	Nevado del Ruiz 5321m stratovolcano	1994			
	Nevado del Huila 5364m stratovolcano	2009			
	Puracé 4650m stratovolcano	1977			
Ecuador *22 volcanoes* **Galápagos Islands** *13 volcanoes*	Tungurahua 5028m stratovolcano	2009	NP	Tungurahua is close to the popular hot spring tourist town Baños (Chapter 1), crater lake with volcanic islands, kayaking, canyoning, mountain biking, horse riding, rock climbing, mountain biking	1976 – **Sangay** (2). 1993 – **Guagua Pichincha** (2). The **Galápagos Islands** are on the UNESCO world heritage list of sites in danger of losing their inscription status due to environmental concerns and problems caused by mass tourism
	Cotopaxi 5911m stratovolcano	1942			
	Reventador 3562m stratovolcano	2008			
	Fernandina 1495m shield volcano	2009	WHA		
	Sierra Negra Volcano 1124m shield volcano	2005			
	Wolf Volcano 1710m shield volcano	1982			
Peru *16 volcanoes*	El Misti 5822m stratovolcano	1784, 1870	NP	Peruvian volcano groups are popular with tourists – unique scenery, adventure tours, organized tours, geotourism, ecotourism, sustainable tourism, trekking, climbing, glaciers, mountaineering, camping, hot springs	1991 – **Sabancaya** (20). Volcanic mountains in Peru require special equipment for ice climbing at higher elevations. Public transport is not considered to be safe in most parts of Peru
	Ubinas 5672m stratovolcano	2008	NR		
	Nevado Chachani 6057m stratovolcano	Dormant			
	Tutupaca 5815m stratovolcano	1902			
	Sabancaya 5967m stratovolcano	2003			
	Yucamane 5550m stratovolcano	1787, 1902			

ASIA

Country	Volcano	Dates	Designation	Tourism	Notes
Arabian Peninsula *15 volcanoes*	Rahat 1744m volcanic field	1256, 1292?	NP	Desert tours	Yebel al Tair island was evacuated in 2007
	Arhab 3100m volcanic field	AD500			
	Dahmar 3500m volcanic field	1937			
	Yebel al Tair 244m stratovolcano	2007–2008			
China *15 volcanoes*	Tengchong 2865m pyroclastic cones	1609	NP	Hydrothermal fields, hot springs, sinter terraces, glaciers, ecotourism, geotourism, global geoparks, national parks	**Baitoushan** is on the China – North Korea border. AD1054 – **Baitoushan** eruption (VEI7)
	Baitoushan 2744m stratovolcano	1702	GGP		
	Wudalianchi 597m volcanic field	1721	NR		

Country or region	Number of volcanoes (examples)	Status (last active)	Protected area type*	Attractions and activities	Information about risk, safety aspects, accidents and number of deaths (in brackets)
India *5 volcanoes*	**Andaman Islands:** Barren Island *305m stratovolcano* Barren 1 *mud volcano* Narcondum *710m stratovolcano* Deccan Traps	2009–ongoing 2003 1900 Ancient lava flows	–	Geothermal features, hot springs The Andaman Islands are a closed military area	
Iran *6 volcanoes*	Taftan *4050m stratovolcano* Bazman *3490m stratovolcano* Damavand *5670m stratovolcano* Qal'eh Hasan Ali Volcano *maars*	1993 Active fumaroles Holocene Holocene	NP GP	Mt Damavand – hiking, mountain climbing, ice climbing, fumaroles, hot springs at summit, climbing trails, shelter huts, guided tours from Teheran	
Indonesia *150 volcanoes* 28 eruptions during last decade 76 historically active	Agung *3142m stratovolcano* Kelut *1731m stratovolcano* Semeru *3676m stratovolcano* Bromo *2329m stratovolcano* Merapi *2911m stratovolcano* Krakatau *813m caldera* Tambora *2850m stratovolcano* Toba *2157m caldera*	1963 2008 2009 2007 1883, 2007 2009–ongoing 1815, 1967	NP WHA	Indonesia is known ̈or the eruption of **Krakatau** in 1883 (VEI6) causing the death of 36,417 people (official figure) as well as for the **Tambora** eruption 1815 (VEI 7) which killed between 71,000 and 117,000 people – figures vary Cultural world heritage sites close to active volcanoes (Borobodur Temple and Mt Merapi) hot springs, jeep tours, horse riding, endangered vegetation, unique volcanic landforms, fumaroles, hiking, mountain climbing	Dangerous volcanoes include: **Semeru** (744 deaths over the last 45 years), **Merapi** (1426 deaths in the last 80 years), **Kelut** (5100 died in 1919), **Agung** (1100 died in 1990), plus many others! 2004 – two tourists died and five were injured More than a dozen volcanoes at alert level 1 with a few at alert level 2 (4 at the time of writing) Some signs, guides mostly without education and geological knowledge; good information only at 'Vogel's Homestay' in Kaliurang (Merapi area), major volcanoes a re monitored
Japan *105 volcanoes*	Mt Aso *1592m caldera* Mt Fuji *3776m stratovolcano* Mt Sakurajima *1117m stratovolcano* Mt Unzen *1500m complex volcano* Mt Usu *731m stratovolcano* Asama *2560m complex volcano* Tsurumi *1584m lava domes* Tokachi *2077m stratovolcano* Kusatsu-Shirane *2176m stratovolcano*	2005 1708 2009–ongoing 1996 2001 2009 867 1989 1989	QNP PP NP GGP	Volcanoes are a very important tourist attraction in Japan and are visited for their cultural/religious aspects as well as for their geological heritage. Every volcanic and geothermal feature possible can be found in Japan including hot springs for spa use, which is usually combined with other recreational activities such as hiking and mountain climbing around the volcanoes.	1741 – Oshima Oshima (1480) 1783 – **Asama** (1200), 1993 (1) 1792 – Unzen (15,000), 1991 (43) 1888 – Bandai (460) 1926 – Tokachi (144) 1976 – Kusatsu Shirane (3) 1977 – Usu (3) 1979 – **Aso** (30, 1997 (2) Japan has excellent systems for emergencies in place – warning signs and announcements are generally in at least four languages, scientific monitoring takes place

Country or region	Number of volcanoes (examples)	Status (last active)	Protected area type*	Attractions and activities	Information about risk, safety aspects, accidents and number of deaths (in brackets)
Kamchatka *114? volcanoes (29 active)*	Avachinsky *2741m stratovolcano* Koryaksky *3456m stratovolcano* Shiveluch *3283m stratovolcano* Klyuchevskoy *4750m stratovolcano* Bezymanny *2882m stratovolcano* Tolbachik *3682m shield volcano* Karymsky *1486m stratovolcano* Maly Semiachik *1560m caldera* Valley of the Geysers	2009 2009 2009–ongoing 2009–ongoing 2008 1976 2009–ongoing 1952	WHA NP Incl. 19 volcanoes	Skiing, hiking, 4WD tours, geotourism, ecotourism, climbing, glaciers, fumaroles, cruise ships, helicopter tours, trekking, bear watching, hot springs, geysers	Essential: mosquito repellent, bear bells, compass, equipment for ice climbing, bad weather gear Mudslide destroyed most of the Valley of the Geysers in 2007, but many hot springs have reappeared since
Korea *(North and South)* *6 volcanoes*	Hallasan, Jeju Island *1950m shield volcano* Baitoushan *2744m stratovolcano* Ulreung *984m stratovolcano*	1007 1702 Holocene	WHA NP	Mt Hallasan – big tourist attraction, lava tubes, tuff rings, lava walls, waterfalls, crater lake, columnar jointed cliffs, unique vegetation, endangered species, mountain climbing, fishing, horse riding, biking, hot springs, geotourism, ecotourism, Baitoushan is located on the border of North Korea and China	
Mongolia *5 volcanoes*	Mount Khorgo Khanuy Gol *1886m volcanic field* Taryatu-Chulutu *2400m volcanic field* Bus-Obo *1162m cinder cone* *Dormant or extinct*	No recent eruptions Holocene	NP GP	Crater lakes in ancient volcanoes, spectacular scenery, Khorgo crater, fumaroles, ice chimneys, caverns, basaltic lava flows, pyroclastic sheets, unique scenery, hot springs	
Philippines *52 volcanoes (plus hundreds of inactive volcanoes)*	Taal *400m stratovolcano* Pinatubo *1486m stratovolcano* Mayon *2420m stratovolcano* Hibok Hibok *1332m stratovolcano* Bulusan *1547m stratovolcano* Apo *2954m stratovolcano*	1977 1992 2009 1953 2007 Active fumaroles	NP	Volcano tourism is actively promoted, hiking to Taal volcano crater, swimming and kayaking in Pinatubo's crater lake, 4WD tours, nature tours, visiting devastation areas, hiking, climbing, mountaineering, unique landforms, fumaroles, hot springs, biodiversity, ecotourism, geotourism	1911 – **Taal** (1334) 1951 – **Hibok Hibok** (500) Wide safety zone on the NE-slope of Mt Hibok-Hibok 1991 – **Pinatubo** (1500+) 1968 – **Mayon** (6), 1981 (40), 1993 (75), 2006 (1266) Currently alert level 2, 6km permanent exclusion zone, 7km extended danger zone 1996 – **Kanlaon** (3)

Country or region	Number of volcanoes (examples)	Status (last active)	Protected area type*	Attractions and activities	Information about risk, safety aspects, accidents and number of deaths (in brackets)
Papua New Guinea (PNG) *47 volcanoes*	Ulawun *2334m stratovolcano* Lamington *1680m stratovolcano* Rabaul *688m caldera* Karkar *1839m stratovolcano* Langila *1330m complex volcano* Bagana *1750m lava cone* Manam *1807m stratovolcano* Ritter Island	2008 1956 (VEI 4) 2009–ongoing 1980 2009 2009 2009 2007	NP	Hot springs, geysers, boiling mud pools, eco tours, wildlife sanctuaries, conservation areas Buried town and historic site Rabaul	1938 – Rabaul (500) 1951 – Lamington (2942) 1979 – Karkar (2) 1996 – Manam (13) 1888 – Ritter (3000) Armed robberies are a possibility
Australia *72 volcanoes, volcanic groups and volcanic centres, mainly dormant or extinct*	Heard Island – Big Ben *2745m stratovolcano* McDonald Island *212m complex volcano, South Indian Ocean* Dormant: Undara Volcanic NP, Crater Lakes NP, Glasshouse Mountains NP, *Queensland* Warrumbungles NP, Mt Kaputar NP, Canabolas, Mt Warning, *New South Wales* Newer Volcanic Provinces, Kanawinka Global Geopark, *Victoria* Mt Gambier, Mt Schank, *South Australia* Lord Howe Island *875m South Indian Ocean* Macquarie Island *433m Southern Ocean*	2008 2005 Holocene 2500BC	Marine Reserve WHA Volcanic NP GGP	The only active volcanism takes place on **Heard and McDonald Islands** which are too remote and therefore very rarely visited other than by scientists. Their geological heritage, outstanding natural values, unique wilderness and wildlife are protected as world heritage. The islands are considered biologically pristine. Elsewhere on the Australian continent many dormant volcanic environments with a range of attractions for leisure and recreation exist: National Parks, State Parks, wildlife viewing, bird watching, ranger guided tours, camping, hiking, trekking, climbing, mountain biking, lava tube/tunnels, maars, crater lakes, columnar joints, volcanic dykes, rock climbing, bushwalking, camping, wildlife, ranger guided tours Heard and McDonald Islands are highly protected Safety guidelines for visitors of National Parks, Rangers, Information Centres, Educational Signboards	
Antarctica *23 volcanoes and volcanic islands*	Mt Erebus, Ross Island *3794m stratovolcano* Deception Island *576m caldera* Buckle Island *1239m stratovolcano* Michael *(S. Sandwich Is.)*	2009 1987 1899 2006	Nature Reserves Protected Areas	Erebus – active lava lake since 1972, strombolian eruptions Hot springs at Deception Island caldera – popular with cruise ship passengers	Sightseeing flight to **Mt Erebus** went wrong in 1979, killing all 237 passengers and 20 crew members on board
New Zealand *25 volcanoes and volcanic fields*	Taranaki *2518m stratovolcano* Tarawera *111m lava domes* Ngauruhoe *2291m stratovolcano* Ruapehu *2779m stratovolcano* White Island *231m stratovolcano*	1755 1973 1977 2007 2001	NP	Hiking, climbing, skiing, Tongariro Crossing, horse riding, boat tours or helicopter flights to White Island and Tarawera, guided tours. Buried Village, hot springs, geothermal parks Ruapehu – ski resorts and lodges on the slopes, campgrounds, visitor centres	1846 - **Taupo** (63), 1910 (1) 1886 - **Tarawera** (between 108 -153, figures differ), 1903 (4), 1917 (2) 1953 - **Ruapehu** (151) 1914 - **White Island** (10), currently alert level 1
Pacific Islands *24 volcanoes*	Raoul Island Tonga Islands Samoa	2006 2009 - ongoing 2005		Observing New Island Forming at Tonga Islands	Tsunami hazard for the entire Pacific because of eruptions.

Country or region	Number of volcanoes (examples)	Status (last active)	Protected area type*	Attractions and activities	Information about risk, safety aspects, accidents and number of deaths (in brackets)
Vanuatu *13 volcanoes*	**Ambrym** *1334m shield volcano* **Yasur** *405m stratovolcano* **Lopevi** *1413m stratovolcano* **Aoba** *1496m shield volcano*	2009 Ongoing activity 2007 2006	NP Nature Reserves	Volcano visiting, hiking, cultural experiences, Yasur – possible to drive within 200m of the crater rim Active lava lake (Ambrym), strombolian eruptions Active fumaroles at Mt Garet's summit crater	Explosive and Strombolian eruptions 1994 – **Yasur** (2), 1995 (1) Dangerous at all times, but volcanoes are an important element of the tourism sector in Vanuatu
Solomon Islands *7 volcanoes*	**Tinakula, Santa Cruz Is.** *851m stratovolcano* **Savo** *510m Stratovolcano* **Nonda** *760m stratovolcano* **Kavachi** *submarine volcano*	2008 1850 Active Vents 2007	-	Hot springs, fumaroles, climbs to caldera ring of Kolombangara	Tsunami hazard for the entire Pacific because of eruptions Tour guides are recommended January to March – rainy season
EUROPE					
France	**Chaine de Puys, Auvergne** **Cap d'Agde**	Dormant - probably no significant Holocene activity	NP	Geological heritage, geotourism, popular for leisure and recreation, Themepark Vulcania, Open Air Museum Lemptegy Cap d'Agde, Mont St Loup, volcanic cliffs, hiking, cycling	Signage around all volcanoes, Guided and unguided tours
Germany *Eifel volcanoes*	**Rhön Mountains** *800–950m* **Vogelsberg** *760–770m* **Vulkaneifel** *400–750m maars (Ulmener Maar, Pulver Maar)*	Ancient volcanoes Some Holocene Activity	NP GGP	Popular holiday destination, Maar lakes, hiking and cycling trails, guided geotours, Vulkangarten Steffeln, Volcano museums, caldera lake, Vulkanpark Brohltal, Vulkanpark Osteifel, Vulkaneifel European Geopark	Interpretive signs in German, but signage includes symbols and pictograms and are easy to recognise
Greece *6 volcanoes*	**Nisyros** *698m stratovolcano* **Santorini** *564m shield volcanoes* **Methana** *760m lava domes* **Milos** *751m stratovolcano* **Kos** *430m hydrothermal field*	1888, 2003 1950 1922 Active fumaroles	-	**Nisyros** - Crater with fumaroles and extreme hot springs, unique volcanic landscape **Santorini** - historical and cultural attractions, volcanic landscape, study tours, educational walking tours, hot springs	**Nisyros** – no warning signs, challenging access to crater, no safety guidelines, brochures inconsistent about state of activity, no steps or handrails on the way down into the crater
Iceland *35 volcanoes*	**Askja** *1516m stratovolcano* **Eldfell** *279m cinder cone* **Laki, Grimsvötn** *1725m caldera* **Hekla** *1491m stratovolcano* **Katla** *1512m subglacial volcano* **Krafla** *650m caldera* **Kverkfjöll** *1764m stratovolcano* **Surtsey** *152m submarine (composite) volcano*	1961 1973 **1785**, 2004 2000 1999 1984 1968 2005	NP Surtsey WHA	Geyser fields, volcanic landscapes, hiking, trekking, mountain biking, hot springs, crater lakes, guided tours, Red Rock Cinema Reykjavik, glaciers,	**Iceland** has a good emergency rescue system, mobile phone connections cover everywhere, signage is usually in several languages around most volcanoes, guided and unguided tours, marked trails, risk management on lower level than in other volcanic areas.

Country or region	Number of volcanoes (examples)	Status (last active)	Protected area type*	Attractions and activities	Information about risk, safety aspects, accidents and number of deaths (in brackets)
Italy *23 volcanoes*	Campi Flegrei *458m caldera* Mt Etna *3350m shield volcano* Ischia *789m complex volcano* Larderello *500m explosion craters* Lipari *602m stratovolcano* Pantelleria *836m shield volcano* Stromboli *926m stratovolcano* Mt Vesuvius *1281m complex volcano* Vulcano *500m stratovolcano*	1538 2008 1302 1282 AD729 1891 2009 1944 1892	NP	**Vulcano** – climbing up to *Grand Cratere Fossa*, fumaroles **Vesuvius** – crater hikes, group tours to summit, Pompeii and Herculaneum **Etna** – climbing, 4WD tours, skiing, camping, eruption viewing by night **Stromboli** – guided night tours – eruption viewing	1906 – **Vesuvius** (350) Warning signs at Etna, Vesuvius, Stromboli and Vulcano. Unguided ascents to Stromboli are strictly prohibited since 2004. Refuge huts
Portugal *14 volcanoes*	Agua de Pau *947m stratovolcano* Faial *1043m stratovolcano* Furnas *805m stratovolcano*	1564 1958 1630	NP	Faial and Pico – caves, spatter cones, hiking trails, climbing, camping, hot springs	Cement posts marking the location of the trails in bad weather
Azores (13) *Madeira (1)*	Pico *2351m stratovolcano* São Jorge *1053m fissure vent* Sete Citades *856m stratovolcano* Terceira *1023m stratovolcano*	1720, 1963 1907, 1964 1880 2001		Madeira – walking trails	
Spain *Canary Islands* *Olot volcanic field*	Fuerteventura *529m fissure vents* Gran Canaria *1949m fissure vents* Hierro *1501m shield volcano* Cumbre Vieja, La Palma *2426m stratovolcano* Lanzarote *670m fissure vents* Mt Teide, Tenerife *3718m stratovolcano* Garrotxa volcanic field (Olot) *893m pyroclastic cones*	Holocene 20BC 1793 1971 1824 1909	NP WHA	**Mt Teide** – UNESCO world heritage site, fumaroles, lava tubes, ice caves, hiking, climbing to the summit, crater rim walks, geotourism, ecotourism	No camping in the national parks
Turkey *13 volcanoes*	Cappadocia *tuff mountains* Mt Hasan *3253m stratovolcano* Mt Erciyes *3916m stratovolcano* Mt Ararat *5137m stratovolcano* Mt Nemrut *2928m stratovolcano* Mt Tendürek *3584m shield volcano*	620BC AD253 1840 1692 1855	NP Special areas of environment protection (e.g. Pamukkale)	**Cappadocia** – Fairy chimneys, hot air ballooning over the volcanic landscape, geotourism, guided tours, hiking, trekking, geological heritage **Erciyes** – skiing, hiking, climbing **Ararat** – highest mountain in Turkey, skiing, climbing, mountaineering, adventure tourism, expeditions, legend of Noah's Ark, summit glacier, camping Sinter terraces of Pamukkale, hot springs	**Mt Ararat** – licensed mountain guides are mandatory, climbers need a permit

Note: *Key: NP – National Park; WHA – World Heritage Area; NR – National Reserve; GGP – Global Geopark; GP – Geopark; QNP – Quasi National Park (Japan); PP – Prefectural Park (Japan).

Source: Table compiled by Patricia Erfurt-Cooper, Jens Edelmann and Christoph Weber

Appendix 3

The following are recommendations for a Fact Sheet that should be made available to all visitors to active volcanic and geothermal environments to provide an overview of the area and emergency shelters etc. The template shown can be adopted for all volcanic regions and should be supplied at points of entry to national parks, through tour operators, information centres and through accommodation providers in the area (Chapter 22).

Hazard maps come in different designs, but should be easy to interpret for inexperienced visitors of active volcanic areas. For example, the island of Hawai'i is divided into coloured and numbered zones according to the degree of hazard from lava flows. Zone 1 is the area of the greatest hazard, Zone 9 of the least. Other maps are colour coded only.

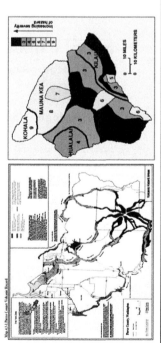

Map indicating possible escape routes

Symbols and pictograms for visual recognition of key points Shelters, First Aid, Emergency Phones etc

Emergency contacts: Names of Rescue Services and Phone Numbers

Appendix 4
Useful Websites

ORGANIZATIONS

Volcano Hazards Program
http://volcanoes.usgs.gov/
USGS Cascades Volcano Observatory (CVO)
http://vulcan.wr.usgs.gov/
USGS Hawaiian Volcano Observatory (HVO)
http://hvo.wr.usgs.gov/
Alaska Volcano Observatory (AVO)
www.avo.alaska.edu/
Philippine Institute of Volcanology and Seismology (PHIVOLCS)
www.phivolcs.dost.gov.ph/
Office of International Earthquake and Volcano Research Promotion
www.eri.u-tokyo.ac.jp/kokusai/english/index
Global Volcanism Program
www.volcano.si.edu/reports/usgs/
World Organization of Volcano Observatories (WOVO)
www.wovo.org/
Volcano Observatories and Research Centres
http://volcanoes.ca/Volcobsv.html
Volcano observatories
www.volcano.group.cam.ac.uk/links.htm
Merapi Volcano Observatory
www.vsi.dpe.go.id/mvohomepage.html
Mount Erebus Volcanic Observatory
www.ees.nmt.edu/Geop/erebus.html
INGEOMINAS Pasto Volcano Observatory, Colombia
www.univalle.edu.co/~ovp/index-e.html
Monitoreo y Vigilancia del Volcan Popocatepetl
http://www.cenapred.unam.mx/mvolcan.html
Maison du Volcan (Piton de la Fournaise)
http://www.runtel.fr/mdv/english/default.htm

Volcano Observatories around the world
http://exodus.open.ac.uk/williamg/volcobsv.html
European Volcanological Society (SVE)
http://www.sveurop.org
International Association of Volcanology and Chemistry of the Earth's Interior (IAVCEI)
www.iavcei.org/
International Volcanic Health Hazard Network (IVHHN)
www.ivhhn.org/
Montserrat Volcano Observatory (MVO)
www.mvo.ms
EOS Volcanology
http://eos.higp.hawaii.edu/index.html

SAFETY RECOMMENDATIONS

Safety recommendations for volcanologists and the public
http://www.iavcei.org/IAVCEI.htm
U.S. Geological Survey – Fact Sheet 2005-3024 – 2005
Steam explosions, earthquakes and volcanic eruptions
http://pubs.usgs.gov/fs/2005/3024/
What to do if a volcano erupts
American Red Cross Safety Information – VOLCANOES – 1998
http://vulcan.wr.usgs.gov/Hazards/Safety/what_to_do.html
What to do if a volcano erupts
Federal Emergency Management Agency (FEMA) – 1998
http://vulcan.wr.usgs.gov/Hazards/Safety/what_to_do_FEMA.html

Mount Aso Ropeway – Warning: Volcanic gases float up from the crater to the rim
www.kyusanko.co.jp/aso/english.html

The Aso Volcano Disaster Prevention Council
www.aso.ne.jp/~volcano/eng/html/history.html

Arenal Volcano safety guidelines
www.wildland.com/wildnews/1000002/cos_wildnews.aspx

Disaster safety – volcano safety
www.thesafetylibrary.com/lib/disastersafety/volcanosafety.php

Volcano safety tips
http://environment.nationalgeographic.com/environment/natural-disasters/volcano-safety-tips.html

University of Alaska Anchorage
http://greenandgold.uaa.alaska.edu/index.php?option=com_content&view=article&id=2572&Itemid=1

Volcano safety
www.volcanolive.com/safety.html

Basic safety guidelines for Kamchatka's visitors
www.kamchatka.travel/tours/guidelines.html

Volcano safety information
www.emergencydude.com/volcano.shtml

Safety on volcanoes: Volcanic risk
www.volcanodiscovery.com/volcano=tours/volcanic_risk.html

Volcano safety
http://www.co.cowlitz.wa.us/dem/pdf/Volcano_Safety.pdf

U.S. Geological Survey Fact Sheet 152-00
http://pubs.usgs.gov/fs/2000/fs152-00/

Lake Eacham, Crater Lakes National Park, environment and resource management
https://www.epa.qld.gov.au/parks_and_forests/safety_in_parks_and_forests.html

VOLCANO TOURISM

www.volcano-tourism.net

VOLCANIC RISKS

What are volcano hazards?
http://pubs.usgs.gov/fs/fs002-97/fs002-97.pdf

Volcano hazards program
http://volcanoes.usgs.gov/vhp/

Volcano hazards – A national threat
http://pubs.usgs.gov/fs/2006/3014/2006-3014.pdf

What to do if a volcano erupts: Volcanic ash and mudflows
http://vulcan.wr.usgs.gov/Hazards/Safety/

Volcanic eruption in Iceland
http://safetravel.is/page.php?idsublink=45

Vulkangefahren (German website)
www.vulkane.net/

Volcanic hazard documentation & logistics research
www.vei.de/vhdl/german/vulkan_gefahr.html

Volcanoes – Volcanic eruptions, their products and their hazards
http://geology.about.com/od/volcanoes/Volcanoes.htm

DESTINATIONS

International Volcanic Sabo Centre – Sakurajima sightseeing
www.qsr.mlit.go.jp/osumi/sivsc/home/english/k01.html

Volcano boarding
www.bigfootnicaragua.com/adventure.html

Yellowstone National Park
Hydrothermal features and how they work www.nps.gov/yell/naturescience/geothermal.htm

Geothermal resources – Yellowstone
www.nps.gov/yell/naturescience/geothermalresources.htm

Geology and Thermal History of Mammoth Hot Springs, Yellowstone National Park, Wyoming by Keith E. Bargar
www.nps.gov/history/history/online_books/geology/publications/bul/1444/index.htm

Yellowstone Volcano Observatory
http://volcanoes.usgs.gov/yvo/

Cascades Volcano Observatory
http://vulcan.wr.usgs.gov/

Welcome to Taupo's Volcanic Activity Centre
www.volcanoes.co.nz/

Welcome to Ruapehu – An all seasons destination
www.visitruapehu.com

Tongariro National Park
www.doc.govt.nz/parks-and-recreation/national-parks/tongariro

Taranaki – Like no other
www.taranakinz.org/noflash/index.php

VOLCANO TOURS

Volcano Expeditions International
www.v-e-i.de/english/start.html

Volcano Discovery Tours
www.decadevolcano.net/travel.htm

Volcano Adventure Travel
www.volcanolive.com/resources.html

New Zealand Tourism Guide: Rotorua volcanic and geothermal tours
www.tourism.net.nz/region/rotorua/tours/volcanic-and-geothermal-tours/

Mt Tarawera Volcano – Rotorua New Zealand volcano tours
www.mt-tarawera.co.nz

White Island Tours
www.whiteisland.co.nz

Geology alive – Special geological tours and geological services
www.geotours.co.nz

Hawaii volcano tours
www.lavatours.com/

Volcano tours in Iceland
www.icelandtotal.com/home/tours_and_activities/volcano_areas/

Arenal Volcano Tours
www.arenalvolcanotours.com/

Vulkanreisen
www.vulkane.net/reisen.html

Vulkan Expeditionen International
www.v-e-i.de/

SummitPost – Climbing, hiking, mountaineering
www.summitpost.org

Index

S

U

V

W

Y

Z

For Product Safety Concerns and Information please contact our EU
representative GPSR@taylorandfrancis.com Taylor & Francis Verlag GmbH,
Kaufingerstraße 24, 80331 München, Germany

Printed and bound by CPI Group (UK) Ltd, Croydon, CR0 4YY

08/05/2025

01864328-0001